Contents

Preface

This book can be used for a one-term or two-term course in Java and for self-study. Chapters 9 and 10 have sufficient material for an introductory course in network programming and distributed systems. The book assumes no prior knowledge of Java or object-oriented programming, but the book does assume programming experience. The reader should be familiar with general programming concepts such as *variable*, *data type*, and *statement*; programming constructs such as statement sequencing, function calls, tests, and loops; and programming practices such as design, coding, and testing. The book makes extensive use of examples, tables, figures, self-study exercises, sample applications, lists of common programming errors and safe practices, and programming exercises. Throughout the book, my goal is to write clear code and to illustrate sound programming practices. All of the code in the book has been compiled and run under Java 2. The book also draws many of its examples from Java's own standard classes so that the Java packages are introduced in a natural, gradual way.

The Special Challenges of Java

This book is based on courses that I have been teaching regularly and on my experience in writing textbooks, with Richard Johnsonbaugh, on C and C++. The Java courses serve three different audiences, which has been helpful in developing pedagogical techniques for presenting the language. One audience consists of undergraduate majors in computer science and information systems with prior coursework in another language, typically C++ or Visual Basic. The second audience consists of graduate students with strong programming skills and fluency in C/C++ or ML. The third audience consists of professional programmers with experience in various languages such as assembler, C, Perl, and COBOL. Despite differences in background, programmers intent on learning Java face challenges that reflect the language's most attractive features:

- Java is a *general-purpose language* with the rich assortment of data types, operators, control structures, and standard packages that befits this status. Although the book offers full coverage of Java, it does so without overwhelming the reader. I focus first on the relatively simple cases before moving to the more complicated ones. To take a basic example, Java has three loop constructs: the for loop, the while loop, and the do while loop. Of the three, the while loop has the simplest syntax and semantics. The while loop is thus presented first and the other loop structures are then clarified with reference to it. To take a more advanced example, Java supports graphics through both the Abstract Window Toolkit (AWT) and the Swing set. Although the Swing set is more flexible and powerful, the Abstract Window Toolkit is simpler; hence, the graphics coverage starts with basic AWT examples then moves to Swing set examples.

- Java is an *object-oriented programming language*. Although Java has primitive types such as int and double, every program requires at least one class. All functions are encapsulated in classes as either constructors or methods, and variables are either encapsulated fields or local variables in constructors and methods. Java has only single inheritance for classes but a class may implement arbitrarily many interfaces; and Java supports multiple inheritance for interfaces. Java also has abstract as well as concrete classes. Further, methods and fields can be associated either with a class itself (static methods and fields) or with class instances or objects (nonstatic methods and fields). Object-oriented constructs such as polymorphism are widely used within Java's own standard classes. Although Java is an elegant object-oriented language, special attention still must be given to the reader who comes to Java from an exclusively or even primarily procedural background. This book addresses object orientation in two ways:

  - The first chapter clarifies the basic concepts, constructs, and benefits of object-oriented design and programming. The chapter explains key terms such as *class*, *object*, *information hiding*, *encapsulation*, *inheritance*, and *message passing*. The chapter also has a section on UML to introduce modern approaches to object-oriented design.
  - The book's short programs and longer sample applications present object-oriented programming as a natural and intuitive approach to programming. The goal is to illustrate the *benefits to the programmer* that object orientation brings.

- Java is a *modern programming language* with standard packages to support graphics, networking, security, persistence, database, reflection, components—and more. Java is large and growing. The standard java packages have been augmented by the javax packages (the x stands for extension) and by many excellent commercial packages. The first seven chapters focus on core language features and the last three chapters then illustrate how these core features support networking in many forms (e.g., sockets, applets, servlets, remote method invocation, and object request brokers), database, security, and component-based programming. All ten chapters draw frequent examples from Java's own standard classes to give the reader an ongoing introduction to Java's rich class libraries.

Chapter Overviews

The book has ten chapters, all of which include self-study exercises at the end of sections. Solutions to odd-numbered section exercises are included in the book, and the instructor CD-ROM has solutions to the even-numbered section exercises. All of the chapters except for the first have programming exercises and a list of common programming errors and safe practices. The book has

- Over 600 end-of-section exercises with answers to odd-numbered exercises.
- Over 140 programming exercises.
- 13 major sample applications and over 150 additional full programs.

Many chapters have a Java Postscript to handle special topics such as the 2's complement representation of integers, the volatile modifier, and deprecated Thread methods. The chapters include short programs as well as longer sample applications. All of the source code for programs and sample applications is available on the book's CD-ROM and at the Web site. The chapters can described as follows:

- **Chapter 1: Object-Oriented Programming**. This chapter explains the basic concepts and advantages of object-oriented design and programming, which are contrasted with top-down design and procedural programming. Central concepts such as *class, object, inheritance, polymorphism, abstract data type, message passing, interface,* and *component* are clarified and illustrated. Although the chapter includes some brief Java examples, the emphasis is on object-oriented programming in general. The chapter includes a section on UML with an overview of the modeling language and various examples of UML diagrams. The section also indicates how UML models can guide coding.
- **Chapter 2: Introductory Programs**. This chapter provides a series of short but realistic programs so that the reader is exposed at once to the "look and feel" of Java code. The sections and the section exercises suggest ways in which the programs can be adapted and expanded so that the reader can gain quick experience with Java programming. The chapter begins with a traditional *Hello, world!* program and then introduces other short programs to illustrate variables

of primitive and class types, variable declarations and assignments, control structures such as tests and loops, constructor and method invocation, and arrays. Writing, documenting, compiling, and running programs is explained carefully. The chapter assumes that the reader compiles and executes from the command line using the JDK for Java 2.

Some of the programs are paired with one program in the pair processing randomly generated numbers and the other reading data from a disk file. The chapter's second introductory program called BigAndSmall is an example. The program selects the largest and smallest integers from a sequence. In one version, the integers are randomly generated using the standard java.util.Random class; in a second version, the integers are read from a local disk file. The two versions together provide the reader with early, alternative examples of generating input data. A similar approach is taken with output: one program in a pair writes to the standard output, whereas the other program writes to a local disk file.

The chapter has a section dedicated to strings, introducing both the String and the StringBuffer classes. The section on the String class also emphasizes how the writing of a *test client* facilitates learning the language.

The three remaining sections cover programmer-defined classes, further basics of the java.io package, and the three sample utility classes: Vector, Hashtable, and StringTokenizer. The sample programs again are short but perform familiar, realistic programming tasks such as sorting.

- **Chapter 3: Programs and Packages**. This chapter explains the role of the Java Virtual Machine and the relationships among program types such as *application*, *applet*, *servlet*, and *bean*. The chapter reviews and extends the coverage of source (*java*) and compiled (*class*) files. The chapter also introduces the package statement and clarifies the CLASSPATH environment variable. The use of subdirectories as subpackages is covered as well. The chapter has a sample application with a programmer-defined package. Many reference figures, including lists of the standard java and javax packages, are included for convenience.

- **Chapter 4: Language Fundamentals**. This chapter covers language fundamentals, including identifiers, primitive and class data types, control structures, operators, arrays, and exceptions. The chapter has a section to review constructors and methods and then to extend coverage of these key topics. The chapter is organized carefully into sections and subsections so that the chapter can be used as a reference as well as an introduction to basic Java. My assumption is that the reader would return repeatedly to selected sections in the chapter. For instance, the reader might delay a careful reading the section on the switch construct until a programming need arises. Some specialized language features such as the bitwise operators are explained in the Java Postscript rather than the chapter's main body. The chapter includes a sample application.

- **Chapter 5: Classes**. This chapter provides a comprehensive and technical coverage of classes. The chapter examines class and member scope, information hiding, encapsulation, constructors, methods, and fields. The chapter explains how technical aspects of class semantics can be used to achieve practical goals. For example, a subsection explains how selective constructor definition can be used to restrict object construction. The chapter also examines the key role of the no-argument constructor.

The chapter includes a section on using class libraries such as Java's own standard libraries. This section reviews the use of test clients to gain fluency in a class, and underscores again the relationship between the *exposed* and *hidden* in a class.

The chapter's first sample application provides two classes, `BasicInput` and `BasicOutput`, that illustrate the usefulness of *wrapper classes*. The two classes support the high-level input and output with intuitive constructors and methods. For instance, `BasicInput` objects can be constructed with either the standard input or a disk file as the source. Methods such as `getRecord` and `getDouble` are straightforward. This sample application, together with the introductory programs in Chapter 2 that use the `java.io` package for both binary and character input/output, provide sufficient examples to write programs that perform realistic input and output operations.

The second sample application has a graphical component to illustrate how graphics is integrated into the language. The early use of graphics underscores that a program can be furnished with graphical components even before the full details of Java's graphics packages are mastered.

- **Chapter 6: Inheritance, Interfaces, and Abstract Classes**. This chapter extends the material covered in Chapter 5 by explaining inheritance, interfaces, and abstract classes. The chapter introduces the technical aspects of polymorphism and underscores its power with a series of short programs and a sample application on polymorphic input and output. The chapter goes into the details of constructors under inheritance, method overriding, and the use of interfaces in object-oriented programming.

  The chapter explains the differences between interfaces and classes, underscoring the object-oriented dictum about "programming to the interface." Examples of standard Java interfaces and programmer-defined interfaces are included. The chapter's last section introduces abstract classes by contrasting these with concrete classes and interfaces. The section emphasizes that abstract classes are bona fide classes with special uses.

- **Chapter 7: Graphics and Event Handling**. This chapter begins with an overview of the Abstract Window Toolkit (AWT) and the Swing set, event-driven programming, and the Java event model. The chapter emphasizes common features between the AWT and the Swing set by focusing on fundamental constructs such as *container* and *component*. The chapter discusses the relationship between "heavyweight" and "lightweight" components and how this distinction relates to the AWT and the Swing set. A section on the model-view-controller architecture presents a foundational view of Swing set graphics. The chapter's many programs and two sample applications illustrate framed windows, dialogs, fonts, colors, layout managers, and controls such as buttons, menus, menu bars and tool bars, lists, checkboxes, and scrollbars. Basic drawing and images are also covered. The emphasis throughout is on practical approaches to graphics programming. For this reason, many short programs are used to focus on particular topics such as closing windows or using popup menus.

The chapter emphasizes Swing set graphics wherever feasible but uses the relatively simpler AWT to illustrate some key ideas. The two sample applications introduce the high-level Swing set components `JTree` and `JTable`.

- **Chapter 8: Three Interfaces**. This chapter examines three key interfaces: `Cloneable`, `Serializable`, and `Runnable`. The first section explains the differences among object construction, the copying of object references, and cloning. The section discusses and illustrates the dangers of cloning objects whose fields include object or array references. There are subsections on overriding the default `clone` method, disabling cloning, and cloning arrays.

  The chapter's second section introduces serialization and object persistence. The section covers not only the basics but also technical details such as serialization for objects whose superclass does not implement `Serializable`, the serial version number, and the dangers of serializing the same object repeatedly to the same stream. The difference between serialization and writing primitive types to binary streams is clarified. Customized serialization is examined and motivated through a series of related examples, all of which are short but complete programs. There are subsections on disabling serialization and implementing `Externalizable`. A sample application on a serializable time card is included to review and consolidate the material. Chapter 9 on networking extends the discussion by covering serialization and sockets, and Chapter 10 covers the relationship between serialization and beans.

  The third section offers a comprehensive introduction to multithreading. The section begins with a detailed examination of the differences between single-threaded and multithreaded applications, using full program examples to illustrate the benefits and basics of multithreading. The section covers thread priorities, the distinction between user and daemon threads, the relationship between `start` and `run`, the recommended way to stop threads, and the use of the `join` method. The section also explains thread groups. Once the basics have been examined, the section then illustrates and discusses the need for thread synchronization. Issues of deadlock, starvation, and fairness are covered in this section and in the sample application on the dining philosophers problem. Basic concepts such as *critical section*, *mutual exclusion*, and *lock* are explained and then illustrated with Java constructs. Chapter 9 on networking extends the discussion with examples of multithreaded servers.

- **Chapter 9: Network Programming**. This chapter covers networking in Java. The chapter begins with an overview section on networking basics, in particular on the TCP/IP protocol suite. Addresses, packets, transport protocols, sockets, firewalls, proxy servers, and other fundamental concepts are explained. A section on sockets follows. This section covers client `Sockets`, `Server-Sockets`, and `DatagramSockets` with various examples. `MulticastSockets` are also clarified. For motivation, the chapter's examples are full programs, some of which implement familiar utilities such as a port tester and a *finger* program. The section highlights the power of serialization over sockets. A sample application illustrates a multithreaded server.

The chapter's third section presents a thorough coverage of applets, including the issue of *sandbox security*. The section begins with elementary examples that can be adapted readily for experimentation. There is a multimedia applet and a discussion of applets and *jar* files. The section illustrates how applets can communicate with one another and how programs other than Web browsers can serve as host programs for applets. There is a sample program, a Java *application*, that downloads and then displays an applet in the application's own framed window. This section also highlights Java's support for URLs and other networking constructs. Although applets can be run on a standalone machine, this section emphasizes their usefulness in a distributed, client/server system. A sample application shows how an applet order form can use a socket to send information back to the server.

The fourth section covers RMI. After motivating RMI, the section provides a step-by-step explanation of setting up an RMI server and client. The section explains the role of the registry and RMI activation. A final subsection introduces Jini, clarifying its relationship to RMI. A sample application on matrix algebra operations reviews and extends the RMI material. In particular, the sample application offers a realistic example of how RMI could be used in a distributed system.

The chapter's final section covers object-request brokers in general and CORBA in particular. Like the RMI section, this section offers a step-by-step explanation of setting up a CORBA server and client. The section covers the IDL file, the *idltojava* utility, CORBA modules and interfaces, language and location transparency, naming services, the dynamic invocation interface, and IIOP with respect to the convergence of RMI and CORBA technologies. The Java Postscript clarifies how an applet can be a CORBA client.

The chapter explains how distributed applications can be developed and tested on a standalone machine using the *localhost* IP address. This chapter together with Chapter 10 has sufficient material for an introductory course in network programming or distributed systems.

- **Chapter 10: Selected Topics**. This chapter covers special topics divided into four sections. The first section is devoted to component-based programming using Java *beans*. The section underscores how bean technology, including Enterprise Java Beans, leverages basic Java constructs such as serialization, interfaces, properties as pairs of *get/set* methods, and the event model. The section introduces and clarifies the *beanbox* utility for developing and testing beans. The section explains how property change events can be used for bean interaction.

  The second section deals with security and cryptography. The security roles of the the compiler, the bytecode verifier, and the security manager are examined. The section emphasizes the use of high-level security constructs such as the access controller and policy files. The subsection on security offers several illustrations of *permissions* for implementing security. Some examples such as the ones on sandbox security review and extend earlier sections. The subsection on cryptography first presents an overview of Java library support and then focuses on authentication. The relationships among message digests, public and private keys, and digital signatures is explained. The approach is a step-by-step discussion and illustration of how digital signatures are used on the sender and the receiver sides. Several short examples and one longer one illustrate Java support for authentication.

The third section, on reflection, is also example-based. This section first presents an overview of Java's support for run-time class information and then illustrates with several examples. For instance, the section shows how basic information about a class can be reconstructed from a *class* file using reflection technology. The section also extends the discussion of beans by showing how reflection technology underlies the dynamic construction of property sheets in utilities such as the *beanbox*.

The fourth section covers servlets and database. Together with the sample application on database webification, this material extends the network programming covered in Chapter 9. After introducing servlet basics, the fourth section offers several short examples that the reader can extend. A subsection then explains how JDBC works and how database and servlet technology are commonly integrated. The examples use the sample Northwind database that comes with Microsoft's Access relational database management system. However, the examples are sufficiently modular so that they could be adapted straightforwardly to other databases. The coverage of JDBC emphasizes the core features such as *connection*, *query*, and *result set*. The sample application then illustrates the integration of servlet and database technology. In the sample application, one servlet presents a list of products in HTML. After the user selects a product, a second servlet generates an HTML list of customers who purchased the product. The data for both lists resides in a database. The application again is designed to be readily adaptable.

Chapter Structure

The basic chapter organization is as follows:

Contents
Overview
Section
Section Exercises
Section
Section Exercises
. . .
Java Postscript
Common Errors and Safe Practices
Programming Exercises

Chapters 3 through 10 have 13 sample applications. A sample application section contains a statement of a problem, sample input and output, a solution to the problem, and a Java implementation of a solution to the problem. The section concludes with an extended discussion of the Java implementation and program development. The sample applications include the following:

- Random number generation through a wrapper class (Section 3.4)
- Basic input and output classes (Section 5.4)
- A graphical utility for file copying (Section 5.5)
- Polymorphic input and output operations (Section 6.3)
- Graphical directory assistance (Section 7.4)
- A graphical table editor (Section 7.6)
- A serializable time card (Section 8.3)
- A multithreaded simulation of the dining philosophers problem (Section 8.5)
- A socketed applet with a membership form (Section 9.5)
- Matrix algebra operations using RMI (Section 9.7)
- Database webification using servlets (Section 10.5)

The *Java Postscript* sections discuss highly specialized parts of the language and give additional technical details about language features.

The *Common Errors and Safe Practices* sections highlight those aspects of the language that are easily misunderstood.

The book contains more than 140 programming exercises drawn from a wide variety of applications. The programming exercises differ in difficulty from the relatively straightforward to the highly challenging.

About this Book

This book includes:

- Examples and exercises that cover a wide range of applications.
- Motivating real-world applications.
- A broad variety of programming exercises. The book contains over 140 programming exercises.
- End-of-chapter lists of common programming errors and safe practices.
- Exercises at the ends of sections so that readers can check their mastery of the sections. The book contains over 600 such exercises. Answers to the odd-numbered section exercises are given in the back of the book, and answers to the even-numbered section exercises are provided on the instructor CD-ROM.
- Figures to facilitate the learning process.

Examples

The book contains 270 numbered examples, which clarify particular facets of Java. Most numbered examples are full programs or class definitions. A box   marks the beginning and end of each example.

Exercises

The book contains over 600 section review exercises, the answers to which are short answers, code segments, and, in a few cases, entire programs. These exercises are suitable as homework problems or as self-tests. The answers to the odd-numbered exercises are given in the back of the book. An accompanying Web site includes additional materials for self-study. My experience teaching Java has convinced me of the importance of these exercises.

Student and Instructor Support Materials

The book includes a CD-ROM with the JBuilder Integrated Development Environment for Java and the source code for all of the sample applications and major examples. The Java source code is also available at

```
http://condor.depaul.edu/~mkalin
```

The Instructor CD-ROM and Web Site provide full instructional support for courses using the text. The Instructor CD-ROM includes

- Solutions to even-numbered Section Exercises.
- Source code for the sample applications and main programs.
- Test suites consisting of multiple-choice questions for each chapter. There are over 160 multiple choice questions.
- A sample syllabus.

The Web site's instructional support includes true/false review questions for each chapter and chapter outlines as Power Point slides. There are over 100 such questions. Source code for all of the sample applications and main programs also is available at the Web site.

Acknowledgments

I wish to thank the following reviewers for their generous help: Sergio Antoy, Portland State University; Chaya Gurwitz, CUNY Brooklyn College; Rex Jaeschke, independent consultant; and Celia Schahczenski, Montana Tech of the University of Montana.

I am indebted to the School of Computer Science, Telecommunications, and Information Systems at DePaul University and its dean, Helmut Epp, for encouraging the development of this book.

Once again I am grateful to Patricia Johnsonbaugh for her patient and insightful copy editing.

I received consistent support from the people at Prentice Hall. Special thanks go to Petra Recter, Senior Acquisitions Editor; Jennie Burger, Senior Marketing Manager; Sarah Burrows, Assistant Editor; and Irwin Zucker, Production Editor.

M.K.

Object-Oriented Programming

Chapter Outline

This chapter introduces the basic concepts, advantages, and constructs associated with object-oriented programming and design. Although some examples use Java, the emphasis is on object-oriented programming in general. Subsequent chapters explain the details of object-oriented programming in Java.

Some of the concepts introduced in this chapter, such as *polymorphism* and *interface*, are among the most technical and challenging in object-oriented programming. Later chapters and sections provide detailed explanations and numerous examples for these and the other object-oriented concepts. This chapter provides only the *first* clarification of the material at the core of object-oriented programming and design.

1.1   Object-Oriented and Procedural Programming

Programs consist of **modules**, which are parts that can be designed, coded, and tested separately and then assembled to form an entire program. In a **procedural language** such as C or Pascal, the modules are procedures. A procedure is a sequence of statements. For example, the pseudocode procedure

```
PROC PRINT_MAX( INT num1, INT num2 )
   INT max;
   IF ( num1 > num2 )
     max = num1;
   ELSE
     max = num2;
   PRINT max;
END_PROC
```

consists of an IF-ELSE statement that tests whether num1 or num2 is the larger integer value, which then is assigned to max, a local variable in the PRINT MAX procedure. A PRINT statement then prints max's value. Because the procedures of traditional languages such as C and Pascal are sequences of imperative statements such as assignment statements, tests, loops, and subprocedure invocations, procedural languages are sometimes called **imperative languages**. In a language such as C, all procedures are **functions**, which map arguments to a return value. The C function

```
int find_max( int num1, int num2 ) {
   if ( num1 > num2 )
     return num1;
   else
     return num2;
}
```

illustrates this. The function find_max takes two integer arguments, named num1 and num2, and returns an integer value. An if-else statement tests for the greater value of the two, which is `returned`. In object-oriented languages such as Java, functions such as `find_max` are called **methods**.

Top-Down Design and Procedural Programming

Procedural programming is associated with a design technique known as **top-down design** in which a *problem* is associated with a *procedure*. For example, consider the problem of producing a schedule for a manufacturing task such as building an automobile. This problem might be labeled *MainProblem*. If we were to code a solution to *MainProblem* in the procedural language C, we would assign *MainProblem* to the C procedure named `main`. Because *MainProblem* is too complicated to solve straightforwardly in `main`, we *decompose* the problem into subproblems such as

- Building the chassis.
- Building the engine.
- Building the drivetrain.
- Assembling the already built components.
- Inspecting the components and their assembly.

We assign each *subproblem* to a *subprocedure*, which is a function that `main` invokes. For example, `main` might invoke the functions `buildChassis`, `buildEngine`, and so on. Just as the problem *MainProblem* decomposes into various subproblems, so the procedure `main` decomposes into various subprocedures to handle the subproblems. The subprograms may be further decomposed, which then is mirrored by a decomposition of the subprocedures (see Figure 1.1.1). This process of **top-down, functional decomposition** continues until a subproblem is straightforward enough that the corresponding subprocedure can solve it. If a procedural program is written in a highly modular style, its primitive procedures (functions) tend to be very simple and short, consisting even of a single statement (for example, the `return` of some value).

Problems with Top-Down Design

Top-down design has the appeal of being intuitive and orderly. Many difficult problems continue to be solved using this design technique. Yet the technique has drawbacks, especially with respect to what is known euphemistically as **software maintenance**, which deals with the testing, debugging, and upgrading of software systems.

Experienced programmers know that the most difficult task is not writing a program in the first place but rather *changing* it afterwards because the program is flawed ("infected by bugs"), the program's requirements change, the program needs to execute more efficiently, and so on. Suppose that we need to change significantly the program that solves *MainProblem*. The change is so significant that we need to change `main`. In particular, suppose that `main` must now pass an additional argument to *each* of the subprocedures that it invokes, and that each of these must pass this additional argument to their subprocedures, and so on until the change has rippled throughout the entire hierarchy sketched in Figure 1.1.1. This phenomenon is known as **cascading changes**: a change in a procedure such as main cascades or ripples down to its subprocedures and to their subprocedures and so on until the change impacts much if not all of the decomposition hierarchy. This is the familiar phenomenon in which a *local* change (e.g., a change to main) has wide-ranging and even global side-effects (e.g., a change to all subprocedures invoked directly or indirectly from main).

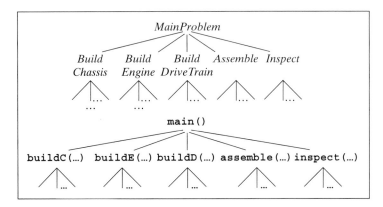

FIGURE 1.1.1   Problem and procedure decomposition.

Object-oriented programming is an alternative to procedural programming. The design technique associated with object-oriented programming is **object-oriented design**. Object-oriented programming and object-oriented design are meant to address major problems associated with procedural programming and top-down design, problems such as cascading changes. In an object-oriented program, the central modules are **classes** rather than procedures.

Classes and Objects

The term *class* has various but related meanings in object-oriented design and programming. In object-oriented design, a **class** is a collection of **objects**. For example, the class *Human* is a collection of objects, that is, human beings such as you, me, and Mary Leakey. In object-oriented programming languages, a class is a *data type* and objects are instances of such a type. A comparison with a primitive data type such as integer may be useful. The declaration

```
int num;
```

specifies that variable num is of primitive type int rather than, for instance, float or boolean, all of which are Java primitive types. Variable num is thus suited to store an *integer* rather than a floating-point or a boolean value. The syntactically similar declaration

```
String greeting;
```

specifies that variable `greeting` is of *class* type `String`. The variables `num` and `greeting` thus differ fundamentally in their data types: `num` is of primitive type `int`, whereas `greeting` is of nonprimitive or class type `String`. In Java, a variable of a class type is called an **object reference** because the variable can refer to an **object**, which in this context is *storage of a class rather than a primitive type*. In the revised declaration

```
String greeting = "hello, world!";
```

the object reference `greeting` now refers to an object, in this case the `String` object that represents the greeting *hello, world!*. Figure 1.1.2 illustrates.

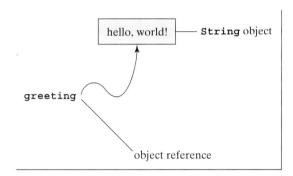

FIGURE 1.1.2   A `String` object reference `greeting` and a `String` object.

In a typical object-oriented program, the programmer uses classes that the programming language provides in its standard libraries (e.g., the `String` class) and builds other classes suited to the application. For example, a program to automate human resource management might have a programmer-defined class named `Emp` to represent an employee, a programmer-defined class `Dept` to represent the department in which the employee works, and so on.

When a class is used as a collection of objects in the design sense, the class name will be italicized. For example, the class *Human* includes you, me, and Mary Leakey. When a class is used as a data type, the class name will appear in a monospace font. For instance, a Java program might use the library class `String` and the programmer-defined class `Human`.

Fields and Methods

Objects in a class share **properties**, **features**, or **attributes**. Humans, for instance, share the properties of being *featherless*, *bipedal*, and *risible*. At the programming level, **fields**—that is, variables contained or **encapsulated** in a class—are used to represent such properties or features. For example, class `Human` might have an `integer` field `feetCount` with its value set to 2 to represent that humans are bipedal and a `String` field `name` to represent the human's name.

Objects need to be **constructed** or created. Object-oriented languages have special functions[†] known as **constructors** for this purpose. In Java, for example, the expression

```
new Human()
```

would construct a Human object. The constructor in this case is Human() and new is an operator that allocates the storage for the appropriate object, in this case a Human object.

A class typically has actions or processes that are distinctive to it. For instance, humans *eat*, *laugh*, *work*, *tango*, and so on. For convenience, we call such actions or processes *operations*. The operations associated with classes are represented by procedures encapsulated within the class. **Methods** are the functions that represent the operations appropriate to a particular class. For example, if the class Human is to model humans, the class needs a method that represents how humans tango; such a method, named tango, might produce a video sequence that shows two humans doing the tango. In any case, classes must combine the appropriate fields and methods to model entities such as humans, automobiles, neutron stars, and Nordic ski teams. Fields and methods are two types of class **members**.

Instance versus Class Members

Class members, whether fields or methods, are of two types: members associated with the class as a whole and members associated with particular instances of the class. Recall that, in object-oriented programming, an **object** is an instance of a class type. In Figure 1.1.2, for example, the object to which the variable greetings refers is an instance of the String class or, in short, a String object.

> ■ **Example 1.1.1.**   An Employee class might have a name field that stores, for example, a string that represents a particular Employee's name. Each Emp object would require its own name field. For example, Emp objects cher and elvis would require distinct name fields in which to store their names (see Figure 1.1.3). A member variable such as name—that is, a variable associated with a particular object—is an **instance variable** because each object or class instance has its own copy of the variable.
>
> An Employee class also might have an integer count field that stores the current count of Emp objects. The count variable would be associated with the Emp class as a whole rather than with any particular Emp object. A variable such as count is known generally as a **class variable** because it is associated directly with the class itself, not with particular class instances.

[†]In object-oriented languages such as C++, the term *method* is typically a synonym for *function* and, therefore, constructors are simply methods used to construct objects. In Java, the distinction between *constructor* and *method* is more formal. For example, Java has a standard class Constructor to represent constructors and a distinct class Method to represent methods. In Java, it is thus preferable to describe constructors and methods as two types of functions.

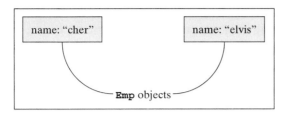

FIGURE 1.1.3   Two Emp objects, each with its own name field.

A similar distinction holds for methods, which can be associated with either the class as a whole (*class methods*) or particular instances (*instance methods*). Object-oriented languages require a syntactic convention to distinguish *instance* members from *class* members. In Java, a member marked as static is associated with the class itself rather than its instances; hence, a static member is a *class* rather than an *instance* member. Any member *not* marked as static is an *instance* member, that is, a member associated with a particular object. Figure 1.1.4 shows

```
class Emp {
   String name;       //*** "instance" member
   static int count;  //*** "class" member
   //...other members
}
```

FIGURE 1.1.4   Java code illustrating static and nonstatic members.

the Java code for an Emp class that has a static member named count and a nonstatic member called name.   ■

A class's constructors are always *instance* members, that is, nonstatic members. In general, classes tend to have more instance (nonstatic) than class (static) members, although there are classes that have only static members. A central decision in class design is whether a particular member should be an instance member or a class member.

Class Design

Object-oriented design, as the name suggests, is the design counterpart of object-oriented programming. Such design is object-oriented in that it focuses on classes as collections of objects. Classes are designed so that they model the entities with which a program deals. Consider again the task of building a scheduling system for manufacturing automobiles. We first need to design classes such as *Automobile*, *Engine*, *Worker*, and *PaintMachine* to represent entities such as automobiles, their engines, and the workers and machines involved in the manufacturing process. The classes are critical because they will serve as the main programming modules. Each class must model the properties and operations of the entities that the class is to represent. Class design is as challenging and creative as the object-oriented programming that depends upon it.

Automated solutions to complex problems typically require complex applications, regardless of the programming language used. Object-oriented programming cannot eliminate the complexity of applications that address large and complicated problems, but the object-oriented approach does offer powerful constructs to *distribute* the complexity so that the application's maintenance avoids the pitfalls so common to large procedural applications. In object-oriented programming, the class is central to the distribution and management of complexity.

Class and Object Relationships

Various relationships can hold among classes and between a class and the objects that belong to it. For instance, there is a *has a* (that is, *has a property*) relationship between a *ComputerSystem* and a *CPU*: a *ComputerSystem has a CPU*. By contrast, there is an *is a* (that is, *is a subclass of*) relationship between a *PersonalComputer* and a *Computer*: a *PersonalComputer is a Computer*. Specifying class relationships is also a central feature of object-oriented design. Between an object and a class there is an *instance of* or *belongs to* relationship: *A Dell PC is an instance of a PersonalComputer*.

Section 1.6 introduces UML (**U**nified **M**odeling **L**anguage), a graphical language for modeling object-oriented software systems. For more on object-oriented design, see J. Rumbaugh, et al., *Object-Oriented Modeling and Design*, (Englewood Cliffs, N.J.: Prentice Hall, 1991), G. Booch, *Object Oriented Analysis and Design With Applications*, 2nd ed., (Reading, Mass.: Addison-Wesley, 1994), and Grady Booch, et. al., *The Unified Modeling Language User Guide*, (Reading, Mass.: Addison-Wesley, 1999).

EXERCISES

1. What are program modules?
2. In a procedural language, what is the basic program module?
3. In an object-oriented language, what is the basic program module?
4. In the context of top-down functional decomposition, what are cascading changes?
5. In the context of top-down functional decomposition, what is a primitive subproblem?
6. What does software maintenance deal with?
7. In object-oriented design, what are classes meant to represent?
8. What is the relationship between a class and an object?
9. In a class such as *Human*, how are human properties such as age and gender typically represented?
10. In a class such as *Human*, how are human operations such as eating and working represented?
11. Design a class *Student* with several properties and operations.
12. Give an example of a *has a* relationship between two classes.

13. Give an example of an *is a* relationship between two classes.
14. What is a constructor?
15. Contrast a constructor and a method.
16. Contrast a class and an instance method.

1.2   Classes and Abstract Data Types

A class is a powerful object-oriented programming construct that directly supports the design, implementation, and use of an abstract data type. This section begins with an overview of the class as a programming construct and then explains what an abstract data type is and how a class supports it. The programmer derives advantages from using abstract rather than primitive data types.

Information Hiding

Consider the challenge that faces modern software products such as browsers, word processors, databases, spreadsheets, and data communications packages. These products undergo rapid development cycles in which a new and perhaps significantly different version replaces an older version. How can users survive such changes? For one thing, the products try to maintain a consistent **interface**. Consider a word processor. From one version to the next, the word processor still supports commands that allow the user to *Open* a new document, *Save* a document, *Print* a document, *Copy* a document, *Format* a document in some special way, perform a *SpellCheck* on the document, and the like. The word processor's *interface* is the functionality made available to the user through commands such as the ones just listed. We say that the interface is **public** to underscore that it is visible or accessible to the user. What is typically *not* public in a modern software product is the underlying **implementation**. An experienced programmer might be able to *guess* how the word processor is implemented, but the vendor deliberately hides these details from the user. For one thing, the product would be too hard to use if the user had to know thousands of technical details. For another, the vendor may be in the process of fixing bugs and would like to leave them hidden until the fix is implemented as a patch or even a new version. We say that the implementation is **private** to underscore that it is *not* visible or accessible to the user. The implementation is *hidden* from the user, whereas the interface is *exposed* to the user. A goal of modern software design is thus to keep a product's public interface constant so that users remain fluent in the product even as its *private* implementation improves or otherwise changes.

In an object-oriented language, a class is a *module that supports information hiding*. In a Java class, we can use reserved words such as `public` and `private` to control access to the class's properties and operations. We can use the reserved word `public` to expose the class's interface and the reserved word `private` to hide its implementation. Object-oriented languages thus have, in the class, a programming construct well suited to building modern software systems.

Encapsulation

In procedural programming, the central modules are procedures, and data are manipulated by procedures. A standard mechanism for this style of data manipulation is passing arguments to and returning a value from a function. In object-oriented programming, the central modules are classes. Data and the procedures to manipulate the data can be **encapsulated** or contained within a class. In different words, the encapsulated data and procedures are the class's members. Imagine a *String* class that can be used to create strings, concatenate them, change the characters they contain, check whether a given character occurs in a *String*, and so on. The *String* class would have fields (variables) to represent the characters in a *String* and, perhaps, such other information as a *String*'s length. Such variables are encapsulated within the class in the sense that every *String* object has access to the variables specified in the *String* class. A *String* class also would have constructors to create *String*s and methods to manipulate *String*s. For example, the *String* class presumably would have a method to search a *String* for a specified character, a method to return the *String*'s length, and so on. Functions, like fields, also are encapsulated within the class. In Java, *all* procedures are encapsulated in classes as either constructors or methods.

A class's encapsulated fields are often hidden so that they provide behind-the-scenes support for constructors and methods that are accessible outside the class. For example, a *String* class might have a public *length* method that gives the *String*'s length. The *String* class might support this public method with a private integer field *len* that records the *String*'s length.

Abstract Data Types

The concepts of information hiding and encapsulation relate closely to that of an abstract data type. Suppose that our goal is to build a *WordProcessor* class that has the functionality of a modern word processor. To make the class easy to use, we distinguish sharply between a public interface consisting of high-level operations such as *Save* and *Print* and a private implementation consisting of low-level details in support of the public interface. In this case, our class is an **abstract data type**. A data type is *abstract* if it exposes in its public interface only high-level operations and hides all low-level implementation details. Java supports classes, which enable information hiding; and information hiding—specifically, the hiding of low-level implementation details—is the key to creating abstract data types. Further, an obvious way to deliver the required functionality in an abstract data type is to encapsulate the appropriate functions as constructors and methods.

■ **Example 1.2.1.** Suppose that we define a *Stack* class whose public interface consists of methods to

- Check whether a *Stack* is empty.
- Check whether a *Stack* is full.

- Insert an object into a *Stack* if the *Stack* is not full. Such an operation is known as a *push*.
- Remove the most recently inserted object from a *Stack* if the *Stack* is not empty. Such an operation is known as a *pop*.
- Inspect the most recently inserted object, if any, but without removing it. Such an object occupies the *top* of a *Stack*.

A *Stack* is called a **LIFO** (**L**ast **I**n, **F**irst **O**ut) **list** because insertions and deletions occur at the same end, known as the *top*. Figure 1.2.1 shows a *Stack* of letters in three states. In the left subfigure, the *Stack* is empty. The middle subfigure shows the *Stack* after the operations *push(A)* and *push(B)* have occurred. Because *B* was inserted last, it is at the top. The right subfigure shows the *Stack* after a *pop* operation, which removes *B*. After *B* has been removed, *A* is at the top.

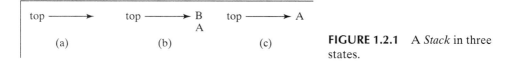

(a)   (b)   (c)   **FIGURE 1.2.1**   A *Stack* in three states.

The *Stack* operations are high-level in that they require no knowledge of the *Stack*'s underlying implementation. Accordingly, the *Stack* as described is an abstract data type. ∎

Abstract data types spare the programmer the job of learning implementation details. The term *abstract* underscores precisely this point: a data type is abstract if it allows the user to abstract from—that is, to ignore—its low-level, implementation details. Further, abstract data types can be studied formally to reveal important properties about them. For example, the *Stack* described in our example cannot overflow or underflow because pushes occur only if a *Stack* is not full, and pops occur only if a *Stack* is not empty. At least one successful push therefore precedes the first successful pop. The number of elements in a *Stack* equals the total number of pushes minus the total number of pops. If the total number of pushes always exceeds the total number of pops, then a *Stack* is empty only before the first *push* but never thereafter.

The use of abstract data types promotes program reliability and robustness. Consider character strings. In a language such as C, a string is represented as an array of the primitive type `char` terminated with a special nonprinting character. The *programmer* must attend to low-level details such as the array's size and the inclusion of the terminating character in the array. By contrast, if the programmer works with a *String* as an abstract data type, the programmer can ignore the implementation details and attend instead to high-level string processing. The Java `String` class is, in effect, an implementation of a string as an abstract data type. The class has constructors and methods to create strings, copy them, compare them, test them for the occurrence of a specified character, extract substrings from a string, and so on. From the programmer's viewpoint, a `String` may be indefinitely long; and the programmer can process `String`s without knowing how the `String`'s characters are stored internally. The `String` class *hides* the implementation details from the programmer, thereby freeing the programmer to focus on the task at hand—string processing.

Abstract data types can be implemented in procedural languages such as C and Pascal, but these languages provide little direct support for abstract data types. By contrast, the class construct of object-oriented languages provides direct support for abstract data types through information hiding and encapsulation. An object-oriented language such as Java is the tool of choice for building abstract data types. Abstract data types, in turn, are the data types of choice in modern programming.

EXERCISES

1. What is a class interface?
2. What is a class implementation?
3. Explain why a class's interface is said to be *public*.
4. Explain why a class's implementation is said to be *private*.
5. How does a class support information hiding?
6. Does a class encapsulate both its fields and its methods?
7. Could a field be either public or private?
8. Could a method be either public or private?
9. What advantages result from keeping a class's implementation details private?
10. What is an abstract data type?
11. Clarify what the term *abstract* means in the phrase *abstract data type*.
12. Suppose that we implement a *Stack* class so that pushes cannot occur on a full *Stack* and pops cannot occur on an empty *Stack*. Show that, at any time, the total number of elements on the *Stack* equals the total number of pushes minus the total number of pops.
13. What is the advantage to the programmer of using an abstract data type such as *Integer* rather than a primitive data type such as `int`?

The Client/Server Model and Message Passing

Well-designed programs have similarities in style regardless of whether the programs are based upon a procedural, an object-oriented, or some other model. For example, such programs tend be modular and to have a flow of control that is clear. Nonetheless, well-designed object-oriented programs have distinctive stylistic features that incorporate key object-oriented constructs such as information hiding and encapsulation. This section sketches some stylistic features of object-oriented programs.

The Client/Server Model

Object-oriented programming is based on a **client/server model** of computing. This model explains the emphasis placed on information hiding in object-oriented programming. For example, the Java language has a `String` class whose public interface includes constructors and methods to create and copy `String`s, concatenate them, search them for characters, and so on. The `String` class is a provider of services for string processing. The `String` class is therefore a **server** that provides string-processing services to applications. An application that uses the `String` class is a **client** that requests services from a `String` object or the `String` class by invoking methods. In this light, method invocation appears as a type of **message passing**. For example, in the code segment

```
String s1 = "The Day the Music Died";
int n = s1.length();
```

s1 refers to a `String` object to which a message is sent requesting its length, which is assigned to the `int` variable n. The `String`'s length is the number of characters in *The Day the Music Died*. The code segment occurs in an application that acts as a *client* of the `String` object, which provides string-processing services.

A good server provides services with a minimum of effort on the client's part. In particular, the client should *not* be required to know *how* the server provides the services. The server's implementation details should be hidden from the client. The client should need to know *only* the server's interface, which typically consists of methods that the client can invoke. Such methods send messages to the server, which are requests for services. The server may send data back to the client, perform actions that the client requests, and so on. Good servers practice information hiding so that clients find the servers easy to use. For example, to get a `String`'s length, a client needs to know only the method `length`. The client does not need to know whether a `String` object stores the length in an encapsulated variable, whose value is returned; whether the `length` method, on each invocation, counts the number of cells in an array until encountering a terminating character; or whether the `length` method uses some other technique to determine the length.

Information hiding also promotes server robustness. For example, suppose that a `String`'s interface consists of well-designed and thoroughly tested methods, with the implementation details hidden. In particular, assume that we test the public `String` methods $m_1, m_2, \ldots, m_n$ until we are confident that no sequence of invocations can "break" a `String` server, that is, cause the `String` server to behave in an inappropriate way. Because a client has access only to these exposed methods and not to the `String`'s underlying implementation, we can be confident that client manipulation of `String` objects cannot "break" such objects. The robustness of a `String` server obviously contributes to the overall robustness of an application that uses such servers.

Message Passing and Method Invocation

A program designed and implemented under the object-oriented model tends to have a distinct coding style. In an object-oriented program, classes and objects behave as servers, and modules that use classes and objects behave as clients. Clients request services in a distinctive manner, which we explore in this subsection.

■ **Example 1.3.1.**   Figure 1.3.1 contains a Java code segment that illustrates method invocation. The code segment contains comments or **documentation**, which is introduced with the double slash //.[†]

```
String s1 = "  Dawn Upshaw, soprano supreme   ";
String s2 = "DawnUpshaw,sopranosupreme";
int len1 = s1.length();            // length() invoked on s1
s1 = s1.toLowerCase();             // "  dawn upshaw, soprano supreme   "
s1 = s1.trim();                    // "dawn upshaw, soprano supreme"
s2 = s2.toUpperCase();             // "DAWNUPSHAW, SOPRANOSUPREME"
if ( s1.equalsIgnoreCase( s2 ) )   // false
  //...
if ( s2.endsWith( "SUPREME" ) )    // true
  //...
```

FIGURE 1.3.1   A Java code segment to illustrate method invocation.

The code segment, which has `String` objects with references `s1` and `s2`, manipulates the `Strings` through assignments and method invocations such as

```
s1 = s1.toLowerCase();
```

The expression

```
s1.toLowerCase()
```

returns a lowercase version of the `String` to which `s1` refers. The assignment statement then makes `s1` refer to the lowercase `String`. The original uppercase `String` is now called **garbage** or **inaccessible storage** because there are no references to this object. Figure 1.3.2 illustrates this.

Some `String` methods, such as `toLowerCase` and `trim`, take no arguments. This is common in object-oriented languages. In general, the fewer the arguments, the easier to use is the method. Other methods, such as `equalsIgnoreCase`, do take arguments. The method names are intuitive, which again makes the `String` class an attractive server to client applications. ■

[†]In Java the double slash // introduces a comment that continues to the end of the line. The slash-star /* introduces a comment that continues until the matching star-slash */.

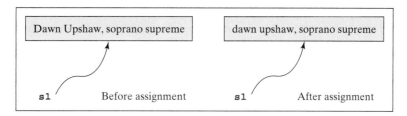

FIGURE 1.3.2   The result of the assignment `s1` `=` `s1.toLowerCase();`.

Because a well-designed class exposes only what a client absolutely needs to request services, such a class's interface usually consists exclusively of constructors and high-level methods. A class's fields typically constitute the class's low-level support of these high-level methods. Client code therefore tends to be correspondingly high-level, as the code segment in Figure 1.3.1 illustrates. The message-passing style also underscores that classes and objects behave as servers whose interfaces are, in effect, a publication of the services provided. If services are hard and cumbersome to request, a class and its objects cannot expect many clients. So a well-designed class is precisely one that delivers appropriate services in a clear, straightforward manner.

EXERCISES

1. Briefly describe how the client/server model relates to object-oriented programming.
2. If a class or an object is a server, what acts as the client?
3. In an object-oriented program, why do clients typically request services from a class by invoking its methods rather than by accessing its data members?
4. How does a client request service from a class or an object?
5. Explain the relationship between message passing and method invocation.
6. How does information hiding contribute to a server robustness?
7. Explain why a well-designed class's interface typically exposes the class's services as *high-level* methods.
8. Does the message-passing style of object-oriented programming eliminate the need for documentation in object-oriented programs?

1.4   Inheritance and Polymorphism

Classes occur in **inheritance hierarchies**, which consist of parent/child relationships among classes. Inheritance is a convenient and efficient way to *specialize* a parent class by creating a child class. For example, given the class *Window*, we could specialize it through inheritance by deriving a child *MenuWin* class. Inheritance also allows the designer to combine features of classes in a common parent. For example, given the classes *Car*, *Motorcycle*, and *Truck*, we could combine their shared features in a common parent class called *Vehicle*.

Polymorphism is a powerful feature of object-oriented programming that exploits the potential of inheritance hierarchies. We cover the details of polymorphism after further clarifying inheritance.

Inheritance

Inheritance supports a form of **code reuse**, which we explain through an example. Suppose that we build a *Win* class to represent windows that appear on a computer's screen. The *Win* class has fields to represent a window's width and height, its x and y screen coordinates, its background and foreground colors, its border width, its style (e.g., framed), and so forth. We encapsulate the appropriate constructors and methods to create and destroy windows, move them, resize and reshape them, change their properties (e.g., background color), and so on. Once the *Win* class is built, we decide to refine or specialize the class by building a *MenuWin* subclass that inherits the *Win* fields and methods but then adds some of its own. For example, the *MenuWin* subclass has fields and methods to support lists of menu items, user choices of menu items, and so on. Other subclasses are possible. Figure 1.4.1 illustrates a possible inheritance hierarchy with *Win* as the parent class. The arrows point from the children to the parent.

FIGURE 1.4.1   An inheritance hierarchy.

Different object-oriented languages support different types of inheritance. All such languages support at least **single inheritance** in which a child class has at most one parent. Under a single-inheritance system, for example, the child class *SportsCar* might have *Car* as its single parent class. Some languages support **multiple inheritance** in which a child class may have multiple parents. Under a multiple-inheritance system, the child class *SportsCar* might have *Car* and *Toy* as parent classes. Whether the inheritance is single or multiple, a child class can inherit fields and methods from each parent. Java supports only *single* inheritance for classes so that every Java class, except `Object`, has exactly one parent class. `Object` is at the top of Java inheritance hierarchy and, therefore, has no parent. Figure 1.4.2 shows inheritance in Java. In this figure, the Java `MenuWin` class `extends`—that is, is a subclass of—the `Win` class, which automatically `extends` the `Object` class because no other superclass is specified. Chapter 6 examines Java inheritance in detail.

```
class Win {                    // superclass is Object by default
  //...members
}
class MenuWin extends Win {    // MenuWin is a subclass of Win
  //...members
}
```

FIGURE 1.4.2   The basic syntax of Java inheritance.

How to design and exploit inheritance hierarchies are central issues in object-oriented design and programming. Inheritance is also a precondition for polymorphism, which we examine in the next subsection.

Polymorphism

The term *polymorphism* is derived from Greek and means *having many forms*. In an object-oriented language, there can be *many methods with the same signature*. A method's **signature** consists of its name and argument types.[†] For example, in the code segment

```
    void print( String s ) { /*...*/ }
    void print( float f ) { /*...*/ }
```

the two methods named `print` have distinct signatures because one expects a `String` argument and the other expects a `float` argument.

For the `Win` class depicted in Figure 1.4.1, an appropriate method is `show`, which displays the `Win` object on the screen. Yet different types of windows display themselves differently. For example, a `MenuWin` presumably displays a list of choices when shown, whereas a `MessageWin` may show only a single string. So there should be various *forms* or versions of the `show` method, presumably a separate one for each class in the `Win` hierarchy. Nonetheless, it is easier on the client (that is, the user of the `Win` hierarchy) to send a *single* show message to any type of `Win`. For example, regardless of whether w refers to a `MenuWin` or a `MessageWin`, we should be able to execute

```
    w.show(); // show yourself
```

If w refers to a `MenuWin`, then this class's `show` method is invoked. If w refers to a `MessageWin`, then this class's `show` method is invoked. The system, not the client, should determine the type to which w refers and, from the type, determine which version of `show` to invoke. In this example, `show` is thus a **polymorphic method.**

[†]A signature also includes modifiers such as `public` and a list of *exceptions* or unexpected conditions that may arise when the body of a constructor or method executes. For now, these parts of the signature can be ignored.

In general, polymorphic methods belong to classes in an inheritance hierarchy. It is common for each class in the hierarchy to provide its own appropriate version of a polymorphic method. In the context of polymorphism, a child class is said to **override** a parent's method of the same signature if the child class provides its own definition of this method. For example, if MenuWin provides its own definition of the show method, then MenuWin overrides the show method available in its parent class Win.

Polymorphism and Recursion

Mastering polymorphism is central to becoming adept at object-oriented programming. Polymorphism has diverse uses. In this subsection, we single out one use to underscore how object-oriented languages offer alternatives to their procedural counterparts in solving certain types of problems.

■ **Example 1.4.1.** Consider the problem of printing each element in a list. Suppose that the list L is

$$(n_1, (n_2, n_3, n_4), n_5)$$

L has three elements: the first element is the node n_1, the second element is the sublist (n_2, n_3, n_4) consisting of three nodes, and the third element is the node n_5. In a procedural language such as C, a function to print lists like L—that is, lists that may contain nested sublists to an arbitrary level—would likely be recursive. Figure 1.4.3 shows what the C function might look like, with Element as a structure to represent list elements. (Even those not familiar with C syntax will see how complex the function's logic is!) An Element structure contains information about whether a structure variable represents a simple node or a nested sublist. For example, the structure member isNode is set to 1 (*true*), if the element is a simple node rather than a sublist, and to 0 (*false*), if the element is a sublist. If an Element is a sublist, the member firstElement points to the first Element in the nested sublist. Although short, the C function in Figure 1.4.3 has complex logic. Recursive functions are notoriously hard to write precisely because they typically require difficult logic.

Now consider the class hierarchy depicted in Figure 1.4.4, which has *Item* as a parent class and *Node* and *List* as two of its child classes. A list's elements may be items that belong to any class in the *Item* hierarchy; in particular, a list may contain any mix of simple *Node*s and sub*List*s nested to arbitrary levels. Assume that the classes *Item*, *List*, and *Node* all have a polymorphic *print* method, which behaves appropriately for each class. For example, the *print* method for a *Node* simply prints the node's contents, whereas the *print* method for a *List* iterates through the list and invokes each element's own *print* method, thereby causing all the *List*'s elements to be printed, including elements that happen to be sub*List*s. Figure 1.4.5 shows how a *List*'s polymorphic *print* method might be coded in Java. We assume that the List class has methods hasMoreElements and next-

```
void printList( Element* e ) {
   if ( e == NULL )  /* an Element? */
      return;           /* base case 1: if not, return */
   else if ( e->isNode )  /* node or sublist? */
      printNode( e ); /* base case 2: if node, just print */
   else { /* else recursively invoke printList */
      Element* temp = e->firstElement;
      while ( temp != NULL ) {
         printList( temp ); /** recurse **/
         temp = temp->nextElement;
      }
   }
}
```

FIGURE 1.4.3   Using recursion to handle nested sublists in C.

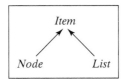

FIGURE 1.4.4   Classes *Item*, *Node*, and *List* in a hierarchy.

```
class List extends Item { //*** List is a subclass of Item
   // print method for List class: public means "exposed"
   public void print() {
      Item next;  // each element is in Item hierarchy
      while ( hasMoreElements() ) {
         next = nextElement(); // get next element, Node or subList
         next.print();         // polymorphic print
      }
   // fields and other methods such as hasMoreElements()
} //*** end of List class
```

FIGURE 1.4.5   The polymorphic `print` method for the `List` class.

Element, which can be used to iterate through list's elements, whether these be simple nodes or nested sublists. Method `hasMoreElements` returns a `boolean` value: `true`, if there are still more elements in the list to process, and `false`, if the iteration has already processed each element. Method `nextElement` returns the list's next element as an `Item` because both a `Node` and a nested `subList` are subtypes of `Item`. When the polymorphic `print` method is invoked in the statement

```
next.print();
```

the system first determines `next`'s actual type, that is, whether `next` refers to a `Node` or a `List`. Once the system determines this type, the system then invokes the appropriate `print` method, in this case either the `print` defined in `Node` or the one defined in `List`. Whenever `next` refers to a nested subList, the effect is the same as recursion in that the `List` method `print` is invoked from within its own body. Yet the syntax remains straightforward rather than complex because the recursion is implicit rather than explicit. The main point is that the system, not the programmer, determines which `print` method to invoke. Contrast this approach with the recursive C function in Figure 1.4.3. In that case, the programmer must determine whether the current list element is a node or a nested sublist. In the polymorphic version, this determination is left to the system, which simplifies the code.   ■

The logic of `List`'s `print` in Figure 1.4.5 is considerably simpler than the recursive logic of `printList` in Figure 1.4.3. The contrast illustrates how polymorphism can be used, in an object-oriented language, to perform tasks that require explicitly recursive or otherwise complex logic in procedural languages. Polymorphism has other uses as well, which Chapter 6 covers in detail. A key challenge of class and hierarchy design is to provide classes in the hierarchy with the appropriate polymorphic methods, that is, with methods that simplify the task of writing client programs.

It should be emphasized again that object-oriented constructs such as polymorphism do not eliminate complexity from programs. Yet object-oriented constructs do allow the programmer to *distribute* a program's complexity in ways not available in traditional, procedural languages. In the case of the `List` class's `print` method, for example, polymorphism allows us to delegate to the system the task of determining whether to invoke `Node`'s version or `List`'s version during each loop iteration. This delegation simplifies the code, which nonetheless performs the same complex task as its recursive C counterpart.

EXERCISES

1. Give an example of single inheritance.
2. Give an example of multiple inheritance.
3. Does Java support multiple inheritance for classes?
4. Briefly describe what polymorphism is and why it is so powerful a programming technique.
5. What does it mean for a child class to *override* a method available in a parent class?
6. Do polymorphic methods have the same signature?
7. What is the relationship between inheritance and polymorphism?
8. Briefly sketch how the system determines which polymorphic method to invoke when control reaches the method invocation.

1.5   **Interfaces and Components**

The distinction between the exposed and the hidden is central to object-oriented programming. A well-designed class typically exposes high-level methods and perhaps some fields. (For example, a `Color` class might have a public field that represents a particular color such as red.) For simplicity, however, we assume a design model in which a class's public part consists of high-level methods and in which the class's private part consists of low-level methods and fields in support of the high-level methods. Recall that a class's interface consists of what it exposes and that its implementation consists of what it hides. Some object-oriented languages, including Java, have `interface` as a reserved word.

■ **Example 1.5.1.**   Suppose that we are designing classes to support input and output operations on files. Presumably the classes would be in a hierarchy to promote code reuse. Assume, further, that we agree that every class in the hierarchy should define this set of methods:

- *Open*. Opens a named file.
- *Close*. Closes a file previously opened.
- *Rewind*. Sets the file's internal position marker to the beginning.

There likely would be other methods as well, for example, a method to rename a file. Some methods might be parameterized. For example, *Open* might take at least two arguments: the name of the file to open, and the mode—input or output—in which to open the named file. Figure 1.5.1 shows the Java code for an interface with these methods.

```
interface StdFile { // StdFile is the interface's name
   public void Open( String name, int mode );
   public void Close();
   public void Rewind();
}                        // end of interface StdFile
```

FIGURE 1.5.1   An interface in Java.

The methods listed in the interface `StdFile` are **declared** but not **defined**. To declare a method is to give its name, return type, and parameter types together with any attributes (for instance, `public`). To define a method is provide its body, that is, the statements that perform whatever operations are appropriate for the method. In Java, method definitions always occur between a left brace { and a matching right brace }. For example, the code segment

```
public void Open(); // declaration
```

declares the method Open, whereas the code segment

```
public void Open() { /*...*/ } // definition
```

defines this method. Within a Java *class*, all methods are *defined.*[†] Within a Java *interface*, all methods are *declared* but not defined.   ■

We can use the Java compiler to enforce the requirement that each of our file classes define the public methods declared in the StdFile interface. The compiler does so if a particular file class implements the StdFile interface.

■ **Example 1.5.2.**   The code segment

```
class Outfile implements StdFile {
  //*** definitions for Open, Close, and Rewind
  //    together with other methods, fields, etc.
}
```

creates a class Outfile that implements the StdFile interface. The class Outfile must define each of the methods declared in the StdFile interface in order for Outfile objects to be constructed. The same holds for any other class, such as Infile or Randomfile, that implements the StdFile interface.   ■

■ **Example 1.5.3.**   The Java Set interface provides methods for high-level operations on a set, that is, an unordered collection of zero or more nonduplicate elements. The Set interface declares 15 methods, which are high level and relatively straightforward to understand. For example, the interface includes the three methods

Method Declaration	*Description*
boolean add(Object obj);	Add an object to a set
void clear();	Remove all elements from a set
boolean isEmpty();	Test whether a set is empty

The method add is used to add an element to a set. If the candidate element is not already in the set, add returns true to signal that the element has been added to the set. If candidate element is already in the set, add returns false to signal that the element cannot be added to the set. The method clear removes all elements from a set. Immediately after clear is invoked on a set, the method isEmpty therefore returns true. If a set has any elements, isEmpty returns false.

Java provides two classes that implement the Set interface, the classes AbstractSet and HashSet. A programmer could create a Set with the statement

```
Set myset = new AbstractSet(); // one implementation
```

[†]To be precise, a *concrete* class defines all of its methods. An *abstract class* need not define all of its methods. An interface defines *no* methods. Chapters 5 and 6 go into the details.

or

```
Set myset = new HashSet(); // another implementation
```

Because the classes `AbtractSet` and `HashSet` share an interface, the programmer could invoke *exactly the same methods* using either implementation. The two implementing classes differ in their efficiency. For example, the `Set` interface declares the method

```
boolean contains( Object obj );
```

which returns `true`, if `obj` is a set element, and `false`, if `obj` is not a set element. An `AbstractSet` requires linear time to determine whether an object is a set element, whereas a `HashSet` requires constant time. For the `contains` operation, therefore, a `HashSet` is more time efficient than an `AbstractSet`. An experienced programmer might surmise how the two implementations differ. The point, however, is that a programmer can operate on either an `AbstractSet` or a `HashSet` implementation by learning their single shared interface—`Set`.

Finally, the syntax

```
// set1 and set2 share the Set interface
Set set1 = new AbstractSet(); // one implementation
Set set2 = new HashSet();     // a different implementation
```

illustrates the dictum that the programmer should code to the *interface*, not to the underlying implementation. To manipulate the `Set`s to which `set1` and `set2` refer, the programmer must learn the `Set` interface rather than the implementation details of an `AbstractSet` or a `HashSet`. ∎

Interfaces, if well built and shared among classes, are a convenience to programmers. Learning a shared interface allows a programmer to request services, using the *same* methods, from a variety of classes. To invoke a method declared in a shared interface, the programmer should not need to know how the method is actually defined in an implementation class. In effect, a method's definition is an implementation detail that could remain hidden. The method's declaration should be sufficient for the programmer to request services by invoking the method. The art of designing high-level, programmer-friendly interfaces is to populate them with methods whose functionality is clear from the declaration together with whatever additional documentation might be appropriate.

Component Technology

A software **component** is a prebuilt part that can be combined with other such parts to build an application. A component is placed in a **container**, a software construct designed to integrate its embedded components. Because a container is itself a component, containers can be embedded in other containers. An application thus can be constructed in an orderly fashion from prebuilt parts able to interact and communicate. A software component is analogous to a hardware component such as a disk drive or printer; and the container is analogous to a computer bus, which integrates components into a single computer system. Calendar components, browser components, e-mail components, database access components, and many other components are already available.

A software component is typically delivered as a binary file and, therefore, its contents are hidden from the programmer who uses it. If the component is well constructed, the user need not know even the language in which the component is written. To be usable, however, a component must expose at least one interface and may expose several interfaces. From the user's viewpoint, then, a component is the *back end* of some front-end interface. A programmer manipulates a component precisely through the methods exposed in its interfaces.

Components play a central role in modern software architecture. They have become a mainstay in the Windows, Unix, and other contemporary systems. Under Windows, for example, even large applications such as *Word* and *Excel* can act as components in some other application. A component extends the object-oriented concept of an object as provider of services exposed in a high-level interface as a collection of methods. In Java, components are called **beans**. Section 10.1 examines beans in detail.

EXERCISES

1. In an interface, are functions declared or defined?
2. What is the difference between a function declaration and a function definition?
3. Does the term `interface` belong to the Java language?
4. Can interfaces be shared?
5. What is a software component?
6. What is a container?
7. Is a container itself a component that can be embedded in another container?
8. Explain the distinction between the *hidden* and the *exposed* with reference to the distinction between a component's implementation and interfaces.

1.6   Object-Oriented Modeling and UML

Modern software systems are complex, which means that ad hoc approaches to system design are inadvisable. The **U**nified **M**odeling **L**anguage (UML) is a popular modeling language meant to facilitate the design, development, deployment, and maintenance of software systems. UML incorporates previous modeling methods such as the Object Modeling Technique (OMT) and Object-Oriented Software Engineering (OOSE). In 1997 the Object Management Group, an international consortium dedicated to object-oriented approaches to software, standardized UML.

As a modeling *language*, UML has a vocabulary in which models are expressed and a syntax that constrains how terms in the vocabulary can be combined. The basic UML vocabulary consists of

- **Things**. Things are the entities or objects to be modeled. If the domain to be modeled is a university, for example, the things might consist of students, professors, curricula, libraries, and the like. If the domain to be modeled is an object-oriented programming language, the things might consist of packages, classes, interfaces, methods, and so on.
- **Relationships**. Relationships are connections among things. An academic department, for example, is *associated with* a university, which is a *subtype of* an institution of higher learning. Relationships, like things, can be concrete or abstract.
- **Diagrams**. Diagrams are graphical depictions of selected things and their relationships. Diagrams provide a visual representation of interrelated things.

The UML vocabulary's basic categories have various subcategories. For example, *structures* and *behaviors* are two subcategories of *thing*. A *structure*, in turn, may be a *class* (a set of objects with shared features), an *interface* (a set of operations that specify a class's services), a *use case* (a sequence of actions that a system performs), and so forth. UML diagrams also have various subcategories such as *class diagram*, *object diagram*, and *deployment diagram*. The point for now is not to provide an exhaustive inventory of UML's vocabulary but rather to sketch its general features. UML is designed to be a general modeling language for software systems, which means that UML must be sufficiently expressive and flexible to support models of widely varied systems.

A thorough introduction to UML would require an entire book. This section illustrates UML's modeling power and presents the UML's "look and feel" through a series of examples, each of which introduces one or more modeling features.

Sample Models

Example 1.6.1.   Figure 1.6.1 is a simple UML model that depicts a *Window* and some of its relationships to other things. The node representing a *Window* lists some window **attributes** such as *location* (e.g., an *x* and *y* coordinate pair) and *size* (e.g., a *width* and *height* pair) as well as standard window **operations** such as *open*, *close*, *resize*, *hide*, and *handleEvent*. The markers such as <<location>>, known as **stereotypes** in UML, are used to organize the attributes and operations. The model has the option of specifying data types for attributes. For example, an attribute such as *borderWidth* might be specified as having a value of type *Integer*.

The UML model indicates that *MainWindow* and *DialogWindow* are two subtypes of *Window* and that *Button* and *MenuItem* are two subtypes of *Control*. The subtype relationship is called **generalization** in UML. The relationship between *DialogWindow* and *Control* is not a subtype relationship but rather an **association**: a dialog window is associated with a control such as a button or a

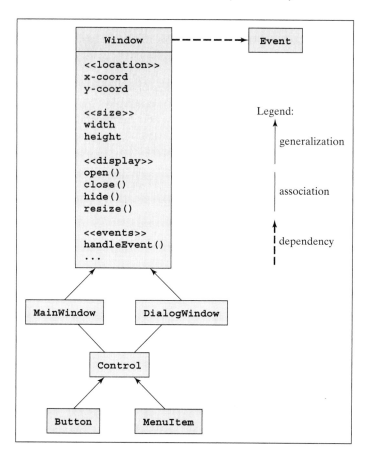

FIGURE 1.6.1   A simple UML model of a window and some
relationships.

menu item in that clicking the button or selecting the menu item opens the dialog
window. An association can specify a **multiplicity**, as Figure 1.6.2 illustrates by
revising part of the UML diagram in Figure 1.6.1. The 1 next to *DialogWindow*

FIGURE 1.6.2   An association with
a specified multiplicity.

and the * next to *Control* represents that one dialog window may be associated
with arbitrarily many controls such as a button, several menu items, and a check
box. The notation for multiplicity is flexible and expressive. For example, 0..1
means *zero or one*, 1...* means *one or more*, and 0..6, 8..* means *any number
except 7*. The default multiplicity is the star *, which represents any number. In
Figure 1.6.1, therefore, the association between *DialogWindow* and *Control* has
the default multiplicity.

In Figure 1.6.1, the dotted line going from *Window* to *Event* is a **dependency**, a relationship in which one thing (in this case, a *Window*) uses another thing (in this case, an *Event*). In this example, a *Window* uses an *Event* by handling the *Event* in some appropriate way. Note that the arrow points *away from* the dependent thing, in this case a *Window*.   ■

In a *generalization*, the two related things differ as *superclass* and *subclass*; for instance, *Physicist* is a subclass of *Scientist*. In an *association*, by contrast, the related things are peers; for instance, an *AcademicDepartment* is associated with a *University* but neither class is the superclass of the other.

An association can be an **aggregation**. For instance, a *University* aggregates or collects together many *AcademicDepartment*s. Figure 1.6.3 illustrates the notation for an association that is likewise an aggregation. In the notation, the diamond represents the *whole* (*University*) that aggregates or collects the *parts* (*AcademicDepartment*s).

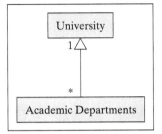

FIGURE 1.6.3   An association that is likewise an aggregation.

■ **Example 1.6.2.**   The model of an athletic team in Figure 1.6.4 introduces new features.

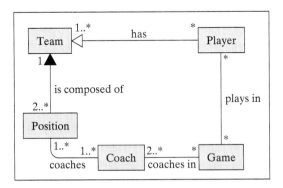

FIGURE 1.6.4   Some structural relationships in a model of an athletic team.

The associations are now labeled to make their meanings clear. The black diamond on the association of *Team* and *Position* represents a special type of association called **composition**. The idea is that a team (e.g., a soccer team) is composed of positions (e.g., midfielder and goal tender) that would not exist apart from the team. In different words, a position such as midfielder is a position *on a team*. By contrast, the open diamond on the association between *Player* and

Team indicates that a team is an aggregation of players but a player as such does not depend on a team. For example, a tennis player need not belong to a team. What the model represents can be stated in words as follows:

- A *Team* is composed of two or more *Position*s, which exist only through association with a *Team*. Further, a particular position (e.g., soccer midfielder) is associated with exactly one team (i.e., a soccer team). In the association between *Position* and *Team*,
  - The multiplicity 2..* next to *Position* means that a *Team* has two or more *Position*s.
  - The multiplicity 1 next to *Team* means that a particular *Position* belongs to exactly one *Team*. The idea is that a vague position such as *goalie* would have to be made precise, for example, *soccer goalie* or *hockey goalie*.

- A *Team* has arbitrarily many *Player*s, who can belong to more than one *Team*. In the association between *Team* and *Player*,
  - The multiplicity 1..* next to *Team* means that a player may play for many teams.
  - The default multiplicity * next to *Player* represents that a *Team* can have many players.

- A *Player* can play in many *Game*s. Each *Game* can have many *Player*s playing in it.
- A *Coach* can coach many *Game*s. Each *Game* has two or more *Coach*es. A *Coach* is associated with a *Position*. For example, a soccer team might have a midfielder coach and a goal tender coach. The same *Coach* could coach many *Position*s. In this model, even a *head coach* is also a coach for a particular position. A *Position* has at least one *Coach* but may have more.
- A *Player* is assigned to exactly one *Position*. Each *Position* may have many associated *Player*s.
- A *Team* plays arbitrarily many *Game*s. Each *Game* requires exactly two *Team*s.

The UML model in Figure 1.6.4 has several advantages over the discursive summary just presented. First, the model is graphical so that it physically represents the things and relationships of interest. Second, the model's meaning is precise. The associations and their multiplicities have a clear-cut interpretation. Third, the model is concise. The entire model can be examined in less time than the summary can be read.

From UML Models to Code

A UML model of a system can serve as a high-level specification for the code that implements the system. Because UML is an object-oriented modeling language, the implementation language of choice is likewise object-oriented. This section sketches how the UML model of Figure 1.6.4 might be implemented in Java. The point of the exercise is not to explain the Java syntax in detail but rather to illustrate the translation of a UML model into code.

■ Example 1.6.3.   The UML diagram of Figure 1.6.4 represents five things: *Team*s, *Player*s, *Position*s, *Coach*es, and *Game*s. Five Java classes of the same names can be used to represent these things:

```
class Team { /*...*/ }
class Player { /*...*/ }
class Position { /*...*/ }
class Coach { /*...*/ }
class Game { /*...*/ }
```

For now, the members of each class are not shown. There are no subtype relationships among the classes. For example, a Coach is *not* a subtype of a Player or vice-versa. Instead, the major relationships are *associations*. For example, a Player is associated with a Team and a Position.

The associations in Figure 1.6.4 have specified multiplicities. For example, a Game requires exactly two teams, which could be represented by adding members to the Game class

```
class Game {
   Team team1;          // one team
   Team team2;          // the other team
   int minTeams = 2;    // Game has at least 2 Teams
   int maxTeams = 2;    // Game has at most 2 Teams
   //...other members
}
```

to implement the association between Team and Game as well as the corresponding multiplicity. The fact that a Team can play in arbitrarily many games might be represented by the members

```
class Team {
   Vector games;
   int gameCount;
   int maxGames = Integer.MAX_VALUE;
   //...other members
}
```

Java provides the symbolic constant Integer.MAX_VALUE that represents the largest integer value $(2,147,483,647)$. A Team presumably would play far fewer than maxGames, but this field still represents that a Team can play many Games. A Vector is a collection of elements that grows and shrinks in size as required.

The idea here is that each Game in which a Team plays would be an element in the Team's Vector field. Other types of collection such as a Set or a Hashtable also might be used.

Other relationships specified in the UML model could be implemented through constructors. For example, the model specifies that a Coach must be associated with a Position, which suggests that the Coach class might be expanded

```
class Coach {
   Coach( Position p ) { pos = p; }
   Position pos;
   int minPos = 1;
   int maxPos = Integer.MAX_VALUE;
   //...other members
}
```

to include fields to represent the association. The constructor

```
Coach( Position p ) { pos = p; }
```

requires a Position argument so that a Coach's position can be specified whenever a Coach object is constructed. The Position argument named p is assigned to the Position field pos in the constructor's body.

Further implementation would proceed in a similar way, with the UML model acting as a guide and a check on particular coding decisions. The UML model is obviously the most beneficial if completed *before* the coding begins. ■

The implementation of a UML model in code is not a mechanical process and many different implementations of the same UML model are possible. The UML model can guide the design of the implementation classes and their members, and the model's diagrams provide an intuitive yet precise articulation of the associations that the implementation must capture. Modern software systems are far too complex to be coded without first creating formal designs. UML has become the dominant modeling language for modern software systems.

EXERCISES

1. What does UML stand for?
2. What are the principal components in a UML model?
3. Is UML a programming language?
4. In a UML relationship, is the default multiplicity 1?
5. List two subcategories of a UML *Thing*.

6. List two subcategories of a UML *Relationship*.

7. Explain what a UML *Diagram* is.

8. Give an example of the difference between a *subtype relationship* and an *association*.

9. Give an example of a multiplicity.

10. Explain the difference between an *aggregation* and a *composition*.

11. For the model in Figure 1.6.4, describe the relationship between a *Player* and a *Team*.

12. For the model in Figure 1.6.4, describe the relationship between a *Player* and a *Position*.

13. According to the model in Figure 1.6.4, must a *Coach* be associated with a *Position*?

14. Accordingly to the model in Figure 1.6.4, is a *Position* specific to a particular *Team*?

15. For a given UML model, is more than one code implementation possible?

16. Add a *Tournament* to the UML model in Figure 1.6.4. Assume that a tournament requires three or more teams.

2

Introductory Programs

Chapter Outline

This chapter introduces basic Java programming to programmers from other languages. The chapter begins with the traditional program that prints a greeting. The first section explains how to write, compile, and execute the program. The program's source code is explained line by line so that the reader can begin to experiment with the code and thereby gain immediate experience with Java.

The chapter's second section focuses on basic programming constructs such as variables, data types, `if` tests, loops, arrays, and parameter passing. Although the source code for each of the sample programs is roughly a page in length, the programs are realistic. The syntactic features of each program are explained in detail so that the reader can adapt the programs. Because classes are the central modules in every Java program, the basic syntax and use of classes are illustrated throughout the first two sections. The second section also introduces input and output operations so that the reader can experiment with reading data from and writing data to disk files. A later section provides more coverage of input and output. Finally, the second section indicates how Java supports familiar programming tasks such as sorting and searching.

Almost all programs use strings. Java's `String` class not only supports high-level string processing but also provides a natural introduction to Java's **standard classes**, that is, classes that are a standard part of the language. The third section thus examines the syntax and use of `Strings`.

A typical Java program is a mix of standard and *programmer-defined* classes. The fourth section thus explains how a programmer defines and then uses the defined classes. This section, like the others, encourages experimentation by providing examples that can be adapted and extended.

Input/output operations are central to any language. Java supports input/output with a rich, flexible assortment of interfaces and classes. The result is a highly modular—but correspondingly rich—library of interfaces and classes. The fifth section therefore focuses on *basic* input and output so that the programmer can begin at once to experiment with programs that perform common input/output operations such as reading and writing characters, numbers, and strings.

Among Java's most attractive features are the standard utility classes that implement familiar abstract data types such as vectors, hashtables, and string tokenizers. The chapter's sixth section illustrates the power and basic syntax of three standard utility classes. Earlier sections introduce other utility classes such as `Date` and `Random`.

Throughout the chapter, the reader should keep in mind that Java is a modern, general-purpose programming language with a complexity that befits this status. Java's object-oriented structure also challenges the new programmer. Yet the key to learning Java is to *program* in the language. This chapter therefore introduces basic programs that can be compiled, executed, studied, and adapted. The programs are explained in detail, although full coverage of the more technical features is left to later chapters. The purpose here is introduce the "look and feel" of Java programs, to explain some basic programming constructs, and to provide code examples with which the reader can experiment. Accordingly, the chapter focuses on complete programs rather than on code segments.

The reader need not understand every syntactic detail introduced in this chapter in order to proceed. Indeed, all of the material in this chapter is reviewed and clarified in subsequent chapters. For example, Chapter 3 provides a thorough and technical discussion of program structure and packages, and Chapter 4 explores the technical details of data types and operators.

2.1   A First Program

Writing and executing a Java program requires three basic steps:

- The programmer creates a text file that contains the **source code**, that is, the code that is **compiled** or translated into binary code, which can be executed. The source code can be written in any text editor, including a text editor that comes with a commercial Java **i**ntegrated **d**evelopment **e**nvironment (IDE). The source code resides in a file that has a *java* extension. For example, the text file for the Hi program of Figure 2.1.1 could be named *Hi.java*.

```
// A first program in Java (This is a one-line comment.)

/* In Java, a program that requires only the interpreter
   to run is called an "application."
   (This is a multiline comment.)
*/

/** This style of multiple-line comment is for the javadoc
 *  utility that generates professional-looking HTML
 *  documentation. The javadoc utility comes with the JDK.
 *  Indentation is optional but, of course,
 *  highly recommended for readability.
 */
class Hi {                                  // line 1
   public static void main( String[ ] a ) { // line 2
     System.out.println( "Hello, world!" ); // line 3
   }                                        // line 4
}                                           // line 5
```

FIGURE 2.1.1   Source code in the file *Hi.java*.

- The source code is compiled or translated using, for example, the compiler that comes with the standard Java software development kit, commonly known as the JDK (**J**ava **D**evelopment **K**it). The current JDK can be downloaded for free from

```
http://java.sun.com/products
```

Assuming that the source code resides in the file *Hi.java*, the command

```
$ javac Hi.java
```

compiles the source code using the JDK compiler called `javac`. (Throughout the book, the $ is the system prompt.) If the source code contains fatal errors, the compiler prints appropriate messages together with the line numbers in the source file at which the errors occur. If the source code contains no errors or only nonfatal errors, the source code compiles into one or more files with a *class* extension. For example, compilation of the source file *Hi.java* shown in Figure 2.1.1 produces the single binary file *Hi.class*.

- The compiled program, which consists of one or more files with a *class* extension, is *executed* using the Java **run-time interpreter**. The JDK includes an interpreter named `java`. For example, the program in the binary file *Hi.class* would be executed with the command

```
$ java Hi
```

Note that the *compiler* command `javac` expects the source file's *java* extension, whereas the *interpreter* command `java` does not expect the binary file's *class* extension.

In summary, if the file *Hi.java* contains the source code for a program, then the two statements

```
$ javac Hi.java
$ java Hi
```

compile and execute the program.

■ **Example 2.1.1.**   Figure 2.1.1 contains the source code for a program that prints

```
Hello, world!
```

followed by a newline to the **standard output**, which defaults to the video display.

The program occurs in a text file named *Hi.java* to underscore that the file contains a definition for the class `Hi`. Although the file could have any name with a *java* extension, *Hi.java* is the preferred name precisely because the file contains a definition for the class `Hi`.

Java supports three styles of documentation, each of which is shown in Figure 2.1.1. The double slash `//` begins a comment that runs to the end of the line. The slash-star combination `/*` begins a comment that runs to the next star-slash combination `*/`. The slash-star style of documentation is suited for multiline comments. The slash-double star `/**` introduces a special type of documentation

that ends with a star-slash combination */ on its own line. The JDK's javadoc
utility produces HTML pages from the third style of documentation. For ease of
reference, single-line comments in Figure 2.1.1 number the program's five lines
beyond the opening documentation.

In the sample greeting program, the first line of code beyond the opening
documentation is

```
class Hi {
```

This syntax defines a class named Hi. The definition runs from the opening brace
{ on line 1 to the matching closing brace } on line 5. The indentation and related
formatting are optional. The entire program could be written on a *single* line if
the comments were eliminated. Of course, indentation and related formatting
should be used to enhance the code's readability.

The program consists of a single class Hi with a single method main. The
method main is the program's **entry point**; that is, execution begins with the first
statement in main. The program terminates when main returns, that is, exits.[†] In
technical language, the program is a Java *application* rather than, for example, an
applet or a *bean*. The distinctions among Java program types are not important
at present. The point for now is that a Java *application* must have a method
named main, which requires the attributes public and static. Such attributes
are called **modifiers**. The modifier public exposes main outside the class Hi.
The modifier static associates main directly with the class Hi rather than with
objects that instantiate the class. In other words, main is a "class" rather than an
"instance" member (see Section 1.1). The order of public and static could
be reversed, but the order in which public precedes static is recommended.

Method main does not return a value, which explains the void in line 1.
If a method does not return a value, then void is used in place of a return type
such as int or float. The void must occur immediately to the left of main.
Following main's name is its argument list in parentheses. All methods have an
argument list, although the list may be empty. Method main expects a single
argument, which is a reference to an array of Strings (see Section 2.3 for the
details on Strings). The array holds any **command-line arguments** passed to the
program when it is executed from the command line. We can ignore the details
for now. The syntax

```
String[ ] args
```

is equivalent to

```
String args[ ]
```

[†]Special methods such as exit in the System class can be invoked to terminate a program. The point
here is that a return from main also terminates a program.

The matching square brackets [ ] signal that `args` is a reference to an *array*. The brackets may occur after the data type (in this case, `String`) or after the parameter's name (in this case, `args`). The parameter's name is arbitrary but it must be present.

The body of `main` is enclosed in the matching braces { and } on lines 2 and 4, respectively. Method `main`'s body consists of the single statement

```
System.out.println( "Hello, world!" );
```

on line 3. A semicolon terminates the statement. Omitting the semicolon would be a compile-time error. We now examine the statement in detail.

The class `System` is a standard Java class that represents the system on which the program executes. The `System` class has a `public` and `static` field named `out`. Because `out` is `static`, this `System` member is associated with the class `System` as a whole rather than with a particular `System` object. The identifier `System.out` uses the **member operator** (the symbol ., the period) to show that `out` is a member of the `System` class rather than some other class. In technical terms, `out` is an **object reference**, that is, an identifier that refers to an object, in this case a `PrintStream` object that represents the standard output. Because `out` refers to a `PrintStream` object, `out`'s data type is `PrintStream`, which in turn is a class that has a `println` method to print a string and a newline (the `ln` stands for newline) to the standard output.

In summary, `System.out` refers to a `PrintStream` object that encapsulates a `println` method for printing to the standard output. Figure 2.1.2

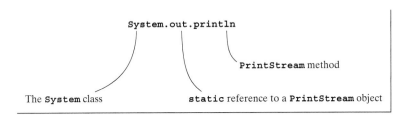

FIGURE 2.1.2   Summary of `System.out.println`.

illustrates the relationships among the `System` class, its public member `out`, and the `PrintStream` object to which `out` refers. The statement

```
System.out.println( "Hello, world!" );
```

thus prints the string `Hello, world!` to the standard output by invoking the `println` method of the `PrintStream` object to which `out` refers, where `out` is a `static` field in the `System` class. After the `println` method returns, the Hi program's `main` returns, which terminates the program.

Finally, note that the string to be printed is enclosed in double quotes, which are *not* printed to the standard output. The double quotes are used to enclose string literals such as the greeting shown in this example. ■

The `Hi` program in Figure 2.1.1 illustrates a key principle in all Java programming:

- Every Java program requires at least one class.

The `Hi` program consists of only a single class with a single method, `main`. However, a program can consist of arbitrarily many classes, each of which can have arbitrarily many members.

Source Files and Class Definitions

The source file *Hi.java* in Example 2.1.1 contains a single class definition; but a source file may contain multiple class definitions, which may occur in any order.

■ **Example 2.1.2.**   The code segment

```
//*** Start of file Foo.java
class Foo {
    //...
}
class Bar {
    //...
}
//*** End of file Foo.java
```

shows source file *Foo.java*, which contains two class definitions. The two class definitions could occur in any order; in particular, class `Bar` could occur first in the file. The file could have been named *Bar.java* or even *x.java*, although the latter name would be confusing because the file does not contain a class named x.
If the source file *Foo.java*, with its two class definitions, is compiled with the javac compiler

```
$ javac Foo.java
```

two *class* files are produced: *Foo.class*, which contains the binary code for class `Foo`, and *Bar.class*, which contains the binary code for class `Bar`. The compiler produces one *class* file for every class defined in a source file.

Java is case sensitive. For example, line 1 in Figure 2.1.1 contains the reserved word `class`. By contrast, neither `CLASS` nor `ClAss` are **keywords**, that is, words reserved for system use. (Figure 2.1.3 lists the Java keywords.)

```
abstract   default   goto        operator   switch
boolean    do        if          outer      synchronized
break      double    implements  package    this
byte       else      import      private    throw
byvalue    extends   inner       protected  throws
case       false     instanceof  public     transient
cast       final     int         rest       true
catch      finally   interface   return     try
char       float     long        short      var
class      for       native      static     void
const      future    new         strict     volatile
continue   generic   null        super      while
```

FIGURE 2.1.3 Java keywords, which cannot be used as class or member names.

■ **Example 2.1.3.**   The code segment

```
class abstract { //***** ERROR: abstract is a keyword!
  //...
}
```

contains an error because it uses the keyword `abstract` as a class's name. ■

■ **Example 2.1.4.**   The code segment

```
class Abstract { // ok: Abstract is not a keyword
  //...
}
```

is correct because `Abstract` is not a keyword, although `abstract` is a keyword. ■

■ **Example 2.1.5.**   The code segment

```
class Hi { // "Hi" is the name
  //...
}
class hi { // "hi" differs from "Hi"
  //...
}
```

defines two distinct classes, one named `Hi` and the other named `hi`. ■

Source files can be compiled one at a time, as the examples so far have illustrated. The command

```
$ javac *.java
```

can be used to compile all *java* files in the current directory.

EXERCISES

1. Adapt the `Hi` program in Figure 2.1.1 so that it prints your name to the standard output.
2. Adapt the `Hi` program in Figure 2.1.1 so that it prints your name to the *standard error*. By default, the standard error is the video display. *Hint:* The `System` class as a `static` member named `err`, which represents the standard error. The `System` member `err`, like the `System` member `out`, is of type `PrintStream`.
3. Adapt the `Hi` program in Figure 2.1.1 so that it prints your full name to the standard output, with each name part on a separate line: your first name on one line, your middle name on another line, and your last name on another line. *Hint:* Although the `println` method could be invoked three times, an alternative is to embed the newline character `\n` in the string to be printed. For example, the statement

```
System.out.println( "Hello,\nworld!" );
```

prints

```
Hello,
world!
```

followed by a newline.
4. Adapt the `Hi` program in Figure 2.1.1 so that it prints your full name (first name, middle initial, last name) to the standard output on one line, with each part separated by a horizontal tab character `\t`. *Hint:* See Exercise 3 on the newline character `\n`.
5. In the statement

```
System.out.println( "hi!" );
```

explain the relationships among `System`, `out`, and `println`.
6. In Exercise 5, are the double quotes around `hi` printed?
7. Amend the `Hi` program of Figure 2.1.1 so that the print statement is

```
System.out.println( "\"Hello, world!\"" );
```

What is the output with these changes?

2.2   Basic Programming Constructs

Java has *primitive data types* such as `int` for integers, `float` for floating-point numbers, `char` for characters, and `boolean` for the truth-values *true* and *false*. Java also has standard *class data types* such as `String` and `Date`, which represent strings and dates, respectively. Programs typically use a mix of primitive and class types.

For convenience, the standard classes such as `String` and `Date` are organized into **packages**, which are collections of related classes. At the conceptual level, a package serves as a *class library*. For example, Java has an input/output library that contains classes for input and output operations and a network library to support networking operations. This section introduces the basic syntax and use of primitive and class types, arrays, and packages. Control constructs such as tests (`if`) and loops (`while`) are also introduced. The material is presented in a series of examples.

Programs commonly process data to produce output. The data to be processed can come from various sources. For example, the data could be entered interactively by the person who runs the program. Data such as random numbers can be generated from within the program. Data also can be read from disk files. Examples throughout this chapter illustrate these three ways of providing input data and the examples also show how output can be written to the standard output or to disk files. This section begins with two programs named `BigAndSmall` and `FillAndSort`, each of which processes numeric data. Each program comes in two versions that differ in how the data are generated and written:

- In one version of the `BigAndSmall` program, the data to be processed are randomly generated numbers. In another version, the data are read from a disk file.
- In one version of the `FillAndSort` program, the output is written to the standard output. In another version of the program, the output is written to a disk file.

The two versions are presented so that the reader can begin experimenting with realistic, interesting programs. After other language features are introduced, Section 2.5 presents a more systematic and technical introduction to Java's input/output package. The emphasis in this section is on basic syntax and usage.

Finding the Smallest and Largest Integers

Example 2.2.1.   The `BigAndSmall` program in Figure 2.2.1 generates 100 random integers and prints the smallest and the largest among them. The program introduces the `import` statement, local variables, tests, loops, and the `Random` utility class.

Java programs often begin with one or more `import` statements. The `BigAndSmall` program begins with the `import` statement

```
import java.util.Random;
```

```
import java.util.Random;              //*** java.util is a package
class BigAndSmall {
   public static void main( String[ ] args ) {
      int max = Integer.MIN_VALUE, //*** the largest number found
          min = Integer.MAX_VALUE; //*** the smallest number found
      Random r = new Random();        //*** construct a Random object
      int i = 0;                      //*** loop counter
      final int n = 100;              //*** n is a constant
      while ( i < n ) {               //*** loop n times
         int next = r.nextInt();      //*** get the next random integer
         if ( next < min )            //*** found something smaller?
           min = next;                //*** if so, save it
         if ( next > max )            //*** found something bigger?
           max = next;                //*** if so, save it
         i = i + 1;                   //*** increment the loop counter
      }                               //*** end of while ( i < n )
      System.out.println( "The maximum found is " + max );
      System.out.println( "The minimum found is " + min );
   }
}
```

FIGURE 2.2.1   A program that prints the largest and smallest of 100
random integers.

The import statement does not physically import anything into the source file
but rather directs the compiler where to find one or more classes, in this class the
Random class. The syntax

java.util.Random

has the general form *package . subpackage . class*. The package named java is the
main Java package and util, short for utilities, is a subpackage. The standard
class Random resides in the java.util package. The import statement is used
for convenience, which can be clarified by considering how the program constructs
a Random number generator.

   The program constructs a Random object to generate random numbers with
the statement

Random r = new Random();

Recall that the term r is an object reference, in this case a reference to a Random
object. The construction of the Random object illustrates the general syntax for
constructing objects:

• The operator new is used with the appropriate constructor to allocate the
  storage required for the object. Because the constructor has the *same name* as

the encapsulating class, the constructor call indicates the object's data type. For example, the construction code

```
new Random()
```

constructs a Random object, whereas the construction code

```
new Date()
```

constructs a Date object.

The Convenience of the import Statement

The role of the import statement now can be explained. If the import statement were omitted in the source code, the program would have to use the **fully qualified name**

```
java.util.Random r = new java.util.Random();
```

for the Random class in constructing the Random object. A fully qualified name specifies the *package* together with the *class*, separating the package, any subpackages, and the class with periods. In the fully qualified name java.util.Random, java is the package, util is the subpackage, and Random is the class. The class always occurs in the rightmost position. An import statement always can be omitted if the programmer is willing to write out a class's fully qualified name.

A single import statement can be used for several classes. For example, the statement

```
import java.util.*;
```

imports all of the classes in the java.util package. The package java.lang, which includes the String class, does not have to be imported explicitly. The statement

```
import java.lang.*; //*** correct but unnecessary
```

illustrates the syntax. Finally, import statements must occur *before* any class definitions. For the BigAndSmall program in Figure 2.2.1, the import statement therefore must occur before the class definition

```
class BigAndSmall {
```

Generating Random Integers

The Random class's objects can be used to generate random numbers of various primitive types such as int and float. In this example, integers are generated by invoking the Random object's nextInt method

```
int next = r.nextInt();
```

Each generated integer is stored in a local int variable named next. The primitive numeric types such as int have standard bit sizes and ranges. For example, an int is 32 bits in size and has a range of $-2,147,483,648$ to $+2,147,483,647$. All integer and floating-point types are signed.

The program contains several local int variables. For example, the code segment

```
int max = Integer.MIN_VALUE, //*** the largest number found
    min = Integer.MAX_VALUE; //*** the smallest number found
```

declares and initializes two int variables named max and min. The variable min is initialized to the constant MAX_VALUE in the java.lang.Integer class, which ensures that none of the randomly generated integers can exceed min's initial value. Of course, it is highly probable that an integer value less than MAX_VALUE will be generated. Similar reasoning accounts for the initialization of max to Integer.MIN_VALUE.

The programmer is responsible for initializing local variables. If max and min were not initialized, this program would not compile. The syntax shows how a variable can be initialized in its declaration. The declaration

```
final int n = 100; //*** n is a constant
```

introduces new syntax. The keyword final is used to mark the int variable named n as a constant. It would be an error to assign n any value after its initialization to 100.

In this example, the integer variable i is used as a *loop counter*, that is, as a variable that tracks how many times a loop's body has been executed. The constant n provides the number of times the loop iterates, in this case 100. Variable i is not a constant because its value must be incremented with each loop iteration.

The while Loop

Once the local int variables are declared and initialized, and the Random object is constructed, the program enters a while loop

```
while ( i < n ) {
```

whose body begins with a left brace { and ends with the matching right brace }. The left brace could occur on a separate line. Recall that indentation and other use of whitespace is generally optional. For example, the space between the `while` and the left parenthesis (could be eliminated. In any case, the loop *condition* is the relational expression

```
i < n
```

enclosed in parentheses. If the expression evaluates to the `boolean` value `true`, the statements in the loop body are executed. If the expression evaluates to `false`, the loop body statements are *not* executed and execution instead resumes at the first statement, in this case a print statement, beyond the loop's body. To begin, the loop condition is `true` because i has an initial value of 0 and n has an initial value of 100. Therefore,

```
i < n
```

evaluates to `true`.

The `if` Statement

After each random integer is generated by invoking the `Random` object's `nextInt` method, the integer is compared against the current values of `min` and `max`. For example, the code segment

```
if ( next < min ) //*** found something smaller?
  min = next;       //*** if so, save it
```

tests whether `next`'s value is less than `min`'s value. If so, `min` is assigned the new smaller value. The `if` condition, like the `while` condition, is enclosed in parentheses. Note that the `if`'s body is not enclosed in braces. If the body of a construct such as an `if` or a `while` consists of a *single* statement, the braces are optional. However, it is always correct to include braces. The revised code segment

```
if ( next < min ) { //*** found something smaller?
  min = next;       //*** if so, save it
}
```

illustrates.

The last statement in the loop's body increments the loop counter i by one. If this statement were omitted, i would always be less than n and, therefore, the loop would be infinite. Once the loop exits, the print statements output the smallest and the largest random integers generated. On a sample run, the output was

```
The maximum found is 2119133254
The minimum found is -2146236930
```

The print statements

```
System.out.println( "The maximum found is " + max );
System.out.println( "The minimum found is " + min );
```

use the string concatenation operator +. The compiler converts the integer values of `max` and `min` to strings so that these strings can be concatenated with the messages. The automatic conversion illustrates how the compiler eases certain programming tasks.

Compiling and Running the `BigAndSmall` Program

The program's source code, which resides in the file *BigAndSmall.java*, was compiled with the command

```
$ javac BigAndSmall.java
```

The compilation produces the single file *BigAndSmall.class* because the source code contains only one class definition. The program was executed with the command

```
$ java BigAndSmall
```                                                                         ■

Reading Input from a Disk File

The `BigAndSmall` program can be revised to read integers from an input file instead of generating random integers. The next example explains the steps.

■ **Example 2.2.2.**   The `BigAndSmallFile` program in Figure 2.2.2 reads integers from an input file but otherwise has the same behavior as the `BigAndSmall` program in Figure 2.2.1. The changes can be clarified as follows:

• The `import` statement changes from

```
import java.util.Random;
```

to

```
import java.io.*;
```

The revised program does not generate random integers and therefore does not require a `Random` object. However, the revised program does require classes

```
import java.io.*;                     //*** java.io is a package
class BigAndSmallFile {
   public static void main( String[ ] args ) throws IOException {
      int max = Integer.MIN_VALUE, //*** the largest number found
          min = Integer.MAX_VALUE; //*** the smallest number found

      //*** Create a BufferedReader whose source is a
      //    the disk file named "input.dat".
      FileReader infile = new FileReader( "input.dat" );
      BufferedReader input = new BufferedReader( infile );

      int i = 0;                            //** loop counter
      final int n = 100;                    //** n is a constant
      while ( i < n ) {                     //** loop n times
         String s = input.readLine();       //** read next record
         s = s.trim();                      //** trim whitespace at ends
         int next = Integer.parseInt( s ); //** convert to int
         if ( next < min )                  //** found something smaller?
           min = next;                      //** if so, save it
         if ( next > max )                  //** found something bigger?
           max = next;                      //** if so, save it
         i = i + 1;                         //** increment loop counter
      }                                     //** end of while ( i < n )
      input.close();                        //** close the reader

      System.out.println( "The maximum found is " + max );
      System.out.println( "The minimum found is " + min );
   }
}
```

FIGURE 2.2.2   A program that reads integer data from a disk file.

from the java.io package. The wildcard character * is used in the import
statement to cover all of the required java.io classes.

- The clause

   throws IOException

now occurs after method main's argument list. An exception is an unusual
condition that arises during a program's execution. For instance, in this example
the specified input file *input.dat* might not exist. The result would be an *input
exception*. Section 2.5 goes into further detail. For now, the basic syntax is
sufficient.

- The program constructs a FileReader, which in turn is used to construct a
  BufferedReader. The syntax is

```
FileReader infile = new FileReader( "input.dat" );
BufferedReader input = new BufferedReader( infile );
```

In Java's input/output terminology, a *reader* is used for the input of *character* or *text* data rather than binary data. In technical terms, the two statements construct a `BufferedReader` whose *source* is a disk file that contains characters ("text") rather than binary data. In this example, the integer data are thus stored in a text file, with one integer per line:

```
88
176
-18
45
```

For efficiency reasons, a *buffered* reader reads data from a memory buffer rather than directly from a disk file. A `BufferedReader` has a `readLine` method that reads a single line of data as a string. Each integer in the input file is thus stored on its own line and read into the program as a string. The input file contains 100 integers.

- The program reads the integers from the input file as `Strings`, which are then converted to `ints`. The code is

```
String s = input.readLine();        //** read next record
s = s.trim();                       //** trim whitespace
int next = Integer.parseInt( s );   //** convert to int
```

The variable `input` refers to the `BufferedReader`, whose `readLine` method is invoked to read a line from the input file. The `parseInt` method in the `java.lang.Integer` class is used to convert a `String` such as `"27"` to the `int` 27. Before the input `String` is converted to an `int`, however, any whitespace is `trimmed` from the ends. Although the `parseInt` method can convert the `String` `"27"` to an `int`, the method *cannot* convert the string `"27  "` to an `int` because of the trailing blank.

- Once an input `String` has been converted to an `int`, the logic in the `while` loop is the same as in the `BigAndSmall` program. After the `while` loop exits, `min` is the smallest integer value and `max` is the largest integer value. Before these values are printed, the program closes the `BufferedReader` because the reader is no longer required.   ∎

Character or text input is generally more intuitive than binary input, which explains why the `BigAndSmallFile` programs read input data as character `Strings` and then convert the input data to `ints`. The conversion of `Strings` to other data types follows the pattern illustrated here. For example, if the input file contained floating-point numbers such as 3.14, then the program could use the statements

```
String s = input.readLine();           //** read next record
s = s.trim();                          //** trim whitespace
double next = Double.parseDouble( s ); //** convert to double
```

to convert a `String` to a `double`. The next program illustrates how output can be written to a disk file instead of the video display.

Filling and Sorting an Array

■ **Example 2.2.3.**   The `FillAndSort` program in Figure 2.2.3 introduces several new programming techniques and constructs. The program can be described as follows:

• The program expects as a command-line argument the number of randomly generated floating-point numbers to place in an array. If the command-line argument is not provided, the program exits with a message about how the program should be invoked.

```
import java.util.*;
class FillAndSort {
   public static void main( String[ ] args ) {
      if ( args.length != 1 ) {
        System.err.println( "java FillAndSort <number of doubles>" );
        return; //*** exits main and, therefore, the program stops
      }
      int n = Integer.parseInt( args[ 0 ] ); //** convert String to int
      double[ ] nums = new double[ n ];
      Random r = new Random();               //** construct a Random
      int i = 0;
      while ( i < n ) {                      //** fill with doubles
         nums[ i ] = r.nextDouble();         //** next random double
         i = i + 1;
      }
      print( nums );                         //** print array
      Arrays.sort( nums );                   //** sort array
      print( nums );                         //** print again
   }
   static void print( double[ ] a ) {
      System.out.println();
      for ( int i = 0; i < a.length; i++ )
         System.out.println( a[ i ] );
   }
}
```

FIGURE 2.2.3   A program that fills and sorts an array.

- The program constructs an array to hold **n** floating-point numbers, where **n** is an **int** variable that stores the integer value entered on the command line. The floating-point numbers are of type **double**. The array is constructed with the statement

  ```
  double[ ] nums = new double[ n ];
  ```

  The array has a reference to it named **nums** and each array element is of type double. The array indexes are 0, 1,. . . , n −1.
- Once the array has been filled with randomly generated **doubles**, the array's values are printed to the standard output. The array is then sorted in ascending order and printed again. Because the array is printed twice, a method is defined to handle the printing so that the printing code needs to be written only once.

  The **FillAndSort** program **imports** all of the classes in the **java.util** package

  ```
  import java.util.*;
  ```

  although only two classes from the package are used: **Random** for generating the random floating-point numbers, and **Arrays** for sorting the array.

Ensuring that a Program is Invoked Properly

The user is expected to invoke the program with a command-line argument that specifies how many floating-point numbers are to be generated. In an invocation such as

```
$ java FillAndSort 100
```

100 is the command-line argument. Recall that the method **main** has as its single argument

```
public static void main( String[ ] args ) {
```

a reference to an array of **Strings**, where each **String** is a command-line argument. Because arrays are indexed starting at 0, the element **args[0]** is the array's *first* element and refers to 100 represented as a **String**. If the program is invoked without a command-line argument

```
$ java FillAndSort
```

the first statement in `main`

```
if ( args.length != 1 ) {
  System.err.println( "java FillAndSort <number of doubles>" );
  return; //*** exits main and, therefore, the program stops
}
```

detects the error, prints a message to the standard error about how the program should be invoked, and `returns` from `main`, which terminates the program. The symbols `!=` mean *not equal*. Every array has a convenient `length` member that stores the number of elements in the array. If the user fails to provide a command-line argument, the array to which `args` refers has a `length` of zero. If a program is invoked incorrectly, it is good practice to provide the invoker with a description of how the program should be invoked.

Command-line arguments are passed to `main` as `Strings`. However, this program needs to convert the command-line argument to an `integer` that specifies how many floating-point numbers are to be generated. Recall that the `Integer` class has a `parseInt` method that converts strings to integers. The statement

```
int n = Integer.parseInt( args[ 0 ] );
```

thus uses `Integer` class's `static` method `parseInt` for the required conversion. If the argument `args[ 0 ]` refers to the string `"100"`, the `parseInt` method converts the string to the `int` value 100.

Constructing, Filling, and Sorting an Array

Once the command-line argument has been converted and assigned to `n`, a `double` array of size `n` is constructed

```
double[ ] nums = new double[ n ];
```

Recall that the square brackets designate an array. The operator `new` allocates sufficient storage for `n` elements in the `double` array to which `nums` refers. Because the array is constructed with the operator `new`, the array's elements are automatically initialized to the appropriate representation of zero, in this case the `double` value 0.0. Figure 2.2.4 depicts the first four array elements. Below each array cell is its index. The program assigns values to each array element immediately after the array has been constructed.

0.0	0.0	0.0	0.0
[0]	[1]	[2]	[3]

FIGURE 2.2.4   Part of the array to which `nums` refers immediately after construction. Indexes are shown below the cells.

Populating, Printing, and Sorting the Array

A while loop is used to populate the array with randomly generated doubles.
The Random class has a nextDouble method that is similar to the nextInt
method except that one method returns a double, whereas the other returns an
int.

The array is printed to the standard output after being filled. The print
method, which expects as its single argument a reference to an array, does the
work. The syntax

```
static void print( double[ ] a ) {
```

indicates that print expects a reference to an *array* of doubles. By contrast, the
syntax

```
static void print( double a ) {
```

indicates that print expects a single double value. Because every array has
a length member, there is no need to pass the array's length as a separate
argument. The print method uses a for loop to print each array element. The
next example explains the syntax of a for loop and also clarifies why print is a
static method. Of immediate interest is the utility class Arrays.

After the initial printing, the array is sorted in ascending order with the
statement

```
Arrays.sort( nums );
```

The java.util.Arrays class has static utility methods for filling, sorting, and
searching arrays. This example invokes the sort method. Once sorted, the array
is again printed to the standard output. A sample run with 8 as the command-line
argument produced the output

```
0.2415222819716782
0.4198495824445776
0.9036491730961306
0.7762009916043142
0.1111115711600756
0.2602584208583781
0.5917780553648082
0.0176780663690463

0.0176780663690463
0.1111115711600756
0.2415222819716782
0.2602584208583781
```

```
0.4198495824445776
0.5917780553648082
0.7762009916043142
0.9036491730961306
```

The first eight doubles are in the original order and the last eight are in the sorted order. ■

Writing Output to a Disk File

The FillAndSort program can be revised to write the output data to a disk file rather than to the standard output. The next example explains the steps.

■ **Example 2.2.4.**   The FillAndSortFile program in Figure 2.2.5 revises the FillAndSort program in Figure 2.2.3 by writing the output to a disk file. The changes can be summarized as follows:

• The import statement

```
import java.io.*;
```

is added so that the required java.io classes such as PrintWriter can be referenced without using their fully qualified names.
• The clause

```
throws IOException
```

follows method main's argument list. This revision, like the earlier revision of the BigAndSmall program, uses the clause to signal that an unusual condition—that is, an exception—may be thrown during the program's execution. For instance, the FillAndSortFile program might lack the permissions needed to create the output file *output.dat*. In such a case, an IOException would be thrown and the program would terminate. Section 2.5 goes into further detail.
• The revised program constructs a PrintWriter from a FileOutputStream, whose destination is the disk file named *output.dat*. The two statements

```
FileOutputStream outfile =
    new FileOutputStream( "output.dat" );
PrintWriter output = new PrintWriter( outfile );
```

show the syntax. In Java input/output terminology, a *writer* writes *character* or *text* output rather than binary output. The revised program thus writes doubles as characters. On a sample run, for instance, the program produced a *output.dat* that begins

```
import java.util.*;
import java.io.*;
class FillAndSortFile {
   public static void main( String[ ] args ) throws IOException {
      if ( args.length != 1 ) {
         System.err.println( "java FillAndSort <number of doubles>" );
         return; //*** exits main and, therefore, the program stops
      }
      int n = Integer.parseInt( args[ 0 ] ); //** convert String to int
      double[ ] nums = new double[ n ];
      Random r = new Random();                  //** construct a Random
      int i = 0;
      while ( i < n ) {                         //** fill with doubles
         nums[ i ] = r.nextDouble();            //** next random double
         i = i + 1;
      }

      //*** Open a writer so that the output can be written to a file.
      FileOutputStream outfile = new FileOutputStream( "output.dat" );
      PrintWriter output = new PrintWriter( outfile );

      print( nums, output );                    //** print array
      Arrays.sort( nums );                      //** sort array
      print( nums, output );                    //** print again
      output.close();                           //** close the writer
   }
   static void print( double[ ] a, PrintWriter out ) {
      out.println();
      for ( int i = 0; i < a.length; i++ )
         out.println( a[ i ] );
   }
}
```

FIGURE 2.2.5   A program that writes output to a disk file.

```
0.9841367599108151
0.4471744920480313
0.0670961742027054
```

Note that each double is written on its own line.

- The method print is revised to take two arguments: a reference to the array of doubles and a reference to the PrintWriter. The PrinterWriter parameter is named out in order to underscore the resemblance between a print statement in the original program such as

```
System.out.println( a[ i ] );
```

and the corresponding print statement in the revised program

```
out.println( a[ i ] );
```

Although System.out refers to a PrintStream object rather than to a PrintWriter object, the two classes share methods such as print and println.
- Once the data have been written to the output file, the PrintWriter is closed. ∎

The FillAndSortFile program uses the same constructs as the original program to fill array with randomly generated doubles and to sort the array. The BigAndSmallFile program and the FillAndSortFile program together illustrate the basics of character input/output operations. Section 2.5 continues the discussion by introducing binary input/output and by further clarifying the java.io package.

Determining the Best Strategy for a Game

The game in question can be described as follows:

- A player is given two black marbles and two white marbles that can be placed in one of two urns. However, each urn must hold at least one marble. There are four possible ways to distribute the four marbles in the two urns (see Figure 2.2.6):

  – Each urn has one black and one white marble.
  – One urn has two black marbles and the other urn has two white marbles.
  – One urn has one white marble and the other urn has two black marbles and one white marble.
  – One urn has one black marble and the other urn has two white marbles and one black marble.

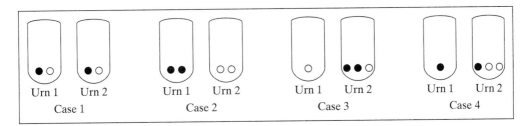

FIGURE 2.2.6   Four possible distributions of the two black and the two white marbles.

- After the player places the marbles in the urns, the player is blindfolded and the referee switches the position of the urns so that the player does not know which urn holds which marbles.
- The blindfolded player then selects one of the urns and draws a marble from it.
- If the marble is black, the player wins $1,000,000. If the marble is white, the player gets to keep the marble but wins no money.

At issue is how the player should distribute the marbles. The `MarbleGame` program in Figure 2.2.7 uses simulation to test which distribution of marbles brings the highest likelihood of a win. Of course, the probabilities of drawing a black marble can be determined analytically for each possible distribution. The best distribution is case 4 in Figure 2.2.6. The probability of selecting the urn with the single black marble is 1/2. If the player selects this urn, the probability that the player will select a black marble is 1 because the urn has only a black marble in it. If the player selects the urn with three marbles, then the probability of the player's picking a black marble is 1/3. Hence, the probability of winning in case 4 is

$$(1/2 \times 1) + (1/2 \times 1/3) = 2/3$$

Determining the probabilities of the remaining cases is left as an exercise.

Example 2.2.5.   The `MarbleGame` program in Figure 2.2.7 simulates the marble game. An array of type `char`, short for `character`, represents an urn. The statement

```
char[ ] urn1_T1 = { 'B', 'W' };
```

declares `urn1_T1` (urn1, Test1) as a reference to an array of `char` and initializes the array in the declaration. The initializing values are enclosed in braces. The character `'B'` represents a black marble, and the character `'W'` represents a white marble. Note that these character constants are enclosed in *single* quotation marks, not double quotation marks. A double-quoted symbol such as `"W"` is a *string literal* rather than a *character constant*. Figure 2.2.8 depicts the array to which `urn1_T1` refers, with the array indexes below each element. Recall that, in Java, array indexes always begin with zero. For an array of N elements, the valid indexes are thus $0, 1, \ldots, N - 1$. In the case of the array to which `urn1_T1` refers, the valid indexes are thus 0 and 1 because the array has two elements.

Two arrays are declared and initialized for each case shown in Figure 2.2.6. The method `simulate` is invoked from `main` to simulate the game. An invocation such as

```
simulate( "Urn1(B,W) Urn2(B,W)", urn1_T1, urn2_T1 );
```

shows that `simulate` expects three arguments: the first argument is a string that describes which case is being simulated; the second argument is an array representing the first urn; and the third argument is an array representing the second urn. Note that an array can be passed as an argument to a method by providing a reference such as urn1_T1.

The method `simulate` is `static` to satisfy an important language condition:

```
import java.util.Random;
class MarbleGame {
   public static void main( String[ ] args ) {
      //**** Define arrays that represent each urn and its
      //      contents. Then simulate drawing a marble from
      //      an urn. The array names also indicate the test
      //      in which the urn participates. For instance,
      //      the first two urns are named urn1_T1 and urn2_T1
      //      where "T1" stands for "Test 1." In the first test,
      //      urn1 has one black and one white marble, as does
      //      urn2. The four cases represent the four different
      //      ways in which two black and two white marbles can
      //      be placed in the urns. Each urn must contain at
      //      least one marble. In each simulation, a marble
      //      is randomly selected 1,000,000 times. If a Black
      //      marble is drawn, the Winning count is incremented; if a
      //      White marble is drawn, the Losing count is incremented.

      //**** Case 1: 1 black, 1 white in each urn
      char[ ] urn1_T1 = { 'B', 'W' };
      char[ ] urn2_T1 = { 'B', 'W' };
      simulate( "Urn1(B,W) Urn2(B,W)", urn1_T1, urn2_T1 );

      //**** Case 2:  urn1 has 2 black, urn2 has 2 white
      char[ ] urn1_T2 = { 'B', 'B' };
      char[ ] urn2_T2 = { 'W', 'W' };
      simulate( "Urn1(B,B) Urn2(W,W)", urn1_T2, urn2_T2 );

      //**** Case 3: urn1 has 1 white, urn2 has 2 black and 1 white
      char[ ] urn1_T3 = { 'W' };
      char[ ] urn2_T3 = { 'B', 'B', 'W' };
      simulate( "Urn1(W)   Urn2(B,B,W)", urn1_T3, urn2_T3 );

      //**** Case 4: urn1 has 1 black, urn2 has 1 black and 2 white
      char[ ] urn1_T4 = { 'B' };
      char[ ] urn2_T4 = { 'B', 'W', 'W' };
      simulate( "Urn1(B)   Urn2(B,W,W)", urn1_T4, urn2_T4 );
   }
}
```

FIGURE 2.2.7   A program to simulate the marble game.

```
    static void simulate( String c, char[ ] u1, char[ ] u2 ) {
        int wins = 0, losses = 0;
        Random r = new Random();           //** to simulate picks

        //*** loop testRun times, each time randomly picking an
        //*** urn and a marble from it
        for ( int i = 0; i < testRun; i = i + 1 ) {
            int whichUrn =
                Math.abs( r.nextInt() ) % 2; //** 0 or 1
            int marble = -1;                 //*** illegal array index
            char selected = ' ';             //*** blank character
            //*** select a marble from an urn
            if ( whichUrn == 0 ) {           //** 1st urn
                marble = Math.abs( r.nextInt() ) % u1.length;
                selected = u1[ marble ];
            }
            else {                           //** 2nd urn
                marble = Math.abs( r.nextInt() ) % u2.length;
                selected = u2[ marble ];
            }
            if ( selected == 'B' )           //** winner
                wins = wins + 1;
            else                             //** loser
                losses = losses + 1;
        } //** end of for loop

        //*** print the result
        System.out.println(c + "\tWins: " + wins + "\tLoss-
es: " + losses);
    }
    static final int testRun = 1000000; //** 1,000,000
}
```

FIGURE 2.2.7   A program to simulate the marble game, *continued.*

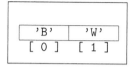

FIGURE 2.2.8   The array to which urn1_T1 refers. Indexes are shown below the cells.

- A static method such as main can access only other static members in the same class. In this example, main can invoke only static methods in the MarbleGame class and access only static fields in this class.

For this reason, the MarbleGame field named testRun is also static. The static method simulate accesses the field testRun, which therefore must be static as well. The field is marked as final to make it a constant. For example, it would be an error for `main` or `simulate` to assign a value to `testRun`, which represents the number of times that a player picks an urn and a marble from it. In the current implementation, `testRun` is initialized to 1,000,000.

The `for` Loop

The method `simulate` uses a `for` loop, which is well suited for *counted loops*, that is, loops that are to iterate a predetermined number of times. In this case, the `for` loop iterates `testRun` times for each case to be simulated. The `for` loop's condition

```
for ( int i = 0;     //** initialization section
       i < testRun;  //** condition section
       i = i + 1 ) { //** post-body section
```

has three sections, which semicolons separate. The sections, written here on separate lines for clarity, are the *initialization section*, the *condition section*, and the *post-body section*.

The *initialization section* contains code that typically initializes and, perhaps, even declares local loop variables. In this example, the `int` variable `i` is declared and initialized to 0. The *initialization section* executes only once, when the loop is first entered. In other words, `i` is initialized to 0 when the loop first starts; thereafter, the initialization code is not executed again until the loop is entered anew with a new invocation of `simulate`.

The *condition section* in the middle is equivalent to the `while` loop condition (see Example 2.2.1). In this example, the *condition section* tests whether `i`'s value is less than `testRun`'s value. If the condition evaluates to `true`, the loop's body is executed. In this example, the body consists of the statements enclosed in braces, which are required because the loop body has multiple statements. If the loop condition evaluates to `false`, the loop body is *not* executed and execution instead resumes at the first statement beyond the loop. In this example, the print statement

```
System.out.println(c + "\tWins: " + wins +
                        "\tLosses: " + losses);
```

is the first (and only) statement beyond the `for` loop. After the print statement executes, `simulate` returns and execution resumes in `main`.

A `for` loop's *condition section* is always executed *before* any statements in the loop's body are executed. If the loop's condition evaluates to `true`, the loop's body is executed, after which the loop's condition is again evaluated, and so on.

The *post-body section* at the right often contains code that, as in this example, increments a loop counter, but code in this section could perform other tasks. The code in the *post-body section* executes immediately *after* the last statement in the loop's body executes. In this example, the *post-body section* uses the assignment expression

```
i = i + 1
```

to increment i. An alternative expression is

```
i++
```

or

```
++i
```

both of which also increment i. The expression ++i illustrates the *preincrement* operator ++, and the expression i++ illustrates the *postincrement* operator ++. Chapter 4 examines the two operators in detail. The point for now is that a for loop's *post-body section* commonly has a preincrement or postincrement expression.

For brevity, let *init* be the initialization section, *cond* the condition section, *body* the loop body, and *post* the post-body section. The for loop's execution then can be depicted as the sequence

init, cond, body, post, cond, body, post, cond, body, post. . .

until the *cond* evaluates to false. Now we turn to the statements in the loop's body.

Absolute Values and Remainders

The first statement in the for loop's body is used to select the first or the second urn. The statement

```
int whichUrn = Math.abs( r.nextInt() ) % 2; //** 0 or 1
```

assigns either 0 or 1 to the int variable whichUrn. The number 0 represents the first urn and the number 1 represents the second urn. The statement can be clarified as follows. The java.lang.Math class has a static method abs, which returns the absolute value of an integer. This method is used because the Random method nextInt returns *signed* integers, which therefore might be negative. Suppose that nextInt returns the integer −98. The method invocation

```
Math.abs( -98 )
```

returns 98. So Math.abs is used to convert negative integers to positive ones. If Math.abs is invoked with a nonnegative integer as an argument, the method returns the argument. The remainder operator % returns the integer remainder of its left operand divided by its right operand. For example, the expression

```
8 % 3
```

evaluates to 2 because 8/3 has an integer remainder of 2. By contrast, the expression

```
8 % 2
```

evaluates to 0 because 8/2 has an integer remainder of zero. In this program, 2 is the right-hand operand for the operator %; hence, the integer remainder is either 0 (first urn) or 1 (second urn).

After an urn has been selected at random, a marble is selected at random from the urn. The code segment

```
//*** select a marble from an urn
if ( whichUrn == 0 ) { //** 1st urn
  marble = Math.abs( r.nextInt() ) % u1.length;
  selected = u1[ marble ];
}
else {                    //** 2nd urn
  marble = Math.abs( r.nextInt() ) % u2.length;
  selected = u2[ marble ];
}
```

simulates the selection. For example, suppose that whichUrn equals 0, which causes the statement

```
marble = Math.abs( r.nextInt() ) % u1.length;
```

to execute. The remainder operation ensures that the randomly generated number is a valid index. Recall that every array has a convenient length field whose value is the number of elements in the array. In this case, u1.length is the length of array u1. Suppose that u1 has three elements. The remainder operation thus ensures that marble is randomly assigned one of the values 0, 1, or 2. Note that marble is initialized to the invalid index value −1, which requires that marble be assigned a valid index value before the variable is used as an index. The statement

```
selected = u1[ marble ];
```

assigns to the local char variable selected either a 'B' or a 'W', the only values stored in any u1 cell.

Once an urn and an index have been selected randomly, an if-else construct

```
if ( selected == 'B' ) //** winner
  wins = wins + 1;
else                    //** loser
  losses = losses + 1;
```

is used to determine whether the player won or lost. If a black marble has been selected, the local `wins` variable is incremented; otherwise, the local `losses` variable is incremented. After the `for` loop exits, the `wins` and `losses` are printed to the standard output. On a sample run, the output was

```
Urn1(B,W) Urn2(B,W)    Wins: 500082   Losses: 499918
Urn1(B,B) Urn2(W,W)    Wins: 500076   Losses: 499924
Urn1(W)   Urn2(B,B,W)  Wins: 333143   Losses: 666857
Urn1(B)   Urn2(B,W,W)  Wins: 666502   Losses: 333498
```

The output confirms that the best strategy for winning is to place one black marble in one urn and the remaining marbles in the other urn. Using this strategy, the player should win approximately two out of three times.

EXERCISES

1. Explain the error:

```
class C {
    public static main( String[ ] args ) { /*...*/ }
}
```

2. In Exercise 1, could `static` occur to the left of `public`?
3. Can a `static` method such as `main` reference both `static` and `nonstatic` members of its encapsulating class?
4. Explain the error:

```
if 2 < 3
   System.out.println( "2 is less than 3" );
```

5. What is the output for this code segment?

```
int n = 10;
int i = 0;
while ( i < n ) {
   System.out.println( i );
   i = i + 1;
}
```

6. Explain the execution sequence for the three expressions in the `for` loop

```
for ( int i = 0; i < 5; i = i + 1 ) {
   System.out.println( i );
}
```

7. If a `while` loop's body consists of a single statement, must the loop's body be delimited by a left brace { and a right brace }?

8. Is it always correct to delimit a `while` loop's body by a left brace { and a right brace }?

9. If a `for` loop's body consists of a single statement, must the loop's body be delimited by a left brace { and a right brace }?

10. If an `if` statement's body consists of a single statement, must the `if` statement's body be delimited by a left brace { and a right brace }?

11. What is printed by the code segment

```
System.out.println( 10 % 3 );
```

12. Test whether the remainder operator % can be applied to floating-point values.

13. Write a statement that allocates a `double` array with 500 elements.

14. Write a statement that prints the number of elements in an array to which `ar` refers.

15. Write a statement that sorts the array `ar` in ascending order.

<h2> 2.3   Strings</h2>

Character strings, or *strings* for short, are common in programs. Java has two primary representations for strings: objects of type `String` and string literals, which are references to `String` objects. The code segment

```
String soprano = new String( "Dawn Upshaw" );
```

illustrates how a `String` object can be constructed from a string literal that is an argument to a `String` constructor. Recall that string literals are enclosed in double quotes. In any case, the constructed `String` object has `soprano` as its reference (see Figure 2.3.1). The object's data type is `String`.

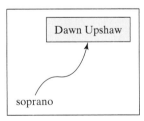

FIGURE 2.3.1   A `String` object with `soprano` as its reference.

Because a string literal such as `"Dawn Upshaw"` is a reference to a `String` object, the statement

```
String soprano = "Dawn Upshaw";
```

makes soprano a reference to the *same* object. After the assignment statement,
"Dawn Upshaw" and soprano refer to the same String. String literals are a convenient way to reference Strings and, therefore, may occur frequently in programs.

■ **Example 2.3.1.**   The PrintStream class's println method is **overloaded**;
that is, the method named println has several definitions, ten in all. The
definitions are distinguished by data types of the arguments. For example, the
two PrintStream methods

```
void println( int x ) { /*...*/ }
void println( float x ) { /*...*/ }
```

are distinguished because one of them expects an int argument, whereas the
other expects a float argument. Included among the println overloads is

```
void println( String s ) { /*...*/ }
```

which allows strings to be printed to the standard output.

For convenience, we say that the PrintStream's ten println methods
have the same name but different **signatures**. Recall that a method's signature
consists of the number, order, and data types of its expected arguments.[†] In the
case of println, the overload that prints only a newline expects no arguments;
and the remaining overloads expect a single argument. Among the single-
argument overloads, the signatures differ because of the expected argument's
data type.   ■

The toString Method

Every object encapsulates a toString method, which returns a String representation
of the object. The method is very useful in situations that require a String.

■ **Example 2.3.2.**   The java.util.Date class represents a date. For
example, on a sample run the statement

```
System.out.println( "Today is " + new Date() );
```

printed

```
Today is Thu Feb 10 21:09:57 CST 2000
```

[†]A method's signature also includes any Exceptions that might be thrown from within the method.
Exceptions are introduced in Section 2.5 and explained in detail in Section 4.6.

Recall that + is the concatenation operator for strings. The problem is that the expression `new Date()` constructs a `Date` rather than a `String`, and string concatenation requires two `Strings`. Nonetheless, the compiler again intervenes in a helpful manner by invoking the `Date` object's `toString` method, which returns the date as a `String` giving the day of week, the month, the day of the month, and so forth. The statement

```
System.out.println( "Today is " + new Date() );
```

is thus shorthand for

```
System.out.println( "Today is " + new Date().toString() );
```

The syntax

```
new Date().toString()
```

deserves further clarification. The `new Date()` constructs an unreferenced date object. Recall that the period . is the member operator. So the unreferenced `Date` object's `toString` method is invoked, which returns a `String` representation of the `Date`.   ■

A Test Client for the `String` Class

One way to gain familiarity with a class such as `String` is to write a **test client**, that is, a program that requests `String` services by constructing `String` objects and invoking their methods. The `String` class has nine *nondeprecated* constructors and more than two dozen methods available to client programs. A **deprecated** language feature such as a class or a method is available but unfit for use. As Java has evolved, various language features have been deprecated as better replacements have been introduced. Figure 2.3.2 lists some `String` constructors and methods. The figure shows the *declaration* rather than the *definition* of the constructors and methods. Recall that a constructor or method **definition** includes the *body*, that is, the statements that perform the constructor or method operations. The principle of information hiding requires that high-level constructors and methods hide implementation details; hence, a programmer should be able to use `String` constructors and methods without having access to their bodies, that is, their definitions. By contrast, a **declaration** describes the constructor or method by giving its name, the data types of its arguments, and, in the case of methods, the return type. The declaration together with documentation should be sufficient for a programmer to use a constructor or method.

    Example 2.3.3.   The `StringClient` program in Figure 2.3.3 is a test client for the `String` class. The program constructs various `Strings` and invokes their methods. Documentation clarifies how the constructors and methods behave.

Declaration	Description
String();	Constructs an empty string
String(String);	Constructs a string as a copy of another
String(char[ ]);	Constructs a string from an array of chars
String(byte[ ]);	Constructs a string from an array of bytes
char charAt(int ind);	Returns the char at the specified index
boolean endsWith(String s);	Tests whether a string ends with s
boolean equals(String s);	Tests whether a string is the same as another
int length();	Returns the number of characters in a string
String substring(int i);	Returns the substring starting at index i
String toLowerCase();	Returns a lowercase copy
String toUpperCase();	Returns an uppercase copy
String trim();	Copies with whitespace trimmed from the ends

FIGURE 2.3.2   Selected String constructors and methods.

Note that the String methods such as toLowerCase and trim have String as the return type. Methods such as these do *not* change the String object on which they are invoked but rather produce a *copy*, which is returned. For example, given a String object

```
String s = new String( "e. e. cummings" );
```

the method invocation

```
s.toUpperCase()
```

does *not* change the String to which s refers but rather returns a *copy* of this String in which lower-case characters have been changed to uppercase characters. The code segment

```
String s = new String( "e. e. cummings" );
String t = s.toUpperCase();
System.out.println( s ); //** e. e. cummings
System.out.println( t ); //** E. E. CUMMINGS
```

illustrates.

By making object reference s the target of an assignment operation, we can change the String to which s refers. The code segment

```
String s = new String( "e. e. cummings" );
System.out.println( s ); //** e. e. cummings
s = s.toUpperCase();
System.out.println( s ); //** E. E. CUMMINGS
```

```
class StringClient {
   public static void main( String[ ] args ) {
      //*** default or no-argument constructor
      String s1 = new String();
      System.out.println( s1 );                    //** should be empty
      //*** String copying constructor
      String s2 = new String( "Dawn Upshaw" );
      String s3 = new String( s2 );
      System.out.println( s2 );
      System.out.println( s3 );                    //* should be same as above
      //*** char[ ] constructor
      char[ ] t1 = {'A', 'B', 'C'};
      String s4 = new String( t1 );
      System.out.println( t1 );
      System.out.println( s4 );                    //* should be same as above
      //*** byte[ ] constructor
      byte[ ] t2 = {65, 66, 67};                   //* ASCII for 'A','B','C'
      String s5 = new String( t2 );
      System.out.println( s5 );                    //* should also be ABC
      //*** charAt
      String s6 = new String( "Mia Hamm" );
      System.out.println( s6.charAt( 1 ) );   //* 'i' in "Mia"
      System.out.println( s6.charAt( 4 ) );   //* 'H' in "Hamm"
      //*** length
      System.out.println( s5.length() );      //* 3 characters
      System.out.println( s6.length() );      //* 8 characters
      //*** substring
      String s7 = new String( "The Bodeans" );
      System.out.println( s7.substring( 6 ) ); //* "deans"
      //*** equals and toLowerCase
      String s8 = new String( "ORSON WELLES" );
      String s9 = s8.toLowerCase();
      String s10 = new String( "orson welles" );
      if ( s9.equals( s10 ) )
        System.out.println( "same" );          //* should print
      //*** toUpperCase
      String s11 = s10.toUpperCase();
      if ( s11.equals( s8 ) )
        System.out.println( "same (2)" );   //* should print
      //*** trim
      String s12 = new String( "  War and Peace  " );
      System.out.println( "!" + s12 + "!" );     // "!  War and Peace  !"
      System.out.println( "!" + s12.trim() + "!" ); // "!War and Peace!"
   }
}
```

FIGURE 2.3.3   Test client for the String class.

```
Dawn Upshaw
Dawn Upshaw
ABC
ABC
ABC
i
H
3
8
deans
same
same (2)
!  War and Peace  !
!War and Peace!
```

FIGURE 2.3.4 Output for the String client in Figure 2.3.3.

uses an assignment statement to make s refer to the uppercase copy of the original lowercase String.

In general, a String object cannot be changed, although an altered copy can be generated through methods such as toLowerCase. For this reason, String objects are sometimes described as being **immutable**. Of course, a *reference* to one String can be changed so that it refers to a different String, as the statement

```
s = s.toUpperCase(); // change String to which s refers
```

illustrates. The code segment

```
String s = "foo"; // s refers to one String
s = "bar";        // s refers to a different String
```

provides another example (see Figure 2.3.5).   ■

String Conversion Methods

Conversions between Strings and other types are common. The String class has various overloads of the static method valueOf to convert some primitive data types such as int and double. The code segment

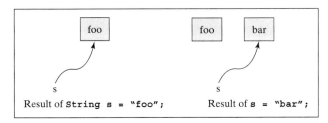

Result of `string s = "foo";`   Result of `s = "bar";`

FIGURE 2.3.5 Changing the String to which s refers.

```
String s1 = String.valueOf( 26 );      // int to String
String s2 = String.valueOf( 3.14 );    // double to String
```

illustrates the syntax. Figure 2.3.6 lists the `valueOf` overloads. As the figure shows, a floating-point constant such as 3.14 is of type `double`, whereas the constant 3.14F or 3.14f is of type `float`. Similarly, an integer constant such as 26 is of type `int`, whereas the integer constant 26L or 26l is of type `long`.

Argument Type	*Example*
boolean	String.valueOf(true)
char	String.valueOf('A')
double	String.valueOf(3.14)
float	String.valueOf(3.14F)
int	String.valueOf(99)
long	String.valueOf(99L)
Object	String.valueOf(new Date())

FIGURE 2.3.6 Overloads of the `String` method `valueOf` for conversions.

Wrapper Classes and Type Conversions

The `java.lang` provides **wrapper classes** for primitive types. For example, the class `Boolean` "wraps" in a class type the primitive `boolean` type; the class `Double` "wraps" in a class type the primitive `double` type; the class `Integer` "wraps" in a class type the primitive `int` type; and so on. The wrapper classes have various uses, including data type conversion. For example, the program in Figure 2.3.5 uses the `Integer` wrapper to convert a command-line `String` to an `int`

```
int n = Integer.parseInt( args[ 0 ] );
```

where `args[ 0 ]` is the command-line argument. The conversion could have been done in another way, as the statement

```
int n = new Integer( args[ 0 ] ).intValue();
```

illustrates. In the second approach, an unreferenced `Integer` object is constructed with a `String` argument, and the `Integer` object's `intValue` method is then invoked to return an `int`. Whether to convert the `String` representation of a `double` using `parseDouble`

```
String s = "3.14";
double d = Double.parseDouble( s );
```

or `doubleValue`

```
String s = "3.14";
double d = new Double( s ).doubleValue();
```

is a question of programming circumstance and style.

The `StringBuffer` Class

Although a `String` is immutable, a `StringBuffer` is mutable. The two classes belong to the `java.lang` package. The `String` class has a constructor that expects a `StringBuffer` as an argument, and the `StringBuffer` class has a constructor that expects a `String` argument. This design means that `String`s and `StringBuffer`s can be converted to one another in a straightforward manner. The code segment

```
//*** construct a String
String s = new String( "test" );
//*** construct a StringBuffer from the String
StringBuffer sb = new StringBuffer( s );
//***...process the StringBuffer
//*** construct a new String from the StringBuffer
s = new String( sb );
```

illustrates the conversion from `String` to `StringBuffer` back to `String`.

The `StringBuffer` class has methods such as `append`, `delete`, `replace`, and `reverse` for changing a `StringBuffer` object. Many of these methods (e.g., `append`) are overloaded. Comparable methods are *not* available in the `String` class. So if a `String` needs to be changed, the approach is to

- Construct a `StringBuffer` from the `String`.
- Alter the characters in the `StringBuffer` as required.
- Get a new `String` from the `StringBuffer` by invoking either a `String` constructor or the `StringBuffer`'s method `toString`.

■ **Example 2.3.4.** The `Reverse` program in Figure 2.3.7 expects as command-line arguments two strings that are appended and then reversed. The `String` class does not have an `append` or a `reverse` method but the `StringBuffer` class has both. Accordingly, a `StringBuffer` is constructed from the first command-line `String` argument; the second command-line `String` is then appended to the `StringBuffer`. Finally, the method `reverse` is used to reverse the `StringBuffer`, after which the `StringBuffer`'s method `toString` is invoked to get a `String`. By the way, the print statement

```
System.out.println( sb.toString() );
```

```
class Reverse {
   public static void main( String[ ] args ) {
      if ( args.length < 2 ) {
         System.err.println( "java Reverse <string1 string2>" );
         return;
      }
      StringBuffer sb = new StringBuffer( args[ 0 ] );
      sb.append( args[ 1 ] );
      sb.reverse();
      System.out.println( sb.toString() );
   }
}
```

FIGURE 2.3.7   A program to illustrate the `StringBuffer` class.

could be simplified to

```
System.out.println( sb );
```

with the same output. If the command-line arguments were `Hello`, and `world!`, the output would be `!dlrow,olleH`. ■

The `String` and `StringBuffer` classes together with the wrapper classes provide high-level constructs for constructing, converting, and otherwise processing strings. The next section has a program that illustrates how individual characters can be processed using the `Character` wrapper class for the primitive `char` data type.

EXERCISES

1. Is the expression `"Upshaw"` of type `String`?
2. Explain the difference between a string constant such as `"A"` and a character constant such as `'A'`.
3. Do the two statements

    ```
    String s = new String( "Howdy!" );
    ```

    and

    ```
    String s = "Howdy!";
    ```

    assign the same `String` to object reference `s`?

4. Explain why the statement

```
System.out.println( new Date() );
```

prints the current date as a String even though the argument to println is a Date rather than a String.

5. Write a short program to confirm that the code segment

```
String s = "FOO";
s.toLowerCase();
System.out.println( s );
```

prints FOO rather than foo.

6. Introduce an assignment statement into the code segment of Exercise 5 that causes foo to be printed.

7. Write a statement that converts the double constant 3.14 to a String.

8. Write a statement that converts the string constant "26" to an integer.

9. Explain briefly the difference between a String and a StringBuffer.

10. Write a statement that converts a String to a StringBuffer.

11. Write a statement that converts a StringBuffer to a String.

12. Write a loop in main that prints to the standard output all of the Strings passed to main as command-line arguments.

2.4   Programmer-Defined Classes

The examples so far have focused on classes such as Date and String from the standard Java packages. Programmer-defined classes have been introduced only to encapsulate main. More realistic programs are a mix of standard and programmer-defined classes. This section introduces the basics of programmer-defined classes so that the reader can begin to experiment with creating classes. Chapter 5 examines classes in detail and Chapter 6 covers the closely related topics of inheritance and interfaces.

■ **Example 2.4.1.**   Figure 2.4.1 contains the programmer-defined Emp class, which represents an employee in an organization. The class is declared as public to make the class available to any Java program that needs to construct Emp objects. The three overloaded Emp constructors are made public so that they, too, are publicly available to Java programs. Three pairs of *get/set* methods, so named because their names begin with either get or set, are public for the same reason. One *get* method does not occur in a pair for reasons given shortly. Methods in the *get/set* style are also called **mutators** and **accessors**. The public method dump prints information about an employee to the standard output.

```
import java.util.Date;
public class Emp {
   //**** constructors
   public Emp() {
      init( "unknown", "unknown", 0 );
   }
   public Emp( String first, String last ) {
      init( first, last, 0 );
   }
   public Emp( String first, String last, int s ) {
      init( first, last, s );
   }
   //**** get/set methods
   public void setFirstName( String first ) { fname = first;}
   public String getFirstName() { return fname; }
   public void setLastName( String last ) { lname = last; }
   public String getLastName() { return lname; }
   public void setSalary( int s ) { sal = s; }
   public int getSalary() { return sal; }
   public Date getStartDate() { return start; }
   //**** print method
   public void dump() {
      System.out.println();
      System.out.println( "First name: " + fname );
      System.out.println( "Last name:  " + lname );
      System.out.println( "Salary:    $" + sal );
      System.out.println( "Start date: " + start );
   }
   //**** low-level method and implementation fields
   private void init( String f, String l, int s ) {
      fname = f;
      lname = l;
      sal = s;
      start = new Date(); //*** today
   }
   private String fname;
   private String lname;
   private int sal;
   private Date start;
}
```

FIGURE 2.4.1   An Emp class to represent an employee.

The method `init` is made `private` because this method is restricted for use *within* the Emp class. The four Emp fields are made `private` for the same reason. In general, the keywords `public` and `private` are used to relax or enforce, respectively, information hiding: `private` is used to hide a particular class member so that the member can be accessed only *inside* the class, whereas `public` exposes a member so that the member can be accessed *outside* the class. The details of information hiding in Java are covered in chapters 5 and 6. For now, the point is to illustrate a common use of `public` and `private` in programmer-defined classes. Finally, because the Emp class is declared `public`, this class *must* reside in a source file called *Emp.java*. A nonpublic class can reside in an arbitrarily named source file, but a public class must reside in a file that bears the class's name.

The Emp class overloads three constructors. The no-argument constructor sets the Employee's first and last names to "`unknown`" and the Employee's salary to zero. Because the salary field `sal` is of type `int`, the field's value defaults to zero; but, for flexibility, all of the constructors invoke the `init` method with values for the Employee's first and last names and salary. The two-argument constructor sets the first and last names to the arguments provided and the salary to zero. The three-argument constructor sets the first and last names and the salary to the arguments provided. The `private` method `init` does the actual assignments of values to the `private` fields fname, lname, and sal. The fname and lname fields are of type `String`. The init method also sets the Employee's starting date to the current date. The `Date` field named `start` represents the starting date.

Properties and Get/Set Methods

Methods that begin with *get* and *set* are used to define properties or features. For example, the pair of methods

```
public void setLastName( String l );
public String getLastName();
```

together specify a `LastName` property that is *readable* because of the `public` method `getLastName` and *writable* because of the `public` method setLastName. Note that the *get* method's return type is the same as the *set* method's argument type, in this case `String`. The Emp class has a public `getStartDate` method but no `setStartDate` method, which means that property `StartDate` is readable but not writable. By design, an Employee's start date is set automatically to the date on which the object is constructed and this date cannot be changed.   ■

■ **Example 2.4.2.** The `EmpClient` program in Figure 2.4.2 is a test client for the Emp class in Figure 2.4.1. The test client constructs various Emp objects, invokes the *get/set* methods, and dumps information about employees to confirm that the Emp class's public methods behave as they should. Test clients should be written to test the functionality of any programmer-defined class. Figure 2.4.3 shows the output for the test client.   ■

```
class EmpClient {
    public static void main( String[ ] args ) {
        //*** construct 3 ways and dump each
        Emp anon = new Emp();
        Emp bruce = new Emp( "Bruce", "Springsteen", 555666777 );
        Emp cindi = new Emp( "Cindi", "Lauper", 777666555 );
        anon.dump();
        bruce.dump();
        cindi.dump();
        //*** test setFirstName
        cindi.setFirstName( "Cynthia" );
        cindi.dump();
        //*** test setLastName
        bruce.setLastName( "Springsteen, Esq." );
        bruce.dump();
        //*** test setSalary
        cindi.setSalary( 999888777 );
        cindi.dump();
        //*** test getStartDate()
        System.out.println( anon.getStartDate() );
    }
}
```

FIGURE 2.4.2   A test client for the Emp class in Figure 2.4.1.

EXERCISES

1. Construct Employee objects with three different constructor invocations.
2. Add a private integer field to the Emp class to represent an employee identification number, and provide public *get/set* methods to access the field.
3. Amend the test client of Figure 2.4.2 to test the methods added in Exercise 2.

Input and Output

Basic text input and output operations were introduced in the BigAndSmallFile (see Figure 2.2.2) and FillAndSortFile (see Figure 2.2.5) programs. This section reviews and extends the coverage of input and output.

Java's library for input and output is highly modular and flexible but also relatively complex. This section thus presents an overview of the input/output facilities together with examples that illustrate basic programming operations such as reading from and writing to binary and text files. The section also explains how **records**, or character sequences terminated by a newline, can be read from the standard input, which is the keyboard by default. The Sample Application Section 5.4 presents a package of two

```
First name: unknown
Last name:  unknown
Salary:    $0
Start date: Sun Feb 13 12:36:17 CST 2000

First name: Bruce
Last name:  Springsteen
Salary:    $555666777
Start date: Sun Feb 13 12:36:17 CST 2000

First name: Cindi
Last name:  Lauper
Salary:    $777666555
Start date: Sun Feb 13 12:36:17 CST 2000

First name: Cynthia
Last name:  Lauper
Salary:    $777666555
Start date: Sun Feb 13 12:36:17 CST 2000

First name: Bruce
Last name:  Springsteen, Esq.
Salary:    $555666777
Start date: Sun Feb 13 12:36:17 CST 2000

First name: Cynthia
Last name:  Lauper
Salary:    $999888777
Start date: Sun Feb 13 12:36:17 CST 2000
Sun Feb 13 12:36:17 CST 2000
```

FIGURE 2.4.3   Output for the test client in Figure 2.4.2.

classes, `BasicInput` and `BasicOutput`, that wrap the more complex Java classes for input and output.

Stream Input/Ouput

The `java.io` package contains the standard classes to support input and output of binary and character data. All input and output operations deal with a **stream**, which is a sequence of data. A stream has an arbitrary number of data but the items in it are ordered: *first, second,. . . , nth*. An **input stream** has a *source* such as the standard input or a disk file, whereas an **output stream** has a *destination* such as the standard output or a disk file. Classes in the `java.io` package are designed to operate on two basic types of stream:

- **Byte stream**. A byte stream is a sequence of 8-bit bytes. The data in a byte stream are of the primitive type `byte`. In the `java.io` naming convention,

byte streams are called *input streams* and *output streams*. For example, the
java.io package has a class named FileInputStream for reading bytes
from a file as the source; and the package has a corresponding class named
FileOutputStream for writing bytes to a stream with a file as the destination.

- **Character stream**. A character stream is a sequence of 16-bit Unicode characters. The data in a character stream are of the primitive type char. In the
java.io naming convention, character streams are called *readers* and *writers*.
For example, the java.io package has a class named FileReader for reading
characters from a stream whose source is a file; and the package has a corresponding class named FileWriter for writing characters to a stream whose
destination is a file.

In addition to these basic stream types, the java.io package supports input and output
operations on special streams, for example, streams associated with primitive data types
such as int and familiar class types such as String. Finally, the standard package
supports **serialization**, which involves the input and output of *objects*. Serialization is
the foundation for components or *beans* and also plays a central role in distributed
computing.

   With respect to input/output, modern applications need to be flexible, portable,
and international. For example, an application may need to read *characters* from a
byte stream or to read *bytes* from a character stream. Applications may need to run
on systems that use different character encodings (e.g., ASCII versus Unicode) or
alphabets (e.g., Russian versus Arabic). The java.io package is therefore highly
flexible and modular by design. Further, this package illustrates sophisticated Java in
its use of classes, interfaces, and other advanced constructs. As a result, the java.io
package is challenging. The goal of this section is to explain and illustrate basic
input/output operations.

The IOException

An **exception** is an unexpected condition that arises during a program's execution.
For example, a program might inadvertently divide an integer by zero, which is
an error. The result is an *arithmetic exception*, in particular a *division by zero exception*. Java has a rich assortment of classes to represent exceptions. For now, it
is enough to be aware that exception-handling constructs occur throughout the input/output classes. Many of the sample programs in this section contain methods of
the form

```
void readFile( String name ) throws IOException { /*...*/ }
```

The throws IOException clause signals that an exception might be generated from
within the method. For example, the file to be read might not exist or the program
might lack the required permissions to read from the file, either of which could cause
an IOException to be generated or **thrown**.

Binary Input: Counting the Bytes in a File

Example 2.5.1.   The ByteCount program in Figure 2.5.1 counts the number of bytes in a pair of files. The program expects as a command-line argument the file pair's name. For example, if the file pair is *Hi.java* and *Hi.class*, the command-line argument should be *Hi*.

```
import java.io.*;
class ByteCount {
   public static void main( String[ ] args ) throws IOException {
      if ( args.length < 1 ) {
         System.err.println( "java ByteCount <file (no extension)>" );
         return;
      }
      String srcName = args[ 0 ] + ".java",
             binName = args[ 0 ] + ".class";
      FileInputStream inSrc = new FileInputStream( srcName ),
                      inBin = new FileInputStream( binName );
      countAndReport( inSrc, srcName );
      countAndReport( inBin, binName ) ;
      inSrc.close();
      inBin.close();
   }
   private static void countAndReport( FileInputStream f, String name )
     throws IOException {
      int n = 0;
      while ( f.read() != -1 )
        n = n + 1;
      System.out.println( name + " has " + n + " bytes." );
   }
}
```

FIGURE 2.5.1   A program that counts the bytes in a pair of files.

The program opens two FileInputStreams to read the bytes from the two files. The constructor used here takes a String argument that represents the file's name. The method countAndReport does the work, after which each FileInputStream is closed by invoking its close method.

The countAndReport method initializes to zero a local variable n, which holds the file's byte count. A while loop

```
while ( f.read() != -1 )
  n = n + 1;
```

is used for the counting, where f refers to the FileInputStream passed as an argument to countAndReport. The while loop is suited to the task at hand because the size of the input file is unknown; hence, the `while` loop executes until there is no more input. The `read` method reads the next `byte` in the file and returns a `byte`-sized positive integer. On end-of-stream, `read` returns -1, which thus serves as the end-of-stream flag. In each loop iteration, the byte count is incremented by one. When the program was invoked

```
$ java ByteCount ByteCount
```

to determine the size of *ByteCount.java* and *ByteCount.class*, the output was

```
ByteCount.java has 845 bytes.
ByteCount.class has 1231 bytes.
```

Distinguishing Letters and Digits

Example 2.5.2.   The `CharacterLog` program in Figure 2.5.2 illustrates a *reader* and a *writer*, which are used for *character* input and output, respectively. The program should be invoked with two command-line arguments: the first is the name of an input file from which to read characters, and the second is the name of an output file that logs information about the characters read. In particular, the program logs whether a character is a letter such as A or a digit such as 9.

A `while` loop is used to read the input characters until end-of-stream. The loop begins

```
while ( (nextInt = infile.read()) != EOS ) {
   char next = (char) nextInt; //** convert to char
```

The variable `nextInt` is of type `int` and `EOS` is an `int` constant initialized to -1, which the `FileReader`'s method `read` returns to signal end-of-stream. Recall that *integer* types such as `int` are signed, which means that an `int` can represent negative as well as positive values. By contrast, the primitive `char` type is *unsigned* because it represents Unicode character codes, all of which are nonnegative. An 32-bit `int` such as `nextInt` can store a 16-bit Unicode character code. So `read` actually returns values that differ significantly in meaning:

- If `read`'s return value is nonnegative, the value represents a character code.
- If `read`'s return value is negative (in particular, -1), the value represents end-of-stream.

Accordingly, the first statement in the `while` loop's body explicitly converts or **casts** the `int` value stored in `nextInt` to a `char` value. The syntax

```
char next = (char) nextInt; //** convert to char
```

```
import java.io.*;
class CharacterLog {
   public static void main( String[ ] args ) throws IOException {
      if ( args.length < 2 ) {
         System.err.println( "java CharacterLog <infile> <logfile>" );
         return;
      }
      FileReader infile = new FileReader( args[ 0 ] );
      FileWriter logfile = new FileWriter( args[ 1 ] );
      int nextInt;                                   //** Note: int
      while ( (nextInt = infile.read()) != EOS ) {
         char next = (char) nextInt;                 //** convert to char
         if ( Character.isDefined( next ) ) {        //** valid Unicode?
            logfile.write( next );
            if ( Character.isLetter( next ) )
               logfile.write( " is a letter\n" );
            else if ( Character.isDigit( next ) )
               logfile.write( " is a digit\n" );
         }                                           //** end of outer if
      }                                              //** end of while
      infile.close();
      logfile.close();
   }                                                 //** end of main
   final static int EOS = -1;                        //*** end of stream
}
```

FIGURE 2.5.2   A program that distinguishes between letters and digits in a file.

illustrates a cast operation. The cast's target type, in this case char, is enclosed in parentheses and placed immediately to the left of the expression to be converted, in this case the int value of nextInt. The cast is required to avoid a compiler error. If the cast is omitted, the program will not compile because an int value cannot be assigned to a char variable without explicit casting.

As each character is read from the input file, the program first checks whether its value is a valid Unicode character encoding

```
if ( Character.isDefined( next ) ) { //*** valid Unicode?
   logfile.write( next );
```

The java.lang.Character class is the wrapper for the char primitive type. The wrapper's isDefined expects a char argument and returns true, if the char's value is a defined code in Unicode, and false otherwise. If the char's value is defined in Unicode, the program writes the character to the log file and then checks whether the character is a letter or a digit

```
if ( Character.isLetter( next ) )
  logfile.write( " is a letter\n" );
else if ( Character.isDigit( next ) )
  logfile.write( " is a digit\n" );
```

and writes the appropriate message in either case. (The program assumes that the input file has only letters and digits.) The `write` method is overloaded and one overload expects a `String` argument. When end-of-stream occurs, the `while` loop terminates and the input and output files are `closed`. For the input file

a1b67deZ0x2

named *input.dat*, the output generated by

$ java CharacterLog input.dat out.log

in the file *out.log* is

```
a is a letter
1 is a digit
b is a letter
6 is a digit
7 is a digit
d is a letter
e is a letter
Z is a letter
0 is a digit
x is a letter
2 is a digit
```
■

The `FileReader` and `FileWriter` classes of Example 2.5.2 are *convenience classes*, that is, classes that are relatively straightforward to use for input/output operations. The `java.io` package has related classes that address issues of efficiency and customize input and output operations. The key point for now is that *reader* and *writer* classes support *text* input and output, whereas *stream* classes support *binary* input and output.

Echoing the Standard Input to the Standard Output

■ **Example 2.5.3.**   The `PromptAndEcho` program in Figure 2.5.3 echoes the standard input to the standard output and to a disk file. The program repeatedly prompts the user for input, which is then echoed. The user terminates the program by entering `exit` in any mix of uppercase and lowercase letters. The sample run

INPUT> What, me worry?

```
import java.io.*;
class PromptAndEcho {
    public static void main( String[ ] args )
        throws IOException {
            if ( args.length < 1 ) {
                System.err.println( "java PromptAndEcho <output file>" );
                return;
            }
            BufferedReader stdin =
                new BufferedReader( new InputStreamReader( System.in ) );
            PrintWriter pw =
                new PrintWriter( new FileOutputStream( args[ 0 ] ) );
            while ( true ) {
                System.out.print( "INPUT> " );
                String s = stdin.readLine();
                if ( s.equalsIgnoreCase( "exit" ) ) //*** terminate?
                    break;
                System.out.println( s );
                pw.println( s );
            }
            pw.close();
            stdin.close();
    }
}
```

FIGURE 2.5.3   A program that echoes the standard input.

```
What, me worry?
INPUT> Say "Hello", Gracie.
Say "Hello", Gracie.
INPUT> exit
```

illustrates. The program should be invoked with the name of the log file as a command-line argument.

The program uses a `BufferedReader` for input and a `PrintWriter` for file output. Echoing the input to the standard output is handled with the now familiar `println` method encapsulated in the `System.out` object. Recall that a **buffered** reader reads characters from a stream source such as a disk file into a memory buffer. The buffering is done for efficiency, as access to a memory buffer can be considerably faster than direct access to a stream source such as a disk file. The `BufferedReader`, in turn, is constructed from an `InputStreamReader`, which in its turn is constructed from `System.in`, which represents the standard input. By default, the keyboard is the standard input. The statement

```
BufferedReader stdin =
    new BufferedReader( new InputStreamReader( System.in ) );
```

illustrates the relatively complex construction of the BufferedReader to which stdin refers. The BufferedReader class has a readLine method to read **records**, or sequences of characters terminated by newline. The method readLine is the input counterpart of println.

Echoing the output to a disk file is handled through a PrintWriter object, which is quite similar to a PrintStream object such as System.out. The PrintWriter is constructed from a FileOutputStream whose target is the disk file named as a command-line argument. The statement

```
PrintWriter pw =
   new PrintWriter( new FileOutputStream( args[ 0 ] ) );
```

constructs the PrintWriter, which encapsulates the print and println methods also available in PrintStream.

Once the input and file output streams have been constructed, the program enters a potentially infinite loop

```
while ( true ) {
```

because the loop condition is the boolean constant true. The loop terminates only if the break statement

```
if ( s.equalsIgnoreCase( "exit" ) ) //*** terminate?
  break;
```

executes. A break statement causes the program to exit a loop that contains the break. In this if statement's condition, s refers to the String that readLine returns. The String method equalsIgnoreCase is used for comparisons so that the user can terminate the program by entering any of exit, eXiT, EXIt, and so on. The loop's body performs five operations:

- The prompt INPUT> is written to the standard output with the print method.
- The user's input is read as a record from the standard input and stored in the String whose reference is s.
- If the record is any variant of *Exit*, the break statement exits the loop, in which case the input and output streams are closed before the program itself exits.
- The user's input is echoed to the standard output and to the log disk file. The method println is used for both purposes, although one println is a PrintStream method and the other is a PrintWriter method. The PrintStream method writes to the standard output, and the PrintWriter method writes to a disk file. ■

EXERCISES

1. Explain briefly what an *input stream* and an *output stream* are.
2. What is the data type of elements in a *byte stream*?
3. What is the data type of elements in a *character stream*?
4. Explain how the Java terminology pairs *reader/writer* and *input stream/output stream* relate to character and binary streams.
5. What is an *exception*?
6. Test the `ByteCount` program of Figure 2.5.1.
7. Give an example of a condition that would cause an `IOException` to be thrown.
8. The `ByteCount` program in Figure 2.5.1 uses a `FileInputStream`'s method named `read` to read `bytes` from a file. What does `read` return to signal the end-of-file condition?
9. What is the basic difference between a `FileInputStream` and a `FileReader`?
10. The `java.lang.Character` class has a `static` method named `isDefined` that returns either `true` or `false`. Explain when the method returns `true` and when it returns `false`.
11. Write a statement that constructs a `BufferedReader` whose source is a disk file named *input.dat*.
12. Write a statement that constructs a `PrintWriter` whose destination is a disk file named *output.dat*.

2.6   Utility Classes

This section introduces three utility classes from the `java.util` package. The classes are `StringTokenizer`, which is used to break a `String` into parts or *tokens*; `Vector`, a collection of objects that grows and shrinks in size as needed; and `Hashtable`, a collection of objects that supports constant-time lookups through a designated value known as a **key** or **hash value**.

The `StringTokenizer` Class

Suppose that a fourth constructor

```
Emp( String initData ) { /*...*/ }
```

were added to the Emp class of Figure 2.4.1. The constructor's single argument would be a string that included, as parts, the employee's first name, last name, and salary separated by blanks. The invocation

```
Emp elvis = new Emp( "Elvis Presley 888777666" );
```

illustrates. The constructor would need to break the string apart into *tokens* or pieces, in this case three pieces: the first name, the last name, and the salary.

■ **Example 2.6.1.**   The constructor

```
public Emp( String allData ) {
    StringTokenizer st = new StringTokenizer( allData );
    init( st.nextToken(),                      //*** first name
          st.nextToken(),                      //*** last name
          Integer.parseInt( st.nextToken() ) ); //*** salary
}
```

enables an Emp to be constructed with a statement such as

```
Emp dawn = new Emp( "Dawn Upshaw 999888777" );
```

The statement

```
StringTokenizer st = new StringTokenizer( allData );
```

constructs a `StringTokenizer` for the `String` parameter `allData`. The `StringTokenizer` constructors are overloaded. The overload shown here uses whitespace such as blanks and tabs as *token delimiters*, that is, as characters that separate the `String`'s tokens. The `nextToken` method returns the tokens in left to right order. Accordingly, the first invocation of `nextToken` returns the first name `Dawn` as a `String`, the second invocation returns the last name `Upshaw` as a `String`, and the third invocation returns the salary `999888777` as a `String`. The `Integer` class's `parseInt` method is used to convert the salary as a `String` to an `integer`. Recall that the `Emp` class's `init` method assigns values to the appropriate fields.

The `StringTokenizer` class belongs to the `java.util` package. Accordingly, the `import` statement in *Emp.java* should be changed to

```
import java.util.*;
```

so that the fully qualified name need not be used for `StringTokenizer`.   ■

■ **Example 2.6.2.**   The `TokenExample` program in Figure 2.6.1 illustrates another constructor for `StringTokenizers`, in this case a constructor whose second argument is a list of *token delimiters*, which can occur in any order. The example's delimiters, the characters !, %, $, #, and @, are the constructor's second argument. The first argument is the `String` to be tokenized. The program uses a `while` loop

```
while ( st.hasMoreTokens() )
    System.out.println( st.nextToken() );
```

```
import java.util.*;
class TokenExample {
   public static void main( String[ ] args ) {
      String s = "This%is!the$way#the@world%ends";
      String delimiters = "!%$#@";
      StringTokenizer st =
         new StringTokenizer( s, delimiters );
      while ( st.hasMoreTokens() )
        System.out.println( st.nextToken() );
   }
}
```

FIGURE 2.6.1   Another StringTokenizer example.

```
This
is
the
way
the
world
ends
```

FIGURE 2.6.2   Output from the
TokenExample program in
Figure 2.6.1.

that tests whether there are more tokens and, if so, prints the next one. The
hasMoreTokens method returns true, if there are more tokens, and false
otherwise. This method together with nextToken is convenient for processing
strings with arbitrarily many tokens. Figure 2.6.2 shows the output when the
program is run.   ∎

The Vector Class

A Vector is a list of elements. A Vector resembles an array in that both can be used
to aggregate or collect items in a single structure, but a Vector differs from an array
in that a Vector grows and shrinks in size automatically as elements are added and
removed. A primitive type such as an int cannot be stored in a Vector. An int value
would have to be wrapped in an Integer or some other class type in order to be a
Vector element.

   ∎ **Example 2.6.3.**   The VectorEx program in Figure 2.6.3 constructs a Vector and adds four strings to it, each the name of a prominent philosopher. The
Vector is empty when first constructed. As elements are added, the Vector
automatically grows in size.
      After the Vector has been populated with strings, the elements are printed
to the standard output. The code segment

```
import java.util.*;                    //*** for Vector and Enumeration
class VectorEx {
   public static void main( String[ ] args ) {
       Vector v = new Vector();        //*** empty to start
       v.addElement( "aristotle" ); //*** add a String
       v.addElement( "descartes" ); //*** add a String
       v.addElement( "hume" );         //*** add a String
       v.addElement( "kant" );         //*** add a String
       //** print the Vector elements using an Enumeration
       Enumeration e = v.elements();
       while ( e.hasMoreElements() )
          System.out.println( e.nextElement() );
   }
}
```

FIGURE 2.6.3   A program to illustrate Vectors and Enumerations.

```
Enumeration e = v.elements();
while ( e.hasMoreElements() )
   System.out.println( e.nextElement() );
```

uses an Enumeration for the printing. An Enumeration has two methods well suited for processing Vectors:

- hasMoreElements. This method returns true, if the Enumeration still has elements to process, and false otherwise. By using this method, the programmer does not need to track the number of elements in the Vector itself.
- nextElement. This method is analogous to the StringTokenizer method nextToken. The method returns the Vector elements in left to right order.

Recall that, as an argument to println, the expression

```
e.nextElement()
```

is shorthand for

```
e.nextElement().toString()
```

The program's output is

```
aristotle
descartes
hume
kant
```

The Vector class has methods to add and remove individual elements, to remove all elements, to access an element at a specified position, to check whether a particular object occurs among the elements, and so on. Vectors are especially useful when the programmer cannot determine beforehand how many elements need to be aggregated.

The Hashtable Class

A **hashtable** is a collection in which expressions known as **keys** map to other expressions known as **values**. For example, the key *gates* might map to the value *microsoft*, whereas the key *wozniak* might map to the value *apple*. Because a hashtable maps keys to values, a hashtable is also called a *map*. In some systems, a hashtable is also called a *dictionary* because of the resemblance between the two. In a dictionary, *words* serve as keys and *definitions* serve as the values to which the keys map. One important difference is that a dictionary's entries are typically arranged in sorted order, but a hashtable's entries are not arranged in sorted order. A hashtable supports *constant-time lookups*; that is, mapping an arbitrary key K_i to its value takes approximately the same time as mapping any other key K_j to its value.

> **Example 2.6.4.**   The HashEx program in Figure 2.6.4 constructs a Hashtable and populates it with the colors of fruits. A fruit name such as banana is the key and its color, in this case yellow, is the value. Values are inserted into the Hashtable with the put method, whose first argument is the key and whose second argument is the value. Any object can serve as a key or a value, although this example uses Strings as keys and values.
> Values are retrieved from a Hashtable in two different ways. First, an Enumeration (see Figure 2.6.3) is used to enumerate the Hashtable's values. Second, a key is used to get a particular value. The get method expects a key as a single argument. For example, the statement

```
ht.get( "banana" );
```

requests the value for the key banana, where ht refers to a Hashtable. If the table contains the key, the corresponding value is returned; otherwise, the special value null is returned.[†] The method containsKey can be used to test whether a Hashtable contains a particular key

```
if ( ht.containsKey( "cherry" ) )
  System.out.println( ht.get( "cherry" ) );
```

[†]The term null represents a null object reference, that is, a reference that does not refer to any object. Later sections examine null more closely.

```
import java.util.*;
class HashEx {
   public static void main( String[ ] args ) {
      String[ ] keys = { "apple",
                         "banana",
                         "kiwi",
                         "plum" };
      String[ ] vals = { "red",
                         "yellow",
                         "green",
                         "purple" };
      //*** Populate a hashtable
      Hashtable ht = new Hashtable();                //*** empty to begin
      for ( int i = 0; i < keys.length; i++ )
         ht.put( keys[ i ], vals[ i ] );

      //*** Test key to value mappings
      System.out.println( "Dumping some arbitrary values..." );
      System.out.println( ht.get( keys[ 1 ] ) );  //** java.io
      System.out.println( ht.get( keys[ 3 ] ) );  //** java.util
      if ( ht.containsKey( "cherry" ) )
         System.out.println( ht.get( "cherry" ) );
      else
         ht.put( "cherry", "cherry red" );

      //*** Use an Enumeration to dump the hashtable values
      System.out.println( "\nDumping through Enumeration..." );
      Enumeration e = ht.elements();
      while ( e.hasMoreElements() )
         System.out.println( e.nextElement() );

      //*** Use the keys to dump the hashtable values
      System.out.println( "\nDumping through keys..." );
      for ( int i = 0; i < keys.length; i++ )
         System.out.println( ht.get( keys[ i ] ) );
   }
}
```

FIGURE 2.6.4   A program to illustrate the Hashtable class.

There is also a containsValue method to test directly whether a Hashtable contains a particular value.

Figure 2.6.5 shows the output for the Hashtable program in Figure 2.6.4. When the hashtable is dumped by directly enumerating its values, the order is

```
cherry red
green
```

```
Dumping some arbitrary values...
yellow
purple

Dumping through Enumeration...
cherry red
green
red
purple
yellow

Dumping through keys...
red
yellow
green
purple
```

FIGURE 2.6.5 Output from the Hashtable program in Figure 2.6.4.

```
red
purple
yellow
```

When the hashtable is dumped by iterating through the keys and using each to get the corresponding value, the order is

```
red
yellow
green
purple
```

The difference in output underscores that the internal order in which the Hashtable stores its values does not reflect the order in which values were inserted. For example, the red value keyed on apple is inserted *first* but does not occur first in the Enumeration. Further, the Hashtable's internal order is not sorted by either key or value. By the way, the cherry red value does not occur in the second output because its key cherry does not occur in the keys array. ∎

EXERCISES

1. For the string constant "a;b!cef;h", what are the tokens if the delimiters are ; and !?

2. Write a statement that constructs a StringTokenizer with the characters ; and ! as delimiters.

3. Write a statement that constructs a `StringTokenizer` with whitespace characters as the delimiters.

4. To which package do utility classes such as `Vector` and `StringTokenizer` belong?

5. Compare and contrast a `Vector` and an array.

6. Can primitive data types such as `int`s be `Vector` elements?

7. Explain how an `int` value could be inserted into a `Vector`.

8. Write a code segment that constructs a `Vector` and adds four `String`s as elements.

9. How does a `Hashtable` differ from a `Vector`?

10. Write a code segment that constructs a `Hashtable`, puts values into the `Hashtable`, and then gets the values from the `Hashtable` using keys.

JAVA POSTSCRIPT

Options to the `javac` Compilation Command

The JDK compiler `javac` can be invoked with various command-line options. For example, the command

```
$ javac -nowarn Hi.java
```

invokes the compiler with the **nowarn** flag to suppress nonfatal errors, which are called *warnings*. Figure A lists the primary compiler flags. Later chapters and sections go into detail.

COMMON ERRORS AND SAFE PRACTICES

1. A Java *application* is a class with a proper definition of `main`

```
class MyApp {
    public static void main( String[ ] args ) { /*...*/ }
}
```

In particular, `main` must be `public` and `static`, have `void` in place of a return data type, and take a single argument that is an array of `String`s, each of which represents a command-line argument. Although the order of `public` and `static` is arbitrary, `void` must occur immediately to the left of `main`. The `String` array data type can be declared with the syntax

```
String[ ] args
```

Option	Description
-g	Generate all debugging information
-g:none	Generate no debugging information
-g:lines,vars,source	Generate specified debugging information
-O	Optimize
-nowarn	Generate no warnings
-verbose	Output messages about what the compiler is doing
-deprecation	Output line numbers of deprecated language features
-classpath <path>	Specify where to find user class files
-sourcepath <path>	Specify where to find input source files
-bootclasspath <path>	Override location of bootstrap class files
-extdirs <dirs>	Override location of installed extensions
-d <directory>	Specify where to place generated class files
-encoding <encoding>	Specify character encoding used in source files
-target <release>	Generate class files for specific compiler version

FIGURE A   Options to the javac compilation command.

or

```
String args[ ]
```

The parameter's name (in this example, args) is arbitrary but must be present.

2. If a program uses a class from a standard library other than java.lang, the class name must be fully qualified unless the appropriate import statement is used. For this reason, the code segment

```
class Alpha {
   String s; // ok, java.lang.String
   Date d;   //***** ERROR
}
```

contains an error, which can be corrected through either a fully qualified name

```
class Alpha {
   String s; // ok, java.lang.String
   java.util.Date d;   // ok
}
```

or an import statement

```
import java.util.Date;
class Alpha {
   String s; // ok, java.lang.String
   Date d;   // ok
}
```

3. An `import` statement must occur *before* any class definitions in a source file. For this reason, the code segment

```
class Alpha { /*...*/ }
import java.util.*; //***** ERROR
class Zeta { /*...*/ }
```

is in error. The code segment

```
import java.util.*;
class Alpha { /*...*/ }
class Zeta { /*...*/ }
```

corrects the error.

4. In an `import` statement, the star `*` can serve as a wildcard character that covers all *classes* (and interfaces) in a particular package. For example, the `import` statement

```
import java.io.*;
```

covers all classes in the `java.io` package. The wildcard character does *not* cover subpackages, however. For example, the syntax

```
import java.*.*; //***** ERROR
```

is in error. The statement presumably is meant to `import` all classes in all subpackages of the `java` package.

5. It is an error to invoke the compiler `javac` on a file that does not have a *java* extension. Assuming that the current directory contains the source file *Emp.java*, the command

```
$ javac Emp
```

illustrates the error. The correct command is

```
$ javac Emp.java
```

6. It is an error to include the file extension *class* when invoking the runtime interpreter `java` on a *class* file that contains a Java application. For example, if the file *Hi.class* contains a Java application, the command

```
$ java Hi.class
```

is an error. The correct command is

```
$ java Hi
```

2.1. Modify the `BigAndSmall` program in Figure 2.2.1 so that program prints to the standard output the biggest, the second biggest, the smallest, and the second smallest of 10,000 randomly generated integers.

2.2. Write a program that generates N random integers and prints the *median*, that is, the integer value below which and above which would be an equal number of values if the N integers were sorted. *Hints*: The `FillAndSort` problem of Figure 2.2.2 fills and sorts an array of randomly generated `doubles`. If N is odd, the median value is the value of the midpoint element in a sorted array.

2.3. The `nextInt` method in the `java.util.Random` class returns an `int`, which is *signed*. Write a program that

- Uses the `Random` class's `nextInt` method to generate 1,000 random integers. This can be done with the loop construct

```
for ( int i = 0; i < 1000; i++ ) {
   /* statements in the loop body */
}
```

- Counts the number of negative and the number of nonnegative integers generated.
- Prints a report to the standard output about how many negative and nonnegative integers were generated.

2.4. Extend Programming Exercise 2.1 so that the program also prints the mean (average) of the nonnegative integers generated and the mean of the negative integers generated.

2.5. The `java.lang.Integer` wrapper class provides three `static` methods for converting decimal integers to binary, octal, and hexadecimal integers. Each method returns a `String` representation of an integer. The code segment

```
int n = 987;                          //*** decimal
System.out.println( n );              // 987
System.out.println(
     Integer.toBinaryString( n ) ); // 1111011011
System.out.println(
     Integer.toOctalString( n ) );  // 1733
System.out.println(
     Integer.toHexString( n ) );    // 3db
```

illustrates the syntax. Amend Programming Exercise 2.1 so that the integers are printed in binary, octal, decimal, and hexadecimal.

2.6. Write a program that generates N random integers and determines

- The sum of the greatest *nondecreasing* sequence.
- The number of integers in the greatest nondecreasing sequence.

For example, suppose that N is 8 and the generated sequence is

$$5, 11, 4, 19, 21, 18, 47, 7$$

The first nondecreasing sequence is

$$5, 11$$

with a sum of 16 and a count of 2. The next nondecreasing sequence is

$$4, 19, 21$$

with a sum of 44 and a count of 3. The largest nondecreasing sequence is

$$18, 47$$

with a sum of 65 and a count of 2. *Hint*: Tracking whether a sequence is nondecreasing requires only a comparison of the *previous* and the *current* integers. In the sample sequence, for instance, if 11 is the *previous* integer and 4 is the *current* integer, a comparison would show that one nondecreasing sequence ends with 11 and another begins with 4. Note, too, that the minimum length of any nondecreasing sequence is 1.

2.7. Write a program that counts how many random integers in total must be generated in order to generate 500,000 *nonduplicate* integers. *Hint*: Although an int array or even a Vector might be used, the java.util package has a Set interface and a HashSet class that are suited to the task. The code segment

```
Set nums = new HashSet();
nums.add( new Integer( 11 ) );
nums.add( new Integer( 78 ) );
System.out.println( nums.size() ); // 2 is printed
```

illustrates how a set can be constructed and how elements can be added to it. The code segment also shows how the size method can be invoked to determine how elements are currently in the set. A Set, like a Vector, grows in size as needed; but a Set, unlike a Vector, does not contain duplicates. For example, if the code segment above were changed to

```
Set nums = new HashSet();
nums.add( new Integer( 11 ) );
nums.add( new Integer( 78 ) );
```

```
nums.add( new Integer( 11 ) );
System.out.println( nums.size() ); // 2 is still printed
```

the set's size would still be 2 because the set cannot hold duplicate Integers.

2.8. Define a Name class with fields to represent a person's first name, middle name,
and last name. Define the constructors

```
public Name(); // name parts default to "unknown"
public Name( String fname, String minit, String lname );
```

and the methods

```
public void setFname( String fname );
public void setMinit( String minit );
public void setLname( String lname );
public String getFname();
public String getMinit();
public String getLname();
```

2.9. Change the Emp class in Figure 2.4.1 by replacing the String fields named
fname and lname with a Name field (see Programming Exercise 2.8). Also,
add public setMiddleInitial and getMiddleInitial methods to the Emp
class. *Hint*: Emp methods such as setFirstName can be revised as *wrappers*
for the corresponding Name methods such as setFName. For convenience, the
Emp wrappers might be renamed. For instance, the Emp method setFirstName
could be changed to setFName.

2.10. Define a public Course class with fields to represent a course taken by a student
for a degree. The class should be able to represent

- The course number.
- The course name.
- A brief description of the course's contents.
- The instructor's name.
- The academic term in which the course was taken.
- The course status as one of *required* or *elective*.
- The final grade received.

All of the fields should be private with public *get/set* methods for access.

2.11. Define a public AcademicRecord class to record all of the courses (see Programming Exercise 2.10) that a student has taken. Provide the appropriate
constructors, fields, and methods to create AcademicRecords and manipulate
their contents. *Hint*: A structure that grows and shrinks automatically in size,
such as a Vector (see Figure 2.6.3) or a Set (see Programming Exercise 2.2),

is well suited to aggregate `Courses`. Further, `Vectors` and `Sets` have high-level methods to add and remove elements and to test whether a specified element occurs in the aggregate.

2.12. Define a public `RegistrarRecords` class that aggregates all of the student `AcademicRecords` for a particular institution. The class should have a one-argument public constructor

```
public RegistrarRecords( String instName );
```

whose argument specifies the institution's name. Add appropriate fields and methods so that `AcademicRecords` can be added, removed, and printed to the standard output. *Hint*: A structure such as `Hashtable` (see Figure 2.6.4) is well suited to the task. A student identification number could be used as the hash key whose corresponding value would be an `AcademicRecord`, which in turn would be a list of `Courses`.

2.13. Define a Company class with at least a dozen members. For example, there should be fields to represent a company's name, a list of its employees (see the `Emp` class of Figure 2.4.1), and its gross income for the year. The class might have a constructor such as

```
public Company( String name ) { /*...*/ }
```

and methods such as

```
public void setName( String name ) { /*...*/ }
public String getName() { /*...*/ }
```

A public dump method should be provided to print pertinent information about Company such as its name, its employees, and its gross income. Write a test client for the Company class.

2.14. Define a `StockExchange` class with `TradingMember`s as well as `Company` instances (see Programming Exercise 2.13). The `Company` class should be amended to include fields to represent a company's current share price, its high price for the year, and its low price for the year. The `StockExchange` should keep track of `Transactions`, which involves a `Sell` by one `TradingMember` and a `Buy` by another. Write a test client to illustrate the functionality of `StockExchange` objects.

2.15. Write a program that echoes the standard input to the standard output except that whitespace characters such as blanks, tabs, and newlines are echoed as non-whitespace characters. For instance, a blank might be echoed as `<blank>`, a tab as `<tab>`, and so on.

Programs and Packages

Chapter Outline

This chapter examines Java's program types and reviews the relationships among *java* files, *class* files, and packages. The chapter revisits the `import` statement, explains the `package` statement, and clarifies the role of the `CLASSPATH` environment variable.

Section 3.1 explains Java's basic program types: *application*, *applet*, *servlet*, and *bean*. Java programs execute on the **J**ava **V**irtual **M**achine (JVM), which is clarified. Section 3.2 reviews the basic relationship between *java* and *class* files and further clarifies the rules for naming source files. The *class* files produced through compilation belong to **packages**, that is, collections of related *class* files. Section 3.3 examines the relationship among source files, compiled files, and packages. For convenience, the chapter includes reference tables that list the classes in the standard packages. The chapter ends with a sample application that uses a programmer-defined package.

3.1   Program Types

Java has several program types, although the differences among them are shallow. Every Java program has at least one class, and the language's basic programming constructs are available in all program types. The program types have evolved. For example, *applications* and *applets* have been a part of Java from the beginning, whereas *servlets* and *beans* are more recent additions to Java's program types. This section introduces the basic program types, which later sections clarify in detail.

The Java Virtual Machine

Java programs, whatever their type, execute on the **J**ava **V**irtual **M**achine (JVM), which is a *virtual* machine, that is, an *abstract* rather than a physical machine. Although the JVM can be implemented in silicon or some other material, the JVM typically is implemented in software as a **runtime interpreter** or **interpreter** for short.[†] When implemented as an interpreter, the JVM acts as a translator of executable instructions called **bytecodes** into the **native instruction codes** of a particular system, for example, a Unix workstation or a Windows personal computer. The programs in this book were executed using the standard interpreter available as the `java` utility, which comes with the JDK (see Section 2.1).

The JVM provides a **runtime environment** or **runtime** that enables a Java program to execute on a particular system and to perform typical programming tasks such as input and output. The runtime interpreter can work with a **security manager** to determine precisely which tasks a program may perform. For example, the security manager may disallow writing to local disks or opening connections to arbitrary machines on a network.

[†]Java also has a KVM, a "lean" version of the JVM suitable for embedded systems.

```
<HTML>
  <HEAD>
    <TITLE> A simple applet</TITLE>
  </HEAD>
  <BODY>
    <APPLET CODE="HiApp.class" WIDTH=400 HEIGHT=400></APPLET>
  </BODY>
</HTML>
```

FIGURE 3.1.1   An HTML document with an APPLET tag.

Applications

An **application** is a *standalone program*, a program that requires only the JVM to execute. By contrast, the other program types—applets, servlets, and beans—require a **host program** to execute. In the case of applets, the host program is typically a *Web browser*. In the case of servlets, the host program is typically a *Web server*. In the case of beans, the host program can be of any other program type—application, applet, servlet, or another bean. A Java application can be run by using the `java` interpreter that comes with the JDK. For example, if the file *Hi.class* contains a Java *application*, the command

    $ java Hi

executes the application.

The term *application* is commonly used outside of Java as a synonym for *program*. In contexts that might lead to confusion, the term *application* is italicized when it refers to a particular Java program type.

Applets

An **applet**, in the original sense, is a *small* program that is typically launched through a Web document and has a Web browser as a host program. However, applets can be launched in other ways, as later examples illustrate. Figure 3.1.1 shows an HTML (**H**yper **T**ext **M**arkup **L**anguage) document with an APPLET tag. When a browser loads this HTML document, the APPLET tag causes the browser to download and execute the program—in this example, the executable file *HiApp.class*—from the server that provided the HTML document. The browser uses the JVM to execute the applet. Of course, the browser itself might be a Java application that runs directly on the JVM. If an applet has graphics, the browser typically provides the applet with an area within the browser's own window to display the graphics. In the typical case, an applet executes on the *client* machine, the machine that is running the browser. The applet code resides originally on the *server* machine, the machine that likewise provides the HTML document to launch the applet. Java first gained widespread attention through the applet.

An applet can originate on the local machine that executes the applet. In other words, applets can be executed *without* network connections. Nonetheless, applets were designed precisely for a client/server environment in which a client machine downloads and executes an applet that resides originally on a remote server machine. Sections 9.4 and 9.5 examine applets in the context of network programming.

Servlets

A **servlet**, like an applet, is typically launched through a Web document. A servlet, however, executes on the *server* machine and, in this respect, differs fundamentally from an applet, which executes on the *client* machine. A servlet's host program is normally a *Web server*, a program on a server machine that handles requests for services from Web clients. Figure 3.1.2 shows an HTML document that launches a servlet named ProcessOrder, which resides on the server machine in the file *ProcessOrder.class*. Such a servlet might be launched from an HTML document that contains an order

```
<HTML>
  <HEAD>
    <TITLE> A simple servlet</TITLE>
  </HEAD>
  <BODY>
    <FORM METHOD=GET ACTION="ProcessOrder">
      Press the button to submit order.
      <INPUT TYPE=SUBMIT>
    </FORM>
  </BODY>
</HTML>
```

FIGURE 3.1.2   An HTML document that launches the servlet named ProcessOrder.

form for merchandise. When the user submits the HTML form by clicking its *Submit* button, the servlet would execute on the server to extract and process the submitted information. The servlet then might update a database and transmit back to the client's browser another HTML document that confirms the order. Servlets are a Java-based alternative to CGI (**C**ommon **G**ateway **I**nterface) scripts and proprietary approaches to server-side processing. Sections 10.4 and 10.5 examine servlets and their use in connection with databases.

Beans

A **bean** is a Java component, that is, a prebuilt and reusable software module that can be integrated into a host program such as a Java application (see Section 1.5). For example, a Java *application* might use a prebuilt LoginBean (see Section 8.2) to validate user names and passwords. A program might use a prebuilt CalendarBean that allows users to enter dates through a graphical user interface with buttons representing the days of a specified month and year. A well-designed bean has an associated GUI (**G**raphical

User Interface) known as a **property sheet**. As the name suggests, the property sheet displays the bean's properties. The user can visually edit selected properties through the GUI. For example, the `LoginBean` might have a property called `CaseSensitive`: if set to `true`, the bean would distinguish between uppercase and lowercase characters in validating a user name and a password; if set to `false`, the `LoginBean` would ignore case during the validation. Section 10.1 examines beans in detail.

Summary of Program Types

On an informal level, Java program types differ mainly in their purpose and functionality. For example, an applet is a program meant to be distributed by a server machine to client machines, where the applet typically executes with a client's Web browser as the host program. A servlet, by contrast, is a program meant to execute on a server machine in response to client requests typically made through a Web browser. Yet an applet and a servlet can use the very same programming constructs. The point is that the distinctions among *application*, *applet*, *servlet*, and *bean* are not deep.

On a technical level, the requirements for being an application, applet, servlet, or bean are straightforward. The requirements allow a given program to be more than one type. For example, a program could be both a servlet and a bean. Every applet is automatically a bean. This section closes with a summary of minimal requirements that a class must satisfy for each program type. Later sections explain these requirements in detail.

- **Application**. Any class that has method named `main` with the appropriate features is thereby an application.
- **Applet**. Any class that is derived from the `Applet` class is thereby an applet.
- **Servlet**. Any class that implements the `Servlet` interface or one of its subinterfaces is thereby a servlet.
- **Bean**. Any class that implements the `Serializable` interface is thereby a bean.

EXERCISES

1. What does JVM stand for?
2. What does *virtual* signify in JVM?
3. Could the JVM be implemented as a *physical* machine?
4. What is a runtime environment?
5. Explain the relationship between the JDK *java* utility and the JVM.
6. What are *bytecodes*?
7. Explain the relationships among bytecodes, the JVM, and native instruction codes.

8. Explain the general responsibility of a *security manager*.

9. What is a Java *application*?

10. What is an *applet*?

11. What is a *servlet*?

12. Does an applet typically execute on a client or a server?

13. Does a servlet typically execute on a client or a server?

14. What is a *bean*?

15. Are the differences among Java's program types deep or shallow?

▮ 3.2 ▮ Review of Source Files and Class Files

This section reviews the relationship between source files and compiled files. The most obvious difference is that source files have a *java* extension and compiled files have a *class* extension.

▮ **Example 3.2.1.**   The Hi program in Figure 3.2.1 is an undocumented copy of the program in Section 2.1. The program occurs in a text file named *Hi.java*.

```
class Hi {
   public static void main( String[ ] a ) {
     System.out.println( "Hello, world!" );
   }
}
```

FIGURE 3.2.1 Source code in the file *Hi.java*.

Recall that Java source files have a *java* extension. This particular source file is named *Hi.java* to underscore that the file contains a definition for the class Hi. Although the file could have any name with a *java* extension, *Hi.java* is the preferred name precisely because the file contains a definition for the class Hi. Compiling *Hi.java* generates the binary file *Hi.class*. The binary or *class* file is automatically named *Hi* because the source file contains the definition of the class named Hi. ▮

Recall that a source file may contain multiple class definitions, which may occur in any order.

▮ **Example 3.2.2.**   The code segment

```
//*** Start of file Alpha.java
class Alpha { /*...*/ }
class Zeta { /*...*/ }
//*** End of file Alpha.java
```

shows source file *Alpha.java*, which contains two class definitions. The two class definitions could occur in any order; in particular, class `Zeta` could occur first in the file. The file could have been named *Zeta.java* or even *foo.java*, although the latter name would be confusing because the file does not contain a class named `foo`.

Compiling the source file *Alpha.java* produces two *class* files, *Alpha.class* and *Zeta.class*, because the source file contains definitions for class `Alpha` and class `Zeta`. Compilation of a source file produces one *class* file per class defined in the source file. ■

Source Files with a `public` Class

If a source file contains a `public` class, the source file *must* have the `public` class's name. Because a source file can have only one name, it follows that a source file can contain one `public` class at most.

Example 3.2.3. The class

```
public class FileUtils { //*** Note: public
  //...
}
```

must occur in a source file named *FileUtils.java* because `FileUtils` is a `public` class. The *FileUtils.java* file can contain definitions of other classes, although none of these can be `public`. ■

The keyword `public`'s meaning is explained in detail later. For now, the important point is that a `public` class must occur in a source file that carries its name. The rules governing source file names can be summarized as follows:

- If a source file contains a `public` class (e.g., `FileUtils`), then the source file must have the `public` class's name (e.g., *FileUtils.java*).
- If a source file contains no `public` classes, the source file can have any name, although the file still requires a *java* extension.
- A source file cannot have more than one `public` class.

EXERCISES

1. What is the extension for source files?
2. What is the extension for compiled source files?
3. If a source file contains the definitions

```
class A { /*...*/ }
class K { /*...*/ }
class Z { /*...*/ }
```

how many *class* files will be produced through compilation of this source file?

4. For Question 3, what will the names of the compiled files be?

5. Do bytecodes occur in files with a *java* or a *class* extension?

3.3   Packages

Files with a *class* extension are aggregated into **packages** or collections of related *class* files. A package thus can serve as a **software library** that groups related classes. For example, Java has a standard network package that aggregates classes useful for networking applications. This section examines standard and programmer-created packages. In particular, the section explains the `import` and `package` statements and the CLASSPATH environment variable.

Java's main package is appropriately named `java` and its main subpackage is named `lang`. There is also a standard extension package named `javax` that contains, for example, classes for GUI programming. Packages can have subpackages to an arbitrary level, although the standard packages stop at three levels. The period . is used to separate package and subpackage names. For example, the `lang` subpackage of the `java` package is named `java.lang`. The input/output output subpackage of the `java` package is named `java.io`.

■ **Example 3.3.1.**   The `java` package has a `security` subpackage, which in turn has an `interfaces` subpackage, whose full name is thus

```
javax.security.interfaces
```

The `java` package has several other subpackages of subpackages (see Figure 3.3.1).   ■

The term *package* covers packages and their subpackages. So, for example, both `java` and `java.lang` are *packages*.

The `import` Statement

■ **Example 3.3.2.**   The `Hi` program in Figure 3.3.3 amends the original `Hi` program of Figure 2.1.1. The output for a sample run of the amended program is

```
Hello, world! on Sun Feb 26 23:59:15 CST 2000
```

Package	Interfaces and Classes for
java.applet	Applets
java.awt	Graphics and graphical user interfaces
java.awt.datatransfer	Cut-and-paste functionality
java.awt.event	Event processing
java.awt.image	Image processing
java.awt.peer	Platform independent graphics
java.beans	Software components
java.io	Input and output
java.lang	Core language functionality
java.lang.reflect	Reflection ("introspection")
java.math	Arbitrary precision arithmetic
java.net	Networking
java.rmi	Remote method invocation
java.rmi.dgc	Support of java.rmi
java.rmi.registry	Support of java.rmi
java.rmi.server	Support of java.rmi
java.security	Security
java.security.acl	Support of java.security
java.security.interfaces	Support of java.security
java.sql	Database
java.text	Internationalization
java.util	Various utilities
java.util.zip	Compression and decompression

FIGURE 3.3.1   The java packages.

Package	Interfaces and Classes for
javax.accessibility	Assistive technology
javax.swing	"Lightweight" graphics and graphical user interfaces
javax.swing.border	Specialized borders
javax.swing.colorchooser	Color selection
javax.swing.event	Event processing extending java.awt.event
javax.swing.filechooser	File selection
javax.swing.plaf	**P**luggable **L**ook **A**nd **F**eel
javax.swing.plaf.basic	Basic look and feel
javax.swing.plaf.metal	Metal look and feel
javax.swing.plaf.multi	Multiplexing look and feel
javax.swing.table	Table representation of data
javax.swing.text	Text representation and processing
javax.swing.text.html	HTML (**H**yper **T**ext **M**arkup **L**anguage) text
javax.swing.text.rtf	RTF (**R**ich **T**ext **F**ormat) text
javax.swing.tree	Tree representation of data
javax.swing.undo	Undo capabilities in text editing

FIGURE 3.3.2   The javax packages.

```
//*** Import all classes (*) in the java.lang subpackage
//    (This import is correct but unnecessary because it
//    represents an implicit import in every Java program.)
import java.lang.*;
//*** Import the Date class from the java.util subpackage
import java.util.Date;
class Hi {
  public static void main( String[ ] a ) {
    String msg = "Hello, world!";  // String is in java.lang
    Date today = new Date();       // Date is in java.util
    // prints "Hello, world!" followed by " on " followed by
    // a String representation of today's date
    System.out.println( msg + " on " + today.toString() );
  }
}
```

FIGURE 3.3.3   Sample packages and the import directive.

The amended program contains the import statements

import java.lang.*;

and

import java.util.Date;

An import statement directs the compiler (javac) where to look—that is, in which *packages* to look—for classes not found in the current directory. So the first import statement directs the compiler to look in the java.lang package. The amended program uses the standard String class but the file *String.class* is not in the current directory. So the first import statement directs the compiler to look in the java.lang package for the definition of String in the appropriate binary file, that is, *String.class*.

The import of the java.lang package is correct but unnecessary because the compiler automatically imports this package. The package java.lang contains the core classes for the language, which explains why it need not be explicitly imported. The import of java.lang is used here only to clarify the syntax and underlying meaning of importing. The program would still compile if this import statement were omitted.

An import statement does *not* import anything physically into the source file that contains the statement. Instead, an import statement acts primarily as a compiler directive. The statement also helps to document the source code, for the statement indicates which packages the code uses. For example, a source file that contains

import java.net.*;

thereby indicates that the program is using classes from the networking package. For convenience, the java package and all its subpackages are called **standard packages** and the classes contained therein are called **standard classes**.

The second import statement in Figure 3.3.1 directs the compiler to use the definition of Date in the java.util package. This import statement is required for the program to compile. If the statement were omitted, then Date's fully qualified name—java.util.Date—would have to be used. ■

Use of the import Statement

In summary, import statements are optional. The programmer can avoid all imports, but at the price of using the fully qualified name of each classes not found in the current directory. The import statement is popular precisely because it is far more convenient to write

```
Date today; // abbreviated name
```

than to write

```
java.util.Date today; // fully qualified name
```

Use of abbreviated names for standard classes requires import statements, except for classes such as String that occur in the java.lang package. (Figure 3.3.1 lists the standard packages with brief descriptions of each. Figure 3.3.2 lists the standard extension packages.) Code generators in commercial integrated development environments commonly use fully qualified names, even if they also have the corresponding import statements.

An import statement must occur in a source file *before* any class definitions. A code segment such as

```
class A { /*...*/ }
import javax.swing.*; //**** ERROR
```

contains an error because a class definition occurs before an import statement. The correct order is

```
import javax.swing.*;
class A { /*...*/ }
```

Finally, the wildcard character * in an import statement covers only *classes* rather than subpackages. For example, the java.awt package has an important subpackage named java.awt.event. The import directive

```
import java.awt.*; //*** all classes in awt
```

covers all of the *classes* in the `java.awt` package but *none* of the classes in the `event` subpackage. To `import` all of the classes in the package and its subpackage, the pair of statements

```
import java.awt.*;       // all awt classes
import java.awt.event.*; // all event classes
```

is required.

Packages and Name Conflicts

Packages are useful not only for aggregating related classes but also for avoiding name conflicts. For example, the standard `java.awt` package (**a**bstract **w**indow **t**oolkit) has a `List` class for graphically displaying choices that can be selected with a mouse click. The `java.util` package has a `List` interface that declares methods for processing an abstract list, that is, a sequence of zero or more elements. Only the fully qualified name can indicate which `List` is meant.

■ **Example 3.3.3.**   The code segment

```
import java.awt.*;   // has a List class
import java.util.*;  // has a List interface
class Sample {
    List list1; //***** ERROR: List is ambiguous
}
```

contains an error because `List` could be `java.awt.List` or `java.util.List`. The error can be avoided by using the fully qualified name for each `List`, as the code segment

```
class Sample {
    java.awt.List  list1; // ok, a gui List
    java.util.List list2; // ok, an abstract List
}
```

illustrates.   ■

Default and Named Packages

Every *class* file occurs in a package, although the package need not be named explicitly. If a source file does *not* begin with a `package` statement, then the classes contained therein reside in a **default unnamed package** when the source file is successfully compiled.

■ **Example 3.3.4.**   The source file

```
//*** start of file SoccerTeam.java
class SoccerTeam {
  // members
}
//*** end of file SoccerTeam.java
```

does not begin with a **package** statement. Therefore, when *SoccerTeam.java* is compiled to produce the file *SoccerTeam.class*, the *class* file belongs to an unnamed default package.   ■

■ **Example 3.3.5.**   Suppose that the directory */java/myprogs*[†] contains the source files

```
//*** start of file SoccerTeam.java
class SoccerTeam {
  // members
}
//*** end of file SoccerTeam.java
```

and

```
//*** start of file SoccerTourney.java
class SoccerTourney {
  // members
}
//*** end of file SoccerTourney.java
```

Neither source file begins with a **package** statement. Now suppose that the files are compiled in this directory with the command

```
$ javac *.java
```

The resulting *class* files also reside in the directory */java/myprogs*. The two files reside in the *same* unnamed default package.   ■

The package Statement

Unnamed packages are adequate for small programs, which may consist of only two or three *class* files in the same directory. Larger programs may consist of tens or even hundreds of *class* files in many different directories. For larger programs, it thus makes

---

[†]This directory is given in Unix style using the slash symbol /. The corresponding Windows directory would use the backslash.

sense *explicitly* to group related classes into packages, regardless of whether these related classes happen to reside in the same directory. The `package` statement serves precisely this purpose.

■ **Example 3.3.6.**   We amend Example 3.3.5 by beginning each source file with an explicit `package` statement. The two source files are now

```
//*** start of file SoccerTeam.java
package soccer; //*** Note: statement starts the file
class SoccerTeam {
  // members
}
//*** end of file SoccerTeam.java
```

and

```
//*** start of file SoccerTourney.java
package soccer; //*** Note: statement starts the file
class SoccerTourney {
  // members
}
//*** end of file SoccerTourney.java
```

After compilation, the resulting *class* files reside in the *same package* regardless of whether they reside in the same directory. The `package` statement ensures that classes `SoccerTeam` and `SoccerTourney` belong to the same package. Two different programmers, working in two different directories, thus could contribute to the same package.

The `package` statement must occur *first* in a source file. For example, a `package` statement must come before any `imports`.

■ **Example 3.3.7.**   The code segment

```
import java.util.*;  // import occurs first
package soccer;      //*** ERROR: package is not first
class SoccerTeam {
  // members
}
```

contains an error because the `package` statement does occur first. The code segment

```
package soccer;      // ok, occurs first
import java.util.*;
```

```
class SoccerTeam {
  // members
}
```

corrects the error.   ■

By convention, third-party packages often begin with `com` or `org`. For example, a statistics package from IBM might be named `com.ibm.stats` and a graphics package from Microsoft might be named `com.ms.wfc` (**w**indows **f**oundation **c**lasses). JDK utilities such as the `javac` compiler can find *standard* packages such as `java.lang`. The next subsection explains what must be done for such utilities to find commercial and *programmer-defined* packages.

The CLASSPATH Environment Variable

JDK utilities such as the compiler (`javac`) and the interpreter (`java`) know where to find standard packages such as `java.lang` and the class files such as *String.class* contained therein. So if a program uses the `String` class, the `javac` compiler and the `java` interpreter can find the *String.class* file. Yet JDK programs such as `javac` may not be able to find *programmer-defined* packages and their classes. Accordingly, the `CLASSPATH` environment variable is used to direct various JDK utilities such as `javac` and `java` where to find programmer-defined packages and classes.

The `CLASSPATH` variable specifies an ordered list of directories and files. Under Windows, items in the list are separated by semicolons; under Unix, the items are separated by colons. On a Windows platform, a sample value of the `CLASSPATH` variable is

```
C:\java\addons;C:\java\printf\hr5.jar
```

Under Unix, the same value would be

```
/java/addons:/java/printf/hr5.jar
```

For simplicity, we focus on how the interpreter `java` uses the `CLASSPATH` environment variable.

■ **Example 3.3.8.**   Suppose that we invoke the interpreter on a Windows system to run the program in the file *Hi.class*:

```
$ java Hi
```

Assume that the file *Hi.class* resides in the current directory, that is, the directory from which the interpreter is invoked. In this example, we assume that the current directory is

```
C:\myprograms\hiprog
```

Invoking the interpreter from the *hiprog* directory makes *hiprog* the *current directory*. If the file *Hi.class* resides in the current directory, the interpreter finds it. Now assume that *Hi.class* does *not* reside in the current directory. Given CLASSPATH value

```
C:\java\addons;C:\java\printf\hr5.jar
```

the interpreter searches in this order for the file *Hi.class*:

1. The current directory, which in this example is

```
C:\myprograms\hiprog
```

2. The directory

```
C:\java\addons
```

which is the first entry in our CLASSPATH list.

3. The file

```
C:\java\printf\hr5.jar
```

which is the second entry in our CLASSPATH list. A *jar* file such as *hr5.jar* is Java's version of the familiar *zip* file.[†]

If the interpreter cannot find *Hi.class* in any of these locations, the interpreter issues a fatal error message to that effect.   ■

If the CLASSPATH environment variable is not set on a particular system, its value defaults to the current directory and the location of the standard classes. The CLASSPATH's value can be overriden with the -classpath option to various commands such as javac and java.

Subdirectories as Subpackages

Because the CLASSPATH environment variable includes the *current directory* among its default settings, a program in the current directory can treat subdirectories as *subpackages* that can be imported in the usual way.

■ **Example 3.3.9.**   Figure 3.3.4 lists the source files *TestHi.java* and *Hi.java*. The file *TestHi.java* resides in a directory named *tester*, and the file *Hi.java* resides in *subdirectory* of *tester* named *hiPkg* (see Figure 3.3.5). The command

```
$ javac TestHi.java
```

[†]Files with *jar* and *zip* extensions are **archives**, that is, collections of other files. An archive is typically compressed for storage efficiency.

```
//**** Start of file
//        tester/TestHi.java  ** Unix path
//        tester\TestHi.java  ** DOS path
import hiPkg.Hi;
class TestHi {
   public static void main( String[ ] args ) {
       Hi hi = new Hi();
       hi.sayHi();
   }
}
//**** end of file TestHi.java

//**** Start of file
//       tester/hiPkg/Hi.java  ** Unix path
//       tester\hiPkg\Hi.java  ** DOS path
package hiPkg;
public class Hi {
   public Hi() {
      message = "**** Hello, world---with fanfare! ***";
   }
   public void sayHi() {
      System.out.println( message );
   }
   private String message;
}
//*** end of file Hi.java
```

FIGURE 3.3.4   Treating a subdirectory as a subpackage.

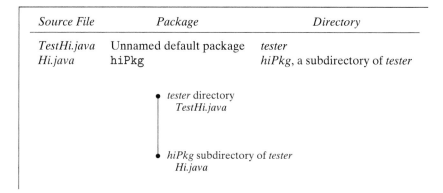

Source File	Package	Directory
TestHi.java	Unnamed default package	*tester*
Hi.java	hiPkg	*hiPkg*, a subdirectory of *tester*

- *tester* directory
  TestHi.java

- *hiPkg* subdirectory of *tester*
  Hi.java

FIGURE 3.3.5   The package/subpackage and directory/subdirectory relationship.

produces the corresponding class files *TestHi.class*, which belongs to an unnamed default package, and *Hi.class*, which belongs to the explicitly named package *hiPkg*. Keep in mind that the subdirectory *hiPkg*, which contains the file *Hi.class*, is an immediate subdirectory of *tester*, which contains the file *TestHi.class*. Note, too, that the two *class* files reside in the same directories as their corresponding source files. Although only the file *TestHi.java* is named in the compilation command, the file *Hi.java* is automatically compiled because a Hi object is referenced inside the TestHi program. The compiler is "smart" enough to note the dependency and to compile *Hi.java* as well, which the compiler finds in subdirectory *hiPkg*.

The TestHi program constructs a Hi object and invokes the object's sayHi method. In effect, Hi is a utility class at the service of applications such as TestHi. Two points need emphasis:

• The source file *Hi.java* uses a package statement that places the Hi class in a package named hiPkg. The package name is the *same* as the directory name—*hiPkg*—in which the file *Hi.class* resides once *Hi.java* has been compiled.

• The source file *TestHi.java* imports the Hi class in the hiPkg package with the statement

```
import hiPkg.Hi;
```

After compilation, the file *TestHi.class* resides in the *tester* directory, which has *hiPkg* as a subdirectory. The javac compiler, in following the import directive, therefore looks for the file *Hi.class* in the subdirectory *hiPkg*, which represents a *subpackage* of the default package to which the file *TestHi.class* belongs.

The fact that the TestHi class happens to reside in an unnamed *default* package has no impact on the example. For example, even if the TestHi class were placed in an explicitly named package

```
package someNameOrOther;
import hiPkg.Hi;
class TestHi {
```

the import statement would remain the same.

The package/subpackage relationship is not confined to physical directory/sub-directory relationships. In other words, a subpackage need not be located in a specific physical subdirectory. Indeed, the CLASSPATH environment variable allows packages and their subpackages to be located anywhere on a system. Yet the use of subdirectories as subpackages is especially convenient for classes that reside in unnamed default packages. The subdirectory approach to subpackages is relatively straightforward and can be used to experiment with subpackaging.

EXERCISES

1. Is a package a collection of *class* files or *java* files?
2. What is the main Java package and subpackage?
3. What does the *x* in javax stand for?
4. Is an import of the java.lang package required to use classes in this package such as the String class?
5. Is it an error explicitly to import the java.lang package?
6. Does an import statement physically import the specified file into the file that contains the statement?
7. What is a *fully qualified name* with respect to a class such as the standard Date class?
8. Suppose that file *Emp.java* contains a definition for an Emp class but no package statement. Does the file *Emp.class* still occur in a package?
9. What is a default or unnamed package?
10. Must two *class* files reside in the same directory to belong to the same package?
11. Explain the purpose of the CLASSPATH environment variable.
12. Explain how a subdirectory can be used to create a subpackage.

3.4   Sample Application: Generating Nonnegative Integers

Problem

Create a utility class to generate nonnegative random integers. The class should reside in a programmer-defined package.

Output

A sample run of the client program in Figure 3.4.1 produced the output

```
i == 0   RandNN == 175139272
i == 1   RandNN == 2068908334
i == 2   RandNN == 695268458
i == 3   RandNN == 2105101720
i == 4   RandNN == 996216726
i == 5   RandNN == 1713894781
i == 6   RandNN == 726285311
i == 7   RandNN == 1531037665
i == 8   RandNN == 160737124
i == 9   RandNN == 1049210161
```

```
import myutils.RandNN;
class MyUtilsClient {
   public static void main( String[ ] args ) {
      RandNN nn = new RandNN();
      int i = 0, n = 10;
      while ( i < n ) {
         System.out.println( "i == " + i +
                            "  RandNN == " + nn.nextInt() );
         i = i + 1;
      }
   }
}
```

FIGURE 3.4.1   Client to test the RandNN class.

Solution

Recall that the java.util package has a Random class whose objects can be used to generate random integers and floating-point numbers. However, the integer types such as int are *signed*, which means that a Random object can generate *negative* random integers. The solution here is a **wrapper class** called RandNN. A wrapper class such as RandNN leverages but modifies the functionality of another class, in this case the standard Random class. In particular, RandNN objects generate only *nonnegative* random integers.

Java Implementation

```
package myutils;            //*** programmer-defined package
import java.util.Random;    //*** utility class for random numbers
public class RandNN {       //*** public class
   public RandNN() {        //*** exposed constructor
      r = new Random();     //*** create Random object
   }
   public int nextInt() {   //*** exposed method
      int t = r.nextInt();  //*** get next integer
      return Math.abs( t ); //*** return a nonnegative integer
   }
   private Random r;         //*** hidden field
}
```

Discussion

The source file *RandNN.java* begins with the package statement that creates a package named myutils. At present, the package contains only the RandNN class, but the package can be expanded to include other programmer-defined utility classes. The class RandNN is public so that it is visible—that is, accessible—outside the myutils package. Indeed, the very point of the myutils package is to populate the package with utility classes that can be accessed from any other package. Because RandNN is a public class, it is said to have **public scope** or **public visibility**. The alternative for classes is **package scope** or **package visibility**. For example, if we change

```
public class RandNN {    //**** public class
```

to

```
class RandNN {           //**** nonpublic class
```

then RandNN would have package scope and, therefore, would be visible only to other classes in the myutils package.

The class RandNN has a public constructor, a public method named nextInt, and a private field named r, which is a reference to a Random object. A class's public members are visible wherever the class is visible; hence, the no-argument constructor and the method nextInt are visible wherever RandNN is visible. By contrast, the private field named r (of type Random) has private scope, which means that r is accessible only within the RandNN class. Accordingly, only RandNN members can access r. Field r is thus *hidden* in the RandNN class, whereas the constructor and the method nextInt are *exposed* by the RandNN class.

Review of Constructors and Methods

Recall that constructors and methods differ in important respects:

- A **constructor** has the same name as the class in which the constructor is encapsulated and has no return type. The keyword void is never used in place of a return type for a constructor.
- A **method** does not have the same name as the class in which the method is encapsulated and does have either a return type or void in place of a return type.

Changing

```
public RandNN() {       //*** exposed constructor
```

to

```
public void RandNN() { //*** ERROR: void not allowed!
```

would be an error because a constructor must not have either a return type or void in place of a return type. Changing

```
public int nextInt() { //*** exposed method
```

to

```
public nextInt() { //*** ERROR: return type missing
```

would be an error because a method must have a return type or void in place of a return type.

As the name suggests, a constructor is used to construct an instance of a class. In particular, a RandNN object is created with the syntax

```
new RandNN() // new operator and constructor call
```

This expression uses the new operator together with the RandNN constructor to allocate sufficient storage for a RandNN object. The expression creates an unreferenced RandNN object. Referencing an object requires an identifier. For example, the statement

```
RandNN nn = new RandNN();
```

creates a RandNN object with a reference named nn. Recall that nn is an *object reference*, that is, an identifier that refers to an object of a class type, in this case type RandNN.

The RandNN constructor invokes a Random class constructor to construct a Random object whose identifier is a private field in RandNN named r. The field r refers to a Random object used to generate random integers that are then converted to nonnegative integers, if required.

A RandNN method such as nextInt does not construct RandNN objects but rather performs some appropriate RandNN operation. In this case, nextInt returns the next randomly generated nonnegative integer. The method has an empty argument list and returns a value of type int. The method's body begins with a left brace { and extends to the matching right brace }:

```
public int nextInt() {   //*** body begins with {
   int t = r.nextInt();   //** get next integer
   return Math.abs( t );  //** return as a nonnegative integer
}                         //*** body ends with }
```

The method uses a local int variable named t to store a random integer generated by the Random object named r, which is a RandNN field. Class Random belongs to the standard java.util package and it, too, has a method named nextInt. Because the Random method named nextInt can return a negative integer, the java.lang.Math class's abs method is invoked to convert a negative integer to a nonnegative one. (The abs stands for absolute value.)

Compiling and Running the Sample Application

For the test client in Figure 3.4.1 to compile and run, the compiler javac and the interpreter java must be able to find the myutils package. Two approaches are possible:

- A subdirectory named *myutils* can be placed immediately below the directory in which the test client resides. The file *RandNN.class* resides in this subdirectory.

- The CLASSPATH environment variable could be set to include the path to the *myutils* package, which at present contains only the *RandNN.class* file. In this case, the file *RandNN.class* need not occur in a subdirectory immediately below the directory that holds the test client.

The CLASSPATH approach is more flexible but likewise more complicated because the environment variable must be set. Regardless of the approach taken, the test client uses an import statement

```
import myutils.RandNN;
```

to import the RandNN class by name, which then allows the client's main to construct a RandNN object

```
RandNN nn = new RandNN();
```

without using the fully qualified name myutils.RandNN. The RandNN object's reference is nn. The identifier nn is not a field in the MyUtilsClient class but rather a local variable in the method main. After constructing the RandNN object, main repeatedly invokes the object's nextInt method

```
while ( i < n ) {
   System.out.println( "i == " + i +
                      "   RandNN == " + nn.nextInt() );
   i = i + 1;
}
```

in a while loop, which in this example executes 10 times. The loop counter i, of type int, is initialized to zero and is incremented at the bottom of the loop so that i's values are $i = 0, 1, \ldots, 9$.

In each loop iteration, i and the next random integer are printed to the standard output. Recall that + applied to strings is the concatenation operator. Although i is an int rather than a string, the concatenation

```
"i == " + i
```

succeeds because the system automatically converts i's value to a string. A similar conversion occurs with the int returned by the method invocation

```
nn.nextInt()
```

Finally, the statement

```
i = i + 1;
```

increments i during each iteration. If this statement were absent, i would always be zero and, therefore, less than n. The result would be an infinite loop.

EXERCISES

1. Explain why the Random field named r can be `private`.

2. How many times does the body of the `for` loop

```
for ( int i = 0; i < 33; i++ )
    System.out.println( i );
```

execute?

3. Add a second method

```
public int nextInt( boolean nonneg ) { /*...*/ }
```

to the RandNN class that returns a nonnegative random integer, if `nonneg` is `true`, and a negative random integer, if `nonneg` is `false`. *Hint*: Code reuse.

COMMON ERRORS AND SAFE PRACTICES

1. If a class does not occur in the current directory or the `java.lang` package, the class must be referenced with its fully qualified name unless the appropriate `import` statement is used. For example, the code segment

```
class A {
    Date d; //***** ERROR
}
```

contains an error. The error can be corrected either by using the fully qualified name

```
class A {
    java.util.Date d; // fully qualified name
}
```

or by using the appropriate `import` statement

```
import java.util.Date;
class A {
    Date d; // ok
}
```

2. It is an error for an `import` statement to occur in a source file *after* a class definition. For example, the code segment

```
class A { /*...*/ }
import javax.swing.*; //***** ERROR
```

contains an error.

3. Fully qualified names are required to resolve ambiguous references. For example, the `java.awt` and the `java.util` packages both have a `List`. If a source file has imports for both packages, a `List` must be referenced with a fully qualified name. The code segment

```
import java.awt.*;
import java.util.*;
class A {
    List l; //**** ERROR: ambiguous
}
```

illustrates the error. The code segment

```
import java.awt.*;
import java.util.*;
class A {
    java.util.List l; // ok
}
```

corrects the error.

4. The package statement, if present, must occur *first* in a source file. The code segment

```
import javax.swing.*; // 1st line in file
package myGraphics;   //***** ERROR
```

illustrates the error. The correct order is

```
package myGraphics;   // 1st line in file
import javax.swing.*; // gui stuff
```

PROGRAMMING EXERCISES

3.1. Suppose that we add the method

```
int nextInt( int k ) {
    int u = Math.abs( k );           //** u is nonnegative
```

```
        int t = Math.abs( r.nextInt() ); //** t is nonnegative
        return (int) (1 + t * (u / (Integer.MAX_VALUE + 1.0)));
    }
```

to the RandNN class (see Section 3.4), where r refers to the Random object used to generate random integers. This version of nextInt returns an integer in the range of 1 through the absolute value of k. For example, if k is 100, the method returns a random integer in the range of 1 through 100. Write a program that

• Uses the method to generate 1,000 random integers within a specified range such as 1 through 100.

• Counts the number of times that the *first* randomly generated integer occurs in the sequence. For example, if 57 is the first randomly generated integer, the program counts how many times 57 occurs among the 1,000 integers generated.

• Prints to the standard output the first randomly generated integer and the number of times that it occurs in the sequence.

3.2. The Random class (see Section 3.4) has a method getLong that returns a random integer of type long, which has a greater range than type int. (A long is a 64-bit integer, whereas an int is a 32-bit integer.) If rand refers to a Random object, the statement

```
        long n = Math.abs( rand.nextLong() );
```

assigns to n the absolute value of the next randomly generated long.
The java.lang.Integer class is a static constant named MAX_VALUE, which is the largest positive value for an int. The code segment

```
        int n;
        // assign some value to n
        if ( n == Integer.MAX_VALUE )
          System.out.println( "n is as big as ints get!" );
```

illustrates the syntax for using Integer.MAX_VALUE.
Write a program that generates and prints random long integers that are less than Integer.MAX_VALUE. A while loop can be used for this purpose. The code segment

```
        while ( true ) { //**** potentially infinite loop
           int x, y;
           // assign values to x and y
           if ( x > y ) {
             System.out.println( x + " > " + y );
             break;      //**** exits the while loop
           }
        }
```

reviews how a `break` statement can be used to terminate a potentially infinite `while` loop, that is, a `while` loop whose test always evaluates to `true`.

3.3. The `java.lang` package has wrapper classes for primitive data types such as `int` and `double`. For example, the class `Integer` is a wrapper for an `int`. The code segment

```
int n = 100;
Integer intWrap = new Integer( n );
int k = intWrap.intValue(); //*** returns 100
```

illustrates how an `Integer` wrapper can be constructed and used to wrap an `int`. Write a program that populates a `Vector` with 1,000 *nonduplicate* random integers. The code segment

```
Integer i = new Integer( 100 );
Vector v = new Vector();
v.addElement( i );
if ( v.contains( i ) ) //**** evaluates to true
  //...
```

shows how the `Vector` method `contains` can be used to determine whether a `Vector` already contains a particular `Integer`. The `Vector` method `size()` returns the `Vector`'s current size as an integer. The code segment

```
if ( v.size() < 100 )
  //...
```

illustrates the syntax.

3.4. Amend Programming Exercise 3.3 so that the nonduplicate integers are printed in *sorted* order. The following hints may be helpful:

- The `Vector` class has a `toArray` method that returns its elements in an array. The code segment

```
Vector v = new Vector();
//...populate v with elements
Object[ ] ar = v.toArray();
```

shows the syntax.
- Recall that the `java.util.Arrays` class has `static` utility methods such as `sort` that expect array arguments. The code segment

```
Arrays.sort( ar );
```

shows the syntax for the array `ar`, which is now sorted in ascending order.

- Recall that every array has a `length` member. The code segment

```
for ( int i = 0; i < ar.length; i++ )
    System.out.println( ar[ i ] );
```

shows how the `length` member can be used in a `for` loop that prints each element in array `ar`. Recall that the square brackets `[ ]` are the subscript or index operator.

3.5. Implement a `SortedList` class for integers that belongs to the `myutils` package (see Section 3.4). The `SortedList` should have public methods to add integer elements, to remove integer elements, and to print the list. *Hint*: See Programming Exercise 3.4.

3.6. Implement a `SortedSet` class for integers that belongs to the `myutils` package (see Section 3.4). A `SortedSet` is like a `SortedList` (see Programming Exercise 3.5) except that a `SortedSet` does not allow duplicate integer elements.

3.7. Implement a `Combination` class that belongs to the `myutils` package (see Section 3.4). The class should have a public two-argument constructor whose arguments are integers:

```
Comb( int n, int r ) {/*...*/}
```

A constructor call such as

```
new Comb( 4, 2 )
```

should evaluate $C(n, r)$ whose value is given by the formula

$$C(n, r) = \frac{n!}{r!(n - r)!}$$

where $n!$ is the factorial of n. For example, $C(4, 2)$ is 6 because there are 6 2-element subsets of a 4-element set. The `Comb` constructor should compute $C(n, r)$ and print the value to the standard output.

3.8. Amend Programming Exercise 3.7 by adding a public `static` method named c that, like the two-argument constructor, computes $C(n, r)$ and prints the value to the standard output. To ensure that the constructor and the `static` method perform the same operation, delegate the computation of $C(n, r)$ to a private method that the constructor and public method c invoke. *Hint*: Recall that a `static` method can access only other `static` members.

3.9. Write a program that determines which of the expressions e^{π} and π^e is larger. The value of π correct to 15 places is 3.141592653589793. The number e is the base of the natural logarithm and its value correct to 15 places is 2.718281828459045. Going from e^{π} to π^e increases the base from about 2.718 to about 3.141, which tends to make π^e larger, but decreases the exponent from about 3.141 to about

2.718, which tends to make π^e smaller. The program thus should determine whether increasing the base or decreasing the exponent has the greater effect. *Hint*: Investigate the `java.lang.Math` class.

3.10. This exercise comes originally from Mitchell Feigenbaum and was adapted by John Allen Paulos in *Beyond Numeracy* (New York: Alfred A. Knopf, 1990). Consider the deceptively simply formula

$$NextYr = Rate \cdot CurrentYr \cdot \left(1 - \frac{CurrentYr}{1,000,000}\right)$$

which calculates next year's population of, say, egrets on the basis of the current population and the growth rate. The variable *Rate* controls the growth rate and takes on values between 0 and 4. The variable *CurrentYr* gives the current value of the egret population and is assumed to have a value between 0 and 1,000,000. The variable *NextYr* gives the value of the egret population one year later. The formula guarantees that *NextYr* also will have a value between 0 and 1,000,000. For example, if *CurrentYr* is 100,000 and *Rate* is 2.6, *NextYr* is 234,000.

Now suppose that we initialize *CurrentYr* to 100,000 and *Rate* to 2.6 and then compute the egret population 25 years hence by solving for *NextYr*, setting *CurrentYr* to *NextYr*, solving again for *NextYr*, and so on for 25 iterations. The egret population turns out to be roughly 615,365. We get the *same* result if we initialize *CurrentYr* to, say, 900,000 but leave *Rate* set to 2.6. In fact, the population stabilizes at roughly 615,385 for *any* positive value of *CurrentYr* so long as *Rate* is 2.6. For some values of *Rate*, however, the population oscillates. For example, if *Rate* is 3.14, then after about 40 years the egret population takes on this pattern from one year to the next: 538,007 to 780,464 to 538,007 to 780,464 and so on indefinitely. For *Rate* equal to approximately 3.57, however, the population does not stabilize or oscillate but rather varies randomly from one year to the next. Write a program that sets an initial *Rate*, an initial *CurrentYr*, and a number of iterations. On each iteration, output the year and the current egret population.

3.11. Amend Programming Exercise 3.8 so that it sets a number of iterations, an initial *Rate*, an initial *CurrentYr*, a *Rate* increase, and a *Rate* limit. For example, if the number of iterations were set to 25, the *CurrentYr* to 100,000, the *Rate* to 3.5, the *Rate* increase to 0.1, and the *Rate* limit to 3.9, then the program iterates 25 times with *Rate* set to 3.5; 25 times for *Rate* set to 3.6; and so on until *Rate* is set to 3.9. On each iteration, output the year, the *Rate*, and the current egret population.

3.12. Algorithms for cryptography often require integers greater than the maximum value of a primitive integer type such as the 64-bit `long`, whose maximum value is $2^{64} - 1$. For example, an implementer of an ElGamal encryption scheme may decide that the encryption key should be 1,024 bits in length.

In general, an ElGamal encryption key is generated from three random integers:

- *M*, whose bit length is the key's length. *M* should be prime.
- *G*, which must be less than *M* but need not be prime.
- *N*, which must be less than *M* but need not be prime.

The encryption key $K = G^N \bmod M$.

The `java.security` package has a `SecureRandom` class that can be used to generate random numbers for cryptographic applications. Further, the `java.math` package has a `BigInteger` class for arbitrary precision integers. The code segment

```
int keyLen = 1024;
int certainty = 16;
SecureRandom sr = new SecureRandom();
BigInteger m = new BigInteger( keyLen, certainty, sr );
```

shows how M might be constructed as a `BigInteger` with a bit length of 1,024. The constructor's `certainty` argument specifies the probability that the resulting `BigInteger` is prime. For certainty C, the probability is $1 - 0.5^C$. In this example, the `certainty` argument is 16; hence, the `BigInteger` is prime with a probability of 0.9999847412109375. Given the `SecureRandom` object named `sr` and a key length `keyLen`, the statement

```
BigInteger g = new BigInteger( keyLen - 1, sr );
```

shows how G might be constructed. Subtracting 1 from `keyLen` ensures that G will be less than M. If g, m, and n refer to `BigInteger`s, the statement

```
BigInteger k = g.modPow( n, m );
```

assigns k the value g^n mod m. Finally, the statement

```
System.out.println( k );
```

prints the key k as a `String` to the standard output.

Write a program that generates and prints 1,000 ElGamal encryption keys of bit length 2,048. For experimentation, vary the `certainty` in the generation of the `BigInteger` modulus M. For a discussion of the ElGamal and other cryptography algorithms, see Bruce Scheier's *Applied Cryptography: Protocols, Algorithms, and Source Code in C*, 2nd edition (New York: Wiley, 1995).

3.13. The class `Convert`

```
import java.util.*;
class Convert {
   public Convert( String exp ) {
      StringTokenizer st = new StringTokenizer( exp );
      Stack stack = new Stack();
      while ( st.hasMoreTokens() )
         stack.push( st.nextToken() );
      while ( !stack.empty() )
         System.out.print( stack.pop() + " " );
      System.out.println();
   }
}
```

reviews the basic functionality of the `StringTokenizer` and `Stack` classes in the `java.util` package. A `StringTokenizer` can be used to extract from a string such as A + B the parts or tokens A, +, and B. The `Stack` class implements a stack as a LIFO (**L**ast **I**n, **F**irst **O**ut) list (see Section 1.2). Together the `StringTokenizer` and `Stack` classes can be used to convert an *infix expression* such as $A * B + C$ into the equivalent *postfix expression*, in this case $AB * C+$. Suppose that a client application

```
class ConvertClient {
   public static void main( String[ ] args ) {
      new Convert( "A * B + C" );
   }
}
```

constructs a `Convert` object, in this case a string that represents the expression $A * B + C$. White space is required between the tokens. If the expression were A*B+C, the `StringTokenizer` would extract the entire expression as a *single* token. At present, the `Convert` constructor creates a `StringTokenizer` named st and then enters a `while` loop that extracts the tokens and pushes each onto a `Stack` named `stack`. A second `while` loop pops each `Stack` element and prints it to the standard output. (The `print` method differs from `println` in *not* printing a newline.) The output in this example is C + B * A.

Amend the `Convert` constructor so that it converts an infix expression to the equivalent postfix expression. *Hint*: Assign *precedence levels* to the operators. For example, operators + and − might be given a precedence of 1, whereas operators * and / might be given a precedence of 2. Push only *operators* or *left parentheses* onto the stack. Operands such as A, B, and C should not be pushed onto the stack. Right parentheses should not be pushed onto the stack. Given these assumptions, there are two cases to consider:

- An infix expression without parentheses such as $A * B + C$. Scan the expression from left to right. If an operator is encountered

  – Pop from the stack any operator with a higher precedence. The `Stack` method **peek** can be used to access the stack's top element without removing it. For example, if operator + were encountered while operator * is at the top of the stack, * would be popped because * has higher precedence than −.
  – Push the operator onto the stack. For example, if + were encountered and only * were currently on the stack, + would be pushed after * had been popped.

  For the infix expression $A * B + C$, the sequence would be

  – Output A, which is an operand rather than an operator.
  – Push * onto an empty stack.

      – Push + onto the stack *after* popping and outputting ∗, which has higher precedence.

      – Output *C*.

      – Pop and output any remaining operators, in this case +.

- A parenthesized infix expression such as $(A+B)*C$. Operators are again pushed and operands are not. A left parenthesis, which should have a *lower* precedence than any operator, is also pushed. When a right parenthesis is encountered, the stack is popped until the corresponding left parenthesis is popped. Given the sample infix expression, the sequence would be

      – Push the left parenthesis (.

      – Output *A*.

      – Push +. The left parenthesis is not popped because every operator has a higher precedence.

      – Output *B*.

      – Pop and output + because a right parenthesis is encountered. Pop but do *not* output the left parenthesis because postfix expressions do not require parentheses.

      – Push ∗ onto a currently empty stack.

      – Output *C*.

      – Push and output any remaining operators, in this case ∗.

Language Fundamentals

Chapter Outline

This chapter examines Java's fundamental programming constructs in a technical and comprehensive fashion so that the chapter can be used for reference. Accordingly, the chapter's sections have many subsections devoted to specific topics. The sections and subsections are kept as independent as possible so that parts of this chapter can be read as needed. For example, the reader who wants more information about exceptions can read Section 4.7 without reading all of the preceding sections. Examples occur frequently to illustrate key language features.

The chapter begins with Java identifiers. An **identifier** is the name of a program component such as a package, a class, and a class member. All languages have rules that govern identifiers and the Java rules are straightforward. Identifiers for variables, either fields or variables local to a constructor or method, must be **declared**, which involves specifying the variable's **data type** or **type** for short. A variable's data type determines the type of values that the variable can store as well as the operations that can be performed on these values.

Java is not a pure object-oriented language because it has **primitive data types**, that is, data types that are not classes. Primitive data types such as `int` and `float` are storage-efficient and closely match the built-in types on which modern computers operate; hence, operations involving primitive data types are also efficient. Java's inclusion of primitive data types shows that it is a practical language with concerns for efficiency. This chapter examines the primitive data types and the operations on them. Primitive and class types can be aggregated into arrays; hence, the chapter also reviews arrays.

Control structures determine a program's flow of control. Statement sequencing, method calls, tests, and loops are the common control structures examined in Section 4.5. The chapter ends with a section on *exceptions*, unusual conditions that may occur while a program executes.

Identifiers, Variables, and Values

An **identifier** is the name of a program component such as a class, a constructor or method, or a parameter. To be a valid identifier, a name must begin with a letter, an underscore (_), or a dollar sign ($). The remaining symbols must be letters, numerals, underscores, or dollar signs.

■ **Example 4.1.1.**   The table

Identifier	Valid?
`taxes`	Yes
`Taxes`	Yes
`TAXES`	Yes
`$taxes99`	Yes
`_taxes_`	Yes
`$taxes_99$$$`	Yes
`____taxes`	Yes

Identifier	*Valid?*
99taxes	No: begins with a numeral, 9
!taxes	No: contains an invalid symbol, !
taxes#99	No: contains an invalid symbol, #
my,taxes	No: contains an invalid symbol, a comma
my taxes	No: contains an invalid symbol, a nested blank

illustrates the rules.   ■

Because compiler-generated identifiers typically include the symbol $, the programmer's own identifiers should exclude this symbol to avoid confusion. There is no length restriction on identifiers.

Variables and Values

A **variable** is a named storage cell that can hold a value of a particular type. A variable must be **declared** before it is used. To declare a variable is to give

- Its name, which must be a valid identifier.
- Its data type, which is either a class type such as `String` or a primitive type such as `int`.

■ **Example 4.1.2.**   The code segment

```
Date    today;
double pi;
```

declares a `Date` variable named `today` and a `double` variable named `pi`. A `Date` is a class type, whereas a `float` is a primitive (nonclass) type. Recall that a variable such as `today` that can refer to a class instance—that is, an *object*—is called an *object reference*.

Once declared, the variables can be used. For example, declared variables can be assigned values. The code segment

```
Date    today;
today = new Date();
double pi;
pi = 3.14;
```

illustrates. After the assignment

```
today = new Date();
```

variable `today` refers to a `Date` object. After the assignment

```
pi = 3.14;
```

variable `pi` stores the floating-point value 3.14.   ■

A variable's data type determines the type of values that can be assigned to it. For example, an `int` variable can be assigned a value of type `int` such as 13, whereas a `boolean` variable can be assigned a value of type `boolean` such as `true`. An `int` variable cannot be assigned `boolean` value, however.

■ **Example 4.1.3.**   The code segment

```
int n;
n = true; //**** ERROR: n is an int, but true is a boolean
```

contains an error because variable n's type is `int` and `true` is a `boolean` constant. Therefore, the `boolean` value `true` cannot be assigned to the `int` variable n. ■

■ **Example 4.1.4.**   The code segment

```
String s = 'Z'; //***** ERROR: 'Z' is a char, not a String
```

contains an error. A single-quoted character such as `'Z'` is of type `char`. A `String` variable such as s cannot be initialized to a `char` value.   ■

In Java, all variables are encapsulated in classes, either directly as fields or indirectly as local variables in a constructor or method.

■ **Example 4.1.5.**   The code segment

```
class C {
   int  n;
   Date today;
   void m() {
     String s;
     float  pi;
     //...
   }
}
```

has four variables: an `int` field named n, a `Date` field named today, a local `String` variable in method m named s, and a local `float` variable also in m named pi. All of the variable names are valid identifiers.   ■

Fields and Default Values

Fields have default values, which are listed in Figure 4.1.1. The default value for a field of a numeric type is the appropriate representation of zero: 0 for integers and 0.0

Data Type	Values	Default Value for Fields
boolean	true, false	false
char	16-bit unicode characters	'\u0000'
byte	8-bit signed integers	0
short	16-bit signed integers	0
int	32-bit signed integers	0
long	64-bit signed integers	0
float	32-bit floating-point numbers	0.0
double	64-bit floating-point numbers	0.0
Class types	Object references	null

FIGURE 4.1.1   Default values for fields.

for floating-point types. The default value for `boolean` fields is `false`. The default value for `char` fields is the nonprinting null character `'\u0000'`. (The \u stands for Unicode, which is clarified in the subsection on the `char` data type).

■ **Example 4.1.6.**   The class declaration

```
import java.util.Date;
class C {
   boolean flag1;    // defaults to false
   boolean flag2 = true;
   char    c1;        // defaults to '\u0000'
   char    c2 = 'A';
   int     z;         // defaults to 0
   int     k = -1;
   double  d1;        // defaults to 0.0
   double  d2 = 3.14;
   String s;          // defaults to null
   Date d;            // defaults to null
}
```

shows the default values for fields of various primitive types. Fields such as `flag2` and `d2` are initialized to nondefault values. The example also shows that a variable of any class type, such as the `String` variable s and the `Date` variable d, default to `null`. ■

The null Default Value for Object References

The default value for a field of any class type such as String or Date is null. In the
code segment

```
class Alpha {
   String s1 = new String( "foo" );
   String s2;  //*** defaults to null
   //...
}
```

the fields s1 and s2 are object references. At the implementation level, an object
reference is a *symbolic pointer* whose default value as a field is null, the traditional
name for the *null pointer*—the pointer that does not point to a valid address. Figure 4.1.2
depicts variable s1 pointing to a String. Object reference s2 does not point to a valid
address because its value is null.

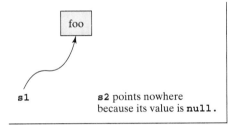

FIGURE 4.1.2   Object references as
symbolic pointers: s1 points to a
String but s2 has a nonpointing
value of null.

Local Variables

Unlike fields, local constructor and method variables do *not* have default values. If
not initialized in their declarations or explicitly assigned a value, such variables have
arbitrary values.

■ **Example 4.1.7.**   The code segment

```
class C {
   void m() {
      int n;          //** Caution: not initialized
      int s = n + n; //** ERROR: n still not assigned a value
      // remaining code
   }
}
```

contains an error because local variable n is used in an arithmetic operation
without having been assigned a value. The code segment will not compile. The
error can be corrected by either initializing n in its declaration

```
void m() {
  int n = 1;      // ok
  int s = n + n;
  //...
```

or explicitly assigning n a value after its declaration

```
void m() {
  int n; //**** Caution: not initialized
  n = 1; // ok
  int s = n + n;
  //...
```

If n were a *field* rather than a local variable, n's value would default to zero. ∎

final Variables

∎ **Example 4.1.8.**   The code segment

```
final double pi = 3.14; // no assignment possible now
```

reviews the keyword final, which can be used to make a variable a *constant*. The keyword final is an example of a **modifier**, that is, a term that signifies an attribute or property. Because variable pi is final, its initialization to 3.14 cannot be overwritten by any subsequent assignment statement. Accordingly, the code segment

```
final double pi = 3.14; // no assignment possible now
pi = 3.1415;            //***** ERROR: pi is final
```

contains an error.

A final variable can be initialized in its declaration (see Example 4.1.8) or assigned a value exactly *once* thereafter.

Example 4.1.9.   The code segment

```
final double pi; // not initialized
pi = 3.14;       // ok, first assignment
pi = 3.1415;     //***** ERROR: pi can be assigned only once
```

illustrates the alternative to initializing a final variable in its declaration. In this example, pi is not initialized in its declaration but rather assigned a value afterwards. The first assignment statement is correct. The second assignment statement is an error precisely because a `final` variable, once given a value, cannot have its value changed.

The modifier `final` also may be used to mark a method parameter as *read only*.

Example 4.1.10.   The code segment

```
void m( final int x ) { // x is read only
    x = x + 2; //***** ERROR: x is read only
    //...
}
```

marks method m's single parameter as *read only*. The attempt to increment x in m's body is therefore an error.

EXERCISES

1. Indicate whether each of the following is a valid identifier:

(a) $x	(e) foo-bar	(i) ###___
(b) $$	(f) foo_bar	(j) ___#
(c) $_$	(g) 2foo	(k) my,name
(d) ___xxx___$	(h) foo2	(l) my name

2. Explain the error:

```
class C {
    void f() {
        int y = x + x + 1;
    }
}
```

3. Explain the error:

```
class C {
    void f() {
        int x;
        int y = 1 + x;
    }
}
```

4. What is the default value for a field of type `char`?

5. What is the default value for a field of type `double`?

6. What is the default value for a field of type `short`?

7. What is the default value of a field that is an object reference?

8. Explain what the keyword `null` means.

9. Explain the error:

```
class C {
   void f() {
      size = 100;
      int n = size * size;
   }
   final int size = 100;
}
```

10. Explain what an *object reference* is and give an example.

4.2   Constructors and Methods

Chapter 5 examines classes and their encapsulated constructors and methods in detail. This section reviews the basic syntax and use of constructors and methods:

- **Constructors**, which must have the same name as their encapsulating class and must not have a return type or `void` in place of a return type. A constructor is used with the operator `new` to construct objects of the class's type.
- **Methods**, which must not have the same name as their encapsulating class and must have a return type or `void` in place of a return type. A method performs operations appropriate to a class or its objects.

A series of examples clarifies constructors and methods.

■ **Example 4.2.1.**   The class

```
class Emp {
   public Emp() {          //*** public constructor
      name = "Unknown";
   }
   private String name;   //*** hidden field
}
```

has a single constructor that expects no arguments. The constructor invoked with no arguments is called the **default constructor** or the **no-argument constructor**. The Emp no-argument constructor would be invoked in a code segment such as

```
Emp e1 = new Emp(); // construct an Emp object
```

The no-argument constructor initializes the private Emp field name to the string "Unknown". In general, a constructor performs whatever initializations are appropriate for an object of the class type. ∎

∎ **Example 4.2.2.**   The code segment

```
class Emp {
   public void Emp() { //***** ERROR
      name = "Unknown";
   }
   private String name;
}
```

contains an error because the no-argument constructor is defined to return void. A constructor never has a return type or void in place of a return type. ∎

Constructor and Method Overloading

Constructors and methods can be **overloaded**; that is, constructors and methods within a class can share a name on the condition that each overloaded version has a distinct **signature**. A constructor's signature includes its name together with the order and data types of its arguments.

∎ **Example 4.2.3.**   The class

```
class Emp {
   public Emp() {
      name = "Unknown";
   }
   public Emp( String n ) {
      name = n;
   }
   private String name;
}
```

has two constructors with different signatures. One constructor takes no arguments, whereas the other constructor takes a single String argument. The signatures make it clear which constructor is being invoked. For example, the code segment

```
Emp who = new Emp(); // no-argument constructor
```

invokes the no-argument constructor, whereas the code segment

```
Emp star = new Emp( "bente" ); // parameterized constructor
```

invokes the parameterized constructor, which assigns the parameter to the private
field name. ■

Classes often have multiple constructors. For example, the java.util package
has a Hashtable class with three constructors and a GregorianCalendar class with
seven constructors.

The Syntax of Methods

Methods perform operations appropriate to a particular class and its instances. With
respect to syntax, methods differ from constructors in two ways: a method *must not*
have the same name as its encapsulating class and a method *must* have a return type or
void in place of a return type if the method does not return a value.

■ **Example 4.2.4.**   The code segment

```
class Emp {
   public Emp() {              //*** public constructor
      name = "Unknown";
   }
   public Emp( String n ) {  //*** public constructor
      name = n;
   }
   public String getName() { //*** public method
      return name;
   }
   private String name;       //*** hidden field
}
```

amends Example 4.2.3 by adding the method getName, which takes no arguments
and returns a reference to a String, in this case the private field name. ■

■ **Example 4.2.5.**   The code segment

```
class Emp {
   public Emp() {              //*** public constructor
      name = "Unknown";
   }
   public Emp( String n ) {  //*** public constructor
      name = n;
   }
   public String getName() { //*** public method
      return name;
   }
```

```
public void sayHi() {      //*** public method
   System.out.println( "Greetings from " + name );
}
private String name;       //*** hidden field
}
```

amends Example 4.2.4 by adding another method sayHi, which takes no arguments and does not return a value. A method that does not return a value has void in place of a return type. It would be an error

```
public sayhHi() { //**** ERROR: no return type!
```

to omit the return type or void because sayHi is a *method*, not a constructor. ■

A method's return type indicates the kind of operations for which it is suitable as a term. Suppose, for example, that class C has a method m:

```
class C {
   public int m() {
      int n = 0;
      //*** statements that process n
      return n; // return n
   }
}
```

The code segment

```
C c1 = new C();  //*** create a C object
int x = c1.m();  // c1.m() returns an int
```

initializes int variable x to the int returned by the method invocation c1.m(). Because c1.m() returns an int, c1.m() can occur wherever an int value is required.

Methods can be static (associated with the class as a whole) or nonstatic (associated with particular objects). Recall that a nonstatic method is also called an *instance method* because it is associated with an object, that is, an instance of a class. Constructors cannot be static.

Distinguishing Methods from One Another

Methods in the same class cannot be distinguished by their return type or void. For example, the code segment

```
char m() { /*...*/ }
byte m() { /*...*/ } //***** ERROR: same signature as above
```

contains an error because the two methods m do *not* have different signatures. The second m must be renamed or take at least one argument

```
byte m( float f ) { /*...*/ } //** ok
```

to differ in signature from the first m.

EXERCISES

1. Explain the error:

```
class C {
    public void C() { /*...*/ }
}
```

2. Explain the error:

```
class K {
    public k() { /*...*/ }
}
```

3. Are all functions encapsulated in Java?

4. Is a method a constructor?

5. Is a constructor a method?

6. What features distinguish a constructor from a method?

7. Must a method have a return type or void in place of one?

8. Do variables local to a constructor or method have default values?

9. Explain the error:

```
class C {
    int m( int x ) {
        int y = x * x;
        int z = y / 2;
    }
}
```

10. Can two methods encapsulated in the same class have the same name?

11. Can two constructors encapsulated in the same class have the same name?

12. Can two methods encapsulated in the same class have the same signature?

13. Do the methods

```
void m( int x, char y ) { /*...*/ }
void m( char x, int y ) { /*...*/ }
```

have different signatures?

14. Explain the error:

```
class C {
    void m( int x ) { /*...*/ }
    char m( int x ) { /*...*/ }
}
```

15. Can a constructor be `static`?

16. Can a method be `static`?

17. Can a field be `static`?

4.3   Primitive Data Types and Operators

The primitive data types have standardized bit sizes and default values for fields of these types. Figure 3.1.1 lists the primitive data types, their bit sizes, and the default values for fields of these types. Figure 4.3.1 repeats the bit sizes and then lists the minimum and maximum values for the character, integer, and floating-point types.

Data Type	Bit Size	Minimum Value	Maximum Value
char	16	`'\u0000'`	`'\uffff'`
byte	8	-128	127
short	16	$-32,768$	$32,767$
int	32	$-2,147,483,648$	$2,147,483,647$
long	64	$-9,223,372,036,854,775,808$	$9,223,372,036,854,775,807$
float	32	$1.40239846E-45$	$3.40282347E+38$
double	64	$4.94065645841246544E-324$	$1.79769313486231570E+308$

FIGURE 4.3.1   Minimum and maximum values for some primitive types.

Java supports standard operations on the primitive types. There are *arithmetic* operators such as binary + (addition), * (multiplication), and % (remainder) that apply to integer and floating-point types alike. There are also *relational* operators such as > (greater than) and == (equals) that also apply to character, integer, and floating-point types. Relational operators such as the equality and inequality operators also apply to the primitive `boolean` data type. The *bit* operators are restricted to integers. For example, the bitwise complement operator ~ and the left shift operator << apply only to integers. The *logical* operators such as && (logical *and*, or conjunction) apply only to `boolean` types. Figure 4.3.2 lists the operators, the appropriate data types for their operands, whether they associate from right to left or from left to right, and their precedence. Operators with a precedence of 1 are the highest, those with a precedence of 2 are the next highest, and so forth. The subsections on specific data types clarify the more important operators for these types.

Prec.	Operator	Operands	Associates	Operation
1	( )	method	NA	method call
1	[ ]	integer	NA	subscript
2	new	any	NA	dynamic storage allocation
3	.	object or class	left	member
4	+ -	numeric	right	unary plus and minus
4	~	integer	right	bitwise complement
4	!	boolean	right	logical negation
4	++ --	numeric	NA	postincrement, postdecrement
4	(type)	any	right	cast
5	* / %	numeric	left	multiplication, division, remainder
5	++ --	numeric	right	preincrement, predecrement
5	(data type)	any	right	cast
6	+ -	numeric	left	addition, subtraction
7	<<	integer	left	left shift
7	>>	integer	left	right shift with sign extension
7	>>>	integer	left	right shift with zero extension
8	< <=	numeric	NA	less than, less than or equal to
8	> >=	numeric	NA	grtr. than, grtr. than or equal to
8	instanceof	any	NA	type comparison
9	==	any	left	equality
9	!=	any	left	inequality
10	&	integer	left	bitwise and
10	&	boolean	left	logical and (conjunction)
11	^	integer	left	bitwise exclusive-or
11	^	boolean	left	logical exclusive-or
12	|	integer	left	bitwise inclusive-or
12	|	boolean	left	logical inclusive-or (disjunction)
13	&&	boolean	left	logical and (conjunction)
14	||	boolean	left	logical inclusive-or (disjunction)
15	? :	boolean, any	right	ternary conditional operator
16	= += -= /= %= *= >>= >>>= <<= &= ^= !=	any	right	assignment

FIGURE 4.3.2   Precedences of operators. (1 is the highest and 16 is the lowest precedence. NA means "not applicable.")

Integer Types

The integer types are all signed but differ in their ranges. For example, a `byte` is an 8-bit signed integer with a range of −128 to 127, whereas an `int` is a 32-bit signed integer with a range of −2, 147, 483, 648 to 2, 147, 483, 647. An integer literal such as 10 is of type `int`. Because `long` is a 64-bit integer type, it should be sufficient for even engineering and scientific applications that require a wide range for integers. An integer literal with letter l or L appended is a `long` literal. For example, 10L is an integer literal of type `long` rather than `int`. If the range of the primitive type `long` is inadequate, the `java.math` package has a `BigInteger` class to support arbitrary-precision integer arithmetic.

Integer literals may be written in decimal (the default), octal, or hexadecimal.

■ **Example 4.3.1.**   The table

Base	Digits	Leftmost Symbol(s)
10 (decimal)	0 to 9	Must *not* be 0
8 (octal)	0 to 7	Must be 0
16 (hexadecimal)	0 to F	Must be 0x or 0X

shows the rules for writing integer constants in decimal, octal, and hexadecimal. The table

Constant	Type	Value in Decimal
27	Decimal	27
033	Octal	27
0x1B	Hexadecimal	27
0X1B	Hexadecimal	27

shows some examples.   ■

■ **Example 4.3.2.**   The code segment

```
int x = 23;    // 23 in decimal, stored in an int
short y = 23;  // 23 in decimal, stored in a short
long z = 123L; // 123 in decimal, a long literal
int p = 0123;  // octal literal == 83 in decimal
int q = 0x1111; // hexadecimal literal == 4,361 in decimal
```

illustrates various integer literals.   ■

The data type `byte` is of the same size, 8 bits, as a JVM instruction. Each *bytecode* in a *class* file thus can be stored in a `byte`, a useful fact illustrated later in several applications.

Java uses the 2's complement binary representation for integers (see the Java Postscript at the end of the chapter). The internal representation of integers is thus standardized, although the programmer can perform the usual arithmetic operations such as addition and division without concern for the internal representation. The fact that the integer types have standard sizes and ranges promotes code portability. Further, the types `byte`, `short`, `int`, and `long` are all signed. The data type `char` is unsigned but is meant to represent *characters*, not integers. By confining integer operations to the standard—that is, signed—integer types, the programmer can avoid the subtle problems that arise when signed and unsigned values are combined in an arithmetic or relational operation. A later example illustrates the problem.

Floating-Point Types

The floating-point types implement the IEEE 754 floating-point standard. (IEEE stands for **I**nstitute of **E**lectrical and **E**lectronics **E**ngineers.) The 32-bit float type implements the IEEE 754 single-precision standard and the 64-bit double type implements the IEEE 754 double-precision standard. Floating-point operations may generate special values such as *positive infinity*, *negative infinity*, and *not a number*. The standard classes java.lang.Float and java.lang.Double provide literals for such values (e.g., POSITIVE_INFINITY and NaN) as well as methods to check for such values (e.g., the method isNaN() in both the Float and Double classes checks whether a value is a valid floating-point number). The Float and Double classes also have the constants MIN_VALUE and MAX_VALUE that can be used in comparisons. By definition, positive infinity is greater than any float or double value. The expression

```
1.0 / 0.0 //*** positive infinity
```

evaluates to positive infinity. Similarly, negative infinity is less than any float or double value. The expression

```
1.0 / -0.0 //*** negative infinity
```

evaluates to negative infinity. Positive zero (0.0) and negative zero (−0.0) are equivalent in all other contexts, however.

■ **Example 4.3.3.**   The expression

```
-0.0 == 0.0 // this equality is true
```

evaluates to true. The == is the equality operator.

A floating-point literal such as 3.14 is a double. A d or D may be appended to such a literal (e.g., 3.14D) to underscore that the literal is a double. Appending an f or an F to such a literal (e.g., 3.14f) makes it a float literal. The compiler does **strict type checking** in variable initializations and assignments involving floating-point types; that is, the compiler checks whether the **target** such as a variable is of exactly the same type as the **source** such as a literal.

■ **Example 4.3.4.**   The code segment

```
float f = 3.14; //**** ERROR: incompatible types!
```

generates a fatal compiler error because the variable f is of type float, whereas the literal 3.14 is of type double. The error can be eliminated in various ways.

For example, f's type could be changed to double or the literal could be made into a float by appending an f or an F. The statements

```
double d = 3.14;   //** ok
float f = 3.14F;   //** ok
```

illustrate. ■

Floating-point literals may be written in scientific notation by using the standard e or E notation.

■ **Example 4.3.5.**   The literals

```
23e4F       // float
23E4f       // ditto
23e4        // defaults to double
.31415e1D   // explicitly double
9.99e+23    // defaults to double
9.99e-23F   // float
```

illustrate floating-point numbers written in scientific notation.

Cast Operations

Example 4.3.4 illustrated the problem of initializing a float variable to a double value and showed different ways to avoid the problem. Yet another way involves the **cast** operation, which is an explicit conversion of one data type to another. For example, the error in the code segment

```
float f = 3.14; //**** ERROR: 3.14 is double
```

can be eliminated by casting the double value 3.14 to a float

```
float f = (float) 3.14; // ok, explicit cast
```

The cast target type, in this case float, is enclosed in parentheses and placed immediately in front of the expression whose value is to be cast, in this case the double literal 3.14.

There are restrictions on casts. For example, a boolean value cannot be cast to any other type. A primitive type such as int cannot be cast to a class type such as String or vice versa. In general, casts should be used with caution, as later examples illustrate.

Arithmetic Operators

Java has the standard arithmetic operators for integers and floating-point numbers:

Operation	Symbol	Example
Addition	+	x + y
Subtraction	-	x - y
Multiplication	*	x * y
Division	/	x / y
Remainder	%	x % y
Plus	+	+x
Minus	-	-x

Figure 4.3.3 shows some operations on integers. Parentheses can be used to control expression evaluation. For example, in the expression

```
(x + y) * z
```

the parentheses force the addition to occur before the multiplication. Otherwise, the multiplication would occur first because * has a higher precedence than +.

Expression	Value
x + y * z	23
(x + y) * z	35
x - y + z	4
x - (y + z)	-6
x % y	3
y % x	1
x * y / z	2
(x * y) / z	2
x * (y / z)	0
x << 1	6
x >> 1	1
-x >> 1	-2
x | y	7
x & y	0
x ^ z	6

FIGURE 4.3.3 Operations on integers for x = 3, y = 4, and z = 5.

All integer arithmetic uses `ints` or `longs`. An integer value of `byte` or `short` is automatically converted to an `int` or a `long`.

■ **Example 4.3.6.**   In the code segment

```
short x = 4;
int y = 5;
int ans = x * y; // x converted to int
```

short integer x's value is converted to an `int` before the multiplication with the `int` value y occurs. ■

All floating-point arithmetic uses `floats` or `doubles`. If a `double` occurs in the operation, all other values are automatically converted to `double`.

■ **Example 4.3.7.**   In the code segment

```
int x = 2;
double y = 3.14;
double ans = x * y; // x converted to double
```

integer x's value is converted to `double` before the multiplication occurs because this operation includes the `double` value y. ■

Integer division by zero is an error and causes an `ArithmeticException` to be thrown. Section 4.7 explains exceptions and how the programmer can handle them. As noted earlier, floating-point division by zero produces either positive infinity or negative infinity. In any case, floating-point division by zero is not an error.

Shift and Bit Operators

The integer shift operators `<<` and `>>` allow bit shifting on integer values. Bitwise *or*, *and*, *exclusive-or*, and *complement* operations are also supported on integers.

■ **Example 4.3.8.**   The code segment

```
byte x = 3; // 00000011 in binary (byte is 8 bits)
x >> 1;     // 00000001 in binary, 1 in decimal
x << 1;     // 00000110 in binary, 6 in decimal
x = -3;     // 11111101 in 2's complement
x >> 1;     // 11111110 in binary, -2 in decimal
x >>> 1;    // 01111110 in binary, 126 in decimal
```

illustrates bit shifting. The right shift operator `>>` preserves the sign, as the second to the last line shows. By contrast, the right shift operator `>>>` does not preserve the sign but rather fills the vacated positions with zeros. As a result, the code segment's last line evaluates to 126. ■

■ **Example 4.3.9.**   The code segment

```
byte x = 3, y = 4, z = 5;
x | y; // 00000011 | 00000100 is 00000111, or 7 in decimal
x & y; // 00000011 & 00000100 is 00000000, or 0 in decimal
```

```
x ^ z; // 00000011 ^ 00000101 is 00000110, or 6 in decimal
~x;    // 11111100 in binary, -4 in 2's complement
```

illustrates bitwise *or* (|), *and* (&), *exclusive-or* (^), and *complement* (~) operations on byte integers.   ∎

Assignment, Increment, and Decrement Operators

Java has a variety of assignment, increment, and decrement operators. Some assignment operators perform arithmetic operations as well.

∎ **Example 4.3.10.**   The code segment

```
int x = 6, y = 2;
x *= y;        // x = x * y: x now equals 12
int z = x++;   // z equals 12; x is postincremented to 13
int w = x;     // w equals 13, x's value after the increment
w = ++x;       // w equals 14, x's incremented value
w--;           // w equals 13
x = --w;       // x equals w equals 12
x = w--;       // x still equals 12; w postdecremented to 11
x += w;        // x = x + w, so x eqauls 23
```

shows some possibilities. The expressions ++x and x++ differ in their *values*, although each expression increments x by 1. If x is initially 3, the value of the expression ++x is 4—x's *incremented* value. If x is initially 3, the value of the expression x++ is 3—x's original value. The predecrement and postdecrement operators work in the same way. Each operator decrements its operand; but the value of x-- is x's *original* value, whereas the value of --x is x's *decremented* value.   ∎

Arithmetic Operators for Floating-Point Numbers

All the arithmetic operators, including %, apply to floating-point numbers. However, the bit operators ~, |, &, ^, <<, >>, and >>> do not apply to floating-point numbers.

Example 4.3.11.   In the code segment

```
double pi = 3.1415, e = 2.7182;
double r = pi % e;
```

r's value is 0.4233. The code segment shows that the remainder operator may be applied to floating-point values.   ∎

If integers and floating-point values are mixed in an arithmetic operation, the integer values are converted to the appropriate floating-point value. For example, if the `int` value 22 and the `float` value 3.14F are multiplied, 22 is converted to the `float` value 22.0F. If the `int` value 22 and the `double` value 3.14D are multiplied, 22 is converted to the `double` value 22.0D.

The `char` Type

The `char` type is based on 16-bit Unicode characters, an international character encoding system. The Unicode character set is compatible with the 7-bit ASCII character set. (Although an ASCII character requires only 7 bits to encode, most systems use an 8-bit byte.) Moreover, the first 256 Unicode characters (encoded in hex as 0x0000 to 0x00FF) correspond to the international ISO8859-1 or Latin-1 character set. There are currently encodings for 38,885 Unicode characters. The `String` and input/output classes hide the implementation details of character encoding from the programmer. In general, the programmer need not know anything about the underlying character encoding.

Character literals are enclosed in single quotes. These literals may contain either the familiar symbol for a character (e.g,. 'A'), an explicit Unicode encoding (e.g., '\u0041', the Unicode code for upper case *A*), or a special symbol sequence that represents a character (e.g., '\r' represents a carriage return).

> **Example 4.3.12.**   The code segment
>
> ```
> char bigA = 'A';
> char littleA = 'a';
> char newline = '\n';
> char cReturn = '\r';
> char oneQuote = '\'';
> char backspace = '\b';
> char tabHoriz = '\t';
> char formFeed = '\f';
> char aleph = '\u05D0';
> ```
>
> illustrates the syntax and shows the symbol sequences for control characters such as the backspace, horizontal tab, form feed, newline, and carriage return. In a character literal, the backslash \ signals the compiler that the character immediately to the control character's right should not be interpreted in the usual manner. So, for example, the lowercase *n* character 'n' is altogether distinct from the newline character '\n'. Each sequence represents a *single* character, even though there are two symbols in the *single* newline character. The last character literal '\u05D0' begins with the sequence \u to signal *Unicode* and is followed by the integer code for the character, in this case 05D0.
>
> A special character such as a new line is typically written '\n'. However, such a character can be written using the Unicode hexadecimal code, in this case '\u000A' or '\u000a'.

The Problem with Mixing `char` Type and Integer Types

The `char` type is technically *not* an integer type. For one thing, all integer types are *signed* and a `char` is unsigned. Caution should be used in combining `char`s and integer or floating-point expressions in the same operation. For example, the assignment of a 16-bit `char` to an 8-bit `byte` would truncate 8 bits from the `char`.

■ **Example 4.3.13.**   The code segment

```
char c = '\u00FF'; // 0000000011111111 in binary
byte b = (byte) c; // 11111111 in binary, -1 in decimal
```

illustrates the problem of combining a `char` and an integer, in this case a `byte`, in a single operation. The example again illustrates the cast operation for converting an expression's data type. Variable b is a `byte`. Therefore, assigning the `char` value `'\u00FF'` to b requires that this value first be cast—that is, explicitly converted—to a `byte`. The problem is that the `char` value `'\u00FF'` is 16 bits, whereas the `byte` variable b is only 8 bits. The assignment operation therefore truncates c's 16-bit value, which becomes 11111111 or c's 8 rightmost bits. In the 2's complement representation of integers, 11111111 in binary is −1 in decimal. (Recall that a 2's complement integer is negative if its leftmost bit is 1.) Consequently, the *unsigned* character value `'\u00FF'` becomes a negative integer when cast to type `byte`. ■

Arithmetic Operations on the `char` Type

Arithmetic operations can be performed on `char`s, although it bears repeating that caution must be used whenever a single arithmetic operation involves mixed types, in particular a `char` and an integer type such as `byte` or `int`.

■ **Example 4.3.14.**   The code segment

```
char bigA = 'A';
char bigB = ++bigA;  // 'B'
char bigC = ++bigB;  // 'C'
int n = bigC - bigA; //  2
```

illustrates how the preincrement operation and subtraction may be applied to the char type. The value of

```
bigC - bigA
```

is 2 because the Unicode code for `'C'` is 67 and the Unicode code for `'A'` is 65. ■

■ **Example 4.3.15.**   The code segment

```
char bigA = 'A';
char bigB = bigA + 1; //***** ERROR: cast needed!
```

contains an error because the addition involves mixed types: the `char` variable `bigA` and the `int` literal 1. To enable the addition, the compiler first converts `bigA`'s value from `char` to `int`. The integer value of `'A'` in decimal is 65. So the sum is 66 and is of type `int`. Therefore, a cast is required to assign 66 to the `char` variable `bigB`:

```
char bigA = 'A';
char bigB = (char) (bigA + 1); // ok
```

Parentheses are required so that the entire expression `bigA + 1` is cast, not simply the term `bigA`.   ■

String Literals

Character string literals are enclosed in double quotes in contrast to single characters, which are enclosed in single quotes.

■ **Example 4.3.16.**   The code segment

```
char bigA = 'A';  // 1 character
String s1 = "A";  // a character string
String s2 = "AB"; // another character string
```

illustrates the difference between a character literal and a character string literal.   ■

Strings are not a primitive type but rather a class. A string literal such as `"Odysseus"` is a *reference* to a `String` object. A string literal can contain control sequences. For example, the string literal

```
"This string has a double quote \" and a newline \n in it"
```

uses the backslash to nest a double quote and a newline character.

The `boolean` Type

The `boolean` type has two values, `true` and `false`. The `boolean` type is *not* an integer type. The `boolean` values `true` and `false` do *not* correspond to integer values such as 1 and 0.

■ **Example 4.3.17.**   The code segment

```
if ( true ) // boolean value
  // body of if statement
if ( 1 )    //***** ERROR: 1 is not boolean
  // body of if statement
```

illustrates that integers cannot be used in place of `boolean`s in an expression. ■

Casts from `boolean` to any other type or from any other type to `boolean` are not allowed.

■ **Example 4.3.18.**   The code segment

```
boolean b;
b = (boolean) 0;    //***** ERROR! no cast allowed
int x = (int) true; //***** ERROR! no cast allowed
```

generates two fatal compiler errors. The `int` value 0 cannot be cast to a `boolean` value; hence, the `int` value 0 cannot be assigned to the `boolean` variable b. Similarly, the `boolean` literal `true` cannot be cast to an `int`. ■

■ **Example 4.3.19.**   The code segment

```
boolean b = true;
int x = 1;
int ans1 = x + b;       //***** ERROR! b won't convert to int
int ans2 = x + (int) b; //***** ERROR! can't cast b to int
```

illustrates again that a `boolean` value cannot be converted, even with an explicit cast, to an `int` value. The first error reflects the compiler's refusal to convert b's value to an `int` value. The second error shows that even an explicit cast cannot accomplish the conversion of a `boolean` value to an `int` value. ■

Relational Operators

The relational operators are used to compare character, integer, and floating-point expressions. Relational expressions such as

```
26.4 < 98.6
```

evaluate to a `boolean` value, that is, to either `true` or `false`. Figure 4.3.4 lists the relational operators and illustrates how they work.

The relational operators can be used to compare Unicode characters. The programmer can use character literals such as `'A'` and `'Z'` in such comparisons.

Operator	Example	true *if*
==	x == y	x and y are equal
!=	x != y	x and y are not equal
>	x > y	x is greater than y
>=	x >= y	x is greater than or equal to y
<	x < y	x is less than y
<=	x <= y	x is less than or equal to y

FIGURE 4.3.4   Relational operators and sample relational expressions.

■ **Example 4.3.20.**   The code segment

```
if ( 'A' < 'Z' ) // true
  // body of if statement
if ( 'a' > 'A' ) // true
  // body of if statement
if ( 'z' - 'a' + 1 == 26 ) // true
  // body of if statement
```

illustrates how relational operators may be used with character expressions. The expression

```
'z' - 'a'
```

subtracts the Unicode character code for 'a' from the Unicode character code from 'z'. Adding 1 thus gives the number of characters between 'a' and 'z' inclusively, which is 26—the number of lowercase letters from 'a' through 'z'. The example again shows that arithmetic operators such as the subtraction operator may be applied to char expressions.

Finally, no parentheses are required in the expression

```
'z' - 'a' + 1 == 26
```

because the arithmetic operators – and + have a higher precedence than the equality operator ==. Accordingly, the unparenthesized expression is equivalent to

```
('z' - 'a' + 1) == 26
```

■

Cautionary Notes on the Equality Operator ==

Caution must be used in comparing floating-point values for equality. In general, it is better to test whether floating-point values differ by some value such as the MIN_VALUE constant provided by the system Float and Double classes.

■ **Example 4.3.21.**   The code segment

```
double d1 = (1.0 / 3.0) * 2.5, // roughly 0.833333
       d2 = 5.0 / 6.0;         // roughly 0.833333
if ( d1 == d2 ) //***** Caution! false
  // body of if statement
```

illustrates the problem. Variables d1 and d2 have *roughly* but not exactly the same value:

```
double d1 = (1.0 / 3.0) * 2.5, // 0.8333333333333333
       d2 = (5.0 / 6.0);       // 0.833333333333334
```

Therefore, the test

```
if ( d1 == d2 ) //***** Caution! false
```

fails. A more appropriate test might be

```
// do d1 and d2 differ by more than Double.MIN_VALUE?
if ( d1 - d2 <= Double.MIN_VALUE ) // true
  // body of if statement
```

The if condition now tests whether d1 and d2 differ by more than the minimum double value. If d1 and d2 do not differ by more than the minimum double value, we may want to consider them as equal.   ■

The Equality Operator == and Object References

The equality operator is typically *not* used to compare object references because every object has an equals method that is generally better suited to the purpose.

Example 4.3.22.   The code segment

```
String s1 = "foo",
       s2 = "foo";
if ( s1 == s2 )
  System.out.println( "s1 == s2" );
else
  System.out.println( "s1 != s2" );
```

prints

```
s1 != s2
```

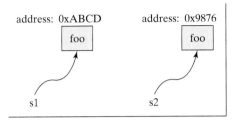

FIGURE 4.3.5   Comparing two object references with the equality operator ==.

Figure 4.3.5 illustrates the situation. Recall that object references such as s1 and s2 are symbolic pointers. Accordingly, their values are the addresses of the objects to which they refer. In Figure 4.3.5, the addresses of the two string objects are depicted in hexadecimal. Variable s1 refers to the `String` at address 0xABCD, whereas variable s2 refers to the `String` at address 0x9876. The expression

```
s1 == s2
```

tests whether the two references are to the same address. In other words, the expression is equivalent to the false expression

```
0xABCD == 0x9876
```

By contrast, the expression

```
s1.equals( s2 )
```

evaluates to `true` because the `equals` method for `Strings` tests whether two `String` objects represent the same string, in this case *foo*.

Logical Operators

There are logical operators for *not*, *and*, *inclusive-or*, and *exclusive-or*. These operators require `boolean` operands such as the values of relational expressions. Of course, the `boolean` literals `true` and `false` also can occur in logical expressions. Figure 4.3.6 lists the operators and shows the basic syntax and meaning for each operator. Logical *not* is **negation**. Logical *and* is **conjunction** and the operands are **conjuncts**. Logical *inclusive-or* is **disjunction** and the operands are **disjuncts**.

■ **Example 4.3.23.**   The code segment

```
int x = -1, y = 999, z = -2, w = 888;
if ( x < y && z < w ) // true AND true?
   // body of if statement
```

Operator	Name	Example	true *if*
&&	*and*	x && y	x and y are both `true`
&	*and*	x & y	x and y are both `true`
||	*inclusive-or*	x || y	x or y (or both) is `true`
|	*inclusive-or*	x | y	x or y (or both) is `true`
^	*exclusive-or*	x ^ y	x and y have opposite truth values
!	*not*	!x	x is `false`

FIGURE 4.3.6   The logical operators. Variables x and y are of type `boolean`.

illustrates the syntax and typical use of a logical operator such as &&. The `if` test evaluates to `true` if *both* of the conjuncts

```
x < y
```

and

```
z < w
```

evaluate to `true`. In this example, the conjunction as a whole evaluates to `true`.   ∎

   In disjunctions and conjunctions involving || and &&, respectively, not all disjuncts or conjuncts may be evaluated. In a disjunction such as

```
x > y || y < z //** x, y, and z are ints
```

left-to-right evaluation halts once a disjunct evaluates to `true`. For example, if x > y evaluates to `true`, the disjunct y < z is *not* evaluated. Recall that a disjunction as a whole is true if any disjunct is true. In a conjunction such as

```
x > y && y < z //** x, y, and z are ints
```

left-to-right evaluation halts once a conjunct evaluates to `false`. For example, if x > y evaluates to `false`, the conjunct y < z is *not* evaluated. Recall that a conjunction as a whole is false if any conjunct is false.

   Operator && has higher precedence than operator ||. Therefore, the expression

```
x > y || y > z && x < 0
```

is equivalent to

```
x > y || (y > z && x < 0)
```

The operators | and & are bitwise operators, if their operands are integers, and logical operators, if their operands are booleans. The Java Postscript explains how | and & differ from | | and && as logical operators.

The instanceof Operator

The instanceof operator can be used with objects to determine the class type that an object instantiates. For example, the code segment

```
Date today = new Date();
if ( today instanceof Date )
  System.out.println( "Object today is of type Date." )
```

prints

```
Object today is of type Date.
```

The expression

```
today instanceof Object
```

evaluates to false because today's type is Date rather than Object. If null occurs on the left side of instanceof, the expression is automatically false. For example,

```
null instanceof Object
```

evaluates to false.

The instanceof operator applies only to *objects* and *class types*. Accordingly, the code segments

```
int x = 0;
if ( x instanceof Object ) //***** ERROR
```

and

```
double d = 3.14;
if ( d instanceof double ) //***** ERROR
```

contain errors. The operator's sole use is to test whether an object is of a particular *class* type.

EXERCISES

1. Is String a primitive data type?
2. Is char a primitive data type?

3. What naming convention seems to be in effect with respect to primitive data types and standard class types?

4. What is the bit size of an `int`?

5. What is the range of an `int`?

6. What is the bit size of a `long`?

7. What is the range of a `long`?

8. What is the bit size of a `float`?

9. What is the range of a `float`?

10. What is the bit size of a `char`?

11. Explain the major differences between integer types such as `byte` and `int` and the `char` type.

12. Is `boolean` an integer type?

13. Can a `boolean` be cast to any other type such as an `int`?

14. Can an integer type such as an `int` be cast to a `boolean`?

15. Write twenty-four as a hexadecimal constant.

16. What is the type of an integer constant such as 10?

17. Explain the error:

```
float pi = 3.1415;
```

18. What is the value of the expression

```
3.1415 / -0.0
```

19. Is the expression

```
-0.0 == 0.0
```

true?

20. Explain the error:

```
double x = 3.1415 / 0.0;
int k = 31415 / 0;
```

21. What is printed in the code segment

```
int x = 1;
System.out.println( x++ );
System.out.println( ++x );
```

22. Is the relational expression

```
'P' < 'Q'
```

true?

23. Do relational expressions all have a `boolean` value?

24. Indicate whether division by zero occurs in the code segment

```
int n1 = 1, n2 = 2, n3 = 3;
if ( n1 < n2 || n3 > n3 / 0 )
```

25. What is printed?

```
String s1 = "hi", s2 = "hi";
if ( s1 == s2 )
  System.out.println( "yes" );
else
  System.out.println( "no" );
```

4.4   Arrays

An **array** groups storage cells of the same type under a single name, the array's identifier. An array's **elements**—the storage cells grouped together under the array's name—are referenced using the array's name and an integer index, which specifies an element's offset from the first element. Figure 4.4.1 depicts an array of five elements. The cell's value (e.g., 111) is written inside of it. Below each cell in square brackets

```
111    222    333    444    555
[ 0 ]  [ 1 ]  [ 2 ]  [ 3 ]  [ 4 ]
```

FIGURE 4.4.1   An array of five elements with indexes below each cell.

is the cell's index. The first cell has an index of 0, the second cell an index of 1, and the third cell an index of 2. For an array of n elements, the valid indexes are therefore $0,1,\ldots,n-1$. Arrays are of arbitrary size and dimensionality. Arrays can aggregate primitive or class data types.

■ **Example 4.4.1.**   The code segment

```
int[ ] a = new int[ 100 ];
```

creates an array of 100 `int`s. The code segment

```
String[ ] strings = new String[ 1000 ];
```

creates an array of 1,000 `String` references.

In a declaration, square brackets [ ] are used to indicate an array. The brackets can occur after the data type

```
int[ ] a;
```

or after the identifier

```
int a[ ];
```

The syntax is equivalent.

An array *declaration* does not allocate storage for the array's elements. There are two ways to allocate such storage:

- The `new` operator can be used to allocate a specified number of array elements. The code segment

```
int[ ] a = new int[ 500 ]; // allocate 500 int cells
```

  illustrates. Here the `new` operator allocates 500 `int` elements.
- The array can be initialized in its declaration by listing values separated by commas. The code segment

```
int[ ] a = { 1, 3, 5, 7, 9 }; // 5 int cells allocated
```

creates an array of five elements by providing five initial values. The array's first element is 1, its second element is 3, and so on.

If an array is created through explicit initialization, its cells store the initializing values. Otherwise, the array's cells are initialized to the appropriate default value; for example, an `int` array allocated with `new` has elements initialized to 0, a `double` array allocated with `new` has elements initialized to 0.0, and a `boolean` array allocated with `new` has elements initialized to `false`.

Arrays cannot grow or shrink in size, although an array identifier can be reused. If a program requires automatic resizing of a collection, the program should use a construct such as a `java.util.Vector` or `java.util.Set`.

Example 4.4.2.   The code segment

```
int[ ] nums;
nums = new int[ 100 ];  // allocate 100 cells
//... process the array
nums = new int[ 15 ];   // new array, same identifier
```

illustrates reuse of the array identifier `nums`. Immediately after its declaration, `nums` refers to an array of 100 elements. Later in the code segment, `nums` refers to an altogether different array, which has 15 elements. Because `nums` is declared as the identifier of an `int` array, both of the arrays must be `int` arrays.

Every array has a `length` member, which gives the number of elements. The `length` member is especially useful in counted loops.

■ **Example 4.4.3.**   The code segment

```
double[ ] nums = new double[ 512 ];
for ( int i = 0; i < nums.length; i++ )
   nums[ i ] = 3.14;
```

creates an array of 512 `doubles` and then uses a `for` loop to assign each element
the value 3.14. The `for` loop's test uses the array's `length` member as one term
in the comparison.   ■

Bounds Checking

Recall that the valid indexes for an array of N elements are 0, 1,. . . , $N - 1$. The
compiler does *not* check whether an index occurs within these bounds.

■ **Example 4.4.4.**   The code segment

```
int[ ] nums = new int[ 10 ];
nums[ -1 ] = 123;  //**** ERROR: out of bounds index
nums[ 10 ] = 321;  //**** ERROR: out of bounds index
```

compiles despite having two indexes that are out of bounds. However, the code
segment does throw an `ArrayIndexOutOfBoundsException` when executed.
The distinction can be summarized by saying that Java does not perform compile-
time bounds checking but does perform run-time bounds checking. In the end,
the programmer is responsible for ensuring that array indexes are inbounds.   ■

Arrays of Arrays

In an array such as

```
int[ ] nums = new int[ 100 ];
```

each element is an `int`. Arrays also can have other *arrays* as elements.

Example 4.4.5.   The code segment

```
int[ ][ ] matrix = new int[ 4 ][ 3 ];
```

creates an array with *four* elements. Each element is itself an array of three `int`
elements. The array thus has 12 `int` cells altogether.

Example 4.4.6.   The code segment

```
int m[ ][ ] = { { 999, 888, 777 }, { 666, 555, 444 } };
```

creates an array m, which has two elements: the first element is itself an array of three elements, each an integer (999, 888, 777); the second element is also an array of three elements, each an integer (666, 555, 444). The array m can be depicted as

	First Element			*Second Element*	
999	888	777	666	555	444
[0][0]	[0][1]	[0][2]	[1][0]	[1][1]	[1][2]

with indexes again given beneath the cells. The array's first element consists of the first three int cells

	First Element	
999	888	777
[0][0]	[0][1]	[0][2]

and its second consists of the second three int cells

	Second Element	
666	555	444
[1][0]	[1][1]	[1][2]

So each of m's two elements is itself an *array* that has int cells as elements. Identifying a particular cell in m therefore requires *two* indexes. The first index (0 or 1) identifies in which of m's elements the cell occurs. The second index (0, 1, or 2) indicates the cell in that element. For example, 888 occupies the second cell in the first element. The index is thus

```
m[ 0 ][ 1 ] // 1st element, 2nd cell
```

where

```
m[ 0 ]  // 1st element
```

refers to the array's first element, and

```
m[ 0 ][ 1 ] // 1st element, 2nd cell
```

then specifies an offset of 1 within the first element, which therefore references the *second* cell in the first element. ■

A simple array such as

```
int[ ] a;  // "one-dimensional"
```

is sometimes called a *one-dimensional* array. An array of arrays such as

```
int[ ][ ] b; // "two-dimensional"
```

or

```
int[ ][ ][ ] b; // "three-dimensional"
```

is sometimes called a *multidimensional* array. A two-dimensional array is also called a *matrix*.

The syntax for arrays is flexible with respect to declaring arrays and passing them as arguments. Method m

```
void m( int[ ][ ] td ) { /*...*/ }
```

expects a single argument, which is a two-dimensional array of ints. The parameter is td. An equivalent (but perhaps more confusing) version is

```
void m( int[ ] td[ ] ) { /*...*/ }
```

Although the latter version does underscore that td is an array of int arrays, this style is uncommon.

Arrays as Return Types

A method's return type can be an array type such as int[ ]. For example, the method

```
int[ ] makeIntArray( int n ) {
    return new int[ n ];
}
```

allocates and returns a reference to an int array. The method could be invoked in a code segment such as

```
int[ ] ar = makeIntArray( 100 );
```

Because the array elements are ints, these elements are initialized to 0.

EXERCISES

1. Explain the two ways in which storage for an array can be allocated.

2. Explain the error:

```
int[ ] ar = new array[ 3 ];
ar[ 3 ] = -999;
```

3. How many *elements* are in the array

```
int[ ] ar = new int[ 10 ];
```

What is the type of each element?

4. How many `ints` are in the array

```
int[ ] ar = new int[ 10 ];
```

5. How many `ints` are in the array

```
int[ ][ ] ma = new int[ 2 ][ 5 ]
```

6. How many *elements* are in the array

```
int[ ][ ] ma = new int[ 5 ][ 2 ];
```

What is the type of each element?
7. Does the compiler do *bounds checking* on arrays?
8. Can a method have an array type such as `int[ ]` as a return type?

4.5   Control Structures

There are control statements for tests, loops, and related constructs. Control statements such as `if`, `for while`, `switch`, and `break` occur *only within constructors and methods*. This section explains the major control constructs and a later section focuses on handling special conditions known as *exceptions*.

Blocks

A **block** is a sequence of zero or more statements enclosed in curly braces. The left brace { begins a block, and a matching right brace } ends the block.

> **Example 4.5.1.**   The class declaration
>
> ```
> class C {
>   void m() { //*** start of m's body, a block
>     int x = 1, y = 2, z;
>     z = x + y * y;
>     //...
>   }           //*** end of m's body, a block
> }
> ```
>
> contains a method m whose body is a block.

Variables defined inside a constructor or method have **block scope**; that is, such variables are visible only within the block that contains their declaration. The containing block may be the constructor's or method's body as a whole

```
void m() {
  int x; //*** containing block is m's body
  //...
}
```

or the body of a control construct such as an `if` statement

```
void m() {
  int x = 9;      //*** containing block is m's body
  if ( x > 0 ) {
    int temp;     //*** if statement's body
    //...
  }
  //...
}
```

In either case, the variable is visible only within its containing block.

■ **Example 4.5.2.**   The code segment

```
class C {
  void m1() {
    int x = -1;  // x visible in m1
    //...
  }
  void m2() {
    x = 999;      //***** ERROR: x not visible in m2!
    //...
  }
}
```

contains an error because variable x is local to method m1's body, the block in which x is declared. In particular, x cannot be referenced in method m2's body, a block altogether distinct from m1's body.   ■

■ **Example 4.5.3.**   The code segment

```
class C {
  void m1() {
    int x = -1;  // x visible in m1
    //...
  }
```

```
    void m2() {
       int x = 999; // ok, x declared inside m2's body
       //...
    }
}
```

amends Example 4.5.2 by declaring two variables named x in two distinct blocks: one x is declared in m1's body and an altogether distinct x is declared in m2's body. The two variables are completely distinct and have completely distinct scopes: the variable x declared in m1 has m1's body as its scope, and the variable x declared in m2's body has m2's body as its scope.   ■

Blocks can be nested to any level. For example, a method's body might contain a test or a loop whose body is a block.

■ **Example 4.5.4.**   In the code segment

```
class C {
   void m() { //*** outer block: m's body
      int x, y;
      // x and y are assigned values
      if ( x > y ) { //** nested block: its body
         x = x - y;   // ok, x and y are visible here
         //...
      } //** end of nested block
   } //*** end of outer block
}
```

method m's body is a block that contains an if statement whose own body is a block. Note that variables x and y are visible *throughout* m's body, which includes the nested block.   ■

Name conflicts among variables are not allowed. For example, a method m cannot contain two local variables named x whose scopes overlap.

Example 4.5.5.   The code segment

```
class C {
   void m() {
      int x = -1;    //*** line 1: outer block's x
      if ( x < 0 ) { //*** nested block
         int x;      //*** line 3: conflicts with x on line 1
         //...
      }              //*** end of nested block
   }                 //*** end of outer block
}
```

illustrates the error. The variable x declared on line 1 is visible throughout method m's body, which includes the nested block that begins on line 3. Therefore, the nested block must not declare a variable named x.   ■

■ **Example 4.5.6.**   We amend Exercise 4.5.5

```
class C {
   void m() {
      int y = -1;
      if ( y < 0 ) {   //** 1st nested block
         int x;         //** x local to 1st nested block
         //...
      }                 //** end of 1st nested block
      if ( y < 100 ) { //** 2nd nested block
         int x;         //** ok, this x does not share scope
                        //** with x in 1st nested block
         //...
      }                 //** end of 2nd nested block
   }                    //*** end of outer block
}
```

by removing the variable x whose scope was m's body. We now have two nested blocks, each the body of an if statement. Each nested block declares a variable named x. Now there is no name conflict between the two variables named x because their scopes do not overlap.   ■

The prohibition against name conflicts also covers parameters. A local variable cannot have the same name as a parameter.

Fields, Parameters, and Local Variables with the Same Name

A local variable or parameter can have the same name as a field. In this case, the object reference this is used to distinguish the field from the local variable or parameter. The keyword this refers to the object involved in the method invocation. Chapter 5 goes into detail. For now, only the basic syntax is important.

■ **Example 4.5.7.**   The code segment

```
class Emp {
   public void setName( String name ) { //*** same as field
      this.name = name; //*** disambiguate with this
   }
   private String name;
}
```

illustrates the syntax. Method `setName` has a parameter `name` and the encapsulating `Emp` class has a field `name`. The expression `this.name` refers to the field,
whereas the expression `name` refers to the parameter.   ∎

Nested Blocks

Nested blocks normally occur as the bodies of `if` statements and loops. However, a
block can be created independently of such constructs.

∎ **Example 4.5.8.**   The code segment

```
class C {
   void m() { //*** start of outer block
      {           //** start of 1st nested block
        int x;
        //...
      }           //** end of 1st nested block
      {           //** start of 2nd nested block
        int x;
        //...
      }           //** end of 2nd nested block
   } //*** end of outer block
}
```

illustrates nested blocks that are not the bodies of `if` statements, loops, or the
like.   ∎

There are also special-purpose blocks associated with `try` and `catch` clauses,
which are used in exception handling (see Section 4.7). (The terms `try` and `catch` are
keywords.) All blocks adhere to the same rules of scope with respect to the variables
declared inside of them.

The `if` Statement

The `if` statement is used to execute a code segment conditionally. The statement has
various forms but all occur *within the body* of a constructor or method.

∎ **Example 4.5.9.**   The code segment

```
int x = -1, y = 999;
if ( x < y )  // if this condition is true
   x = x * y; // then execute this code
y = 0;        //*** 1st statement beyond if statement's body
```

shows the simplest form of the `if` statement. The parenthesized expression that follows the `if` is called the **test** or **condition** and its value must be `boolean`. In this case, the test is the relational expression

```
x < y
```

If the expression evaluates to `true`, the statement

```
x = x * y;
```

executes. If the test evaluates to `false`, the statement does *not* execute and execution resumes at the first statement beyond the `if` statement's body

If an `if` statement's body consists of a *single* statement, as in this example, the body need not be enclosed in curly braces. If the body consists of *multiple* statements, the body must be enclosed in curly braces. It is always permissible to enclose the body in curly braces, however. The code segment

```
int x = -1, y = 999;
if ( x < y ) { // braces optional: body is 1 statement
  x = x * y;
}
if ( x < y ) { // braces required: body is two statements
  x = x * y;
  y = y / x;
}
```

illustrates.

Indentation and whitespace are optional. Our original `if` statement could have been written

```
if(x<y)x=x*y; //**** valid but hard to read
```                                                    ■

The `if` statement with an `else` can be used as a two-way decision structure.

Example 4.5.10.   The code segment

```
boolean jupiterAlignedWithMars, myLuckIsGood;
// jupiterAlignedWithMars is assigned a boolean value
if ( jupiterAlignedWithMars )
  myLuckIsGood = true;
else
  myLuckIsGood = false;
```

illustrates the basic `if-else` structure. If the test evaluates to `true`, the `boolean` variable `myLuckIsGood` is assigned `true` as its value; otherwise, this variable is assigned `false` as its value. The bodies of both the `if` and `else` parts consist of single statements, which means that the curly braces are optional.

The `if` statement can be used as a *multiway* decision structure by using the `else if` and `else` constructs together.

■ **Example 4.5.11.**   The code segment

```
char academicYear = '3';
if ( academicYear == '1' )         //*** 1st test
   // freshman-appropriate action
else if ( academicYear == '2' )  //*** 2nd test
   // sophomore-appropriate action
else if ( academicYear == '3' )  //*** 3rd test
   // junior-appropriate action
else if ( academicYear == '4' )  //*** 4th test
   // senior-appropriate action
else                              //*** default
   // default action: none of the above
```

illustrates a multiway decision structure using `if`, `else if`, and `else`. There are four `if`s in the construct and, therefore, as many as four tests may be performed. If each of four tests evaluates to `false`, the `else` at the bottom ensures that a default action occurs. Further, only *one* of the four `if` tests can succeed. For example, if `academicYear`'s value is `'3'`, the first two tests fail, the third test succeeds, and the fourth test is not performed at all. Instead, the body of the third test (the junior-appropriate action) executes and then execution resumes at the first statement beyond the entire multiway decision structure.   ■

The condition of an `if` statement must evaluate to a `boolean` but there are no other restrictions. Further, there are no restrictions on what the body of an `if` or an `else` statement may contain. For example, the body may contained nested `if` constructs, loops, and method calls. The Java Postscript explains how the conditional operator may be used for two-way tests.

The `switch` Statement

The `switch` statement is a multiway decision structure based on the value of an integer expression.

■ **Example 4.5.12.**   Figure 4.5.1 contains a code segment that illustrates the `switch` statement and reviews the `break` statement. The `switch` condition, like an `if` condition, is enclosed in parentheses. The difference is that a `switch` condition is an *integer* rather than a `boolean` expression. In particular, the data type of the `switch` condition must be `byte`, `short`, `int`, or `char`. If the

```
char who;
String team; // String to contain name of team
//*** code to assign who a value
switch ( who ) { //*** start of switch block
case 'J':    // Michael Jordan
   team = "Chicago Bulls";
   break;
case 'P':    // Scottie Pippen
   team = "Chicago Bulls";
   break;
case 'S':    // John Stockton
   team = "Utah Jazz";
   break;
default:     // anything other than 'J', 'P', 'S'
   team = "??????";
   break;
} //*** end of switch block
```

FIGURE 4.5.1   A code segment illustrating the `switch` statement.

expression's type is not `int`, the compiler converts the expression to `int`. In this example, therefore, the value of the `char` variable `who` is converted to an `int`. Recall that a `boolean` cannot be converted, even with an explicit cast, to any other type. Accordingly, a `switch` condition must not be of type `boolean`.

A `switch` statement's body must be enclosed in curly braces. The body typically includes multiple `case` labels and their associated constants followed by colons. For example, this example's first `case` label is

```
case 'J': // case label
```

and the associated constant is `'J'`. The associated constant is a possible value for the `switch` condition's variable, in this case `who`. If `who`'s value is `'J'`, the statements following this `case` label execute in sequence until

- The `switch` statement's body is exited.
- A `break` statement occurs, which automatically exits the `switch` statement's body.

In our example, only one statement executes after each `case` label before a `break` statement occurs.

The `default` label is optional but, if present, introduces statements that execute if none of the `case` label constants matches the `switch` condition. In this example, if the `switch` condition's variable `who` were set to any value other than `'J'`, `'P'`, or `'S'`, the `default` statement would execute. We include a `break` in the `default` section only to maintain a consistent style. Because the `default` section occurs last in the body of a `switch`, exiting this section also exits the `switch`'s body.

Example 4.5.13.   In the code segment of Figure 4.5.1, two `case` labels result in having the `String` variable `msg` assigned the value `"Chicago Bulls"`. We can simplify the relevant code to

```
switch ( who ) { //*** start of switch block
case 'J': // Michael Jordan
case 'P': // Scottie Pippen
   team = "Chicago Bulls";
   break;
//...
```

Two `case` labels now occur together so that variable `team` is assigned the value `"Chicago Bulls"` if the `switch` condition's value is either `'J'` or `'P'`. ■

■ **Example 4.5.14.**   The code segment in Figure 4.5.2, which uses an `if` statement instead of a `switch` statement, is logically equivalent to the code segment in Figure 4.5.1. ■

```
char who;
String team; // String to contain name of team
//*** code to assign who a value
if ( who == 'J' || who == 'P' )
   team = "Chicago Bulls";
else if ( who == 'S' )
   team = "Utah Jazz";
else
   team = "??????";
```

FIGURE 4.5.2 A code segment with `if` instead of `switch` that is logically equivalent to the code segment of Figure 4.5.1.

The `while` and `do while` Loops

The `while` and `do while` statements are suited for **conditional looping**, that is, for looping as long as a specified condition is `true`. The two statements differ with respect to where the test or condition occurs in the loop. In a `while` loop, the condition occurs at the *top*; in a `do while` loop, the condition occurs at the *bottom*.

■ **Example 4.5.15.**   The code segment

```
int i = 0;
final int n = 100;
```

```
while ( i < n ) { //*** loop while i is less than n
   System.out.println( i * i ); // print i's square
   i++;                          // increment i
}
```

illustrates a `while` loop. The condition is the expression

```
i < n
```

This condition is evaluated *before* the loop's body is executed. So if i were initialized to 100 in this example, the loop's body would not execute. The loop's body is a block of two statements.

■ **Example 4.5.16.**   The code segment

```
int next;
do {
   next = promptAndReadPosInt();
} while ( next <= 0 );
```

illustrates a `do while` loop. The method `promptAndReadPosInt` prompts the user for a positive integer, reads an integer from the standard input, and returns the integer. The loop's body assigns the user's input to `next`; the loop's condition then tests whether the input is positive. The loop repeats until `next`'s value is greater than zero.

  As the example shows, a `do while` is convenient for validating user input. The loop test occurs at the *bottom*, which ensures that the loop's body is entered at least once. If the user input is correct the first time, the loop exits.   ■

A `while` or `do while` loop can be made an **infinite loop** by setting the loop condition to the `boolean` literal `true`. In this case, a `break` statement can be used to exit the loop's body.

■ **Example 4.5.17.**   We rewrite Example 4.5.15 by using an infinite `while` loop:

```
int next;
while ( true ) {
   next = promptAndReadPosInt();
   if ( next > 0 )
      break; // exit the loop's body
}
```

The code segment in Example 4.5.16 is simpler and clearer. The two loops are logically equivalent, however.   ■

The `for` Loop

The `for` statement is suited for **counted loops**, that is, loops that iterate a predetermined number of times.

■ **Example 4.5.18.**   The code segment

```
final int n = 100;
for ( int i = 0; i < n; i++ )
   System.out.println( i * i );
```

illustrates a `for` loop. The `for` loop's condition section consists of three **clauses** or parts, separated by semicolons. The first clause contains the variable declaration and initialization

```
int i = 0
```

Because variable `i` is declared *inside* the `for` loop, the variable's scope is the `for` loop's body. Variable `i` could have been declared above the `for` loop

```
int i;
final int n = 100;
for ( i = 0; i < n; i++ )
   printSquare( i * i );
```

in which case the first clause merely assigns `i` a value. If `i` is declared above the `for` loop, `i`'s scope is not confined to the loop's body.

The condition's first clause may contain multiple expressions. An example is

```
int i;
final int n = 100;
for ( int i = 0, int j = i + 1; i < n; i++ )
   //...
```

In any case, the first clause is executed *once* only and at the very beginning. If there are multiple expressions in the first clause, they evaluate in a left-to-right sequence. In this example, therefore, `j` is assigned the value `i + 1`.

Once the first clause completes, the loop enters a *test/action/post-body* pattern. In this example,

• The *test* is the second clause

```
i < n
```

If the test evaluates to `true`, the loop's body executes. Otherwise, the loop terminates and execution resumes at the first statement beyond the loop's body.

- The *action* is the loop's body, in this case the `println` statement. If the loop's body consists of multiple statements, these must be enclosed in curly braces.
- The *post-body* is the third clause in the condition

```
i++
```

which executes *after* the loop's body executes. In this example, the *post-body* clause adds 1 to the loop counter `i`. ∎

Any of the three `for` loop clauses may be empty, but the two semicolons must be present. The loop

```
for ( ; ; ) { // infinite loop
   //...
}
```

illustrates. Because the *test* is empty, its value is `true` and so the loop's body repeatedly executes until a `break` or comparable statement is executed.

∎ **Example 4.5.19.**   The `for` loop

```
int next;
for ( next = 0; next <= 0; ) // empty 3rd clause
   next = promptForPosInt();
```

is logically equivalent to the `do while` loop of Example 4.5.16. However, the `for` loop's logic is somewhat obscure. For example, `next` is assigned 0 in the loop condition's first clause to ensure that the *test*

```
next <= 0
```

succeeds before the *first* iteration. The loop's body then assigns a user-provided `int` to `next`. The *post-body* clause is empty; hence, the *test* repeats immediately after each iteration of the loop's body. By contrast, the logic of the `do while` loop in Example 4.5.16 is straightforward. ∎

EXERCISES

1. Is a local variable visible outside the constructor's or method's body in which it is declared?

2. If a variable is declared inside the body of a `while` loop, what is the variable's scope?

3. Assume that every adult is either *never married* ('n'), *married* ('m'), *divorced* ('d'), or *widowed* ('w'). Write an `if` construct to test whether `char` variable `c` has either one of the `char` values shown or none of these values.

4. Explain the error in the method:

```
void m() {
   int x = 4, y = 16;
   if ( x < y ) {
      int x = x + 1;
      //...
   }
}
```

5. Explain and then correct the error:

```
int x = 1, y = 2;
if ( x > y )
   x = x * 2;
   y = y * 3;
else
   x = 0;
```

6. Must the body of a `while` loop be entered at least once?

7. Must the body of a `do while` loop execute at least once?

8. Explain the behavior of the loop

```
for ( ; ; )
   System.out.println( "What, me worry?" );
```

9. What does the code segment print?

```
int x = 1;
while ( true ) {
   System.out.println( x++ );
   if ( x > 3 )
      break;
}
System.out.println( x + 1 );
```

10. What does the code segment print?

```
char c1 = 'M', c2 = 'K', c3;
if ( c1 > c2 )
   c3 = c2;
else
```

```
    c3 = c1;
switch ( c3 ) {
case 'M':
   System.out.println( c1 );
case 'K':
   System.out.println( c2 );
default:
   System.out.println( "none of the above" );
}
```

4.6   Sample Application: Generating Nonduplicate Integers

Problem

Generate a series of reports about how many integers have to be generated in order to generate N nonduplicate integers within a specified range. After each report, increase the range of integers from which the nonduplicate integers are selected. Given an initial goal of 100, for example, the first attempt might report on how many random integers in the range of 0 through 110 had to be generated in order to generate 100 nonduplicate integers. The second attempt might generate integers in a range of 0 through 120, the third attempt might generate integers in a range of 0 through 130, and so forth. A client should have the option of printing the reports with or without the nonduplicate integers.

Output

A sample run of the client in Figure 4.6.1 produced the output

```
List size: 10000
   Tries for 0 through 11000: 26695
   Tries for 0 through 12000: 21732
   Tries for 0 through 13000: 19144
   Tries for 0 through 14000: 17475
   Tries for 0 through 15000: 16423
   Tries for 0 through 16000: 15855
   Tries for 0 through 17000: 14940
```

```
class GenNonDupsClient {
   public static void main( String[ ] args ) {
      new GenNonDups( 10000 ); //*** 10,000
   }
}
```

FIGURE 4.6.1   Test client for the GenNonDups class.

```
Tries for 0 through 18000: 14544
Tries for 0 through 19000: 14098
Tries for 0 through 20000: 13845
Tries for 0 through 21000: 13604
Tries for 0 through 22000: 13422
Tries for 0 through 23000: 13176
Tries for 0 through 24000: 12946
Tries for 0 through 25000: 12828
Tries for 0 through 26000: 12643
Tries for 0 through 27000: 12576
Tries for 0 through 28000: 12359
Tries for 0 through 29000: 12225
Tries for 0 through 30000: 12144
```

for a goal of 10,000 nonduplicate integers. The initial range is 0 through 11,000 and the final range is 0 through 30,000.

The output confirms the theoretical expectation that a broader range of random integers tends to require fewer random integers to be generated in order to reach the goal of N nonduplicate integers. For example, the range of 0 through 11,000 requires the generation of 26,695 random integers, whereas the range of 0 through 30,000 requires the generation of only 12,144 random integers.

Solution

The class GenNonDups has four public constructors. The no-argument constructor

```
new GenNondups()
```

sets the goal to a default number (currently 100) and does *not* print the nonduplicate integers. By contrast, the two-argument constructor in an invocation such as

```
new GenNonDups( 3000, true )
```

sets the goal to 3,000 nonduplicate integers and does print the integers in each report. The random integers are generated using the utility class Random, with negative integers converted to nonnegative ones.

The first report is on integers selected from a range of 0 through 110% of the goal. Subsequent reports select integers from ranges whose upper bounds are 120%, 130%,. . . , 300% of the goal. For a goal of 100, for instance, the upper bounds are 110, 120,. . . , 300.

Java Implementation

```
import java.util.*;
class GenNonDups {
  //** no-argument constructor: goal defaults to defaultGoal
  public GenNonDups() {            //*** no-argument constructor
```

```java
      test( defaultGoal );
}
public GenNonDups( boolean d ) { //*** true means print numbers
      details = d;
      test( defaultGoal );
}
public GenNonDups( int n ) {       //*** n is list's size
   if ( n > 0 )
     test( n );
   else
     test( defaultGoal );
}
public GenNonDups( int n, boolean d ) {
      details = d;
      if ( n > 0 )
        test( n );
      else
        test( defaultGoal );
}
//*** run the tests
private void test( int n ) {
   goal = n;
   nums = new HashSet();
   generateReports();
}
private void generateReports() {
   double percent = 1.1,
          percentLimit = 3.1;
   System.out.println( "List size: " + goal );
   while ( percent < percentLimit ) {
      int ub = (int) (goal * percent);
      populateSet( ub );
      percent += 0.1;
   }
}
//** fill the Set nums with random integers
private void populateSet( final int ub ) {
   Random r = new Random();
   tries = 0;                        // tries required
   if ( !nums.isEmpty() )            // if not empty
     nums.clear();                   // then remove all elements
   while ( true ) {                  // potentially infinite loop
      int next = Math.abs( r.nextInt() ) % ub;
      tries++;
      nums.add( new Integer( next ) );
```

```
          // Exit if n nonduplicate integers are generated
          if ( nums.size() == goal )
             break;
      }
      report( ub );
   }
   private void report( int ub ) {
      System.out.println( "   Tries for 0 through " +
                           ub + ": " + tries );
      if ( details ) {
        //*** sort the numbers into ascending order
        Object[ ] temp = nums.toArray();
        Arrays.sort( temp );
        for ( int i = 0; i < temp.length; i++ )
           System.out.println( temp[ i ] );
      }
   }
   //*** private fields
   private int goal;              // how many random ints
   private int tries;             // how many tries required
   private Set nums;              // set to hold the integers
   private boolean details;       // print the numbers in report?
   private static final int defaultGoal = 100;
}
```

Discussion

The GenNonDups class's only public members are the four constructors. The constructors invoke private methods to generate the nonduplicate integers and to report on the total number of integers generated. The constructors are

- GenNonDups(). Generates defaultGoal nonduplicate integers but does *not* print them in the reports. The private field defaultGoal is currently set to 100.
- GenNonDups(boolean f). Like the no-argument constructor, generates defaultGoal nonduplicate integers but prints them if f is true.
- GenNonDups(int n). Generates n nonduplicate integers, if n is greater than zero; otherwise, generates defaultGoal nonduplicate integers. Does *not* print the nonduplicate integers in the reports.
- GenNonDups(int n, boolean f). Generates n nonduplicate integers, if n is greater than zero; otherwise, generates defaultGoal nonduplicate integers. Prints the nonduplicate integers if f is true.

Each constructor invokes the private method test, which in turn invokes the private method generateReports in order to populate a set with numbers in the range of 0 through ub for upper bound.

The Set Interface and HashSet Implementation

The populateSet method uses a HashSet to collect the integers. The HashSet class defines all of the methods declared in the Set interface. For example, the Set interface declares a method add for adding elements to a set; and HashSet defines add. (For a review of interfaces, see Section 1.5.) The syntax

```
Set nums = new HashSet();
```

signals that nums refers to an object—in this case, a HashSet object—that implements or defines the methods declared in the Set interface.

A Set is useful for this application because a Set has *no duplicates*. For example, the code segment

```
String s = new String( "foo" );
Set sample = new HashSet();
sample.add( s );                        //*** 1 element in Set
sample.add( s );                        //*** still 1 element
System.out.println( sample.size() ); //*** 1
```

tries but fails to add the same String twice to a Set. The method add returns true, if an element is added to the Set, and false, if an element cannot be added to the Set because, for example, the Set already contains the element. In summary, a Set is well suited for the task at hand by solving the problem of how to avoid duplicates. As each candidate integer is generated, the counter tries is incremented so this value can be included in the report.

Collections such as Sets and Lists can hold references to class instances such as Integers but not primitive types such as ints. Accordingly, the next randomly generated int is wrapped in an Integer

```
nums.add( new Integer( next ) );
```

before being added to the Set called nums.

Once the set has been populated with the required number of nonduplicate integers, the report method checks whether the invoker specified that the integers should be printed to the standard output. If so, report invokes the Set's method toArray, which returns the set elements as an array of Objects. The syntax is

```
Object[ ] temp = nums.toArray();
```

where nums is a reference to the HashSet object. The conversion is done so that the static method sort

```
Arrays.sort( temp );
```

of the `java.util.Arrays` class can be invoked to sort the array in ascending order. The `Arrays` class also has methods to fill and search arrays. The `Collections` class, which likewise belongs to the `java.util` package, has various utility methods to fill, sort, reverse, shuffle, and otherwise process collections such as `Lists`. Utility classes such as `Arrays` and `Collections` are particularly helpful in performing standard programming tasks such as sorting and searching.

EXERCISES

1. Run the sample application to test its behavior.
2. Amend the application so that it uses a `List` rather than a `Set`. Although a `List` can hold duplicates, it has a method

```
boolean contains( Object o );
```

that returns `true`, if the object already occurs in the `List`, and `false`, if the object does not occur in the `List`. Also, `List` is an interface and class `Vector` implements this interface.

4.7   Exceptions

An **exception** is an unexpected condition that arises while a program executes. For example, a program might try to read from a nonexistent file or to divide an integer by zero. **Exception handling** is a mechanism for handling exceptions in a disciplined, robust, and uncluttered way. When an exception occurs, it is said to be *thrown*. Once thrown, an exception is *caught* by either a `catch` clause in the code or by a default exception-handler. (`catch` is a keyword.)

The runtime environment *implicitly* throws an exception when a program violates some condition such as trying to read from a nonexistent file or dividing an integer by zero. A program can *explicitly* throw an exception with a `throw` statement. (`throw` is a keyword.) After an exception has been thrown in either way, control transfers from the current point of execution to a `catcher` associated with a `try` clause, or a `finally` clause, or the system's default exception-handler. (`try` and `finally` are keywords.)

■ **Example 4.7.1.**   The code segment

```
int x = 26 / 0; //*** arithmetic exception
```

throws an exception because it divides an integer by zero. The code segment does not catch—that is, handle—the exception. The system therefore handles the exception. The system's default action is to print a message about the exception before terminating the program that threw it. The message is informative. For example, when the code segment executed as part of an application, the default exception-handler printed

```
Exception in thread "main" java
        at Ex.main(Ex.java:3)
```

before terminating the program. The division-by-zero statement occurs in source file *Ex.java* on line 3, which is in method `main`. ∎

■ **Example 4.7.2.**   The code segment

```
int n, d;
n = promptUserForNumber();
d = promptUserForDivisor();
try {
   System.out.println( "The remainder is " + n % d );
}
catch( ArithmeticException e ) {
   System.err.println( e );
}
System.out.println( "Beyond the catcher..." );
```

illustrates the basic syntax for handling exceptions. We assume that the method calls return integers, which then are assigned to the two `int` variables n and d. The block associated with the `try` clause is commonly called the `try` block. In this example, there is a single statement in the `try` block but, in general, a `try` block can contain arbitrarily many statements. Statements are placed in a `try` block to enable exception handling through `catch` clauses. In this case, the remainder operation is placed inside the `try` block to prepare for division by zero.

If variable d has zero as its value, the runtime environment throws an exception of type `ArithmeticException`. There is a hierarchy of exception classes rooted in the `Throwable` class to represent exceptions that can be thrown and handled. The `catch` clause immediately below the `try` block handles arithmetic exceptions such as integer division by zero. If d is zero, the remainder operation n % d causes an `ArithmeticException` to be thrown. Control immediately transfers to the `catch` clause. In particular, the `System.out.println` statement inside the `try` block does *not* complete. Instead, the `catch` clause prints the exception to the standard error. The printed exception is generally informative. For example,

```
java.lang.ArithmeticException: / by zero
```

is printed when integer division by zero occurs. Because our own code rather than the system handles the exception, the division by zero does *not* cause the program to terminate. By providing our own exception-handler, we thereby make integer division by zero a *recoverable* rather than a fatal error.

A `catch` clause can have arbitrarily many statements. In particular, a statement in a `catch` clause might throw an exception or even terminate the program. In this example, the `catcher` merely prints an error message. Control then resumes at the statement beyond the `catch` block and the message

```
Beyond the catcher...
```

is printed to the standard output.

Finally, a `catch` clause requires a parameter type and a parameter identifier. In this example, the type is `ArithmeticException` and the parameter is named e. The `catch` parameter must be a valid identifier and must be present. ∎

The `finally` Clause

A `try` clause requires at least one `catch` or `finally` clause. The body of a `catch` clause executes if the appropriate exception is thrown from inside the accompanying `try` clause. By contrast, the body of a `finally` clause executes regardless of whether such an exception is thrown.

■ **Example 4.7.3.**   We amend Example 4.7.2

```
int n, d;
n = promptUserForNumber();
d = promptUserForDivisor();
try {
   System.out.println( "The remainder is " + n % d );
}
catch( ArithmeticException e ) {
   System.err.println( e );
}
finally {
   System.out.println( "n == " + n + " and d == " + d );
}
```

by adding a `finally` clause, whose body executes regardless of whether an arithmetic exception is thrown from inside the `try` block. If an arithmetic exception is thrown, the statements in both the `catch` clause and the `finally` clause execute. If such an exception is not thrown, the statement in the `finally` clause still executes. So, in either case, the statement

```
System.out.println( "n == " + n + " and d == " + d );
```

executes.

A `finally` clause can be used for clean-up operations such as closing files or resetting variables to appropriate values. ■

Statements in a `try` block might generate different types of exception. In this case, there could be several `catch`ers at the end of the `try` block.

■ **Example 4.7.4.**   The code segment

```
try {
  // statements that might cause different
  // exception types to be thrown
}
catch( ArithmeticException e ) {
   // handle arithmetic exception
}
catch( ArrayIndexOutOfBoundsException e ) {
   // handle out of bounds exception
}
catch( IllegalArgumentException e ) {
   // handle illegal argument to a method exception
}
//...other catchers, if needed
```

shows a `try` block with three `catch` clauses. As the example also shows, the names of the standard exception classes are intuitive. ■

Deliberately Throwing an Exception in a Program

A program can throw exceptions of its own. Here we illustrate the basic syntax and leave more compelling examples to later chapters.

■ **Example 4.7.5.**   The program in Figure 4.7.1 uses a `while` loop to generate and print random integers. If an integer greater than 1,000,000,000 is generated, the program throws an `Exception`, which transfers control to the corresponding `catch`er. The standard class `Exception` is an immediate subclass of `Throwable`. The `Exception` class has a constructor that takes a string argument, which we invoke with a message.

The `catch`er prints the `Exception`—including message used to construct it—to the standard error. Because the `catch` clause occurs in `main`, a `return` in the clause terminates the program. A sample run produced the output

```
-1521738988
-1698674194
-801440189
854048706
```

```
import java.util.Random;
class ThrowTest {
   public static void main( String[ ] args ) {
      Random r = new Random();
      try {
         while ( true ) {             //** potentially infinite loop
            int next = r.nextInt();
            if ( next < 1000000000 ) //** 1,000,000,000
              System.out.println( next );
            else
              throw new Exception( "Generated " + next +
                                   " and exiting..." );
         }
      }
      catch( Exception e ) {
         System.out.println( e );
         return;                     //** return from main is an exit
      }
   }
}
```

FIGURE 4.7.1   A program that throws an exception.

```
406063147
381542129
121347371
java.lang.Exception: Generated 1780798452 and exiting...
```

The throws Clause

There is an alternative to placing statements that may generate exceptions within a try clause. A constructor or method can contain a throws clause that lists the exceptions that may be thrown by statements in the constructor's or method's body. (throws is a keyword.)

Example 4.7.6.   The ByteCount program in Figure 4.7.2 repeats the program in Figure 2.5.1. The program expects as a command-line argument the name of a file pair. In an invocation such as

```
$ java ByteCount Login
```

the ByteCount program assumes that the command-line argument Login names the file pairs *Login.java* and *Login.class*. The program tries to open two FileInputStreams, one for the source file (e.g., *Login.java*) and the other for the *class* file (e.g., *Login.class*). The class FileInputSteam in the java.io package is used to read bytes from the two files.

```
import java.io.*;
class ByteCount {
   public static void main( String[ ] args ) throws IOException {
      if ( args.length != 1 ) {
         System.err.println( "java ByteCount <file (no extension)>" );
         return;
      }
      String srcName = args[ 0 ] + ".java",
             binName = args[ 0 ] + ".class";
      FileInputStream inSrc = new FileInputStream( srcName ),
                      inBin = new FileInputStream( binName );
      countAndReport( inSrc, srcName );
      countAndReport( inBin, binName ) ;
      inSrc.close();
      inBin.close();
   }
   private static void countAndReport( FileInputStream f, String name )
    throws IOException {
      int n = 0;
      while ( f.read() != -1 ) //*** read until EOF
         n++;
      System.out.println( name + " has " + n + " bytes." );
   }
}
```

FIGURE 4.7.2 The throws clause.

The method main contains several statements that might throw exceptions. In particular, the attempt to open the files for reading might fail because, for example, the files do not exist. In such a case, the constructor calls

```
FileInputStream inSrc = new FileInputStream( srcName ),
                inBin = new FileInputStream( binName );
```

would throw a FileNotFoundException, which is a subtype of an IOException. The attempts to close the files

```
inSrc.close();
inBin.close();
```

might also throw IOExceptions. Nonetheless, method main does not place the constructor calls or the close invocations within a try block. Instead, main has a throws clause to signal that IOExceptions of various types might be thrown from within main. If such exceptions are thrown, the system's default exception-handler handles the exceptions because main makes no provision to handle them. The default exception-handler would print a message about the exception (e.g., `FileNotFoundException`) and then terminate the program. The method `promptAndReport` also `throws` an `IOException` because the `read` operation could throw an exception.   ∎

Exceptions and Debugging

Every `Exception` class has a `printStackTrace` method well suited for debugging. The method prints a "backtrace" of the method calls leading to the `Exception`.

∎ **Example 4.7.7.**   The program in Figure 4.7.3 illustrates how `printStack-Trace` might be used. Method `main` invokes method `divide` with an integer and an integer divisor, in this example 6 and 0, respectively. Method `divide`

```
class StackTraceEx {
   public static void main( String[ ] args ) {
      divide( 6, 0 ); //**** Will generate an exception
   }
   static void divide( int num, int div ) {
      divideAux( num, div ); //**** call another method
   }
   static void divideAux( int n, int d ) {
      try {
         System.out.println( n + " divided by " + d + " is " + n / d );
      }
      catch( ArithmeticException e ) {
         e.printStackTrace();
      }
   }
}
```

FIGURE 4.7.3   A program to illustrate the `printStackTrace` method.

then invokes `divideAux` with the same arguments. This second invocation is contrived in order to have three methods in the invocation sequence. Dividing 6 by 0 throws an `ArithmeticException`, which the `catch` clause in `divideAux` handles. The `catch` clause

```
catch( ArithmeticException e ) {
   e.printStackTrace();
}
```

invokes the `printStackTrace` method, which outputs

```
java.lang.ArithmeticException: / by zero
        at StackTraceEx.divideAux(StackTraceEx.java:10)
```

```
at StackTraceEx.divide(StackTraceEx.java:6)
at StackTraceEx.main(StackTraceEx.java:3)
```

in this example. The output's first line specifies the type of `Exception`, in this case division by zero. The next output line reports that source code line 10 in `divideAux` caused the `Exception` to be thrown. The third output line reports where in the source code `divide` invokes `divideAux`, and the fourth output line specifies where in the source code `main` invokes `divide`.   ■

EXERCISES

1. What is an exception?
2. Explain the relationships among a `try` block, an exception, and a `catch` clause.
3. If a program does not `catch` a thrown exception, what happens?
4. Can more than one `catch` clause follow a `try` clause?
5. What does a `throws` clause indicate in the definition of a constructor or method?
6. Explain the purpose of a `finally` clause.
7. Must a `try` clause have at least one `catch` or `finally` clause?

JAVA POSTSCRIPT

2's Complement Representation of Integers

In the 2's complement system, an integer is represented as a sequence of 0s and 1s in which the *leftmost* bit represents its sign and the remaining bits represent its magnitude. The principal features of 2's complement representation are

- Zero has a single representation, that is, a bit sequence consisting of all 0s. For example, zero is represented in a `byte` as 00000000.
- An integer is nonnegative if its leftmost bit is 0. For example, the integer 3 as a `byte` has the representation 00000011. The leftmost bit is 0, thus indicating a nonnegative integer.
- An integer is negative if its leftmost bit is 1. To represent an integer such as −3 in 2's complement as a `byte`, we

  1. Represent 3 as the nonnegative binary integer 00000011.
  2. Complement (invert) the bits: 11111100. This is called the *1's complement* of 3.
  3. Add 1: 11111101. This is called the *2's complement* of 3, which therefore represents −3.

Using 2's complement representation, −3 in binary is thus 11111101. Applying the same procedure to 11111101 yields 00000011 because the 2's complement of −3 is 3.

- The most negative value does not have a positive equivalent. For example, the most negative value for a `byte` integer is −128 but the most positive value is 127. The most negative value for a `short` integer is −32, 768 but the most positive value is 32,767.

Garbage Collection

The `new` operator is used with constructors to allocate storage for class instances such as `Dates`, `Strings`, `Hashtables`, and `Random` number generators. This operator also is used to allocate storage for arrays. Although Java provides the operator `new` to allocate storage at run time, Java does not provide an operator to deallocate or free dynamically allocated storage because the JVM has a **garbage collector**, which automatically reclaims *unreferenced* storage.[†] The term *garbage* refers to dynamically allocated storage that a program can no longer use because the program no longer has a reference to the storage. The garbage collection process is commonly abbreviated as *gc*.

■ **Example**   The method `printDate`

```
class Alpha {
   void printDate() {
      java.util.Date today = new java.util.Date();
      System.out.println( today );
   } //*** gc performed on Date object
}
```

dynamically allocates a `Date` object whose reference is `today`, which is visible or accessible only *within* the `printDate` method. Once the `printDate` method returns, the `Date` object is therefore inaccessible or *unreferenced*. The JVM's garbage collector automatically reclaims or deallocates the storage for the `Date` object once `printDate` returns.

Automatic garbage collection benefits the programmer, who does not have to deallocate dynamically allocated storage. The `java.lang.Runtime` and `java.lang.System` classes do provide a method called gc, which requests that the garbage collector deallocate any unreferenced storage. The code segment

```
//*** one way to request garbage collection
Runtime rt = Runtime.getRuntime();
```

[†]By contrast, C++ has a `delete` operator to deallocate dynamically allocated storage using the C++ `new` operator.

```
rt.gc();
//*** another way
System.gc();
```

illustrates the syntax. (Note that the System method gc is static, whereas the Runtime method of the same name is nonstatic.) The applications programmer typically does not need to worry about garbage collection, and the invocation of either gc method is accordingly uncommon in Java programs.

The Bitwise/Logical Operators

The operators & and | are *bit* operators, if the operands are integers, and *logical* operators, if the operands are booleans.

■ **Example**   The code segment

```
int x = 1, y = 2, z;
int b1 = true, b2 = false, b3;
z = x & y;     // bitwise AND
b3 = b1 & b2;  // logical AND
```

illustrates the different meanings of the operator &. In the assignment involving the int variables x, y, and z, the operator & is the *bitwise and* operator. By contrast, in the assignment involving the boolean variables b1, b2, and b3, the operator & is the *logical and* operator.   ■

The operators | and & have higher precedence than || and &&, and & has a higher precedence than | just as && has a higher precedence than ||. However, the operator pairs differ in how they evaluate:

- In a disjunction involving ||, the left-to-right evaluation of the disjuncts stops once a true disjunct is encountered. For example, in the code segment

```
boolean b1 = true, b2 = true, b3;
b3 = b1 || b2;  //*** only b1 evaluated
```

  only disjunct b1 is evaluated in the assignment statement. Because b1 is true, the disjunction as a whole is true.
- In a disjunction involving |, *all* disjuncts are evaluated.
- In a conjunction involving &&, the left-to-right evaluation of the conjuncts stops once a false conjunct is encountered. For example, in the code segment

```
boolean b1 = false, b2 = true, b3;
b3 = b1 && b2;  //*** only b1 evaluated
```

only conjunct `b1` is evaluated in the assignment statement. Because `b1` is `false`, the conjunction as a whole is `false`.

- In a conjunction involving &, *all* conjuncts are evaluated.

The logical operators `||` and `&&` can thus be more efficient with respect to evaluation than their counterparts `|` and `&`, respectively. The operators `|` and `&` are more flexible in ensuring the evaluation of *all* terms in the disjunction or the conjunction.

■ **Example**   In the code segment

```
int x = 9, y = 8, p = 1, q = 2, r = 0;
if ( x > y || p > q / r ) //**** no run-time error
  //...
```

the `if` test is a disjunction using `||`. The first disjunct evaluates to `true` because 9 is greater than 8. The evaluation stops at the first disjunct because `||` rather than `|` is used. Evaluating the second disjunct would cause a run-time error because `r`'s value is 0 and integer division by zero is an error. If `||` were replaced by `|`, a run-time error would occur because the second disjunct would then be evaluated. ■

The Conditional Operator

The conditional operator `? :` can be used for two-way tests. For example, the code segment

```
int x, y, z;
// ...assign values to x and y
z = (x > y) ? x : y;
```

assigns to `z` the larger of `x` and `y`. The *test expression* occurs to the left of the question mark `?`. If the test evaluates to `true`, the conditional expression's value is the expression immediately after the question mark. If the test evaluates to `false`, the conditional expression's value is the expression following the colon `:`. Because `? :` is an *operator*, it can occur in contexts where an `if` construct could not occur. For example, the conditional operator can be used to initialize a variable *in its declaration*

```
int x = 1, y = 2, z = (x < y) x ? y;
```

whereas an `if` construct could not be used in this way.

1. The names of programming constructs such as classes, their members, local variables, and parameters must be valid identifiers. Such identifiers must begin with an underscore _, a dollar sign $, or an alphabetic character. The remaining characters may be any of these together with numerals.

2. It is an error to reference an undeclared field or variable. The code segment

```
class A {
   void f() {
      z = 23; //***** ERROR: z not declared
      //...
   }
}
```

illustrates the error.

3. Although *fields* have default values, local variables do not. A local variable must be initialized in its declaration or assigned a value before the variable is otherwise used. The code segment

```
void m() {
   int x, y;      //***** caution: not initialized
   f( x );        //***** ERROR: x not initialized
   int z = 2 * y; //***** ERROR: y not initialized
   //...
}
```

illustrates the error.

4. It is an error to reference a local variable outside the block that contains its declaration. The code segment

```
void f() {
   int x = 1, y = 2;
   if ( x < y ) {
      int t = x * y;
      //...
   }
   System.out.println( t ); //**** ERROR: t not visible
}
```

illustrates the error.

5. Name conflicts among local variables or between local variables and parameters is not allowed. Within the same scope, every parameter and local variable must have a distinct identifier. Accordingly, the code segment

```
void m() {
   int x = -1; //*** scope is m's body
   if ( x > 0 ) {
```

```
int x; //***** ERROR: x already used as an identifier
//...
```

contains an error. A local variable or parameter may have the same name as a field, however. The code segment

```
class Alpha {
   void m( int x ) { //*** same as field
      this.x = x;
   }
   private int x;
}
```

illustrates how the local variable and field are distinguished.

6. In a control statement with a boolean test or condition such as if and while, the condition occurs in parentheses. The error

```
if x > y // ****** ERROR: no parentheses
```

is corrected by

```
if ( x > y ) //** ok, parentheses
```

7. Only boolean expressions may occur as tests or conditions in if, do while, while, and for loops. In particular, integer expressions do *not* have a boolean value. The code segment

```
int x = 1;
if ( x ) //***** ERROR: x is not boolean
```

illustrates the error.

8. The boolean type cannot be cast to any other type and no other type, primitive or class type, can be cast to boolean. The code segment

```
int x = 1;
boolean b = (boolean) x; //***** ERROR: invalid cast
```

illustrates the error.

9. Integer division by zero throws an ArithmeticException. Floating-point division by zero does not throw any exception.

10. Caution should be used in comparing object references with the equality operator ==. For example, in the code segment

```
String s1 = new String( "hi" ), s2 = new String( "hi" );
if ( s1 == s2 )           //*** false
```

```
//...
if ( s1.equals( s2 ) ) //*** true
//...
```

the first if condition tests whether s1 and s2 refer to the *same object*, whereas the second if condition tests whether the Strings to which s1 and s2 refer have the same contents, in this case *hi*.

11. Caution should be used in operations that mix integer types with the char type because integer types such as int are signed, whereas char is unsigned. For example, the code segment

```
char c = '\u00FF'; // 0000000011111111 (255 in decimal)
byte b = (byte) c; // 11111111 (-1 in decimal)
```

truncates the 16 bits stored in c in the assignment to b.

12. Caution should be used in comparing floating-point values with the equality operator ==. The code segment

```
double d1 = (1.0 / 3.0) * 2.5, // 0.8333333333333333
       d2 = (5.0 / 6.0);       // 0.8333333333333334
if ( d1 == d2 ) //*** false
```

illustrates the problem. A more appropriate test might be

```
if ( d1 - d2 <= Double.MIN_VALUE ) // true
```

13. It is an error for a try clause not to be followed by at least one catch clause or a finally clause. The code segment

```
try {
    //...
}
```

illustrates the error. The code segment

```
try {
    //...
} catch( ArithmeticException e ) { /*...*/ }
```

corrects the error by adding a catcher.

PROGRAMMING EXERCISES

4.1. Write a program that

- Generates an array of *N* random integers.

- Uses the appropriate `sort` method in the `java.util.Arrays` class to sort only the first half of the array.

Separate methods should be used to populate the array with random integers and to print the array before and after sorting.

4.2. Write a program that generates the first 500 Unicode characters and prints the digits, whitespace characters, and letters with their numeric values. *Hint*: The `java.lang.Character` class has `static` methods to test characters. The code segment

```
char c = 'A';
++c; //*** 'B'
```

reviews how a `char` variable may be incremented.

4.3. Write a program that converts a two-dimensional array such as

```
int rows = 10, cols = 20;
int[ ][ ] matrix = new int[ rows ][ cols ]
```

into a one-dimensional array `ar` such that

```
matrix[ i ][ j ] == ar[ i * cols + j ];
```

Use separate methods to

- Populate the two-dimensional array with random integers.
- Generate the one-dimensional array.
- Copy the values from the two-dimensional array into the corresponding elements of the one-dimensional array.

4.4. The 16 bits in the `short` integer s

```
short s = 0x7A4E; // 31,310 in decimal
```

could be stored in two different ways. The figure

```
7A4E // "big endian"
```

depicts an internal representation in which the *high-order* bits come first, whereas the figure

```
4E7A // "little endian"
```

depicts the situation in which the *low-order* bits come first. Computers that store the high-order bits first are known as **big-endian** machines, and machines that store the low-order bits first are known as **little-endian** machines. The terms come from Jonathan Swift's novel *Gulliver's Travels* in which a war breaks out over whether hard-boiled eggs should be opened at the big or the little end. Most Unix systems are big-endian, whereas most Windows systems are little-endian. Write a utility that converts big-endian `shorts` to little-endian `shorts`. *Hint*:

```
short s = 0x7A4E;
short mask = 0x00FF; // 0000000011111111 in binary
short t = (short) ((s >> 8) & mask); //** t is 0x007A
```

The entire conversion can be done in one statement.

4.5. An International Standard Book Number (ISBN) is a code of 10 characters separated by dashes such as 0-670-82162-4. An ISBN consists of four parts: a group code, a publisher code, a code that uniquely identifies the book among the publisher's offerings, and a check character. For the ISBN 0-670-82162-4, the group code is 0, which identifies the book as one from an English-speaking country. The publisher code 670 identifies the book as a Viking Press publication. The code 82162 uniquely identifies the book among the Viking Press publications (Homer: *The Odyssey*, translated by Robert Fagles). The check character is computed as follows:

1. Compute the sum of the first digit plus two times the second digit plus three times the third digit. . . plus nine times the ninth digit.

2. Compute the remainder of this sum divided by 11. If the remainder is 10, the last character is X; otherwise, the last character is the remainder.

For example, the sum for ISBN 0-670-82162-4 is

$$0 + 2 \times 6 + 3 \times 7 + 4 \times 0 + 5 \times 8 + 6 \times 2 + 7 \times 1 + 8 \times 6 + 9 \times 2 = 158$$

The remainder when 158 is divided by 11 is 4, the last character in the ISBN. Write a program that prompts the reader for an IBSN number and then checks whether candidate ISBN is valid. An appropriate message should be printed to the standard output. *Hint*: The `PromptAndEcho` program in Figure 2.5.3 reads `Strings` from the standard input and echoes them to the standard output. The `java.lang.Character` class has `static` methods to test whether a character is a digit.

4.6. Write a program that converts Roman numerals into decimal equivalents. The program prompts the user for a Roman numeral, which is entered as a string. After converting the Roman numeral to decimal, the program prints the decimal numeral. The program halts with an error message if the user enters a string that is not a valid Roman numeral. Assume that each Roman numeral has a maximum length of 10. The following table gives the Roman symbols and their decimal equivalents:

Roman	Decimal
M	1,000
D	500
C	100
L	50
X	10
V	5
I	1

The algorithm for converting a Roman numeral

$$R_1, R_2, \ldots, R_n$$

to decimal is

1. Set i to 1, where i is the position of the symbol currently being scanned.
2. Set *convert* to 0. At the conclusion of the algorithm, *convert* is the decimal value of the Roman numeral.
3. If $i = n$, add the decimal value of R_n to *convert* and stop.
4. If $R_i \geq R_{i+1}$ in decimal, add the decimal value of R_i to *convert*, set i to $i + 1$, and go to step 3.
5. If $R_i < R_{i+1}$ in decimal, subtract the decimal value of R_i from *convert*, set i to $i + 1$, and go to step 3.

Example: The decimal value of the Roman numeral XIV is 14. Initially, *convert* is 0. Because X's value is greater than I's, we add 10 to *convert* so that *convert* now equals 10. Because I's value is less than V's, we subtract 1 from *convert*, which now equals 9. Because V is the last numeral, we add 5 to *convert* to obtain 14.

4.7. John H. Conway (*Scientific American*, October 1970, p. 120) invented a game called *Life* to model the process of birth, survival, and death. The idea is that organisms required others to survive and procreate but that overcrowding results in death.

A square matrix can be used to implement the game. We start with a 10×10 array:

```
final int n = 10;
char[ ][ ] life = new char[ n ][ n ];
```

Each cell holds an asterisk * or a blank. The asterisk represents the presence of an organism and the blank its absence. The game starts with an initial generation, which consists of any mix of asterisks and blanks. However, the game becomes interesting only with certain mixes of asterisks and blanks. The game progresses as generations succeed one another.

Three rules govern the transition from one generation to the next:

- *Birth Rule*: An organism is born into an empty cell that has exactly three living neighbors.
- *Survival Rule*: An organism with either two or three living neighbors survives from one generation to the next.
- *Death Rule*: An organism with four or more neighbors dies from overcrowding. An organism with fewer than two neighbors dies from loneliness.

A *neighbor* of cell C is any cell that touches C. For example, the cells labeled N are neighbors of A:

N	N	N
N	A	N
N	N	N

A cell that does not lie along an edge has exactly eight neighbors. Because of the rules, it is relatively easy for an organism along an edge to die and relatively hard for either an edge organism to survive or a new organism to be born into an edge cell.

Write a program that reads an initial generation into the array `life` and then produces N new generations, $N > 20$. Print each generation to the standard output.

4.8. A **binary** (**digital**) **picture** is a two-dimensional array, each of whose elements is 0 or 1. The image is interpreted as light (1) on a dark (0) background. For example, here is a binary picture of a football:

```
0  0  0  0  0  0  0
0  0  1  1  1  0  0
0  1  1  1  1  1  0
0  0  1  1  1  0  0
0  0  0  0  0  0  0
```

In analyzing the picture, it is often necessary to identify the edges. A **pixel** (**pic**ture **el**ement) is an edge pixel if it is 1 and at least one of the pixels immediately above, below, left, or right is 0. We can show the edges by setting each edge pixel to 1 and all other pixels to 0. After identifying the edges in the preceding picture, we obtain

```
0  0  0  0  0  0  0
0  0  1  1  1  0  0
0  1  0  0  0  1  0
0  0  1  1  1  0  0
0  0  0  0  0  0  0
```

Write a program that displays a binary picture and then displays the picture showing the edges.

4.9. Simulate the Monty Hall puzzle, which gets its name from the host of the television game show, "Let's Make a Deal." The puzzle involves a game played as follows. A contestant picks one of three doors; behind one of the doors is a car, and behind the other two are goats. After the contestant picks a door, the host opens an unpicked door that hides a goat. (Because there are two goats, the host can open a door that hides a goat no matter which door the contestant first picks.) The host then gives the contestant the option of abandoning the picked door in favor of the still closed and unpicked door. The puzzle is to determine which of three strategies the contestant should follow:

- Always stay with the door initially picked.
- Randomly stay or switch (e.g., by flipping a coin to decide).
- Always switch to the unpicked and unopened door.

The user should be prompted as to which strategy he or she wishes to follow as well as for how many times the game should be played. Use a random number generator to place the car at the start and to simulate the contestant's initial pick. If the contestant follows the second strategy, use a random number generator to determine whether the contestant stays or switches. The program should print the number of games played and the percentage of games won. (A game is won if the contestant gets the car.) Before running the simulation, try to determine whether any of the three strategies is better than the others. You then can use the simulator to test your answer. The results may surprise you. (For a technical discussion of this puzzle, see L. Gillman, "The car and the goats," *Amer. Math. Mo.* 99 (1992): 3–7.)

4.10. This programming exercise is based on Lewis Carroll's system for encoding and decoding text. We assume ASCII representation of characters. The encoding and decoding use the following table:

	bl	!	"	#	···	|	}	~
bl	bl	!	"	#	···	|	}	~
!	!	"	#	$	···	}	~	bl
"	"	#	$	%	···	~	bl	!
#	#	$	%	&	···	bl	!	"
⋮					⋮			
|	|	}	~	bl	···	y	z	{
}	}	~	bl	!	···	z	{	|
~	~	bl	!	"	···	{	|	}

Across the top and along the side we list, in order, the (printable) ASCII characters blank (`bl`) through `~`. The first row inside the table is identical to the list across the top. Thereafter, each row is the same as the previous row, except that each character is shifted one position to the left, and the last character of a row is the first character of the preceding row.

To encode text, a string, called a *code string*, is chosen arbitrarily. To illustrate the encoding method, we assume that the code string is `Walrus` and the text to encode is

```
Meet me in St. Louis
```

Characters other than blank through ~ are not altered. We write the code string, repeated as often as necessary, on top of the text to be encoded:

```
WalrusWalrusWalrusWa
Meet me in St. Louis
```

The pairs of characters WM, ae, le, ..., one on top of the other, are used as indexes into the preceding table. The encoded text results from finding the entries in the table that correspond to these pairs. The entry in row W and column M is %, so the first character of the encoded text is %. The entry in row a and column e is G; the entry in row l and column e is R; and so on. Thus the text is encoded as

```
%GRgua=aVauGLol?eiAU
```

To decode text, we reverse this process.

Write a program that repeatedly prompts the user to encode text, decode text, or quit. If the user chooses either to encode or decode text, he or she is prompted for a code string, a file to encode or decode, and an output file. *Hint*: For code to read `Strings` from the standard input and to convert a `String` to a `char` array, see Programming Exercise 4.5.

4.11. Generate a 5 × 5 table of random integers, each of which has five digits. For example, the table's first row might be

```
06551 84537 54467 33184 58320
```

Once the table has been generated, count the occurrences of the digits 0,1,...,9 in the random integers. In the first row, for example, the digit 6 occurs twice: once in 06551 and again in 54467. Print a report that lists the frequency with which each digit occurs. *Hint*: The `String` and `Integer` classes have useful conversion methods, including a method that returns a `String`'s characters as an array of `char`.

4.12. Modify Programming Exercise 4.11 by reporting on the frequency with which specific two-digit opening sequences and two-digit ending sequences occur. For example, the program would report on the frequency of the opening sequences 00, 01, 02, and so on.

5

Classes

Chapter Outline

Classes are at the center of object-oriented programming. In Java *every* program requires at least one class. An object-oriented programmer not only creates new classes but also uses prebuilt classes. This chapter focuses on the creation and use of **concrete classes**, that is, classes that can be instantiated as objects. The examples so far have involved only concrete classes. The chapter also reviews and refines material introduced earlier and then extends the coverage of classes. Chapter 6 extends the discussion by covering inheritance, interfaces, and abstract classes.

5.1   Class and Member Scope

Scope pertains to the accessibility or visibility of program constructs such as classes and their members. For example, a class with **public scope** is visible *outside* its containing package, whereas a class with **package scope** is visible only *inside* its containing package. A class member with public scope is visible wherever its encapsulating class is visible, whereas a member with private scope is visible only within its encapsulating class.

Class Scope

A **top-level class** is one that is not nested inside another class; a **nested class** or **inner class** is defined inside another class (see Java Postscript). All of the examples so far have used top-level classes, whether these were standard classes such as `String` and `Date` or programmer-defined classes such as `Emp`. Top-level classes have either *public* or *package* scope. By default, such a class has *package* scope. For a class to have *public* scope, it must be declared with the keyword `public`.

Example 5.1.1.   The classes

```
package sample;
class C1 {        //*** defaults to package scope
  //...members
}
public class C2 { //*** explicitly declared public
  //...members
}
```

belong to the `sample` package. Because class `C1` is not explicitly declared public, the class has *package* scope. By contrast, class `C2` is explicitly declared `public` and, therefore, `C2` has public rather than package scope.

Because class `C1` has package scope, `C1` is visible only within package `sample`. Because `C2` has public scope, `C2` is visible not only within package `sample` but also *outside* this package.

206Chap. 5   Classes

■ **Example 5.1.2.**   The class `java.lang.Object` is the ultimate ancestor class for *every* Java class, standard or programmer-defined. The class `Object`'s declaration

```
public class Object {
  //...members
}
```

gives it public rather than package scope. Because `Object` has public scope, the class is visible in packages other than its own home package `java.lang`.   ■

■ **Example 5.1.3.**   The class Emp

```
package empPkg;
public class Emp {  //*** public scope
  // members
}
```

belongs to the programmer-defined `empPkg` package. The class Emp is declared public, which means that Emp is visible *outside* the empPkg package. For example, a class such as `Firm`

```
package businessPkg;
import empPkg.*;
class Firm {
   Emp e;   //*** Emp is public, hence accessible
   //...other members
}
```

in another package could have an Emp field.   ■

■ **Example 5.1.4.**   The class EmpId

```
package empPkg;
class EmpId {  //*** package scope
   //...members
}
```

has *package* scope because it is *not* declared with the keyword `public`. Therefore, EmpId is visible only *inside* the empPkg package. The code segment

```
package businessPkg;
import empPkg.*;
class FirmOfficer {
```

```
EmpId eId;   //***** ERROR: EmpId is not accessible
//...other members
}
```

contains an error because `EmpId` is not visible outside the `empPkg` package. In particular, `EmpId` is not visible in the `businessPkg` package. ∎

■ **Example 5.1.5.**   Given this declaration for class `EmpId`

```
package empPkg; //*** Note: empPkg package
class EmpId {
   //...members
}
```

the declaration of class `Emp`

```
package empPkg;      //*** Note: same package as EmpId
public class Emp {
   EmpId id;         //*** therefore, EmpId member is ok
   //...other members
}
```

contains no errors. Although class `EmpId` has package rather than public scope, class `Emp` is in the same package as `EmpId`, that is, the package `empPkg`. Therefore, `EmpId` is accessible to `Emp`. ∎

Figure 5.1.1 summarizes the two possible scopes, public and package, available for top-level classes. Although the examples so far have used explicitly named packages for clarity, even classes in *default* packages have either public or package scope.

Sample Declaration	Scope	Meaning
`public class A {/*...*/}`	Public	Visible outside containing package
`class Z {/*...*/}`	Package	Visible only inside containing package

FIGURE 5.1.1   Scope for top-level classes: package or public.

■ **Example 5.1.6.**   The class `A`

```
class Alpha { //*** default package and package scope
   //...members
}
```

has package scope. Because the source file does not begin with a `package` statement, class `Alpha` belongs to a default package. ∎

■ **Example 5.1.7.**   The class Zeta

```
public class Zeta { //*** default package and public scope
   //...members
}
```

has public scope and belongs to a default package.   ■

Member Scope

A class has either public or package scope. A class *member*—whether constructor, method, or field—has one of four possible scopes:

- **Private scope.** A member with private scope is visible only within its encapsulating class. Private scope thus represents maximum information hiding. To have private scope, a member must be declared explicitly as `private`. In the class declaration

```
class C {
    private int num;
    //...other members
}
```

  field `num` has private scope.

- **Package scope.** A member with package scope is visible only within the package to which its encapsulating class belongs. To have package scope, a member is declared *without* any of the keywords `private`, `protected`, and `public`. In the class declaration

```
class C {
    int num;
    //...other members
}
```

  field `num` has package scope.

- **Protected scope.** A member with protected scope is visible

  – In the package to which its encapsulating class belongs.
  – In any subclass of its encapsulating class, regardless of whether the subclass is in the same package as the encapsulating class.

  To have protected scope, a member must be declared explicitly as `protected`. In the class declaration

```
class C {
    protected int num;
    //...other members
}
```

field `num` has protected scope. Note that protected scope is broader than package scope. For example, assume that class Z is a subclass of C but that the two classes reside in *different* packages. In this case, a protected C member such as num would be visible in Z, whereas a package C member would *not* be visible in Z. Within a package, members with package and protected scope have *equal* visibility.

• **Public scope**. A member with public scope is visible wherever its encapsulating class is visible. To have public scope, a member must be declared explicitly as `public`. In the declaration

```
public class C {
    public int num;
    //...other members
}
```

field `num` has public scope. The encapsulating class C need not have public scope for member num to have public scope. In the declaration

```
class C {
    public int num;
    //...other members
}
```

member `num` still has public scope. However, a member with public scope typically occurs in a class with public scope because the public member is visible only where its encapsulating class is visible. If a class has *package* scope, then even its *public* members are visible only within the package and, therefore, these public members have the same visibility as members with package scope.

Figure 5.1.2 summarizes member scope. We illustrate the different member scopes with a series of examples that use a mix of fields and methods.

Scope	Keyword	Visible Where?
Private	`private`	In encapsulating class
Package	None	In encapsulating class's package
Protected	`protected`	In encapsulating class's descendants or package
Public	`public`	Wherever encapsulating class is visible

FIGURE 5.1.2   Member scope: private, package, protected, or public.

■ **Example 5.1.8.**   The two classes A and Z in Figure 5.1.3 belong to the same package. Class Z's method m invokes object a1's get method, where a1 refers to an A object. Because get is an A member with *package* scope, get is visible to other classes in the same package such as Z. By contrast, the A member num has *private* scope. Therefore, num is not accessible outside of A. In particular, num is not visible in Z's method m.   ■

```
//**** start of source file A.java
package samplePkg;
class A {
   private int num;          //*** private
   int get() { return num; } //*** package
}
class Z {
   A a1 = new A();        //*** package
   void m() {             //*** package
     int t = a1.get(); // ok, get is visible
     int s = a1.num;   //***** ERROR: num is private in A
   }
}
//**** end of source file A.java
```

FIGURE 5.1.3   An example of class and member scope.

■ **Example 5.1.9.**   The two classes P and Q in Figure 5.1.4 belong to the same package. Class P has a *public* method get and a *package* field num. However, P has only *package* scope. Therefore, P's public method m and package field num effectively have the same visibility. Each is visible *only* in the package

```
//**** start of source file P.java
package samplePkg;
class P {   //*** Note: package scope
   int num;                       //*** package
   public int get() { return num; } //*** public
}
class Q {
   P p1 = new P();        //*** package
   void m() {             //*** package
     int t = p1.get(); // ok, get is visible
     int s = p1.num;   // ok, num is visible
   }
}
//**** end of source file P.java
```

FIGURE 5.1.4   Another example of class and member scope.

samplePkg. Both members are visible in class Q, which also belongs to package samplePkg. If class P had public scope

```
public class P { //*** public scope
```

then its method get would be visible wherever P were visible. The package member num still would be visible only within package samplePkg. ∎

∎ **Example 5.1.10.**   The class Parent

```
package parentPkg;
public class Parent { //*** class: public scope
   protected int x;   //*** member: protected scope
}
```

resides in one package and its subclass Child

```
package childPkg;
import parentPkg.Parent;
class Child extends Parent { //*** subclass of Parent
   public Child() {
      x = -1;                 //*** x is inherited from Parent
   }
}
```

resides in a different package. The syntax

```
class Child extends Parent { //*** subclass of Parent
```

makes Child a subclass of Parent, which means that Child inherits all of the fields in Parent, in this case the single int field x. The Child no-argument constructor can access the inherited x because x has protected scope in Parent. If x had either private or package scope, the constructor Child() would not be able to access the inherited x. Note that class Parent has public scope to ensure that this class is visible in other packages, in particular in the package childPkg in which its subclass Child resides.

Chapter 6 examines inheritance in detail. For now, the goal is to clarify how protected scope differs from package scope. ∎

Summary of Class and Member Scope

Restricting class and member scope contributes to information hiding, a key principle in object-oriented programming. Classes and their members therefore should be given the *narrowest* possible scope appropriate to the functionality that they provide. Of course, sometimes the very nature of a class or member requires that broad scope.

For example, utility classes such as RandNN (see Section 3.4) need to be public so that classes in other packages can use these utility classes. An applet class must be public. In the sample applications and longer examples, we clarify how decisions about scope follow from object-oriented principles and practices.

EXERCISES

1. Explain the error:

```
protected class Alpha { /*...*/ }
```

2. What is the default scope for a class?
3. What scopes can a top-level class have?
4. Explain package scope for a class.
5. What is the default scope for a class member?
6. Explain the difference between protected and package scope for a member.
7. If a class has package scope, where are its private members visible?
8. If a class has public scope, where are its private members visible?
9. If a class has package scope, where are its protected members visible?
10. If a class has package scope, where are its public members visible?
11. Explain the error:

```
class Alpha {
   private int x;
}
class Beta {
   public void m() {
     Alpha al = new Alpha();
     al.x = -999;
   }
}
```

5.2   Constructors, Methods, and Fields

We begin with a review of terminology and related issues. Class members are of three types:

- **Constructors**. A constructor is a function member that has the *same name* as the class that encapsulates it and *no return type* or void in place of a return type. In class Alpha, for example, a constructor would be named Alpha. Constructors are used with the new operator to construct objects of a class type. For example, an `Alpha` object might be constructed with the syntax `new Alpha()`. Recall that a constructor invoked with no arguments is the default constructor or no-argument constructor. A constructor invoked with one or more arguments is a parameterized constructor.

- **Methods**. A method is a function member that has a *different name* than the class that encapsulates it and *a return type* or `void` in place of a return type. In class `Alpha`, for example, no method can be named `Alpha` and every method has either a return type such as `int` or `void` in place of a return type. Methods provide the processing or operations appropriate to a class and its objects. For example, a `BarGraph` class might have a `draw` method that draws a bar graph in a window, whereas an `AccountsRcv` class might have a `save` method that saves accounts receivable records in a database.
- **Fields**. A field is a variable or an array member encapsulated in a class. Fields provide storage appropriate to a class and its objects. For example, a `BarGraph` class might have `width` and `height` variables that store the width and height of the window that displays the bar graph. An `AccountsRcv` class might have an array of `Strings`, with each element storing the name and address of a customer.

Constructors

Constructors are used with the operator `new` to construct objects. Constructors also typically initialize fields and perform other processing appropriate to constructing objects. In their role as object initializers, constructors can contribute greatly to program robustness.

Example 5.2.1.   The class `Emp`

```
class Emp {
    public void setName( String n ) {
        name = n;
    }
    //**** Caution! setName should have been called first!
    public void printName( boolean upper ) {
        if ( upper )
            System.out.println( name.toUpperCase() );
        else
            System.out.println( name.toLowerCase() );
    }
    private String name;
}
```

has a private `name` field and two public methods. Method `setName` sets the field to a `String` and method `getName` prints the name in either upper or lower case, depending on the value of `getName`'s parameter. Recall that fields of class types such as `name` have `null` as their default value. If `name` has `null` as its value, the statement

```
System.out.println( name.toUpperCase()  );
```

throws a `NullPointerException`. A `String` method such as `toUpperCase` or `toLowerCase` cannot be invoked with a `null` object reference.

Class `Emp` is not robust in that the class does not ensure a nonnull value for field `name`. If a programmer invokes `printName` before first invoking `setName` with a `String` object as an argument, an exception is thrown.   ■

■ **Example 5.2.2.**   We amend Example 5.2.1

```
class Emp {
   public Emp() { setName( "Anonymous" ); }
   //...
}
```

by adding a no-argument constructor that invokes `setName`, thus ensuring that `setName` is invoked at least once before `printName` is invoked. As a result, an object's `name` field will not have a value of `null` when the object is first constructed. Through this initializing behavior, the default constructor makes the `Emp` class robust.   ■

■ **Example 5.2.3.**   Next we amend Example 5.2.2

```
class Emp {
   public Emp() { setName( "Anonymous" ); }
   public Emp( String n ) { setName( n ); }
   //...
}
```

by **overloading** the constructors, that is, by providing the class with more than one constructor. The parameterized constructor takes a single `String` argument and invokes `setName` with this argument, which is assigned to the `name` field.   ■

Constructor overloading is common. In class `Emp` of Example 5.2.3, for example, the no-argument constructor and the method `setName` have different names—identifiers—and, therefore, different signatures. The `Emp` no-argument and parameterized constructors take a different number of arguments: none for the default constructor and one for the parameterized constructor. The two constructors thereby have different signatures. The `Emp` constructors

```
Emp( String s, boolean b ) { /*...*/ } // one signature
```

and

```
Emp( boolean b, String s ) { /*...*/ } // another signature
```

differ in signature because one of them takes a `String` argument followed by a `boolean` argument, whereas the other takes a `boolean` argument followed by a `String` argument. Recall that, in the case of methods, a return type or `void` in place of a return type does *not* contribute to a method's signature. Accordingly, the declarations

```
class C {
  void m() { /*...*/ }
  char m() { /*...*/ } //**** ERROR: same as void m()
}
```

generate an error because the two methods have the same signature.

The No-Argument Constructor

The no-argument constructor is the simplest constructor to invoke because it takes no arguments. However, this constructor is complicated in other respects. For example, a class can get a no-argument constructor in one of two ways:

- The programmer defines a no-argument constructor.
- The programmer defines *no constructors whatever*. In this case, the compiler supplies a no-argument constructor with public scope.

■ **Example 5.2.4.**   The class `Alpha`

```
class Alpha {
   public Alpha() { /*...*/
}
```

defines a no-argument constructor, which happens to have public scope. A constructor can have any of the four scopes for members: private, package, protected, or public.   ■

■ **Example 5.2.5.**   Because the class `Zeta`

```
class Zeta {
  //...members, but no constructors
}
```

defines *no* constructors, the compiler provides a no-argument constructor with public scope. Wherever class `Zeta` is visible, a `Zeta` object therefore can be constructed with the syntax

```
new Zeta()
```
■

■ **Example 5.2.6.**   The class `Delta`

```
package samplePkg;
class Delta {
   Delta() { /*...*/ } // package scope
}
```

defines a no-argument constructor with package scope. Therefore, within the package `samplePkg`, a `Delta` object can be constructed with the syntax

```
new Delta()
```

The no-argument constructor also could have been defined with private, protected, or public scope.   ■

■ **Example 5.2.7.**   The class `Alpha`

```
class Alpha {
   Alpha( int x ) { /*...*/ } // a parameterized constructor
   //...other members but no no-argument constructor
}
```

defines a parameterized constructor but does not define a no-argument constructor. Therefore, the compiler does *not* supply a no-argument constructor and the expression

```
new Alpha() //***** ERROR
```

is therefore an error. An error would occur even if the no-argument constructor were invoked *inside* an `Alpha` method. For example, in this version of `Alpha`

```
class Alpha {
   Alpha( int x ) { /*...*/ } // a parameterized constructor
   void m() {
     Alpha a = new Alpha(); //***** ERROR
     //...
   }
   //...other members, no no-argument constructor
}
```

method m tries to invoke the nonexistent no-argument constructor, thus generating an error. If the parameterized constructor were eliminated, the error would be eliminated because the compiler then would provide a public no-argument constructor.

Restricting Object Creation through Constructors

Constructors can be used to restrict how objects are constructed. Suppose, for example, that we want every Employee object to be constructed with a name. This policy can be enforced through selective constructor definition.

■ **Example 5.2.8.**   Because the class declaration

```
public class Emp {
   public Emp( String n ) {
     name = n;
   }
   //...members, but no other constructors
   private String name;
}
```

defines a parameterized Emp constructor, the compiler does *not* provide a no-argument constructor. Accordingly, a statement such as

```
Emp elvis = new Emp(); //**** ERROR
```

does not compile. The one constructor available for constructing Emp objects requires a String argument, which represents the Emp's name. The Emp class's design thus requires syntax such as

```
Emp cher = new Emp( "Cher" );
```

to construct Emp objects.   ■

■ **Example 5.2.9.**   The java.awt package has a Color class whose objects represent different colors. The class does not have a no-argument constructor. The three parameterized constructors

```
public Color( int r, int g, int b ) { /*...*/ }
public Color( int rgb ) { /*...*/ }
public Color( float r, float g, float b ) { /*...*/ }
```

expect numeric arguments that specify the red, green, and blue components of the color. For example, the syntax

```
Color red = new Color( 255, 0, 0 );
```

constructs an object that represents red. This particular constructor expects integers in the range of 0 through 255.   ■

Constructors and Unreferenced Objects

The statement

```
Date today = new Date();
```

constructs a `java.util.Date` object to which `today` refers. The statement thus constructs a *referenced object* with `today` as the reference. At times, however, an *unreferenced object* is as useful as a referenced one. For example, suppose that we are generating a report that is to begin with today's date. We could use the pair of statements

```
Date today = new Date();
System.out.println( "Today is " + today.toString() );
```

Yet we can accomplish the same thing with the single statement

```
System.out.println( "Today is " + new Date().toString() );
```

The expression `new Date()` constructs a `Date` object whose `toString` method is then invoked. The constructed `Date` object is unreferenced. Because the `new` operator has higher precedence than the member operator `.`, no parentheses are required.

■ **Example 5.2.10.**   The `java.awt.Dialog` class supports dialog box windows. The class does not have a public no-argument constructor but does have a constructor that takes a `java.awt.Frame` object as an argument, where a `Frame` represents a framed window. The statement

```
Dialog d = new Dialog( new Frame() );
```

shows how to construct a `Dialog` object by constructing an unreferenced `Frame` object, which is passed as an argument to the `Dialog` constructor.   ■

■ **Example 5.2.11.**   The `java.awt.Component` class is the ancestor class for various graphical components such as `Containers` and `TextComponents`, which are also classes in the `java.awt` package. A component's font can be set with the `setFont` method, which expects a `java.awt.Font` object as an argument. The statement

```
setFont( new Font( "Dialog", Font.BOLD, 14 ) );
```

illustrates the syntax. Method `setFont` is invoked with an unreferenced `Font` object as the argument. The `Font` object is constructed with the expression

```
new Font( "Dialog", Font.BOLD, 14 )
```

The Font constructor's first argument is the font name, its second argument is the font style, and its third argument is the font size.   ■

Methods

Methods, like constructors, are encapsulated functions. Methods, unlike constructors, do not have the same name as the class in which they are encapsulated and do have a return type or void in place of a return type. Methods provide the *operations*, *behavior*, or *processing* appropriate to a class and its objects.

■ **Example 5.2.12.**   The java.util package has a Stack class that represents a **LIFO** (**L**ast **I**n **F**irst **O**ut) list (see Section 1.2). The class has five public methods:

- Method empty() returns true, if a Stack is empty, and false, if a Stack has elements.
- Method peek returns the Stack's top element but without removing it.
- Method pop returns the Stack's top element and removes it.
- Method push inserts an element at the top of the Stack.
- Method search searches for an element.

Together the methods provide the operations appropriate to a Stack.   ■

Properties and Get/Set Methods

Recall that fields can be used to represent *properties* or *features* shared by objects that belong to a class. Fields that represent low-level implementation details are typically hidden by declaring them private. Nonetheless, a client typically requires access to properties. In such cases, it is common to define nonprivate method pairs called **get/set methods**, also called **accessors** or **mutators**, which provide access to the hidden fields that implement properties.

■ **Example 5.2.13.**   The java.net package has a Datagram class that represents a special type of communications **packet**—a package containing arbitrary binary data—that can be sent from an application running on one machine to an application running on another machine. The datagrams are addressed using an internet address, which the java.net package represents with the InetAddress class. The class has four pairs of public *get/set* methods:

- Method setAddress sets the datagram's InetAddress, and method getAddress returns the datagram's InetAddress.
- Method setData sets the datagram's data as an array of bytes, and method getData returns the datagram's data as an array of bytes.
- Method setLength sets the length of byte array that holds the datagram's data, and method getLength returns this length.

- Method `setPort` sets the port number on the receiving machine to which the datagram should be sent, and method `getPort` returns the port number.

Example 5.2.14. The `java.util.Date` class has various methods, including several pairs of *get/set* methods. Among the *get/set* pairs are the methods `getTime` and `setTime`. The `setTime` method takes a `long` argument, which represents the number of elapsed *milliseconds* since midnight on January 1, 1970. The `getTime` method returns a `Date` object's time value as a `long`. The code segment

```
Date d1 = new Date();  //*** time set to now
long oneHourFromNow =  d1.getTime() + 60 * 60 * 1000;
d1.setTime( oneHourFromNow );
```

shows how the methods can be used. The `Date` class's no-argument constructor initializes the `Date` object's time to a numeric representation of *now* in Coordinated Universal Time (UTC), an international standard for keeping time on atomic clocks.[†] The constructor thus initializes the `Date` object's time to the elapsed milliseconds from midnight on January 1, 1970 to now. On a sample run, this value was 931895719215. The `Date`'s method `getTime` then is invoked to retrieve the time in milliseconds, which is incremented by the number of milliseconds in an hour. The object's `setTime` method is invoked with this new value, which updates the time to an hour from now. The *get/set* pair of methods thus provides access to a `Date` object's time-in-milliseconds property.

Example 5.2.15. A `javax.swing.JToolBar` is a graphics container that can hold components such as buttons, check boxes, text fields, and menus. The class has a public `getComponentAtIndex` method but does not have a public `setComponentAtIndex` method. Therefore, the property *ComponentAtIndex* is *read only*; that is, the property's value can be retrieved but not set. ■

Methods and Miscellaneous Functionality

The *get/set* methods that access properties have a distinctive role. Other methods define miscellaneous operations or behaviors appropriate to a particular class.

■ **Example 5.2.16.** The `java.io` package has an `ObjectOutputStream` class for **serializing** objects, that is, writing in-memory objects to an output stream. The method `writeObject` is used to write an object to an output stream. The `ObjectInputStream` class provides a `readObject` method to **deserialize** previously serialized objects. Section 8.2 examines serialization in detail. ■

[†]UTC is similar to Greenwich Mean Time (GMT), but the two standards use slightly different algorithms for keeping time.

Invoking Methods from Constructors

A constructor often invokes methods, a practice that can contribute to modular programming and class robustness.

Example 5.2.17.   The class Emp

```
class Emp {
   public Emp( String n ) { setName( n ); }
   public void setName( String n ) { name = n; }
   private String name
}
```

has a parameterized constructor that invokes the `setName` method rather than simply assigning its `String` parameter to the `String` field name, as the method does. Given the current design, a code segment such as

```
Emp e1 = new Emp( "the artist formerly known as prince" ),
    e2 = new Emp( "the artist formerly known as prince" );
```

could result in two employees having the same name. Suppose that we redesign the class so that `setName` somehow ensures unique names for all Employees. In this case, the constructor would not have to be rewritten at all, as the constructor simply invokes `setName`. Having the constructor invoke `setName` ensures that the statement

```
Emp surprised = new Emp( "The Man Who Knew Too Much" );
```

and the subsequent statement

```
surprised.setName( "The Man Who Knew Too Much" );
```

set the name in the same way.   ■

Returning Values from Methods with Return Types

If a method has a return type such as `int` or `Date`, the method must explicitly `return` a value of the specified type.

Example 5.2.18.   The code segment

```
class Alpha {
   int m( int k, int n ) {
      int t = k % n;
   } //***** ERROR: must return an int!
}
```

illustrates the error of a method's not returning a value of the appropriate type. Method m's return type is int but m fails to return an int value. ∎

A method with void in place of a return type can but need not contain an explicit return statement. An explicit return may be useful for control purposes.

∎ **Example 5.2.19.**   In the code segment

```
void m( int[ ] a, int n ) {
   if ( n <= 0 || n > a.length )
     return;
   // otherwise,...
}
```

method m's return type is void, which means that m need not contain an explicit return statement. Nonetheless, m returns if the if-test fails. By the way, it would be an error for m to return a value. The code segment

```
void m( int[ ] a, int n ) {
   if ( n <= 0 || n > a.length )
     return -1; //***** ERROR
   // otherwise ...
}
```

illustrates.

Object Construction through Factory Methods

Although many classes expose *constructors* to construct objects, a class may provide special methods commonly known as **factory methods** to construct objects.

Example 5.2.20.   The java.net.InetAddress class represents an Internet Protocol (IP) address. Although the class exposes no constructors, it does expose three static methods that can be used to instantiate an InetAddress. For example, the statement

```
InetAddress c = InetAddress.getByName( "condor.depaul.edu" );
```

invokes the factory method getByName to instantiate an InetAddress whose reference is c. The getByName method constructs an InetAddress object and returns a reference to this object. ∎

Later chapters offer other examples of factory methods. The point for now is that Java supports object construction through constructors and specially designed methods.

Fields

Fields are encapsulated variables and arrays that are class *members*. Field variables differ from parameters and local variables in constructors and methods.

■ **Example 5.2.21.**   The class `Alpha`

```
class Alpha {
   public void m( double x ) {
      int i;  //*** local variable
      //...
   }
   private int n;    //*** int field
   private Date d;   //*** Date field
}
```

has two fields. Variable `n` is of primitive type `int`, whereas variable `d` is of nonprimitive type `Date`. Method `m` has a local `int` variable named `i`, which is not a field. Method `m` also has a `double` parameter `x`, which is likewise not a field.   ■

Fields, unlike local variables, have default values. Fields of primitive numeric types such as `int` and `double` have a default value of zero. Fields of type `char` have a default value of `'\u0000'`, a nonprinting character sometimes called the *null character*. Fields of type `boolean` default to `false`. Fields that are object references or array references default to `null`.

■ **Example 5.2.22.**   The class `Beta` in Figure 5.2.1 illustrates the default values of various fields. Figure 4.1.1 lists the default values for different field types.   ■

Instance Fields and an Object's State

Instance fields (i.e., fields that are not `static`) allow objects within a class to be individuated by the values of their fields, which is their **state**.

Example 5.2.23.   Given the class Emp

```
class Emp {
   public Emp( int d ) {
      dept = d;
   }
   private int dept;
}
```

```
import java.util.*;
class Beta {
   public void m( double x ) {
      int i;  // local variable, no default value
      //...
   }
   private int      n; // defaults to 0
   private double   d; // defaults to 0.0
   private char     c; // defaults to '\u0000'
   private boolean  b; // defaults to false
   private Random   r; // defaults to null
   private String   s; // defaults to null
   private int[ ]   a; // defaults to null
   private Date[ ]  z; // defaults to null
}
```

FIGURE 5.2.1   Default values for fields.

the code segment

```
Emp e1 = new Emp( 1 );   // 1 == accounting department
Emp e2 = new Emp( 9 );   // 9 == marketing department
```

constructs two Emp objects that differ in state, that is, in the values of their fields. The Employee e1's dept field has a value of 1, whereas the Employee e2's dept field has a value of 9 (see Figure 5.2.2). ■

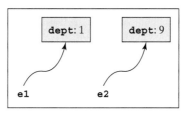

FIGURE 5.2.2   Two Emp objects that differ in state, the values of their dept fields.

Field Initialization

Constructors often initialize fields, as various examples have shown. Fields also can be initialized in their declarations.

■ **Example 5.2.24.**   The program in Figure 5.2.3 generates the *Fibonacci sequence*, which begins

$$1, 1, 2, 3, 5, 8, 13, 21, 34, 55, 89, 144, 233, 377, 610, \ldots$$

The sequence is named in honor of the great Italian mathematician Leonardo Fibonacci (ca. 1170-1250). The ith Fibonacci number f_i is $f_{i-1} + f_{i-2}$, for

```
class FibSeq {
   public FibSeq() {
      generateFibs( maxFibs );
   }
   public FibSeq( int n ) {
      if ( n < minFibs )
        generateFibs( minFibs );
      else if ( n > maxFibs )
        generateFibs( maxFibs );
      else
        generateFibs( n );
   }
   public void dumpFibs() {
      System.out.println( "\nThe first " + fibs.length +
                          " Fibonacci numbers are:" );
      for ( int i = 0; i < fibs.length; i++ )
        System.out.println( fibs[ i ] );

   }
   private void generateFibs( int n ) {
      fibs = new long[ n ];
      fibs[ 0 ] = fibs[ 1 ] = 1;
      for ( int i = 2; i < n; i++ )
        fibs[ i ] = fibs[ i - 1 ] + fibs[ i - 2 ];
   }
   private long[ ] fibs;
   private final int minFibs = 8;
   private final int maxFibs = 64;
}
class FibsTest {
   public static void main( String[ ] args ) {
      new FibSeq( 32 ).dumpFibs();
   }
}
```

FIGURE 5.2.3   A program that generates Fibonacci sequences.

$i >= 2$. For example, the seventh Fibonacci number is $8 + 5$ or 13, where 8 is the sixth Fibonacci number and 5 is the fifth Fibonacci number. The sequence is originally a response to Fibonacci's whimsical question about how many pairs of rabbits there will be after one year if, starting from an initial pair, each pair produces an offspring pair that then becomes reproductive after one month and no deaths occur. The sequence turns out to have many illustrations in nature and important roles in mathematics, science, and engineering.

The class `FibSeq` has a private array of `long`s to store the integers in the Fibonacci sequence. The class also has two private `int` fields named `minFibs` and maxFibs, which are initialized in their declarations. The fields are constants that represent the minimum and the maximum length of the Fibonacci sequence that a client can generate. These constants could be initialized in the public constructors or the private generateFibs method that the constructors invoke to generate the sequence. Initializing these two fields in their declarations underscores that they serve as constants and makes it relatively easy for a reader to see their values.   ■

static Methods and Fields

Recall that only methods and fields, not constructors, can be static. A field or method not marked as static is an *instance member* precisely because it is associated with an object as an instance of a class type. Recall, too, that a field or method marked as static is called a *class member* because it is associated with the class itself rather than with a class instance.

■ **Example 5.2.25.**   The java.awt.Color class has 13 public static fields that represent various color constants. Some examples are

```
Color.black
Color.blue
Color.magenta
Color.red
```

For example, if win refers to a Framed window, the statements

```
win.setForeground( Color.black );
win.setBackground( Color.yellow );
```

would set the window's foreground color to black and its background color to yellow.   ■

■ **Example 5.2.26.**   The class java.beans.Introspector has five methods, all of which are static. The class is a utility for building tools to manipulate components or *beans*. For example, the static method getBeanInfo can be used to get information about a bean's properties and methods. The code segment

```
MyBean b = new MyBean(); //** a programmer-defined Bean
BeanInfo info = Introspector.getBeanInfo( b.getClass() );
```

shows how this static method might be used. The class BeanInfo, which also belongs to the java.beans package, has members to store and process information about beans. The getClass instance method returns a reference to an object that represents the invoker's class. In this case, getClass would return a reference to an object that represents the MyBean class.   ■

A nonstatic method can access static members, although the preferred way to access static members is directly through the class. For example, the code segment

```
Frame f = new Frame();     // framed window
Color c = new Color();     // Color object
f.setBackground( c.red );  // use c to access static red
```

uses the Color object to which c refers to access the Color class's static field named red. This is not recommended practice. The code segment

```
Frame f = new Frame();
f.setBackground( Color.red );
```

uses the Color class directly to access its static field named red. The second code segment is more straightforward.

A Workaround for Accessing static Members

A static method can access *only* other static members, whether these be fields or methods.

   ■ **Example 5.2.27.**   The HiWorld program in Figure 5.2.4 contains two errors. Because method main is static, this method cannot access the nonstatic field n or invoke the nonstatic method sayHi.

```
class HiWorld {
   public static void main( String[ ] args ) { //*** static!
      n = 3;                  //***** ERROR: n is not static
      sayHi();                //***** ERROR: sayHi is not static
   }
   private void sayHi() {  //*** nonstatic
      for ( int i = 0; i < n; i++ )
         System.out.println( "Hello, world!" );
   }
   private int n;           //*** nonstatic
}
```

FIGURE 5.2.4   A static method trying to access nonstatic members.

   There are two ways to correct the errors. First, the nonstatic members n and sayHi could be made static. Suppose, however, that class HiWorld had tens of members. For main to have access to these members—either directly or indirectly by invoking other static methods—all members would have to be static. An alternative is to have main construct an object of the class type in which `main` itself occurs. The constructed object then can access *all* members in the encapsulating class, `static` or `nonstatic`. The revised `HiWorld` program in Figure 5.2.5 illustrates. Method `main` now constructs an object of type `HiWorld`

```
class HiWorld {
   public static void main( String[ ] args ) { //*** static!
      HiWorld hw = new HiWorld(); // create a HiWorld object
      hw.n = 3;                   // set its field n to 3
      hw.sayHi();                 // invoke its sayHi method
   }
   private void sayHi() {  //*** nonstatic
      for ( int i = 0; i < n; i++ )
         System.out.println( "Hello, world!" );
   }
   private int n;               //*** nonstatic
}
```

FIGURE 5.2.5   A class that instantiates an object of its own type.

to which `hw` refers, where `HiWorld` is the very class that encapsulates `main`. The object to which `hw` refers then is used to access the `HiWorld` members, neither of which needs to be `static` because `main` itself does not access these members. ■

Uses for `static` Members

■ **Example 5.2.28.**   The `Emp` class in Figure 5.2.6 ensures that every Employee has a unique identifying name, the `String` field called `id`. An `Emp` object is constructed by specifying the object's name. For example, the statement

```
Emp e1 = new Emp( "Janet" );
```

constructs an `Emp` object with *Janet* as the specified name. The problem, however, is that an `Emp` named *Janet* may have been created already. The method `setName`, which can be used to change the name of an existing Employee, also raises the problem of ensuring a unique name for each Employee. The private method `validateID` solves the problem by generating a new name if the name requested in a constructor call or a `setName` call is already in use. All `Emp` names are stored in a `static` field of type `java.util.Vector`.

     To see how `validateID` works, suppose that an `Emp` client tries to construct two objects with the same name. For simplicity, assume that these are the first two `Emp` objects constructed:

```
Emp e1 = new Emp( "Janet" );
Emp e2 = new Emp( "Janet" ); //*** name already in use
```

```
import java.util.*; // Random and Vector
class Emp {
   public Emp( String n ) {
      setID( n );
   }
   public void setID( String name ) {
      validateID( name );
   }
   public String getID() {
      return id;
   }
   public static void list() {
      Enumeration e = allIDs.elements();
      while ( e. hasMoreElements() )
         System.out.println( e.nextElement() );
   }
   private void validateID( String name ) {
      while ( allIDs.contains( name ) )
         name += delimiter + Math.abs( r.nextInt() );
      id = name;
      allIDs.addElement( id ); //*** add id to list
   }
   private static Vector allIDs = new Vector();
   private static Random r = new Random();
   private static final String delimiter = "#";
   private String id;
}
```

FIGURE 5.2.6   An Emp class that ensures unique object names.

Since the e1-object is constructed first, the name *Janet* as a String is added to the Vector called allIDs. When the e2-object is then constructed, the while loop's test in validateID

```
while ( allIDs.contains( name ) ) {
```

detects that *Janet* is already in the Vector. The Vector method contains returns true, if an object is already an element, and false, if the object is not an element. In each loop iteration, name is changed by appending a delimiter

```
Janet#
```

and then a random integer

```
Janet#8761234651
```

to it. This process is repeated as necessary. In the end, for example, the Employee's unique identifier might be

```
Janet#8761234651#198762652#45129875
```

Once a unique name has been generated, it is assigned to the field `id`

```
id = name;
```

and then added to the `Vector`.

In order to track the names of *all* `Emp` objects, the vector `allIDs` must be associated with the `Emp` class itself rather than with a particular `Emp` object. Accordingly, `allIDs` is `static`. The random number generator used to generate the random integers that are appended to names to make them unique is likewise `static`. After all, the class itself rather than any particular object is responsible for generating unique names. Further, it is unnecessary and thus inefficient for every object to have its own `Random` field. The public method `list` prints the names of all `Emp`s to the standard output by iterating through the `allIDs` vector. Because the `allIDs` vector is `static`, the method `list` must be `static` as well. Recall that a `static` member may access only other `static` members. By contrast, the method `getName` is nonstatic because it prints the name of a *particular* `Emp` object. The field `id` clearly must be nonstatic so that each `Emp` object can have its own unique name.

The `Emp` class illustrates how a mix of `static` and `nonstatic` members can contribute to the overall functionality that a class provides to its clients. This functionality could not be provided easily or efficiently with only `nonstatic` members.   ■

Deprecated Features

Java has undergone significant development in its relatively brief history. The development is reflected in successive JDKs (**J**ava **D**evelopment **K**its). The transition from JDK 1.0 to JDK 1.1 is particularly significant because it brought fundamental changes in areas such as event handling. In the JDK 1.0 to JDK 1.1 transition, a significant number of language constructs such as constructors and methods were **deprecated**, that is, marked as unfit for continued use. Language features may continue to be deprecated as Java evolves.

■ **Example 5.2.29.**   The objects to which `System.out` and `System.err` refer are of type `PrintStream`, a standard class that supports text output for `Strings` and the primitive data types. In JDK 1.0, the `PrintStream` class does not properly handle 16-bit Unicode characters, which are truncated to 8 bits. JDK 1.1 fixes this problem with `PrintStream` but also introduces the `PrintWriter` class, which is meant to supersede the `PrintStream` class. All of the public `PrintStream` methods are available with the same signatures in `PrintWriter`, which has additional public methods not present in `PrintStream`. The `PrintStream` class itself could not be deprecated because the `System` class has the references `out` and `err` to `PrintStream` objects. However, the public `PrintStream` constructors have been deprecated to discourage construction of `PrintStream` objects.   ■

■ **Example 5.2.30.**   The `java.util.Date` class has six public constructors, four of which have been deprecated in JDK 1.1. For example, the `Date` constructor that takes a single `String` argument representing a formatted date was deprecated. Various public `Date` methods such as `parse`, which returns as a `long` an integer representation of a `Date`, also were deprecated. The reason is that JDK 1.1 added a `Calendar` class whose functionality either replaces or supercedes the functionality of the `Date` class. The `Date` still has two nondeprecated constructors and several nondeprecated methods such as `getTime`, which returns an integer representation of a `Date`.   ■

The examples in this book avoid deprecated language features. Robust code requires that deprecated constructs be eliminated in favor of nondeprecated replacements.

EXERCISES

1. Is a constructor a function?

2. Is a constructor a method?

3. What are a constructor's main roles?

4. Can a constructor have private, package, protected, or public scope?

5. Explain the error:

```
class Alpha { public void Alpha() { /*...*/ } }
```

6. If a class defines no constructors at all, does the compiler provide a public no-argument constructor?

7. Explain the error:

```
class Alpha {
   public Alpha( int x ) { num = x; }
}
class Beta { int x; }
class Zeta {
   public Zeta() {
     Alpha a1 = new Alpha();
     Beta b1 = new Beta();
   }
}
```

8. Can a constructor be `static`?

9. Is a constructor always invoked with the operator `new`?

10. Why is the expression

```
new java.util.Date()
```

said to construct an *unreferenced* object?

11. Explain the error:

```
class Alpha { m() { /*...*/ } }
```

12. Suppose that the class `Emp` has a private `name` field that stores an Employee's name. Explain how the class designer can nonetheless make *name* a public property of Employees.

13. If the main purpose of constructors is to create objects, what is the main purpose of methods?

14. Can a method's scope be private, package, protected, or public?

15. Do fields have default values?

16. What is the default value, if any, for a field of any class type?

17. What is the default value for an `int` field?

18. Explain the error:

```
class Zeta {
    static void setX( int n ) { x = n; }
    int x;
}
```

19. Explain how the correct syntax in the code segment

```
java.awt.Color background = java.awt.Color.red;
```

makes it clear that `red` is a `static` field in the `Color` class.

20. Can a method be `static`?

21. Can a constructor be defined with a return type or `void` in place of one?

22. The code segment

```
class Alpha {
    public void m( int x ) { x = x; }
    private int x;
}
```

assigns m's parameter x to itself. Change the code so that m assigns the parameter x to the field x.

23. What does it mean for a language feature to be *deprecated*?

5.3   Learning Library Classes

Programming in an object-oriented language requires a variety of skills. Two basic skills are building classes and using prebuilt classes. A prebuilt class belongs to a package, which can serve as a **class library**, that is, a collection of prebuilt classes that support specific programming tasks such as input/output, text processing, graphics, security, and so on. The standard java packages, the javax packages, and the rapidly growing number of commercial packages serve as class libraries. This section focuses on learning the functionality provided in such libraries.

A client might use a prebuilt class as is or derive a subclass from it. If a prebuilt class is used as is, its *public* members are of interest precisely because these members have been exposed for general client use. If a prebuilt class is used as a superclass, its *protected* members are also of interest because these members, like the public ones, are accessible in the subclass. Because private members are inaccessible outside the class, a client should not need to know anything about them—including even their existence. Chapter 6 focuses on inheritance and, accordingly, on the importance of protected members in a superclass. Package members are of interest to a narrow group of clients, that is, clients within the *same* package as the prebuilt class. Our focus here is on *general clients*, that is, clients that need not be in the same package as the class from which these clients request services. Our focus is thus on a prebuilt class's *public* members, which are typically high-level methods.

If a class is designed according to object-oriented principles, a client should not need to know implementation details to use the class. Such implementation details include the bodies of even high-level methods. A client should need to know only

- The method's name.
- The method's argument types and what the arguments represent.
- The method's return type or void in place of a return type.
- Any exceptions that the method may throw.

In other words, a client that understands a method's *declaration* but not its *definition* still should be able to use the method productively.

■ **Example 5.3.1.**   The java.util.Date class has a public method named after that takes a single Date argument. If d1 and d2 refer to two Date objects, the method call

```
d1.after( d2 )
```

returns true, if the d1-date occurs after the d2-date, and false, if the d1-date does not occur after d2-date. The method's declaration is

```
public boolean after( Date );
```

Understanding this declaration should enable us to use the method productively. ■

Test Clients

Professionally designed and implemented libraries include documentation beyond constructor and method declarations, of course. Yet test clients for a class can be written even from declarations alone. Indeed, writing a test client is an excellent first step towards fluency in a class.

■ **Example 5.3.2.**   The `java.util.Stack` class has one public constructor and five public methods (see Figure 5.3.1). Figure 5.3.2 shows a test client for the `Stack` class and Figure 5.3.3 shows the output for the test client.

Public Member	*Description*
`Stack();`	Constructs an empty stack
`boolean empty();`	Tests if the stack is empty
`Object peek();`	Returns the top element without removing it
`Object pop();`	Returns and removes the top element
`Object push( Object obj );`	Inserts an element at the top
`int search( Object obj );`	Returns an object's position in the stack

FIGURE 5.3.1   The public members of the `java.util.Stack` class.

The `Stack` class has a no-argument constructor that creates an empty stack. The class exposes no other constructors. The `empty` instance method returns `true`, if the `Stack` is empty, and `false`, if the `Stack` has one or more elements. The `push` method inserts objects such as `Strings` onto the `Stack` and the `pop` method returns and removes the `Stack`'s top element. The `peek` method returns the `Stack`'s top element but without removing it. It is an error to invoke `peek` or `pop` on an empty `Stack`, which explains why the `StackClient` program `peeks` at the top of a `Stack` from within a `try` block.

A `Stack` can be `searched` for an object. If the object is on the `Stack`, `search` returns its position with 1 as the position of the top element, 2 as the position of the element immediately below the top, and so on. If an object is not on the `Stack`, the `search` method returns -1. ■

■ **Example 5.3.3.**   The `java.math` package has classes for arbitrary-precision arithmetic: `BigInteger` for arbitrary-precision integer arithmetic and `Big-Decimal` for arbitrary-precision floating-point arithmetic. Figure 5.3.4 lists the public constructors and some public methods for the `BigDecimal` class. The `BigE` program in Figure 5.3.5 computes the value of the constant *e*, the base of the natural logarithm, to 60 decimal places. The constant *e* is the sum of the infinite series

$$1/0! + 1/1! + 1/2! + 1/3! + \dots$$

The `BigE` program computes the series until the precision is not improved in a loop iteration, at which point the program halts. Figure 5.3.6 shows the output.

The `BigE` program initially constructs four `BigDecimal` objects from `String` representations of 0 and 1. Then the `BigDecimal` methods add,

```
import java.util.*;
class StackClient {
   public static void main( String[ ] args ) {
      //*** construction
      Stack s1 = new Stack();
      System.out.println( s1.empty() );     // true
      try {
         Object top = s1.peek();                //**** ERROR: empty stack!
      }
      catch( EmptyStackException e ) {
         System.err.println( e );
         System.err.println( "Continuing test of Stack methods..." );
      }

      //*** insertions
      s1.push( "anna" );
      s1.push( "otto" );
      s1.push( "ada" );
      System.out.println( s1.empty() );     // false

      //*** inspections and removals
      System.out.println( s1.peek() );      // ada
      System.out.println( s1.pop() );       // ada
      System.out.println( s1.pop() );       // otto
      System.out.println( s1.peek() );      // anna

      //*** search
      s1.push( "abba" );
      s1.push( "ebbe" );
      System.out.println( s1.search( "ebbe" ) ); // 1
      System.out.println( s1.search( "anna" ) ); // 3
      System.out.println( s1.search( "abba" ) ); // 2
      System.out.println( s1.search( "fred" ) ); // -1 == not in stack
   }
}
```

FIGURE 5.3.2   Test client for the java.util.Stack class.

multiply, and divide are used to compute the expressions in the series. The series' current value, stored in the BigDecimal to which currVal refers, is repeatedly compared with the BigDecimal value from the previous loop iteration to determine whether the precision has improved. If the precision has not improved, the computation of the series halts.

The BigE program illustrates how a client application can leverage the services that BigDecimal class provides. Writing a client is a key step in learning how to use the services that a class exposes through its public members. ∎

```
true
java.util.EmptyStackException
Continuing test of Stack methods...
false
ada
ada
otto
anna
1
3
2
-1
```

FIGURE 5.3.3 Output for the StackClient program in Figure 5.3.2.

Public Member	Description
BigDecimal(BigInteger n);	Constructed from a BigInteger
BigDecimal(BigInteger n, int scale);	Constructed from a BigInteger
BigDecimal(double n);	Constructed from a double
BigDecimal(String n);	Constructed from a String
BigDecimal abs();	Returns the absolute value
BigDecimal add(BigDecimal n);	Returns this + n
BigDecimal subtract(BigDecimal n);	Returns this - n
BigDecimal multiply(BigDecimal n);	Returns this * n
BigDecimal divide(BigDecimal n);	Returns this / n
BigDecimal negate();	Returns -this
BigInteger toBigInteger();	Converts to a BigInteger

FIGURE 5.3.4 Some public members of the java.math.BigDecimal class.

All of the forthcoming sample applications build classes. The applications always include a test client that illustrates how objects can be constructed and how the public methods can be used. Test clients not only test a class to ensure that it behaves as advertised but also are a natural first step to learning how the class might be used in larger applications.

EXERCISES

1. How are class libraries implemented in Java?
2. Name two Java class libraries and briefly describe the type of programming task that each supports.
3. Can a programmer derive classes from the prebuilt ones in a library?
4. Under what conditions would a client application be concerned with a library class's protected members?

```
import java.math.*;
public class BigE {
   public static void main( String[ ] args ){
      BigDecimal one     = new BigDecimal( "1" ),
                 fact     = new BigDecimal( "1" ),
                 factMult = new BigDecimal( "1" ),
                 currVal  = new BigDecimal( "0" );
      BigDecimal last = one;
      // number of desired decimal places
      final int places = 60;
      // Compute series until precision not improved in an iteration
      while ( true ) {
        // divide 1 by the current factorial
        // ROUND_HALF_EVEN rounds towards the nearest digit, up or down,
        // and towards an EVEN digit in case of a tie. For example,
        // 755 / 100 = 7.6 (7.5 and 7.6 are equidistant, round toward 6)
        // 745 / 100 = 7.4 (7.4 and 7.5 are equidistant, round toward 4)
        // The goal is minimize rounding errors.
        BigDecimal t =
           one.divide( fact, places + 1, BigDecimal.ROUND_HALF_EVEN );
        // add the result to the accumulated value
        currVal = currVal.add( t );
        // move to the next factorial value
        fact = fact.multiply( factMult );
        factMult = factMult.add( one );
        // check convergence of the current value
        if ( currVal.equals( last ) )
          break;
        else
          System.out.println( currVal );
        last = currVal;
      }
   }
}
```

FIGURE 5.3.5   A program to illustrate the BigDecimal class.

5. Under what conditions would a client application be concerned with a library class's public members?

6. Should a client application be concerned with a library class's private members?

7. What should a client need to know about a public method in a class library in order to use the services that the method provides?

8. Run the StackClient program in Figure 5.3.2.

9. Run the BigE program in Figure 5.3.5.

10. Adapt the BigE program in Figure 5.3.5 so that places can be initialized to a value passed to the program as a command-line argument.

```
1.0000000000000000000000000000000000000000000000000000000000000
2.0000000000000000000000000000000000000000000000000000000000000
2.5000000000000000000000000000000000000000000000000000000000000
2.6666666666666666666666666666666666666666666666666666666666667
2.7083333333333333333333333333333333333333333333333333333333334
2.7166666666666666666666666666666666666666666666666666666666667
2.7180555555555555555555555555555555555555555555555555555555556
. . .
2.7182818284590452353602874713526624976385970411900203714065180
2.7182818284590452353602874713526624977537603973977398742123868
. . .
2.7182818284590452353602874713526624977572470936999595749669675
2.7182818284590452353602874713526624977572470936999595749669676
```

FIGURE 5.3.6   Output from the `BigE` program in Figure 5.3.5 that computes *e*.

11. Is the `BigDecimal` field `ROUND_HALF_EVEN` a static or nonstatic member?

5.4   Sample Application: Basic Input and Output Classes

Problem

Provide utility classes for the input and output of records, strings, integers, and floating-point types. The input class should support input from the standard input or a disk file, and the output class should support output to the standard output or a disk file.

Input/Output

If the standard input is

```
26 A 3.14
this is the way the world ends
not -999
```

and the file *input.dat* is

```
1 2 3
4  5  6
7
8
9
```

```
import java.io.*;
import basicIO.BasicInput;
class BasicInputTester {
   public static void main( String[ ] args ) throws IOException {
      //*** test reading from the standard input
      BasicInput stdin = new BasicInput();
      System.out.println( stdin.getInt() );
      System.out.println( stdin.getChar() );
      System.out.println( stdin.getDouble() );
      System.out.println( stdin.getRecord() );
      System.out.println( stdin.getString() );
      System.out.println( stdin.getInt() );
      System.out.println();
      //*** test reading until end-of-file
      BasicInput inFile = new BasicInput( "input.dat" );
      while ( !inFile.eof() )
         System.out.println( inFile.getInt() );
      inFile.close();
   }
}
```

FIGURE 5.4.1   Test client for the BasicInput class.

the program in Figure 5.4.1 outputs

```
26
a
3.14
this is the way the world ends
not
-999

1
2
3
4
5
6
7
8
9
```

Given the same input file *input.dat*, the program in Figure 5.4.2 prints

```
1 2 3 4 5 6 7 8 9
```

```
import basicIO.*;
import java.io.*;
class BasicOutputTester {
   public static void main( String[ ] args ) throws IOException {
      BasicInput in = new BasicInput( "input.dat" );
      BasicOutput out = new BasicOutput( "output.dat" );
      BasicOutput stdout = new BasicOutput();
      while ( !in.eof() ) {
         int t = in.getInt();
         out.putln( t );
         stdout.put( t );
         stdout.put( ' ' );
      }
      stdout.put( '\n' );
      in.close();
      out.close();
   }
}
```

FIGURE 5.4.2   Test client for the `BasicOutput` class.

to the standard output and

```
1
2
3
4
5
6
7
8
9
```

to the file *output.dat*.

Solution

We provide two wrapper classes, one for input and another for output. Recall that a wrapper class repackages other classes to make them less challenging to use, more robust, and the like. The `BasicInput` class supports the input of records, strings, integers, and floating-point types from either the standard input or a specified disk file. The `BasicOutput` class supports the output of records, strings, integers, floating-point types to either the standard output or a specified disk file. The two classes belong to the user-defined `basicIO` package.

Java Implementation

```java
//******************* start of BasicInput.java
package basicIO;
import java.io.*;
import java.util.StringTokenizer;

public class BasicInput {
   public BasicInput() throws IOException {
      init( new InputStreamReader( System.in ) );
   }
   public BasicInput( String f ) throws IOException {
      init( new InputStreamReader( new FileInputStream( f ) ) );
      diskFile = true;
   }
   public void close() throws IOException {
      if ( diskFile && input != null )
        input.close();
   }
   public boolean eof() throws IOException {
      resetBuffer();
      return !st.hasMoreTokens();
   }
   public String getRecord() throws IOException {
      resetBuffer();
      st = null;     // forces a read on next resetBuffer()
      return buffer;
   }
   public String getString() throws IOException {
      resetBuffer();
      return st.nextToken();
   }
   public byte getByte() throws IOException {
      resetBuffer();
      return Byte.parseByte( st.nextToken() );
   }
   public int getInt() throws IOException {
      resetBuffer();
      return Integer.parseInt( st.nextToken() );
   }
   public double getDouble() throws IOException {
      resetBuffer();
      return Double.parseDouble( st.nextToken() );
```

```
      }
      public char getChar() throws IOException {
         resetBuffer();
         return st.nextToken().charAt( 0 ); //*** 1st char in String
      }
      private void init( InputStreamReader in ) throws IOException {
         close();
         input = new BufferedReader( in );
         st = null;
         resetBuffer();
      }
      private void resetBuffer() throws IOException {
         if ( st == null || !st.hasMoreTokens() ) {
           buffer = input.readLine();
           if ( buffer != null )
             st = new StringTokenizer( buffer );
         }
      }
      protected BufferedReader input;
      private String buffer;
      private StringTokenizer st;
      private boolean diskFile;
}
//****************** end of BasicInput.java

//****************** start of BasicOutput.java
package basicIO;
import java.io.*;
public class BasicOutput {
      public BasicOutput() {
         output = new PrintWriter( System.out, true );
      }
      public BasicOutput( String f ) throws IOException {
         output =
          new PrintWriter( new FileOutputStream( f ), true );
         diskFile = true;
      }
      public BasicOutput( String f, boolean a ) throws IOException {
         if ( a ) //*** append mode?
           output =
            new PrintWriter( new FileOutputStream( f, true ), true );
         else
           output =
            new PrintWriter( new FileOutputStream( f ), true );
         diskFile = true;
```

```
     }
     public void flush() throws IOException {
        output.flush();
     }
     public void close() throws IOException {
        if ( diskFile && output != null )
          output.close();
     }
     public void put( String s ) {
        output.print( s );
        output.flush();
     }
     public void putln( String s ) {
        output.println( s );
     }
     public void put( byte b ) {
        output.print( b );
        output.flush();
     }
     public void putln( byte b ) {
        output.println( b );
     }
     public void put( int i ) {
        output.print( i );
        output.flush();
     }
     public void putln( int i ) {
        output.println( i );
     }
     public void put( double d ) {
        output.print( d );
        output.flush();
     }
     public void putln( double d ) {
        output.println( d );
     }
     public void put( char c ) {
        output.print( c );
        output.flush();
     }
     public void putln( char c ) {
        output.println( c );
     }
     public void putln() {
        output.println();
```

```
    }
    protected PrintWriter output;
    private boolean diskFile;
}
//****************** end of BasicOutput.java
```

Discussion

Stream Input/Output

Recall that the `java.io` package contains the standard classes to support input and output of binary and character data (see Section 2.5). All input and output operations are based on a **stream**, which is a sequence of data. A stream has an arbitrary number of data but the items in it are ordered: *first, second,. . . , nth*. An input stream has a *source* such as the standard input or a disk file, whereas an output stream has a *destination* such as the standard output or a disk file. Classes in the `java.io` package are designed to operate on two basic types of stream: byte streams, or sequences of 8-bit bytes, and character streams, or sequences of 16-bit `chars`. The `java.io` package also provides constructs for handling the input and output of specific data types such as `int`, `double`, and `String`.

The `java.io` package is highly flexible and modular by design and exemplifies sophisticated Java in its use of regular classes, interfaces, abstract classes, and other advanced constructs. As a result, the `java.io` package is challenging. The `basicIO` package is therefore designed to provide high-level, relatively easy-to-use classes for input and output. The package's two classes, `BasicInput` and `BasicOutput`, repackage or wrap `java.io` classes so that programmers can perform basic input and output operations without first becoming fluent in the `java.io` package.

The `BasicInput` Class

The `BasicInput` class has two public constructors. The public no-argument constructor creates a `BasicInput` object that reads from the standard input, whereas the public parameterized constructor creates a `BasicInput` object that reads from a specified disk file. The statements

```
    BasicInput stdin = new BasicInput(); // standard input
    BasicInput file = new BasicInput( "in.dat" ); // disk file
```

illustrate.

The `BasicInput` class also has a `close` method to close a file and an `eof` method to test for end-of-file. The method `eof` returns `true` to signal that the end of the file has been reached and, therefore, no further input from the file is possible. The class's other public methods are:

- getRecord. A record is a sequence of characters terminated by a newline. The method returns a record as a `String`. If the method reads from the standard input

      This is the way

  it returns *This is the way* as a `String`.
- getString. The method reads characters until encountering whitespace and returns these characters as a `String`. If the method reads from the standard input

      This is the way

  it returns *This* as a `String`.
- getByte. The method reads an integer, using whitespace as a delimiter. If the method reads from the standard input

      -8 This is the way

  it returns −8 as a `byte`.
- getInt. The method reads an integer, using whitespace as a delimiter. If the method reads from the standard input

      -8 This is the way

  it returns −8 as an `int`.
- getDouble. The method reads a floating-point number, using whitespace as a delimiter. If the method reads from the standard input

      3.141 This is the way

  it returns 3.141 as a `double`.
- getChar. The method reads a non-whitespace character. If the method reads from the standard input

      ␣␣␣This␣is␣the␣way

  it returns *T* as a `char`.

The *get* methods throw an `IOException` to handle unexpected conditions such as attempting to read from an empty input stream. The programmer can provide exception handling by placing `BasicInput` statements within a `try` block. The code segment

```
try {
    BasicInput bi = new BasicInput( "input.dat" );
```

```
        String r = bi.getRecord();
        //...
    }
    catch( IOException e ) { System.err.println( e ); }
```

illustrates.

The `BasicInput` class's hidden implementation consists of two private methods, a protected field, and three private fields. We focus on how the `BasicInput` class uses its private implementation to leverage the underlying functionality provided in the `java.io` package.

End of File

The `BasicInput` method `eof` can be used to test for the end of the file, which occurs under two conditions in this implementation:

- The last file in the record has been read. For example, if the input file were

```
        The Caine Mutiny
        The High and the Mighty
```

  a `BasicInput` object would read two records and then detect end-of-file.
- A blank record has been read, although there are still nonblank records beyond the blank one. For example, if the input file were

```
        The Caine Mutiny
        The High and the Mighty

        Rear Window
```

  a `BasicInput` object would read two records and then detect end-of-file because of the blank record. In short, the last record would be ignored.

Buffered Input and Output

Input and output are often **buffered** for efficiency. For example, if an application reads a single character from a file, the system may actually read a larger number of characters in anticipation of further reads. The additional characters are stored temporarily in a *buffer* or memory area. The `java.io` package has classes that support buffered input/output. For example, the package's `BufferedReader` class supports buffered input for character streams. A `BufferedReader` can be constructed out of a `InputStreamReader` by invoking the constructor

```
    public BufferedReader( InputStreamReader )
```

An InputStreamReader, in turn, can be constructed from an InputStream such as System.in, which represents the standard input, or from a FileInputStream that represents a disk file.

The BufferedReader class has a readLine method that reads a record from a buffered character stream and returns the record as a String. The BasicInput class leverages this underlying functionality by storing the returned String. The BasicInput class has a private String field named buffer, which represents an input buffer encapsulated in a BasicInput object, and a protected BufferedInput field named input. The BufferedInput field is declared protected so that it can be accessed in any subclass or copackage class of BufferedInput. In the body of the private resetBuffer method, the statement

```
buffer = input.readLine();
```

uses the BufferedReader object to which input refers to read a record, if the input stream is not empty, and to store the record in the String object to which buffer refers. For example, if the input stream is

```
This is 3.141
```

the statement would store *This is 3.141* in the String to which buffer refers.

The BasicInput methods such as getDouble read directly from the internal String buffer named buffer. In particular, the *get* methods use a StringTokenizer object (see Section 2.6) to read appropriate tokens or parts from a string. The details can be illustrated with method getDouble.

Suppose that the BasicInput object's internal String buffer contains the string *3.141 Miles Davis*, which has been read as a record (i.e., a String) by using the getLine method. From this string, we construct a StringTokenizer object to which st refers. When getDouble is called, the StringTokenizer is used to extract the next token, in this case *3.141*, as a String. Next, the extracted String must be converted to type double so that getDouble can return a double:

```
public double getDouble() throws IOException {
    resetBuffer();
    return Double.parseDouble( st.nextToken() );
}
```

The method resetBuffer is invoked to check whether the internal String buffer to which buffer refers still has tokens. If not, resetBuffer tries to read another record into the internal buffer and to create a StringTokenizer to extract tokens from this buffer. The Double class's static method parseDouble is then invoked with the next token, a String that is converted to a double and returned. The other *get* methods take a similar approach. By the way, the methods getRecord and getString are the simplest because they return Strings and, therefore, need not convert a String to a primitive type.

Error Checking

The BasicInput class's *get* methods do no error checking or exception handling of their own. For example, the code segment

```
BasicInput stdin = new BasicInput(); //*** standard input
int x = stdin.getInt();
```

throws a NumberFormatException if the standard input is

```
foo
```

because the string *foo* cannot be converted to an int. The code segment

```
BasicInput file = new BasicInput( "input.dat" );
String s = file.getString();
```

throws a FileNotFoundException if *input.dat* does not exist. The BasicInput class does not prevent a client from trying to read from an empty file; indeed, the method eof is provided so that a client can check whether a file is empty before trying to read from the associated stream.

The BasicOutput **Class**

The BasicOutput class has three public constructors. The no-argument constructor creates a BasicOutput object for writing to the standard output. The two parameterized constructors create BasicOutput objects for writing to a specified disk file in either **overwrite** or **append** mode. If a BasicOutput object is constructed in *overwrite* mode, the specified disk file overwrites or replaces an already existing file. If a BasicOutput object is constructed in *append* mode, an already existing file is not overwritten; instead, any characters written are appended to the end of the already existing file. The statements

```
BasicOutput stdout = new BasicOutput(); // standard output
BasicOutput fw =
   new BasicOutput( "out.dat" );        // overwrite mode
BasicOutput fa =
   new BasicOutput( "out.dat", true );  // append mode
BasicOutput fo =
   new BasicOutput( "out.dat", false ); // overwrite mode
```

illustrate.

The BasicOutput class also has five pairs of public, parameterized *put* methods. In each pair, a method called put writes the parameter without adding a newline, whereas the method called `putln` writes the parameter and adds a newline. For example, the code segment

```
BasicOutput stdout = new BasicOutput();
stdout.put( 26 );
stdout.put( ' ' );
stdout.put( 999 );
```

writes

```
26 999
```

to the standard output, whereas the code segment

```
BasicOutput stdout = new BasicOutput();
stdout.putln( 26 );
stdout.put( 999 );
```

writes

```
26
999
```

to the standard output. The *put* methods mimic the syntax of the `print` and `println` methods familiar from the `System.out` and `System.err` objects. Accordingly, the `putln` method that takes no argument simply writes a newline, as does `println` with no argument.

Recall that overloaded functions within a class, such as the `put` and `putln` methods in `BasicOutput`, must have distinct signatures. For example, the `put` methods

- `put( String )` writes a `String` without a newline.
- `put( byte )` writes a `byte` without a newline.
- `put( int )` writes an `int` without a newline.
- `put( double )` writes a `double` without a newline.
- `put( char )` writes a `char` without a newline.

differ in the data type of their single parameter. For each of these types, the corresponding `putln` method writes the argument and appends a newline. All of the `put` and `putln` methods have `void` in place of return type.

Buffer Flushing

The `BasicOutput` class, like the `BasicInput` class, has a `close` method for closing a stream whose destination is a disk file. Closing a file automatically flushes an associated system buffer. The `BasicOutput` class also has a `flush` method that can be invoked to ensure that a system buffer is flushed during an output operation. Buffer flushing is also an issue with respect to the put and putln methods in each pair. We clarify by explaining the implementation details of the BasicOutput class.

The BasicOutput class wraps the java.io.PrintWriter class, which has pairs of print and println methods for writing primitive types and Strings. The BasicOutput class's put and putln methods invoke the corresponding print and println methods. A PrintWriter object can be constructed with *auto-flushing*, which means that writing a newline character '\n' automatically flushes a system buffer even if the buffer is not full. The println methods write newlines and, therefore, perform auto-flushes. The PrintWriter object encapsulated within a BasicOutput object is constructed with auto-flushing, which means that the putln methods automatically flush the system output buffer. However, the put methods do not perform auto-flushing because these methods do not append a newline to the output. Therefore, the put methods explicitly flush the system buffer by invoking the PrintWriter class's flush method. For example, the method

```
public void put( int i ) {
   output.print( i );
   output.flush();
}
```

writes an int to the output stream and then flushes the buffer. The field output refers to a PrintWriter. The corresponding putln method

```
public void putln( int i ) {
   output.println( i );
}
```

does not need to flush the system buffer because the PrintWriter object named output has been constructed with auto-flushing enabled.

Summary of the Basic Input/Output Classes

The java.io package has a rich assortment of classes for flexible, powerful input and output. The complexity of the standard package results from its power and flexibility. The user-defined basicIO package thus offers the relatively simple utility classes BasicInput and BasicOutput so that programs can perform input and output operations before the programmer becomes fluent in the java.io package.

EXERCISES

1. Explain why BasicInput and BasicOutput are called *wrapper classes*.
2. What are the two basic stream types supported by java.io classes?

3. What is the basic distinction between *readers* and *writers*, on the one hand, and *input streams* and *output streams*, on the other hand?

4. Explain what it means for input and output to be *buffered*.

5. Write a client that tests all of the public BasicInput constructors and methods.

6. Write a client that tests all of the public BasicOutput constructors and methods.

7. Add public methods to BasicInput to read the primitive data types not currently covered.

8. Add public methods to BasicOutput to write the primitive data types not currently covered.

5.5   Sample Application: A Utility Class for File Copying

Problem

Create a utility class to copy files, whether binary or text. The utility should have a graphical interface that allows the user to select the source and the destination file. The utility class should be able to produce a log of the copying operation.

Sample Output

The program in Figure 5.5.1 is a test client for the CopyFile utility class. On a sample run that copied the file *CopyUtil.class* to *CopyUtil.bak*, the test client produced the log file

```
import java.io.*;
public class FileCopyClient {
   public static void main( String[ ] args ) throws IOException {
     CopyUtil cu = new CopyUtil();
     cu.copy( true );  //*** true == create a log file
     cu.cleanup();
   }
}
```

FIGURE 5.5.1   Test client for the CopyFile class.

```
**** Log entry for source file named CopyUtil.class.
### Entry made at Sat May 13 00:20:01 CDT 2000
Path:      D:\jbook\code\ch4\copy\CopyUtil.class
Byte size: 3042

**** Log entry for destination file named CopyUtil.bak.
### Entry made at Sat May 13 00:20:01 CDT 2000
Path:      D:\jbook\code\ch4\copy\CopyUtil.bak
Byte size: 3042
```

Solution

The CopyUtil class encapsulates methods and fields to copy a source file to a destination file, which are required to be different so that a file cannot be copied to itself. To provide the user with a graphical interface, we use a java.awt.FileDialog object to prompt for the source and destination files. Figure 5.5.2 shows the FileDialog on a Windows system. The copying is done byte by byte so that either text or binary files can be copied. The user can request creation of a log file, which records basic information about the copying such as the time that the copying began and the full path names of the source and destination files.

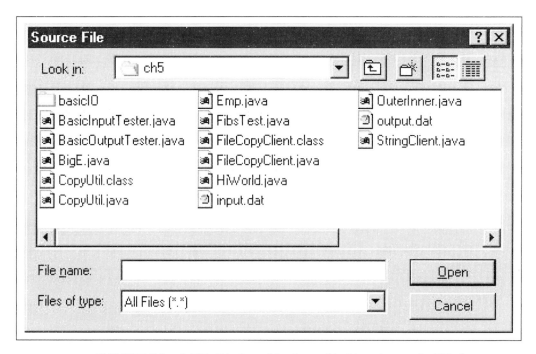

FIGURE 5.5.2   A FileDialog object's graphical interface under Windows.

Java Implementation

```
import java.io.*;
import java.awt.*;
import java.util.*;
import basicIO.BasicOutput;
public class CopyUtil {
   public void copy( boolean writeLog ) throws IOException {
      //*** Prompt for source and destination files
      fd = new FileDialog( new Frame(), "Source File" );
      fd.show();
```

```
    src = fd.getFile();
    if ( !ok( src, "source" ) )
      return;
    fd.setTitle( "Destination File" );
    fd.show();
    des = fd.getFile();
    if ( !ok( des, "destination" ) )
      return;
    if ( src.equals( des ) ) { //*** copying a file to itself?
      cleanup();
      return;
    }
    //*** Copy bytes from source to destination
    in = new FileInputStream( src );
    out = new FileOutputStream( des );
    int next;
    while ( (next = in.read()) != -1 )
       out.write( next );
    cleanup();
    if ( writeLog ) {
      logCopy();
      log.close();
    }
  }
  public void cleanup() throws IOException {
    if ( fd != null )
      fd.dispose();
    if ( in != null )
      in.close();
    if ( out != null )
      out.close();
  }
  private boolean ok( String file, String type )
   throws IOException {
    if ( file == null ) {
      System.err.println( "No " + type + " file name given." );
      cleanup();
      return false;
    }
    return true;
  }
  private void logCopy() throws IOException {
    String logName = "LOG_" + des +
                      new Date().getTime() + ".log";
    System.err.println( "Log file name is " + logName );
```

```
        log = new BasicOutput( logName, true ); //** append mode
        logAux( src, "source" );
        logAux( des, "destination" );
    }
    private void logAux( String name, String which )
      throws IOException {
        if ( name == null )
            return;
        File f = new File( name );
        if ( !f.exists() || !f.isFile() )
            return;
        log.putln( "**** Log entry for " + which +
                   " file named " + name +
                   ".\n\t### Entry made at " +
                   new Date().toString() );
        log.putln( "Path:       " + f.getCanonicalPath() );
        log.putln( "Byte size: " + f.length() );
        log.putln();
    }
    private FileDialog fd;
    private FileInputStream in;
    private FileOutputStream out;
    private BasicOutput log;
    private String src;
    private String des;
}
```

Discussion

Because the application introduces a graphical component, we begin with an overview of graphics. We then explain how the copying and logging work.

The Abstract Window Toolkit and the Swing Set

There are two related packages that support graphics. The `java.awt` package contains the standard classes that comprise the **A**bstract **W**indow **T**oolkit (AWT). The AWT has shortcomings. AWT components such as the `FileDialog` in the sample application use **native components**, that is, components that are specific to the runtime platform. Accordingly, a `FileDialog` on a Windows platform differs from a `FileDialog` on a Unix platform. AWT's reliance on native components thus raises portability issues, including issues of "look and feel." Further, the AWT components are useful but rudimentary. For example, the AWT has no direct support for split-pane windows and other advanced graphical features that have become common in user interfaces. Finally, the AWT is not built upon a **model-view-controller** architecture, which has become the standard software architecture for graphical user interfaces.[†] The `javax.swing` package, called the **Swing set**, was designed to overcome these and other shortcomings in the AWT. In short, the Swing set supercedes the AWT. Swing set components are more portable, powerful, and flexible than their AWT counterparts.

Despite the Swing set's advantages, the AWT is still worth studying. For one thing, learning AWT is a good way to learn the Swing set, particularly because AWT components are generally simpler. The AWT's event-handling model has been incorporated into the Swing set. Further, some AWT components are more flexible, if less sophisticated, than their Swing counterparts. Chapter 7, which covers basic graphics and event-handling, emphasizes Swing set graphics.

The `FileDialog` Component

The `java.awt.FileDialog` class has three public, parameterized constructors. For each constructor, the first argument is a parent window, which we provide as a `java.awt.Frame`. For the two-argument and the three-argument constructors, the second argument is the `FileDialog`'s title, given as a `String`. For the three-argument constructor, the third argument is a `boolean` value that indicates whether the `FileDialog` is **modal**. If a dialog is modal, no other window can be active while the dialog is displayed. The one-argument and two-argument constructors create modal dialogs. The three-argument constructor creates a modal dialog if the third argument is `true`.

The sample application invokes the two-argument constructor with a **Frame** parent and a title

```
fd = new FileDialog( new Frame(), "Source File" );
```

to inform the user about which file is to be selected first. The private field `fd` is encapsulated in the `CopyUtil` class. The sample application later invokes the method `setTitle`

```
fd.setTitle( "Destination File" );
```

to change the dialog's title.

Once constructed, a `FileDialog` is not displayed on screen until its `show` method is invoked. The `show` method **blocks**; that is, the method does not return until the user has either selected a file or canceled. Because of this blocking behavior, we can simply sequence the two statements

```
fd.show();
src = fd.getFile()
```

[†]The model-view-controller architecture was popularized in Smalltalk but has been adapted to other application frameworks such as Motif and the Microsoft Foundation Classes.

where `src` refers to a `String` that names the source file. When the user selects a file or cancels, `show` returns and the `getFile` method returns either the selected file's name or `null`, if the user cancels the dialog operation. Once `show` returns, the `FileDialog` is no longer visible, although the underlying object still exists. If the user selects a source file, we reset the title and again show the dialog so that the user can select the destination file.

Graphics components can be relatively expensive with respect to system resources such as memory. Accordingly, graphics components have a `dispose` method to signal that these resources are no longer needed. The `CopyUtil` class has a `cleanup` method that invokes `dispose`

```
if ( fd != null )
  fd.dispose();
```

for the `FileDialog` object to which `fd` refers. The `cleanup` method also closes any open files.

The `CopyUtil` Class

The `FileDialog` object provides the `CopyUtil` class with a graphical user interface for selecting the source and destination files. The copying itself, which is done byte by byte so that either binary or text files can be copied, uses two classes from the `java.io` package:

- `FileInputStream`. This stream has a file as a source. The method

  ```
  int read();
  ```

  reads a single byte and returns the byte's value as an `int`. The byte's value is returned as an *unsigned* integer, which is thus a number in the range of 0 through 255. On end-of-file, the method returns −1 as an `int`. In the code segment

  ```
  int next;
  while ( (next = in.read()) != -1 )
  ```

  in refers to a `FileInputStream` object. The `while` loop's test illustrates how the value returned by `read` can be used to detect end-of-file.
- `FileOutputStream`. This stream has a file as a destination. The method

  ```
  void write( int );
  ```

  writes a byte whose value should be in the range of 0 through 255. Because the parameter is of type `int`, however, a number out of this range could be passed to `write`. In such a case, the argument is first reduced to modulo 256 and then is written. The method `write` is thus ideal for writing the bytes that have been read by `read`. The actual file-copying code is therefore

```
int next;
while ( (next = in.read()) != -1 )
    out.write( next );
```

where `in` refers to a `FileInputStream` and `out` refers to a `FileOutput-Stream`.

To copy a file, a client of `CopyUtil` creates an object and then invokes the `copy` method with a `boolean` argument. If `copy` is invoked with `true` as the argument, a log file is created. If the method is invoked with `false` as the argument, no log file is created. Our sample client (see Figure 5.5.1) creates a `CopyUtil` object and invokes its `copy` method with logging enabled

```
CopyUtil = new CopyUtil();
cu.copy( true ); //*** true == create log
```

The log file shown in Figure 5.5.2 is named

LOG_CopyUtil.bak933399122169.log

All log files begin with *LOG* and have a *log* extension. The rest of the name is the integer representation of the current time appended to the destination file's name. This naming convention makes it relatively straightforward to find log files and helps to avoid name conflicts among log files. Because log files contain only text, the `BasicOutput` class (see Section 5.4) is used to create them.

The `CopyUtil` class uses the `java.io.File` to represent files, including directories. The `CopyUtil`'s private `logAux` method, which writes the information about the copying to a log file, creates a `File` object from the file's `String` name. The `File` class has methods such as `exists` and `getCanonicalPath` to gain information about a file. The `File` method `length` returns a file's size in bytes. The log file records the lengths of the source and destination files so that these can be compared.

Program Development

The `CopyUtil` class has a `cleanup` method that disposes of the `FileDialog` when this component is no longer needed and also closes the source and destination files of the copy operation. Several `CopyUtil` methods such as the public `copy` method and the private `ok` method invoke `cleanup`. Indeed, method `copy` is designed so that any execution path through the method invokes `cleanup`. The `cleanup` method is made public and thus available to the client because a copying operation may abort in unexpected ways. For example, the `FileInputStream` and `FileOutputStream` constructors and methods may throw exceptions. If a client catches such an exception, the exception handler should invoke `cleanup` to ensure that the `FileDialog` is disposed and that the source and destination files are closed.

1. In the `java.awt` package, what does `awt` stand for?

2. Run the test client for the `CopyUtil` class in order to confirm its advertised functionality.

JAVA POSTSCRIPT

Inner Classes

An **inner class** or a **nested class** is defined within another class, which is its **enclosing class**. There are various subtypes of inner class, including an unnamed inner class. Inner classes are particularly useful in the context of event-driven programs for defining **callback methods** on the fly. A *callback method* is a method invoked by the system in response to an event such as a mouse click. Chapters 6 and 7, which deal with interfaces, event-driven programming, and graphics, have various examples to illustrate the power of inner classes. The purpose of this section is to introduce the basic syntax.

■ **Example.**   The declaration

```
class Outer {
   class Inner {
      //...Inner's members
   }
   //...Outer's other members
}
```

shows the basic syntax for an inner class. The class `Outer` could enclose arbitrarily many inner classes, although each inner class requires its own identifier. An inner class cannot have the same name as its enclosing class.

Example.   The program in Figure A produces the output

```
*** Inner.print()
Inner
Inner
Inner
Outer
```

```
class Outer {
   class Inner {
      private void print() { //**** Inner's print is private
         System.out.println( "*** Inner.print()" );
         System.out.println( name );              //** Inner's name
         System.out.println( this.name );         //** ditto
         System.out.println( Inner.this.name );   //** ditto
         System.out.println( Outer.this.name );   //** Outer's name
      }
      private String name = "Inner";
   }
   public void print() { //**** Outer's print is public
      new Inner().print(); //*** delegate to Inner's print
   }
   private String name = "Outer";
}
public class OuterInner {
   public static void main( String[ ] args ) {
      new Outer().print();
   }
}
```

FIGURE A   A program to illustrate inner classes.

Method `main` constructs an unreferenced `Outer` object and invokes the object's public `print` method. The `Outer` class's `print` method delegates the actual printing to an unreferenced `Inner` object whose private `print` method is invoked. Note that class `Outer` has access to the inner class's private members, in this case `Inner`'s private method `print`:

```
public void print() {   //**** Outer's print is public
   new Inner().print(); //*** delegate to Inner's print
}
```

The inner class also can access the enclosing class's private members. In this example, the enclosing `Outer` class has a private field `name` to which the `Inner` class's `print` method has access using special syntax with `this`:

```
private void print() {
   System.out.println( "*** Inner.print()" );
   System.out.println( name );              //** Inner's name
   System.out.println( this.name );         //** ditto
   System.out.println( Inner.this.name );   //** ditto
   System.out.println( Outer.this.name );   //** Outer's name
}
```

The `Inner` class's `print` method refers to the `Inner` class's own `name` field in three ways:

- By using only the field name: `name`.
- By using `this` together with the field name: `this.name`.
- By using the class name, `this`, and the field name: `Inner.this.name`.

The special syntax for `this` is needed. Because class `Inner` is a *member* of class `Outer`, the reference `this` within `Inner` could refer to either an `Outer` object or an `Inner` object. By prepending the class name, the reference `this` is disambiguated.

COMMON ERRORS AND SAFE PRACTICES

1. A class can have only package or public scope:

```
class A { /*...*/ } // ok, package scope
public class B { /*...*/ } // ok, public scope
protected class D { /*...*/ } //***** ERROR
private class E { /*...*/ }   //***** ERROR
```

2. A class with package scope cannot be referenced outside its containing package. Therefore, the code segment

```
//*** start of file Alpha.java
package p1;
class Alpha { /*...*/ }
//*** end of file Alpha.java
//*** start of file Zeta.java
package p2;
class Zeta {
   public Zeta() {
     new Alpha(); //***** ERROR
   }
}
//*** end of file Zeta.java
```

contains an error. Because class `p1.Alpha` has package scope, this class cannot be accessed outside of package `p1`.

3. If a `package` statement occurs, it must come *before* any `import` statements or class declarations. The code segment

```
import java.util.*;
package p1; //***** ERROR: must come first
class A { /*...*/ }
```

illustrates the error. The correct order is

```
package p1;
import java.util.*;
class A { /*...*/ }
```

4. If import statements occur, they must come *before* class declarations. The code
segment

```
class A { /*...*/ }
import java.io.File; //***** ERROR
```

illustrates the error. The correct order is

```
import java.io.File;
class A { /*...*/ }
```

5. If a class member has private scope, the member cannot be accessed outside its
encapsulating class. The code segment

```
//*** start of source file
package p1;
class Alpha {            // package scope
   Alpha() { /*...*/ } // package scope
   private int n;        // private scope
}
class Zeta {
   Zeta() {
      Alpha a = new Alpha(); //*** ok
      a.n = 0; //***** ERROR n is private in Alpha
   }
}
//*** end of source file
```

illustrates the error.

6. If a class member has package scope, the member cannot be accessed outside the
package that contains the encapsulating class. The code segment

```
//*** start of Alpha.java
package p1;
class Alpha {               // package scope
```

```
      Alpha() { /*...*/ } // package scope
      private int n;        // private scope
}
//*** end of Alpha.java
//*** start of Zeta.java
package p2;
class Zeta {
   Zeta() {
      Alpha a = new Alpha(); //***** ERROR
      //...
   }
}
//*** end Zeta.java
```

illustrates the error. Because constructor `Alpha` has *package* scope, this constructor cannot be invoked outside the containing package p1.

7. If a class member has protected scope, the member cannot be accessed outside the package that contains the encapsulating class C except for subclasses of C. The code segment illustrates

```
//*** start of Alpha.java
package p1;
class Alpha {              // package scope
   Alpha() { /*...*/ } // package scope
   private int n;        // private scope
}
//*** end of Alpha.java
//*** start of Zeta.java
package p2;
class Zeta extends Alpha { // Zeta subclasses Alpha
   Zeta() {
      Alpha a = new Alpha(); // ok, Zeta is a subclass
      //...
   }
}
//*** end Zeta.java
```

by revising the example in Common Errors and Safe Practices 6. Class `Zeta` can now access the protected constructor `Alpha` despite the fact that `Alpha` and `Zeta` occur in different packages. The reason is that `Zeta` is a *subclass* of `Alpha`.

8. If a class has package scope, even its *public* members are visible only in the containing package where the class itself is visible. The code segment

```
//*** start of Alpha.java
package p1;
```

```
class Alpha {                        // package scope
   public Alpha() { /*...*/ } // public scope
}
//*** end of Alpha.java
//*** start of Zeta.java
package p2;
class Zeta {
   Zeta() {
      Alpha a = new Alpha(); //***** ERROR
      //...
   }
}
//*** end Zeta.java
```

illustrates the rule. Although constructor `Alpha` has public scope, the encapsulating class has only *package* scope. The constructor's visibility is thus restricted to package `p1`, where the encapsulating class `Alpha` is visible.

9. A constructor has *no return type* or `void` in place of a return type. The code segment

```
class Alpha {
   int Alpha() { /*...*/ }        //***** ERROR
   void Alpha( int x ) { /*...*/ } //***** ERROR
   Alpha( float f ) { /*...*/ }    // correct
}
```

illustrates.

10. All methods have a return type or `void` in place of a return type. The code segment

```
class Alpha {
   m() { /*...*/ } //***** ERROR: no return type
   void alpha() { /*...*/ } // ok
}
```

illustrates. Note that function `alpha` is a method rather than a constructor because its name is not the encapsulating class's name, `Alpha`.

11. If a method has a return type, the method must explicitly `return` a value of the specified type. The code segment

```
class Alpha {
   int m() { //*** should return an int
      int x = 2, y = 4;
      int z = x * x + y;
   } //***** ERROR: no int returned
}
```

illustrates the error.

12. A method with `void` in place of a return type can but need not have an explicit `return` statement. In any case, the `return` statement must *not* return a value of any type. The code segment

```
void m( int m, int n ) { //*** void return type
   if ( m > n )
     return; // ok, explicit return
   //...
   return m; //***** ERROR: void is the return type
}
```

illustrates the error.

13. If a class defines *any* constructor, the compiler does *not* provide a no-argument constructor. Therefore, the code segment

```
class Alpha {
   Alpha( int n ) { /*...*/ }
}
class Beta {
   Beta() {
      Alpha a = new Alpha(); //***** ERROR
      //...
   }
}
```

contains an error. If a class defines no constructors at all, the compiler provides a *public* no-argument constructor.

14. A constructor cannot be `static`.

15. A `static` method cannot access a nonstatic member. The code segment

```
class Alpha {
   static void m() { n = 0; } //***** ERROR
   int n;
}
```

illustrates the error with `static` method m accessing nonstatic field n.

PROGRAMMING EXERCISES

5.1. Implement a `Car` class that includes data members to represent a car's make (e.g., Honda), model (e.g., Civic), production year, and price. The class should include methods that provide appropriate access to the fields (e.g., a method to set the car's model or to get its price). In addition, the class should have a method

```
public void compare( Car otherCar ) { /*...*/ }
```

that compares a `Car` against another using whatever criteria seem appropriate. The `compare` method prints a short report of its comparison.

5.2. Implement a `CollegeStudent` class with appropriate data members such as `name`, `year`, `expectedGrad`, `major`, `minor`, `GPA`, `coursesAndGrades`, `maritalStatus`, and the like. The class should expose at least a half-dozen methods. For example, there should be a method to compute GPA from `coursesAndGrades` and to determine whether the GPA merits honors or probation. There also should be methods to display a `CollegeStudent`'s current course load and to print remaining required courses.

5.3. Implement a `Deck` class that represents a deck of 52 cards. The class should include methods to shuffle, deal, display hands, do pairwise comparisons of cards (e.g., a Queen beats a Jack), and the like. To simulate shuffling, use the `Random` utility class.

5.4. Implement a `Profession` class with fields such as `name`, `title`, `credentials`, `education`, and `avgIncome`. The class should include methods that compare `Professions` across the fields. The class should have at least a dozen fields and a dozen methods.

5.5. A **queue** is a list of zero or more elements. An element is added to a queue at its **rear**; an element is removed from a queue at its **front**. If a queue is **empty**, a removal operation is an error. If a queue is **full**, an add operation is an error. Implement a `Queue` class for arbitrary `Objects`.

5.6. A **deque** is a list of zero or more elements with insertions and deletions at either end, its front or its rear. Implement a `Deque` class whose elements are arbitrary `Objects`.

5.7. A **semaphore** is a mechanism widely used in computer systems to enforce synchronization constraints on shared resources. For example, a semaphore might be used to ensure that two processes cannot use a printer at the same time. The semaphore mechanism first grants exclusive access to one process and then to the other so that the printer does not receive a garbled mix from the two processes. Implement a `Semaphore` class that enforces synchronization on files so that a process is ensured exclusive access to a file. The class should have methods that *set* a semaphore for a specified file, that *release* a semaphore protecting a specified file, and that *test* whether a semaphore is currently protecting a specified file.

5.8. Implement an interactive `Calculator` class that accepts as input an arithmetic expression such as

    25 / 5 + 4

and then evaluates the expression, printing the value. In this example, the output would be

    9

There should be methods to validate the input expression. For example, if the user inputs

    25 / 5 +

then the output should be an error message such as

```
ERROR: operator-operand imbalance.
```

5.9. Implement a Bag class. A **bag** is like a set except that a bag may have duplicates. The Bag class should have methods to insert and remove elements, to test whether the Bag is empty, to get a count of how many elements are in the Bag, and to search the Bag for a specified element.

5.10. Create a Spaceship class suitable for simulation. One of the constructors should allow the user to specify the Spaceship's initial position in 3-dimensional space, its trajectory, its velocity, its rate of acceleration, and its target, which is another Spaceship. The simulation should track a Spaceship's movement every clock tick (e.g., every second), printing such relevant data as the Spaceship's identity, its trajectory, and so forth.

5.11. Implement a Database class where a Database is a collection of *tables*, which in turn are made up of *rows* and *columns*. For example, the employee table

Employee ID	Last Name	Department	Boss
111-11-1234	Cruz	ACC	Werdel
213-44-5649	Johnstone	MIS	Michaels
321-88-7895	Elders	FIN	Bierski

has three records, each of which has four fields (*Employee ID*, *Last Name*, *Department*, and *Boss*). The class should have methods to

• Create a table.
• Change a table's structure by adding or removing fields.
• Delete a table.
• Add records to a table.
• Remove records from a table.
• Retrieve information from one or more tables using a suitable query language.

5.12. Implement a BankTransaction class that allows the user to

• Open an account.
• Close an account.
• Add funds to an already open account.
• Remove funds from an already open account.
• Transfer funds from one open account to another.
• Request a report on one or more open accounts.

There should be no upper bound on the number of accounts that a user may open. The class also should contain a method that automatically issues a warning if an account is overdrawn.

5.13. Introduce appropriate classes to simulate the behavior of a **local area network**, hereafter **LAN**. The network consists of **nodes**, which may be devices such as personal computers, workstations, FAX machines, telecommunications switches, and so forth. A LAN's principal job is to support data communications among its nodes. The user of the simulation should, at a minimum, be able to

- Enumerate the nodes currently on the LAN.
- Add a new node to the LAN.
- Remove a node from the LAN.
- Configure a LAN by specifying which nodes are directly connected.
- Specify packet size, which is the size in bytes of a message sent from one node to another.
- Send a packet from one specified node to another.
- Broadcast a packet from one node to all others.
- Track LAN statistics such as the average time it takes a packet to reach the most distant node on the LAN.

5.14. Implement a `Schedule` class that produces a conflict-free, maximum-size subset of activities given an input set of activities together with the start and finish times for each activity. The conflict-free subset, together with the start and finish times, is a schedule. The schedule is conflict-free when, given any two distinct activities, one finishes before the other starts. For example, given the input set

Activity	Start Time	Finish Time
A1	6	10
A2	1	5
A3	1	6
A4	9	12
A5	5	7
A6	6	14
A7	3	7
A8	10	14
A9	13	16

an optimal `Schedule` is

Activity	Start Time	Finish Time
A2	1	5
A5	5	7
A4	9	12
A9	13	16

Given the input set, it is impossible to produce a `Schedule` of five or more non-conflicting activities. The class should include methods for creating, destroying, revising, and combining Schedules. *Hint*: Iterate through the activities, picking in each iteration the activity with the minimum finish time that does not conflict with any previously selected activity for the Schedule.

5.15. Implement a SymbolTable class. A **symbol table** lists all identifiers (e.g., function and variable names) in a program's source code together with pertinent information such as the identifier's data type, its role within the program (e.g., whether the identifier is a function name, variable name, or a label), and its position in a source code file (e.g., a line number designating the line in which the identifier occurs). The class should have methods to allow the user to specify one or more source files from which the SymbolTable is to be built. There also should be methods for displaying and editing a SymbolTable.

5.16. Implement a RegExp class to represent **regular expressions**, which are used in pattern matching. A regular expression is a character string that consists of ordinary and special characters. For example, the regular expression

        aRgT

matches only other strings with exactly these four characters in this order. Regular expressions are more interesting and useful when they include special characters such as these:

Special Character	What It Matches
.	Any character.
[<list>]	Any character in list. For instance, [aBc] matches a, B, or c.
[^<list>]	Any character not in list.
[<X>-<Y>]	Any character in range X to Y. For instance, [a-c] matches a, b, or c.
*	Zero or more occurrences of the preceding RegExp. For instance, ab* matches ab, abb, abbb, etc.

The class should include methods to create RegExps and to match them against strings.

5.17. Implement an Employee class. The class should restrict construction to Employees with an identifier such as a social security number. The class should represent Employee properties or features such as *last name, first name, marital status, home address, home phone number, salary, office, office phone number, title(s), current projects*, and the like. The class should include methods to access and, where appropriate, to change Employee properties.

5.18. Implement a Product class. The class should allow construction of Products with only a name; with a name and price; and with a name, price, and shelf life in days. A Product also has a manufacturer; a description; flags to signal whether the Product is fragile or edible; and an availability date, which indicates when the Product will first be available for consumer purchase. Add at least three other features to the class implementation. The class interface should include methods to access the implementation.

5.19. The `java.util.Set` interface specifies methods for manipulating a set as an unordered collection of nonduplicate elements. Implement the interface's methods but, for this exercise, ignore the four methods that have a `Collection` as a parameter type and the method that returns an `Iterator`. Also, provide a no-argument constructor and a constructor that creates a set from an array of `Objects`. Use the `java.util.Vector` class for implementation.

5.20. The `java.util.List` interface specifies methods for manipulating a list as a sequence of elements. Implement the interface's method but, for this exercise, ignore the methods that have a `Collection` as a parameter type or that return a `ListIterator`. Also, provide a no-argument constructor and a constructor that creates a list from an array of `Objects`. Use the `java.util.Vector` class for implementation.

6

Inheritance, Interfaces, and Abstract Classes

Chapter Outline

Inheritance in Java has two forms: class inheritance and interface inheritance. The first section explains inheritance for classes, and the third section extends the explanation to interfaces. The basic relationship in class inheritance is between a parent class or **superclass** and a child class or **subclass**. For example, we might design a class called *ProgLang* to represent any programming language and derive one class named *OOProgLang* and another named *PProgLang* to represent object-oriented and procedural languages, respectively. Class inheritance supports a basic form of *code reuse* in that a subclass inherits superclass methods and their supporting fields. Inheritance also enables a powerful construct in object-oriented programming, **polymorphism**. In polymorphism, distinct methods within an inheritance hierarchy have the same signature but class-specific functionality.

An interface is a construct that exemplifies the object-oriented principle of information hiding. A typical interface is a list of methods *declarations* as opposed to *definitions*. Any class that **implements** the interface does so by defining the declared methods in a class-appropriate way. A well-designed object-oriented library allows programmers to "program to the interface"; that is, programmers can focus on the functionality specified in an interface's methods without concern for the implementation details. Interfaces are also a powerful design mechanism that allows distinct classes to have a similar "look and feel." For example, an interface might declare methods named `init` and `cleanup`. Any class that implements the interface would define the two methods to provide functionality appropriate to the particular class. For instance, the `cleanup` method for a window class `MyWin` might dispose of all graphical components, whereas the `cleanup` method for an output class `MyOut` might flush buffers and close files. The programmer who uses the two classes benefits by being able to invoke `cleanup` with the very same high-level goal—disposing of system resources in some appropriate way—and the very same syntax. The code segment

```
MyWin w = new MyWin();
MyOut o = new MyOut();
//...
w.cleanup();
o.cleanup();
```

illustrates the syntax. This chapter examines the general details and uses of interfaces. Chapter 8 studies three important standard interfaces: `Cloneable`, `Runnable`, and `Serializable`.

The emphasis so far has been on **concrete classes**, that is, classes that can be instantiated as *objects*. The standard `Date`, `String`, and `Vector` classes are examples of concrete classes. An **abstract class** cannot be instantiated as an object. An abstract class, like a concrete class, can define methods; but an abstract class, like an interface, can merely declare but not define other methods. The chapter also clarifies the syntax and uses of abstract classes.

6.1   Inheritance Basics

The keyword `extends` is used to derive a subclass from a superclass or a subinterface from a superinterface. This section clarifies basic inheritance by focusing on classes rather than interfaces.

■ **Example 6.1.1.**   The declaration

```
class Mang extends Emp {
  //...members
}
```

illustrates the syntax for `extends`. In this example, `Mang` is a subclass of `Employee`, which in turn is the superclass of `Mang`.   ■

For brevity, we use the term *subclass* to mean *direct subclass* and *superclass* to mean *direct superclass*. For example, the `Mang` class of Example 6.1.1 is a (direct) subclass of `Emp`, which is the (direct) superclass of `Mang`. Because class `Object` is the root of any inheritance hierarchy, `Object` is an **ancestor class** or **ancestor** of `Emp` and `Mang`, and `Emp` and `Mang` are **descendant classes** or **descendants** of `Object`. A superclass is an *immediate* or *direct* ancestor, and a subclass is an *immediate* or *direct* descendant. Figure 6.1.1 illustrates the inheritance relationships of Example 6.1.1, with arrows going from a class to its superclass.

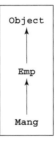

FIGURE 6.1.1   The inheritance relationships among `Mang`, `Emp`, and `Object`.

A subclass inherits the fields and methods of its superclass, which in turn may have inherited fields and methods from its own superclass. A class typically has **local members**, that is, members that are not inherited but rather added locally to the class. Most classes have a mix of inherited and local members.

■ **Example 6.1.2.**   The `Emp` hierarchy in Figure 6.1.2 shows that a subclass inherits the fields and methods of its superclass. Class `Mang` inherits method `setName` and field `name` from `Emp`. Class `Emp`'s public `setName` method assigns a `String` to the private field `name`. The constructors for class `Mang` invoke the inherited `setName` to assign a manager's name to the inherited `name` field. In addition to the inherited members, class `Mang` has one local member, the field `rank`, which represents a manager's executive level within an organization.   ■

```
class Emp {
   Emp() { setName( "Unknown employee" ); }
   Emp( String n ) { setName( n ); }
   public void setName( String n ) { name = n; }
   private String name;
}
class Mang extends Emp {
   Mang() { setName( "Unknown manager" ); }
   Mang( String n ) { setName( n ); }
   private int rank;
}
```

FIGURE 6.1.2   An Emp/Mang inheritance hierarchy.

Constructors are *not inherited*. A constructor is used to construct an object of the particular class that encapsulates the constructor. A later subsection explains the special relationship between subclass constructors and superclass constructors. For now, the main point is that only *fields* and *methods* are inherited.

Although a class can have arbitrarily many ancestor classes, a class can have only *one* superclass or immediate ancestor.

■ **Example 6.1.3.**   The declaration

```
class FunnyNum extends Short, Float { //**** ERROR!
  //...
}
```

contains an error because it tries to derive FunnyNum as a subclass of two classes. Java supports only *single* inheritance for classes, which means that a class cannot have more than one superclass. Java does allow multiple inheritance for *interfaces* so that a subinterface can have more than one superinterface.   ■

■ **Example 6.1.4.**   The class FileDialog (see Section 5.5) is a subclass of Dialog, which is a subclass of Window, which is a subclass of Container, which is a subclass of Component, which is a subclass of Object. The class FileDialog thus has Dialog as its superclass and Dialog, Window, Container, Component, and Object as its ancestors (see Figure 6.1.3).   ■

The Class Object

Every class except java.lang.Object has a superclass. Because Object does not have a superclass, Object is the **root** or **top** of the inheritance hierarchy. Further, every class is derived directly or indirectly from Object. If a class is

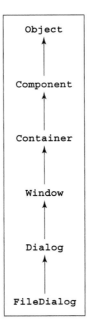

FIGURE 6.1.3   Class `FileDialog` and its ancestors.

defined without an explicit superclass, the default superclass is `Object`. A declaration such as

```
class Alpha { // implicitly extends Object
  //...
}
```

is thus equivalent to

```
class Alpha extends Object { // explicitly extends Object
  //...
}
```

Among the standard classes, some are derived directly from `Object`, whereas others are derived indirectly from `Object`. For example, the class `String` is a subclass of `Object`, whereas the class `Double` is a subclass of `Number`, which in turn is a subclass of `Object` (see Figure 6.1.4).

Some Important `Object` Methods

The class `Object` has nine public methods and two protected methods, which every subclass inherits. Among the nine public methods is `toString`, which returns an appropriate `String` representation of an object. Recall that this method is particularly convenient because the compiler invokes the method to convert arguments of arbitrary class types to `Strings` in function calls that require a `String` argument.

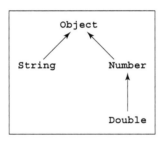

FIGURE 6.1.4 Inheritance relationships among Object, String, Number, and Double.

■ **Example 6.1.5.**   On a sample run of a test program, the statement

```
System.out.println( new Random() );
```

printed

```
java.util.Random@fd78d6b6
```

The only type of object suitable as a `println` argument is `String`. Therefore, the compiler invokes the `toString` method that the `Random` class inherits from `Object`. The `println` statement is thus shorthand for

```
System.out.println( new Random().toString() );
```

The inherited `toString` method prints the object's class, in this case the `Random` class in the `java.util` package, followed by an *at* symbol @ and a hexadecimal integer, which is the value returned by the `Object` method `hashCode`.[†] The important point is that, because of inheritance, *every* object encapsulates a method with the signature

```
public String toString();
```
■

The class `Object` has a `getClass` method that returns a reference to an object of type `Class`, an object that provides information about a particular class. For example, the `Class` instance method `getSuperclass` provides information about a superclass. Because *every* class derives directly or indirectly from `Object`, every object has a `getClass` method.

■ **Example 6.1.6.**   The program

```
import java.awt.*;
class Super {
    public static void main( String[ ] args ) {
```

[†]The `hashCode` method returns an integer suitable for use as a hashtable key. For an object of any class type, the `hashCode()` method must return the *same* integer during an application's execution. However, the integer returned need not be the same from one execution of the application to another. Further, it is possible but highly unlikely that two different objects might have the same hash code.

```
Class c = new FileDialog( new Frame() ).getClass();
while ( c != null ) {
   System.out.println( c );
   c = c.getSuperclass();
}
   }
}
```

prints

```
class java.awt.FileDialog
class java.awt.Dialog
class java.awt.Window
class java.awt.Container
class java.awt.Component
class java.lang.Object
```

The program begins by invoking the getClass method of a FileDialog. A while loop then iterates through the FileDialog's ancestor classes by invoking getSuperclass repeatedly. Initially, local variable c refers to a Class object that represents the FileDialog class. The first output is thus

```
class java.awt.FileDialog
```

After the statement

```
c = c.getSuperclass();
```

executes for the first time, c refers to a Class object representing the superclass of FileDialog, which is Dialog. On the loop's last iteration, c refers to a Class object that represents Object. Because Object has no superclass, the statement

```
c = c.getSuperclass();
```

assigns null to c and the loop terminates.

Scope and Inheritance

The rules of scope apply to inheritance. For example, the class declaration of Mang

```
class Mang extends Emp {
   //...members
}
```

requires that superclass Emp be visible to subclass Mang. If superclass Emp has *package* scope, then Emp must be in the same package as Mang for the declaration to work.

If classes Emp and Mang are *not* in the same package, then superclass Emp must have *public* scope to be visible in Mang's declaration.

■ **Example 6.1.7.**   Given the class declaration

```
package basicEmp;
class Emp { //*** Note: package scope
  //...members
}
```

the declaration

```
package bigBucksPkg;
import basicEmp.Emp;
class Mang extends Emp { //***** ERROR
  //...members
}
```

generates an error because superclass Emp has only *package* scope and subclass Mang is not in the same package as Emp. The import statement does not remove the error because this statement does not change Emp's scope. The error can be eliminated in two ways. The first way is to make Emp's scope *public*

```
package basicEmp;
public class Emp {
  //...members
}
```

rather than package. The second way is to place Mang in the same package as superclass Emp

```
package basicEmp; //** same package as Emp
class Mang extends Emp {
  //...members
}
```

In the second way, Emp can still have package scope.   ■

Inherited members retain their scope. For example, a public member in a superclass Alpha is likewise public in every Alpha subclass. Recall that a *private* member is visible only with its encapsulating class. Therefore, an inherited private member is *not visible* in the subclass that inherits the member.

■ **Example 6.1.8.**   The code segment

```
class Alpha {
   public void set( int p ) { n = p; }
   private int n;
}
class Zeta extends Alpha {
   public void m() {
      n = 0; //***** ERROR: n is private in Alpha
   }
}
```

contains an error because method m in subclass Zeta tries to access the inherited field n, which is *private* in superclass Alpha. Class Zeta can access n only indirectly, in this case by invoking the public set method also inherited from Alpha. The revised definition of Zeta

```
class Zeta extends Alpha {
   public void m() {
      set( 0 ); // ok, set is public in Alpha
   }
}
```

illustrates.   ■

Scope and Inheritance

To summarize how scope and inheritance interact, we use a sample inheritance hierarchy of three classes (see Figure 6.1.5). The superclass Emp has four members, one apiece with private, package, protected, and public scope. The Emp subclass Temporary employee resides in the same package as Emp, whereas the other Emp subclass Mang resides in a different package. Subclasses Temp and Mang inherit the very same members from superclass Emp but the visibility of these members differs in the subclasses because of package considerations. We consider the Emp members one at a time.

- setName. This public member is visible wherever Emp is visible. Superclass Emp and subclass Temp reside in the same package; hence, Emp and its public method setName are visible in Temp. Although subclass Mang resides in a different package than superclass Emp, superclass Emp has public scope. Therefore, Emp and its public method setName are visible in Mang. Note that Mang has an import statement to avoid using the fully qualified name p1.Emp.

- secCode. This protected member is visible to classes in the same package as Emp, which includes Temp. The protected member is likewise visible to subclasses of Emp, regardless of whether the subclass resides in the same package as Emp. Because p2.Mang is a subclass of p1.Emp, the Emp field secCode is visible in Mang despite the different packages of the two classes.

```
//*** start of Emp.java
package p1;
public class Emp {
   //...constructors
   public void setName( String n ) { name = n; } //** public
   protected int secCode;                         //** protected
   int dept;                                      //** package
   private String name;                           //** private
}
//*** end of Emp.java

//*** start of Temp.java
package p1; //*** same package as Emp
public class Temp extends Emp {
   //...constructors
   public void setWage( double w ) { wage = w; }
   public double getWage() { return wage; }
   private double wage;
   //...other local members
}
//*** end of Temp.java

//*** start of Mang.java
package p2; //*** different package than Emp
import p1.Emp;
public class Mang extends Emp {
   //...constructors
   public void setRank( int r ) { rank = r; }
   public int getRank() { return rank; }
   private int rank;
   //...other local members
}
//*** end of Mang.java
```

FIGURE 6.1.5   A sample inheritance hierarchy with superclass members of different scopes.

- dept. This package member is visible only to classes in the same package as p1.Emp. Therefore, dept is visible in p1.Temp but not in p2.Mang.
- name. This private member is visible only in its encapsulating class, Emp. The member is not visible in any subclass, including Temp and Mang. To access a private member such as name, a subclass requires access to an *inherited* method such as setName.

Figure 6.1.6 summarizes the visibility of inherited members in the subclasses of Figure 6.1.5.

Member	Scope in `p1.Emp`	Visible in `p1.Temp`?	Visible in `p2.Mang`?
setName	Public	Yes	Yes
secCode	Protected	Yes	Yes
dept	Package	Yes	No
name	Private	No	No

FIGURE 6.1.6   Visibility of members in the sample hierarchy of
Figure 6.1.5.

Changing the Scope of an Inherited Member

A subclass can redefine or **override** an inherited method, which thereby enables
polymorphism (see Section 6.2). Of interest here is how a subclass can change the
scope of any inherited member, whether method or field. The general principle is that
a subclass can *increase* rather than *decrease* the scope of an inherited member.

■ **Example 6.1.9.**   The code segment

```
class Alpha { //**** superclass
   private void m() { /*...*/ } //*** private scope
   public void p() { /*...*/ }  //*** public scope
}
class Beta extends Alpha { //**** Alpha subclass
   public void m() { /*...*/ }   //** ok, private to public
   private void p() { /*...*/  } //**** ERROR!
}
```

illustrates the error of reducing the scope of an inherited member, in this case
the method p, which is `public` in the superclass `Alpha` but then redefined as
`private` in the subclass `Beta`. The superclass method m is `private` in `Alpha`
but redefined as `public` in the subclass `Beta`. Because m's scope is increased
rather than decreased in the subclass, the redefinition is allowed.   ■

The scope of superclass members is typically *not* changed in a subclass. Chapter 8
clarifies a common exception by explaining why a subclass of `Object` might redefine
the `clone` method as `public`. In class `Object`, the `clone` method is `protected`.

Constructors under Inheritance

The `Tester` program in Figure 6.1.7 outputs

```
Top()
Mid()
Bot()
```

```
class Top {
   public Top() { System.out.println( "Top()" ); }
}
class Mid extends Top {
   public Mid() { System.out.println( "Mid()" ); }
}
class Bot extends Mid {
   public Bot() { System.out.println( "Bot()" ); }
}
public class Tester {
   public static void main( String[ ] args ) {
      new Bot();
   }
}
```

FIGURE 6.1.7   A program to illustrate constructors under inheritance.

The hierarchy consists of three classes: superclass Top has a subclass Middle, which in turn has a subclass Bottom. Each class has a public no-argument constructor with a print statement for tracing flow of control. After explaining the output, we modify the hierarchy to highlight how constructors behave under inheritance.

Although method main creates an unreferenced Bot object, the Bot constructor's print statement does not execute until *after* the print statements of its two immediate ancestors have executed. In particular, the Top print statement executes first, which is followed by the Mid print statement, which is then followed by the Bot print statement. The reason is that the compiler in effect changes the Bot constructor's body from

```
public Bot() {
   System.out.println( "Bot()" );
}
```

to

```
public Bot() {
   super(); //**** invoke superclass no-argument constructor
   System.out.println( "Bot()" );
}
```

Similarly, the Mid no-argument constructor's body changes, in effect, from

```
public Mid() {
   System.out.println( "Mid()" );
}
```

to

```
public Mid() {
   super();
   System.out.println( "Mid()" );
}
```

Recall that super is a reference to an object's superclass. The syntax

```
super();
```

invokes the no-argument constructor of an object's superclass. Accordingly, the statement

```
super();
```

in a Bot constructor invokes Mid(), whereas the same statement in a Mid constructor invokes Top().

The class Top's constructor also invokes its superclass's no-argument constructor. The Top no-argument constructor is changed in effect from

```
public Top() {
   System.out.println( "Top()" );
}
```

to

```
public Top() {
   super();
   System.out.println( "Top()" );
}
```

Class Top is declared without an explicit superclass, which therefore defaults to Object. In the body of Top constructor, the statement

```
super();
```

thus invokes Object's no-argument constructor. Note that the invocation of super() occurs as the *first* statement in each constructor's body. The underlying rule now can be stated explicitly:

- *All* constructors (except for the Object constructor) must invoke a superclass constructor. The invocation must occur as the *first statement* in the constructor's body. If the programmer does not include such a statement, the compiler, in effect, inserts

  ```
  super();
  ```

  as the first statement in the constructor's body.

This rule ensures that, in the construction of a subclass object, a superclass constructor will be invoked to construct and initialize the superclass-part of the object before the subclass constructor constructs and initializes the subclass-part of the object. For example, consider the simple hierarchy shown in Figure 6.1.8, which sketches a two-level hierarchy consisting of superclass Book and a subclass Textbook. A Textbook

```
class Book {
    public Book() { /*...*/ }
    public Book( String TITLE,
                 String ISBN,
                 String PUB,
                 Date    PUBDATE ) { /*...*/ }
    //...methods
    private String title;
    private String ibsn;
    private String publisher;
    private Date dateOfPub;
    //...other fields
}
class Textbook extends Book {
    //...constructors
    //...methods
    private String level;        // freshman, sophomore, etc.
    private String academicArea; // biology, computer science, etc.
    //...other fields
}
```

FIGURE 6.1.8   A Book-Textbook hierarchy.

object is a *composite object* in that it has a Book-part and a local Textbook-part (see Figure 6.1.9). When a Textbook object is constructed, a Book constructor should

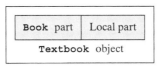

FIGURE 6.1.9   Depiction of a Textbook object as a composite object.

construct the specifically Book-part of the object and initialize such Book-specific fields as title and publisher. The Textbook constructors should construct the specifically Textbook-part of the object and initialize Textbook-specific fields such as level. Further, the Book construction and initialization should occur *first*. For instance, we can imagine how a Textbook constructor might determine a textbook's academicArea by looking up its title in a database table that contains title/area pairs. In this case, a Book constructor must initialize title before a Textbook constructor initializes academicArea.

■ **Example 6.1.10.**   The revised `Tester` program in Figure 6.1.10 amends the program in Figure 6.1.7 by adding a parameterized constructor to the classes Top, Mid, and Bot. Method `main` now creates an unreferenced Bot object by invoking

```
class Top {
   public Top() { System.out.println( "Top()" ); }
   public Top( String s ) { System.out.println( "Top( " + s + " )" ); }
}
class Mid extends Top {
   public Mid() { System.out.println( "Mid()" ); }
   public Mid( String s ) { System.out.println( "Mid( " + s + " )" ); }
}
class Bot extends Mid {
   public Bot() { System.out.println( "Bot()" ); }
   public Bot( String s ) { System.out.println( "Bot( " + s + " )" ); }
}
public class Tester {
   public static void main( String[ ] args ) {
       new Bot( "foo" );
   }
}
```

FIGURE 6.1.10   A revision of the program in Figure 6.1.7.

the parameterized rather than the no-argument constructor. The revised program outputs

```
Top()
Mid()
Bot( foo )
```

Once again

```
super();
```

executes as the *first* statement in all of the constructors because none of the constructors explicitly invokes a superclass constructor. Therefore, the parameterized Bot constructor invokes the Mid no-argument constructor, which in turn invokes the no-argument Top constructor.   ■

■ **Example 6.1.11.**   Figure 6.1.11 shows a final revision of the `Tester` program. In this version, the parameterized Bot and Mid constructors explicitly invoke their parameterized superclass constructors, passing along the `String` parameter. Method `main` again constructs an unreferenced Bot object by invoking the Bot parameterized constructor. The program outputs

```
class Top {
   public Top() { System.out.println( "Top()" ); }
   public Top( String s ) { System.out.println( "Top( " + s + " )" ); }
}
class Mid extends Top {
   public Mid() { System.out.println( "Mid()" ); }
   public Mid( String s ) {
      super( s ); //**** explicitly invoke a superclass constructor
      System.out.println( "Mid( " + s + " )" );
   }
}
class Bot extends Mid {
   public Bot() { System.out.println( "Bot()" ); }
   public Bot( String s ) {
      super( s ); //**** explicitly invoke a superclass constructor
      System.out.println( "Bot( " + s + " )" );
   }
}
public class Tester {
   public static void main( String[ ] args ) {
      new Bot( "foo" );
   }
}
```

FIGURE 6.1.11   A revision of the Figure 6.1.7 program so that constructors
explicitly invoke superclass constructors.

```
Top( foo )
Mid( foo )
Bot( foo )
```

■ **Example 6.1.12.**   Consider the class

```
class MyDialog extends java.awt.Dialog {
   public MyDialog() {
      title = "My own dialog"; //*** Note: 1st statement
      //...other statements
   }
   private String title;
   //...other members
}
```

The statement

```
MyDialog md = new MyDialog(); //***** ERROR
```

generates an error. The `MyDialog` no-argument constructor does not explicitly invoke a superclass constructor as the first statement in its body. Therefore,

```
super();
```

executes as the first statement in the `MyDialog` no-argument constructor. The problem is that the superclass `Dialog` does not have a public no-argument constructor. The problem can be fixed by having the `MyDialog` constructor explicitly invoke a superclass constructor. For example, the change to

```
class MyDialog extends java.awt.Dialog {
   public MyDialog() {
      super( new Frame(), title = "My own dialog" );
      //...other statements
   }
   private String title;
   //...other members
}
```

eliminates the error because the `Dialog` class has a public constructor that expects a `Frame` window and a `String` title as arguments. Recall that an assignment such as

```
title = "My own dialog"
```

is an *expression* whose value is the `String` representation of *My own dialog*. ■

Name Hiding

Within a class, every field must have a unique name and every method must have a unique signature. *Within an inheritance hierarchy*, however, fields in different classes can have the same name; and methods in different classes can have the same signature. A possible result is **name hiding** in which a class and an ancestor have a field with the same name or a method with the same signature. Name hiding may be deliberate or inadvertent. In either case, the reference `super` can be used to resolve the matter.

■ **Example 6.1.13.**   The classes `Alpha` and `Zeta`

```
class Alpha {
   int x = -999;
}
class Zeta extends Alpha {
   public void m() {
      System.out.println( x ); //*** 1234
   }
   int x = 1234; //** caution: hides super.x
}
```

have fields named x. The local x in Zeta hides the x inherited from Alpha. Therefore, the statement

```
new Zeta().m(); //*** prints 1234
```

outputs 1234, the value of Zeta local field named x. To print both fields, the Zeta method m would have to use the super reference to access the inherited x. For example, given this change to m

```
public void m() {
   System.out.println( x );         //*** 1234
   System.out.println( super.x ); //*** -999
}
```

the statement

```
new Zeta().m(); //*** prints 1234 and -999
```

now prints 1234 and −999.   ■

Name hiding can be overcome by using the reference super to access a superclass member with the same name or signature as a local subclass member. The next section explains why superclass and subclass methods may be given the same signature on purpose.

Disabling Inheritance with the final Modifier

The keyword final has several related uses, two of which have been seen so far. In a field declaration such as

```
final int double pi = 3.1415;
```

the keyword final is used to make the double field pi a constant. A related use such as

```
void m( final String s ) { /*...*/ }
```

marks a parameter as *read-only*. Classes and methods also can be marked as final. We explain final methods in the next section. This subsection explains how subclassing can be disabled by marking the class as final.

■ **Example 6.1.14.** The class SquareMatrix in Figure 6.1.12 represents a **square matrix**, that is, a two-dimensional array in which each dimension has the same size known as the *matrix side*. For purposes of the example, a Square-Matrix's elements are ints. The class is marked as final, thus preventing subclasses of SquareMatrix. The declaration

```
class Zeta extends SquareMatrix { /*...*/ }
```

```
public final class SquareMatrix {
   public SquareMatrix() {
      smatrix = new int[ defaultSide ][ defaultSide ];
   }
   public SquareMatrix( int side ) {
      if ( side <= 0 )
         smatrix = new int[ defaultSide ][ defaultSide ];
      else
         smatrix = new int[ side ][ side ];
   }
   //...other members
   private static final int defaultSide = 4;
   private int[ ][ ] smatrix;
}
```

FIGURE 6.1.12   A class marked as final to disable subclassing.

generates an error because a final class such as SquareMatrix cannot be
extended.   ■

Marking a class as final to prevent subclassing reflects a design decision. The
SquareMatrix class of Figure 6.1.12 is not designed as a potential superclass but
rather as a standalone class for creating square matrices of various sides. By marking
a class as final, a designer thereby notifies potential clients about how the class is
designed to be used.

■ **Example 6.1.15.**   The standard String class is final. Therefore, the
declaration

```
class MyString extends String { /*...*/ } //**** ERROR!
```

is in error because String cannot be extended. The standard System class
is likewise final but the standard Runtime class is not final. Accordingly,
Runtime can be extended but System cannot be extended.   ■

Casting and Type Safety

Inheritance restricts casts among class types. The rules about casting class types can be
explained in terms of object references. In general,

- An object reference of a *superclass type* can refer to a superclass object or
  any subclass object. For example, the class Object has Date as a subclass.
  Therefore, an assignment such as

```
Object obj = new Date(); //*** ok, no cast needed
```

requires no cast. Of course, we ordinarily would use a variable of type `Date` to refer to a `Date` object; but polymorphism requires a superclass reference that may refer to either a superclass or some subclass object.

- An object reference of a *subclass type* cannot refer to a superclass object without explicit casting. The statement

```
Date d = new Object(); //***** ERROR!
```

is therefore in error. An explicit cast

```
Date d = (Date) new Object(); // dangerous
```

is required. Casting a superclass type such as `Object` to a subclass type such as `Date` is known as a **down cast**. Although allowed, a down cast is dangerous. The code segment

```
Date d = (Date) new Object(); // dangerous
long now = d.getTime();        //****** run-time error
```

causes a run-time exception because the object to which d refers is of type `Object`, which does not encapsulate a `getTime` method. Specifically, the code's execution causes a `ClassCastException` to be thrown. In object-oriented terminology, a down cast is not **type safe** and thus may cause a run-time error.

- If two class types are peers—that is, neither is the ancestor or descendant of the other—one type cannot be cast directly to the other. For example, the classes `Date` and `String` are peers in that neither is an ancestor of the other. Therefore, the statement

```
Date d = new String();        //***** ERROR!
```

is in error. An explicit cast

```
Date d = (Date) new String(); //***** ERROR!
```

does not eliminate the error.

The Danger of Down Casts

Although a down cast does not cause a *compile-time* error, such a cast remains dangerous because it can cause a *run-time* error.

■ **Example 6.1.16.**   The code segment

```
String s1 = (String) new Object(); //*** Caution!
String s2 = s1.toLowerCase();      //***** Run-time error
```

compiles but causes a run-time error. The cast in the first statement enables s1 of type String to refer to an Object. The second statement causes a run-time error because an Object does *not* encapsulate the String method toLowerCase. ■

EXERCISES

1. Can a class be created that does not have Object as an ancestor?

2. What is unique about the class Object with respect to inheritance?

3. Declare a class that explicitly extends Object.

4. Explain the error:

```
class Zeta extends Alpha, Kappa { /*...*/ }
```

5. Are constructors inherited?

6. Are fields and methods inherited?

7. Although no overload of the println method expects a Vector argument, the statement

```
System.out.println( new Vector() );
```

compiles and executes without error. Explain how this occurs.

8. Explain why every class has a getClass method.

9. Suppose that a superclass has a public field named num. Does the field remain public when inherited by subclasses?

10. How does *name hiding* occur?

11. Change the code segment

```
class Alpha {
   protected int n;
}
class Zeta extends Alpha {
   public void m( int p ) { n = p; }
   protected int n;
}
```

so that Zeta's method m assigns p to the inherited and the local n.

12. Explain the error:

```
String s = new Object();
```

13. Explain the error:

```
Vector v = (Vector) new Date();
```

14. Change the declaration of class `Alpha`

```
class Alpha { /*...*/ }
```

so that `Alpha` cannot be extended.

15. For the hierarchy

```
class Alpha {
    public Alpha() { print( "Alpha" ); }
    public void print( String s ) { System.out.println( s ); }
}
class Beta extends Alpha {
    public Beta() { print( "Beta" ); }
}
```

what is the output when the statement

```
new Beta();
```

executes?

16. Give an example of why a *down cast* is not type safe?

6.2   Polymorphism

Inheritance enables a powerful object-oriented mechanism known as **polymorphism**, which comes from Greek and means *many forms*. An inheritance hierarchy can have arbitrarily many methods *with the same signature*, although within a class each method requires its own signature. The different polymorphic methods can be invoked using the same syntax.

Polymorphism has two basic requirements. After stating the requirements, we clarify them with a series of examples.

- **Method overriding**. A subclass method must be defined with the *same signature* as a superclass method. The subclass method thereby **overrides** the superclass method. For example, if a superclass defines a no-argument method named m, a subclass also defines a no-argument method named m. The methods have the *same signature* but *different scopes*, as each method is encapsulated in a different class. The definitions of the superclass and subclass versions of m presumably differ so that each class's m performs class-appropriate operations. Method overriding is *deliberate* name-hiding.

- **Method invocation through a superclass reference**. A superclass reference is used to invoke one of the polymorphic methods in a hierarchy. The system determines which method to execute from the data type of the object to which the reference refers.

■ **Example 6.2.1.**   Figure 6.2.1 is the code for the employee hierarchy shown in Figure 6.2.2. The superclass Emp has Temp and Mang as subclasses, and class Mang has CorpOff as a subclass. Each class in the hierarchy defines a no-argument method named hi. The subclasses Temp, Mang, and CorpOff thus *override* the method hi in their respective superclasses.

```
class Emp {
   public void hi() { System.out.println( "Emp greetings." ); }
}
class Temp extends Emp {
   public void hi() { System.out.println( "Temp greetings." ); }
}
class Mang extends Emp {
   public void hi() { System.out.println( "Mang greetings." ); }
}
class CorpOff extends Mang {
   public void hi() { System.out.println( "CorpOff greetings." ); }
}
```

FIGURE 6.2.1   A class hierarchy with overrides of the method hi.

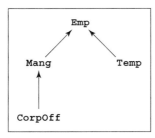

FIGURE 6.2.2   Inheritance hierarchy for the code in Figure 6.2.1.

The program in Figure 6.2.3 randomly constructs objects in the employee hierarchy of Figure 6.2.1. The objects are inserted into a Vector named v. After the object construction, a while loop is used to iterate through the Vector of objects, polymorphically invoking each object's hi method:

```
Enumeration e = v.elements();
while ( e.hasMoreElements() ) {
   Emp t = (Emp) e.nextElement(); // superclass reference
   t.hi(); //**** polymorphic invocation
}
```

```
import java.util.*;
class PolyTest {
    public static void main( String[ ] args ) {
        Random r = new Random();
        Vector v = new Vector();
        //*** generate objects randomly
        for ( int i = 0; i < 12; i++ ) {
            int n = Math.abs( r.nextInt() );
            n = n % 4;      // n = 0, 1, 2, or 3
            switch( n ) {
            case 0: //*** Emp
                v.addElement( new Emp() );
                break;
            case 1: //*** Temp
                v.addElement( new Temp() );
                break;
            case 2: //*** Mang
                v.addElement( new Mang() );
                break;
            case 3: //*** CorpOff
                v.addElement( new CorpOff() );
                break;
            }
        }
        //*** invoke polymorphic hi method
        Enumeration e = v.elements();
        while ( e.hasMoreElements() ) {
            Emp t = (Emp) e.nextElement();
            t.hi(); //**** polymorphic invocation
        }
    }
}
```

FIGURE 6.2.3   Polymorphism in the hierarchy of Figure 6.2.1

In the loop body's first statement, the expression

`e.nextElement()`

returns a reference to an `Object`. Because the class `Object` does not have a `hi` method, the reference must be cast to an appropriate type, in this case to `Emp`, which is the data type of the object reference `t`. The critical point is that `t` can refer to an object of *any type* in the `Emp` hierarchy. Accordingly, `t` can refer to a superclass `Emp` object or to subclass objects of types `Temp`, `Mang`, and `CorpOff`. In the polymorphic method invocation

`t.hi();`

the system determines the data type of the object to which t refers and invokes this object's hi method. On a sample run, the program output

```
CorpOff greetings.
Mang greetings.
Emp greetings.
Temp greetings.
Temp greetings.
Mang greetings.
Emp greetings.
Temp greetings.
Mang greetings.
CorpOff greetings.
CorpOff greetings.
Mang greetings.
```

In the loop's first iteration, therefore, t refers to a CorpOff object, whose hi method is invoked. In the second iteration, t refers to a Mang object, whose hi method is invoked, and so forth.

Example 6.2.2. The program in Example 6.2.1 can be modified to exploit the fact that a Vector holds references of type Object, although a particular reference can refer to *any* type of object because every object's type is a subclass of Object. Two modifications are in order:

- Throughout the Emp hierarchy, the hi method is replaced by an override of toString, a method defined in class Object. For example, the Temp class becomes

```
class Temp extends Emp {
   public String toString() {
      return "Temp greetings.";
   }
}
```

The toString method takes no arguments and returns a String reference.
- The while loop in the main method of PolyTest changes to

```
Enumeration e = v.elements();
while ( e.hasMoreElements() )
   System.out.println( e.nextElement().toString() );
```

where v refers to the Vector that holds references to objects in the Emp hierarchy. If the Vector's next element is of type Temp, then Temp's override of toString is invoked. If the next element is of type Mang, then Mang's override of `toString` is invoked, and so forth. Recall that the `println` statement can be simplified to

```
System.out.println( e.nextElement() );
```                                    ■

The power of polymorphism becomes evident by considering how the `PolyTest` program in Figure 6.2.3 would have to change if polymorphism were not available. The *programmer* would need to include code that determines the data type—`Emp`, `Temp`, `Mang`, or `CorpOff`—of each object as the object is taken from the `Vector`. A test construct such as a `switch` statement then would be used to invoke the class-appropriate greeting method for each object. Polymorphism shifts this work from the programmer to the system, which automatically determines the object's data type and then invokes the corresponding version of `hi`. Polymorphism is a construct that has the run-time system do work that the programmer would otherwise have to do.

Overriding the `toString` Method

Because class `Object` is the ancestor of every class, the methods encapsulated in `Object` are especially important candidates for overrides. One such method is `toString`, whose use has been illustrated several times already. This subsection looks more closely at the advantages to be derived from overriding `toString`.

■ **Example 6.2.3.**   On a sample run, the `CompTester` program in Figure 6.2.4 output

```
Comp@f217ea80
Comp@f237ea80
```

Class Computer, like all subclasses, inherits the `toString` method from its superclass `Object`. The `Object` version of `toString` returns a class name such as `Comp` followed by an @ sign and the object's hash code. Yet the inherited `toString` is not very informative with respect to `Comp` objects. A `Comp`-specific version should be provided so that information about a particular `Comp` object is printed whenever the object's `toString` method is invoked. In other words, class `Comp` should *override* the inherited `toString` method by providing a `Comp`-appropriate definition. A sample override is

```
public String toString() {
    return "\n**************************\n" +
            "Vendor: " + vendor + "\n" +
            "\tProcessor: " + processorVendor + "\n" +
            "\tProcessor speed: " + processorSpeed + "\n" +
            "\tCache size (Kbits): " + cacheSize + "\n" +
            "\tRam size (Mbytes): " + ramSize;
}
```

```
class Comp {
   public Comp( String v,     // vendor
                String p,     // processor vendor
                int    s,     // processor speed in MHz
                int    c,     // total on-chip cache in kilobits
                int    r ) {  // RAM size in megabytes
      vendor = v;
      processorVendor = p;
      processorSpeed = s;
      cacheSize = c;
      ramSize = r;
   }
   //...methods and other members
   private String vendor;
   private String processorVendor;
   private int    processorSpeed;
   private int    cacheSize;
   private int    ramSize;
}
public class CompTester {
   public static void main( String[ ] args ) {
      System.out.println( new Comp( "dell", "intel", 340, 512, 128 ) );
      System.out.println( new Comp( "hp", "hp", 620, 1024, 512 ) );
   }
}
```

FIGURE 6.2.4   A program to illustrate the inherited toString method.

Given this override of toString, a sample run now outputs

```
**************************
Vendor: dell
   Processor vendor: intel
   Processor speed: 340
   Cache size (Kbits): 512
   Ram size (Mbytes): 128

**************************
Vendor: hp
   Processor vendor: hp
   Processor speed: 620
   Cache size (Kbits): 1024
   Ram size (Mbytes): 512
```

■ **Example 6.2.4.**   On a sample run of a program, the statement

```
System.out.println( new java.util.Date() );
```

output

```
Thu Apr 06 22:22:19 CDT 2000
```

because the Date class overrides the toString method inherited from its super-class Object. The override provides a human-readable, string representation of a date.   ■

■ **Example 6.2.5.**   On a sample run of a program, the statement

```
System.out.println( new FileOutputStream( "out.dat" ) );
```

output

```
java.io.FileOutputStream@ad73e564
```

because neither the FileOutputStream class nor its non-Object ancestors override the toString method inherited from Object.   ■

Overriding and Name Hiding

To override an inherited method is to hide it. Invoking the inherited method then requires the reference super.

■ **Example 6.2.6.**   The Comp overload of the toString method inherited from Object (see Figure 6.2.4) can be modified

```
public String toString() {
    return "\n**************************\n" +
            super.toString() + "\n" + //** Object's toString
            "\tVendor: " + vendor + "\n" +
            "\tProcessor: " + processorVendor + "\n" +
            "\tProcessor speed: " + processorSpeed + "\n" +
            "\tCache size (Kbits): " + cacheSize + "\n" +
            "\tRam size (Mbytes): " + ramSize;
}
```

to invoke the superclass—that is, the Object—version. Because Comp extends Object, the expression

```
super.toString()
```

invokes the Object version. On a sample run, the output from the statement

```
System.out.println( new Comp( "hp", "hp", 620, 1024, 512 ) );
```

was

```
**************************
Comp@fcd72497
   Vendor: hp
   Processor: hp
   Processor speed: 620
   Cache size (Kbits): 1024
   Ram size (Mbytes): 256
```
■

Method Overrides Invoking the Superclass Method

Method overrides commonly invoke, as the *first* statement in their bodies, the overriden superclass method. This style mimics the way a subclass constructor invokes a superclass constructor. The underlying idea is the same: superclass-specific tasks should be delegated to a superclass constructor or overriden method, and subclass-specific tasks should be handled by a subclass constructor or method override.

■ **Example 6.2.7.**   Consider the Emp-Mang hierarchy in Figure 6.2.5. Neither class has a public no-argument constructor; hence, the subclass Mang's parameterized constructor explicitly invokes the superclass Emp's parameterized constructor by using the `super` reference. The Emp class has a `writeLog` method, which writes basic Employee information to a file. The Mang class overrides this method to write Mang-specific information, such as the manager's rank and stock options, to a file. The first statement in the Mang's `writeLog` override is

```
super.writeLog();
```

so that the Emp superclass can first write Emp-specific information to the log file. At present, Emp writes only two fields to the log file. More fields might be added to the Emp class, which would require changes to the Emp's `logFile` method. The key point is that such changes should be confined to Emp's version of `logFile`. Subclass versions would simply continue to invoke Emp's version of `logFile` as the first statement in their own overloads. ■

Disabling Overrides with the `final` Modifier

Not all methods can be overridden. For example, methods in a `final` class cannot be overriden because a `final` class cannot be extended. Also, `static` and `private` methods cannot be overriden. If a method otherwise eligible for overriding is marked as `final`, the method cannot be overridden.

■ **Example 6.2.8.**   The `java.lang.Thread` class, whose objects represent independent threads of control running on the JVM, has various `final` methods. For example, the `getName` method, which returns a Thread's name as a `String`, is `final`. The deprecated `stop` method, which stops a Thread from further execution, is also `final`. ■

```
import java.io.*;
import basicIO.BasicOutput;
class Emp {
   Emp( String i, String d ) {
      id = i;
      dept = d;
   }
   public void writeLog() throws IOException {
      if ( logFile == null )
         logFile = new BasicOutput( logName, true );
      logFile.put( id );
      logFile.put( ' ' );
      logFile.putln( dept );
   }
   public void closeLog() throws IOException {
       logFile.close();
   }
   private String id;
   private String dept;
   private static final String logName = "empLog.log";
   protected BasicOutput logFile;
}
class Mang extends Emp {
   Mang( String i, String d, String r, double so ) {
      super( i, d );
      rank = r;
      stockOptions = so;
   }
   public void writeLog() throws IOException {
      super.writeLog(); //*** first invoke superclass writeLog
      logFile.put( rank );
      logFile.put( ' ' );
      logFile.putln( stockOptions );
      logFile.putln( "***************" );
   }
   private String rank;
   private double stockOptions;
}
```

FIGURE 6.2.5   A method override invoking the superclass method.

■ **Example 6.2.9.**   The code segment

```
class Alpha {
   public final void m() { /*...*/ }
}
```

```
class Zeta extends Alpha {
   public void m() { /*...*/ } //***** ERROR!
}
```

contains an error because subclass `Zeta` tries to override a method declared as
`final` in superclass `Alpha`.   ■

Most methods eligible for overriding are not marked `final`. Because polymorphism is such a powerful programming technique, class designers typically encourage
the overriding of the class's eligible methods. If a design decision requires that a particular method not be overridden, the method can be marked as `final` to implement
the decision.

Overriding versus Overloading

Constructor and method *overloading* differs fundamentally from the method *overriding*
that enables polymorphism. We conclude with a summary of the differences:

- *Overloaded* constructors and methods have the *same name* but *different signatures*. The code segment

  ```
  class Alpha {
     public void print( byte b ) { /*...*/ }
     public void print( char c ) { /*...*/ }
  }
  ```

  illustrates an overload of a `print` method. By contrast, *overriden* methods
  have the *same signature*. The code segment

  ```
  class Alpha {
     public void print( byte b ) { /*...*/ }
  }
  class Zeta extends Alpha {
     public void print( byte b ) { /*...*/ }
  }
  ```

  illustrates an override of a `print` method.
- Inheritance is required for *overriding* but not for overloading. A class overrides
  a method precisely by providing a class-specific definition of an inherited
  method with the same signature.
- Constructors can be and often are overloaded because a class typically provides
  several ways to construct objects. Recall, for example, that the `String` class
  overloads its constructors. Some examples are
```
```

```
String();
String( String s );
String( char[ ] value );
String( char[ ] value, int offset, int count );
```

By contrast, constructors *cannot* be overridden because they are not inherited. Methods may be overloaded and overridden.

EXERCISES

1. If a descendant of Object defines the method

```
public String toString() { /*...*/ }
```

does the descendant class thereby *override* the inherited toString?

2. Does the code segment

```
Object t = new Date();
System.out.println( t );
```

invoke the Object or the Date version of toString?

3. What is the output?

```
class Alpha {
   public void m() { System.out.println( "Alpha" ); }
}
class Zeta extends Alpha {
   public void m() { System.out.println( "Zeta" ); }
}
class Tester {
   public static void main( String[ ] args ) {
      Alpha obj1 = new Alpha(),
            obj2 = new Zeta();
      obj1.m();
      obj2.m();
   }
}
```

4. What is the output?

```
class Alpha {
   public void m() { System.out.println( "Alpha" ); }
}
class Zeta extends Alpha {
   public void m() {
      super.m();
      System.out.println( "Zeta" );
   }
}
class Tester {
   public static void main( String[ ] args ) {
      Alpha obj1 = new Alpha(),
            obj2 = new Zeta();
      obj1.m();
      obj2.m();
   }
}
```

5. In the code segment

```
class Alpha {
   public void m() { System.out.println( "Alpha" ); }
}
class Zeta extends Alpha {
   public void m( int p ) { /*...*/ }
}
```

does Zeta's method m override the m inherited from Alpha?

6. State the two conditions for polymorphism.

7. Can a constructor be overloaded?

8. Can a constructor be overridden?

9. Can a method be overloaded?

10. Can a method be overridden?

11. Rewrite the class declaration

```
class Alpha {
   public void m() { /*...*/ }
}
```

so that m cannot be overridden in any Alpha subclass.

12. Explain why a programmer should not be able to override a private method.

Problem

Construct objects in an Employee hierarchy from records in a text input file, where each record represents a particular Emp object. Allow in-memory Emp objects to be written to a text output file with the same format as the input file. The input and output operations should be polymorphic.

Sample Input/Output

On a test run, the input file

```
E AC98 Hampsten Andy mkt
M B718 Hamm Mia acc VPSales 504
M 449A Rubin Chandra mis director 781
T 22WR Kerr Steve mkt 110.25 234.75
C AA89 Graf Steffie cio mis 9000 500 3000
T 9871 Balboa Rocky acc 8.45 17.05
C GFD1 Daehlie Bjoern org ceo 10000 4500 1000
E 4561 Armstrong Lance mis
E 0091 Belmondo Stefania acc
T 2323 Jordan Michael grd 5001.24 25876.42
E 4431 DiCenta Manuela mis
```

was used to generate eleven employees of different types. In each record, the first field represents the employee type: E for regular employee, M for manager, T for temporary employee, and C for corporate officer. Once constructed, the employees were then written as text records to an output file that was identical in contents to the input file.

In the variable-length input records, fields two through five are present in all records: a 4-character identification code, last name, first name, and department. Manager records have a title field and a count of direct reports, that is, employees who report directly to the manager. Corporate executive records have all of the manager fields and two additional fields: the amount of corporate funds, in millions of dollars, at the executive's discretion for business deals; and the value of annual stock options in thousands of dollars. Temporary employee records have the regular employee fields and, in addition, an hourly and overtime wage. Figure 6.3.1 shows the inheritance relationships.

Solution

The application has four classes in an Employee hierarchy (see Figure 6.3.1), which correspond to the four types of input records. The class EmpRW initiates input and output operations by invoking the polymorphic read and write methods in the Emp hierarchy.

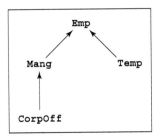

FIGURE 6.3.1 The employee inheritance hierarchy.

Java Implementation

```
//**************************** Begin EmpRW.java
import java.util.*;
import java.io.*;
import basicIO.*;
public class EmpRW {
   //**** Construction: The no-argument constructor prompts
   //      for input and output file names.
   //      The one-argument constructor prompts for output file name.;
   //      The two-argument constructor tries to create the files.
   public EmpRW() {
      inName = promptForFile( "infile" );
      outName = promptForFile( "outfile" );
      allEmps = new Vector();
   }
   public EmpRW( String in ) {
      inName = in;
      outName = promptForFile( "outfile" );
      allEmps = new Vector();
   }
   public EmpRW( String in, String out ) {
      inName = in;
      outName = out;
      allEmps = new Vector();
   }
   //**** Read table records from input file until end-of-file.
   public void read() {
      createInfile();
      try {
         while ( !infile.eof() ) {
            String code = infile.getString().toUpperCase();
            Emp t = null;
            if ( code.equals( "E" ) )
              t = new Emp();
            else if ( code.equals( "M" ) )
              t = new Mang();
            else if ( code.equals( "C" ) )
              t = new CorpOff();
```

```
                    else if ( code.equals( "T" ) )
                      t = new Temp();
                    allEmps.addElement( t );
                    t.read( infile );              //*** polymorphic
                }
            }
            catch( IOException e ) {
                System.err.println( "Can't read  " + inName );
                System.err.println( e );
            }
            try {
                infile.close();
            }
            catch( IOException e ) {
                System.err.println( "Can't close " +  inName );
                System.err.println( e );
            }
        }
        public void write() {
            createOutfile();
            Enumeration e = allEmps.elements();
            while ( e.hasMoreElements() ) {
                Emp t = (Emp) e.nextElement();
                t.write( outfile );
                outfile.putln();
            }
            try {
                outfile.close();
            } catch( IOException ex ) { System.err.println( ex ); }
        }
        public void writeRecords( Vector v ) {
            createOutfile();
            Enumeration rows = v.elements();
            while ( rows.hasMoreElements() )
                outfile.putln( (String) rows.nextElement() );
            try {
                outfile.close();
            } catch( IOException ex ) { System.err.println( ex ); }
        }
        //**** write records to standard error
        public void dump() {
            Enumeration e = allEmps.elements();
            while ( e.hasMoreElements() )
                System.err.println( e.nextElement() );
        }
        //**** set/get for Vector of Employees
        public Vector getEmps() { return allEmps; }
        public void setEmps( Vector v ) { allEmps = v; }
        //**** private methods to prompt for file names and
```

```java
   //     create the files.
   private String promptForFile( String which ) {
      String fname = null;
      try {
         BasicInput stdin = new BasicInput();
         System.out.println( "Please enter the " + which +
                             " file's name: " );
         fname = stdin.getString();
      }
      catch( IOException e ) { System.err.println( e ); }
      finally { return fname; }
   }
   private void createInfile() {
       try {
          infile = new BasicInput( inName );
       }
       catch( IOException e ) {
          System.err.println( "Can't open " + inName +
                              "Please try again." );
       }
   }
   private void createOutfile() {
      try {
         outfile = new BasicOutput( outName );
      }
      catch( IOException e ) {
         System.err.println( "Can't open " + outName +
                             "Please try again." );
      }
   }
   //*** instance fields
   private String inName;
   private String outName;
   private BasicInput infile;
   private BasicOutput outfile;
   private Vector allEmps;
}
//************************** End EmpRW.java

//************************** Begin Emp.java
import java.util.*;
import java.io.*;
import basicIO.*;
public class Emp {
   //*** construction
   public Emp() {
      init( unknown, unknown, unknown, unknown );
   }
   public Emp( String ID ) {     //** unique identifier
```

```
      init( ID, unknown, unknown, unknown );
   }
   public Emp( String ID,        //** unique identifier
               String LNAME,     //** last name
               String FNAME,     //** first name
               String DEPT ) {   //** department
      init( ID, LNAME, FNAME, DEPT );
   }
   //*** overrides
   public String toString() {
      return id + " " + fname + " " + lname + " in " + dept;
   }
   //*** input/output
   public void read( BasicInput in ) throws IOException {
      setId( in.getString() );
      setLname( in.getString() );
      setFname( in.getString() );
      setDept( in.getString() );
      setFieldValues();
   }
   public void write( BasicOutput out ) {
      out.put( "E " );  //*** Emp code
      writeFields( out );
   }
   public void writeFields( BasicOutput out ) {
      out.put( getId() + " " );
      out.put( getLname() + " " );
      out.put( getFname() + " " );
      out.put( getDept() + " " );
   }
   //*** get/set methods
   public void setId( String ID ) {
      id = ID.toUpperCase();
   }
   public String getId() {
      return id;
   }
   public String getLname() {
      return lname;
   }
   public String getFname() {
      return fname;
   }
   public String getDept() {
      return dept;
   }
   public void setLname( String s ) {
     lname = s.toUpperCase();
   }
```

```java
    public void setFname( String s ) {
      fname = s.toUpperCase();
    }
    public void setDept( String s ) {
      dept = s.toUpperCase();
    }
    public String getCode() { return code; }
    public void setCode( String c ) { code = c; }
    public String[ ] getFieldValues() { return fields; }
    protected void setFieldValues() {
        fields[ 0 ] = getCode();
        fields[ 1 ] = getId();
        fields[ 2 ] = getLname();
        fields[ 3 ] = getFname();
        fields[ 4 ] = getDept();
        fields[ 5 ] = NotApplicable;
        fields[ 6 ] = NotApplicable;
        fields[ 7 ] = NotApplicable;
        fields[ 8 ] = NotApplicable;
        fields[ 9 ] = NotApplicable;
        fields[ 10 ] = NotApplicable;
    }
    //*** implementation methods
    private void init( String id, String ln, String fn, String de ) {
        setId( id );
        setLname( ln );
        setFname( fn );
        setDept( de );
        setCode( "E" );
        fields = new String[ totalFieldCount ];
    }
    //*** instance fields
    protected String[ ] fields;
    protected String code;
    private String id;
    private String lname;
    private String fname;
    private String dept;
    //*** class fields
    public static final String NotApplicable = "NA";
    public static final int totalFieldCount = 11;
    protected static final String unknown = "???";
}
//*************************** End Emp.java

//*************************** Begin Temp.java
import java.util.*;
import java.io.*;
import basicIO.*;
```

```
public class Temp extends Emp {
  //*** construction
  public Temp() {
    init( 0.0, 0.0 );
  }
  public Temp( String ID ) {     //** unique identifier
    super( ID );
    init( 0.0, 0.0 );
  }
  public Temp( String ID,        //** unique identifier
               String LNAME,     //** last name
               String FNAME,     //** first name
               String DEPT,      //** department
               double HR,        //** hourly wage
               double OVR ) {    //** overtime wage
    super( ID, LNAME, FNAME, DEPT );
    init( HR, OVR );
  }
  //*** overrides
  public String toString() {
    return super.toString() + " " + getHourly() +
           " " + getOvertime();
  }
  public void read( BasicInput in ) throws IOException {
    super.read( in );
    setHourly( in.getDouble() );
    setOvertime( in.getDouble() );
    setFieldValues();
  }
  public void write( BasicOutput out ) {
    out.put( "T " );
    writeFields( out );
  }
  public void writeFields( BasicOutput out ) {
    super.writeFields( out );
    out.put( getHourly() + " " );
    out.put( getOvertime() + " " );
  }
  //*** get/set methods
  public void setHourly( double h ) {
    hourly = h;
  }
  public double getHourly() {
    return hourly;
  }
  public void setOvertime( double o ) {
    overtime = o;
  }
  public double getOvertime() {
```

```
      return overtime;
   }
   protected void setFieldValues() {
      super.setFieldValues();
      fields[ 9 ] = new Double( getHourly() ).toString();
      fields[ 10 ] = new Double( getOvertime() ).toString();
   }
   //*** implementation methods
   private void init( double h, double o ) {
      setHourly( h );
      setOvertime( o );
      setCode( "T" );
   }
   //*** instance fields
   private double hourly;        //** regular hourly wage
   private double overtime;      //** overtime hourly wage
}
//************************** End Temp.java

//************************** Begin Mang.java
import java.util.*;
import java.io.*;
import basicIO.*;
public class Mang extends Emp {
   //*** construction
   public Mang() {  //*** super() invoked automatically
      init( unknown, 0 );
   }
   public Mang( String ID ) {    //** unique identifier
      super( ID );
      init( unknown, 0 );
   }
   public Mang( String ID,       //** unique identifier
                String LNAME,    //** last name
                String FNAME,    //** first name
                String DEPT,     //** department
                String TITLE,    //** title
                int    RPTS ) {  //** direct reports
      super( ID, LNAME, FNAME, DEPT );
      init( TITLE, RPTS );
   }
   //*** overrides
   public String toString() {
      return super.toString() + " " + title + " " + dirReports;
   }
   //*** input/output
   public void read( BasicInput in ) throws IOException {
      super.read( in );
      setTitle( in.getString() );
```

```
        setDirectReports( in.getInt() );
        setFieldValues();
     }
     public void write( BasicOutput out )  {
        out.put( "M " );
        writeFields( out );
     }
     public void writeFields( BasicOutput out ) {
        super.writeFields( out );
        out.put( getTitle() + " " );
        out.put( getDirectReports() + " " );
     }
     //*** get/set methods
     public void setTitle( String t ) {
        title = t.toUpperCase();
     }
     public String getTitle() {
        return title;
     }
     public void setDirectReports( int n ) {
        dirReports = n;
     }
     public int getDirectReports() {
        return dirReports;
     }
     protected void setFieldValues() {
        super.setFieldValues();
        fields[ 5 ] = getTitle();
        fields[ 6 ] = new Integer( getDirectReports() ).toString();
     }
     //*** implementation methods
     private void init( String t, int dr ) {
        setTitle( t );
        setDirectReports( dr );
        setCode( "M" );
     }
     //*** instance fields
     private String title;        //** official company title
     private int dirReports;      //** number of direct reports
  }
  //*********************** End Mang.java

  //*********************** Begin CorpOff.java
  import java.util.*;
  import java.io.*;
  import basicIO.*;
  public class CorpOff extends Mang {
     //*** construction
     public CorpOff() {
```

```java
        init( 0.0, 0.0 );
    }
    public CorpOff( String ID ) {     //** unique identifier
        super( ID );
        init( 0.0, 0.0 );
    }
    public CorpOff( String ID,        //** unique identifier
                    String LNAME,     //** last name
                    String FNAME,     //** first name
                    String DEPT,      //** department
                    String TITLE,     //** title
                    int    RPTS,      //** direct reports
                    double DISC,      //** discretionary funds
                    double OPTS ) {   //** options value
      super( ID, LNAME, FNAME, DEPT, TITLE, RPTS );
      init( DISC, OPTS );
    }
    //*** overrides
    public String toString() {
        return super.toString() + " " + getDiscretionary() +
                              " " + getOptions();
    }
    public void read( BasicInput in ) throws IOException {
        super.read( in );
        setDiscretionary( in.getDouble() );
        setOptions( in.getDouble() );
        setFieldValues();
    }
    public void write( BasicOutput out ) {
        out.put( "C " ); //*** CorpOff code
        writeFields( out );
    }
    public void writeFields( BasicOutput out ) {
        super.writeFields( out );
        out.put( getDiscretionary() + " " );
        out.put( getOptions() + " " );
    }
    //*** get/set methods
    public void setDiscretionary( double n ) {
        disc = n;
    }
    public double getDiscretionary() {
        return disc;
    }
    public void setOptions( double n ) {
        opts = n;
    }
    public double getOptions() {
        return opts;
```

```
   }
   protected void setFieldValues() {
      super.setFieldValues();
      fields[ 7 ] = new Double( getDiscretionary() ).toString();
      fields[ 8 ] = new Double( getOptions() ).toString();
   }
   //*** implementation methods
   private void init( double d, double o ) {
      setDiscretionary( d );
      setOptions( o );
      setCode( "C" );
   }
   //*** instance fields
   private double disc; // discretionary funds in millions
   private double opts; // options per year in thousands
}
//************************** End CorpOff.java
```

Discussion

The application's class is EmpRW, which provides methods to read and write records
that represent objects in an Employee hierarchy. The polymorphic input and output
operations can be clarified by focusing on three sample classes in the hierarchy:

- Emp, which is at the root of the employee inheritance hierarchy and which
  defines read for reading records and write and writeFields for writing
  records.
- Mang, which is an Emp subclass that overrides read, write, and writeFields.
  Each Emp descendant overrides read, write, and writeFields.
- EmpRW, which opens the input and output files and initiates the polymorphic
  input and output operations on these files.

The EmpRW class has three constructors. The two-argument constructor expects
the names of the input and output files. The one-argument constructor expects the
name of the input file and prompts for the name of the output file. The no-argument
constructor prompts for the input and output file names. The constructors invoke the
private method createFiles to create a BasicInput object and a BasicOutput
object (see Section 5.4) associated with a disk file.

The public EmpRW method named read initiates the polymorphic input operations. The method reads a record from an input file and then checks the first field,
which is a code: E for Emp, M for Mang, and so on. The code segment

```
   String code = infile.getString().toUpperCase();
   Emp t = null;
   if ( code.equals( "E" ) )
      t = new Emp();
   else if ( code.equals( "M" ) )
      t = new Mang();
```

```
else if ( code.equals( "C" ) )
  t = new CorpOff();
else if ( code.equals( "T" ) )
  t = new Temp();
allEmps.addElement( t );
t.read( infile );
```

occurs in a loop that reads input records until end-of-file. Note that object reference
t is of type Emp, the root class in the inheritance hierarchy, so that t can refer to an
instance of any class in the hierarchy. The field allEmps refers to a Vector in which
the employee objects are stored. The statement

```
t.read( infile );
```

invokes the polymorphic read method defined in each class within the Emp hierarchy.
    Consider the case in which t refers to a Mang object. The Mang class's override
of read

```
public void read( BasicInput in ) throws IOException {
   super.read( in );
   setTitle( in.getString() );
   setDirectReports( in.getInt() );
}
```

first invokes the superclass read, in this case the Emp version, which is responsible
for reading from the current input record the four fields common to every Employee:
identification number, last name, first name, and department. The Mang override of
read then reads from the current input record the Mang-specific fields: the manager's
title and the number of employees who report directly to the manager. In all of the
descendant classes, the override of read first invokes the superclass version and then
performs subclass-specific input operations.
    The polymorphic output is handled in a similar manner. The EmpRW method
named write iterates through a Vector of employees, polymorphically invoking each
employee object's write method. For example, the Mang class's write first writes the
code M to the output file and then invokes writeFields to write the remaining fields
to the output record:

```
public void writeFields( BasicOutput out ) {
   super.writeFields( out );
   out.put( getTitle() + " " );
   out.put( getDirectReports() + " " );
}
```

The pattern is similar to the polymorphic read: first the superclass version of write-
Fields is invoked and then Mang-specific fields are written.

If additional classes are added to the Emp hierarchy, the resulting complexity of input and output operations can be distributed as follows:

- The EmpRW method named read must be changed to construct instances of the new classes. For example, if a Consultant class were added, the code

```
else if ( code.equals( "O" ) )
    t = new Consultant();
```

would be added. However, the polymorphic invocation of an employee object's read method would not change at all. Further, the EmpRW method named write would not change.
- The newly added class would override read, write, and writeFields in the appropriate manner. For example, the Consultant class would override these methods to handle Consultant-specific input and output operations. No changes would be required to the input and output methods in the other classes.

The EmpRW class and the classes in the Emp hierarchy have public methods designed to support graphical editing of employee records (see the Sample Application in Section 7.6). For example, the EmpRW method named write writes employee records by iterating through a Vector of object references in the Emp hierarchy and creating a string record to represent each object. By contrast, the EmpRW method named writeRecords expects a Vector of references to Strings, each of which already represents an employee record. Each class in the Emp hierarchy also has the method pair getFieldValues and setFieldValues, which will be useful later in building a graphical editor for Employee records.

EXERCISES

1. Run a client to test the sample application.
2. In the Emp hierarchy, are the read and write methods both polymorphic?
3. In the Emp hierarchy, the polymorphic read methods in the subclasses first invoke the superclass read method before performing their own input. Explain the design considerations that motivate this programming practice.

6.4   Interfaces

A fundamental concept in object-oriented programming is information hiding, which rests upon the distinction between a *hidden* implementation and an *exposed* interface. Java formalizes this distinction with the interface construct. (interface is a keyword.) An interface typically consists of *declarations* of related methods, although an interface also may contain `static` and `final` fields, that is, fields that represent constants. In any case, all interface members are *public*. A class that `implements` an interface typically provides *definitions* for the methods declared in the interface. (`implements` is a keyword.) If a class implements an interface by defining all of the methods declared in the interface, these methods are then part of what the class *exposes* rather than hides.

■ **Example 6.4.1.**   The `java.lang.Runnable` interface

```
public abstract interface Runnable {
   public abstract void run();
}
```

declares a single method named `run`. The keyword `abstract` occurs twice. In the interface declaration, the term `abstract` signals that the interface contains only `abstract` methods, that is, methods that are *declared but not defined*. For emphasis, the interface's single method is also marked as `abstract`. Both occurrences of `abstract` are optional. All `interface` methods are `abstract` regardless of whether the term `abstract` occurs. In more basic terms, an interface is abstract because an interface cannot be instantiated as an object.

The standard class `java.lang.Thread` implements the `Runnable` interface:

```
public class Thread extends Object implements Runnable {
  public void run() { /*...*/ }  //** implementation
  //...
}
```

Class `Thread` defines the method `run` by providing a method body. A `Thread` object represents a thread of control running on the JVM; hence, `Thread` objects can be used to build multithreaded applications. For a `Thread` to run is for the statements in its `run` method to execute. The `run` method is a **pure callback**, that is, a method that the *system* rather than the program itself invokes. Section 8.4 examines the `Runnable` interface and the `Thread` class in more detail.   ■

■ **Example 6.4.2.**   The `java.io.DataInput` interface

```
public abstract interface DataInput {
    public abstract boolean readBoolean() throws IOException;
    public abstract byte readByte() throws IOException;
    //...other method declarations
}
```

contains 15 method declarations. The class `java.io.DataInputStream`

```
public class DataInputStream extends FilterInputStream
                                implements DataInput {
   //...
}
```

implements the `DataInput` interface and provides definitions for the 15 methods listed in this interface. The `java.io` class `RandomAccessFile` also implements the `DataInput` interface. ■

■ **Example 6.4.3.**   The `java.awt.Adjustable` interface

```
public abstract interface Adjustable {
    public static final int HORIZONTAL;
    public static final int VERTICAL;
    //...method declarations
}
```

illustrates that an interface may contain field constants, that is, variables that are `static` and `final`. The `java.awt.Scrollbar` class implements this interface, whose declared methods contain the core functionality of a scrollbar.

The `Runnable`, `DataInput`, and `Adjustable` interfaces shown in Example 6.4.1, Example 6.4.2, and Example 6.4.3 have public scope. An `interface`, like a class, has either package or public scope. For example, the interface

```
interface Sample {
   //...
}
```

has package scope because the interface is not explicitly declared public.

Interfaces and Inheritance

One interface can extend another, with the subinterface inheriting the members of the superinterface. The code segment

```
interface Inter1 {
   //...
}
interface Inter2 extends Inter1 {
   //...
}
```

illustrates. In this example, interface `Inter2` now includes all of `Inter1`'s members together with any local members of its own.

One interface cannot implement another. Indeed, an *interface* never implements—that is, defines—any methods at all. The code segment

```
interface Inter1 {
    //...
}
interface Inter2 implements Inter1 { //***** ERROR
    //...
}
```

illustrates the error of trying to have one interface implement rather than extend another.

Although Java supports only *single inheritance* for *classes*, Java supports *multiple inheritance* for *interfaces*. A subinterface thus can have multiple superinterfaces, although a subclass can have only one superclass.

■ **Example 6.4.4.**   The code segment

```
interface FileReadIF { /*...*/ }
interface FileWriteIF { /*...*/ }
interface FileIF extends FileReadIF, FileWriteIF {
    //...
}
```

illustrates the syntax. In this example, the `FileIF` interface inherits whatever method declarations and constants are present in the `FileReadIF` and `FileWriteIF`. As usual, the `FileIF` also may add local method declarations and constants to the inherited ones.   ■

Every class except `Object` extends exactly one other class. However, a class may *implement* arbitrarily many interfaces. For example, the `java.util.GregorianCalendar` class does not implement any interfaces. Some classes implement more than one interface. For example, the `java.util.Date` class implements the `java.io.Serializable` and the `java.lang.Cloneable` interfaces. Many standard classes implement both the `Cloneable` and `Serializable` interfaces, which Sections 8.1 and 8.2 discuss in detail.

Interfaces as Reference Data Types

An interface is not a class and, therefore, cannot be instantiated as an object. For example, the `java.util.Set` interface declares methods to model a **set**, which is a collection of elements with no duplicates.[†] The expression

---

[†]Although a mathematical set can be infinite and has unordered elements, the `Set` implementations are obviously finite and the `TreeSet` implementation sorts the elements in natural order (e.g., strings are sorted lexicographically).

```
new Set()  //***** ERROR: Set is an interface, not a class
```

is thus in error. However, an interface can be the data type of an *object reference*.

■ **Example 6.4.5.**   Recall that the `java.util` package has two classes that implement the `Set` interface, `HashSet` and `TreeSet`. The statements

```
Set s1 = new HashSet();
Set s2 = new TreeSet();
```

declare two object references s1 and s2 of the interface type `Set`. Reference s1 refers to a `HashSet` object, whereas reference s2 refers to a `TreeSet` object. Because s1 and s2 are of the *same* type, each can be used to invoke exactly the same methods. The code segment

```
Set s1 = new HashSet();
Set s2 = new TreeSet();
//...insert elements into the Sets
// get the size of each Set
int n1 = s1.size();
int n2 = s2.size();
```

illustrates how s1 and s2 can be used to invoke the `size` method declared in the `Set` interface.

References s1 and s2 could have been declared as `HashSet` and `TreeSet` types, respectively. However, the two classes `HashSet` and `TreeSet` are merely *different implementations* of the `Set` interface. Neither `HashSet` nor `TreeSet` exposes any public members other than constructors and the methods declared in the `Set` interface. In effect, these two classes represent hidden implementations of their shared—and public—`Set` interface. Declaring references s1 and s2 as `Sets` signals that `Set` methods are sufficient for manipulating whichever `Set` implementation the programmer selects. Recall, too, that the `HashSet` and `TreeSet` implementations differ in the efficiency of certain operations such as `add` (a `HashSet` adds in constant time but a `TreeSet` does not) and in whether the elements are ordered (a `TreeSet`'s elements are ordered but a `HashSet`'s are not). Nonetheless, both implementations support the very same operations specified in the `Set` interface.

The `Set` represents a (finite) set as an abstract data type. A `Set` client needs to be proficient only in the high-level methods declared in this interface. The choice of `Set` implementations rests exclusively on issues of efficiency and sorted order of elements rather than on functionality.   ■

■ **Example 6.4.6.**   The `java.util.Enumeration` interface declares two methods

```
boolean hasMoreElements();
Object nextElement();
```

The `java.util.StringTokenizer` class implements the interface, and various other classes have methods that return an `Enumeration`. For example, both the `Vector` and `Hashtable` table classes in the `java.util` package age have an `elements` method that returns an `Enumeration`. The code segment

```
Hashtable ht = new Hashtable();
ht.put( "fiorina", "hp" );
ht.put( "gates", "microsoft" );
ht.put( "ellison", "oracle" );
Enumeration e = ht.elements();
while ( e.hasMoreElements() )
   System.out.println( e.nextElement() );
```

reviews how an `Enumeration` can be used to iterate through a `Hashtable`'s elements.   ■

Nested Interfaces

An interface can be nested inside a class or another interface. A nested interface is `static` by default but may be declared so explicitly for emphasis. When the enclosing class is compiled, the nested interface is likewise compiled and occupies a separate *class* file. Nested interfaces are a way to summarize for clients a class's key methods, that is, its public and protected methods. Methods with private and package scope cannot occur in a nested interface. Also, methods declared in a nested interface must be nonstatic. A nested interface, like a regular interface, never contains constructor declarations.

■ **Example 6.4.7.**   The `BasicInput` class of Section 5.4 has eight public methods. The class declaration can be amended to include a nested interface that lists these methods (see Figure 6.4.1). The nested interface, which could occur anywhere in the enclosing class, provides a convenient summary of the methods available to a client.   ■

Application Program Interfaces

This section has emphasized the convenience of interfaces for applications programmers. The acronym API (**A**pplication **P**rogram **I**nterface) has become the common term to describe an interface designed specifically for application programmers. Java's standard packages such as `java.io` provide APIs as collections of particular Java `interfaces` such as `DataInput`, `DataOutput`, and `FileFilter`. Java also provides specialized APIs. For example, the JNI (**J**ava **N**ative **I**nterface) is an interface for C functions that Java programs can invoke to manipulate a particular system's hardware devices.

```
public class BasicInput {
   public BasicInput() throws IOException {
      init( new InputStreamReader( System.in ) );
   }
   public BasicInput( String f ) throws IOException {
      init( new InputStreamReader( new FileInputStream( f ) ) );
      diskFile = true;
   }
   interface BasicInputInterface { //*** implicitly static
      public void close() throws IOException;
      public boolean eof() throws IOException;
      public String getRecord() throws IOException;
      public String getString() throws IOException;
      public byte getByte() throws IOException;
      public int getInt() throws IOException;
      public double getDouble() throws IOException;
      public char getChar() throws IOException;
   }
   //...remaining members
}
```

FIGURE 6.4.1   The BasicInput class with a nested interface.

EXERCISES

1. What are the possible scopes for an interface?
2. Is the keyword abstract required in an interface declaration?
3. What does the keyword abstract signal in an interface declaration?
4. Given that java.lang.Runnable is an interface, why is the statement

        java.lang.Runnable r = new java.lang.Runnable();

in error?
5. Does an interface contain method definitions or declarations?
6. Does a class implement or extend an interface?
7. Can one interface extend another?
8. Is multiple inheritance supported for interfaces?
9. Explain why an interface cannot implement another interface.
10. Can an interface be an object reference's data type?
11. Given that v refers to a Vector, write a code segment that iterates through v and prints each of its elements by using the methods in the Enumeration interface.
12. Must an interface nested inside a class be declared static explicitly?
13. What does API stand for?

14. List the Java `interfaces` that make the API for the input and output operations provided by the `java.io` package.

15. What is JNI?

6.5   Abstract Classes

The focus so far has been on **concrete classes**, that is, classes that can be instantiated as objects by using the `new` operator and a constructor. A concrete class defines or implements *all* of its methods. A class is `abstract` if it fails to define all of its methods. An abstract class cannot be instantiated as an object. In this regard, an abstract class resembles an interface. If class `Abst` is abstract, then any attempt to create an instance such as

```
new Abst()  //***** ERROR: abstract class!
```

is in error.

An abstract class can selectively implement or define methods and, in this regard, resembles a concrete class. So an abstract class can contain a mix of method declarations and definitions. An abstract class, also like a concrete class, can have fields that are `nonstatic` and `nonfinal`.

■ **Example 6.5.1.**   The `java.lang.Number` class

```
public abstract class Number extends Object
                   implements Serializable {
    //...
}
```

is an abstract class that serves as the superclass for such concrete wrapper classes as `java.lang.Byte` and `java.lang.Double`. Although the Double class can be instantiated

```
new Double()  //*** ok, a concrete class
```

the Number class cannot be instantiated

```
new Number()  //***** ERROR: abstract class!
```

Example 6.5.2.   The `java.util.Dictionary` class

```
public abstract class Dictionary extends Object {
    //...members
}
```

is an abstract class. The expression

```
new Dictionary()  //***** ERROR: abstract class!
```

is therefore in error. The `java.util.Hashtable` class extends `Dictionary`. The `Hashtable` class is concrete and, therefore, must implement all of the abstract methods in `Dictionary` such as `isEmpty` and `remove`.   ■

Three Ways to Make a Class Abstract

An abstract class is a bona fide class. For example, every abstract class has `Object` as ancestor. An abstract class can serve as a superclass for another class, abstract or concrete. There are three basic ways for a class to be abstract:

- The keyword `abstract` occurs in the class declaration

```
abstract class Sample { //** abstract
  //...
}
```

or in a method declaration

```
class Sample {
  public abstract m();
  //...
}
```

or in both

```
abstract class Sample {
  public abstract m();
  //...
}
```

- A class implements an interface but fails to define *all* of the methods declared in the interface. For example, the class `Sample`

```
class Sample implements Runnable {
  public void m() { /*...*/ }
  int x;
}
```

does not define the method `run`, which is declared in the interface `Runnable`. Therefore, class `Sample` is abstract and any attempt to instantiate it

```
new Sample()   //***** ERROR: abstract class!
```

is in error. For `Sample` to be a concrete class, it must either define `run` or not implement the `Runnable` interface.
- A class extends an abstract class but fails to define *all* of the undefined methods in this abstract superclass. For example, the class `Sample`

```
class Sample extends Dictionary {
   public void m() { /*...*/ }
   int x;
}
```

is abstract because it fails to define abstract `Dictionary` methods such as `isEmpty` and `get`.

Abstract methods must be public, regardless of whether they occur in an abstract class or an interface. Because abstract classes combine features of concrete classes and interfaces, they tend to have very specialized uses. A good way to learn about their usefulness is to study the standard packages, which are a mix of concrete classes, abstract classes, and interfaces.

Summary of Concrete Classes, Abstract Classes, and Interfaces

Concrete classes, abstract classes, and interfaces represent three different constructs for encapsulating fields and functions. The three constructs present options in the design and implementation of programs and class libraries. The differences among the three can be summarized as follows:

- **Concrete class**. A concrete class encapsulates only *defined* methods and, therefore, can be instantiated as an object. Every concrete class (except `Object`) extends some superclass, whether concrete or abstract, and can implement an arbitrary number of interfaces, including none. A program requires at least one concrete class.
- **Abstract class**. An abstract class can encapsulate a mix of defined and merely declared methods, which means that such a class cannot be instantiated as an object. An abstract class extends a superclass, whether concrete or abstract, and can implement an arbitrary number of interfaces, including none. A program does not require any abstract classes.
- **Interface**. An interface can contain only method declarations and field constants. Because an interface is not a class, an interface cannot be instantiated as an object. Nonetheless, one interface can extend another. A program does not require any interfaces.

EXERCISES

1. What is the difference between an abstract and a concrete class?
2. If `Alpha` is an abstract class, is the expression

```
new Alpha()
```

an error?

3. Can the keyword `abstract` be used to declare a class abstract?

4. If a class has even one abstract method, is the class abstract?

5. Change the declaration

```
class Kappa {
    public Kappa() { /*...*/ }
    public void m() { /*...*/ }
}
```

so that `Kappa` becomes an abstract class.

6. Can an abstract class *define* methods?

7. Can an abstract class *declare* methods?

8. Find at least two abstract classes in the system classes.

9. Is every abstract class a descendant of `java.lang.Object`?

10. Summarize the similarities and differences among a concrete class, an abstract class, and an interface.

11. Suppose that the keyword `abstract` does not occur anywhere in the declaration of class `Alpha`. Explain how `Alpha` still could be an abstract class.

JAVA POSTSCRIPT

Interface Types, Anonymous Classes, and Unreferenced Objects

In a statement such as

```
java.util.Set s = new java.util.HashSet();
```

the interface `Set` is the data type of the object reference `s`, which refers to a `HashSet` object. Because `HashSet` is a *concrete class* and `Set` is an *interface*, it must be `HashSet` that is instantiated as the object to which `s` refers. Nonetheless, the statement illustrates that an interface type can be used in the construction of a *referenced* object, in this case the `HashSet` object to which `s` refers. Interface types also can be used in the construction of an *unreferenced* object.

■ **Example.** The `ActionListener` interface in the `java.awt.event` package declares the method `actionPerformed`, which serves as a callback for *action events* such as button pushes and menu selections. Because `ActionListener` is an *interface*, the statement

```
new ActionListener(); // ERROR: can't instantiate interface
```

is in error. However, the statement

```
new ActionListener() {
   public void actionPerformed( ActionEvent e ) {
      //...body of the method
   }
};
```

is correct. The statement does *not* instantiate an interface as an object but rather constructs an *unreferenced object* of an *unnamed class* that implements the `ActionListener` interface by defining the `actionPerformed` method. Code segments such as

```
import javax.swing.JButton;
import java.awt.event.*;
class Alpha {
   void someMethod() {
      JButton b = new JButton( "Exit" );
      b.addActionListener( new ActionListener() {
         public void actionPerformed( ActionEvent e ) {
            System.exit( 0 ); //*** exit application
         } } );
   }
   //...
}
```

are common. In this example, an unreferenced object is constructed to listen to pushes on the JButton to which b refers. The unreferenced object belongs to an *unnamed class* that implements the `ActionListener` interface by defining the `actionPerformed` method. This unnamed class is an *inner class* (see Java Postscript, Chapter 5) because it is defined inside class `Alpha`.

When the JButton to which b refers is pushed, the unreferenced object's `actionPerformed` method is invoked to terminate the application by calling the `exit` method in the `System` class. The key point is that the code segment does *not* instantiate an interface but rather an object of an anonymous class that implements the `ActionListener` interface. An interface cannot be instantiated as an object.

COMMON ERRORS AND SAFE PRACTICES

1. It is an error to declare a class with more than one superclass. The code segment

```
class Emp extends Person, Worker { /**** ERROR
```

illustrates. Java supports only *single* inheritance for classes but does support multiple inheritance for interfaces.

2. A private member is accessible only in its encapsulating class. It is therefore an error for a subclass to access a private member in its superclass. The code segment

```
class Alpha {
   //...
   private int n;
}
class Zeta extends Alpha {
   Zeta() {
      n = -1; //***** ERROR: n is private in Alpha
   }
}
```

illustrates that inherited private members are accessible in subclasses only through inherited methods that are nonprivate.

3. An inherited member's scope cannot be reduced. In the code segment

```
class Alpha {
   public int n;
}
class Zeta extends Alpha {
   private int n; //***** ERROR
}
```

the subclass Zeta redeclares as private the inherited n, which is public in the superclass. If n had been declared as private in the superclass, subclass Zeta then could redeclare n in any way that increased n's scope. For example, n then could be redeclared as public.

4. If a subclass member has the same name as a member inherited from its superclass, the reference super must be used to disambiguate. The code segment

```
class Alpha {
   protected int n;
}
class Zeta extends Alpha {
   Zeta() {
      super.n = -1; //*** inherited n
      n = -999;     //*** local n or this.n
   }
   protected int n; //*** hides Alpha's n
}
```

illustrates the syntax.

5. A subclass constructor must invoke, as the *first* statement in its body, a superclass instructor. If the superclass has an accessible *no-argument* constructor, the compiler will invoke the no-argument constructor automatically; otherwise, a superclass constructor must be invoked explicitly. Because class `Alpha`

```
class Alpha {
   Alpha( int n ) { /*...*/ }
}
class Zeta extends Alpha {
   Zeta() {
      n = 1; //*** ERROR: no Alpha constructor invoked
   }
   private int n;
}
```

does not have a no-argument constructor, the `Zeta` constructor must explicitly invoke `Alpha`'s parameterized constructor. The code segment

```
class Zeta extends Alpha {
   Zeta() {
      super( -1 ); //** ok, Alpha constructor invoked
      n = 1;
   }
   private int n;
}
```

makes the correction.

6. A `final` class such as `java.lang.String` cannot be extended.

7. A superclass method marked as `final` cannot be overriden in a subclass.

8. Although an object reference of a *superclass type* can refer to a subclass object without casting, the opposite is not the case. The code segment

```
//** Object is the superclass, String the subclass
Object o = new String();          //** ok
String s1 = new Object();         //***** ERROR
String s2 = (String) new Object(); //***** DANGEROUS
```

illustrates. The third statement, although not an error, is dangerous because it is not *type safe*. For example, the statement

```
String s3 = s2.toLowerCase(); //** s2 refers to an Object!
```

would cause a run-time error because `s2` refers to an `Object`, which does not encapsulate the `String` method `toLowerCase`.

9. It is an error to try to instantiate an interface. The code segment

```
interface Sample { /*...*/ }
new Sample(); //***** ERROR: Sample is an interface
```

illustrates.

10. It is an error for one interface to `implement` another interface. However, one interface can `extend` another.

11. It is an error to try to instantiate an `abstract` class. The code segment

```
abstract class AC { /*...*/ }
new AC(); //***** ERROR: AC is abstract
```

illustrates. A class is abstract if declared so explicitly, as in this example; if any of its methods is declared `abstract`; or if the class fails to define a method in any of the interfaces that the class implements.

12. It is an error for one class to `implement` another class, even an abstract class. One class `extends` another but `implements` an interface.

PROGRAMMING EXERCISES

6.1. Implement a `Library` hierarchy with at least a half dozen classes. Consider a *library* to be a collection of literary or artistic materials that is not for sale. In addition to the constructors, the classes should include methods that describe the classes much in the way that a human librarian might describe a class or subclass of materials among the library's holdings. For example, a library might have *rare books* and *modern sculpture* collections.

6.2. Implement a `CardGame` class that represents an ordinary 52-card deck with four suits (hearts, clubs, diamonds, and spades) and 13 cards per suit: ace, king, queen, jack, 10, ..., 2. Represent the deck in any convenient way. Derive a `Bridge` class that includes a method `deal` to divide the deck into four 13-card hands. Derive a `Poker` class that includes a method `deal` to divide the deck into a specified number (between 2 and 7, inclusive) of 5-card hands. After creating the classes, write a test client for the hierarchy.

6.3. For the `CardGame` hierarchy of Programming Exercise 6.2, design an interface `CardGameIFace` that declares methods appropriate for any class in the hierarchy.

6.4. Implement a `Vehicle` class that includes data members to represent a vehicle's make, model, production year, and price. The class interface includes methods that provide appropriate access to the data members. Derive a `Car` class and a `Truck` class from `Vehicle`. Each of these derived classes should add appropriate data members and methods. Also, derive two classes from `Car` that represent particular cars and two classes from Truck that represent particular trucks. Implement a test client to test the hierarchy. Propose other classes to derive from Vehicle.

6.5. Create a Book hierarchy with subclasses such as Reference, Fiction, Periodical, and Textbook. Add appropriate fields and methods to each of these classes. Implement a test client to test the hierarchy.

6.6. Implement a Person class that includes fields to represent name, address, and identification number. The class should have an associated interface with methods that provide appropriate access to the fields. Derive a CollegeStudent class and a Professor class from Person. Each of these derived classes should add appropriate fields and methods. Implement a test client to test the hierarchy.

6.7. Design and implement a Film hierarchy with at least six classes. Provide polymorphic methods to handle input and output so that objects can be created from a file and later saved to a file. Derive from Film additional classes such as ForeignFilm, DirectorCut, SongAndDance, and GreekMyth. Implement a test client to test the hierarchy and, in particular, the overrides.

6.8. Implement an index hierarchy with a base class Entry to represent entries in a book's index. The base class represents a basic index entry such as

```
quark, 234, 512, 901
```

A basic entry consists of a term such as quark followed by the page numbers on which the word occurs. Here are samples of other entry types that should be included in the hierarchy:

```
//*** Sample: proper name followed by pages
Gauss, Carl, 67, 69, 106

//*** Sample: entry with multiple subentries
topology, 46, 78-80
   map-coloring problems, 45-47
   Mordell's conjecture, 107

//*** Sample: entry with descriptive subentry
music, harmony in, 37
```

The hierarchy should have a polymorphic format method that correctly formats a particular entry type as the entry is printed. Write a test client that has an array of references, each of which refers to an Entry or subclass object.

6.9. The No Guarantees Dating Service (hereafter, NGDS) includes, for an extra charge, a breakup service in which NGDS generates a form letter to announce the breakup and handles any subsequent correspondence from the dumpee. The form letter is based on a personality profile that NGDS social scientists put together for each client. The personality categories are

- Normal.
- Slightly Neurotic.
- Passive/Aggressive.
- Comatose.
- Beavis or Butthead.
- Loose Cannon.
- Freddy.

Create an inheritance hierarchy to represent the personality profiles. The base class should have a pure `virtual` method called `dearJohn` that, when invoked, generates a breakup letter appropriate for the personality profile. Write a test client to generate letters for a mix of objects that belong to the different personality classes.

6.10. Design a `Shape` interface that declares methods `draw` and `resize`. Implementing concrete classes should include `Point`, `Line`, `Circle`, `Triangle`, and `Rectangle`. Each concrete class implements the `draw` method to draw an appropriate representation of an object in the class and the `resize` method to change an object's initial size. If you are familiar with Java graphics, provide a graphical implementation of `draw`; otherwise, simulate the actual drawing by printing an appropriate formula for drawing the object.

6.11. Administrative software for computer networks provides various services that require **hosts**—that is, machines on the network—to be polled. A polled host typically responds with its network address and other pertinent information. Create a hierarchy with `Host` as a superclass with an abstract `poll` method whose declaration is

```
public HostInfo poll();
```

The returned `HostInfo` reference contains pertinent information about a host such as its network address; its type (e.g., *applications server, file server, workstation, router, personal computer, print server*, etc.); most recent connect time to network; status (e.g., *active* or *idle*); and the like. Classes derived from `Host` are different types of host such as `Workstation`, `FileServer`, and so forth. Each class derived from `Host` overrides `poll` to return, as a `HostInfo` object, appropriate information about itself. Because `Host` is an abstract class rather than an interface, `Host` can *define* methods. Provide `Host` definitions of `toString` and at least one other method. After creating the necessary hierarchy and auxiliary classes such as `HostInfo`, write a test client.

6.12. Design and implement a `Computer` hierarchy with subclasses such as PC, Work-station, DSP (digital signal processor), and `SuperComputer`. Provide su-percomputer subclasses such as SISD (**S**ingle **I**nstruction stream, **S**ingle **D**ata stream), and MIMD (**M**ultiple **I**nstruction stream, **M**ultiple **D**ata stream). The `Computer` class and its subclasses should provide an override of `toString` and polymorphic methods such as `boot`, which provides instructions for starting the computer, and `shutdown`, which provides instructions for gracefully shutting down the computer.

6.13. Provide an abstract superclass for the `BasicInput` class of Section 4.2. The ab-stract superclass should provide a default implementation for all of the `BasicIn-put` methods with the exception of `getRecord`. To be concrete, `BasicInput` must therefore define `getRecord`. Test alternative definitions of `getRecord`. In one definition a newline character *is* returned as part of the record, where-as in the other definition a newline character *is not* returned as part of the record.

6.14. The `java.util.Iterator` interface declares three methods

```
boolean hasNext(); // tree if iteration has more elements
Object next();     // next object in iteration
void remove();     // removes from underlying collection
                   //   the last Object returned by next()
```

Define a class `DefaultIteration` that implements the three methods. Provide a test class with a method that returns a `DefaultIteration` and write a client to confirm that a `DefaultIteration` object behaves appropriately.

6.15. The abstract `java.lang.Dictionary` class serves as the superclass for con-crete classes such as `java.util.Hashtable` that map keys to values. De-rive a concrete `CoursesAndGrades` class from `Dictionary`. The code seg-ment

```
String courseNum = "CS334"; // Java in a Nutshell
String grade = "A-";        // no one's perfect
CoursesAndGrades cag = new CoursesAndGrades();
cag.put( courseNum, grade );
System.out.println( cag.get( courseNum ) ); // prints: A-
```

illustrates how the put and get methods might be used. Write a test client to show the functionality of `CoursesAndGrades` objects.

Graphics and Event Handling

Chapter Outline

Users of modern applications such as spreadsheets, databases, word processors, browsers, e-mail systems, and communications packages have come to expect a powerful and sophisticated yet straightforward GUI (**G**raphical **U**ser **I**nterface). Because a GUI can be challenging to design and to implement, and because the applications that use a GUI often migrate across computer platforms, GUI portability is highly desirable. Java, unlike many other general-purpose languages, has standard packages for graphics. GUIs written with the standard packages are thereby portable. This chapter examines the fundamental constructs for developing GUIs in Java.

7.1   Overview of the AWT and the Swing Set

Two related packages and their subpackages support graphics. The two main packages are `java.awt` and `javax.swing`, known as the AWT (**A**bstract **W**indow **T**oolkit) and the Swing set, respectively. Many AWT components such as panels rely on **native components**, that is, underlying graphical components that are native to the runtime platform. For this reason, an AWT component on a Unix system may have a different "look and feel" and different behavior than the same AWT component on a Windows NT system or an IBM mainframe.

At the implementation level, an AWT component such as a drawing `Canvas` has a peer graphical object native to the host platform. Yet an AWT component may not need to be identical in appearance and behavior to its peer. In this sense, the peer object carries extra baggage that the AWT component does not need. AWT components with peers thus became known as **heavyweight components**. AWT components on the whole are rudimentary and many of them are heavyweight because their underlying peers are not rudimentary. The Swing set, too, has heavyweight components but only four of them: `JApplet`, `JFrame`, `JDialog`, and `JWindow`. These four components are **top-level windows** in that each serves as a window container for other components.

Although heavyweight components dominate in the AWT, the AWT does have classes such as `Component` and `Container` for building **lightweight components**, that is, components that are not bound directly to native peers. A lightweight component renders itself graphically by drawing lines, filling rectangles with patterns or colors, and performing other primitive graphics operations. A lightweight component thus has more control over its behavior and appearance than does a heavyweight component. Although the AWT can be used to *build* sophisticated lightweight components, the Swing set offers portable, flexible, and powerful lightweight components that are *prebuilt*.

The lightweight Swing set components are derived from the Swing set's JComponent class, which in turn is derived from the AWT's `Component` class. Every descendant of `JComponent` is lightweight. The Swing set's `JButton` and `JTree` classes are two examples. By contrast, the Swing set's `JFrame` extends the AWT's `Frame` rather than the Swing set's `JComponent` class. Figure 7.1.1 sketches the contrast.

Although a GUI can contain any mix of AWT and Swing set components, caution should be used. The problem is that heavyweight components are rectangular in shape and **opaque**, that is, nontransparent. A heavyweight component therefore

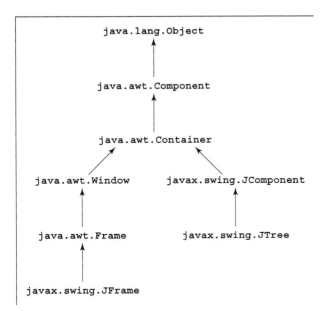

FIGURE 7.1.1   Inheritance of the heavyweight JFrame and the lightweight JTree.

can "show through" a transparent lightweight component that sits on top of it. This chapter emphasizes the use of the Swing set wherever possible, although introductory examples often rely upon the relatively simpler AWT components. At times AWT and Swing set components are deliberately mixed to illustrate how this can be done safely.

The Swing set belongs to the **J**ava **F**oundation **C**lasses or JFC, which also includes support for 2D graphics, printing, accessibility, and "drag and drop" functionality. Swing set classes, especially ones that extend or supercede AWT classes, often begin with the letter J to signal the link between the Swing set and the JFC. For example, the AWT Frame class becomes the Swing set JFrame class and the AWT Button class becomes the Swing set JButton class. Many Swing set components without AWT counterparts also begin with J, however. For example, the Swing set's JOptionPane has no direct counterpart in AWT.

The Model-View-Controller Architecture

The Swing set adapts the **model-view-controller** architecture popularized by Smalltalk and adapted by other major class libraries such as the Microsoft Foundation Classes. Under this architecture, a component such as a button or a list has three main parts: a model, a view, and a controller. The terms can be clarified as follows:

- **Model**. A component's model consists of *state information* that determines how the component behaves. For example, a Swing set JList can be used to present graphically a list of items from which the user can choose. A JList has a *selection model* that determines whether the user can select one or more items at a time. If the selection model is *single selection*, for example, then the user may choose only one item at a time.

- **View**. A component's view consists of its graphical representation. A JList, for example, can have different *look-and-feels* such as the Motif look-and-feel and the Windows look-and-feel. A JList might appear with or without a scrollbar.
- **Controller**. A component's controller consists of the mechanisms that handle events such as mouse clicks and keyboard pushes. A component's controller can be constructed to ignore certain events and to respond in appropriate ways to other events. For example, clicking the mouse on one particular panel in a window might change the panel's background color, whereas clicking the mouse on another panel might be ignored. In summary, the controller is responsible for handling events often generated from a view (GUI) in order to change the underlying model (state).

Common Features in the AWT and the Swing Set

The AWT and Swing set components share architectural features despite the differences between the two packages. These features can be divided roughly into four groups:

- **Constructors**. Almost all of the components have overloaded constructors. For example, the AWT's MenuItem has three public constructors and the Swing set's JMenuItem has five public constructors. Component constructors provide the same underlying functionality—construction and initialization—as constructors in nongraphics classes.
- **Properties**. Recall that pairs of *get/set* methods define a property. For example, all graphical components have the methods

```
public void setBackground( Color background );
public Color getBackground();
```

Together these methods define a background property, which is the component's background color. Recall too that the *set* method's argument is the same type as the *get* method's return type, in this example Color. For boolean properties, the *get* method's prefix changes to *is*. For example, every component has a *visible* property that the methods

```
public void setVisible( boolean f );
public boolean isVisible(); //*** Note: is, not get
```

define. If both methods in a *get/set* pair are public, the property is *read/write*. If the *get* method is public but the *set* method is nonpublic, the property is *read only*. If the *get* method is nonpublic but the set method is public, the property is *write only*—peculiar but possible.
- **Operations**. Not all methods define properties, of course. For example, the Swing set's JMenuItem class has an insertSeparator method for adding

a horizontal separator. The class also has other `insert` methods for adding menu items and `remove` methods for removing them. Methods such as these, which do not define properties but rather provide miscellaneous functionality, define class-appropriate operations.

- **Events**. Components are capable of generating various types of events. For example, clicking a button or selecting a menu item generates an `ActionEvent`, whereas iconifying or deiconifying a window generates a `WindowEvent`. Components can interact by generating and handling events, as the next section explains.

Next we examine event-driven programming in general and the **event model** at the core of AWT and Swing set graphics. The event model is foundational for graphics and for *beans* (see Section 10.1). We then examine various components and some useful containers that can embed then. After a sample application, we focus on the model-view-controller architecture to gain a deeper understanding of how Swing set components work.

EXERCISES

1. What is meant by a *heavyweight component*?
2. What is meant by a *lightweight component*?
3. Explain what role a *native peer* plays in graphics.
4. What does AWT stand for?
5. What does JFC stand for?
6. Are the Swing set and JFC synonymous?
7. What is the main package for AWT components?
8. What is the main package for Swing set components?
9. Does a subclass of `JComponent` instantiate lightweight or heavyweight components?
10. Clarify the basic roles of *model*, *view*, and *controller*.
11. Give an example of a *get/set* pair that defines a graphical property.

7.2   Event-Driven Programming

Modern windows systems, such as Microsoft's Win32 or Motif under Unix, employ an **event-driven programming model**. In this model, an application typically has a GUI to facilitate interaction with the application through, for example, mouse clicks on an application window or selections from an application menu. A user-generated action such as a mouse click generates an **event**. The system queues up such events and then **dispatches** them to procedures known as **event handlers**. An event handler is a callback procedure, that is, a procedure that the programmer writes but the system invokes ("calls back"). Although many events are user-generated, others may be system-generated. For example, if the system shuts down, it typically generates events that any currently executing application may need to handle. The general process in which the system queues up events and later dispatches them to event handlers is known as the **event loop**. Figure 7.2.1 sketches what an event loop might look like at the code level.

```
while ( theApp.isRunning() ) { //** theApp is the application
   Event e = nextEvent();        //** get the next Event from the queue
   int id = e.getId();           //** getId returns an Event's integer id
   switch( id ) {
   case Event_MouseClick:
      theApp.handleMouseClick( e );
      break;
   case Event_MouseMove:
      theApp.handleMouseMove( e );
      break;
   case Event_ButtonPush:
      theApp.handleButtonPush( e );
      break;
   case Event_KeyPush:
      theApp.handleKeyPush( e );
      break;
   //... other events
   default:
      ignoreEvent( e );
      break;
   }                             //** end switch
}                                //** end while( theApp.isRunning() )
```

FIGURE 7.2.1   A code sketch of the main event loop's logic.

When an event-driven application begins execution, it usually enters an **initialization phase** for setting graphical features such as fonts and colors and for other processing such as reading command-line arguments or opening files. Once the initialization phase ends, the application enters its event loop where the application waits for the system to notify it that some event has occurred. Such notification occurs when the system dispatches an event to the application's appropriate callback procedure, which then handles the event. For example, the application might wait for the user to click a mouse in a particular region of the application's GUI. The system notifies the application of such a click by invoking a callback provided by the application to handle this event. A callback then does whatever processing is appropriate for handling the event.

The event-driven programming model has obvious implications for how an applications programmer works. Much of the applications programmer's own code may consist of callbacks. A callback may be a *pure callback*, that is, a method invoked *exclusively* by the system as it dispatches an application's events. An applications programmer may write many pure callbacks, which are never invoked in the programmer's *own* code. This callback-style of coding is among the first skills to be mastered for applications programming in a modern windows environment.

The Event-Delegation Model

The Swing set adapts and extends the basic model for event handling that the AWT provides. This **delegation model** of event handling can be clarified by listing its main parts:

- **Event source**. An event source is an object such as a button or a scrollbar that can generate an event. For example, clicking a button or moving a scrollbar generates an event. An event source has methods that allow objects to be registered as **listeners**, that is, as objects that should be notified whenever the event occurs. For example, a button has an `addActionListener` method that registers listeners for button clicks.

- **Event listener**. An event listener is an object notified about events. When an event source generates an event, the registered listeners are notified when the system invokes the appropriate callback method encapsulated in a listener. For example, the listener for a button-click event would implement the appropriate callback, in this case the `actionPerformed` method declared in the `ActionListener` interface. When the button is clicked, the listener's `actionPerformed` method is invoked to handle the event.

- **Event object**. Information about the event is passed to an event listener's callback as an argument of some type in the `Event` hierarchy. For example, information about a button click is passed to a callback as an `ActionEvent` argument. The `actionPerformed` method thus has the signature

```
public void actionPerformed( ActionEvent e );
```

The callback can use the argument to gain information about the event such as the identity of the object that generated the event.

This event model is flexible in allowing any object to be registered as listener for various types of event. Event sources delegate handling of the generated events to the appropriate callbacks encapsulated in registered listeners. Figure 7.2.2 lists event types in the `java.awt.event` package together with the corresponding listener interface and callback methods declared in the interface. Figure 7.2.3 lists AWT components and the events that each generates. The Swing set event model extends the AWT model.

Event Class	Listener Interface	Listener Callback
`ActionEvent`	`ActionListener`	`actionPerformed`
`AdjustmentEvent`	`AdjustmentListener`	`adjustmentValueChanged`
`ComponentEvent`	`ComponentListener`	`componentHidden`
		`componentMoved`
		`componentResized`
		`componentShown`
`ContainerEvent`	`ContainerListener`	`componentAdded`
		`componentRemoved`
`FocusEvent`	`FocusListener`	`focusGained`
		`focusLost`
`ItemEvent`	`ItemListener`	`itemStateChanged`
`MouseEvent`	`MouseListener`	`mouseClicked`
		`mouseEntered`
		`mousePressed`
		`mouseReleased`
	`MouseMotionListener`	`mouseDragged`
		`mouseMoved`
`TextEvent`	`TextListener`	`textValueChanged`
`WindowEvent`	`WindowListener`	`windowActivated`
		`windowClosed`
		`windowClosing`
		`windowDeactivated`
		`windowDeiconified`
		`windowIconified`
		`windowOpened`

FIGURE 7.2.2   Events, listener interfaces, and callbacks for `java.awt.event` types.

Learning the basic AWT event model is the natural first step to learning the Swing set extension.

■ **Example 7.2.1.**   The `BasicButtons` class in Figure 7.2.4 has three `Buttons` and a `Label`, components from the `java.awt` package. After each button b is created in the `addButton` method, a listener is registered

`b.addActionListener( this );`

for button clicks. The listener is `this`, the `BasicButtons` object that has a `Frame` window member, which in turn holds the buttons and the label. The `BasicButtons` class implements the `ActionListener` interface to signal that `BasicButtons` can listen for action events such as button clicks. The `BasicButtons` class implements the `actionPerformed` method, which is the callback for action events declared in the `ActionListener` interface.

Component	Event Generated	Generated When
Button	ActionEvent	Clicked
Checkbox	ItemEvent	Selected or deselected
CheckboxMenuItem	ItemEvent	Selected or deselected
Choice	ItemEvent	Selected or deselected
Component	ComponentEvent	Moved, resized, hidden, or shown
	FocusEvent	Gains or loses focus
	KeyEvent	Pressed or released
	MouseEvent	Pressed, released, moved, dragged, etc.
Container	ContainerEvent	Added or removed
List	ActionEvent	Double clicked
	ItemEvent	Selected or deselected
MenuItem	ActionEvent	Selected
Scrollbar	AdjustmentEvent	Moved
TextComponent	TextEvent	Changed
TextField	ActionEvent	Completed editing
Window	WindowEvent	Opened, closed, iconified, deiconified, etc.

FIGURE 7.2.3   Events generated by AWT components.

When a button is clicked, the `actionPerformed` callback is automatically invoked with an `ActionEvent` argument that encapsulates information about the button, including the button's name. The callback performs different operations depending on the name. For example, if the button's name is `Exit`, the callback invokes the `System.exit` method to terminate the application.

Finally, the `BasicButtons` class shows how basic graphics features such as fonts, colors, and sizes can be set. The `init` and `addButton` methods contain the relevant code. ∎

∎ **Example 7.2.2.**   The `Delegate` code in Figure 7.2.6 shows how handling an event such as a button click can be delegated to an object other than the container that actually holds the button. A `TwoButtons` object has two buttons. If either is clicked, a message dialog from the Swing set appears. If the exit button is clicked, the application terminates after the message dialog is closed. A `TwoButtons` object does *not* listen for button clicks, however. Instead, a `TwoButtons` object has a `Delegate` member named d. The `Delegate` class implements the `ActionListener` interface and defines an `actionPerformed` callback for button clicks. As each button is created, a `Delegate` object named d is registered as the listener

```
b.addActionListener( d ); // delegate to object d, not this
```

for button clicks. So a button need not have the object that embeds it, in this case a `TwoButtons` object, handle the events that the button generates.

The example uses a Swing set class to display a message dialog. The `JOptionFrame` class has various `static` methods for displaying dialog boxes.

```
import java.awt.*;
import java.awt.event.*;
class BasicButtons implements ActionListener {
  public BasicButtons() {
     win = new Frame( "Event Handling Example" );
     init();
     win.show();
  }
  public void actionPerformed( ActionEvent e ) {
     String cmd = e.getActionCommand();
     if ( cmd.equals( hi ) )
       msg.setText( hi );
     else if ( cmd.equals( huh ) )
       msg.setText( huh );
     else if ( cmd.equals( bye ) )
       System.exit( 0 );
  }
  private void init() {
     win.setLayout( new FlowLayout() );
     addButton( hi ); addButton( huh ); addButton( bye );
     msg = new Label( "    This is a label.    " );
     msg.setFont( new Font( "Dialog", Font.BOLD, 14 ) );
     msg.setBackground( Color.green );
     msg.setAlignment( Label.CENTER );
     win.add( msg );
     win.setSize( 600, 100 );
  }
  private void addButton( String name ) {
     Button b = new Button( name );
     b.setFont( new Font( "Helvetica", Font.BOLD, 14 ) );
     b.addActionListener( this );   //*** BasicButton object
     win.add( b );
  }
  private Frame win;
  private Label msg;
  private static final String hi = " Hello, world! ";
  private static final String huh = " What, me worry? ";
  private static final String bye = " Exit ";
}
```

FIGURE 7.2.4   Basic event handling using the `ActionListener`
interface.

Figure 7.2.6 shows the dialog box. In this example, an *information* dialog is
displayed. There are also `JOptionPane` methods for displaying warning, input,
confirmation, and other dialogs. ▪

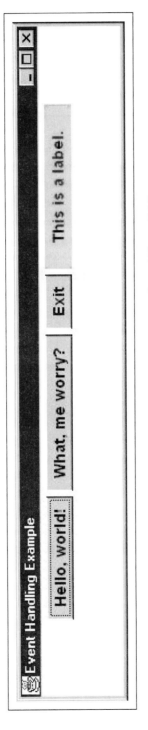

FIGURE 7.2.5 The GUI for the BasicButtons class of Figure 7.2.3.

```
import java.awt.*;
import java.awt.event.*;
import javax.swing.*;
class Delegate implements ActionListener {
   public void actionPerformed( ActionEvent e ) {
      JOptionPane.showMessageDialog(
                     new JFrame(),                         //*** parent
                     "Keep your chin up!",                 //*** message
                     "Delegate Example",                   //*** title
                     JOptionPane.INFORMATION_MESSAGE ); //*** type
      if ( e.getActionCommand().equals( TwoButtons.EXIT ) )
        System.exit( 0 );
   }
}
class TwoButtons { //*** note: does not implement ActionListener
   public TwoButtons() {
      win = new Frame( "Event Delegation Example" );
      d = new Delegate(); //*** Delegate implements ActionListener
      init();
      win.show();
   }
   private void init() {
      win.setLayout( new FlowLayout() );
      addButton( click );
      addButton( EXIT );
      win.setSize( 400, 100 );
   }
   private void addButton( String name ) {
      Button b = new Button( name );
      b.setFont( new Font( "Dialog", Font.BOLD, 14 ) );
      b.addActionListener( d ); //*** delegate to object d, not this
      win.add( b );
   }
   private Delegate d; //*** d will provide the callback
   private Frame win;
   private static final String click = " Click me, please. ";
   public static final String EXIT = " Exit ";
}
```

FIGURE 7.2.6   How an object can delegate event handling to another
object.

The Action Interface

The Swing set builds upon the AWT event model in various ways. For example, the
Swing set's Action interface extends the AWT ActionListener interface but has
declarations for methods besides actionPerformed. The additional Action methods

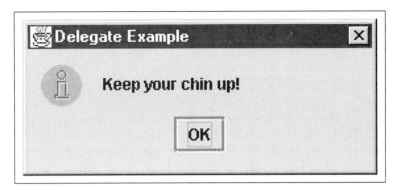

FIGURE 7.2.7   The information dialog for the code in Figure 7.2.6.

support **property change events**, that is, events that fire automatically when designated properties change in an object. The BasicButtons code in Example 7.2.4 uses the ActionListener interface because only button clicks are of interest. Swing set interfaces such as TableModelListener are designed for Swing-specific components, in this case the TableModel component. The javax.swing.event package contains the interfaces for events fired by Swing set components.

Almost all GUIs require event handling. This section introduces the basic event model. Later examples and applications examine the event model in more detail.

EXERCISES

1. What is a *pure callback* method?
2. Explain the relationships among an event *source*, an event *listener*, and an event *object*.
3. What is a *delegate* in the event model?
4. If a class such as a JFrame embeds an event source such as a JButton, must the JFrame object be the listener for the JButton's pushes?
5. Which methods are declared in the ActionListener interface?
6. Which methods are declared in the WindowListener interface?
7. What is the argument type for the componentAdded callback in the Container-Listener interface?
8. What is the argument type for the textValueChanged callback in the TextListener interface?
9. Complete the code segment

```
class Alpha {
    public Alpha() {
```

```
        JButton b1 = new JButton( "Hi" );
        //...
    }
}
```

so that an `Alpha` object that embeds `b1` is the action event listener for `b1` pushes.

10. Explain the relationship between the `ActionListener` interface, a class that implements the interface, and the `actionPerformed` method.

11. What package contains the core classes for event handling?

12. Explain the relationships among the `ActionListener` interface and the `Action` interface.

7.3   Components and Containers

Powerful graphics packages are likewise complex. Understanding a package's **architecture**—its parts and subparts together with the interactions among them—is critical to mastering this complexity. The event delegation model is basic to Java graphics in both the AWT and the Swing set. These two packages share other architectural features as well. For both packages, the relationship between **components** and **containers** is basic. We begin with a brief clarification of each term.

- **Component**. A component is a prebuilt part of a larger application. Among *graphical* components are such familiar items as menus, buttons, scrollbars, text fields, labels, and check boxes. Components can interact through events. For example, clicking a button might cause a message to appear in a text field or on a label. Editing a text field might cause a label to change. A scrollbar might generate events that cause some other control to grow or shrink in size. Components range from the relatively simple such as AWT `Button`s or Swing set `JButton`s to the relatively complex such as the Swing set's `JTable` (see Section 7.6) and `JTree` (see Section 7.4).

- **Container**. A container is a component that can embed other components. A container has a **layout manager** that determines how the embedded or contained components are organized and arranged. For example, one container might use a `FlowLayout` to arrange buttons and labels in a left-to-right and top-to-bottom fashion, whereas another container might use a `BorderLayout` to place the same components in one of a container's five regions *north*, *south*, *east*, *west*, and *center*. Figure 7.3.1 lists the available layout managers.

  Window *panes* and *panels* are common container types. For example, the Swing set's `JSplitPane` is a container that allows exactly two components to be placed side by side. However, each of these components could itself be a *container*, thus allowing arbitrary splitting of a single top-level pane. Because the `Container` class `extends` the `Component` class, every container is likewise a component and, therefore, containers can be nested in other containers to

Layout Manager Class	Package	How Container's Components Are Arranged
BorderLayout	AWT	Along four borders and in the center
BoxLayout	Swing	In boxes along a horizontal or vertical axis
CardLayout	AWT	One at a time taking up the whole container
FlowLayout	AWT	Left to right and top to bottom
GridBagLayout	AWT	In a complex grid of rows and columns
GridLayout	AWT	In a simple grid of rows and columns
OverlayLayout	Swing	On top of one another using alignment points

FIGURE 7.3.1   The layout managers.

arbitrary levels. Containers as components can interact through events. For example, resizing one container might cause another container's background color to change. A *framed window* is a familiar type of container in GUI applications.

Although the AWT and Swing set share an underlying architecture, they differ in implementation detail. For example, the AWT Frame and the Swing set JFrame classes are both descended from the AWT Window class, which in turn is a subclass of Container. Accordingly, Frame and JFrame objects are containers that can hold other components such as buttons and labels. Yet the code for adding a component to a Frame differs from the code for adding the same component to a JFrame.

Example 7.3.1.   The code segment

```
Frame f = new Frame();
f.setLayout( new FlowLayout() );
f.add( new Button( "foo" ) );
f.setSize( 400, 400 );
```

creates a Frame window named f, sets the Frame's layout manager to a FlowLayout, and adds an unreferenced Button labeled *foo*. The Frame's size is then set to 400 by 400 device units. By contrast, the code segment

```
JFrame jf = new JFrame();
Container c = jf.getContentPane(); //*** note well
c.setLayout( new FlowLayout() );   //*** ditto
c.add( new Button( "foo" ) );      //*** ditto
f.setSize( 400, 400 );             //*** same as for Frame
```

does not add the button to the JFrame but rather to a special Container, a **content pane**, that is embedded in the JFrame. A JFrame's content pane includes all of the frame's real estate except for parts such as its title bar and any menu bars or tool bars. In this example, the JFrame content pane's layout manager is likewise set to a `FlowLayout`. In both code segments, the frame window's size is set by invoking the frame's `setSize` method.   ∎

The `JFrame` Window

A window is a basic container for any GUI. In the Swing set, the `JFrame` is the most commonly used *general* window. A `JFrame`, which is a top-level rather than a nested window, has a title, a border, and such platform-specific features as button or menu selections for minimizing, maximizing, and closing the window. Figure 7.3.2 shows an empty `JFrame`. The code segment

```
JFrame f = new JFrame();
f.setSize( 250, 250 );
f.show();
```

shows how the `JFrame` is constructed, sized, and then shown on the screen. The constructor creates an *invisible* framed window. To make the `JFrame` visible, the `show` method is invoked as shown here; or the `setVisible` method is invoked with an argument of `true`.

   A `JFrame` can be **instrumented**—that is, embedded with components—in arbitrarily complex ways. The `JFrame`'s content pane can be partitioned as needed into other containers, which then can be populated with the Swing set's rich assortment of controls. Menu bars, tool bars, and other constructs can be added to the `JFrame`. AWT components also could be added to the `JFrame`, although the recommended practice is not to mix AWT and Swing set components.

   ∎ **Example 7.3.2.**   The `MaceGUI` class in Figure 7.3.3 creates a GUI application form for the nonprofit organization MACE (**M**idwest **A**ssociation for **C**harisma **E**nhancement). Figure 7.3.4 shows the GUI before user input.
   The class `MiscGUI` extends `JFrame` and implements the `ActionListener` interface by defining `actionPerformed` to serve as the callback for clicks on three control buttons. Recall that `JFrames` come with a content pane container. The `MiscGUI` class sets the content pane's layout manager to a `BorderLayout`, which allows components to be placed in one of five regions: top (`NORTH`), bottom (`SOUTH`), left (`WEST`), right (`EAST`), and center (`CENTER`). In this example, the top, left, and bottom regions are paneled with `JPanels`, which are themselves containers that can hold other components. The center region holds a `JTextArea` component, which can be used as a multiline text editor. The right region is not used. Use of the regions deserves further clarification:

- **Top**. The `JPanel` at the top has a `FlowLayout` manager that organizes three `JButtons` in left to right order. Clicking the `Submit` button causes the user's application form to be submitted to the MACE organization's server. At present, the `post` method simulates submission of the application form. After sockets are clarified, the `post` method will be rewritten to transmit the data

FIGURE 7.3.2 An empty JFrame on a Windows platform.

```
import javax.swing.*;
import java.awt.*;
import java.awt.event.*;

class MaceGUI extends JFrame implements ActionListener {
   public MaceGUI() {
      super( "Midwest Association for Charisma Enhancement" );
      pane = getContentPane();
      buttons = new JPanel( new FlowLayout() );
      misc = new JPanel( new FlowLayout() );
      stList = new JPanel();
      married = new JRadioButton( "Married", false );
      email = new JTextField( promptE );
      name = new JTextField( promptN );
      reasons = new JTextArea( promptR );
      list = new JList( states ); //** Midwest state names
      init();
      setVisible( true );
   }
   public void actionPerformed( ActionEvent e ) {
      String cmd = e.getActionCommand();
      if ( cmd.equals( submit ) )
        submitForm();
      else if ( cmd.equals( clear ) )
        clearForm();
      else if ( cmd.equals( exit ) )
        System.exit( 0 );
   }
   private void submitForm() {
      String t = (list.getSelectedValue() == null) ? "none" :
                   list.getSelectedValue().toString();
      post( name.getText(), email.getText(), t,
           (married.isSelected()) ? "married" : "not married",
           reasons.getText() );
   }
   private void clearForm() {
      reasons.setText( promptR );
      name.setText( promptN );
      email.setText( promptE );
      married.setSelected( false );
      list.getSelectionModel().clearSelection();
   }
   //*** For now, a stub function that prints to the standard error.
   private void post( String n, String e, String s,
                      String m, String r ) {
```

FIGURE 7.3.3   An instrumented JFrame.

```
      System.err.println( n + " " + e + " " + s + "\n" + m + "\n" + r );
  }
  private void init() {
     JLabel j;
     Font f = null;
     pane.setLayout( new BorderLayout() );
     buttons.setBackground( Color.gray );
     email.setFont( f = new Font( "Dialog", Font.BOLD, 12 ) );
     name.setFont( f );
     reasons.setFont( f );
     reasons.setLineWrap( true );
     misc.add( name ); misc.add( email ); misc.add( married );
     list.setFont( f );
     list.setBackground( Color.cyan );
     list.getSelectionModel().setSelectionMode(
        ListSelectionModel.SINGLE_SELECTION );
     stList.setLayout( new BoxLayout( stList, BoxLayout.Y_AXIS ) );
     stList.add( j = new JLabel( "Home state   " ) );
     j.setFont( f );
     j.setForeground( Color.black );
     stList.add( list );
     addButton( submit ); addButton( clear ); addButton( exit );
     pane.add( buttons, BorderLayout.NORTH );
     pane.add( reasons, BorderLayout.CENTER );
     pane.add( stList, BorderLayout.WEST );
     pane.add( misc, BorderLayout.SOUTH );
     pack();
  }
  private void addButton( String name ) {
     JButton b = new JButton( name );
     b.setFont( new Font( "Dialog", Font.BOLD, 14 ) );
     b.addActionListener( this );
     buttons.add( b );
  }
  //*** instance fields
  private Container pane;
  private JPanel buttons, misc, stList;
  private JList list;
  private JRadioButton married;
  private JTextField email, name;
  private JTextArea reasons;
  //*** class fields
  private final static String submit = "  Submit  ";
  private final static String clear = "  Clear   ";
```

FIGURE 7.3.3   An instrumented JFrame, *continued.*

```
private final static String exit = "  Exit   ";
private final static String promptN =
    "First and last name           ";
private final static String promptE =
    "E-mail address                ";
private final static String promptR =
    "   My charisma needs enhancement because";
private final static String[ ] states =
    { "Illinois", "Indiana", "Iowa", "Kansas", "Minnesota",
      "Michigan", "Missouri", "Nebraska", "Ohio", "Wisconsin" };
}
```

FIGURE 7.3.3 An instrumented JFrame, *continued.*

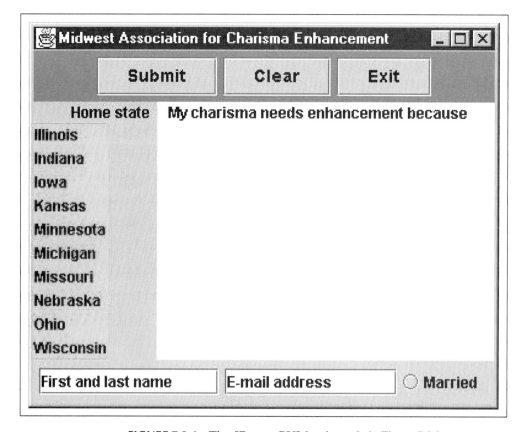

FIGURE 7.3.4 The JFrame GUI for the code in Figure 7.3.3.

to the server (see Section 9.5). Clicking the Clear button causes the GUI to be restored to its initial condition, that is, its condition before any user input. Clicking the Exit button terminates the application. A later subsection introduces an alternative to this method of termination. The top panel has a gray background to distinguish it from the neighboring panels.

- **Left**. The JPanel at the left has a BoxLayout manager that organizes a JLabel and a JList vertically so that the JLabel appears above the JList. The JList contains a list of names for the Midwestern states. Only *single* selection is enabled on the list, although the user need not select any state to submit the form. A JList encapsulates a **selection model** that has methods for specifying, among other things, whether the list is enabled for single or multiple selections. This example uses the default selection model and invokes its clearSelection method to restore the list to its original condition whenever the Clear button is clicked. The list has a cyan background so that it stands out from the rest of the form.

- **Bottom**. The JPanel at the bottom has a FlowLayout manager that arranges two JTextFields and a JRadioButton in left to right order. The text fields are for the user's name and e-mail address, whereas the radio button is for marital status.

- **Center**. The center region is not paneled but rather holds a JTextArea component in which the user can type reasons for wishing to join MACE.

The MaceGUI constructor creates the panels and other components. The constructor invokes super with a String so that the superclass JFrame's constructor can set the window's title. The JFrame class also has a public setTitle method for the same purpose. The private init method performs relatively low-level graphics tasks such as setting fonts and colors, specifying layout managers, and adding components to containers. After instrumenting the framed window, the init method invokes the pack method so that the window is automatically sized to accommodate all of its components.

Finally, the constructor invokes setVisible with an argument of true to display the GUI. Recall that JFrames are constructed as *invisible*. The JFrame method show also makes the window visible. The statement

```
new MaceGUI();
```

causes the GUI in Figure 7.3.4 to appear on the screen.   ■

Terminating an Application by Closing Its Top-Level Window

The JFrame examples so far have relied upon a clicked Exit button to terminate an application. The click event's handler has been the actionPerformed callback, which usually has been implemented in the same class that holds the Exit button. Other approaches are possible.

The WindowListener interface in the java.awt.event package declares seven methods to be implemented by classes meant to handle window events (see Figure 7.3.5). The WindowAdapter class provides a **trivial implementation** of the WindowListener interface; that is, the WindowAdapter class provides an *empty body*

Callback	Invoked When the Window Is
windowActivated	Activated to receive keyboard events.
windowClosed	Closed through a call to dispose.
windowClosing	Closed through the window's system menu.
windowDeactivated	Deactivated for keyboard events.
windowDeiconified	Changed from minimized to normal state.
windowIconified	Changed from normal to minimized state.
windowOpened	Made visible for the first time.

FIGURE 7.3.5   The seven methods declared in the `WindowListener` interface.

for each method in the interface. If a *concrete* class implements the `WindowListener` interface, the class must implement *each* of the seven methods. By contrast, a class that extends the `WindowAdapter` class can selectively *override* whatever callbacks are of interest. For example, a subclass of `WindowAdapter` might override `window-Closed` but none of the other trivial method implementations in the `WindowAdapter` class.

> **Example 7.3.3.**   The code in Figure 7.3.6 creates a `WinCloser` class as a subclass of `WindowAdapater` and overrides the `windowClosing` callback, which is invoked when the user clicks the *Close* entry on the window's system menu. The

```
import java.awt.event.*;
import javax.swing.*;
class WinCloser extends WindowAdapter {
   public void windowClosing( WindowEvent e ) {
      e.getWindow().dispose();
      System.exit( 0 );
   }
}
class WinEventEx extends JFrame {
   public WinEventEx() {
      super( "Window closing example." );
      addWindowListener( new WinCloser() ); //*** register listener
      setSize( 400, 400 );
      show();
   }
}
```

FIGURE 7.3.6   Terminating an application by closing its top-level window.

override is required explicitly to hide or dispose of the window. In this example, the `dispose` method is invoked but invoking `setVisible` with an argument of `false` also would work. Once the window is disposed, the application itself is terminated with a call to the `System` class's `exit` method.

The `WinEventExample` class registers an unreferenced `WinCloser` object as a *listener* for window events such as closing. When a `WinEventEx` window is closed from the system menu, this listener's override of the `windowClosing` callback is invoked. The callback closes the window and then terminates the underlying application.

The `Action` Interface and `AbstractAction` Class

The `WindowAdapter` class's trivial implementation of the `WindowListener` interface is convenient in permitting selective overrides of methods. However, a *trivial implementation*—that is, an implementation that provides *empty* method bodies—differs from a *default implementation*, which provides a *basic* implementation that subclasses may override. For example, the Swing set's `Action` interface extends the `ActionListener` interface but also declares callbacks for property changes, that is, changes in fields that represent object features or properties. The Swing set's `AbstractAction` class provides a default implementation for all of `Action`'s methods *except* for `actionPerformed`. A *concrete* class that extends `AbstractAction` therefore must implement `actionPerformed` but still can use `AbstractAction`'s default implementations of the remaining `Action` methods.

■ **Example 7.3.4.**   The `ColorButton` code in Figure 7.3.7 creates `Action-Handler` as a subclass of the abstract class `AbstractAction`. For `Action-Handler` to be concrete, this class must implement `actionPerformed`. The program's GUI has two buttons, one to terminate the application and another to change the GUI's background color. In the `ColorButton` private method `init`, an `ActionHandler` object is registered as the listener for clicks of the application's two `JButton`s.

Example 7.3.5.   To illustrate how an *anonymous class* can be used to construct an event listener, the `ColorButton` code in Figure 7.3.8 amends the code in Figure 7.3.7. Each of the two `JButton`s now has an instantiation of an anonymous class as its own click listener. For the `JButton` named `setBk`, for example, the code segment

```
setBk.addActionListener( new AbstractAction() {
    public void actionPerformed( ActionEvent e ) {
      ((JButton) e.getSource()).setBackground(Color.green);
    }
  } );
```

adds an `ActionEvent` listener that sets the button's background color to green. By contrast, the unreferenced event listener for the `EXIT` button's click terminates

```
import javax.swing.*;
import java.awt.*;
import java.awt.event.*;

class ActionHandler extends AbstractAction {
   public void actionPerformed( ActionEvent e ) {
      if ( e.getActionCommand().trim().equalsIgnoreCase( "EXIT" ) )
        System.exit( 0 );
      else
        ((JButton) e.getSource()).setBackground( Color.green );
   }
}
class ColorButton extends JFrame {
   public ColorButton() {
      super( "Action Example" );
      init();
      show();
   }
   private void init() {
      ActionHandler ah = null;
      Font f = null;
      Container c = getRootPane();
      c.setLayout( new FlowLayout() );
      JButton setBk = new JButton( " Change My Background, Please! " );
      setBk.setBackground( Color.pink );
      JButton exit = new JButton( " EXIT " );
      setBk.setFont( f = new Font( "Dialog", Font.BOLD, 12 ) );
      setBk.addActionListener( ah = new ActionHandler() );
      exit.setFont( f );
      exit.addActionListener( ah );
      c.add( setBk );
      c.add( exit );
      setSize( 350, 200 );
   }
}
```

FIGURE 7.3.7   Extending the `AbstractAction` class to handle `ActionEvents`.

the application. Anonymous classes are thus a convenient way to customize event listeners. Recall that anonymous classes are one type of **inner class**, that is, a class defined inside another class.

The syntax for constructing an object instance of an anonymous class deserves a close look particularly because `AbstractAction` is an *abstract* class. Therefore, a statement such as

```
new AbstractAction();
```

```
import javax.swing.*;
import java.awt.*;
import java.awt.event.*;

class ColorButton extends JFrame {
    public ColorButton() {
        super( "Action Example" );
        init();
        show();
    }
    private void init() {
        Font f = null;
        Container c = getRootPane();
        c.setLayout( new FlowLayout() );
        JButton setBk = new JButton( " Change My Background, Please! " );
        setBk.setBackground( Color.pink );
        JButton exit = new JButton( " EXIT " );
        setBk.setFont( f = new Font( "Dialog", Font.BOLD, 12 ) );
        setBk.addActionListener( new AbstractAction() {
                public void actionPerformed( ActionEvent e ) {
                    ((JButton) e.getSource()).setBackground( Color.green );
                }
            } );
        exit.setFont( f );
        exit.addActionListener( new AbstractAction() {
                public void actionPerformed( ActionEvent e ) {
                    System.exit( 0 );
                }
            } );
        c.add( setBk );
        c.add( exit );
        setSize( 350, 200 );
    }
}
```

FIGURE 7.3.8   The use of anonymous classes to customize event callbacks.

is in error. In this example, however, the syntax is

```
new AbstractAction() { //*** left brace begins body
        //...implementation body
    }                              //*** right brace ends body
```

So the constructor call is followed by an *implementation* in which the method `actionPerformed` is indeed defined. The anonymous class is not abstract but concrete because only `actionPerformed` needs to be defined. ∎

Menus, Popup Menus, and Submenus

Menus, like buttons and checkboxes, are a convenient way to present choices graphically. Menus have the advantage of being particularly space-efficient. Tool bars are relocatable elements that can be "docked" in various positions within a GUI. This subsection examines both.

A menu consists of items to be selected. In the Swing set, the items represented can be a mix of text, icons, and Swing set components in general. A menu resides in a **menu bar**, which is a component designed to hold menus. The Swing set has intuitively named classes to represent the basic components that go into building a menu: JMenuBar, JMenu, and JMenuItem.

> **Example 7.3.6.** The code in Figure 7.3.9 creates two menus for a JFrame. The first menu lists the names of colors. Selecting an item such as Pink from this list causes the content pane's background to change to the selected color. The second menu has two items: Restore, which restores the content pane's background to white; and Exit, which terminates the application. The menus are added to a JMenuBar, which in turn is added to the JFrame window. Figure 7.3.10 shows the window with the first menu opened. ∎

The class JMenu is a *subclass* of JMenuItem, which means that menus can contain submenus to arbitrary levels. A JMenu is simply added as item in another JMenu.

> ∎ **Example 7.3.7.** The ColorMenuEx program in Figure 7.3.9 can be revised so that the color menu includes a submenu. The sample revision takes these steps:
>
> • A JMenu named colorSubMenu is constructed and populated with two colors, orange and pink. The original colorMenu now has four items: three colors (blue, cyan, and grey) and the color submenu, which has two colors (orange and pink).
> • After colorSubMenu is created, it is added to the colorMenu with the statement
>
>   colorMenu.add(colorSubMenu);
>
> The event handling remains the same. Figure 7.3.11 shows the revision with the submenu open for selection. ∎

Keyboard Shortcuts

Menu items can be selected with mouse clicks. However, each item also can be paired with a **keyboard shortcut** so that pressing the appropriate key likewise selects the item

```
import javax.swing.*;
import java.awt.event.*;
import java.awt.*;
class ColorMenuEx extends JFrame implements ActionListener {
   public ColorMenuEx() {
      menuBar = new JMenuBar();
      colorMenu = new JMenu( "Colors" );
      controlMenu = new JMenu( "Control" );
      init();
      setSize( 300, 150 );
      getContentPane().setBackground( orig );
      setVisible( true );
   }
   public void actionPerformed( ActionEvent e ) {
      String s = e.getActionCommand();
      if ( s.equals( "Exit" ) )
        System.exit( 0 );
      else if ( s.equals( "Restore" ) )
        getContentPane().setBackground( orig );
      else
        setColor( s );
   }
   private void init() {
      initMenu( colorMenu, colorNames );
      initMenu( controlMenu, controls );
      menuBar.add( colorMenu ); menuBar.add( controlMenu );
      setJMenuBar( menuBar );
    }
   private void initMenu( JMenu menu, String[ ] items ) {
      for ( int i = 0; i < items.length; i++ ) {
        JMenuItem item = new JMenuItem( items[ i ] );
        item.addActionListener( this );
        menu.add( item );
      }
   }
   private void setColor( String c ) {
      for ( int i = 0; i < colorNames.length; i++ )
        if ( c.equals( colorNames[ i ] ) ) {
          getContentPane().setBackground( colors[ i ] );
          break;
        }
   }
   private JMenuBar menuBar;
   private JMenu colorMenu;
   private JMenu controlMenu;
```

FIGURE 7.3.9   A window with a menu bar and two menus.

```
    private static final Color orig = Color.white;
    private static final String[ ] colorNames =
      { "Blue", "Cyan", "Gray", "Orange", "Pink" };
    private static final Color[ ] colors =
      { Color.blue, Color.cyan, Color.gray, Color.orange, Color.pink };
    private static final String[ ] controls = { "Restore", "Exit" };
}
```

FIGURE 7.3.9   A window with a menu bar and two menus, *continued.*

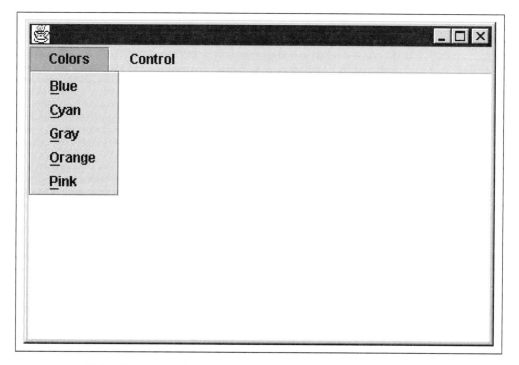

FIGURE 7.3.10   The GUI created by the `CodeMenuEx` code in Figure 7.3.9.

whenever the menu is open. For the menu in Figure 7.3.9, for instance, the key B could be associated with the menu item `Blue`, the key C with the menu item `Cyan`, and so on.

Example 7.3.8.   Adding keyboard shortcuts to the menus created in Figure 7.3.9 requires one small change to the code. In the method `initMenu`, the `JMenuItem` constructor call changes from

```
JMenuItem item = JMenuItem( items[ i ] );
```

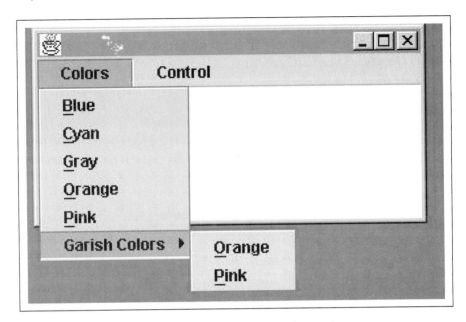

FIGURE 7.3.11   A menu with a submenu item.

to

```
JMenuItem item = JMenuItem( items[ i ],
                           items[ i ].charAt( 0 ) );
```

The constructor call now has two arguments, the second of which is a character that represents the keyboard shortcut: C for Cyan, P for Pink, and so on. The code segment

```
JMenuItem item = new JMenuItem( items[ i ] );
item.setMnemonic( items[ i ].charAt( 0 ) );
```

is another way to achieve the same result.

Note that all of the menu items in both menus start with distinctive characters, which enables this simple change to the code. If two colors started with the same letter (e.g., Black and Blue), only one of them could be associated with the key B. A different keyboard shortcut would have to be specified for the other. ■

Popup Menus

The Swing set also supports **popup menus**, that is, menus that are "free floating" rather than attached to a menu bar. The JPopupMenu class also can be populated with items that are JMenuItems, arbitrary Components, and Actions. Popup menus are typically displayed through a **mouse trigger**, that is, a mouse event such as click.

Example 7.3.9.   The `ColorMenuEx` code in Figure 7.3.12 amends the code in Figure 7.3.9 by making the color menu a popup menu. Several changes are needed:

```java
import javax.swing.*;
import javax.swing.border.*;
import java.awt.event.*;
import java.awt.*;
class ColorMenuEx extends JFrame implements
                            ActionListener, MouseListener {
   public ColorMenuEx() {
      menuBar = new JMenuBar();
      colorMenu = new JPopupMenu( "Colors" );
      controlMenu = new JMenu( "Control" );
      init();
      setSize( 300, 150 );
      getContentPane().setBackground( orig );
      addMouseListener( this );
      setVisible( true );
   }
   public void actionPerformed( ActionEvent e ) {
      String s = e.getActionCommand();
      if ( s.equals( "Exit" ) )
        System.exit( 0 );
      else if ( s.equals( "Restore" ) )
        getContentPane().setBackground( orig );
      else
        setColor( s );
   }
   public void mousePressed( MouseEvent e ) { checkTrigger( e ); }
   public void mouseClicked( MouseEvent e ) { checkTrigger( e ); }
   public void mouseEntered( MouseEvent e ) { checkTrigger( e ); }
   public void mouseExited( MouseEvent e ) { checkTrigger( e ); }
   public void mouseReleased( MouseEvent e ) { checkTrigger( e ); }
   private void checkTrigger( MouseEvent e ) {
      if ( e.isPopupTrigger() )
        colorMenu.show( this, e.getX(), e.getY() );
   }
   private void init() {
      colorMenu.setBorder( new BevelBorder( BevelBorder.RAISED ) );
      initMenu( colorMenu, colorNames );
      initMenu( controlMenu, controls );
      menuBar.add( controlMenu );
      setJMenuBar( menuBar );
   }
```

FIGURE 7.3.12   Revision of Figure 7.3.9 to use a popup menu for colors.

```
private void initMenu( JComponent menu, String[ ] items ) {
   for ( int i = 0; i < items.length; i++ ) {
      JMenuItem item = new JMenuItem( items[ i ] );
      item.addActionListener( this );
      menu.add( item );
   }
}
private void setColor( String c ) {
   int i = 0;
   while ( i < colorNames.length )
      if ( c.equals( colorNames[ i ] ) ) {
         getContentPane().setBackground( colors[ i ] );
         break;
      }
      else
         i++;
}
private JMenuBar menuBar;
private JPopupMenu colorMenu;
private JMenu controlMenu;
private static final Color orig = Color.white;
private static final String[ ] colorNames =
   { "Blue", "Cyan", "Gray", "Orange", "Pink" };
private static final Color[ ] colors =
   { Color.blue, Color.cyan, Color.gray, Color.orange, Color.pink };
private static final String[ ] controls = { "Restore", "Exit" };
}
```

FIGURE 7.3.12   Revision of Figure 7.3.9 to use a popup menu for colors,
continued.

- The colorMenu's type changes from JMenu to JPopupMenu, which in turn
  requires that the first parameter in initMenu change from JMenu to JComponent, a common ancestor of JMenu and JPopupMenu.

- Because colorMenu is a *popup* menu, it is *not* added to the JFrame's menu
  bar. The controlMenu remains on the menu bar.

- The ColorMenuEx class now implements the MouseListener interface in
  addition to the ActionListener interface. The MouseListener interface
  declares five methods, each of which is implemented to check whether a
  particular mouse event such as a click is a platform-specific *trigger* for a popup
  menu. A **trigger** in this sense is an event that displays the popup menu. On a
  Windows platform, for example, a *right* mouse click is a trigger. Covering all of
  the possible mouse events promotes portability.

- The ColorMenuEx class registers this as a MouseListener so that Color-
  MenuEx objects are notified of mouse events.

- The popup menu's `show` method is invoked to display the menu. Two `MouseEvent` methods, `getX` and `getY`, are used to get the horizontal and vertical coordinates of the mouse event such as a right click that triggers the popup menu. The popup menu is then shown at these coordinates.
- The code uses the `javax.swing.border` package to ornament the popup menu with a beveled border.

The remaining code is the same as in Figure 7.3.9.   ■

Tool Bars

Tool bars, unlike menu bars, can float freely and dock at various locations within a container. A tool bar is itself a container that can be instrumented with controls such as buttons and labels. A tool bar typically is added to a container with a *border* layout so that the tool bar can be conveniently docked in any of the five standard border layout positions: top, bottom, left, right, and center.

■ **Example 7.3.10.**   The code in Figure 7.3.13 uses a `JToolBar` as the container for control buttons such as the `Exit` button. Figure 7.3.14 shows the tool bar docked on the left side of the content pane. The `Exit` and `Restore` choices are now available as `JButtons` on the `JToolBar`.   ■

Dialog Windows

The `JWindow` class is rarely used because it lacks the convenient `JFrame` features such as a border and a title. The `JDialog` class `extends` the AWT `Dialog` class but does not significantly enhance functionality already available in the AWT superclass; hence, `JDialogs` are not widely used. The `JOptionPane` class is better suited for applications that require **dialog windows**, which are special-purpose windows that appear for a short amount of time. Dialog windows typically have standard controls such as an *OK* button that closes the window when clicked. A **message dialog** can be used to post a message graphically; a **file selection dialog** can be used to prompt the use to select a file graphically.

■ **Example 7.3.11.**   Figure 7.3.15 shows an input dialog that the code segment

```
Object ans =
   JOptionPane.showInputDialog(
      new JFrame(),                  //** parent window
      "Favorite exercise?",          //** prompt
      "Input Dialog Example",        //** title
      JOptionPane.QUESTION_MESSAGE,  //** option type
      new ImageIcon( "swing.jpg" ),  //** image displayed
```

```
import javax.swing.*;
import java.awt.event.*;
import java.awt.*;
class ColorMenuEx extends JFrame implements ActionListener {
   public ColorMenuEx() {
      menuBar = new JMenuBar();
      colorMenu = new JMenu( "Colors" );
      controls = new JToolBar();
      init();
      setSize( 300, 150 );
      getContentPane().setBackground( orig );
      setVisible( true );
   }
   public void actionPerformed( ActionEvent e ) {
      String s = e.getActionCommand();
      if ( s.equals( exitString ) )
        System.exit( 0 );
      else if ( s.equals( restoreString ) )
        getContentPane().setBackground( orig );
      else
        setColor( s );
   }
   private void init() {
      initMenu( colorMenu, colorNames );
      menuBar.add( colorMenu );
      setJMenuBar( menuBar );
      addButton( exitString ); addButton( restoreString );
      getContentPane().add( controls, BorderLayout.SOUTH );
   }
   private void addButton( String n ) {
      JButton j = new JButton( n );
      controls.add( j );
      j.addActionListener( this );
   }
   private void initMenu( JMenu menu, String[ ] items ) {
      for ( int i = 0; i < items.length; i++ ) {
         JMenuItem item = new JMenuItem( items[ i ],
                                         items[ i ].charAt( 0 ) );
         item.addActionListener( this );
         menu.add( item );
      }
   }
   private void setColor( String c ) {
      int i = 0;
      while ( i < colorNames.length )
```

FIGURE 7.3.13   The colors example revised to include a tool bar.

```
        if ( c.equals( colorNames[ i ] ) ) {
          getContentPane().setBackground( colors[ i ] );
          break;
        }
        else
          i++;
    }
    private JMenuBar menuBar;
    private JToolBar controls;
    private JMenu colorMenu;
    private JButton exit;
    private JButton restore;
    private static final String exitString = " Exit ";
    private static final String restoreString = " Restore ";
    private static final Color orig = Color.white;
    private static final String[ ] colorNames =
        { "Blue", "Cyan", "Gray", "Orange", "Pink" };
    private static final Color[ ] colors =
        { Color.blue, Color.cyan, Color.gray, Color.orange, Color.pink };
}
```

FIGURE 7.3.13   The colors example revised to include a tool bar, *continued.*

```
        new Object[ ] {                          //** list of choices
            "Running",   "Cycling",
            "Swimming",  "Blading",
            "XC Skiing", "Climbing" },
          "XC Skiing" );                         //** default selection
    System.out.println( "You choose " + ans );
```

creates and then prints the user's selection to the standard output. If the user clicks the option pane's OK button, a selection is returned as an Object reference. For an input dialog, a selection is returned as a String reference. If the user clicks the Cancel button, null is returned.

The JOptionPane class has static methods to open input, message, option, and confirmation dialogs. The dialogs can be instrumented with lists, buttons, check boxes, and other components. The static methods are provided for dialogs that are used just once. For repeated use of a dialog, the JOptionPane class can be instantiated as an object with methods appropriate for the dialog type. For example, there is a getValue method for getting a user's selection from a JOptionPane input or selection dialog.

Finally, the example shows how an ImageIcon can be constructed, in this case from a JPEG file. The ImageIcon constructor also accepts GIF and other popular graphical file types.

FIGURE 7.3.14 The tool bar of Figure 7.3.13 docked on the container's left border.

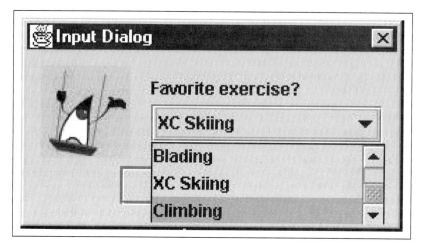

FIGURE 7.3.15   A JOptionPane opened as an input dialog.

EXERCISES

1. What is a *component*?
2. What is a *container*?
3. Is a *container* likewise a *component*?
4. Can one *container* be nested inside another?
5. What is the purpose of a *layout manager*?
6. Explain the difference between a *flow layout* and a *border layout* manager.
7. What sort of component has a *layout manager*?
8. Provide a code segment that instantiates a JFrame, sets its size to 400 by 400, and shows it.
9. Does a JFrame constructor create a visible or invisible framed window?
10. Instrument a JFrame window with a label, text field, and radio button and then display the framed window.
11. In a JFrame, components are not added directly to the JFrame object but rather to a special container known as the *content pane*. For the JFrame named jf, provide the expression that accesses jf's content pane.
12. Explain the relationship between the WindowListener interface and the WindowAdapter class.
13. What is the difference between a *trivial implementation* and a *default implementation* of an interface such as Action?
14. Give an example of an anonymous class used to instantiate a listener for pushes on a JButton.
15. What is the distinction between a Menu and a PopupMenu?

16. Can a JMenu contain submenus?
17. Explain what a *keyboard shortcut* is.
18. What is the purpose of a *tool bar*?
19. Can a toolbar hold menus?
20. What is a *dialog window*?
21. A JOptionPane has `static` methods to display various types of dialog window as well as constructors to create dialog objects. Explain the rationale behind supporting dialog windows in two ways.
22. Provide a statement that constructs an `ImageIcon` from the image file *beverages.gif*.

7.4   Sample Application: Directory Assistance

Problem

Create a utility that uses a graphical tree structure to represent a computer's hierarchical file system. By clicking on a node that represents a directory, the user should be able to view the directory's properties (for instance, whether the directory is readable) together with a list of the files in the directory. By clicking on a node that represents a nondirectory file, the user should be able to view the file's properties together with its size in bytes.

Sample Output

Figure 7.4.1 shows the utility's graphical representation of a computer's floppy disk drive. In Figure 7.4.2, the directory `A:\ch5\code` has been expanded through a mouse click to display the individual files in the directory.

Solution

The application constructs a graphical `JTree` using a `DefaultTreeModel` to represent the hierarchical arrangement of directories and files in a platform's file system. If the user clicks on a `JTree` node after checking a `JCheckBox` labeled ShowDetails, a message dialog displays information about the directory or file that the node represents.

Java Implementation

```
import javax.swing.*;
import javax.swing.tree.*;
import java.io.*;
```

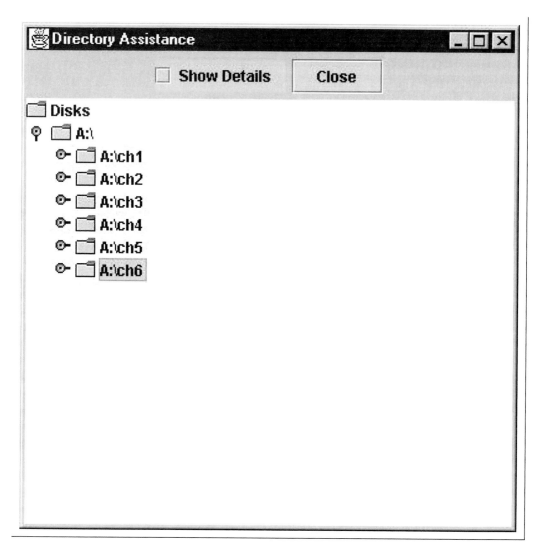

FIGURE 7.4.1   The JTree representation of a computer's floppy disk drive.

```java
import java.awt.*;
import java.awt.event.*;
import javax.swing.*;
import javax.swing.tree.*;
public class DirTree extends JFrame implements ActionListener {
    public DirTree() {
        super( "Directory Assistance" );
        Container c = getContentPane();
        //*** Build the tree and a mouse listener to handle clicks
```

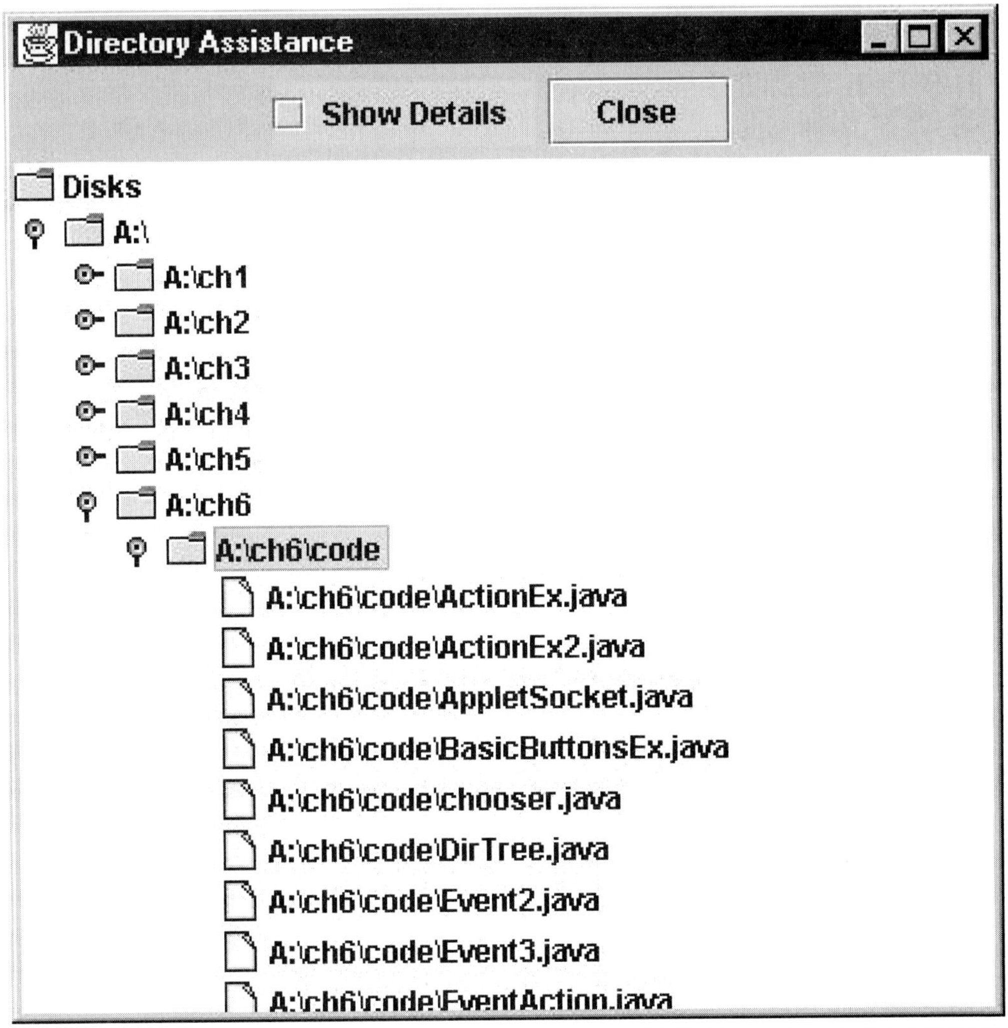

FIGURE 7.4.2   The details of the ch6 directory from Figure 7.4.1.

```
root = new DefaultMutableTreeNode( "Disks" );
treeModel = new DefaultTreeModel( root );
tree = new JTree( treeModel );
MouseListener ml =
  new MouseAdapter() {
    public void mouseClicked( MouseEvent e ) {
      if ( box.isSelected() )
        showDetails( tree.getPathForLocation( e.getX(),
                                              e.getY() ) );
    }
```

```
      };
   tree.addMouseListener( ml );
   //*** build the tree by adding the nodes
   buildTree();
   //*** panel the JFrame to hold controls and the tree
   controls = new JPanel();
   box = new JCheckBox( showString );
   init(); //** set colors, fonts, etc. and add buttons
   c.add( controls, BorderLayout.NORTH );
   c.add( tree, BorderLayout.CENTER );
   setVisible( true ); //** display the framed window
}
public void actionPerformed( ActionEvent e ) {
   String cmd = e.getActionCommand();
   if ( cmd.equals( closeString ) )
      dispose();
}
private void init() {
   tree.setFont( new Font( "Dialog", Font.BOLD, 12 ) );
   controls.add( box );
   addButton( closeString );
   controls.setBackground( Color.lightGray );
   controls.setLayout( new FlowLayout() );
   setSize( 400, 400 );
}
private void addButton( String n ) {
   JButton b = new JButton( n );
   b.setFont( new Font( "Dialog", Font.BOLD, 12 ) );
   b.addActionListener( this );
   controls.add( b );
}
private void buildTree() {
   File[ ] list = File.listRoots();
   for ( int i = 0; i < list.length; i++ )
      if ( list[ i ].exists() )
         buildTree( list[ i ], root, i );
}
private void buildTree( File f,
                        DefaultMutableTreeNode parent,
                        int where ) {
   DefaultMutableTreeNode n =
      new DefaultMutableTreeNode( f.toString() );
   treeModel.insertNodeInto( n, parent, where );
   if ( f.isDirectory() ) {
     String list[] = f.list();
```

```
            for ( int i = 0; i < list.length; i++ )
                buildTree( new File( f, list[ i ] ), n, i );
        }
    }
    private void showDetails( TreePath p ) {
        if ( p == null )
            return;
        File f = new File( p.getLastPathComponent().toString() );
        JOptionPane.showMessageDialog( this, f.getPath() +
                                       "\n    " +
                                       getAttributes( f ) );
    }
    private String getAttributes( File f ) {
        String t = "";
        if ( f.isDirectory() )
            t += "Directory";
        else
            t += "Nondirectory file";
        t += "\n    ";
        if ( !f.canRead() )
            t += "not ";
        t += "Readable\n    ";
        if ( !f.canWrite() )
            t += "not ";
        t += "Writeable\n    ";
        if ( !f.isDirectory() )
            t += "Size in bytes: " + f.length() + "\n    ";
        else {
            t += "Contains files: \n       ";
            String[ ] contents = f.list();
            for ( int i = 0; i < contents.length; i++ )
                t += contents[ i ] + ", ";
            t += "\n";
        }
        return t;
    }
    private JCheckBox box;
    private JTree tree;
    private DefaultMutableTreeNode root;
    private DefaultTreeModel treeModel;
    private JPanel controls;
    private String file;
    private static final String closeString = " Close ";
    private static final String showString = " Show Details ";
}
```

Discussion

The application has a single class, the public `DirTree` class that extends the `JFrame` class and implements the `ActionListener` interface. A client can construct and display a `DirTree` with the statement

```
new DirTree();
```

The `DirTree`'s GUI includes a `JButton` for closing it. All of the `DirTree`'s graphical and support components come from the Swing set. How the directory tree is constructed can be summarized as follows:

- `JTree`. This `JComponent` can be used to represent hierarchical data in a visually intuitive fashion. A `JTree` consists of **nodes**, which are its elements. The **root node** is at the top of the hierarchy and is distinguished by having no ancestor nodes. **Leaf nodes** are at the bottom of the hierarchy and are distinguished by having no descendant nodes. **Intermediate nodes** have a parent, arbitrarily many ancestors, and arbitrarily many descendants. A direct descendant is a **child node**. Given these informal definitions, it follows that a `JTree` could be used to illustrate an *inheritance hierarchy*. The `JTree` is suited to a graphical representation of a **hierarchical file system**, which consists of **directories** and **files**. Conceptually, a directory is a special file that collects other files, often including other directories. A file system has a **root directory** that typically includes subdirectories and perhaps nondirectory files, which are leafs.
- `DefaultMutableTreeNode`. For nodes, the application uses the Swing set's `DefaultMutableTreeNode`. Such a node is *mutable* in that, for example, child nodes may be added and removed as desired. A node that represents a directory can be viewed in either *collapsed* or *expanded* form: a collapsed node *hides* its children, whereas an expanded node *displays* them. In Figure 7.4.1, the node representing the ch5 directory is expanded, whereas the node representing the other chapter directories such as ch1 and ch2 are collapsed.
- `DefaultTreeModel`. A `JTree` provides a graphical view of a tree model, which consists of the data to be viewed. The `DefaultTreeModel` is a convenient Swing set class for representing tree data. The class implements the `TreeModel` interface, which includes methods for standard tree operations such as getting the tree's root or a particular node's children. A tree model requires at least one node, which is thereby the root. Accordingly, the `DefaultTreeModel` does not have a public no-argument constructor. Our `DefaultTreeModel` is constructed from a `DefaultMutableTreeNode` labeled Disks, which serves as the root. Each child is one of the computer's disk drives. On a PC, for example, the children might be the A, C, and D drives. The code segment

```
root = new DefaultMutableTreeNode( "Disks" );
treeModel = new DefaultTreeModel( root );
tree = new JTree( treeModel );
```

in the `DirTree` constructor first constructs the root node, then the tree model from this node, and finally the `JTree` from the tree model. The `JTree` is placed at the center of the `JFrame` under a border layout manager, which gives the `JTree` room to grow wider and deeper as needed.

Building Tree Structures

Trees are ideal structures for processing recursively precisely because tree *parts* are likewise trees, that is, subtrees. Even a single leaf node is a subtree whose one and only node, the root, is the leaf node itself. The application uses recursion to construct the tree, starting from the root labeled `Disks`. The private overloaded methods named `buildTree` do the work. The `buildTree` with no arguments

```
private void buildTree() {
   File[ ] list = File.listRoots();
   for ( int i = 0; i < list.length; i++ )
      if ( list[ i ].exists() )
         buildTree( list[ i ], root, i );
}
```

is nonrecursive and is invoked in the `DirTree` constructor. The `java.io` package's `File` class has a `static` method named `listRoots` that returns a list of a computer system's root directories. The `if` inside the `for` loop tests whether a given root directory `exists` and is accessible. If the directory does exist and is accessible, the recursive `buildTree` is invoked for each root directory. The three arguments are

- `list[ i ]`. This is the *i*th root directory. On a PC, for example, the first root directory is typically the root directory of the floppy disk.
- `root`. This is the root node in the tree, the one labeled `Disks`.
- `i`. This is the index that indicates *which* node is being added to the root node: the first, second, and so on. The order in which the nodes are added determines the left to right order in which they are displayed in the `JTree`.

The parameterized `buildTree`

```
private void buildTree( File f,
                        DefaultMutableTreeNode parent,
                        int where ) {
   DefaultMutableTreeNode n =
      new DefaultMutableTreeNode( f.toString() );
   treeModel.insertNodeInto( n, parent, where );
   if ( f.isDirectory() ) {
      String list[ ] = f.list();
      for ( int i = 0; i < list.length; i++ )
         buildTree( new File( f, list[ i ] ), n, i );
   }
}
```

first constructs a `DefaultMutableTreeNode` from the `File` parameter's name and then inserts the node into the tree as a *child* of some parent node, which is the second parameter. The third parameter specifies which child is being added: the first, the second, and so on. If the `File` is a directory, its contents—other files, including subdirectories—are recursively added to the directory by invoking `buildTree` with the appropriate arguments. Recursive logic tends to be complex but the corresponding code also tends to be short.

Event Handling

The application needs to handle two types of events: clicks on the `Close` button, which closes the `DirTree` GUI by invoking `dispose`, and clicks on the various `JTree` nodes. To handle the button click, `DirTree` implements `ActionListener` and defines `actionPerformed`. To handle mouse clicks on the `JTree` nodes, the application implements the `MouseListener` with an inner `MouseAdapter` class

```
MouseListener ml =
  new MouseAdapter() {
    public void mouseClicked( MouseEvent e ) {
      if ( box.isSelected() )
        showDetails( tree.getPathForLocation( e.getX(),
                                               e.getY() ) );
    }
  };
```

and then adds this listener to the `JTree`

```
tree.addMouseListener( ml );
```

The field `box` refers to a `JCheckBox`, which the user checks in order to see details about a clicked directory or file. The `JTree` method `getPathForLocation` returns the selected node's path as a `Vector` such as

```
[Disks, A:\, A:\ch5, A:\ch5\code\, A:\ch5\code\Zeta.java]
```

The `DirTree` private method `showDetails` extracts the last component

```
A:\ch5\code\Zeta.java
```

and converts this component to a `String`, which is then used to construct a `File` object. This `File` object is used to display information about a file such as *Zeta.java*. The information includes the file's size in bytes and whether the file is readable and writable.

Because the underlying Swing set components are powerful, the `DirTree` utility requires only about two pages of source code. The Swing set's modular architecture encourages customization and expansion of GUIs. For example, the `DirTree` might be expanded so that a mouse click on a node that represents a text file would open the file for editing.

EXERCISES

1. Why is a `JTree` well suited to represent a modern file system?
2. What is the basic distinction between a `JTree` and its tree model, in this example the `DefaultTreeModel`?
3. In the code segment

   ```
   MouseListener ml = new MouseAdapter() { /*...*/ }
   ```

   explain the relationship between `MouseListener` and `MouseAdapter`.
4. The `DirTree` class overloads the `buildTree` method. Explain the functionality of each overload.
5. The `DirTree`'s method `showDetails` uses a `static` method in the `JOption-Pane` class to display a message dialog. Amend the application by providing a `JOptionPane` object to provide the same functionality.

7.5   The Model-View-Controller Architecture

The model-view-controller architecture is a modular, intuitive organization of graphical components. Understanding this architecture can shorten the learning curve for the Swing set. Although Swing set components such as the `JTable` and the `JTree` may seem quite different at first glance, they share an underlying organization that eases the task of programming either component. We begin with an example.

Example 7.5.1.   The `ScrollColor` code in Figure 7.5.1 creates a framed window with a black background and a horizontal scrollbar (see Figure 7.5.2). As the bar is moved from left to right, the window's background changes from black to red; as the bar is moved right to left, the background changes from red to black.

A scrollbar has various parts, including a *thumb* that can moved left and right in a horizontal scrollbar or up and down in a vertical scrollbar. An integer value represents the thumb's position. In a horizontal scrollbar, for example, a thumb might have a value of 0 in the leftmost position and a value of 100 in the rightmost position. A `JScrollBar` object has the standard scrollbar features and functionality. As a Swing set component, a `JScrollBar` falls under the the model-view-controller architecture:

```java
import java.awt.*;
import java.awt.event.*;
import javax.swing.*;
class ScrollColor extends JFrame {
   public ScrollColor() {
      cont = getContentPane();
      setSize( 300, 300 );
      sb = new JScrollBar( JScrollBar.HORIZONTAL );
      sb.addAdjustmentListener(
        new AdjustmentListener() {
          public void adjustmentValueChanged( AdjustmentEvent e ) {
            colorPane( e.getValue() );
          }
        } );
      oldPos = sb.getMinimum();
      cont.add( sb, BorderLayout.NORTH );
      cont.setBackground( Color.black );
      scale = 3;
      setVisible( true );
   }
   private void colorPane( int newPos ) {
      int red = cont.getBackground().getRed();
      red += (newPos - oldPos) * scale;
      if ( red > 0 && red < 255 )
        cont.setBackground( new Color( red, 0, 0 ) );
      oldPos = newPos;
   }
   private Container cont;
   private JScrollBar sb;
   private int oldPos;
   private int scale;
}
```

FIGURE 7.5.1   Using a scrollbar to change a window's background color.

- **Model**. A JScrollBar has a getModel method that returns a reference to its model, a DefaultBoundedRangeModel object. The model encapsulates *state information* about the scrollbar such as its current position within a range of possible values. In particular, the model has methods that return the thumb's minimum position (typically 0 by default), its maximum position (typically 100 by default), and the thumb's own extent (typically 10 units by default).
- **View**. A JScrollBar's view depicts the component's underlying state (model) graphically and also allows the user to *change* the component's state graphically. For example, if a horizontal scrollbar's initial value is 0 in a range of 0 through 100, the thumb is displayed in the leftmost position. If the thumb is moved to the rightmost position, the scrollbar's state changes to a value of 100. The

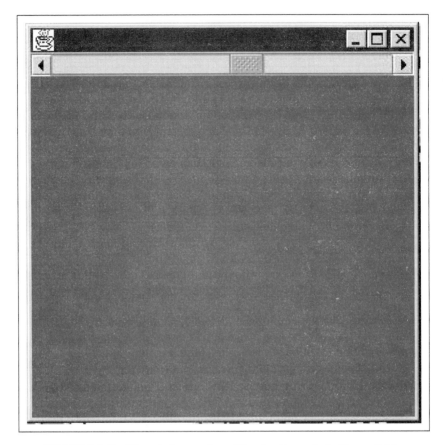

FIGURE 7.5.2   The window and scrollbar for the code in Figure 7.5.1.

view *reflects* the state information stored in the model but manipulating the view—in this case, moving the scrollbar—changes the scrollbar's state.

- **Controller**. The scrollbar's controller is the component's event handler. A scrollbar is a relatively simple component in that it generates only *adjustment events*, that is, events resulting from moving the thumb. As the user manipulates the scrollbar by moving the thumb, the controller determines how the events should be handled. In the obvious case, moving the thumb in the component's view causes the component's position to change, and the change must be stored in the component's model. For example, as the scrollbar moves right from its initial position of 0, the position values are 1, 2, . . . ,99, 100 given the standard range of 0 through 100. In general, the controller manages interactions between the component's model and view.

In the Swing set, components such as JLists, JTables, and JTrees have default models that implement an appropriate interface.

Example 7.5.2. A JList (see Figure 7.3.3) has an implementation of a ListModel, an interface with list-appropriate methods to add and remove elements, to access arbitrary elements, to determine whether an element occurs in the list, and so on. The DefaultListModel class implements the interface and is sufficient for most list processing. However, a programmer could provide a customized implementation of the ListModel for an application that required specialized list processing. In any case, the JList has a getModel method that returns the list's underlying model. The getModel method is standard for components in the model-view-controller architecture.

Example 7.5.3. If a JTree (see Section 7.4) is constructed without an explicit TreeModel, the tree has a DefaultTreeModel, a concrete class that implements the TreeModel interface. Figure 7.5.3 lists the methods in the TreeModel interface. The DefaultTreeModel class uses several fields to support its implementation of the TreeModel interface. For example, the field root refers to the JTree's root node and the listenerList is a list of event listeners for JTree-specific events. In any case, some of the methods in the TreeModel interface are designed specifically to obtain state information about a tree, for example, whether a particular tree node is a leaf. A JTree's underlying model is updated automatically as nodes are added and deleted.

A programmer can construct a JTree using a customized tree model that implements the TreeModel interface. Such customization might be appropriate for particularly large trees or for trees that require special processing.   ∎

Method	Comment
void addTreeModelListener(TreeModelListener l)	Tree change events
Object getChild(Object parent, int i)	Parent's *i*th child
int getIndexOfChild(Object parent, Object child)	Index of child
Object getRoot()	Tree's root node
boolean isLeaf()	A leaf node?
void removeTreeModelListener(TreeModelListener l)	Remove listener
void valueForPathChanged(TreePath p, Object n)	Replace p with n

FIGURE 7.5.3   Methods in the TreeModel interface.

∎ **Example 7.5.4.** A JTable can be constructed with a DefaultTable-Model (see Section 7.6), a concrete class that implements the TableModel interface. The DefaultTableModel class has methods for adding and removing rows and columns, for getting the name of a specified column, for determining whether a specified table cell is editable, and for other table-appropriate operations. Rows are not added directly to a JTable but rather to the underlying model. In effect, the JTable integrates the underlying model with an appropriate view or GUI.

The Swing set also has a `TableColumnModel` interface and the `Default-TableColumnModel` concrete class as a default implementation. A `JTable` can be constructed not only with an explicit table model but also with an explicit column model for the table. ∎

Components such as `JLists`, `JTables`, and `JTrees` can be constructed with explicit models and have a `getModel` method to access their underlying model. Although every Swing set component has a model, not every such component has a public `getModel` method. For example, a relatively simple component such as a `JButton` does not expose its model to clients. Further, every component type has a unique model that is appropriate to precisely that type. For example, a `JList` model differs from a `JTable` model.

Integration of a Component's View and Controller

A Swing set component's *view* and *controller* are integrated in a single object called the **UI delegate** (**UI** stands for **U**ser **I**nterface). Figure 7.5.4 depicts the relationships among a component, a model, a view, a controller, and a UI delegate.[†] Although models must differ among subclasses in the `JComponent` hierarchy, UI delegates need not differ because all of the Swing set's lightweight components are rendered graphically in the same basic way, that is, by using graphics primitives. Accordingly, the *same* UI delegate could be used to display all of the components in the `JComponent` hierarchy. An issue for the programmer is whether to use different built-in UI delegates or whether to customize a UI delegate.

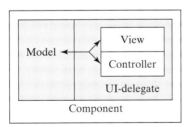

FIGURE 7.5.4   A component, its model, and its UI delegate.

A component's UI delegate plays two roles, although in a particular case one role may be more pronounced than the other. The two roles are

- To draw the component on the screen in a manner that suitably reflects the component's state, which is stored in the component's model.
- To handle events that the component generates. Such event handling may result in changes to the component's model.

[†]The integration of the view and the controller has become popular. The Microsoft Foundation Classes offer a C++ example of the same integration.

In the event-handling role, the UI delegate supplements rather than replaces AWT event handling. For example, a relatively complex component such as a **JTree** generates highly specialized events such as *tree expansion*, which were not anticipated in the AWT's event package. The underlying event handling remains the same, however: registered listeners for events such as tree expansion are notified whenever such events occur so that the listener's appropriate callback can handle the event.

The UI delegate's most obvious service to clients involves a component's *look and feel*. The programmer can manipulate a component's view through various UI delegate methods.

Component Look and Feel

The acronym PLAF stands for **P**luggable **L**ook **A**nd **F**eel, a Swing set architecture that allows the programmer to control a component's look and feel regardless of the underlying platform. The PLAF architecture includes classes from the **javax.swing** package, the **plaf** subpackage, and several subpackages of **plaf**.

In technical terms, PLAF functionality allows the programmer to control how a component is *rendered*, that is, displayed graphically. In less technical terms, PLAF allows a component's view to take on distinct graphical styles. For example, a particular component displayed in a Windows environment has a distinctively Windows look and feel. The same component displayed in a Unix environment under XWindows/Motif has a different look and feel. The PLAF architecture makes it possible for the component to have the *same* look and feel whatever the platform. Further, PLAF enables the programmer to build a customized look and feel.

> ■ **Example 7.5.5.**   The LandF code in Figure 7.5.5 creates a simple GUI class with various Swing set components: a button, a check box, a label, and a text field. The private method **buildMenu** constructs a menu of *look and feels* supported on a particular platform. For example, when statement
>
> new LandF();
>
> executes on Windows NT platform, the menu has three items:
>
> Metal
> CDE/Motif
> Windows
>
> The Metal look and feel is the default for Swing set components. The CDE/Motif[†] look and feel is standard on many Unix systems and is quite similar to the look and feel of Windows 3.1. The Windows look and feel is standard on more recent Windows versions such as Windows 98 and Windows

---

†CDE stands for **C**ommon **D**esktop **E**nvironment.

```java
import javax.swing.*;
import java.awt.*;
import java.awt.event.*;
class LandF extends JFrame {
   public LandF() {
      super( "Look and Feel Example" );
      Font f = new Font( "Dialog", Font.BOLD, 14 );
      cont = getContentPane();
      cont.setLayout( new FlowLayout() );
      close = new JButton( "Close" );
      happy = new JCheckBox( "Happy?" );
      namePrompt = new JLabel( "Field for name ===>" );
      name = new JTextField( "  Please enter your name  " );
      menuBar = new JMenuBar();
      lookAndFeelMenu = new JMenu( "Look and Feel" );
      lookAndFeelMenu.setFont( f );
      buildMenu();
      menuBar.add( lookAndFeelMenu );
      setJMenuBar( menuBar );
      close.setFont( f );
      close.addActionListener( new ActionListener() {
         public void actionPerformed( ActionEvent e ) {
            dispose();
         } } );
      happy.setFont( f );
      namePrompt.setFont( f );
      namePrompt.setForeground( Color.black );
      name.setFont( f );
      cont.setLayout( new FlowLayout() );
      cont.add( close );
      cont.add( happy );
      cont.add( namePrompt );
      cont.add( name );
      setSize( 600, 200 );
      setVisible( true );
   }
```

FIGURE 7.5.5   A simple GUI with a menu to change its look and feel.

NT. Figure 7.5.6 shows the Metal look and feel on a Windows NT platform, and Figure 7.5.7 shows the Motif look and feel on the same platform.

The LandF's private buildMenu method invokes static methods from the utility UIManager and SwingUtilities classes:

• UIManager.getInstalledLookAndFeels(), which returns a list of look and feels available on the platform. The Metal, Motif, and Windows are typically available on desktop systems.

```
private void buildMenu() {
   final UIManager.LookAndFeelInfo[ ] lfs =
         UIManager.getInstalledLookAndFeels();
   for ( int i = 0; i < lfs.length; i++ ) {
      String name = lfs[ i ].getName();
      final UIManager.LookAndFeelInfo lf = lfs[ i ];
      JMenuItem item = new JMenuItem( name, name.charAt( 0 ) );
      lookAndFeelMenu.add( item );
      item.addActionListener( new ActionListener() {
         public void actionPerformed( ActionEvent e ) {
            try {
               UIManager.setLookAndFeel( lf.getClassName() );
            }
            catch( Exception ex ) { System.err.println( ex ); }
            SwingUtilities.updateComponentTreeUI( LandF.this );
         } } );
   }
}
private Container cont;
private JButton close;
private JCheckBox happy;
private JTextField name;
private JLabel namePrompt;
private JMenuBar menuBar;
private JMenu lookAndFeelMenu;
}
```

FIGURE 7.5.5   A simple GUI with a menu to change its look and feel,
continued.

- `UIManager.setLookAndFeel( String name )`, which sets a component's look and feel to the named one.
- `SwingUtilities.updateComponentTree( Component c )`, which invokes `updateUI` for each child component in a container component such as a `JFrame`. For example, if our goal were to change only the check box's look and feel, we would replace this call with

```
happy.updateUI(); // JCheckBox
```

The `updateUI` updates a component's look and feel to the current one. After a look and feel has been changed, `updateUI` causes a particular component to be *displayed* with the new look and feel. The `updateComponentTree` is thus a convenient shortcut in cases where `updateUI` would otherwise be invoked on *all* components in a container. ∎

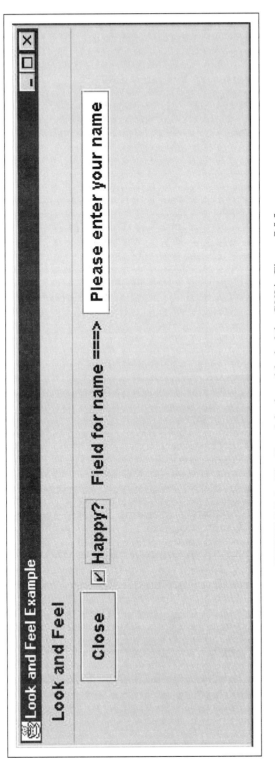

FIGURE 7.5.6 The Metal look and feel of the GUI in Figure 7.5.5.

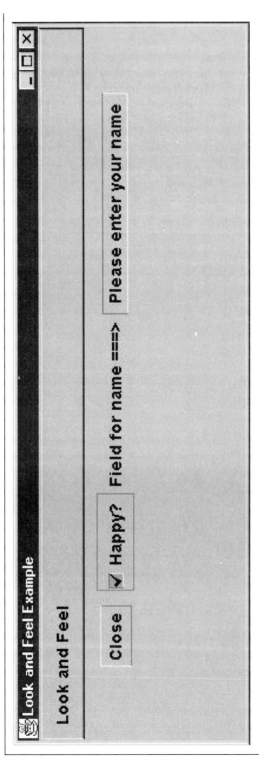

FIGURE 7.5.7 The Motif look and feel of the GUI in Figure 7.5.5.

Painting and Repainting

When a component is first shown, it needs to be **painted**, that is, rendered graphically. The Component class has a paint method, which expects a Graphics argument. The abstract class Graphics serves as the superclass for all **graphics contexts**, which are objects that encapsulate information used in drawing operations. For example, the Graphics class has a setColor method that sets the particular color for all subsequent graphics operations, such as drawing lines or ovals, using a particular graphics context. Figure 7.5.8 lists the Graphics methods.

Once drawn, a component may later need to be redrawn. Suppose, for example, that a string is drawn on a component using the drawString method of the Graphics class. If the string is later changed, the component needs to be *repainted* so that the new string is displayed. Although the programmer might invoke paint directly, it is easier to invoke repaint, which expects no arguments. Method repaint calls update with an appropriate graphics context, and update then invokes paint.

> **Example 7.5.6.**   The OneButton class in Figure 7.5.9 overrides the paint method to draw one of two strings inside a colored 3D rectangle. Each time the user clicks the JButton, the string and the rectangle's color are changed. The original string, Hello, world!, is displayed in a white 3D rectangle (see Figure 7.5.10). If the user clicks the button, the string changes to What, me worry? and the rectangle's color changes to cyan. To display the new string and to change the rectangle's color, the actionPerformed callback invokes repaint, which causes paint to be invoked:

```
public void paint( Graphics g ) {
    super.paint( g ); //*** to clear the pane
    g.draw3DRect( 50, 70, 150, 70, true );
    g.setColor( fillColor );
    g.fill3DRect( 50, 70, 150, 70, true );
    g.setColor( Color.black );
    g.setFont( f );
    g.drawString( displayedMsg, 70, 100 );
}
```

> The call to the superclass's paint clears the component. Next the 3D rectangle is drawn and filled with the appropriate color. The Graphics color then must be set to black so that the string is not drawn in the same color as the rectangle. The Graphics font also is set. Finally, the string is drawn at the specified x and y coordinates. In general, an override of paint should invoke the superclass's paint in order to clear the drawing area before any new drawing occurs. ■

Method	Description
`void clearRect(int x, int y,` `int w, int h)`	Restore rectangle to current background.
`void clipRect(int x, int y,` `int w, int h)`	Intersect clip region and rectangle.

`void copyArea(int x, int y,`
`int w, int h`
`int dx, int dy)`
	Copy area to specified destination (dx,dy).

`void create()`	Create a copy of this graphics context.
`void dispose()`	Free resources of this graphics context.

`void draw3DRect(int x, int y,`
`int w, int h,`
`boolean raised)`
	Draw 3-D outline of rectangle.

`void drawArc(int x, int y,`
`int w, int h,`
`int startAngle,`
`int arcAngle)`
	Draw outline of circular or elliptical arc.

`void drawBytes(byte[ ] b,`
`int st, int len,`
`int x, int y)`
	Draw text bytes at (x,y).
	(*Method* `drawChars` *is similar.*)

`boolean drawImage(Image i, int x,`
`int y, Color c,`
`ImageObserver io)`
	Draw image at (x,y).
	(*Six overloads.*)

`void drawLine(int x1, int y1,` `int x2, int y2)`	Draw line from (x1,y1) to (x2,y2).
`void drawOval(int x, int y,` `int w, int h)`	Draw oval of specified width and height.
`void drawPolygon(Polygon p)`	Draw polygon. (*Two overloads.*)

`void drawPolyline(int[ ] xPts,`
`int[ ] yPts,`
`int count`
	Connect pairs of points (xPts,yPts).

`void drawRect(int x, int y,` `int w, int h)`	Draw rectangle of specified width and height.

`void drawRoundRect(int x, int y,`
`int w, int h)`
`int aw, int ah)`
	Draw rounded rectangle of specified width, height, arc width, and arc height.

`void drawString(String s, int x,` `int y)`	Draw string at (x,y). (*Two overloads.*)

`void fill3DRect(int x, int y,`
`int w, int h,`
`boolean raised)`
	Fill 3D rectangle with graphics context current color.

`void fillArc(int x, int y,`
`int w, int h,`
`int sa, int aa)`
	Fill arc with graphics context current color.

`void fillOval(int x, int y,` `int w, int h,`	Fill oval with graphics context current color.

FIGURE 7.5.8   Methods in the abstract `Graphics` class.

Method	Description
void fillPolygon(Polygon p)	Fill polygon. (*Two overloads.*)
void fillRect(int x, int y, int w, int h)	Fill rectangle with graphics context current color.
void fillRoundRect(int x, int y, int w, int h, int aw, int wh)	Fill rounded rectangle with graphics context current color.
void finalize()	Dispose of graphics context once not referenced.
Shape getClip()	Get the current clipping area.
Rectangle getClipBounds()	Get clip area's bounding rectangle.
Color getColor()	Get graphics context current color.
Font getFont()	Get the font.
FontMetrics getFontMetrics()	Get the font's metrics. (*Two overloads.*)
boolean hitClip(int x, int y, int w, int h)	Return true if clip area's bounding rectangle intersects specified rectangle.
void setClip(Shape s)	Set the clip area to s. (*Two overloads.*)
void setColor(Color c)	Set the color to c.
void setFont(Font f)	Set the font to f.
void setPaintMode()	Set paint mode to overwrite in current color.
void setXORMode(Color c)	Set xor to alternate between c and current color.
String toString()	Return a String representation.
void translate(int x, int y)	Translate origin to point (x,y).

FIGURE 7.5.8   Methods in the abstract Graphics class, *continued.*

Validating and Invalidating

Every component has a pair of methods, validate and invalidate, that can be invoked to ensure that any change to a component property is reflected in how the component is displayed. For example, suppose that we amend the OneButton code in Figure 7.5.9 so that every fifth click of the button adds a new JLabel to the GUI. The revised actionPerformed

```
public void actionPerformed( ActionEvent e ) {
    displayedMsg = (toggle) ? msg1 : msg2;
    fillColor = (toggle) ? Color.white : Color.cyan;
    toggle = !toggle;
    repaint();
    if ( ++count > 4 ) {
        c.add( new JLabel( "Wow!" ) );
        c.validate();
        count = 0;
    }
} } );
```

shows how this could be done. After the JLabel is added to the container, the container's validate method is invoked to ensure that the newly added label is

```
import javax.swing.*;
import java.awt.*;
import java.awt.event.*;
class OneButton extends JFrame {
    public OneButton() {
        super( "Repaint Example" );
        c = getContentPane();
        displayedMsg = msg1 = "Hello, world!";
        msg2 = "What, me worry?";
        b = new JButton( " Toggle " );
        b.addActionListener( new ActionListener() {
            public void actionPerformed( ActionEvent e ) {
                displayedMsg = (toggle) ? msg1 : msg2;
                fillColor = (toggle) ? Color.white : Color.cyan;
                toggle = !toggle;
                repaint(); //*** invokes update, which invokes paint
            } } );
        c.setLayout( new FlowLayout() );
        c.add( b );
        c.setFont( f = new Font( "Dialog", Font.BOLD, 14 ) );
        setSize( 300, 200 );
        setVisible( true );
    }
    public void paint( Graphics g ) {
        super.paint( g ); //*** to clear the pane
        g.draw3DRect( 50, 70, 150, 70, true );
        g.setColor( fillColor );
        g.fill3DRect( 50, 70, 150, 70, true );
        g.setColor( Color.black );
        g.setFont( f );
        g.drawString( displayedMsg, 70, 100 );
    }
    private Container c;
    private JButton b;
    private String msg1, msg2, displayedMsg;
    private Color fillColor = Color.white;
    private boolean toggle;
    private Font f;
    private int count;
}
```

FIGURE 7.5.9   Example of overriding paint and invoking repaint.

indeed arranged and displayed in the proper way. If the call to validate is removed,
the new JLabel may not be displayed.

A component's invalidate method signals that the component has changed in
some way that would impact its display. For example, if a labeled JButton's font is made

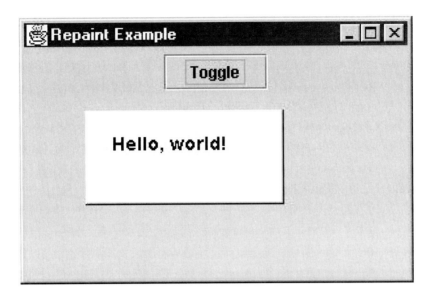

FIGURE 7.5.10   The initial string drawn by the code in Figure 7.5.9.

larger, the JButton typically needs to be resized so that the entire label fits properly within the button. If jb refers to a button whose font is changed dynamically, the call

```
jb.invalidate(); //*** I need redrawing!
```

signals that the button needs redrawing. For safety, the validate method of the button's container also might be invoked to signal that the container has changed in some way, in this case by a change in a button's font. The validate call would cause the container to redraw itself and its components.

A component's invalidate method is usually invoked automatically whenever a GUI-impacting property is changed. The programmer can still invoke the method explicitly if this invocation does not occur automatically.

EXERCISES

1. Explain the *model*, the *view*, and the *controller* of a sample component such as a JScrollBar or a JTree.
2. The Swing set's JList class has a ListModel. Explain why the list's *selection mode*—whether the list is enabled for single or multiple selections—is set in the ListModel rather than the JList itself.
3. Java does not have a pure model-view-controller architecture in that two of three parts are integrated into one. Which two?

4. What is the `UIDelegate` in a Swing set component?

5. What is a *graphics context*?

6. What are the three look and feels commonly available on desktop systems?

7. Explain the relationship between a `Component`'s `paint` and `repaint` methods.

8. Why does an override of `paint` typically invoke the superclass's version as the first statement in the override's own body?

9. Explain the purpose of the methods `validate` and `invalidate`.

10. Is `java.awt.Graphics` a concrete class, an abstract class, or an interface?

7.6   Sample Application: A Graphical Table Editor

Problem

Provide a graphical interface for the `EmpRW` utility of Polymorphic Input and Output sample application (see Section 6.3). The interface should support the record-based display of the data and the editing of all fields in a record.

Sample Input

Figure 7.6.1 shows the GUI for the data from the `EmpRW` Sample Application in Section 6.3.

ID	LNAME	FNAME	DEPT	TITLE	RPTS	DISC	OPTS	HR	OT
AC98	HAMPSTEN	ANDY	MKT	NA	NA	NA	NA	NA	NA
B718	HAMM	MIA	ACC	VPSALES	504	NA	NA	NA	NA
449A	RUBIN	CHANDRA	MIS	DIRECTOR	781	NA	NA	NA	NA
22WR	KERR	STEVE	MKT	NA	NA	NA	NA	110.25	234.75
AA89	GRAF	STEFFIE	CIO	MIS	9000	500.0	3000.0	NA	NA
9871	BALBOA	ROCKY	ACC	NA	NA	NA	NA	8.45	17.05
GFD1	DAEHLIE	BJOERN	ORG	CEO	14000	4500.0	1000.0	NA	NA
4561	ARMSTRONG	LANCE	MIS	NA	NA	NA	NA	NA	NA
0091	BELMONDO	STEFANIA	ACC	NA	NA	NA	NA	NA	NA
2323	JORDAN	MICHAEL	GRD	NA	NA	NA	NA	5001.24	25876.42
4431	DICENTA	MANUELA	MIS	NA	NA	NA	NA	NA	NA

FIGURE 7.6.1   The `JTable` with employee records for editing.

Solution

The application uses the Swing set's `JTable`, which displays data in a two-dimensional table format. A `JFileChooser` component allows the user to select an input file, and a button click saves the edited records to an output file. The `EmpRW` utility of Section 6.3 handles the underlying input/output operations.

Java Implementation

```java
import java.util.*;
import java.awt.*;
import java.awt.event.*;
import javax.swing.*;
import javax.swing.table.*;
public class EmpGUI extends JFrame {
   //** Construct the GUI, including controls and a JTable,
   //    and display the GUI automatically.
   //    Syntax: new EmpGUI()
   public EmpGUI() {
      super( "Employee Edit Application" );
      setSize( 900, 350 );
      cont = getContentPane();
      initControls();
      initTable();
      show();
   }

   //** Add buttons to read, write, and exit.
   //    Add action listeners per button.
   private void initControls() {
      JButton b;
      JPanel controls = new JPanel();
      controls.setLayout( new FlowLayout() );
      b = addButton( controls, readString );
      b.addActionListener( new ActionListener() {
         public void actionPerformed( ActionEvent e ) { read(); }
      } );
      b = addButton( controls, writeString );
      b.addActionListener( new ActionListener() {
         public void actionPerformed( ActionEvent e ) { write(); }
      } );
      b = addButton( controls, exitString );
      b.addActionListener( new ActionListener() {
         public void actionPerformed( ActionEvent e ) {
            System.exit( 0 ); }
      } );
      cont.add( controls, BorderLayout.NORTH );
   }

   //** Create an empty JTable to hold the employee records
   private void initTable() {
      String[ ] cols = { "CODE", "ID", "LNAME", "FNAME", "DEPT",
```

```java
                    "TITLE", "RPTS", "DISC", "OPTS", "HR", "OT" };
    dm = new DefaultTableModel( cols, 0 );
    table = new JTable( dm );
    table.getTableHeader().setFont( new Font( "Dialog",
                                         Font.BOLD, 12 ) );
    cont.add( new JScrollPane( table ), BorderLayout.CENTER );
}


//** Add the named button to a panel
private JButton addButton( JPanel p, String name ) {
    JButton b = new JButton( name );
    b.setFont( new Font( "Dialog", Font.BOLD, 14 ) );
    p.add( b );
    return b;
}


//** Use an EmpRW object to read records from a
//   specified input file. Add the records to the JTable.
private void read() {
    clearRows();
    JFileChooser fc = new JFileChooser();
    int choice = fc.showOpenDialog( new JFrame() );
    if ( choice == JFileChooser.APPROVE_OPTION )
      infileName = fc.getSelectedFile().getName();
    else
      return; //*** user hit CANCEL button
    String outfileName = "OutputFor_" + infileName;
    empRW = new EmpRW( infileName, outfileName );
    empRW.read();
    Enumeration e = empRW.getEmps().elements();
    while ( e.hasMoreElements() ) {
      Emp t = (Emp) e.nextElement();
      dm.addRow( t.getFieldValues() ); //*** polymorphic
    }
}


//** Use an EmpRW object to write records from the JTable
//   to a specified file.
private void write() {
    Enumeration e = dm.getDataVector().elements();
    Vector records = new Vector();
    while ( e.hasMoreElements() ) {
      Vector fields = (Vector) e.nextElement();
      String t = "";
      Enumeration e2 = fields.elements();
```

```
        while ( e2.hasMoreElements() ) {
            String s = (String) e2.nextElement();
            if ( !s.equals( Emp.NotApplicable ) )
              t += s + " ";
        }
        records.addElement( t );
    }
    empRW.writeRecords( records );
}

//** Clear the JTable's rows before a read.
private void clearRows() {
    int n = dm.getRowCount();
    for ( int i = dm.getRowCount() - 1; i >= 0; i-- )
        dm.removeRow( i );
}
//*** instance fields
private Container cont;
private JTable table;
private DefaultTableModel dm;
private EmpRW  empRW;
private String infileName;
private String outfileName;
//*** class fields
private static final String readString  = " Read File ";
private static final String writeString = " Write File ";
private static final String exitString  = " Exit ";
}
```

Discussion

A JTable is a lightweight component that is derived directly from JComponent and falls under the model-view-controller architecture. A JTable thus has a model, and the Swing set provides a DefaultTableModel for clients that do not need a customized table model. The JTable also supports view customization but again provides a default so that a two-dimensional table can be constructed straightforwardly.

The current application constructs a DefaultTableModel with 11 columns or fields, each representing a feature of an object in the Emp hierarchy of Section 6.3. For example, there are columns to represent an employee's first and last name, department, and title. The code segment

```
String[ ] cols = { "CODE", "ID", "LNAME", "FNAME", "DEPT",
        "TITLE", "RPTS", "DISC", "OPTS", "HR", "OT" };
dm = new DefaultTableModel( cols, 0 );
table = new JTable( dm );
```

first constructs an empty `DefaultTableModel` by specifying the column names and the number of rows (0) in the model. The table is empty to begin because records are added during the input operation by invoking the table model's `addRecord` method with an array of `Strings`, with each `String` representing a particular field's value. The `JTable` is constructed from the `DefaultTableModel` and placed within a `JScrollPane` so that a scrollbar is available if the `JTable` cannot display on the screen all of the records in the underlying table model.

Editing Employee Records

The Swing set's `JFileChooser` is a specialized dialog for selecting a file. Once the user has selected a text input file with the help of this dialog, an `EmpRW` object is constructed to perform the input operations. The current application thus leverages the functionality of the `EmpRW` object, which in turn delegates specific input operations to the polymorphic `read` methods in the `Emp` hierarchy. Before the input operations begin, any records currently in the table model are removed.

Employees do not share all features. For instance, a `CorpOff` (corporate officer) does not have an overtime wage but a `Temporary` worker does. If a particular feature does not apply to a particular employee, NA (**N**ot **A**pplicable) appears as the field value. The user completes an editing session by clicking a button, which saves the records to a separate file from the input file. The application thus prevents the input file from being accidentally overwritten during a session. The records are written in the same format in which they were read so that the output file can be used as the input file in a subsequent session.

Because the `JTable` and `DefaultTableModel` classes hide so many implementation details, the application itself is only about a page and a half of source code. Finally, the application uses only Swing set components. For example, `JButtons` and a `JPanel` are used instead of AWT `Buttons` and the AWT `Panel`.

EXERCISES

1. Compile and run the sample application.
2. Explain why the `TableModel` rather than the `JTable` itself has methods to add and remove records.
3. Why is the `JTable` placed inside a `JScrollPane`?
4. A `JFileChooser` has an `APPROVE_OPTION` field that indicates whether the user selected a file or canceled the operation. Is the `APPROVE_OPTION` a `static` field?

COMMON ERRORS AND SAFE PRACTICES

1. The package for AWT components is `java.awt`, but the package for Swing set components is `javax.swing`. Accordingly, the statement

```
import java.swing.*; //***** ERROR: javax, not java
```

is in error.

2. The package for basic event handling is `java.awt.event`. The statement

```
import java.awt.*; //*** does not import subpackages
```

imports AWT classes but *not* classes of AWT subpackages such as the event subpackage. The code segment

```
import java.awt.*;
class Alpha implements WindowListener { //**** ERROR
```

is in error. The error can be corrected by either the proper `import` statement

```
import java.awt.event.*;
class Alpha implements WindowListener {  // ok
```

or a fully qualified name

```
class Alpha implements java.awt.event.WindowListener {
```

3. To be concrete, a class that implements an event-listener interface such as `ActionListener` must define all of the methods declared in the interface. The code segment

```
import java.awt.event.*;
import javax.swing.*;
class MyGUI extends JFrame implements ActionListener {
   // actionPerformed is not defined
}
class MyGuiDriver {
   public static void main( String[ ] args ) {
      new MyGUI(); //**** ERROR: MyGUI is abstract
   }
}
```

illustrates the error.

4. Top-level windows such as `JFrame`s are *invisible* when constructed. The code segment

```
JFrame myWin = new JFrame(); //*** invisible
myWin.show(); // == myWin.setVisible( true )
```

illustrates how such windows can be made visible.

5. Components are added directly to a java.awt.Frame container but to the *content pane* of a javax.swing.JFrame container. The code segment

```
Frame f1 = new Frame();
f1.add( new Button( "foo" ) ); // ok

JFrame f2 = new JFrame();
f2.add( new Button( "bar" ) ); //***** ERROR
f2.getContentPane().add( new Button( "bar" ) ); // ok
```

illustrates the difference. The getContentPane method returns a Container to hold JFrame components.

6. An override of the paint method should invoke the superclass version to clear the painting surface. The code segment

```
public void paint( Graphics g ) {
    super.paint( g ); //*** invoke superclass version
    //...local customization
}
```

illustrates.

7. If controls are added dynamically to a container, the container's validate method should be invoked after the additions to ensure that the container is rendered properly with its newly embedded components.

PROGRAMMING EXERCISES

7.1. Provide a GUI for the FillAndSort program of Figure 2.2.3. The GUI should display the generated integers before and after they have been sorted.

7.2. Provide a GUI for the nondecreasing sequence program of Programming Exericse 2.6. The GUI should display the original sequence, each of the nondecreasing sequences, and the nondecreasing sequence with the largest sum.

7.3. Users of modern applications such as browsers sometimes complain that the graphical interfaces are too complex. Provide a GUI that meets your needs and expectations for a browser. Chapter 9 on networking covers some tools to make your browser functional.

7.4. Provide a GUI for the program in Programming Exercise 3.10, which tracks the population of a species given an initial population and a growth rate. In particular, provide a graphical representation of the population over a user-specified time period. Also, allow the user to set the initial population and the growth rate.

7.5. Build a graphical application in which a user enters a sequence of letters. The program permutes the letters and uses a dictionary to determine whether a particular permutation is a word. Once the process completes, the application displays the original sequence of letters together with a list of words and a separate list of nonwords.

7.6. Provide a GUI for the `Convert` program in Programming Exercise 3.13. The user should be able to enter an infix expression and see the equivalent postfix expression displayed.

7.7. Build a graphical calendar that allows the user to select a year and a month. The calendar should then display the month with buttons representing each day. The user then can specify a particular date by clicking the appropriate button.

7.8. Provide a GUI for the Roman numeral conversion program of Programming Exercise 4.6. The user should be able to enter either a Roman or a decimal numeral and then click a button to convert to the other format. The GUI also should allow a user to perform addition and subtraction on Roman numerals. *Hint*: For the arithmetic operations, first convert the Roman numerals to their decimal equivalents, perform the operation, and convert the result, if possible, back to a Roman numeral.

7.9. Provide a GUI for John Conway's game of *Life* (see Programming Exercise 4.7).

7.10. The Swing set package `javax.swing.text` has classes for building text editors. Use the package to build a basic test editor that supports standard editing operations such as creating, opening, and saving text files, adding and deleting text, changing fonts, and putting text into italics or bold type.

7.11. Extend Programming Exercise 7.10 by providing a *structured editor* for writing Java source code. A structured editor provides language-specific support. For example, such an editor might display general keywords such as `static` in one color (e.g., blue), data types such as `int` in another color (e.g., red), programmer-selected variable names in another color (e.g., black), and documentation in yet another color (e.g., green). The editor also might provide automatic indentation and alignment.

7.12. Define a `Spreadsheet` class and any required auxiliary classes to create a spreadsheet application, which should have a GUI that allows users to enter three types of data into a spreadsheet cell:

- **Label**: A label is used for documentation. For example, the first cell in a column could contain the label *Monthly Sales* and each of the cells under it would have a label such as *Jan* or *Feb* to its left in order to represent the month.
- **Signed numeric constant**: A signed numeric constant represents an integer or a floating-point number. For example, the signed numeric constant -47 represents negative forty-seven.

- **Formula**: A formula allows a cell's numeric value to be computed from values in other cells. Assuming that the spreadsheet's rows have unique identifiers $R1, R2, \ldots$ and that the spreadsheet's columns have unique identifiers $C1, C2, \ldots$, a formula has the syntax

$$= R1C10 + R14C37 * 2$$

A formula begins with an equals sign $=$ and may contain the standard binary arithmetic operators. The formula's terms may be cell references (e.g., $R1C10$) or numerical constants (e.g., 2).

The spreadsheet should have instruments (e.g., buttons or menu items) to clear the spreadsheet, to copy a region from one location to another, and to compute the spreadsheet by computing the value of every cell. *Hint*: Computing the spreadsheet can be simplified if each cell has a `contents` property of an appropriate numeric type (e.g., `int` or `double`). If a cell contains a label, its `contents` is set to some special value to reflect this fact. Otherwise, the value of the `contents` reflects either the constant displayed in the cell (e.g., 47) or the value of the formula displayed in the cell (e.g., $= R1C10 + R14C37 * 2$). Each cell also maintains a list of other cells whose values depend on it. For example, if cell $R2C2$ contains the formula

$$= R1C10 + R14C37 * 2$$

then each of the cells $R1C10$ and $R14C11$ would have $R2C2$ as an entry in the dependency list. If $R1C10$'s contents were changed, for example, then the spreadsheet would automatically update $R2C2$'s contents to reflect $R1C10$'s new value.

7.13. Build a graphical application that plays a tic-tac-toe board game against a human opponent. Each cell on the game's 3×3 board can hold either an X or an O, two symbols that are assigned to each of two players. The players flip a coin to determine who goes first and then place symbols in open board cells. The first player to have three symbols in a row, a column, or a diagonal wins the game. If both opponents play well, the game ends in a draw. The application should have a *play back* facility that displays the history of each game as a sequence of moves.

7.14. Build a card-playing application for a game such as solitaire or poker. The application's GUI should simulate shuffling, dealing, and other standard operations in card games. If appropriate, the application should display scores, wins, losses, and the like. *Hint*: Various third-party packages with card graphics are available through the Internet. Also, see Programming Exercise 6.2.

7.15. Provide a GUI for the `Calculator` class of Programming Exercise 5.8.

7.16. Provide a GUI for the `Spaceship` class of Programming Exercise 5.10 and animate basic spaceship operations.

7.17. Provide a GUI for the index hierarchy in Programming Exercise 6.8. The user should be able to enter index entries through a text field, to recompute the index, to search the index for a particular entry, and to view the index as a whole through, for example, a scrolled window.

7.18. Build a graphical application that draws the shapes specified in the `Shape` interface of Programming Exercise 6.10.

7.19. The package `javax.swing.text.html` has classes to support text editors for HTML (**H**yper **T**ext **M**arkup **L**anguage) documents, which is pertinent because the JDK itself includes HTML documentation for the Java language. Use the Swing set package to build an editor that can at least display HTML documents.

7.20. Provide a GUI for the `MarbleGame` of Figure 2.2.7. The GUI should allow a user to move marbles into urns through mouse clicks or mouse drags. The user also should determine the number of simulations to run in order to determine the probability of winning with the specified distribution of marbles.

7.21. Build a graphical application that simulates the behavior of chip-gathering ants. In the simulation, a rectangular grid represents the *range* in which ants search for chips suitable for building a nest. For example, a 25 × 25 range would have 625 cells. In the simulation's initial state, individual chips are randomly distributed in a specified percentage of the range's cells. For example, if .75 were the specified percentage of chip coverage for a 25 × 25 range, then 469 randomly selected cells would hold one chip apiece. In the simulation's initial state, individual ants are also randomly distributed in a specified percentage of the range's cells. For example, if .50 were the specified percentage of ant coverage for a 25 × 25 range, then 313 randomly selected cells would hold one chip apiece. In the initial state, however, a cell should not hold both an ant and a chip.

Once the simulation begins, randomly selected ants move into randomly selected *neighboring cells*, where a neighboring cell is immediately above, below, to the left, or to the right of an ant's current cell. Cells in the grid's corners have only two neighbors, cells along the grid's edges but not in the corners have three neighbors, and cells in the grid's interior have four neighbors. The following rules constrain the movements. For ease of reference, an *empty-handed ant* is one that is not carrying a chip and a *chip-bearing ant* is one that is carrying a single chip.

- A cell can hold only one ant at a time; that is, an ant cannot move into a cell that another ant already occupies.
- If an empty-handed ant enters a cell that holds any chips, the ant picks up a single chip for its next move.
- If a chip-bearing ant enters a cell that holds any chips, the ant deposits the chip but does *not* pick up a chip.
- If a chip-bearing ant enters a cell without any chips, the ant holds onto the chip for its next move.

Under these rules, the chips tend to congregate in a relatively small number of cells. The simulation should run a specified number of *moves*, where a move consists of an ant's moving from one cell to another.

Three Interfaces: **Cloneable, Serializable,** and **Runnable**

Chapter Outline

This chapter examines three important standard interfaces. The Cloneable[†] and Serializable interfaces are empty or **marker** interfaces, which signal that an implementing class has a distinctive feature. A class that implements Cloneable thereby signals a policy about the cloning—this is, copying—of its objects. A class that implements Serializable thereby signals that its in-memory objects can be **serialized**, that is, transformed to a byte stream and later reconstructed in memory to the same state from a byte stream. The Runnable interface, which pertains to Threads, declares a single method run. A Thread represents a **thread of control**, a sequence of instructions that executes in the JVM. After a Thread is constructed, its start method is invoked to signal that the thread is *ready* to run. The JVM invokes the object's run method to execute the instructions in the method's body. The Runnable interface's run method thus serves as a *callback* for executing threads. Any thread started with the start method executes the code in a run method.

The chapter has two sample applications, one on serialization and the other on multithreading, as well as various shorter programs to illustrate the three standard interfaces.

8.1   Cloning Objects

Cloning objects differs from copying *object references*. The code segment

```
Date d1 = new Date(), d2;
d2 = d1; // two references to one object
```

constructs a single Date object that has two references to it: d1 and d2 (see Figure 8.1.1).

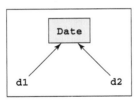

FIGURE 8.1.1   Two references to a single Date object.

The code segment does not clone—that is, create an exact copy of—a Date object.

An object is not cloned by duplicating references to it but rather by invoking its clone method, if the method is available.

■ **Example 8.1.1.**   The code segment

```
Date today = new Date();
Date todayClone = (Date) today.clone();
```

[†]The language designers are aware that Cloneable should be spelled Clonable. The former spelling may be deprecated eventually.

constructs a Date object named today and then clones the object by invoking its clone method. The cast to type Date is required because Object is clone's return type. After the clone, there are two distinct but identical Date objects (see Figure 8.1.2). ■

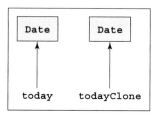

today   todayClone

FIGURE 8.1.2 Cloning a Date object.

The Default Implementation of the clone Method

The class Object has a *protected* method named clone, which is therefore the default implementation of clone. Recall that protected members are visible only *within* the superclass's package and its descendants. Of course, no programmer-defined class is in the same package, java.lang, as Object. For a programmer-defined class, the clone inherited from Object is thus visible only *within* the class and its descendants.

■ **Example 8.1.2.**   The program

```
class Emp {
   public Emp( int ID ) { id = ID; }
   private int id;
}
public class CloneTest  {
   public static void main( String[ ] args ) {
      Emp e1 = new Emp( 1 );
      Emp e2 = (Emp) e1.clone(); //***** ERROR
   }
}
```

contains an error because CloneTest is not a descendant of Emp. Therefore, the protected clone that Emp inherits from Object is *not* visible in CloneTest. ■

The error in Example 8.1.2 can be eliminated by having Emp implement Cloneable and override clone so that it has public scope:

```
class Emp implements Cloneable {
   public Emp( int ID ) { id = ID; }
   public Object clone() throws CloneNotSupportedException {
```

```
            return super.clone();
        }
        private int id;
    }
```

This revision of Example 8.1.2 makes two changes. First, the class Emp now implements Cloneable to signal that the class has a policy for cloning Emp objects. Second, the override of clone redeclares the method as public. The override simply invokes the clone in superclass Object, which returns an exact copy of an object. If the CloneTest program were run with the revised version of Emp, references e1 and e2 would refer to *distinct* objects (see Figure 8.1.3) whose id fields have the same value. Finally, the default clone method can throw a CloneNotSupportedException, which explains the throws clause in the Emp override.

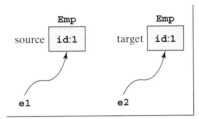

FIGURE 8.1.3   The Emp source and target objects in the cloning of an Emp object.

Problems with the Default clone Method

The cloning of objects can lead to subtle problems if the object encapsulates object or array *references*. The difficulty can be illustrated with an example.

■ **Example 8.1.3.**   The CloneProblem program in Figure 8.1.4 clones a Zeta object, which has a field named al that refers to an Alpha object. The Zeta override of clone simply invokes the superclass's clone, in this case the Object class's clone, which copies the field values from the source to the cloned object. Class Zeta's only field is an *object reference* to an Alpha object; hence, the source and the cloned Zeta objects have fields that refer to the *same* Alpha object (see Figure 8.1.5). Invoking the cloned object's set method changes the shared Alpha object; hence, a change to the cloned object also changes the source object. The point is that the source and the cloned objects be *independent* after the cloning.

Example 8.1.4.   The CloneProblemFix program of Figure 8.1.6 corrects the CloneProblem of Figure 8.1.4. In particular, the Zeta class's clone method now

- Invokes the superclass clone (in this case, Object's version) to create an exact copy of itself, including a copy of the reference al to an Alpha object.

```
class Alpha implements Cloneable {
   public void set( int i ) { n = i; }
   public int get() { return n; }
   public Object clone() throws CloneNotSupportedException {
     return super.clone();
   }
   int n;
}
class Zeta implements Cloneable {
   public void set( int i ) { al.set( i ); }
   public int get() { return al.get(); }
   public Object clone() throws CloneNotSupportedException {
      return super.clone(); //***** Caution!
   }
   Alpha al = new Alpha();
}
class CloneProblem {
   public static void main( String[ ] args ) throws
                     CloneNotSupportedException {
      Zeta z1 = new Zeta();          //*** create one Zeta object
      z1.set( 1 );                   //*** z1.alpha == 1
      Zeta z2 = (Zeta) z1.clone();   //*** clone the object
      z2.set( 2 );                   //*** z2.alpha == 2
      System.out.println( z1.get() ); //***** Note well: z1.alpha == 2!
   }
}
```

FIGURE 8.1.4   A program to illustrate problems with the default `clone` method.

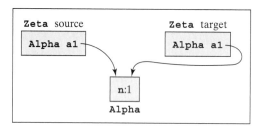

FIGURE 8.1.5   The result of cloning in the `CloneProblem` program of Figure 8.1.4.

- Invokes the `Alpha` field's `clone` to create an exact—and distinct—copy of the `Alpha` field, which is then assigned as the newly cloned `Zeta` object's `Alpha` field.
- Returns a reference to the newly and properly cloned `Zeta` object.

As a result, a change to either the original or the cloned object does not affect the other object (see Figure 8.1.7).

```
class Alpha implements Cloneable {
   public void set( int i ) { n = i; }
   public int get() { return n; }
   public Object clone() throws CloneNotSupportedException {
     return super.clone();
   }
   int n;
}
class Zeta implements Cloneable {
   public void set( int i ) { al.set( i ); }
   public int get() { return al.get(); }
   public Object clone() throws CloneNotSupportedException {
      Zeta t = (Zeta) super.clone();   //** 1st use the superclass clone
      t.al = (Alpha) al.clone();       //** 2nd invoke Alpha's clone
      return t;                        //** 3rd return the exact copy
   }
   Alpha al = new Alpha();
}
class CloneProblemFix {
   public static void main( String[ ] args ) throws
                     CloneNotSupportedException {
      Zeta z1 = new Zeta();            //*** create one Zeta object
      z1.set( 1 );                     //*** z1.alpha == 1
      Zeta z2 = (Zeta) z1.clone();     //*** clone the object
      z2.set( 2 );                     //*** z2.alpha == 2
      System.out.println( z1.get() );  //*** ok, z1.alpha == 1
   }
}
```

FIGURE 8.1.6   A program that corrects the CloneProblem of Figure 8.1.4.

Finally, note that the correct implementation of clone in Zeta does *not* involve any constructor calls. Instead, the implementation first invokes the superclass clone and then makes appropriate adjustments to local fields, in this case the assignment statement

```
t.al = (Alpha) al.clone();
```

The revised Zeta class of Figure 8.1.6 has a proper override of clone, which should be invoked, in turn, by the clone method of any class that encapsulates a Zeta object. The code segment

```
class C implements Cloneable {
    public Object clone() throws CloneNotSupportedException {
        C t = super.clone();     // invoke super.clone()
        t.z = (Zeta) z.clone(); // invoke Zeta field's clone()
```

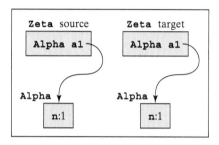

FIGURE 8.1.7   The result of cloning in the `CloneProblemFix` program of Figure 8.1.6.

```
        return t;
    }
    Zeta z = new Zeta();
}
```

illustrates. Because class `C` has a reference to a `Zeta` object, the `C` class's override of `clone` invokes the encapsulated `Zeta` object's `clone`, which in turn invokes the encapsulated `Alpha` object's `clone`. The result is the proper cloning of a `C` object; that is, the source and cloned `C` objects have references to *distinct* `Zeta` objects.

Cloning Arrays

The `clone` method can be invoked on arrays. The clone of an array has the same number of elements as the original array and each element in the cloned array has the same value as the corresponding element in the original array. The code segment

```
int[ ] a1 = { 1, 2, 3 };
int[ ] a2 = (int[ ]) a1.clone();
a2[ 0 ] = -999;                       //** a2[ 0 ] == -999
System.out.println( a1[ 0 ] ); //** a1[ 0 ] == 1
```

illustrates.

If a class encapsulates an array, the array's `clone` should be invoked in the class's override of `clone`. The code segment

```
class C implements Cloneable {
    public Object clone() throws CloneNotSupportedException {
        C t = (C) super.clone();           //** default clone
        t.nums = (int[ ]) nums.clone(); //** array's clone
        return t;
    }
    int[ ] nums = new nums[ 10 ];
}
```

illustrates.

Disabling Cloning

The default `clone` restricts cloning because of the method's protected scope. Recall that an inherited member's visibility cannot be further restricted. For instance, an inherited protected member cannot be redeclared as private. Cloning therefore cannot be disabled by redeclaring the default `clone` as private. To disable cloning, a public override of the default `clone` can throw a `CloneNotSupportedException`.

Example 8.1.5.   The class `Zeta`

```
class Zeta implements Cloneable {
   public Object clone() throws CloneNotSupportedException {
      throw new CloneNotSupportedException(); //*** disable
   }
   //...
}
```

disables the cloning of `Zeta` objects by throwing an exception in the `clone` override.   ■

EXERCISES

1. Explain the difference between copying a reference to an object and cloning it.

2. Explain the error:

```
class Alpha { int x; }
class Beta {
   public void m() {
      Alpha a1 = new Alpha();
      Alpha a2 = (Alpha) a1.clone();
   }
}
```

3. What is printed?

```
class Engine { int hPower; }
class Car implements Cloneable {
   public Object clone() {
      try {
         return super.clone();
      } catch( CloneNotSupportedException e ) { }
      return null;
   }
```

```
        Engine e = new Engine();
    }
    class Test {
        public static void main( String[ ] args ) {
            Car c1 = new Car();
            c1.e.hPower = 125;
            System.out.println( c1.e.hPower );
            Car c2 = (Car) c1.clone();
            c2.e.hPower = 512;
            System.out.println( c1.e.hPower );
        }
    }
```

  4. What is `clone`'s return type?
  5. Give an example of a cloned object that is not independent of the source object from which it was cloned.
  6. Explain the problem with the code in Exercise 3.
  7. Explain how cloning can be disabled.
  8. How many methods are declared in `Cloneable`?
  9. Why is `Cloneable` known as a *marker interface*?
  10. Are `java.util.Hashtable`s clonable?
  11. What advantages result from having `Object`'s definition of `clone` be `protected` rather than `public`?

8.2   Serialization

Serialization is the process of transforming an in-memory object to a byte stream. **Deserialization** is the inverse process of reconstructing an object in memory from a byte stream to the same state in which the object was serialized. Serialization also is described as *serializing out* and deserialization is also described as *serializing in*. The term *serialization* is commonly used in a general sense to cover the complementary operations of *serializing out* and *serializing in*.

Serialization has various uses. If the serialization byte stream has a disk file as its target, then serialization supports **object persistence**, which is the preservation of an object in its current state so that the object later can be reconstructed in the same state. Recall that an object's **state** is determined by the values of its `nonstatic`, `nontransient` fields. (The keyword `transient` is explained shortly.) Serialization is also useful in networking. An application on one machine can serialize an object to a network stream so that an application running on another machine then can deserialize the same object. Section 9.2 examines serialization and sockets in the context of networking. This section focuses on serialization with local disk files. The syntax and behavior of serialization remain the same regardless of how serialization is used.

Serialization Basics

The requirements and syntax for serialization are relatively straightforward:

- Only *objects*—that is, class instantiations—can be serialized. Although primitive types such as `ints` can be written to and read from binary streams, primitive types technically cannot be serialized and deserialized.
- For an object to be serializable, its class or some ancestor class must implement the `java.io.Serializable` interface.
- An object is serialized by writing it to an `ObjectOutputStream` and deserialized by reading it from an `ObjectInputStream`. The code segment

```
Date today = new Date();
FileOutputStream fos = new FileOutputStream("save.ser");
ObjectOutputStream oos = new ObjectOutputStream( fos );
oos.write( today );
```

illustrates the serialization of a `Date` object. The code segment

```
FileInputStream fis = new FileInputStream("save.ser");
ObjectInputStream ois = new ObjectInputStream( fis );
Date today = (Date) ois.readObject();
```

illustrates the syntax of deserializing the same `Date` object. The cast to `Date` is required because `readObject`'s return type is `Object`.

The following subsections further clarify serialization and deserialization.

Rules for Serialization

An object is serializable if its class or any ancestor class implements the interface `java.io.Serializable`. For example, the Swing set's JButton class has JComponent as an ancestor. Because JComponent implements `Serializable`, every JButton object is thereby serializable.

■ **Example 8.2.1.**   The class Alpha

```
class Alpha implements Serializable { /*...*/ }
```

explicitly implements `Serializable` because its superclass `Object` does *not* implement this interface. For **Alpha** objects to be serializable, the explicit `implements Serializable` is therefore required.   ■

■ **Example 8.2.2.**   The class `MyTreeModel`

```
class MyTreeModel extends DefaultTreeModel
            implements Serializable { /*...*/ }
```

explicitly implements `Serializable`, although this is not necessary because the superclass `DefaultTreeModel`, in the `javax.swing.tree` package, already implements `Serializable`. However, there is no harm in having `MyTreeModel` explicitly implement the interface.   ■

Serialization and Object Graphs

If an object has references to other objects as fields, the entire **object graph** is serialized when the object is serialized. A serialized object graph consists of the object directly serialized and any other objects to which the serialized object has direct or indirect references.

■ **Example 8.2.3.**   When a `Firm` object

```
class Emp implements Serializable {
  //...
  private Vector clients;
}
class Firm implements Serializable {
  //...
  private Emp ceo;
}
```

is serialized, the `Emp` object to which `ceo` refers also is serialized. The `Emp` class has a reference `clients` to a `Vector`, which is likewise serialized. Serializing a `Firm` object thus involves serializing an object graph.

Nonserializable Superclasses with Serializable Subclasses

Object graphs that consist exclusively of serializable objects can be serialized without qualification. Yet a serializable class might have a *nonserializable superclass*. Recall that any direct subclass of `Object` has a nonserializable superclass because `Object` does not implement `Serializable`. A subclass of a nonserializable class is still serializable if

- The subclass implements `Serializable`.
- The superclass has a no-argument constructor that is accessible for deserialization.

The nonserializable `Object` class has a public no-argument constructor, which allows `Object` subclasses to be serializable.

■ **Example 8.2.4.**   In the hierarchy

```
class Alpha {                   // Note: not serializable
    public Alpha() { /*...*/ } // but no-argument constructor
    //...
}
class Zeta extends Alpha implements Serializable { /*...*/ }
```

superclass `Alpha` is not serializable but subclass `Zeta` is serializable because `Zeta` implements `Serializable` and its superclass `Alpha` has an accessible no-argument constructor. When a `Zeta` object is serialized in, the `Alpha` no-argument constructor is invoked to construct and initialize the `Alpha`-part of the object.   ■

The Object Input and Output Streams

The `java.io` package provides the `Serialization` interface and the input/ouput classes that support serialization. The two main methods for serialization are

- `writeObject( Object obj )` of the `ObjectOutputStream` class. An `ObjectOutputStream` can be constructed from a `FileOutputStream` for serialization to disk files.
- `readObject()` of the `ObjectInputStream` class. An `ObjectInputStream` can be constructed from a `FileInputStream` for deserialization from a disk file.

■ **Example 8.2.5.**   The `SerialTest` program in Figure 8.2.1 puts `Integers` in a `Vector` and then serializes the `Vector` out to a file named *save.ser*, where *ser* is the recommended extension for files that hold serialized objects. The program constructs an `ObjectOutputStream` to which oos refers from a `FileOutputStream` and then invokes the stream's `writeObject` method

```
oos.writeObject( orig );
```

to serialize the `Vector` to which `orig` refers. The program then constructs an `ObjectInputStream` object to which `ois` refers from a `FileInputStream` and invokes the stream's `readObject` method

```
Vector restore = (Vector) ois.readObject();
```

to deserialize the `Vector`. The cast to type `Vector` is required because `readObject`'s return type is `Object`.

Finally, method `main` throws a general `IOException` to handle conditions such as *file not found*. The method also throws a `ClassNotFoundException` because the deserialization stream might not contain bytes that represent an instance of a specified class, in this case an instance of a `Vector`. ■

```java
import java.util.*;
import java.io.*;
class SerialTest {
   public static void main( String[ ] args )
           throws IOException, ClassNotFoundException {
      //** populate a Vector with some Integers
      Vector orig = new Vector(); // serializable
      for ( int i = 0; i < 5; i++ )
         orig.addElement( new Integer( i + 1 ) );
      //** serialize the Vector out
      String fileName = "save.ser";
      ObjectOutputStream oos =
         new ObjectOutputStream( new FileOutputStream( fileName ) );
      oos.writeObject( orig );
      oos.close();
      //** serialize the Vector in
      ObjectInputStream ois =
         new ObjectInputStream( new FileInputStream( fileName ) );
      Vector restore = (Vector) ois.readObject();
      ois.close();
      //** print the elements to confirm deserialization
      Enumeration e = restore.elements();
      while ( e.hasMoreElements() )
         System.out.println( e.nextElement() );
   }
}
```

FIGURE 8.2.1   A program to illustrate serialization and deserialization.

Serialization, Arrays, and Primitive Types

With respect to serialization, arrays behave like objects. An array of any type is serialized out with `writeObject` and serialized in with `readObject`.

Example 8.2.6.   The code segment

```java
String file = "array.ser";
ObjectOutputStream oos =
   new ObjectOutputStream( new FileOutputStream( file ) );
int[ ] array = new int[ 10 ];
```

```
for ( int i = 0; i < 10; i++ )
   array[ i ] = i;
oos.writeObject( array );
```

creates and populates an `int` array that is then serialized out with the `writeObject` method. The code segment

```
String file = "array.ser";
ObjectInputStream ois =
   new ObjectInputStream( new FileInputStream( file ) );
int[ ] a = (int[ ]) ois.readObject();
```

serializes in the array. The cast to type `int[ ]` is required because `readObject`'s return type is `Object`.   ■

Primitive Types and Object Streams

The `writeObject` and `readObject` are aptly named because they serialize *objects* out and in, respectively. Primitive types such as `ints` and `doubles` cannot be serialized with these methods. However, the `DataInput` and `DataOutput` interfaces provide method pairs such as `writeInt` and `readInt` for writing primitive types to and reading primitive types from binary streams. The `ObjectOutput` interface, which `ObjectOutputStream` implements, extends the `DataInput` interface. In effect, then, primitive types can be written with the appropriate methods to an `ObjectOutputStream`. A similar relationship holds among the `DataInput` interface, the `ObjectInput` subinterface, and the `ObjectInputStream` class.

■ **Example 8.2.7.**   The code segment

```
String file = "test.ser";
ObjectOutputStream oos =
   new ObjectOutputStream( new FileOutputStream( file ) );
oos.writeObject( new Date() ); //*** serialize
oos.writeInt( 9876 );
oos.writeDouble( 3.14 );
oos.writeChar( 'A' );
```

shows how an object such as a `Date` and various primitive types can be written to an `ObjectOutputStream`. The code segment

```
String file = "test.ser";
ObjectInputStream ois =
   new ObjectInputStream( new FileInputStream( file ) );
Date d = (Date) ois.readObject(); //*** deserialize
```

```
int n = ois.readInt();
double d = ois.readDouble();
char c = ois.readChar();
```

shows how the Date object and miscellaneous primitive types then can be read from the corresponding ObjectInputStream. Note that the data are read in the same order in which they are written: first the Date object, next the int, and so on. ∎

Serialization and Strings

Because Strings are objects, they can be serialized in and out with the methods writeObject and readObject, respectively. Special methods also are available for writing Strings to and reading them from binary streams: writeUTF and readUTF, where UTF stands for **U**nicode **T**ransmission **F**ormat. UTF is a format designed to encode 16-bit Unicode characters as 8-bit bytes for applications that require such byte coding. For example, many network applications assume 8-bit encoding.

■ **Example 8.2.8.**   The code segment

```
String file = "string.ser";
ObjectOutputStream oos =
   new ObjectOutputStream( new FileOutputStream( file ) );
oos.writeUTF( new String( "Hello, world!" ) );
```

shows how a String can be written to an ObjectOutputStream using write-UTF. The code segment

```
String file = "string.ser";
ObjectInputStream ois =
   new ObjectInputStream( new FileInputStream( file ) );
String s = ois.readUTF();
```

shows how a String can be read from an ObjectInputStream using readUTF. The writeUTF method writes each Unicode character in a String to the designated binary stream. The method also writes the total number of characters needed to represent the String. A String written using writeUTF should be read using readUTF. A String written using writeObject should be read using readObject. ∎

Serialization and static and transient Fields

An object's state is determined by the values of its *instance fields*, that is, its nonstatic fields. Serialization and deserialization therefore ignore static fields. An instance field declared as transient is also ignored in serialization and deserialization. (transient is a keyword.) During deserialization, `transient` fields are restored to their default values.

■ **Example 8.2.9.**   The program in Figure 8.2.2 serializes an `Alpha` object with three `int` members:

- Field x, initialized to 9, is `nonstatic` and `nontransient`. Therefore, x should be 9 after deserialization.
- Field y, initialized to −555, is `transient`. Therefore, y should be 0—the default value for `int` fields—after deserialization.
- Field z, initialized to 1, is `static`. Therefore, z should not be affected by serialization or deserialization.

When the `Alpha` object is serialized, the `static` field z has a value of 1. Before the `Alpha` object is deserialized, `static` field z is incremented to 2. The output

```
import java.io.*;
class Alpha implements Serializable {
   int x = 9;
   transient int y = -555;
   static int z = 1;
}
class SerialTestForTransientAndStatic {
   public static void main( String[ ] args )
           throws IOException, ClassNotFoundException {
      String fileName = "save.ser";
      ObjectOutputStream oos =
         new ObjectOutputStream( new FileOutputStream( fileName ) );
      //*** serialize an Alpha object: x == 9, y == -555, z == 1
      oos.writeObject( new Alpha() );
      oos.close();
      //*** increment static z to 2
      Alpha.z++;
      ObjectInputStream ois =
         new ObjectInputStream( new FileInputStream( fileName ) );
      //*** deserialize the Alpha object
      Alpha a2 = (Alpha) ois.readObject();
      ois.close();
      System.out.println(
         "   a2.x == " + a2.x +    //*** 9 (x is nonstatic, nontransient)
         "   a2.y == " + a2.y +    //*** 0 (y is nonstatic, transient)
         "   Alpha.z == " + Alpha.z ); //*** 2 (z is static)
   }
}
```

FIGURE 8.2.2 Deserializing an object with `transient` and `static` fields.

confirms that the `transient` field y has the default value of 0 and that the `static` field z is unaffected by the deserialization. Only the `nontransient`, nonstatic field x is restored to its serialized value of 9. ∎

Customizing Serialization

Serialization can be customized to meet a particular class's needs. Such a class still implements `Serializable` and, in addition, implements the two methods

```
private void writeObject( ObjectOutputStream os )
    throws IOException;
private void readObject( ObjectInputStream os )
    throws IOException, ClassNotFoundException;
```

Note that the two methods are `private`.

The private `writeObject` and `readObject` are *callback* methods. The relationship of these methods to the public versions can be clarified with an example.

∎ **Example 8.2.10.**   Given a serializable class `Zeta` that implements a private `writeObject` and a private `readObject`

```
class Zeta implements java.io.Serializable {
   //...
   private void writeObject( ObjectOutputStream os )
      throws IOException { /*...*/ }
   private void readObject( ObjectInputStream os )
      throws IOException, ClassNotFoundException { /*...*/ }
}
```

the code segment

```
ObjectOutputStream os =
  new ObjectOutputStream( new FileOutputStream("out.ser") );
os.writeObject( new Zeta() );
```

invokes the `ObjectOutputStream`'s public `writeObject` method with a `Zeta` object as the argument. This public `writeObject` then invokes Zeta's private `writeObject` with the object output stream os as the argument. The private `writeObject` in Zeta is thus "called back" from the public `writeObject` in `ObjectOutputStream`. In effect, the public `writeObject` defers to the private `writeObject` because the latter is designed to perform customized rather than default serialization.

In deserialization, the public and private `readObject` methods behave in a similar fashion: the public `readObject` in `ObjectInputStream` "calls back" the private `readObject` in Zeta with the object input stream object as the argument. ∎

Customized serialization typically augments rather than replaces default serialization. Accordingly, the private `writeObject` typically has the structure

```
private void writeObject( ObjectOutputStream os )
            throws IOException {
  os.defaultWriteObject(); // default serialization
  //...customized serialization
}
```

The call to `defaultWriteObject` handles default serialization after which the customized serialization can occur. Similarly, the private `readObject` typically has the structure

```
private void readObject( ObjectInputStream os )
            throws IOException, ClassNotFoundException {
  os.defaultReadObject(); // default deserialization
  //...customized deserialization
}
```

The call to `defaultReadObject` handles the default deserialization after which the customized deserialization can occur.

Example 8.2.11.   The Emp class in Figure 8.2.3 illustrates customized serialization. The Emp class has four fields:

- The `String` field named `id`, which is `transient`, represents the Emp's identification code. The code is generated from the return value of the default `toString` method and a randomly generated hexadecimal integer. Recall that the default `toString` is based upon an object's hash code, which is returned by the `Object` method `hashCode`. It is possible for two different objects to have the same hash code. Accordingly, the Emp class's `makeId` method generates a random integer that is appended to the hash code, which reduces the probability that two different Emps would have the same `id`. We assume that an Emp does not require the *same* identification code before and after serialization but only that such an object's identification code be unique with high probability. For this reason, the `id` is declared as `transient` and regenerated in a customized deserialization.
- The `int` field named `ran`, which is `nonstatic` and `nontransient`, stores the random integer appended as a hexadecimal string to an Emp object's default `toString` value. This integer is serialized and deserialized.
- The `String` field called `name`, which is `nonstatic` and `nontransient`, represents the Employee's name. This field is serialized and deserialized.
- The `Random` field named `r`, which is `static`, is used to generate the random integers that contribute to an Emp object's `id`. As `static`, this field is unaffected by serialization.

```
import java.io.*;
import java.util.*;
class Emp implements Serializable {
   public Emp( String NAME ) {
      makeId( ran = r.nextInt() );
      setName( NAME );
   }
   public String getId() { return id; }
   public String getName() { return name; }
   public void setName( String NAME ) { name = NAME; }
   private void makeId( int n ) {
      id = toString() + "-" + Integer.toHexString( n );
   }
   private void writeObject( ObjectOutputStream os )
            throws IOException {
      os.defaultWriteObject(); // default serialization
   }
   private void readObject( ObjectInputStream is )
            throws IOException, ClassNotFoundException {
      is.defaultReadObject(); // default deserialization
      makeId( ran ); //*** reconstruct the deserialized object's id
   }
   private transient String id;
   private int ran;
   private String name;
   private static Random r = new Random();
}
```

FIGURE 8.2.3 A class to illustrate customized serialization and deserialization.

The program in Figure 8.2.4 populates a `Vector` with `Emp` objects and then serializes and deserializes the `Vector`. A sample run produced the output

```
Preserialized Emps:
Emp@f25b2f0d-12c0a00b
Emp@fca32f0d-4cba88ac
Emp@fc372f0d-83a16ede
Emp@fce72f0d-e9326e09

Deserialized Emps:
Emp@e3f32f0d-12c0a00b
Emp@e3b32f0d-4cba88ac
Emp@e2c32f0d-83a16ede
Emp@e2832f0d-e9326e09
```

```
import java.io.*;
import java.util.*;
class EmpSerial {
   public static void main( String[ ] args ) throws
                         IOException, ClassNotFoundException {
      String file = "save.ser";
      Vector v = new Vector();
      ObjectOutputStream os =
         new ObjectOutputStream( new FileOutputStream( file ) );
      System.out.println( "Preserialized Emps:" );
      for ( int i = 0; i < 4; i++ ) {
         Emp t = null;
         v.addElement( t = new Emp( "fred" + i ) );
         System.out.println( t.getId() );
      }
      os.writeObject( v );
      os.close();
      ObjectInputStream is =
         new ObjectInputStream( new FileInputStream( file ) );
      Vector x = (Vector) is.readObject();
      is.close();
      System.out.println( "\nDeserialized Emps:" );
      Enumeration e = x.elements();
      while ( e.hasMoreElements() )
         System.out.println( ((Emp) e.nextElement()).getId() );
   }
}
```

FIGURE 8.2.4   A program to test customized serialization of Emp objects in Figure 8.2.3.

The values returned by toString have indeed changed, but the serialized random integers at the end of each identification code remain the same.

Only the deserialization needs to be customized. Accordingly, the private writeObject simply invokes defaultWriteObject, although customization might be appropriate if the class changes. The private readObject first invokes defaultReadObject to deserialize the nontransient fields named ran and name and then invokes makeId to regenerate the Emp object's identification code. ■

Cautionary Notes on Serialization

Serialization is powerful and straightforward but still requires caution. Consider, for example, the situation in which the same object is serialized repeatedly and then deserialized the same number of times.

```
import java.io.*;
class C implements Serializable {
   public C( int n ) { x = n; }
   public void set( int n ) { x = n; }
   public int get() { return x; };
   int x;
}
class SerialCaution {
   public static void main( String[ ] args ) throws Exception {
      C c1 = new C( 1 );
      //*** serialize the same C object twice
      ObjectOutputStream os =
       new ObjectOutputStream( new FileOutputStream( "c.ser" ) );
      os.writeObject( c1 );          //*** write the object once
      os.writeObject( c1 );          //*** write the same object again
      os.close();
      //*** deserialize the same C object twice
      ObjectInputStream is =
       new ObjectInputStream( new FileInputStream( "c.ser" ) );
      C t1 = (C) is.readObject();  //*** assign to reference t1
      C t2 = (C) is.readObject();  //*** assign to reference t2
      is.close();
      if ( t1 == t2 )                //*** Note well: true
        System.out.println( "t1 and t2 refer to the same object." );
   }
}
```

FIGURE 8.2.5   A program that serializes and deserializes the same object twice.

■ **Example 8.2.12.**   The SerialCaution program of Figure 8.2.5 serializes the *same* object twice and then deserializes the object twice. In the deserialization, two references t1 and t2

```
C t1 = (C) is.readObject();  //*** reference t1
C t2 = (C) is.readObject();  //*** reference t2
```

occur as assignment targets for readObject's return value. The critical point is that readObject twice returns a reference to the *same* object precisely because the same object was serialized out twice. References t1 and t2 thus refer to the *same* object, not to distinct objects. The fact that t1 and t2 are two references therefore may be misleading. Difficulties obviously could arise if the programmer mistakenly assumed that two distinct objects had been deserialized. ■

The Serial Version Number

Another potential problem involves changes to a class between the serialization and deserialization of its objects. When an object is serialized, a 64-bit `long` integer known as its **serial version unique identifier** is written with the object. The version number identifies the object's class.

■ **Example 8.2.13.**   Object instances of the `SerialUID` class

```
class SerialUID implements java.io.Serializable {
    int x;
}
```

are serializable. The JDK *serialver* utility can be used to get a class's serial version number. On a sample run, the command

```
$ serialver SerialUID
```

printed

```
static final long serialVersionUID = 8009999899228719149L;
```

The class was then changed to

```
class SerialUID implements java.io.Serializable {
    int x;
    float y;   //*** Note well: a new field
}
```

and the *serialver* utility was run again with the output

```
static final long serialVersionUID = -3206817158915123701L;
```

If a `SerialUID` object were serialized with the first version number, then an attempt to deserialize the object after the class definition changed would fail. In particular, an `InvalidClassException` would be thrown during the deserialization.

The programmer can explicitly set a serial version number so that, for example, `SerialUID` objects serialized under one class definition can be deserialized even if the class definition changes. The redefinition

```
class SerialUID implements java.io.Serializable {
    int x;
    static final long serialVersionUID = 8009999899228719149L;
}
```

illustrates the syntax. It is clearly preferable *not* to change a class's definition in between the serialization and deserialization of its objects.   ∎

The `Externalizable` Interface

The `java.io.Externalizable` interface is available for completely customized serialization and deserialization. The interface declares the two methods

```
public void writeExternal( ObjectOutput out )
     throws IOException;
public void readExternal( ObjectInput in )
     throws IOException;
```

If a subclass of an externalizable class overrides `writeExternal` and `readExternal`, the subclass should invoke the superclass versions of these methods during serialization and deserialization, respectively.

Disabling Serialization

To disable serialization for a class derived from a `Serializable` ancestor, the private `writeObject` method can throw a `NotSerializableException`. Because serialization is so powerful and useful, disabling it for a class is unusual. Customized serialization is generally adequate to handle special requirements.

EXERCISES

1. How many methods are declared in the `Serializable` interface?
2. Which standard package has the `Serializable` interface?
3. Explain the difference between serialization and deserialization.
4. The `java.util.Date` class implements `Serializable`. Are objects of the class `MyDate`

```
class MyDate extends Date { /*...*/ }
```

serializable?
5. Suppose that class `Alpha` is a direct subclass of `Object`. What is required for `Alpha` objects to be serializable?
6. Explain an *object graph* with respect to serialization.
7. Suppose that class `Alpha` does not implement `Serializable`. What is required for objects of a direct subclass of `Alpha` to be serializable?
8. Can arrays be serialized and deserialized?
9. Can primitive types be serialized and deserialized?

10. Can primitive types be written to and read from byte streams?

11. What is the connection between `ObjectOutputStream` and serialization?

12. What is the connection between `ObjectInputStream` and deserialization?

13. Suppose that a `String` is written to a byte stream using `writeObject`. Which method should be used to read the `String` from the byte stream?

14. Suppose that a `String` is written to a byte stream using `writeUTF`. Which method should be used to read the `String` from the byte stream?

15. What happens to `static` fields in serialization?

16. What happens to `transient` fields in serialization?

17. Explain the keyword `transient`.

18. In customized serialization, the `private` methods `writeObject` and `readObject` serve as callbacks. From where are these methods called back?

19. Explain the role of the `Externalizable` interface.

20. Explain how serialization can be disabled for objects of a particular class.

21. What is the *serial version unique identifier*?

22. Can the same object be serialized repeatedly to an output stream?

8.3   Sample Application: A Serializable Time Card

Problem

Implement a serializable time card that can be used, for example, to track the amount of time that an application runs. The graphical user interface should display the start time, the current time, and the duration. The serialization should be storage efficient; that is, as little state information as possible should be saved and restored.

Sample Output

Figure 8.3.1 shows a test application with a `TimeCard` object. The test client allows the user to create a new `TimeCard`, to serialize the currently open `TimeCard`, or to deserialize a previously saved `TimeCard`.

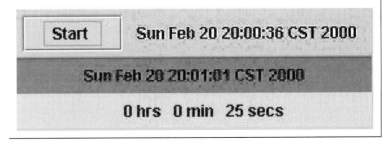

FIGURE 8.3.1   The `TimeCard`.

Solution

The TimeCard class has three private fields:

- Field `start` is a reference to a Date object that represents the TimeCard's start time. The start time can be reset to the current time by pressing a button. Only the `start` field is nontransient. When a TimeCard is first constructed, the start time is initialized to the current time. Thereafter, the start time is restored through deserialization.
- Field `now` is a reference to a Date object that represents the current time. This field is `transient` because the current time is recomputed each time a TimeCard is constructed or deserialized.
- Field `gui` is a reference to a TimeCardGUI object that provides the graphical user interface. This field is transient because a TimeCardGUI object is constructed anew each time a TimeCard is constructed or deserialized.

A client constructs a TimeCard by invoking the no-argument constructor. The class has a private `readObject` to initialize the `transient` fields and build the GUI during deserialization.

Java Implementation

```java
import java.io.*;
import java.awt.*;
import java.awt.event.*;
import javax.swing.*;
import java.util.Date;
public class TimeCard implements Serializable {
   public TimeCard() {
      initGUI();
      start = now = new Date();
      setGUITimes();
   }
   public void setStart() {
      gui.setStart( start = new Date() );
   }
   public Date getStart() { return start; }
   public void setNow() {
      gui.setNow( now = new Date() );
   }
   public Date getNow() { return now; }
   private void writeObject( ObjectOutputStream os )
                                    throws IOException {
      os.defaultWriteObject();
   }
```

```
      private void readObject( ObjectInputStream is )
            throws IOException, ClassNotFoundException {
         is.defaultReadObject();
         now = new Date();
         initGUI();
         setGUITimes();
      }
      private void initGUI() { gui = new TimeCardGUI( this ); }
      private void setGUITimes() {
         gui.setStart( start );
         gui.setNow( now );
      }
      private Date start;
      private transient Date now;
      private transient TimeCardGUI gui;
   }
   class TimeCardGUI extends JFrame {
      public TimeCardGUI( TimeCard tc ) {
         super( "Time Card" );
         host = tc;
         init();
         show();
      }
      public void setStart( Date d ) {
         startL.setText( getFormattedTime( d ) );
      }
      public void setNow( Date d ) {
         nowL.setText( getFormattedTime( d ) );
      }
      private void init() {
         Container cont = getRootPane();
         cont.setFont( new Font( "Dialog", Font.BOLD, 12 ) );
         JPanel top = null, mid = null, bot = null;
         Date d = null;
         cont.setLayout( new BorderLayout() );
         cont.add( top = new JPanel(), BorderLayout.NORTH );
         cont.add( mid = new JPanel(), BorderLayout.CENTER );
         cont.add( bot = new JPanel(), BorderLayout.SOUTH );
         top.setLayout( new FlowLayout() );
         top.setBackground( Color.green );
         mid.setLayout( new FlowLayout() );
         mid.setBackground( Color.red );
         bot.setLayout( new FlowLayout() );
         bot.setBackground( Color.orange );
         JButton startB = new JButton( "  Start   " );
```

```
        startB.addActionListener( new AbstractAction() {
            public void actionPerformed( ActionEvent e ) {
                host.setStart(); }
        } );
        startL = new JLabel( getFormattedTime( d = new Date() ) );
        startL.setForeground( Color.black );
        JButton nowB = new JButton( "   Now   " );
        nowB.addActionListener( new AbstractAction() {
            public void actionPerformed( ActionEvent e ) {
                host.setNow(); }
        } );
        nowL = new JLabel( getFormattedTime( d ) );
        nowL.setForeground( Color.black );
        JButton durB = new JButton( "Duration" );
        durB.addActionListener( new AbstractAction() {
            public void actionPerformed( ActionEvent e ) {
                setDuration();
            }
        } );
        durL = new JLabel( getFormattedTime( d ) );
        durL.setForeground( Color.black );
        top.add( startB );
        top.add( startL );
        mid.add( nowB );
        mid.add( nowL );
        bot.add( durB );
        bot.add( durL );
        pack();
    }
    private void setDuration() {
        long secsPerHr = 60 * 60, h, m, s;
        long dur =  Math.round( (host.getNow().getTime() -
                    host.getStart().getTime()) / 1000.0 );
        h = dur / secsPerHr;
        dur -= h * secsPerHr;
        m = dur / 60;
        s = dur - m * 60;
        s = (s < 0) ? 0 : s;
        durL.setText( "      " + h + " hrs    " +
                    m + " min    " + s + " secs" );
    }
    private String getFormattedTime( Date d ) {
        return "   " + d.toString() + "   ";
    }
    private TimeCard host;
```

```
    private JLabel startL;
    private JLabel nowL;
    private JLabel durL;
}
```

Discussion

The key to deserialization is to restore nontransient fields to their serialized values. Deserialization thus should be viewed as an alternative to initial construction. In the case of the TimeCard class, the constructor

```
    public TimeCard() {
        initGUI();
        start = now = new Date();
        setGUITimes();
    }
```

first constructs the GUI, then initializes the start and now fields to the current time, and finally causes the start and now times to be displayed in the GUI. The customized readObject

```
    private void readObject( ObjectInputStream is )
            throws IOException, ClassNotFoundException {
        is.defaultReadObject();
        now = new Date();
        initGUI();
        setGUITimes();
    }
```

first invokes defaultReadObject to restore the serialized start value, which allows the serialized TimeCard to "remember" its initial start time. The customized readObject, like the constructor, then sets now to the current time, constructs the GUI, and causes the GUI to display the deserialized start time and the current time. The GUI computes and displays the duration by subtracting the start time from the current time.

The customized writeObject simply invokes defaultWriteObject to serialize the TimeCard's only nontransient field, start. Because the GUI consists of a JFrame that embeds various objects such as panels, buttons, labels, and fonts, serializing the GUI would not be storage efficient. For example, serializing only the start time results in a roughly 100 byte file, whereas serializing the start time and the GUI results in a roughly 11,000 byte file. The design decision is thus to serialize the minimum number of bytes necessary for the TimeCard to function correctly.

The TimeCard application could benefit from the multithreading introduced in the next section. At present, the user must push a button to update the current time and to display the current duration. These tasks could be automated (see the Programming Exercises).

EXERCISES

1. Run the sample application and confirm that the `TimeCard` can be serialized and deserialized correctly.

2. List the `TimeCard` fields that contribute to a `TimeCard` object's *state*.

3. Explain why the sample application can use default serialization but needs customized deserialization.

8.4   Multithreaded Programs

A **thread of execution** or **thread of control** is a sequence of instructions. For example, the code segment

```
int i = 0;                                  //*** 1
while ( i++ < 3 )                           //*** 2
   System.out.println( "Hello, world!" );   //*** 3
System.out.println( "Goodbye, world!" );    //*** 4
```

illustrates a sequence of instructions that starts with a variable declaration and initialization. The second statement is a `while` statement whose body consists of a single print statement. A thread of execution would execute the declaration/initialization first, the loop test next, the print statement next, the loop test again, the print statement again, and so on until the loop exits. The print statement beyond the `while` loop then executes once. The source code lines have been labeled for reference. The sequence of execution is

$$1, 2, 3, 2, 3, 2, 3, 2, 4$$

So far our sample programs have been **single-threaded**; that is, the JVM runs the program by executing a *single* sequence of instructions. In equivalent terms, such a program has a *single thread of execution*. In Java applications, the thread begins execution at the first statement in `main`.

From Single-Threaded to Multithreaded Execution

A program *begins* as single-threaded and becomes multithreaded if this single thread constructs and `starts` a second `Thread` of execution, where `Thread` is a class in the `java.lang` package. The first thread can construct and `start` arbitrarily many `Threads`, each of which can construct and `start` arbitrarily many `Threads`. A `started` thread executes the body of the `run` method, which is declared in the interface `Runnable` as

```
public void run();
```

The method `run` is a *pure callback*. If `t` refers to a `Thread`, a program invokes

```
t.start(); //*** invoked in program
```

to start the Thread. In effect, the JVM then invokes

```
t.run(); //**** invoked by JVM, not in program
```

to execute the Thread's sequence of statements. The program does *not* invoke t.run().

■ **Example 8.4.1.**   The code segment

```
Thread t = new Thread();
t.run(); //***** INCORRECT!
```

contains an error. The programmer *never* invokes run on a Thread object. Instead, the programmer invokes start:

```
Thread t = new Thread();
t.start(); //** correct                                           ■
```

■ **Example 8.4.2.**   The program in Figure 8.4.1 is multithreaded. For reference, the thread that executes main is the *main thread*. The *main thread* begins execution at the first statement in main, which checks whether the program was invoked with a command-line argument that determines how many times two for loops will iterate. The *main thread* eventually executes the statements in doIt, which is invoked from main.

Method main constructs an instance of ThreadEx1 to which theApp refers and then uses theApp to invoke the instance method doIt. The reason is that the program constructs a Thread using the reference this; and main, as a static method, cannot use the *instance* reference this. Instance method doIt, by contrast, does have access to this.

When main exits, the *main thread* stops. Once stopped, a thread of execution is completed and cannot be restarted.

Method doIt, which the *main thread* executes, constructs and starts a second thread. The statement

```
Thread t = new Thread( this );
```

constructs the thread. The argument this refers to a **runnable target**, that is, an object whose class implements the Runnable interface by defining the run method. In the current example, this and theApp refer to the same ThreadEx1 object, which encapsulates a ThreadEx1 implementation of the run method. The newly constructed thread to which t refers thus will execute the statements in the ThreadEx1 implementation of run. Once the Thread to which t refers exits run, the Thread stops. A thread stops if it exits the run method.

```
class ThreadEx1 implements Runnable {
    public static void main( String[ ] args ) throws Exception {
        if ( args.length < 1 )
            throw new Exception(
              "\n\nInvoke as: ThreadEx1 <how many iterations>\n" );
        howMany = new Integer( args[ 0 ] ).intValue();
        ThreadEx1 theApp = new ThreadEx1();
        theApp.doIt();
    } //*** main Thread stops when main exits
    private void doIt() {
        Thread t = new Thread( this );
        t.start(); //*** start the newly constructed Thread
        for ( int i = 0; i < howMany; i++ )
            System.out.println( "First thread" );
    }
    public void run() { //*** implementation of run()
        for ( int i = 0; i < howMany; i++ )
            System.out.println( "Second thread" );
    } //*** t stops when t exits run
    private static int howMany;
}
```

FIGURE 8.4.1   An example of a multithreaded program.

Interleaved Thread Execution

The *main thread* and the thread to which t refers execute *separate* sequences of instructions, in each case a for loop with the print statement. The order in which the JVM executes these statements is *indeterminate*. On a sample run with howMany set to three, the output was

```
First thread
First thread
First thread
Second thread
Second thread
Second thread
```

The first thread completed its execution *before* the second thread completed its execution. On a sample run with howMany set to 3,000, the output was

```
First thread
First thread
...
Second thread
Second thread
...
```

```
First thread
First thread
```

In the second run, the execution of the two threads is interleaved: the first thread begins execution first; then the second thread happened to execute until completion; then the first thread resumed execution to completion. For larger values of howMany, the interleaving is even more pronounced. ■

Summary of Thread Execution

The thread that executes main (the *main thread*) differs in an important respect from started threads:

- The *main thread* executes main and whatever other methods are invoked from main. In particular, the *main thread* does *not* execute run. Recall that the programmer should never invoke run but only start.
- A started thread executes the run method and whatever other methods are invoked from run. A started thread was started either directly by the *main thread* or by some other thread started ultimately by the *main thread*.

Benefits of Multithreading

Multithreading has various benefits. Consider the familiar situation of using a browser to download a document that has several large images associated with it. The user can abort the download by clicking a *Stop* button on the browser's toolbar or selecting a comparable command from a browser menu. The browser is multithreaded. There is a thread dedicated to handling user inputs such as button clicks and menu selections, and there are other threads dedicated to the various tasks associated with downloading documents and their associated images. If the browser were a *single-threaded* application, then the same thread would handle user inputs and download documents. Once a document download began, the user might click the *Stop* button in vain until the download completed because the single thread would be consumed with the downloading tasks. Multithreading allows an application to perform multiple tasks concurrently. An application can have multiple threads $T_1, T_2, \ldots, T_n$ handle multiple tasks $Task_1$, $Task_2, \ldots, Task_n$, with each thread dedicated to a single task. A single thread also might handle a group of related tasks. Multithreading is flexible and powerful.

> **Example 8.4.3.**   The program in Figure 8.4.2 implements an algorithm named the *sieve of Eratosthenes* in honor of the ancient Greek mathematician Eratosthenes. The algorithm, which is used to construct lists of prime numbers, can be described as follows:

1. List the integers from 2 through N. If N is 20, the list is

$$2, 3, 4, 5, 6, 7, 8, 9, 10, 11, 12, 13, 14, 15, 16, 17, 18, 19, 20$$

```
import java.awt.*;
import java.awt.event.*;
import javax.swing.*;
import java.util.Vector;
class SieveErat {
   public static void main( String[ ] args ) {
      new SieveGui();
   }
}
class SieveGui extends JFrame implements Runnable {
   public SieveGui() {
      super( "Sieve of Eratosthenes" );
      init(); pack(); show();
   }
   public void run() {
      boolean[ ] multiple = new boolean[ n ];
      int i = 2;
      while ( i < n ) {  //*** determine which integers are primes
         boolean repeat = false;
         for ( int j = i + 1; j < n; j++ )
            if ( j % i == 0 ) {
               multiple[ j ] = true;
               repeat = true;
            }
         if ( !repeat ) //*** any more numbers eliminated?
           break;        //*** if not, search for primes is finished
         while ( ++i < n && multiple[ i ] ) //*** else get next element
            ;
         pause();                           //*** sleep a bit...
      }
      Vector v = new Vector();
      for ( i = 2; i < n; i++ ) { //*** add primes to an answer list
        if ( !multiple[ i ] )
          v.addElement( String.valueOf( i ) );
      }
      addAnsList( v );
      threadRunning = false;
   }
   private void addAnsList( Vector v ) {
      JList l = new JList( v ); l.setFont( font );
      c.add( ansPane = new JScrollPane( l ) ); pack();
   }
   private void pause() { // pauses the sieve thread
      try { Thread.sleep( 2 ); } catch( InterruptedException e ) { }
   }
```

FIGURE 8.4.2   A multithreaded program for the Sieve of Eratosthenes.

```
   private void init() {
      c = getContentPane();
      c.setFont( font = new Font( "Dialog", Font.BOLD, 12 ) );
      c.setLayout( new FlowLayout() );
      JButton start = new JButton( "Start" );
      start.addActionListener( new ActionListener() {
         public void actionPerformed( ActionEvent e ) {
            startSieve();
         } } );
      JButton exit = new JButton( "Exit" );
      exit.addActionListener( new ActionListener() {
         public void actionPerformed( ActionEvent e ) {
            System.exit( 0 );
         } } );
      Vector v = new Vector();
      int k = 100;
      for ( int i = 0; i < 6; i++ ) {
         v.addElement( String.valueOf( k ) );
         k *= 10;
      }
      numList = new JList( v );
      numList.setFont( font );
      c.add( exit ); c.add( start ); c.add( numList );
   }
   private void startSieve() {
      String s = (String) numList.getSelectedValue();
      if ( s == null || threadRunning )
        return;
      if ( ansPane != null ) {
        c.remove( ansPane ); pack();
      }
      n = Integer.parseInt( s );
      threadRunning = true;
      new Thread( this ).start();
   }
   private Container c;
   Font font;
   private JList numList;
   private JScrollPane ansPane;
   private int n;
   private boolean threadRunning;
}
```

FIGURE 8.4.2   A multithreaded program for the Sieve of Eratosthenes, *continued*.

2. Start with the first element 2 and eliminate any other number that is a multiple of 2. The sample list becomes

$$2, 3, \checkmark, 5, \checkmark, 7, \checkmark, 9, \checkmark, 11, \checkmark, 13, \checkmark, 15, \checkmark, 17, \checkmark, 19, \checkmark$$

3. Take the next element 3 and eliminate any remaining number that is a multiple of 3. The sample list becomes

$$2, 3, \checkmark, 5, \checkmark, 7, \checkmark, \checkmark, \checkmark, 11, \checkmark, 13, \checkmark, \checkmark, \checkmark, 17, \checkmark, 19, \checkmark$$

4. Continue in this manner until an iteration does not eliminate a number. For the sample list, the procedure thus ends with a search for multiples of 5, which fails to eliminate any more numbers. The remaining numbers

$$2, 3, 5, 7, 11, 13, 17, 19$$

are the primes from 2 through 20.

For large N the algorithm is time-consuming because of the repeated iterations through the list. The program in Figure 8.4.2 is multithreaded so that an impatient user can terminate the program before it computes all of the primes from 2 to a large N such as $1,000,000$. For reference, the two threads are the *main thread*, which executes the statements in `main`, and the *sieve thread*, which executes the statements in `run`.

- The *main thread* handles user interactions such as the selection of N from a list of numbers or a click on the `Exit` button, which terminates the application.
- The *sieve thread* generates the list of numbers $2, 3, \ldots, N$ and determines which elements are prime numbers. This thread also generates a scrollable `JList` that lists the primes. After each iteration through the list to eliminate multiples of the next prime P, the *sieve thread* pauses briefly so that the *main thread* has a chance to run and, therefore, to detect an impatient user's click on the `Exit` button. Without this pause, the user's clicks might not be processed in a timely manner.

The event handler for a click on the `Start` button invokes the `startSieve` method, which returns if the user has failed to pick N from a list of six numbers or if the *sieve thread* is already computing primes for a previously selected N. Otherwise, the `startSieve` method removes an answer list, if any, from a previous computation; converts the selected N from a `String` to the `integer n`; and starts a thread to compute the primes from 2 through n. The `run` method computes the primes and exits, which stops the *sieve thread*. At this point, the program is single threaded until the user again selects N and clicks the `Start` button. ■

■ **Example 8.4.4.**   The program in Figure 8.4.3 produces a fractal image known as the Mandelbrot set and Figure 8.4.4 shows the image produced. Although the test for inclusion in the Mandelbrot set involves relatively simple arithmetic, the set plays a foundational role in branches of modern mathematics

```
import javax.swing.*;
import java.awt.*;
import java.awt.event.*;
class MandelThread extends Thread {
   public MandelThread( MandelPanel p ) { mp = p; }
   public void run() {
      drawMandel( mp.getGraphics() );
   }
   public Thread getThread() { return this; }
   private void drawMandel( Graphics g ) {
      mp.repaint();
      double xstep, ystep, x, y, real, imag, spread;
      int i, j, iter, k = 0;
      Complex c1 = new Complex(), c2 = new Complex();
      xstep = div / mp.getWidth(); ystep = div / mp.getHeight();
      Color[ ] colors = mp.getColors();
      int MaxColors = colors.length - 1;
      for ( y = start, j = 0; y <= limit; y += ystep, j++ ) {
         for ( x = start, i = 0; x <= limit; x += xstep, i++ ) {
            c1.real = x; c1.imag = y;
            c2.real = c2.imag = 0.0;
            for ( iter = 0; iter < MaxColors; iter++ ) {
               real = c1.real + c2.real;
               imag = c1.imag + c2.imag;
               c2.real = real * real - imag * imag;
               c2.imag = 2 * real * imag;
               spread = c2.real * c2.real + c2.imag * c2.imag;
               if ( spread > MaxSpread )
                  break;
            }
            g.setColor( colors[ iter ] );
            g.fillRect( i, j, 1, 1 );
            if ( ++k % 4 == 0 ) {
               try {
                  sleep( 1 ); //*** one millisecond
               } catch( InterruptedException e ) { }
               k = 0;
            }
         }
      }
   }
   class Complex { //** utility class for drawing the set
      double real;
      double imag;
   };
```

FIGURE 8.4.3   A multithreaded program to display the Mandelbrot set.

```
      private MandelPanel mp;
      private static final double MaxSpread = 4.0;
      private static final double limit = 1.0;
      private static final double start = -1.0;
      private static final double div = 2.0;
}
class MandelPanel extends JPanel {
   public MandelPanel() { makeColors();  }
   protected void paintComponent( Graphics g ) {
      super.paintComponent( g );
      setBackground( Color.white );
   }
   public void draw() { new MandelThread( this ).start(); }
   public Color[ ] getColors() { return colors; }
   private void makeColors() {
      int maxRGB = 255, r = 0, g = 0, b = 0;
      colors = new Color[ MaxColors + 1 ];
      for ( int i = 0; i < MaxColors; i++ ) {
         colors[ i ] = new Color( r, g, b );
         r += MaxColors;
         if ( r > maxRGB ) {
           r = 0;
           g += MaxColors;
           if ( g > maxRGB ) {
             g = 0;
             b += MaxColors;
           }
           if ( b > maxRGB )
             b = 0;
         }
      }
      colors[ MaxColors ] = Color.white;
   }
   private static Color[ ] colors;
   private static final int MaxColors = 64;
}
class MandelSet {
   public MandelSet() { makeWin(); }
   private void makeWin() {
      win = new JFrame( "Mandelbrot Set" );
      Container c = win.getContentPane();
      c.setBackground( Color.white );
      c.setLayout( new BorderLayout() );
      JMenuBar menuBar = new JMenuBar();
```

FIGURE 8.4.3 A multithreaded program to display the Mandelbrot set, *continued.*

```
            JMenu menu = new JMenu( "Menu" );
            JMenuItem draw = new JMenuItem( "Draw", 'D' );
            draw.addActionListener( new AbstractAction() {
                public void actionPerformed( ActionEvent e ) {
                  canvas.draw();
                } } );
            JMenuItem exit = new JMenuItem( "Exit", 'E' );
            exit.addActionListener( new AbstractAction() {
                public void actionPerformed( ActionEvent e ) {
                  System.exit( 0 );
                } } );
            menu.add( draw ); menu.add( exit );
            menuBar.add( menu );
            canvas = new MandelPanel();
            win.setJMenuBar( menuBar );
            c.add( canvas, BorderLayout.CENTER );
            win.setSize( 400, 400 );
            win.show();
        }
        private JFrame win;
        private MandelPanel canvas;
    }
```

FIGURE 8.4.3   A multithreaded program to display the Mandelbrot set,
continued.

known as fractal geometry and chaos theory. For more on the Mandelbrot set
and related topics, see Manfred Schroeder, *Fractals, Chaos, Power Laws: Minutes
from an Infinite Paradise* (New York: W. H. Freeman, 1991).

The fractal image is visually stunning and, of interest here, relatively
time-consuming to produce. The program in Figure 8.4.2 uses three nested
for loops to draw the image. Drawing the image in a window that is approximately 500×500 requires about six million iterations of the innermost
loop.

The program has a menu with two selections: Draw, which causes the
image to be drawn, and Exit, which terminates the application. When the user
selects Draw, the application starts a MandelThread, which extends Thread.
The statement occurs in the draw method of the MandelPanel class, which
provides the JPanel in which the image is drawn:

```
public void draw() { new MandelThread( this ).start(); }
```

The MandelThread constructor assigns the argument this to a MandelPanel
field mp so that the MandelThread object can obtain the panel's Graphics
object and also invoke the panel's repaint method. The class MandelThread
overrides the run method inherited from its superclass Thread

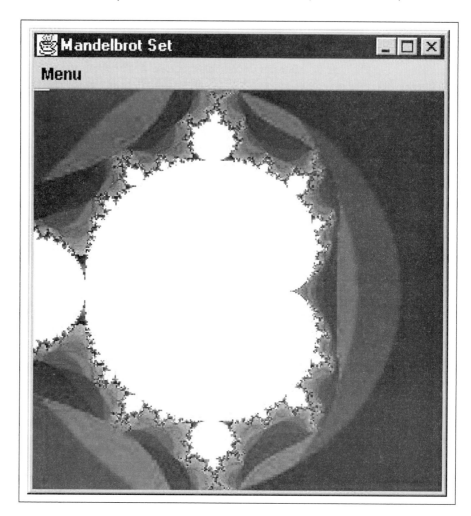

FIGURE 8.4.4   The image produced by the Mandelbrot program in
Figure 8.4.3.

```
public void run() {
   drawMandel( mp.getGraphics() );
}
```

so that `run` invokes the private `drawMandel` method, which does the drawing. To
slow down the drawing so that the viewer can watch the image being constructed,
the `drawMandel` method invokes the `Thread` class's `static` method named
`sleep`

```
if ( ++k % 4 == 0 ) {
   try {
```

```
        sleep( 1 ); //*** one millisecond
    } catch( InterruptedException e ) { }
    k = 0;
}
```

with an argument of 1, which represents one millisecond. Invoking the `sleep` method suspends the thread for the specified duration, after which the thread resumes. Increasing the `sleep` argument to 2 would slow down the drawing even more. The sleep occurs every fourth iteration of the innermost loop.

   The application's initial thread does *not* do any drawing so that this thread can handle user inputs. In particular, the user might tire of the relatively slow rendering of the image and decide to `Exit` the application. ■

Two Ways to Make a Program Multithreaded

Finally, the program illustrates a second way in which the application can be multithreaded. Here is a summary of the two basic approaches to multithreading:

- A class implements `Runnable` and defines the `run` method. Threads constructed and started within the class with a statement such as

  ```
  new Thread( this ).start();
  ```

  execute the statements in the class's implementation of `run`. The `ThreadEx1` program in Figure 8.4.1 takes this approach to multithreading.
- A class extends the `Thread` class and overrides the inherited `run` method. Given `MyThread` as a subclass of `Thread`, the statement

  ```
  new MyThread().start();
  ```

  constructs and starts a `MyThread` thread, which executes the body of `MyThread`'s overridden `run` method. The `SieveErat` program in Figure 8.4.2 takes this approach to multithreading. By the way, if `MyThread` fails to override `run`, the `run` inherited from `Thread` returns immediately. So if `MyThread` fails to define `run`, all `MyThread` objects will stop immediately.

Multithreading and Program Termination

Termination of a single-threaded application is relatively straightforward. For example, the application

```
class TermEx {
    public static void main( String[ ] args ) {
```

```
      for ( int i = 0; i < 3; i++ )
         System.out.println( "Hello, world!" );
   } //*** main exits, Thread stops, application halts
}
```

terminates when main exits. Program termination becomes more complicated under multithreading because a program now has *multiple* threads to sustain its execution.

■ **Example 8.4.5.** The RunForever program in Figure 8.4.5 constructs a Thread whose run method has an infinite loop in it. The output begins

```
class RunForever implements Runnable {
   public static void main( String[ ] args ) {
      RunForever me = new RunForever();
      System.out.println( "main thread about to exit!" );
      new Thread( me ).start();
   } //*** main exits so main Thread stops
   public void run() {
      while ( true ) {
         System.out.println( "2nd Thread says 'hi!'..." );
         try {
            Thread.sleep( 10 ); // pause 10 milliseconds
         } catch( InterruptedException e ) { System.err.println( e ); }
      }
   }
}
```

FIGURE 8.4.5   An application that continues to run after main exits.

```
main thread about to exit!
2nd Thread says 'hi!'...
2nd Thread says 'hi!'...
2nd Thread says 'hi!'...
...
```

Although the main thread exits, the second Thread started in main continues to execute indefinitely—and, therefore, the application continues to execute indefinitely. Recall that method main in class RunForever instantiates a RunForever object

```
RunForever me = new RunForever();
```

and then uses this object as the Runnable target in the thread's construction

```
new Thread( me ).start();
```

because the `static` method `main` cannot access the `nonstatic` object reference
`this`.   ■

User and Daemon Threads

■ **Example 8.4.6.**   The `NotRunForever` program in Figure 8.4.6 amends the
`RunForever` program in Figure 8.4.5 in an important way. Method `main` still con-

```
class NotRunForever implements Runnable {
   //*** main thread is user, not daemon, thread
   public static void main( String[ ] args ) {
      NotRunForever me = new NotRunForever();
      Thread t1 = new Thread( me );
      t1.setDaemon( true ); //*** t1 is a daemon, not a user, thread
      t1.start();
      try {
         Thread.sleep( 50 ); //*** main thread
      } catch( InterruptedException e ) { System.err.println( e ); }
      System.out.println( "main thread about to exit!" );
   } //*** main exits, t1 stops, application halts
   public void run() {
      while ( true ) {
         System.out.println( "2nd Thread says 'hi!'..." );
         try {
            Thread.sleep( 10 ); // pause 10 milliseconds
         } catch( InterruptedException e ) { Sys-
tem.err.println( e ); }
      }
   }
}
```

FIGURE 8.4.6   A program to contrast a daemon thread and a user thread.

structs a `Thread` but marks the `Thread` as a **daemon** before starting it. A daemon
thread is one that serves **user threads**. An application continues to run as long as
at least one of its *user threads* is alive. When a user thread stops in an application,
the JVM checks whether any other user threads are still alive. If so, the application
continues. If not, the application terminates because the JVM itself halts.

The program sleeps the `main` thread, which is a *user* thread, to give the
daemon thread to which `t1` refers a chance to run. On a sample application run,
the output was

```
2nd Thread says 'hi!'...
2nd Thread says 'hi!'...
```

```
2nd Thread says 'hi!'...
main thread about to exit!
```

Because the `main` thread is the application's only *user* thread, the application terminates when `main` returns.   ■

A *user* thread constructs other *user* threads, whereas a *daemon* thread constructs other *daemon* threads. A constructed thread's `setDaemon` method can be invoked to change its status. The `setDaemon` method must be invoked *before* the thread is `started`. In Example 8.4.6, the *main thread* constructs the thread to which `t1` refers, which is thus a user thread as well. The thread to which `t1` refers has its status changed to daemon by invoking the `setDaemon` method with an argument of `true`. The `isDaemon` method returns `true` for a daemon thread and `false` for a user thread. By the way, the JVM's garbage collector runs as a daemon thread because the JVM itself should terminate if no user threads are alive.

Thread Priorities

The JVM implements **preemptive, priority-based scheduling** for threads. Every `Thread` has an `integer` priority in the range of `MIN_PRIORITY` to `MAX_PRIORITY`, which are public `static` members of the `Thread` class. A thread is constructed with the default priority of `NORM_PRIORITY`. The integer values for `MIN_PRIORITY`, `NORM_PRIORITY`, and `MAX_PRIORITY` are not standardized; but common values are 1, 5, and 10, respectively.

A thread's priority can be adjusted with the `setPriority` method. The code segment

```
Thread t = new Thread();
System.out.println( t.getPriority() ); // NORM_PRIORITY
t.setPriority( t.getPriority() + 1 ); // higher priority
if ( t.getPriority() > Thread.NORM_PRIORITY ) //** true
   System.out.println( "t has higher than normal priority" );
```

illustrates the syntax of the `getPriority` and `setPriority` instance methods. When a thread *T* enters a runnable state by, for instance, being `started`, the JVM checks whether the currently executing thread *C* has a lower priority than *T*. If so, the JVM preempts *C* in favor of *T*.

■ **Example 8.4.7.**   The `ThreadPriority` program in Figure 8.4.7 constructs two `Threads`. The `Thread` to which `t1` refers has the default priority, whereas the one `Thread` to which `t2` refers has the maximum priority. The lower-priority thread is started first. Once the higher-priority thread is started, however, it immediately preempts the lower-priority one. On a sample run, the program's output was

```
class ThreadPriority implements Runnable {
   public static void main( String[ ] args ) {
      ThreadPriority tp = new ThreadPriority();
      tp.testPriority();
   }
   public void run() {
      while ( true )
         System.out.println( Thread.currentThread().getName() );
   }
   private void testPriority() {
      Thread t1 = new Thread( this, "Normal Priority" );
      t1.start(); //*** starts first
      Thread t2 = new Thread( this, "Max Priority" );
      t2.setPriority( Thread.MAX_PRIORITY );
      t2.start();
   }
}
```

FIGURE 8.4.7   Starting threads with different priorities.

```
Max Priority
Max Priority
Max Priority
Max Priority
. . .
```

The maximum-priority thread immediately preempts the normal-priority thread, which then *starves*, that is, never runs.

In this program, a two-argument `Thread` constructor is used. The first argument is the `Runnable` target and the second argument is the constructed `Thread`'s name. The statement

```
Thread t1 = new Thread( this, "Normal Thread" );
```

has the same effect as

```
Thread t1 = new Thread( this );
t1.setName( "Normal Thread" );
```

The `getName` method returns a thread's name.   ∎

∎ **Example 8.4.8.**   If the `run` method in the `ThreadPriority` program of Figure 8.4.7 is changed to

```
public void run() {
   while ( true ) {
```

```
      System.out.println( Thread.currentThread().getName() );
      try {
        Thread.sleep( 10 );
      } catch( InterruptedException e ) { }
    }
  }
```

the normal-priority thread has the opportunity to run because of the `sleep`, which causes the currently executing thread to pause for the specified amount of time. During this pause, other threads in the JVM's scheduling queue have an opportunity to run. After this change, a sample run produced the output

```
Max Priority
Normal Priority
Max Priority
Normal Priority
...
```

■

A constructed thread has the same priority as the thread that constructs it. The `setPriority` method then can be used to change the constructed thread's priority *before* the thread is started.

Thread States

A `Thread` is always in exactly one of four possible states. The states can be described as follows:

- **Initial state**. A newly constructed thread is in its initial state until `started`. Once a thread leaves the initial state, the thread never returns to the initial state.
- **Runnable state**. Once `started`, a thread is *runnable* or ready for execution. A runnable thread need not be actually running, however. In Figure 8.4.6, the thread to which `t1` refers enters the runnable state once started. A higher-priority thread such as the `Thread` to which `t2` refers can prevent the `t1`-Thread from ever actually running. Besides being started, there are other ways for a thread to enter the runnable state. For example, a sleeping thread becomes runnable once the sleep is over.
- **Blocked state**. A thread enters a blocked state when waiting for some event to occur. A standard networking example involves a client thread waiting to read data from a server that has not yet provided the data. Later subsections illustrate other ways for a thread to be blocked.
- **Stop state**. A thread enters the stop state whenever its `run` method returns. There is also a deprecated `stop` method that explicitly stops a thread. Once

stopped, a thread cannot enter any other state. For example, a stopped thread cannot be restarted to enter the runnable state.

Thread states are a convenient way to characterize how `Thread` methods work. For example, `start` takes a thread from the initial to the runnable state, whereas exiting `run` takes a thread from the runnable to the stop state. Note that a thread is in the initial state between being constructed and started. Once started, a thread never again enters the initial state. Once stopped, a thread never leaves this state. Threads can and commonly do make transitions between the runnable and blocked states, as subsequent examples illustrate.

Thread Groups

Every thread belongs to a **thread group**, which is a set of threads. Thread groups are a convenient way to organize threads and to invoke methods on the group as whole rather than on individual threads.

■ **Example 8.4.9.**   The code segment

```
Thread t1 = new Thread();
t1.setDaemon( true );
Thread t2 = new Thread();
t2.setDaemon( true );
Thread t3 = new Thread();
t3.setDaemon( true );
```

constructs three threads and then makes a daemon thread. By contrast, the code segment

```
ThreadGroup tg = new ThreadGroup( "A sample thread group" );
Thread t1 = new Thread( tg ); // t1 belongs to tg
Thread t2 = new Thread( tg ); // as does t2
Thread t3 = new Thread( tg ); // as does t3
tg.setDaemon(); // t1, t2, and t3 are now daemon threads
```

first constructs a `ThreadGroup` and then three `Threads` as members of the group. The three `Threads` are made daemons with the single method call

```
tg.setDaemon();
```

on the group as a whole.   ■

If a `Thread` is constructed without an explicit `ThreadGroup`, the `Thread` belongs to a **default thread group**. Otherwise, the thread belongs to the thread group specified in the constructor.

■ **Example 8.4.10.**   The `ThreadGroupEx` program in Figure 8.4.8 constructs four referenced threads. The threads with references `mt1` and `mt2` belong to a

```
class ThreadGroupEx {
  public static void main( String[ ] args ) {
    ThreadGroup tg = new ThreadGroup( "Test Group" );
    MyThread mt1 = new MyThread( "mt1" ), mt2 = new MyThread( "mt2" ),
     mt3 = new MyThread( tg, "mt3" ), mt4 = new MyThread( tg, "mt4" );
    mt1.start(); mt2.start(); mt3.start(); mt4.start();
  }
}
class MyThread extends Thread {
  public MyThread( String n ) { super( n ); }
  public MyThread( ThreadGroup tg, String n ) { super( tg, n ); }
  public void run() {
    System.out.println( getName() + " in " + getThreadGroup() );
  }
}
```

FIGURE 8.4.8   A program to illustrate a default and a specified `ThreadGroup`.

default thread group because no `ThreadGroup` is specified in the constructor. By contrast, the threads with references `mt3` and `mt4` belong to an explicitly specified `ThreadGroup`. The program's output is

```
mt1 in java.lang.ThreadGroup[name=main,maxpri=10]
mt2 in java.lang.ThreadGroup[name=main,maxpri=10]
mt3 in java.lang.ThreadGroup[name=Test Group,maxpri=10]
mt4 in java.lang.ThreadGroup[name=Test Group,maxpri=10]
```

The default thread group is named after the method `main` in which the threads are constructed.

A thread group can be constructed as a subgroup of another group, which thus allows the grouping of thread groups in a hierarchy. For example, in the code segment

```
ThreadGroup p = new ThreadGroup( "parent" );
ThreadGroup c = new ThreadGroup( p, "child" );
```

the `ThreadGroup` to which c refers is constructed with the `ThreadGroup` to which p refers as its parent. Figure 8.4.9 lists the `ThreadGroup` public constructors and nondeprecated methods with a brief description of each.

Declaration	Description
`ThreadGroup( String n );`	Constructs a thread group
`ThreadGroup( ThreadGroup p, String n);`	Constructs a parented thread group
`int activeCount();`	Returns estimated count of active threads in group
`int activeGroupCount();`	Returns estimated count of active groups in group
`void checkAccess();`	Checks if current thread has permission to modify group
`void destroy();`	Destroys thread group and its subgroups
`int enumerate( Thread[ ] list );`	Copies references to active threads in group and subgroup into array
`int enumerate( Thread[ ] list,` `            boolean recurse );`	Copies references to active threads in group and subgroups into array
`int enumerate( ThreadGroup[ ] list );`	Copies references to active subgroups into array
`int enumerate( ThreadGroup[ ] list,` `            boolean recurse );`	Copies references to active subgroups into array
`int getMaxPriority();`	Returns maximum priority of group threads
`String getName();`	Returns group's name
`ThreadGroup getParent();`	Returns group's parent
`void interrupt();`	Interrupts all threads in group
`boolean isDaemon();`	Checks whether group is a daemon group
`boolean isDestroyed();`	Checks whether group has been destroyed
`void list();`	Prints group information to standard output
`boolean parentOf( ThreadGroup tg );`	Checks for parent relationship
`void setDaemon( boolean tf );`	Sets group's daemon status
`void setMaxPriority( int p );`	Sets group's maximum priority
`String toString();`	Returns group's string representation

FIGURE 8.4.9   The `ThreadGroup` constructors and nondeprecated methods.

Thread Synchronization

Threads execute independently in the JVM, although there are ways to coordinate or **synchronize** thread execution. Further, each thread has its *own copy* of local variables in whatever methods the thread happens to execute. Assume, for example, that two threads execute the `run` method

```
public void run() {
   int i = 0;
   while ( i++ < 3 )
      System.out.println( "hi" );
}
```

Each thread has its own copy of `i` and neither thread can access the other's variable `i`. In this sense, local variables such as `i` are **thread safe**; that is, the programmer is not required to provide any special thread synchronization to prevent one thread from accessing another thread's local variables. However, there are cases in which the programmer needs to synchronize threads so that a multithreaded program behaves correctly.

■ **Example 8.4.11.**   The SyncEx1 program in Figure 8.4.10 illustrates the need for thread synchronization. The program has three threads: the *main*

```
class SyncEx1 {
   public static void main( String[ ] args ) {
      if ( args.length < 1 ) {
        System.err.println( "java SyncEx1 <loops per thread>" );
        System.exit( -1 );
      }
      int n = Integer.parseInt( args[ 0 ] ); // iterations per thread
      MyThread plus =  new MyThread( +1, n ), // plus increments
               minus = new MyThread( -1, n ); // minus decrements
      plus.start(); minus.start();
      // wait for both threads to complete before printing result
      try {
         plus.join(); minus.join();
      } catch( InterruptedException e ) { }
      System.out.println( n + " iterations each: " + MyThread.shared );
   }
}
class MyThread extends Thread {
   MyThread( int type, int howMany ) { t = type; n = howMany; }
   public void run() {
      for ( int i = 0; i < n; i++ )
         if ( t > 0 )
           shared = shared + 1;
         else
           shared = shared - 1;
   }
   static int shared; //*** shared by all MyThread objects
   private int n;
   private int t;
}
```

FIGURE 8.4.10   A program to illustrate the need for thread synchronization.

thread, which executes the statements in main; and two MyThread objects, where MyThread extends Thread and overrides run. The *main thread* constructs and starts the two MyThread objects, which share access to the MyThread class's static integer field named shared. The MyThread object to which plus refers increments shared, whereas the MyThread object to which minus refers decrements `shared`. The increments and decrements of field `shared` occur the *same number of times*. For example, if the `plus` thread increments `shared` 10,000 times, then the `minus` thread decrements `shared` 10,000 times as well. Once the two `MyThreads` stop, therefore, `shared`'s value should be zero.

The `join` Method

After constructing and starting the two `MyThread` objects with references `plus` and `minus`, the *main thread* invokes the `join` method on each

```
try {
  plus.join(); minus.join();
} catch( InterruptedException e ) { }
```

The thread that invokes `join` waits for the thread on which `join` is invoked to stop before continuing itself. The *main thread* thus waits for the threads with references `plus` and `minus` to stop before the *main thread* continues and prints `shared`'s value to the standard output. By the way, no harm results from invoking `join` on a thread that has already stopped. The point is that the *main thread* must not print `shared`'s value until all increments and decrements of `shared` have finished. Having the *main thread* invoke `join` on the other two threads provides the required coordination.

The program is invoked with a command-line argument N that determines how many times the `plus` thread increments and the `minus` thread decrements `shared`. If N is relatively small, `shared`'s value is typically zero after the `plus` and `minus` threads have stopped. As N becomes relatively large, however, `shared`'s final value may vary in unpredictable ways. For example, running the program four times in a row with N set to 10,000,000 each time produced four different outputs

```
10000000 iterations each: 0
10000000 iterations each: 8579655
10000000 iterations each: 9452129
10000000 iterations each: -3738118
```

The Need for Thread Synchronization

The synchronization problem in the `SyncEx1` program can be clarified by focusing on the apparently innocent statements

```
shared = shared + 1; // done by plus thread
```

and

```
shared = shared - 1; // done by minus thread
```

Neither statement maps to an **atomic**—that is, noninterruptible—operation in the JVM. Instead, each statement corresponds to a *pair of operations*. For example, the statement

```
shared = shared + 1; // done by plus thread
```

corresponds to an *addition operation* followed by an *assignment operation*.

The underlying problem now can be described more precisely and then illustrated. While running, the `plus` and `minus` threads perform two operations on each loop iteration: an arithmetic operation (addition for the `plus` thread and subtraction for the `minus` thread) followed by an assignment operation. These operations can be interleaved in different ways, which leads to unpredictable results. For example, the JVM might perform an addition operation followed by a subtraction operation followed by two assignment operations. To illustrate, consider the following scenario with successive operation times listed as T_0, T_1, T_2, and T_3. At T_0, assume that `shared`'s value is zero.

- T_1: The `plus` thread completes the addition operation but does *not* complete the assignment operation before relinquishing execution on the JVM to the `minus` thread. The `plus` thread has computed the value of 1 to assign to `shared` but has not yet assigned the value. Therefore, `shared`'s value is still zero.
- T_2: The `minus` thread completes the subtraction operation, which computes the value of -1.
- T_3: The `minus` thread completes the assignment operation so that `shared`'s value becomes -1.
- T_3: The `plus` thread completes the assignment operation, which assigns 1 to `shared`.

At this point, the statements

```
shared = shared + 1; // done by plus thread
```

and

```
shared = shared - 1; // done by minus thread
```

have executed *once apiece*. Nonetheless, `shared`'s value is 1 rather than 0. As the number of operations increases, so does the likelihood of their interleaving in inappropriate ways.

Critical Sections and Mutual Exclusion

The `SyncEx1` program in Figure 8.4.10 illustrates a *critical section problem*, where a **critical section** is a segment of code to which a thread must have *exclusive access* in

order for a program to behave correctly. The critical section in the `SyncEx1` program
is code segment

```
if ( t > 0 )
   shared = shared + 1; //** plus thread
else
   shared = shared - 1; //** minus thread
```

in the `run` method. Whenever one of the threads begins to execute the code segment, the thread should *finish* executing the code segment before the other thread
begins to execute the code segment. In different but equivalent terms, the entire
code segment should behave as if it were *atomic* or *uninterruptible*. The synchronized keyword can be used to lock code segments and entire methods so that
the code segments and methods behave as if they were atomic, uninterruptible
operations.

■ **Example 8.4.12.**   The `SyncEx1` program in Figure 8.4.10 can be revised to
enforce mutual exclusion on its critical section code by revising the `run` method.
The new version has an `Object` field

```
class MyThread extends Thread {
   //...
   private Object lock = new Object(); //*** the lock
}
```

that serves as a lock for the critical `if-else` construct

```
synchronized( lock ) {
  if ( t > 0 )
    shared = shared + 1;
  else
    shared = shared - 1;
}
```

The new version thus nests the `if-else` statement in a `synchronized` statement,
which allows one thread to **lock** an `Object` and thereby prevent any other thread
from executing the body of the `synchronized` statement.[†] The locking is
an atomic operation. In this example, either the `plus` thread or the `minus`
thread—but not both—locks the `Object`. Suppose that the `minus` happens to
lock first. The `minus` thread then has exclusive access to the `if-else` statement.
Only after the `minus` thread completes the code segment in the `synchronized`
block can the `plus` thread enter this block. The `synchronized` block thus
ensures that the statements

[†] A *lock* is also called a *monitor*, a term that has various and even inconsistent uses.

```
shared = shared + 1; //** plus thread
```

and

```
shared = shared - 1; //** minus thread
```

will be executed as if they were atomic operations. With this revision to the
SyncEx1 program, shared's value at the end is always zero.   ■

The object (class instance) in a synchronized statement is required, although the
object need not be used within the synchronized statement itself, as Example 8.4.12 illustrates. The key point is that a thread first must gain a lock on the object specified in the
synchronized clause before the thread can execute the body of the synchronized
clause, and only one thread at a time can hold the lock on the specified object.

>   **Example 8.4.13.**   The SyncEx1 program revision in Example 8.4.12 uses a
> synchronized statement to enforce mutual exclusion. An entire method also
> can be synchronized, as this revision

```
private synchronized void addOrSubtract() {
    if ( t > 0 )
        shared = shared + 1;
    else
        shared = shared - 1;
}
```

> of the addOrSubtract method illustrates. Because the entire method is now
> synchronized, one thread at a time has exclusive access to the method's body.
> This revision also ensures that the SyncEx1 variable shared's printed value is
> zero.   ■

Communication among Synchronized Threads

Synchronization prevents threads from interfering with one another by enforcing mutual exclusion on critical section code. However, an application may require synchronized
threads to cooperate in some manner. Consider the case of two threads T_1 and T_2, each
of which needs to invoke the synchronized method M. Whichever thread gains the
lock required to execute M's body thereby prevents the other thread from executing
M's body. Suppose that an application requires T_1 and T_2 to *alternate* execution of M's
body. Synchronization by itself cannot ensure this behavior. Such cooperation requires
further mechanisms.

>   ■ **Example 8.4.14.**   The SyncWaitEx program in Figure 8.4.11 shows how
> synchronized threads can interact in a cooperative way. The program can be
> described as follows:

- Method `main` constructs and starts N threads, with N currently set to 8. The threads are `MyThread` objects and class `MyThread` has a `static` array of `char` that its objects share by writing characters into the array.

- Each `MyThread` has an integer identifier field and a `char` field that the thread writes into the shared `char` array, which holds 8 characters. The `MyThread` with an `id` of 0 writes the character `'A'`, the `MyThread` with an `id` of 1 writes the character `'B'`, and so on. The writing and related operations (e.g., printing the array once it fills) are synchronized, thus ensuring that only one thread at a time can write its character at the current array position.

- The threads are started in this order of their `id`s: $7, 6, \ldots, 0$. The thread with an `id` of 7 writes the character `'H'`. However, the program coordinates the threads to ensure that `'A'` (written by `MyThread-0`) is written at the array's first position, `'B'` (written by `MyThread-1`) is written at the array's second position, and so on. Although `MyThread-7` starts first, this thread does not write its character until the seven `MyThread`s started afterwards write their characters. The threads are thus synchronized, that is, *coordinated*.

The `MyThread` override of `run` consists of an infinite loop in which the `writeChar` method is repeatedly invoked on the current thread

```
public void run() {
   while ( true )
     writeChar();
}
```

Method `writeChar` is `synchronized` to ensure that only one thread at a time is writing to the shared array called `queue`. To coordinate the order in which the threads write to the `queue`, the `writeChar` method uses the `wait` and `notifyAll` methods inherited from `Object`.

The `wait` Method and Notification

The `wait` method is invoked as

```
private synchronized void writeChar() {
   //*** release lock and wait until it's your turn
   while ( turn != id )
      try {
        wait( 20 ); // 20 milliseconds
      } catch( InterruptedException e ) { }
```

Suppose that `MyThread-7` first gains the lock on the synchronized `writeChar` method. At this point, `turn`'s value is 0. The `while` expression is thus `false` and, therefore, `MyThread-7` invokes the `wait` method inside the `try` block. This version of `wait` pauses the thread for the specified number of milliseconds or

```
class SyncWaitEx {
   public static void main( String[ ] args ) {
      final int n = 8;
      MyThread[ ] mt = new MyThread[ n ];
      char c = 'A';
      //*** construct and initialize the threads
      for ( int i = 0; i < n; i++ )
         mt[ i ] = new MyThread( i, c++ );
      //*** start the threads, in reverse order
      for ( int i = n - 1; i >= 0; i-- )
         mt[ i ].start();
   }
}
class MyThread extends Thread {
   public MyThread( int i, char ch ) { id = i; c = ch; }
   public void run() {
      while ( true )
         writeChar();
   }
   //*** synchronized to ensure only 1 thread at a time
   //    writes to the queue, etc. Threads wait their turn, however.
   private synchronized void writeChar() {
      //*** release lock and wait until it's your turn
      while ( turn != id )
         try {
            wait( 20 ); // 20 milliseconds
            } catch( InterruptedException e ) { }
      queue[ turn++ ] = this.c;
      if ( turn == n ) { //*** queue full?
         System.out.println( queue ); //** if so, print it
         turn = 0;                     //    and reset turn to zero
      }
      notifyAll(); //*** awaken any waiting threads
   }
   private int id; //*** identifier
   private char c; //*** character to write to shared array
   private static int turn = 0;
   private static final int n = 8;
   private static char queue[ ] = new char[ n ]; //** shared array
}
```

FIGURE 8.4.11   A program to illustrate the wait and notifyAll
methods.

until notification occurs, whichever is first. (Notification is explained shortly.)
Invoking the wait method *releases* the lock on the synchronized method. The
thread that invokes wait performs an atomic operation in which the thread

pause and the lock release are conceptually simultaneous. In effect, MyThread-7 releases the lock on writeChar to some other MyThread that is trying to gain the lock. So, in this example, a thread that gains the lock first checks whether it is that thread's turn to write to the shared array. If so, the thread continues and writes the character. If not, the thread waits and thereby releases the lock.

The wait occurs within a while statement because there is no guarantee that a waiting thread's turn will occur immediately after the thread has emerged from the wait. Suppose, for example, that MyThread-7 awakens but that turn's value is now 2. MyThread-7 therefore must wait again.

The notify and notifyAll Methods

A thread that gets beyond the wait writes its character to the shared array and, if the array is full, prints the array to the standard output. The thread then invokes notifyAll immediately before exiting writeChar

```
private synchronized void writeChar() {
    //...
    notifyAll(); //*** awaken any waiting threads
}
```

This notification awakens *all* waiting threads, even if the specified pause of 20 milliseconds has not elapsed for a particular thread. By invoking notifyAll, the current also releases its lock on the synchronized method. For this reason, the method is invoked as the *last* statement in writeChar. The method notify is like notifyAll except that the former notifies a *single*, arbitrary thread. In this example, notifyAll is used because *several* threads may be waiting. All of the waiting threads should be awaken so that each of them can test whether the turn is now set to its id.

Because the program coordinates the synchronized threads with the wait and notifyAll methods, the program's output is

```
ABCDEFGH
ABCDEFGH
ABCDEFGH
...
```

regardless of the order in which the MyThreads invoke the writeChar method.

Finally, the methods wait, notify, and notifyAll are inherited from Object. These methods are designed for use only within synchronized blocks or methods. The method wait has three overloads, which can be described as follows:

- wait(long ticks) pauses the current thread for ticks milliseconds or until the current thread is notified, whichever occurs first. If ticks is zero, the waiting does not time out on its own but rather ends only with notification.

- `wait( long ticks, int moreTicks )` has the same behavior as the single-argument version except that the pause interval is now `ticks` milliseconds plus `moreTicks` nanoseconds.
- `wait()` is equivalent to `wait( 0 )`. ∎

Deadlock

Thread synchronization must be programmed with care to avoid **deadlock**, a situation in which two or more threads wait endlessly for one another to release locks. At a minimum, deadlock requires two threads. A single thread cannot deadlock an application. As a general example, suppose that

- Threads T_1 and T_2 hold locks L_1 and L_2, respectively.
- T_1 cannot continue executing unless it acquires L_2, and T_2 cannot continue executing unless it acquires L_1.
- T_1 will not release L_1 until *after* it acquires L_2. Similarly, T_2 will not release L_2 until *after* it acquires L_1.

T_1 and T_2 thus wait endlessly for the other thread to release its lock. The situation is also called **deadly embrace**.

■ **Example 8.4.15.** The `DeadlockEx` program in Figure 8.4.12 deadlocks. The relationship between `wait` and `notify` (or `notifyAll`) contributes directly to the deadlock. For a `notify` to awaken a waiting thread, the `wait` must occur *before* the `notify` because a notification awakes only a thread that is *already* waiting. A notification that occurs *before* a thread `waits` cannot awaken this thread.

In the deadlocking program, the `foo` thread executes the synchronized method `fooM` first and then the synchronized method `barM`, and the `bar` thread executes the synchronized method `barM` first and then the synchronized method `fooM`. However, each thread *waits* in the method that has the other thread's name. For instance, the `foo` thread waits in the `barM` until the `bar` thread executes `notify` to awaken the `foo` thread.

The `MyThread` override of `run` ensures that the `foo` thread invokes the method `fooM` and the `bar` thread invokes `barM`. The `foo` thread bypasses the `fooM` method's `wait` because the thread's name is `foo` rather than `bar`. The first `fooM` statement beyond the `try` block that contains the `wait` is

```
barM();
```

So the `foo` thread now invokes the synchronized method `barM`. There are two possibilities:

- The `foo` thread gains the lock on `barM` and `waits`. The `foo` thread now can be awoken only by the `bar` thread's subsequent invocation of `notify` in method `barM`.

```
class DeadlockEx {
   public static void main( String[ ] args ) {
      new MyThread( "foo" ).start();
      new MyThread( "bar" ).start();
   }
}
class MyThread extends Thread {
   public MyThread( String name ) { super( name ); }
   public void run() {
      while ( true )
         if ( getName().equalsIgnoreCase( "foo" ) )
           fooM();
         else
           barM();
   }
   private synchronized void fooM() {
      System.out.println( getName() + " entering fooM." );
      while ( getName().equalsIgnoreCase( "bar" ) )
        try {
           wait(); // wait indefinitely
        } catch( InterruptedException e ) { }
      barM();  // invoke other synchronized method
      System.out.println( getName() + " exiting fooM." );
      notify(); // awaken the other thread, if it's waiting
   }
   private synchronized void barM() {
      System.out.println( getName() + " entering barM." );
      while ( getName().equalsIgnoreCase( "foo" ) )
        try {
           wait(); // wait indefinitely
        } catch( InterruptedException e ) { }
      fooM();  // invoke other synchronized method
      System.out.println( getName() + " exiting barM." );
      notify(); // awaken the other thread, if it's waiting
   }
}
```

FIGURE 8.4.12   A program that deadlocks.

- The foo thread does not gain the lock on barM because the bar thread currently holds the lock. When the foo thread does gain the lock, the thread will wait for a subsequent notification by the bar thread.

The foo thread eventually waits in method barM for a bar thread notification in the same method, whereas the bar thread eventually waits in method fooM for a foo thread notification in the same method. Each thread thus waits indefinitely for the other thread to awaken it. The two threads are deadlocked. The program's output is

```
foo entering fooM.
foo entering barM.
bar entering barM.
bar entering fooM.
```

Note that neither thread exits the methods that it enters.   ■

The `DeadlockEx` program in Figure 8.4.12 is contrived in that the deadlock is deliberate. Deadlocks in real-world applications are typically inadvertent and the program logic that leads to such deadlocks may be very subtle. The JVM provides no help with respect to deadlock; that is, the JVM does not detect, prevent, or recover from deadlock. Avoiding deadlock is the programmer's responsibility.

Summary of Nondeprecated `Thread` Constructors and Methods

Figure 8.4.13 lists the public `Thread` constructors, with a brief description of each. Figure 8.4.14 lists the major public instance methods, and Figure 8.4.15 lists the public `static` methods. In the descriptions, the *current thread* refers to the currently executing thread.

Declaration	Description
`Thread();`	Unnamed and default runnable target.
`Thread(String n);`	Named and default runnable target.
`Thread(Runnable target);`	Unnamed but specified runnable target.
`Thread(Runnable t, String n);`	Named and specified runnable target.
`Thread(ThreadGroup tg, String n);`	Named and specified thread group.
`Thread(ThreadGroup tg, Runnable t);`	Unnamed but specified thread group and runnable target.
`Thread(ThreadGroup, Runnable t, String n);`	Named and specified thread group and runnable target.

FIGURE 8.4.13   The `Thread` class's constructors.

EXERCISES

1. What is a thread?
2. When an application first begins, is it single threaded or multithreaded?
3. Must the *main thread* (i.e., the thread that executes `main`) directly construct all of the other threads in a multithreaded application?
4. What code does a `started` thread execute?
5. Does the *main thread* (i.e., the thread that executes `main`) execute `run`?

Declaration	Description
`void checkAccess();`	Checks whether current thread can modify this thread.
`String getName();`	Returns the thread's name.
`int getPriority();`	Returns the thread's priority.
`ThreadGroup getThreadGroup();`	Returns the thread's thread group.
`void interrupt();`	Interrupts the thread.
`boolean isAlive();`	Tests whether the thread is alive (not yet stopped).
`boolean isDaemon();`	Tests whether the thread is a daemon.
`boolean isInterrupted();`	Tests whether the thread has been interrupted.
`void join();`	Waits for the thread to die.
`void join( long t );`	Waits at most t milliseconds for the thread to die.
`void join( long t, int n );`	Same as above plus n nanoseconds.
`void run();`	Callback executed by thread.
`void setDaemon( boolean d );`	Sets the thread's daemon status.
`void setName( String n );`	Sets the thread's name.
`void setPriority( int p );`	Sets the thread's priority.
`void start();`	Makes the thread runnable.

FIGURE 8.4.14   The `Thread` class's important instance methods.

Declaration	Description
`int activeCount();`	Counts the active threads in the thread's group.
`Thread currentThread();`	Returns a reference to the current thread.
`void dumpStack();`	Prints a stack trace for the current thread.
`void enumerate( Thread[ ] a );`	Copies thread group members into the `Thread` array.
`boolean interrupted();`	Tests whether current thread has been interrupted.
`void sleep( long n );`	Sleeps the current thread for n milliseconds (ms).
`void sleep( long n, int m );`	Sleeps the current thread for n ms + m nanoseconds.

FIGURE 8.4.15   The `Thread` class's `static` methods.

6. Explain the error:

```
Thread t = new Thread( this );
t.run();
```

7. Explain why applications with a GUI are commonly multithreaded.

8. Rewrite the *sieve of Erastosthenes* as a single-threaded program and test its responsiveness to user input after the program begins computing primes up to a large number such as 10,000,000.

9. How many methods are declared in the `Runnable` interface?

10. Explain why `run` is a *pure callback*.

11. Suppose that class `MyThread` extends `Thread` but fails to override the inherited `run` method. What is the behavior of the *inherited* `run` method?

12. Explain the error:

```
class MyThread extends Thread {
    protected void run() { /*...*/ }
}
```

13. Explain the difference between a user thread and a daemon thread.

14. If thread *T* is a user thread, are other threads constructed by *T* also user threads by default?

15. Explain the error:

```
Thread t = new Thread( this );
t.start();
t.setDaemon( true );
```

16. Does an application necessarily terminate if `main` returns?

17. Does a single-threaded application exit if `main` returns?

18. Write a code segment that constructs a thread and changes its status to a daemon thread.

19. Explain how thread priority impacts thread scheduling within the JVM.

20. At what priority does the *main thread* (i.e., the thread that executes `main`) run?

21. When is a thread in the initial state?

22. When is a thread in the runnable state?

23. When is a thread in the stop state?

24. When is a thread in the blocked state?

25. If a thread is *runnable*, does this imply that the thread is currently executing?

26. Explain the error:

```
Thread t = new Thread( this );
t.start();
//... the Thread to which t refers has stopped
t.start(); //*** restart the Thread
```

27. What is a thread group?

28. Does every thread belong to a thread group?

29. Must every thread be constructed with a specified `ThreadGroup`?

30. Explain the behavior of the `join` method with reference to this code segment:

```
Thread t = new Thread( this );
t.start();
t.join();
```

31. Explain the error:

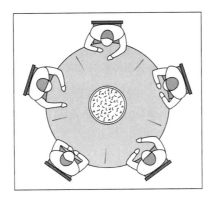

FIGURE 8.5.1   Dijkstra's dining philosophers.

```
int x = -1;
synchronized( x ) { /*...*/ }
```

32. Explain what a *critical section* is.

33. Explain what *mutual exclusion* means.

34. Explain what it means for a `synchronized` block or method to behave as if it were *atomic* or *uninterruptible*.

35. Explain the relationship between `wait`, on the one hand, and `notify` and `notifyAll`, on the other hand.

36. Explain deadlock.

37. Can a single-threaded application deadlock?

8.5   Sample Application: The Dining Philosophers Problem

Problem

Simulate the dining philosophers problem and offer a solution that prevents deadlock. E. W. Dijkstra first stated and solved the dining philosophers problem ("Cooperating Sequential Processes," *Technical Report EWD-123*, Technological University, Eindhoven, The Netherlands, 1965). The problem has become a classic by illustrating a large class of concurrency control problems. Despite the whimsical description that Dijkstra offers, the problem is of great practical importance for operating systems in particular and concurrent systems in general.

Dijkstra's original paper has five philosophers seated around a circular table in the middle of which is a bowl of rice. On the table are five chopsticks, one between each pair of philosophers (see Figure 8.5.1). The philosophers either think or eat but do not communicate with one another. When a philosopher gets hungry, the philosopher tries to pick up the chopsticks to the immediate left and the immediate right. The chopsticks are picked up *one at a time*. Once a philosopher picks up a chopstick, the chopstick is not released until the philosopher has finished eating, at which time both chopsticks are put back in their original positions. The situation is deadlock-prone. In the same instant, for example, each philosopher might pick up the chopstick to his or her immediate left. In this case, no one would ever eat again because no one can eat with a single chopstick and a chopstick, once grabbed, is not released until the philosopher has eaten. The philosophers would be deadlocked.

The dining philosophers can represent processes running on a system and the chopsticks can represent resources that the processes require. Suppose, for example, that the processes P_1 and P_2 are currently running and that each process requires three tape drives to complete its execution. Assume that the system has three tape drives D_1, D_2, and D_3. Now suppose that processes gain tape drives one at a time and that a process does not release any gained tape drive until all three have been gained and the process has finished executing. The sequence

- P_1 gets D_1.
- P_1 gets D_2.
- P_2 gets D_3.

now deadlocks the processes: each process waits indefinitely for the other to release tape drives, but neither process will release a tape drive until gaining all three and thereby completing its execution.

Sample Output

A sample run with 16 dining philosophers produced the output in Figure 8.5.2. Each philosopher has an integer identifier and is implemented as a `Thread`. The philosopher threads are `start`ed in random order. The remaining output consists of two bit strings per row, each 16 bits in length. The first bit string represents the philosophers: the leftmost bit represents philosopher 0, the next bit philosopher 1, and so on. A 1 means that the philosopher is eating and a 0 that the philosopher is thinking. For the chopstick bit string, a 1 signifies that the chopstick has been taken and a 0 that the chopstick is still free.

The output can be checked for errors in the simulation. The philosopher bit string should never show two adjacent 1s, as this would indicate that two philosophers seated next to one another were both eating, which is impossible. The leftmost bit and the rightmost bit should not both be 1s because these bits also represent philosophers seated next to one another. (Recall that the table is circular.) Given N philosophers, only $N/2$ can be eating at any one time.

Solution

The philosophers are represented as threads and the chopsticks as booleans. A chopstick's value is `true`, if the chopstick is taken, and `false`, if the chopstick is available. The philosopher threads run at the same priority. Eating and thinking are

```
### Philosopher 4 started.
### Philosopher 8 started.
### Philosopher 7 started.
### Philosopher 5 started.
### Philosopher 13 started.
### Philosopher 9 started.
### Philosopher 10 started.
### Philosopher 11 started.
### Philosopher 3 started.
### Philosopher 15 started.
### Philosopher 14 started.
### Philosopher 1 started.
### Philosopher 6 started.
### Philosopher 0 started.
### Philosopher 12 started.
### Philosopher 2 started.

Philosophers                Chopsticks
(1 = eating 0 = thinking)   (1 = taken 0 = free)
0000000000000000            0000000000000000
0000100000000000            0000110000000000
0000100010000000            0000110011000000
0000100010000100            0000110011000110
0000100010100100            0000110011110110
0000100010100101            1000110011110111
0100100010100101            1110110011110111
0100101010100101            1110111111110111
                      . . .
```

FIGURE 8.5.2   Output from a sample run with 16 philosophers.

simulated by `sleeping` for a randomly generated interval, currently in the range of 1 to 4 seconds. The `synchronized` method `grabChopsticks` coordinates the threads and prevents deadlock by ensuring that a hungry philosopher gets either both chopsticks or neither of them. A hungry philosopher that cannot grab both chopsticks `waits` until the chopsticks are free. A philosopher who manages to get both chopsticks notifies any waiting philosophers before exiting the `synchronized` method.

Java Implementation

```
import java.util.Random;
public class DiningPhils {
   public static void main( String[ ] args ) {
      if ( args.length < 1 ) {
         System.err.println( "DiningPhils <# of philosophers>" );
```

```
         System.exit( -1 );
      }
      DiningPhils self = new DiningPhils();
      self.init( Integer.parseInt( args[ 0 ] ) );
   }
   public int getCount() {
      return n;
   }
   public boolean getChopstick( int i ) {
      return chops[ i ];
   }
   public void setChopstick( int i, boolean v ) {
      chops[ i ] = v;
   }
   private void init( final int N ) {
      r = new Random();
      n = (N < 0 || N > maxPhils) ? maxPhils : N;
      chops = new boolean[ n ];
      phils = new Philosopher[ n ];
      initPhils();
      dumpStatus();
   }
   //*** Create phil threads and start them in random order.
   private void initPhils() {
      for ( int i = 0; i < n; i++ ) {
         phils[ i ] = new Philosopher( this, i );
         phils[ i ].setTimeSlice( generateTimeSlice() );
         phils[ i ].setPriority( Thread.NORM_PRIORITY - 1 );
      }
      while ( moreToStart() ) {
         int i = Math.abs( r.nextInt() ) % n;
         if ( !phils[ i ].isAlive() ) {
           System.out.println( "### Philosopher " +
                String.valueOf( i ) + " started." );
           phils[ i ].start();
         }
      }
      System.out.println(
        "\nPhilosophers                 Chopsticks" +
        "\n(1 = eating 0 = thinking)  (1 = taken 0 = free)" );
   }
   private boolean moreToStart() {
      for ( int i = 0; i < phils.length; i++ )
         if ( !phils[ i ].isAlive() )
            return true;
```

```
              return false;
           }
           public int generateTimeSlice() {
              int ts = Math.abs( r.nextInt() ) % (maxEat + 1);
              if ( ts == 0 )
                 ts = minEat;
              return ts;
           }
           public void dumpStatus() {
              for ( int i = 0; i < n; i++ )
                 System.out.print( (phils[ i ].getEat()) ? 1 : 0 );
              for ( int i = n; i < maxPhils + 4; i++ )
                 System.out.print( " " );
              for ( int i = 0; i < n; i++ )
                 System.out.print( (chops[ i ]) ? 1 : 0 );
              System.out.println();
           }
           private int n;
           private Philosopher[ ] phils;
           private boolean[ ] chops;
           private Random r;
           private static final int maxPhils = 24;
           private static final int maxEat = 4; // seconds
           private static final int minEat = 1; // seconds
        }
        class Philosopher extends Thread {
           public Philosopher( DiningPhils HOST, int i ) {
              host = HOST; index = i;
           }
           public void setTimeSlice( int TS ) { ts = TS; }
           public boolean chopsticksFree() {
              return !host.getChopstick( index ) &&
                     !host.getChopstick( (index + 1) % host.getCount() );
           }
           public void setLeftChopstick( boolean flag ) {
             host.setChopstick( index, flag );
           }
           public void setRightChopstick( boolean flag ) {
             host.setChopstick( (index + 1) % host.getCount(), flag );
           }
           private void releaseChopsticks() {
             host.setChopstick( index, false );
             host.setChopstick( (index + 1) % host.getCount(), false );
           }
```

```
public void run() {
   while ( true ) {
      grabChopsticks();
      eat();
      think();
   }
}
private synchronized void grabChopsticks() {
   while ( !chopsticksFree() )
     try {
        wait();
     } catch( InterruptedException e ) { }
   takeChopsticks();
   notifyAll();
}
private void takeChopsticks() {
   setLeftChopstick( true );
   setRightChopstick( true );
   setEat( true );
   host.dumpStatus();
}
private void eat() {
   pause();
   setEat( false );
   releaseChopsticks();
}
private void think() {
   pause();
}
private void pause() {
   setTimeSlice( host.generateTimeSlice() );
   try {
     sleep( ts * 1000 );
   } catch ( InterruptedException e ) { }
}
private void setEat( boolean f ) {
   isEating = f;
}
public boolean getEat() {
   return isEating;
}
private DiningPhils host;
private boolean isEating;
private int index;
private int ts;
}
```

Discussion

The application has two classes, DiningPhils with main and Philosopher, which extends Thread. For reference, the thread that executes main is called the *main thread*. The *main thread* converts to an int a command-line argument that specifies how many philosophers are to dine. The DiningPhils class's static field maxPhils, currently set to 24, specifies the maximum number of dining philosophers. The *main thread*, which runs at normal priority, constructs an array of Philosophers, each of which will run at a lower priority. Because the *main thread* starts the philosopher threads in random order, fairness dictates that all of the philosopher threads be started before any one of them begins executing. Having the *main thread* run at a higher priority ensures that its task of starting the philosopher threads will be completed before any philosopher thread begins the endless cycle of thinking and eating. After the *main thread* starts all of the philosopher threads, the *main thread* stops as main returns. The philosopher threads then sustain the application because they are *user* rather than *daemon* threads.

Each philosopher thread executes an overridden run that has an infinite loop

```
public void run() {
    while ( true ) {
        grabChopsticks();
        eat();
        think();
    }
}
```

in which the thread tries to get the two chopsticks required for eating. After eating, the thread then thinks and repeats the process. The eating and thinking occur for a randomly generated interval, currently between 1 and 4 seconds. The sleep method is used to simulate both eating and thinking. The only synchronization occurs in the synchronized method grabChopsticks

```
private synchronized void grabChopsticks() {
    while ( !chopsticksFree() )
      try {
        wait();
      } catch( InterruptedException e ) { }
    takeChopsticks();
    notifyAll();
}
```

A thread that gains the lock on the method checks whether the two chopsticks are free. The simulation is faithful to Dijkstra's original statement of the problem in that the chopsticks are checked one at a time for availability and picked up one at a time. An array of booleans represents the chopsticks: a value of true means that a chopstick is taken and a value of `false` means that a chopstick is free. If a thread cannot get the two chopsticks required for eating, the thread `waits` indefinitely for notification, thereby releasing the lock on `grabChopsticks` so that another thread can try to eat. A thread whose chopsticks are free takes them one at a time and then notifies all waiting threads immediately before exiting the `synchronized` method. The method `takeChopsticks` is not `synchronized` because it is invoked from within a `synchronized` method. In effect, then, the `synchronized` method ensures that this sequence of operations

- Check whether the two chopsticks required for eating are available.
- Pick up the chopsticks, one at a time, when both become available.
- Notify any waiting threads to check again on the availability of their chopsticks.

is executed by a *single* thread as if the sequence were atomic or uninterruptible. Note, too, that the `eat` method is not synchronized and is not invoked from within the synchronized `grabChopsticks`. The critical section should not include the code that simulates eating because more than one philosopher can eat at the same time. The critical section needs to include only the code that simulates getting the chopsticks required for eating.

Solutions to Critical Section Problems

Proposed solutions to a critical section problem are judged on four criteria. It may be helpful to summarize the application by describing whether and how it satisfies the four criteria:

- **Progress**. If a critical section is unlocked, a thread should be able to enter it. The `synchronized` construct automatically supports this behavior. If a `synchronized` block or method is unlocked, a thread can gain the lock and enter the block or method.
- **Mutual Exclusion**. At most one thread can hold the lock on a critical section. The `synchronized` construct automatically supports this behavior. Because only one thread at a time can hold the lock on a `synchronized` block or method, only one thread at a time can execute the critical section code.
- **Starvation**. None of the threads that are trying to execute critical section code should be permanently prevented from doing so. The `synchronized` construct by itself does not address this issue. The sample application makes no explicit provision to avoid starvation but rather depends upon three factors:

    – All of the threads contending to execute the critical section code run at the same priority, which eliminates priority as a factor that might cause a thread to starve.

- Each thread eats for a finite interval and, after eating, immediately relinquishes the two chopsticks. A thread that stops eating immediately increases the likelihood that a hungry thread can eat.

- Threads endlessly think and eat for random intervals. Chance thus plays a decisive role in determining which threads gain the chopsticks and when these threads gain them. In the long run, each thread has roughly the same opportunity to eat as any other.

- **Fairness**. Each of the N threads should eat approximately the same amount of time. The synchronized construct by itself does not address this issue. The sample application does promote fairness in a small way but mainly relies upon the same three factors listed under **Starvation**. The small way has to do with how the philosopher threads are started. Recall that each philosopher thread's priority is set to NORM_PRIORITY−1 by the *main thread*, which runs at NORM_PRIORITY. The *main thread*, immediately before exiting, starts the philosopher threads in random order. The philosopher threads thus do not run until the *main thread* has started all of them and then exited itself. Accordingly, the philosopher threads are at least started fairly.

The Programming Exercises suggest ways to analyze and improve the sample application with respect to starvation and fairness.

EXERCISES

1. Run the sample application and inspect the output to confirm that adjacent philosophers do not eat simultaneously.

2. Explain the relationship between Dijkstra's philosophers and chopsticks, on the one hand, and a system's processes and resources, on the other hand.

3. Although the code that simulates taking the chopsticks belongs to the application's critical section, the takeChopsticks method is not synchronized. Explain why this method is not synchronized.

4. Explain why, in the synchronized method grabChopsticks, notification to waiting threads is given by notifyAll rather than by notify.

5. Does the *main thread* (i.e., the thread that executes main) stop or run indefinitely?

6. Why are the philosopher threads not made daemons?

7. Why is the priority of each constructed philosopher thread set lower than the priority of the constructing thread?

8. Does the simulation implement *progress*?

9. Does the simulation implement *mutual exclusion*?

10. Does the simulation *guarantee* that no philosopher thread will starve?

11. To what extent does the simulation implement *fairness*?

JAVA POSTSCRIPT

Deprecated Thread Methods

The `Thread` methods `stop`, `suspend`, `resume`, and `countStackFrames` have been deprecated. Invoking the `stop` method on a `Thread` immediately releases any locks that the `Thread` may hold, thereby allowing another `Thread` to execute the unlocked `synchronized` code. Because `stop` can be invoked anywhere, a stopped `Thread` that holds a lock may not have performed the appropriate cleanup operations. The `stop` method thus may leave an application in an unsafe state. The preferred way to stop any `Thread` that has been `started` is to have the `Thread` exit the `run` method.

The `suspend` method suspends a `Thread`'s further execution until `resume` is invoked on the same `Thread`. A suspended `Thread` does *not* release any locks that it may hold. If a suspended `Thread` is not eventually resumed, deadlock thus may result. So `suspend` has been deprecated because its use is inherently deadlock-prone. Methods `resume` and `countStackFrames` are used only in conjunction with `suspend`; hence, these methods also have been deprecated.

Threads, Compiler Optimization, and the `volatile` Modifier

Suppose that a class has a field such as the `int` variable `winks`

```
class C {
  void m1() {
    for ( int i = 0; i < winks; i++ )
      //...
  }
  void m2() {
    if ( x == y ) winks++;
    //...
  }
  int winks = 10, x, y;
}
```

that is accessed in nonsynchronized methods. The compiler may assume that `winks` in method `m1` can be replaced by the integer constant 10. Yet suppose that a *multithreaded* application uses a `C` object, in particular that one thread T_1 executes `m1` while another thread T_2 executes `m2`. If T_2 increments `winks` in `m2` but the compiler has substituted 10 for `winks` in `m1`, the program does not behave correctly. By marking a variable such as `winks` as `volatile`

```
volatile int winks = 10;
```

the programmer cautions the compiler not to replace `winks` by its initial value. By contrast, marking `winks` as `final` would signal the compiler that the variable could be replaced by its initial value.

COMMON ERRORS AND SAFE PRACTICES

1. The `clone` inherited from `Object` is `protected` and, therefore, is not visible outside a class or its descendants. The code segment

```
class Alpha { /** clone not redeclared public **/ }
class Zeta {
   public Zeta() {
      Alpha a1 = new Alpha();
      Alpha a2 = (Alpha) a1.clone(); //***** ERROR
   }
}
```

thus contains an error because `Zeta` is not an `Alpha` descendant. The error can be eliminated by redefining the inherited `clone` as public:

```
class Alpha {
   public Object clone() {        //** public
      try {
         return super.clone();  //** protected
      } catch( CloneNotSupportedException e ) { }
      return null;
   }
}
```

2. A redefinition of `clone` that invokes the superclass version must deal with the `CloneNotSupportedException`. The code segment

```
class Alpha {
   public Object clone() {
      return super.clone();   //**** ERROR
   }
}
```

is thus in error. The error can be corrected, for example, by placing the call to the superclass's `clone` in a `try` block:

```
class Alpha {
   public Object clone() {
```

```
            try {
               return super.clone();   //*** ok
            } catch( CloneNotSupportedException e ) { }
            return null;
         }
      }
```

3. Method `clone`'s return type is `Object`, which must be cast the appropriate target type. The code segment

```
      String s1 = new String( "Howdy" );
      String s2 = s1.clone();         //***** ERROR
      String s3 = (String) s1.clone(); //** correct
```

illustrates.

4. A class that redefines `clone` as a public method also must implement the `Cloneable` interface to enable the cloning of its objects. The class `Kappa`

```
      class Kappa { //**** ERROR: needs to implement Cloneable!
         public Object clone() { /*...*/ }
      }
```

illustrates.

5. A redefinition of `clone` should ensure that the source and target objects are *independent* after the cloning operation. The program in Figure 8.1.4 illustrates the error of not making the source and target objects independent, and Figure 8.1.6 illustrates how the error can be corrected.

6. A redefinition of `clone` should *not* clone the object by invoking constructors but rather by first invoking the inherited `clone` and then customizing as required.

7. It is an error to serialize or deserialize an object whose class does not implement `Serializable` and is not derived from a class that implements this interface. The code segment

```
      class Alpha { /*...*/ }
      Alpha a1 = new Alpha();
      os = new ObjectOutputStream(
            new FileOutputStream( "out.ser" ) );
      os.writeObject( a1 ); //***** ERROR
```

illustrates the error, which can be corrected by having `Alpha` implement `Serializable`:

```
      class Alpha implements java.io.Serializable { /*...*/ }
      Alpha a1 = new Alpha();
      os = new ObjectOutputStream(
```

```
            new FileOutputStream( "out.ser" ) );
    os.writeObject( a1 ); // ok
```

8. Primitive types such as `ints` and `doubles` cannot be serialized. The code segment

```
class Alpha implements java.io.Serializable { /*...*/ }
int x = -1;
os = new ObjectOutputStream(
        new FileOutputStream( "out.ser" ) );
os.writeObject( x ); //***** ERROR
```

thus contains an error. However, the `DataOutput` and `DataInput` interfaces declare methods such as `writeInt` and `readInt` to write primitive types to and read primitive types from binary streams. These methods are available in `ObjectOutputStreams` and `ObjectInputStreams`.

9. A `String` that is serialized out with `writeObject` should be serialized in with `readObject`. A `String` that is written to a binary stream with `writeUTF` should be read from the binary stream using `readUTF`.

10. It is an error to assume that the values of `static` or `transient` are saved when an object is serialized out and restored to these values when an object is serialized in. Deserializing an object has no effect on its `static` fields, and the `transient` fields of a deserialized object are initialized to their default values (e.g., 0 for integers and `null` for object references).

11. Given the hierarchy

```
class Alpha {
    public Alpha( int x ) { /*...*/ }
}
class Zeta extends Alpha implements Serializable {
    //...
}
```

it is an error to serialize `Zeta` objects even though `Zeta` implements `Serializable`. The problem is that `Zeta`'s superclass does not implement this interface, or extend a class that implements this interface, or have an accessible no-argument constructor. The error can be corrected by having `Alpha` implement `Serializable`, or extend a class that implements this interface, or define an accessible no-argument constructor.

12. If a class customizes serialization by defining `writeObject` and `readObject`, these methods must be defined as *private*. The code segment

```
class Alpha implements java.io.Serializable {
    public void writeObject( Object obj )
        { /*...*/ } //***** ERROR
```

```
public Object readObject()
   { /*...*/ } //***** ERROR
}
```

illustrates the error. In this type of customized serialization, the private `writeObject` and `readObject` serve as *callbacks* rather than as directly invoked methods.

13. If a class customizes serialization by implementing the `Externalizable` interface, the methods `writeObject` and `readObject` must be defined as *public*.

14. If a class implements `Runnable`, the class must define

```
public void run();
```

to be concrete.

15. It is an error to invoke a `Thread`'s `run` method. The code segment

```
Thread t = new Thread( this );
t.run(); //***** ERROR
```

is thus in error. Because `run` is a pure callback, it should never be invoked. A `Thread` should be `started` rather than `run`:

```
Thread t = new Thread( this );
t. start(); // ok
```

16. If a `Thread` is constructed without a runnable target and then started

```
new Thread().start(); //*** Caution: no runnable target
```

the `Thread` stops immediately because the default `run` returns immediately.

17. It is an error to change a `Thread`'s daemon status *after* the `Thread` is started. The code segment

```
Thread t = new Thread( this );
t.start();
t.setDaemon( true ); //***** ERROR
```

thus contains an error. Changing a `Thread`'s daemon status must be done *before* the `Thread` is started.

18. It is an error to try to restart a `Thread` that has stopped. The code segment

```
Thread t = new Thread( this );
t.start();
//...
if ( !t.isAlive() )
   t.start(); //***** ERROR: can't restart a Thread!
```

illustrates the error.

19. It is an error to attach a `synchronized` lock to a primitive type. For example, the code segment

```
int x;
synchronized( x ) { /*...*/ } //***** ERROR
```

contains an error because x is a primitive type. Only an instance of a class type can be used.

20. If a `synchronized` block or method contains an indefinite `wait` statement, the block or method also should contain a `notify` or `notifyAll` statement to awaken any waiting threads. The code segment

```
public void synchronized m() {
   while ( !yourTurn() )
      wait(); //*** same as wait( 0 ), indefinite wait
      doWhatever(); // contains no notify() or notifyAll()
} //***** ERROR: threads may still be waiting
```

thus in error. This code violates the standard of *progress*: once a thread that holds the lock on method m exits the method, some waiting thread should be able to gain lock and execute m.

21. In a multithreaded application, *critical section code* should be placed inside a `synchronized` block or method because such code requires *mutual exclusion* for its proper execution.

22. Various `Thread` methods such as `sleep` and `join` throw an `Interrupted-Exception`; hence, these method calls must occur inside `try` blocks or methods that have the appropriate `throws` clause.

PROGRAMMING EXERCISES

8.1. Implement a `RecordSet` class with a GUI for entering and viewing records, where a **record** is any of sequence characters. A `RecordSet` should have a unique identifying name such as *Employees* or *Inventory*, and the GUI should provide a list available `RecordSet`s to edit. The GUI also should allow a user to build a new `RecordSet`. The `RecordSet`s should be serializable so that the set can be serialized with `writeObject` and deserialized with `readObject`. *Hint*: See the graphical table editor application of Section 7.6.

8.2. Implement a `Database` class whose objects are sets of `RecordSet`s (see Programming Exercise 8.1). A `Database` should have a unique identifying name. Provide a GUI so that users can create and delete `Database`s, add `RecordSet`s to and delete them from a `Database`, and display a selected `RecordSet` in a selected `Database`.

8.3. Files are a basic but effective structure for interapplication communication. Design a `WReport` class that represents an hourly weather report from a field station. The class should encapsulate fields that represent the last hourly and the current temperature, humidity, dew point, and precipitation. A `WReporter` object should serialize a `WReport` object to a file, and a `WRecorder` object should deserialize and then process all of the `WReports` from the last hour. The `WRecorder`'s processing might consist of, for example, a statistical analysis or trend analysis of the submitted `WReports`. The multiple `WReporters` and the single `WRecorder` should execute as separate Java applications.

8.4. Amend the `TimeCard` class (see Section 8.3) so that a separate thread automatically updates the current time.

8.5. Provide a GUI for the Dining Philosophers application of Section 8.5. The user should be able to determine the number of dining philosophers and the time ranges for eating and thinking. (In the current application, philosophers eat and think from one to four seconds.) A separate thread should manage GUI controls such as buttons and menu items.

8.6. Amend the Dining Philosophers application of Section 8.5 to prevent starvation, that is, to prevent the possibility that a philosopher never has a chance to eat.

8.7. Amend the Dining Philosophers application of Section 8.5 to promote fairness, that is, to promote the situation in which each of the N dining philosophers eats approximately $1/N$th of the time. *Hint*: Track the amount of time that each philosopher has eaten and compare this amount against a constant that represents the maximum difference in amounts that the application will tolerate before ensuring that an underfed philosopher eats.

8.8. Build a multithreaded version for John Conway's game of *Life* (see Programming Exercises 4.7 and 7.9). Separate threads should manage user inputs to the GUI, on the one hand, and the computation and display of successive generations, on the other hand.

8.9. Build a multithreaded version of the `Spreadsheet` application of Programming Exercise 7.12. Begin with a design that specifies a thread and the tasks for which the thread is responsible.

8.10. Build a multithreaded version of the chip-gathering ant simulation in Programming Exercise 7.21. In particular, a separate thread should simulate each ant. *Hint*: The ant-threads must be synchronized because a cell can hold only one ant at a time.

8.11. A steel company has a warehouse that can hold up to 500 ingots, which the company's various manufacturing divisions use to make finished steel products. Various ingot producers $P_1, P_2, \ldots, P_n$ ship ingots to the warehouse, and various consumers $C_1, C_2, \ldots, C_m$ (which are divisions within the steel company) draw from the warehouse's inventory of ingots to manufacture finished products. The producers ship ingots in lots of 10 to 30 units and the consumers consume ingots in lots of 15 to 70 units. Build a multithreaded graphical simulation with a specified number of producers and consumers. Each producer continually ships ingots to the warehouse, and each consumer continually draws ingots from the warehouse's inventory. The number of ingots shipped to the warehouse should be a random number in the range of 10 to 30, and the number of ingots drawn from the warehouse should be a random number in the range of 15 to 70. A consumer never draws less than the desired number of ingots. For example, if a consumer needs 15 ingots but only 10 are available, the consumer waits until 15 ingots are available before drawing them from inventory.

After each ingot shipment, a producer should *sleep* (that is, stop shipping) for a random interval. In similar fashion, a consumer should sleep for a random interval after drawing ingots from the warehouse. If the warehouse is full, a producer waits in a queue to unload the ingots into the warehouse. If the warehouse does not contain the desired number of ingots, a consumer waits in a queue to draw ingots from the warehouse. The graphics should depict the producers, the consumers, the warehouse, a time line, and the movement of ingots into and out of the warehouse.

8.12. Extend Programming Exercise 8.11 to support scenarios in which the user specifies different rates of production and consumption. A scenario should record pertinent information such as the number of producers and consumers, the rates of production and consumption, the number of productions and consumptions during the simulation, the state of the warehouse after each production and consumption, and the like. The scenarios should be serialized to a log file for later analysis. *Hint*: The different rates of production and consumption could be simulated by varying the number of producers and consumers, the amount of time that the producers and the consumers sleep, the lot ranges for the producers and the consumers, and so on.

8.13. Modern operating systems such as Unix and Windows support multiprocessing even on machines with a single CPU (**C**entral **P**rocessing **U**nit) by allowing processes $P_1, P_2, \ldots, P_n$ to share the CPU by allowing threads associated with the processes to share the CPU. One approach is to give each thread a *time slice* or *quantum* (e.g., 20 milliseconds) for execution. If the thread does not complete before the time slice expires, the operating system *preempts* the thread by returning it to a wait queue so that another thread can execute. In this manner, multiple threads, typically from multiple processes, can share a single CPU. Build a multithreaded application that simulates CPU scheduling. The application should simulate a platform with a single CPU and a time-shared CPU scheduling algorithm. The user should be able to specify through a GUI the number of processes, the number of threads per process, and the time slice for each thread. Nonexecuting but alive threads should wait in a queue. The application should use graphics to display the executing and waiting threads. *Hint*: See the Dining Philosophers application of Section 8.5.

8.14. Modify Programming Exercise 8.13 by assigning each thread a priority between 1 and N, where N is

```
Thread.MAX_PRIORITY - Thread.MIN_PRIORITY + 1
```

The system has N waiting queues, one for each priority. For example, a thread with priority P would wait in $Queue_P$. When the CPU becomes available, the operating system now dispatches the first process in $Queue_1$ to the CPU. If $Queue_1$ is empty, the operating system dispatches the first process in $Queue_2$ to the CPU, and so on. If a thread waits for more than P time slices (where P is the queue's priority) without gaining the CPU, the operating system moves the thread to a queue with a higher priority. For example, if a thread in $Queue_6$ waits 6 time slices without gaining the CPU, the operating system moves the thread to $Queue_5$. Moving waiting threads to higher-priority queues promotes fairness.

8.15. Modify Programming Exercise 8.14 by simulating a platform with multiple CPUs. Any waiting thread may execute on any available CPU. Nonexecuting but alive threads wait in a global queue for an available CPU. A system of this type is called an SMP (**S**ymmetric **M**ulti**P**rocessor) computer. In this context, the term *symmetric* signals that any thread may execute on any CPU.

Network Programming

Chapter Outline

A modern application is commonly designed as a **distributed system**, that is, a software system whose modules can execute on physically distinct machines. The Internet itself is an example of a distributed system. Various standard packages such as `java.applet`, `java.net`, and `java.rmi` provide excellent support for building flexible and robust distributed systems. This chapter examines basic networking tools such as datagrams, sockets, internet addresses, and uniform resource locators. The chapter also has a section on the *applet*, a basic program type well suited for Web-based client/server applications. The chapter concludes with sections on two relatively advanced constructs: RMI (**R**emote **M**ethod **I**nvocation) and object request brokering under CORBA (**C**ommon **O**bject **R**equest **B**roker **A**rchitecture). Chapter 10 continues the coverage of distributed applications with one section on servlets and databases, another section on security and encryption, and a sample application on database webification.

Basic Concepts

Modern data communications networks have a layered representation in which a **layer** represents a family of protocols for transmitting and receiving data. The Internet Protocol (IP) from which the Internet takes its name is a four-layered protocol suite (see Figure 9.1.1) Network professionals also use the seven-layered OSI (**O**pen **S**ystems **I**nterconnect) model, which subdivides the IP's transport and internet layers. Because the protocol layers are stacked, a protocol suite is also called a **protocol stack**. For example, the phrase *IP stack* is commonly used to describe the protocols that belong to the IP family. This family of protocols is commonly called TCP/IP after the IP network-level protocol and the TCP transport-level protocol. The layers in the TCP/IP stack can be clarified as follows:

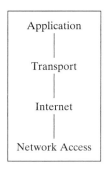

FIGURE 9.1.1   The Internet Protocol layers.

- **Application Layer**. This is the top layer, which provides high-level protocols such as *ftp* (**f**ile **t**ransfer **p**rotocol) for transferring files between applications running on physically distinct machines, *telnet* for remote login, and *smtp* (**s**imple **m**ail **t**ransfer **p**rotocol) for exchanging electronic mail. The protocol names are written in uppercase, lowercase, and mixed case. They are written

---

†Readers with a background in networking may wish to skip this section.

in lowercase here to signal that protocols such as *ftp* correspond to *service utilities*.

- **Transport Layer**. This layer's two main protocols are TCP (**T**ransmission **C**ontrol **P**rotocol) and UDP (**U**ser **D**atagram **P**rotocol). The layer provides *host to host* or *end to end* data delivery services. Any device on a network such as a personal computer, a mainframe, or a handheld device is called a **host**.

- **Internet Layer**. This layer consists of the IP (**I**nternet **P**rotocol) itself, which is responsible for basic **internetworking**, that is, communications among different networks. The IP's primary responsibility is the routing of **packets** or packages of data from one host to another.

- **Network Access Layer**. This layer consists of protocols that govern access to a particular physical network such as an Ethernet.

The IP protocol stack has become the *de facto* industry standard. Although the `java.net` and related packages abstract from the technical details of the IP protocol stack, the standard packages do reflect their close ties to the IP suite.

IP Addresses

In the IP suite, hosts communicate with one another through **addresses**, which are currently 32-bits in length.[†] The standard 32-bit address has four fields, each 8 bits in length. Because of their bit length, the fields are called *octets*. A sample address in binary is

10001100.11000000.00000001.00000110

When the address is represented in decimal

140.192.1.6

it is called a *dotted-decimal address*. For convenience, the IP protocol supports symbolic addresses such as

condor.depaul.edu

that map to 32-bit IP addresses. Although symbolic addresses typically consist of fields separated by dots, such addresses do not have a standard format. As the current example shows, a symbolic address need not have four fields.

IP addresses belong to classes such as *A*, *B*, and *C* that determine the default interpretation of the 32-bit address. In the interpretation of an address, the distinction between the *host portion* and the *network portion* of the address is critical. For example, the 32-bit address

10001100.11000000.00000001.00000110

is a class B address because its leftmost bits are 10, which means that the leftmost octet represents an unsigned integer in the range of 128 through 191. Under the default

---

[†]Under the *next generation* initiative, an IP address expands to 128 bits.

interpretation of a class B address, the two leftmost octets represent the *network* and the two rightmost octets represent the *host*. The dotted-decimal address

140.192.1.6

thus represents host 1.6 on network 140.192. Recall that the symbolic version

condor.depaul.edu

does not have a standard IP interpretation. In this case, the symbolic address represents the host named *condor* (1.6) on the *depaul.edu* network (140.192). Figure 9.1.2 lists the three primary address classes.

Class	Leftmost Bit(s)	Leftmost Octet	Example	Network	Host
A	0	Less than 128	18.69.0.41	18	69.0.41
B	10	128 to 191	140.192.3.19	140.192	3.19
C	110	192 to 223	195.4.12.2	195.4.12	2

FIGURE 9.1.2   Sample IP address classes.

Packet Structure

The data packets through which hosts exchange information have two primary parts. The packet's **header** contains required overhead information such as the packet's source and destination addresses and the quality of service. The packet's **cargo** or **payload** consists of the informational data to be exchanged such as text or various types of binary data: programs, digitized audio or video, and so forth. Under the IP protocol, a packet header is between 20 and 60 bytes and packet cargo can be as large as 65,515 bytes.

As a packet moves *down* a protocol stack—for example, from the Transport to the Internet layer—the packet is *encapsulated* as the cargo at the lower level. A TCP or UDP packet (see Figure 9.1.1) is thus encapsulated as cargo in an IP packet. As a packet moves *up* a protocol stack, a given layer removes the cargo—an encapsulated packet—and sends the cargo up to the next layer for further processing. For example, the IP layer removes an encapsulated TCP packet and sends this packet up to the TCP layer. Figure 9.1.3 illustrates packet encapsulation.

Port Numbers

An IP address identifies a host, which could be a **server**, that is, a machine that provides some service to clients. A **port number** or **port** identifies a particular service. For example, the *http* (**h**yper **t**ext **t**ransfer **p**rotocol) service at the heart of the World Wide Web typically runs on port 80, whereas *telnet* usually runs on port 23. An IP address together with a port number identifies an application on a particular machine. Port numbers range between 0 and 65,535. Port numbers between 0 and 1023 are typically reserved for *well-known services* such as *ftp* or *telnet* (see Figure 9.1.4).

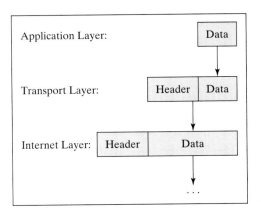

FIGURE 9.1.3   A sketch of packet encapsulation.

Service	Port	Description
echo	7	Verifies that two hosts can talk: one host echoes the other's input.
daytime	13	Text representation of the current time.
ftp-data	20	File transfer.
ftp	21	FTP commands such as *get* and *put*.
telnet	23	Remote login.
smtp	25	Simple mail transfer protocol.
time	37	Elapsed seconds from a fixed instant.
finger	79	Gets information about users.
http	80	Hyper text transfer protocol.
nntp	119	Network news transfer protocol.

FIGURE 9.1.4   Sample well-known port assignments.

Sockets

A **socket** is a network construct, first implemented as part of Berkeley Unix, that allows a programmer to treat a network connection as a stream. An application can write to and read from a socket as if the socket were, for example, a stream associated with a disk file. A socket hides the low-level implementation details of network connections so that applications can exchange data at a high level. Sockets, in turn, can serve as infrastructure for even higher level distributed services such as *ftp*. Socket-based communications has a client/server architecture in that a communicating host is either a client requesting services or a server handling service requests from clients.

Reliable versus Best-Try Transport

The transport layer in the IP suite (see Figure 9.1.1) has two primary protocols, UDP (**U**ser **D**atagram **P**rotocol) and TCP (**T**ransmission **C**ontrol **P**rotocol). UDP is an example of a **best-try**, **unreliable**, or **connectionless** protocol, whereas TCP is an example of a **reliable** or **connection-oriented** protocol. The main differences between the protocol types can be clarified with an example. Suppose that sender *S* sends packets P_1, P_2, and P_3 to receiver R in that order. Under UDP, R is not guaranteed to receive the packets at all or in the right order. If a packet is lost, R may not be aware of it. Under TCP, R is guaranteed to receive the packets or at least notification of failure; and if R does receive all of the packets, the protocol stipulates that the packets must be rearranged, if necessary, in the order in which they were sent.

Reliable protocols have obvious advantages. Yet unreliable protocols such as UDP do have the advantage of very low overhead. An unreliable protocol is typically used for relatively small packets whose loss is not critical and whose order or reception is unimportant. A later example illustrates.

Firewalls and Proxy Servers

Access from local area networks (LANs) to external networks such as the Internet is often protected with a hardware/software configuration known as a **firewall** that sits between the LAN and the external network. The firewall's purpose is to screen packets as they move between the LAN and the external network, filtering out packets deemed inappropriate. Local networks that employ firewalls often employ **proxy servers** as well. A proxy server, as the name suggests, is a host that acts as a proxy for a real server. Suppose, for example, that host H on a LAN requests a document from an *http* server but that a firewall prevents H from directly accessing the server. The LAN may instead provide a local proxy server to which H makes the request. The proxy server is presumably able to bypass the firewall, get the document, and then deliver the document to H.

Java's standard packages draw freely from the concepts and terminology associated with the IP stack. The following sections further clarify the material introduced here and also extend the coverage of basic networking constructs.

EXERCISES

  1. What does *IP* stand for?
  2. What are the four layers of the so-called TCP/IP protocol suite?
  3. Give an example of an *Application Layer* protocol under TCP/IP.
  4. Give an example of a *Transport Layer* protocol under TCP/IP.
  5. What is the main responsibility of the *Network Access Layer* under TCP/IP?
  6. Explain the difference among class A, B, and C IP addresses.
  7. What is the bit size of an IP address?
  8. Into how many fields is a class B IP address formatted?
  9. Indicate the network and host portions of the IP address 140.192.1.1.
  10. Must a symbolic IP address have four fields?
  11. Explain the role of a port number in distributed applications.
  12. Explain the difference between a *connection-oriented* and a *connectionless* transport protocol.

13. What is a firewall?

14. What is a proxy server?

9.2   Sockets

The `java.net` package has three main socket classes, which reflect the original Berkeley Unix implementation that has migrated to most platforms:

- The class `ServerSocket` represents server sockets that wait for client requests for services.
- The class `Socket` represents client sockets through which requests for services are made to servers. A server, too, can use a client socket to send response data back to a client.
- The class `DatagramSocket` represents datagram sockets for UDP (**U**ser **D**atagram **P**rotocol) transport.

The section first examines client `Socket`s before introducing `ServerSocket`s, `DatagramSocket`s, and `MulticastSocket`s.

Client Sockets

The `Socket` class provides high-level constructors and methods for constructing and using client sockets. The abstract `SocketImpl` class is the superclass for underlying socket implementations. Programmers who need to deal with firewalls and proxy servers extend `SocketImpl` to handle their particular situation. Programmers who need not deal with firewalls and proxy servers simply create `Socket` instances, which are known as *plain sockets*.

The `Socket` class has four public and two protected constructors (see Figure 9.2.1).[†] The constructors require either the server's symbolic name or its IP address and the port number of the desired service.

Declaration	Socket Connected To
`Socket( String host, int port );`	Named host on specified port.
`Socket( InetAddress a, int port );`	IP address on specified port.
`Socket( String host, int sPort,`	Named host on specified port,
`InetAddress a, int cPort );`	providing client IP address and port.
`Socket( InetAddress s, int sPort )`	IP address on specified port,
`InetAddress c, int cPort );`	providing client IP address and port.

FIGURE 9.2.1   The public `Socket` constructors.

[†]Two additional public constructors are deprecated in favor of `DatagramSocket`s.

Example 9.2.1. The PortTester program in Figure 9.2.2 tests for service availability on eight well-known ports on a specified host. On the sample run, the program produced the output

```
import java.net.*;
import java.io.IOException;
public class PortTester {
   public static void main( String[ ] args ) {
      if ( args.length < 1 ) {
        System.err.println( "PortTester <host name>" );
        return;
      }
      InetAddress addr = null;
      try {
        addr = InetAddress.getByName( args[ 0 ] );
      }
      catch( UnknownHostException e ) {
        System.err.println( e );
        return;
      }
      System.out.println( "Testing ports on " + args[ 0 ] );
      // well-known ports for echo, daytime, ftp-data,
      // smtp, time, http, and nttp
      int[ ] ports = { 7, 13, 20, 23, 25, 37, 80, 119 };
      int i = 0;
      for ( i = 0; i < ports.length; i++ ) {
         Socket s = null;
         try {
            if ( s != null ) //** socket already open?
              s.close();      //** if so, close
            s = new Socket( addr, ports[ i ] );
            System.out.println( "  Server listening on port " +
                              ports[ i ] );
         }
         catch( IOException e ) {
            System.err.println( "  Server not listening on port " +
                              ports[ i ] );
            continue;
         }
      }
   }
}
```

FIGURE 9.2.2   A program to test some well-known ports on a specified host.

```
Testing ports on athena-dist.mit.edu
   Server listening on port 7
   Server listening on port 13
   Server not listening on port 20
   Server listening on port 23
   Server listening on port 25
   Server listening on port 37
   Server not listening on port 80
   Server not listening on port 119
```

The host's name is given as a command-line argument. The `InetAddress` class's `static` method `getByName` is then invoked to get the host's IP address from the host's name. The other argument to the `Socket` constructor is the number of a well-known port. On each loop iteration, an already opened `Socket` is `closed`. Note that the `close` method for `Socket`s has the same syntax as for input/output streams. The `Socket`'s method `close` also can throw an `IOException`, which again underscores the similarity between sockets and other streams. It is important to `close` a `Socket` that is no longer needed because otherwise the `Socket` may remain open indefinitely.   ■

■ **Example 9.2.2.**   The `Finger` program in Figure 9.2.3, which opens a client socket at a specified server's *finger* port, shows how a `Socket`'s input and output streams can be used, respectively, to send information to and receive information from a server. A client socket is **full duplex** or **bi-directional** in that the socket can be used to read from and write to a server.

After constructing a `Socket` with the specified host and user name, the program invokes the `Socket`'s `getOutputStream` method

```
PrintWriter ask = new PrintWriter( s.getOutputStream() );
```

to construct a `PrintWriter` named `ask` for sending the required *finger* information to the server. This information can be described as the *finger query* because, in effect, the client asks the server for information about a user. The *finger* service requires that the query be formatted as follows: host name followed by user's name followed by a carriage return (`\r`) and a newline (`\n`) character. The query is written to the `Socket`'s output stream

```
ask.print( host + " " + user + "\r\n" ); //*** finger query
ask.flush();
```

after which the stream is flushed to ensure that any buffered output is indeed sent to the server.

Next the program constructs a `BufferedReader` named `ans` using the `Socket`'s associated `InputStream`. The `BufferedReader` has a `readLine` method that returns a `String` reference, if there is more input to read, and `null`,

```
import java.net.*;
import java.io.*;
public class Finger {
   public static void main( String[ ] args ) {
      if ( args.length < 2 ) {
        System.err.println( "Finger <host name> <user>" );
        return;
      }
      Finger self = new Finger();
      self.finger( args[ 0 ], args[ 1 ] );
   }
   private void finger( String host, String user ) {
      try {
         Socket s = new Socket( host, port );
         PrintWriter ask = new PrintWriter( s.getOutputStream() );
         ask.print( host + " " + user + "\r\n" ); //*** finger query
         ask.flush();
         BufferedReader ans = new BufferedReader(
                     new InputStreamReader( s.getInputStream() ) );
         String t = null;
         while ( (t = ans.readLine()) != null )
            System.out.println( t );
         ask.close();
         ans.close();
      } catch( IOException e ) { System.err.println( e ); }
   }
   private static final int port = 79; //*** well-known finger port
}
```

FIGURE 9.2.3   A client program for the *finger* service.

if end-of-stream has been reached. A for loop is thus used to print repeatedly the information sent back from the server to the client. Afterwards, the PrintWriter and the BufferedReader are closed. Note that the input/output operations on the Socket streams are the same as any other streams. On a sample run, the program was run as

```
java Finger condor.depaul.edu epp
```

and the output was

```
Login    Name          TTY     Idle    When           Where
sepp     Susanna S Epp  pts/0           <Nov 30 12:44> junior40.dp
hepp     HELMUT P EPP   pts/45          <Dec 12 11:56> csslip42.cs
```

A flawed implementation of the *finger* utility on VAX computers running the Unix 4BSD operating system allowed the infamous Internet Worm of 1988 to cause widespread mischief. The worm exploited a buffer overflow that the C language input function `gets` does not detect. The worm's creator was caught and the *finger* utility on VAX computers was quickly fixed by replacing `gets` with a different C library function named `fgets`. For security reasons, many hosts do not support the *finger* service.

Server Sockets

The `ServerSocket` class provides high-level constructors and methods for constructing and using server sockets. For `ServerSocket`s as for client `Socket`s, the abstract `SocketImpl` class is the superclass for actual socket implementations. Programmers who need to deal with firewalls and proxy servers extend `SocketImpl` to handle their particular situation. Programmers who need not deal with firewalls and proxy servers simply create `ServerSocket` instances, which are known as *plain server sockets*.

The `ServerSocket` class has three public constructors (see Figure 9.2.4). The `int` parameter `maxQ` specifies the maximum number of clients that can

Declaration	Server Socket Created on
`ServerSocket( int port );`	Specified port.
`ServerSocket( int port, int maxQ );`	On specified port with at most `maxQ` clients waiting.
`ServerSocket( int port, int maxQ,` `            InetAddress bindAddr );`	On specified port at specified address with at most `maxQ` clients waiting.

FIGURE 9.2.4   The public `ServerSocket` constructors.

be queued for service before the server refuses a connection. For example, the statement

```
ServerSocket sv = new ServerSocket( 1234, 100 );
```

constructs at server socket on port 1234 that accommodates up to 100 client connections before the server refuses a connection. The three-argument constructor is designed for servers that have several IP addresses. For example, the statement

```
ServerSocket sv = new ServerSocket( 1234, 100,
    InetAddress.getHostByName( "condor1.depaul.edu" ) );
```

constructs a server socket that listens to connections only at the address *condor1.depaul.edu*. The same underlying machine may have other IP addresses such as *condor2.depaul.edu*, a common practice for Web servers.

Once constructed, a server socket typically sits in an infinite loop and waits for connections, which then are handled in the appropriate way. The method `accept`, which is used for this purpose, blocks until a client connects. When the connection occurs, `accept` returns a reference to a client `Socket` that represents a particular client connection.

```
import java.net.*;
import java.io.*;
class JustListen {
   public static void main( String[ ] args ) {
      try {
         ServerSocket sSock = new ServerSocket( 1234 );
         while ( true ) {
            Socket sock = sSock.accept();
            printInfo( sock );
            sock.close();
         }
      } catch( IOException e ) { System.err.println( e ); }
   }
   private static void printInfo( Socket s ) {
      System.out.println( "Remote (server) port: " + s.getPort() );
      System.out.println( "Local (client) port:  " + s.getLocalPort() );
      System.out.println( "Server IP addr:    " + s.getInetAddress() );
      System.out.println( "Client IP addr:    " + s.getLocalAddress() );
   }
}
```

FIGURE 9.2.5   A basic server socket program.

■ **Example 9.2.3.**   The JustListen program in Figure 9.2.5 above constructs a ServerSocket, which then blocks by invoking its accept method until a client connection occurs. The server socket's accept method returns a reference to a client Socket that represents the client connection. The method printInfo illustrates the informational client socket methods getPort, getLocalPort, getInetAddress, and getLocalAddress. For a client socket, the *local* port and address are those on the *client* machine.   ■

■ **Example 9.2.4.**   The Reverse program in Figure 9.2.6 opens a Server-Socket and waits for clients to send Strings, which are reversed and returned. Figure 9.2.7 shows a test client that can connect to the server. The input and output operations on the client and the server are intuitive: *writing* is done to an *output* stream, and *reading* is done from an *input* stream. Note, too, that a client Socket is used on both the server and the client side for information exchange. The ServerSocket is used only to wait for client connections.   ■

Datagram Sockets

The client Socket and ServerSocket constructs use *reliable* transport; that is, these constructs are TCP-based (see Section 8.1). The DatagramSocket construct uses *unreliable* transport; that is, this construct is UDP-based. A DatagramSocket is used to send and receive DatagramPackets.

```
import java.net.*;
import java.io.*;
public class Reverse {
   public static void main( String[ ] args ) {
      ServerSocket sSock = null;
      try {
         sSock = new ServerSocket( 1234 );
      }
      catch( IOException e ) {
         System.err.println( e );
         return;
      }
      System.out.println( "Server running..." );
      while ( true ) {
         try {
            Socket sock = sSock.accept();
            BufferedReader in = new BufferedReader(
                new InputStreamReader( sock.getInputStream() ) );
            String t = in.readLine();
            if ( t != null ) { // something read?
              PrintWriter ps = new PrintWriter(sock.getOutputStream());
              ps.println(new String(new StringBuffer(t).reverse()));
              ps.flush();
            }
            sock.close();
         } catch( IOException e ) { System.err.println( e ); }
      }
   }
}
```

FIGURE 9.2.6   A server socket program that reverses and returns a client string.

Both the sender and the receiver of `DatagramPacket`s use a `DatagramSocket`. The construction of `DatagramPacket`s differs slightly on the sender and receiver sides:

- **Receiver side**. The receiver constructs a `DatagramPacket` of an appropriate `byte` size. For example, a receiver that expects packets of up to 1,000 bytes in size could construct a `DatagramPacket` with the code segment

   ```
   byte[ ] info = new byte[ 1000 ];
   DatagramPacket dp =
       new DatagramPacket( info, info.length );
   ```

- **Sender side**. The sender also constructs a `DatagramPacket` of an appropriate `byte` size. In addition, the sender provides the IP address and the port number to which the packet is to be sent. Specifying the IP address and the port number can be done either in constructors or in the appropriate `set` methods. The code segment

```
import java.net.*;
import java.io.*;
public class ReverseClient {
    public static void main( String[ ] args ) {
        if ( args.length < 1 ) {
          System.err.println( "ReverseClient <IP address of server>" );
          return;
        }
        try {
            String s = "In the Quiet Morning";
            Socket sock = new Socket( args[ 0 ], 1234 );
            PrintWriter out = new PrintWriter( sock.getOutputStream() );
            out.println( s );
            out.flush();
            BufferedReader in = new BufferedReader(
                  new InputStreamReader( sock.getInputStream() ) );
            String t = in.readLine();
            if ( t != null )
              System.out.println( "To server:    " + s +
                                  "\nFrom server: " + t );
            sock.close();
        } catch( IOException e ) { System.err.println( e ); }
    }
}
```

FIGURE 9.2.7   A test client for the server socket program of Figure 9.2.6.

```
InetAddress addr =
  InetAddress.getByName( "140.192.6.77" );
int port = 1111;
String s = "stuff to send to a client";
byte[ ] cargo = s.getBytes();
DatagramPacket dp =
 new DatagramPacket( cargo, cargo.length, addr, port);
```

illustrates how a sender might construct a datagram packet.

Example 9.2.5.   The DateBCast program in Figure 9.2.8 uses a Datagram-Packet and a DatagramSocket to broadcast the the string representation of the current Date every five seconds. The program is invoked with command-line arguments that are the IP addresses of receivers to which the Date is broadcast. After creating the datagram socket with the no-argument constructor

```
ds = new DatagramSocket();
```

the program constructs a datagram packet whose cargo is the string representation of the current date

```
import java.net.*;
import java.util.*;
import java.io.*;
public class DateBCast {
  public static void main( String[ ] args ) {
    if ( args.length < 1 ) {
      System.err.println( "TimeBCast <list of target IP addresses>" );
      return;
    }
    DateBCast db = new DateBCast();
    db.broadcast( args );
  }
  private void broadcast( String[ ] hosts ) {
    InetAddress addr = null;
    DatagramSocket ds = null;
    try {
      ds = new DatagramSocket();
    }
    catch( SocketException e ) {
      System.err.println( e );
      return;
    }
    while ( true ) {
      byte[ ] buff = new Date().toString().getBytes();
      DatagramPacket cargo =
        new DatagramPacket( buff, buff.length, addr, port );
      for ( int i = 0; i < hosts.length; i++ ) {
        try {
          cargo.setAddress( InetAddress.getByName( hosts[ i ] ) );
          ds.send( cargo );
        }
        catch( UnknownHostException e ) { System.err.println( e ); }
        catch( IOException e ) { System.err.println( e ); }
      }
      try {
        Thread.sleep( winks );
      } catch( InterruptedException e ) { System.err.println( e ); }
    }
  }
  private static final int port = 1313;
  private static final int winks = 5000; // 5 seconds
}
```

FIGURE 9.2.8 A datagram server to broadcast the current date and time.

```
byte[ ] buff = new Date().toString().getBytes();
DatagramPacket cargo =
  new DatagramPacket( buff, buff.length, addr, port );
```

The program assumes that all receivers connect on the same port. Of course, the receivers have different IP addresses. In the body of a `for` loop, the program sets the datagram's address to each receiver's IP address

```
cargo.setAddress( InetAddress.getByName( hosts[ i ] ) );
```

The reference `cargo` is to the datagram and `hosts` is an array of command-line arguments, which are IP addresses as strings.

The `DateClient` program in Figure 9.2.9 is a test receiver for the sender. The test receiver prints out the date repeatedly. The receiver constructs a datagram socket on the port to which the sender broadcasts

```
ds = new DatagramSocket( port );
```

```
import java.net.*;
import java.io.*;
public class DateClient {
  public static void main( String[ ] args ) {
    DateClient dc = new DateClient();
    dc.listen();
  }
  private void listen() {
    DatagramSocket ds = null;
    try {
      ds = new DatagramSocket( port );
    }
    catch( SocketException e ) {
      System.err.println( e );
      return;
    }
    DatagramPacket dp = new DatagramPacket( new byte[ bLen ], bLen );
    while ( true ) {
      try {
        ds.receive( dp );
      } catch( IOException e ) { System.err.println( e ); }
      System.out.println( "\nCurrent time: " +
                          new String( dp.getData() ) +
                          "\nfrom          " + dp.getAddress() );
    }
  }
  private static int port = 1313;
  private static int bLen = 128; // length of byte buffer
}
```

FIGURE 9.2.9   A sample receiver for the date sender in Figure 9.2.8.

and a datagram packet of appropriate size

```
DatagramPacket dp =
    new DatagramPacket( new byte[ bLen ], bLen );
```

In this example, bLen is initialized to 128 for good measure. The DataSocket's receive method is invoked with the packet as an argument

```
ds.receive( dp );
```

to receive the packet from the sender. On a sample run, the test receiver's output was

```
Current time: Wed May 24 14:07:05 CST 2000
from          condor.depaul.edu/140.192.1.6

Current time: Wed May 24 14:07:10 CST 2000
from          condor.depaul.edu/140.192.1.6
...
```

A Datagram socket is appropriate for this application. If a packet is lost, another is broadcast five seconds later. Even if the packets are received out of sequence, the receiver presumably could recover from the error by checking the dates against one another. The roughly sixty bytes of data also fit easily into a single packet.   ■

Serialization and Sockets

The Date-server program in Figure 9.2.8 requires a sender continually to broadcast the date and receivers continually to receive the broadcasted Date in order to remain current. The receiver is permanently dependent on the sender because the receiver receives *string representations of the date and time* rather than a Date object that the receiver could use to compute the current date and time locally, thus offloading a task from the sender (server) to the receiver (client). Because sockets have associated byte streams suitable for serialization, an alternative is to have a server serialize a Date object to any client that requests one. Once the client deserializes this object, the client no longer needs a connection to the server because the Date then can be used locally to get the current date and time.

■ **Example 9.2.6.**   The server program in Figure 9.2.10 constructs a Date object and a ServerSocket that awaits client connections. When a client connects, the server serializes the Date object to a byte stream

```
Socket sock = sSock.accept();
ObjectOutputStream os =
```

```
import java.net.*;
import java.io.*;
import java.util.Date;
public class DateServer {
   public static void main( String[ ] args ) {
      ServerSocket sSock = null;
      try {
         sSock = new ServerSocket( 9876 );
      }
      catch( IOException e ) {
         System.err.println( e );
         return;
      }
      Date d = new Date();
      while ( true ) {
         try {
            Socket sock = sSock.accept();
            ObjectOutputStream os =
              new ObjectOutputStream( sock.getOutputStream() );
            os.writeObject( d );
            os.flush();
            sock.close();
         } catch( IOException e ) { System.err.println( e ); }
      }
   }
}
```

FIGURE 9.2.10   A server that serializes a Date to a socket.

```
new ObjectOutputStream( sock.getOutputStream() );
os.writeObject( d );
```

so that the client then can deserialize the Date. Once the client has the Date object, the client needs no further contact with the server. The program is written so that all clients receive the *same* Date object, which thus coordinates dates and times across clients. Standardizing on a server's date may be useful in a world-wide distributed application that requires, for example, the uniform time-stamping of documents.

The program in Figure 9.2.11 is a test client, which opens a socket on the appropriate server port and then deserializes a Date object from the socket's byte stream. The command-line argument args[0] refers to the server's IP address as a string. The code is remarkably straightforward:

```
Socket sock = new Socket( args[ 0 ], 9876 );
ObjectInputStream ois =
  new ObjectInputStream( sock.getInputStream() );
Date d = (Date) ois.readObject();
```

```
import java.net.*;
import java.io.*;
import java.util.Date;
public class DateSerialClient {
    public static void main( String[ ] args ) {
        if ( args.length < 1 ) {
            System.err.println( "DateClient <IP address of server>" );
            return;
        }
        try {
            Socket sock = new Socket( args[ 0 ], 9876 );
            ObjectInputStream ois =
                new ObjectInputStream( sock.getInputStream() );
            Date d = (Date) ois.readObject();
            sock.close();
            System.out.println( "The date is " + d );
        }
        catch( IOException e ) { System.err.println( e ); }
        catch( ClassNotFoundException e ) { System.err.println( e ); }
    }
}
```

FIGURE 9.2.11   A test client for the Date server in Figure 9.2.10.

Sockets and serialization are a straightforward, powerful, and flexible way for distributed applications to exchange objects. Later sections introduce other high-level mechanisms, remote method invocation and object request brokers, that also allow distributed applications to share objects rather than arbitrary data. Serialization over sockets is especially attractive because of its simplicity.

Multicast Sockets

In addition to the primary address classes A, B, and C (see Figure 9.1.2), the IP suite also provides a class D address for **multicasting**, that is, sending packets to groups of hosts. In a class D address, the leftmost bits are 111 so that the leftmost octet represents an unsigned integer in the range of 224 through 239.

■ **Example 9.2.7.**   The code segment in Figure 9.2.12 illustrates the basic syntax of multicasting. A multicast socket is opened on the appropriate port, and the participating program joins a group associated with an IP address

```
int port = 7777;
InetAddress myGroup = InetAddress.getByName( "228.1.2.3" );
MulticastSocket s = new MulticastSocket( port );
s.joinGroup( myGroup );
```

```
//**** send a message to a group
byte[ ] cargo = new String( "Hello, world!" ).getBytes();
int port = 7777;
InetAddress myGroup = InetAddress.getByName( "228.1.2.3" );
MulticastSocket s = new MulticastSocket( port );
s.joinGroup( myGroup );
DatagramPacket msg =
   new DatagramPacket( cargo, cargo.length, group, port );
s.send( msg );
//*** receive a response back
byte[ ] ans = new byte[ 1000 ];
DatagramPacket recv = new DatagramPacket( ans, ans.length );
s.receive( recv );
s.leaveGroup( myGroup ); //*** all done for now
s.close();
```

FIGURE 9.2.12   A code segment to illustrate the syntax of multicasting.

A datagram packet is constructed in the usual way and then sent to the group

```
s.send( ans );
```

where `ans` refers to a `DatagramPacket`. The program receives multicasts from other hosts in the group by invoking the socket's `receive` method, which expects a `DatagramPacket` as its argument

```
s.receive( recv );
```

Once a session is completed, a program can leave the multicast group by invoking the multicast socket's `leave` method

```
s.leaveGroup( myGroup );
```

with the group's IP address as the argument.

Java Secure Sockets Extension

The Java Secure Sockets Extension (JSSE) is a package that supports secure Internet communications by implementing two protocols in the TCP/IP family: Secure Sockets Layer (SSL) and Transport Layer Security (TLS). JSSE supports data encryption, server and client authentication, and message integrity in applications that use standard protocols such as *http, telnet, nntp,* and *ftp*. The URL for JSSE is

```
http://java.sun.com/products
```

Section 10.2, which focuses on security, clarifies some of the underlying mechanisms in JSSE.

Testing Distributed Applications on a Standalone Machine

The distributed applications illustrated in this section can be tested on standalone machines running modern operating systems such as Unix and Windows. The IP address 127.0.0.1 represents the *localhost*, that is, a local machine that can be used as both a client and a server.

■ **Example 9.2.8.** The DateBcast and DateClient applications of Figure 9.2.8 and 9.2.9, respectively, can be tested on a standalone machine. The sender can be started with the command

```
$ java DateBCast localhost
```

or

```
$ java DateBCast 127.0.0.1
```

and the receiver with the command

```
$ java DateClient
```

The reserved *localhost* IP address is useful for preliminary testing of distributed applications. Eventually, of course, a distributed application must be tested on a network in order to gain a realistic assessment of the application's performance.

EXERCISES

1. Write a statement that opens a client Socket to IP address 140.192.1.1 on port 23.
2. Explain what is meant by a *plain client socket*.
3. Test the PortTester application of Figure 9.2.2.
4. Test the Finger application of Figure 9.2.3.
5. Write a statement that creates an InetAddress from the name *140.192.1.1*.
6. Write a statement that opens a ServerSocket on port 9999 that accepts up to 10 client connections.
7. Explain what is meant by a *plain server socket*.
8. Test the Reverse and ReverseClient applications in Figures 9.2.6 and 9.2.7, respectively.

9. What is the basic difference between a `Socket` and a `DatagramSocket`.

10. Characterize the types of application that are suited for `DatagramSockets`.

11. Test the `DateBcast` server and the `DateClient` of Figures 9.2.8 and 9.2.9, respectively.

12. What is a `MulticastSocket` used for?

Sample Application: A Multithreaded Cliche Server

Problem

Implement a multithreaded, socket-based distributed system in which a client can request *cliches of the day* from a server, which reads the cliches from a file. A multithreaded server is also called a **concurrent server**, which contrasts with a single-threaded or **iterative server**. The server should allocate a thread to handle each client request. The server can limit the number of client connections that can be open at a time.

Sample Input/Output

Using the server cliche file

```
Absence makes the heart grow fonder.
Out of sight, out of mind.
A penny saved is a penny earned.
Penny wise and dollar foolish.
Live hard, die young.
Only the good die young.
As you sow so shall you reap.
Nice guys finish last.
```

the test client in Figure 9.3.1 produced the output

```
Cliches of the day:
Only the good die young.
As you sow so shall you reap.
Nice guys finish last.
```

Solution

The server program is multithreaded. The *main thread* (i.e., the thread that executes `main`) reads the cliches from an input file and then waits, using a `ServerSocket`, for a maximum of `maxQ` client connections. The *main thread* starts a `ClientHandler`

```java
import java.net.*;
import java.io.*;
import java.util.Random;
class ClicheClient {
   public static void main( String[ ] args ) {
      if ( args.length < 2 ) {
         System.err.println( "ClicheClient <IP address> <Port>" );
         return;
      }
      try {
         Socket sock = new Socket( args[ 0 ],    //** IP address
                Integer.parseInt( args[ 1 ] ) ); //** port
         DataOutputStream out =
                new DataOutputStream( sock.getOutputStream() );
         int n = Math.abs( new Random().nextInt() ) % 10 + 1;
         out.writeInt( n );
         out.flush();
         BufferedReader in = new BufferedReader(
                 new InputStreamReader( sock.getInputStream() ) );
         System.out.println( "Cliches of the day:" );
         String t = null;
         while ( (t = in.readLine()) != null )
            System.out.println( t );
         sock.close();
      } catch( IOException e ) { System.err.println( e ); }
   }
}
```

FIGURE 9.3.1   A test client for the `ClicheServer`.

thread to service each client. The `ClientHandler` uses a client `Socket` to send back
however many cliches the client requests. Once the `ClientHandler` thread has sent
the cliches and closed the `Socket`, the thread stops.

Java Implementation

```java
import java.io.*;
import java.net.*;
import java.util.*;
import basicIO.BasicInput;
public class ClicheServer {
   public static void main( String[ ] args ) {
      if ( args.length < 1 ) {
         System.err.println( "ClicheServer <input file>" );
         return;
      }
```

```
        new ClicheServer().handleClients( args[ 0 ] );
   }
   private void handleClients( String infile ) {
      cliches = new Vector();
      readInput( infile, cliches );
      try {
        ServerSocket servSock = new ServerSocket( port, maxQ );
        while ( true ) {
           Socket sock = servSock.accept();
           new ClientHandler( sock, cliches ).start();
        }
      } catch( IOException e ) { System.err.println( e ); }
   }
   private void readInput( String infile, Vector cliches ) {
      try {
         BasicInput in = new BasicInput( infile );
         while ( !in.eof() )
            cliches.addElement( in.getRecord() );
         in.close();
      } catch( IOException e ) { System.err.println( e ); }
   }
   private static final int port = 9999;
   private static final int maxQ = 100;
   private Vector cliches;
}
class ClientHandler extends Thread {
   public ClientHandler( Socket s, Vector c ) {
      sock = s;
      cliches = c;
   }
   public void run() {
      try {
         Random r = new Random();
         int s = cliches.size();
         DataInputStream req =
           new DataInputStream( sock.getInputStream() );
         int n = Math.abs( req.readInt() );
         n = (n > s) ? s : n;
         PrintWriter ans =
           new PrintWriter( sock.getOutputStream() );
         //*** Pick a random starting index in the vector and
         //    send the next N cliches
         int k = Math.abs( r.nextInt() ) % s;
         for ( int i = 0; i < n; i++ ) {
            ans.println( cliches.elementAt( k ) );
```

```
            k = (k + 1) % s;
        }
        ans.flush();
        sock.close();
    } catch( IOException e ) { System.err.println( e ); }
    }
    private Socket sock;
    private Vector cliches;
}
```

Discussion

The server uses the BasicInput class (see Section 5.4) to read cliches as records from an input file whose name is given as a command-line argument. The server then opens a ServerSocket that accommodates a maximum of maxQ client connections, which is currently set to 100. The server then waits for clients

```
    while ( true ) {
        Socket sock = servSock.accept();
        new ClientHandler( sock, cliches ).start();
    }
```

and starts a new ClientHandler thread to select and send N cliches, where N is an integer that the client sends as part of its request for service. By start-ing a separate ClientHandler thread to handle each client, the *main thread* is thus dedicated to *listening* for client connections rather than *servicing* the actual client requests. This division of labor is common in industrial-strength client/server applications. The *main thread* constructs a ClientHandler with two arguments: references to the client Socket returned from accept and to the Vector of cliches.

The ClientHandler class extends Thread and overrides run. A Client-Handler performs two basic tasks before stopping:

- The thread reads an int from client Socket's input stream. The integer n specifies how many cliches the client would like.
- The thread selects the cliches by picking a random start index in the Vector of cliches and then selecting n elements, wrapping around to the start of the Vector if necessary. Each element, a String, is then sent to the Socket's output stream. Because println is used, each cliche is followed by a newline character \n, which allows the client to read the cliches as records by using the readLine method.

Immediately after flushing the output stream and closing the socket, a client-handling thread exits run and, therefore, stops.

The Client

The test client in Figure 9.3.1 is invoked with two command-line arguments: the server's IP address and the appropriate port number. After constructing a client `Socket`, the client then sends the server an integer

```
DataOutputStream out =
new DataOutputStream( sock.getOutputStream() );
int n = Math.abs( new Random().nextInt() ) % 10 + 1;
out.writeInt( n );
```

that specifies how many cliches the client would like back. The client uses the `Socket`'s input stream to reads and prints the cliches sent back

```
BufferedReader in = new BufferedReader(
   new InputStreamReader( sock.getInputStream() ) );
System.out.println( "Cliches of the day:" );
String t = null;
while ( (t = in.readLine()) != null )
   System.out.println( t );
```

before closing the socket and terminating. Because the server uses `println` to send the cliches, the client can use `readLine` to read them; that is, each cliche is sent as a `String` followed by a newline character.

EXERCISES

1. What advantages derive from dividing the server's labor between a *main thread* (i.e., a thread that executes `main`) and client-handling threads?
2. Set `maxQ` to a small number such as 2 and then test what happens when more than `maxQ` clients try to connect to the server.
3. Suppose that the server used `print` rather than `println` to send the cliche `Strings` to the client. How might the client separate one cliche from another?

9.4   **Applets**

An **applet** is small application embedded in another application, typically a Web browser, that acts as a **host program**. The host program provides an environment or **applet context** in which the applet executes. The host program is responsible for such tasks as loading, initializing, starting, and stopping the applets embedded in it. An applet is typically launched when a browser downloads an HTML or other document that references the applet, which is then downloaded and executed by the browser acting as the host program. At a more technical level, an applet is an embeddable `Panel`, which in turn is a simple `Container` window. An applet has special methods such as `init`, `start`, and `paint` that support interaction between the applet and the host program. Any program, including another Java program, can serve as the host program for an applet. A later example illustrates by having a Java *application* download and launch an applet.

Applets are well suited for a client/server environment, particularly one in which browsers provide the graphical user interface for a distributed system. An applet resides originally on a server, typically a server of HTML or other documents that can be used to launch the applet. Once an applet is downloaded, it executes on the client, thus using client rather than server resources such as CPU cycles. Applets are thus a natural way, in a client/server environment, to offload tasks from a server to clients. Other technologies such as client-side scripting in languages such as JavaScript[†] provide similar capabilities. After explaining the basics of applets, this section focuses on the ways in which applets provide distinctive capabilities in a client/server environment.

The `Applet` and `JApplet` Classes

To create an applet, the programmer extends the `java.awt.Applet` class or the `javax.swing.JApplet` class, which in turn extends `Applet`. The `JApplet` class allows special paned windows to be children of the `Applet` window. Further, the `JApplet` class, unlike the `Applet` class, supports the Swing set's menu bars. Because `JApplet`s are essentially specialized `Applet`s and because some Web browsers do not handle `JApplet`s correctly, this section focuses on `Applet`s. It should noted that a `JApplet`, like an `Applet`, is a heavyweight rather than a lightweight component (see Section 7.1).

■ **Example 9.4.1.**   The program in Figure 9.4.1 is a simple applet named `HelloWorld`. At a minimum, an applet must be a `public` class that extends `Applet` or `JApplet`. The `HelloWorld` applet overrides the `init` method inherited from `Applet` in order to place a label with a greeting in the applet window. After the host program loads the applet, the host program invokes `init` before invoking `show`, which makes the applet window and its controls visible.

The HTML (**H**yper **T**ext **M**arkup **L**anguage) document in Figure 9.4.2 launches the applet. The document contains an APPLET tag, which requires WIDTH and HEIGHT attributes that specify the width and height, respectively, of the applet window. A browser typically gives the applet part of the browser's own framed window for display. Figure 9.4.3 shows the applet launched from a commercial browser.   ■

[†]Although there are some syntactic and semantic similarities between Java and JavaScript, the languages are altogether distinct. In particular, JavaScript is *not* "lightweight Java."

```
import java.awt.*;
import java.applet.*;
public class HelloWorld extends Applet {
   public void init() {
      Label l = new Label( "Hello, world!" );
      add( l );
   }
}
```

FIGURE 9.4.1 The source code for the Hello, world! applet.

```
<HTML>
<HEAD>
  <TITLE> Hello World Applet </TITLE>
</HEAD>
<BODY>
  <APPLET CODE="HelloWorld.class" WIDTH=200 HEIGHT=50></APPLET>
</BODY>
</HTML>
```

FIGURE 9.4.2 The HTML document that launches the applet of Figure 9.4.1.

■ **Example 9.4.2.** The HelloWorldWillTravel applet in Figure 9.4.4 responds to mouse clicks by moving a displayed message to the point at which the mouse was clicked. The program also toggles the background color between green and orange. When the user clicks the mouse

- The mouseClicked callback is invoked with a MouseEvent argument. The callback is encapsulated in a MyMouseAdapter object, which is designated as the applet's listener for mouse events. Class MyMouseAdapter extends java.awt.MouseAdapter.
- The mouseClicked callback invokes the applet's setXY method with the x and y coordinates of the mouse click. The callback also invokes the applet's toggleBGround method to change the applet's background color.
- The mouseClicked callback invokes the applet's repaint method. Recall that repaint calls update, which then calls paint with a Graphics argument. The applet's paint method sets the applet's background color and draws the greeting String at the x and y coordinates.

The applet's init method invokes the getParameter method to read a parameter, in this case the greeting to display, from the HTML document that launched the applet. In this example, the call is

```
String t = getParameter( "Message" );
```

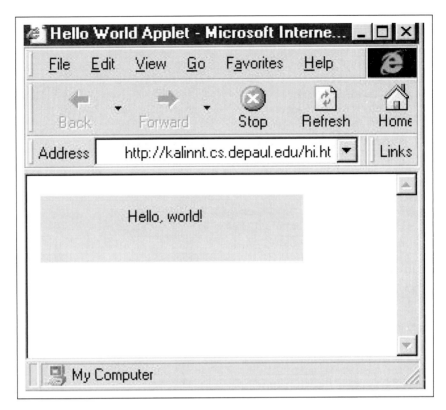

FIGURE 9.4.3   The applet of Figure 9.4.1 displayed in a commercial browser.

and the related HTML code is

```
<APPLET CODE="HelloWorldWillTravel.class"
    WIDTH=400 HEIGHT=400>
    <param name="Message" value="What, me worry?">
</APPLET>
```

Because `getParameter`'s argument `Message` matches the parameter named `Message`, the method returns the parameter's value, in this case the string `What, me worry?`. If there were no HTML parameter named `Message` (in uppercase, lowercase, or mixed case), then `getParameter` would return `null`. An applet can read an arbitrary number of values from the HTML document that launched the applet, including none as the applet in Figure 9.4.1 illustrates. ■

■ **Example 9.4.3.**   The `NavURL` applet in Figure 9.4.5 presents a list of URLs (Uniform Resource Locators), which are references to resources such as documents on the World Wide Web. When the user selects from the list a string such as IBM or `Hewlett Packard` and then clicks the *Load Document* button, the

```
import java.awt.*;
import java.awt.event.*;
import java.applet.*;
public class HelloWorldWillTravel extends Applet {
    public void init() {
        String t = getParameter( "Message" );
        msg = (t == null) ? "Hello, world!" : t;
        x = y = 20;
        setFont( new Font( "Dialog", Font.BOLD, 18 ) );
        bground = Color.green;
        addMouseListener( new MyMouseAdapter( this ) );
    }
    public void paint( Graphics g ) {
        setBackground( bground );
        g.drawString( msg, x, y );
    }
    public void setXY( int X, int Y ) { x = X; y = Y; }
    public void toggleBGround() {
        bground = (bground == Color.orange) ? Color.green : Color.orange;
    }
    private String msg;
    private int x, y;
    private Color bground;
}
class MyMouseAdapter extends MouseAdapter {
    public MyMouseAdapter( HelloWorldWillTravel h ) { host = h; }
    public void mouseClicked( MouseEvent e ) {
        host.setXY( e.getX(), e.getY() );
        host.toggleBGround();
        host.repaint();
    }
    private HelloWorldWillTravel host;
}
```

FIGURE 9.4.4   An applet that reads an HTML parameter and responds to mouse clicks.

loadDocument method executes. This method gets the index of a selected string such as IBM and then uses the index to reference the corresponding URL as a string, in this case

```
http://www.ibm.com
```

A URL object is then constructed and used as the first argument to the applet context method showDocument

```
getAppletContext().showDocument( u, "right" );
```

to display the specified document, in this case IBM's home page document. In the two-argument version of showDocument, the second argument indicates where the document should be displayed, in this case to the applet's right. The

```java
import java.awt.*;
import java.awt.event.*;
import java.applet.*;
import java.net.*;
import java.io.*;
public class NavURL extends Applet {
    public void init() {
        setFont( new Font( "Dialog", Font.BOLD, 14 ) );
        setLayout( new FlowLayout() );
        list = new List( prompts.length );
        list.setSize( getPreferredSize() );
        for ( int i = 0; i < prompts.length; i++ )
          list.add( prompts[ i ] );
        add( list );
        Button b = new Button( prompt );
        b.addActionListener( new ActionListener() {
          public void actionPerformed( ActionEvent e ) {
             loadDocument();
          } } );
        add( b );
    }
    private void loadDocument() {
       URL u = null;
       int index = list.getSelectedIndex();
       try {
          getAppletContext().showStatus( "Trying hard..." );
          u = new URL( urls[ index ] );
       } catch( MalformedURLException ex ) {
           System.err.println( ex );
           return;
         }
       getAppletContext().showDocument( u, "right" );
    }
    private List list;
    private String[ ] urls = { "http://www.compaq.com",
                               "http://www.dell.com",
                               "http://www.hewlettpackard.com",
                               "http://www.ibm.com",
                               "http://www.microsoft.com",
                               "http://www.sun.com",
                               "http://www.yahoo.com" };
```

FIGURE 9.4.5   An applet with URLs of documents to browse.

```
private String[ ] prompts = { "Compaq Computer",
                              "Dell Computer",
                              "Hewlett Packard",
                              "IBM",
                              "Microsoft",
                              "Sun Microsystems",
                              "Yahoo" };
private final String prompt = " Load Document ";
}
```

FIGURE 9.4.5   An applet with URLs of documents to browse, *continued.*

applet context method `showStatus` displays a string in the browser's status window, which is typically at the bottom.

If the URL were for an audio clip rather than an HTML document, the `play` method could be invoked with the URL object as its argument to play the audio clip. An URL also might reference an image, which can be fetched with the `loadImage` method. A later example illustrates a multimedia applet. ■

Initializing, Starting, and Stopping Applets

The applet methods `init`, `start`, and `stop` are three important callbacks that a browser or other applet host invokes. The methods are commonly overriden in `Applet` or `JApplet` subclasses. The applet host typically invokes `init` once the applet has been loaded but *before* the applet has been shown. The `init` method is thus suited for initialization tasks such as setting fonts or colors and instrumenting the applet with the appropriate controls such as lists, labels, and buttons. The host invokes `start` to start the applet's execution and `stop` to terminate the applet's execution. If an applet is multithreaded, `start` is the natural method in which to construct and start the additional threads and `stop` is the natural method in which to stop such threads.

Example 9.4.4.   The multimedia `JugglerApplet` in Figure 9.4.6 is multithreaded. The `init` method populates an `Image` array with GIF images that together depict Sun's ubiquitous Duke juggling coffee beans (see Figure 9.4.7). The method

```
private Image loadImage( String name ) {
   try {
      return getImage( getDocumentBase(), name );
   } catch( Exception e ) { return null; }
}
```

retrieves each image using the URL for the HTML document that launched the applet. The assumption is that the GIF files reside in the same directory on the server as the HTML document and the applet's *class* file. In any case,

```
// Adaptation of Sun's juggler bean in which the ubiquitous
// Duke juggles coffee beans.
// Adaptation of Sun's juggler bean in which the ubiquitous
// Duke juggles coffee beans.
import java.applet.Applet;
import java.awt.*;
import java.awt.event.*;
import java.awt.image.*;
import java.net.URL;
public class JugglerApplet extends Applet implements Runnable {
    public void init() {
        beansCount = 5;
        images = new Image[ beansCount ];
        for ( int i = 0; i < beansCount; i++ ) {
            String imageName = "Juggler" + i + ".gif";
            images[ i ] = loadImage( imageName );
            if ( images[ i ] == null ) {
              System.err.println( "Couldn't load image " + imageName );
              return;
            }
        }
    }
    public void start() {
        if ( jt == null || !isAnimating ) {
          jt = new Thread( this );
          isAnimating = true;
          jt.start();
        }
    }
    public void stop() {
        isAnimating = false;
    }
    public void run() {
        while ( isAnimating ) {
          repaint();
          try { Thread.sleep( pause ); }
          catch( InterruptedException e ) { System.err.println( e ); }
        }
    }
    public void paint( Graphics g ) {
        super.paint( g );
        for ( int i = 0; i < images.length; i++ ) {
          g.drawImage( images[ i ], x, y, this );
        }
    }
```

FIGURE 9.4.6   A multithreaded multimedia applet.

```
    private Image loadImage( String name ) {
      try {
         return getImage( getDocumentBase(), name );
      } catch( Exception e ) { return null; }
    }
    private Image[ ] images;
    private int beansCount;
    private Thread jt;
    private boolean isAnimating;
    private static final int x = 15;
    private static final int y = 25;
    private static final int pause = 250;  //*** 1/4 of a second
}
```

FIGURE 9.4.6   A multithreaded multimedia applet, *continued*.

FIGURE 9.4.7   The ubiquitous
Duke juggling coffee beans.

the method `getDocumentBase()` returns a reference to a URL object that
represents the HTML document's URL. The URL object and the GIF file's name
(e.g., `Juggler0.gif`) are the arguments to `getImage`, which returns each GIF
file as an `Image` object. Images in other formats such as JPEG would work as
well.

The applet method `start` is overriden to construct and start a `Thread`
that controls the animation by repainting the panel window by displaying each
juggling image. The override of `paint`

```
public void paint( Graphics g ) {
   super.paint( g );
   for ( int i = 0; i < images.length; i++ ) {
     g.drawImage( images[ i ], x, y, this );
   }
}
```

loops through the images, invoking the drawImage method of the Graphics object on one of the images. The animating thread pauses briefly after each repaint so that the animation is not too fast. The pause, currently set to 1/4 of a second, can be shortened to make the animation faster and lengthened to make the animation slower. The applet method stop causes the juggling thread to return from run and, therefore, to stop. The Programming Exercises request additional multimedia features such as audio.

The Appletviewer Utility

The JugglerApplet in Figure 9.4.7 was launched from the **appletviewer**, a JDK utility designed specifically for running applets. Given the HTML file

```
<HTML><HEAD>
<TITLE>The Duke Juggles Coffee Beans</TITLE>
</HEAD><BODY>
<APPLET CODE="JugglerApplet.class"
        WIDTH=150 HEIGHT=150></APPLET>
</BODY></HTML>
```

named *juggle.html*, the command

```
$ appletviewer juggle.html
```

launches the applet.

The appletviewer is an alternative to commercial browsers for developing and testing applets. Although the appletviewer does *not* display HTML or related documents, the viewer properly displays and executes applets. ■

Communicating Applets

Multiple applets can be launched from a single HTML document, which has multiple APPLET tags. The applets can communicate with one another because they thereby occur in the same applet context.

■ **Example 9.4.5.**   The HTML document in Figure 9.4.8 launches two applets, FooApplet and BarApplet. Figure 9.4.9 shows the code for the FooApplet, which has a button to change the background of the BarApplet. The BarApplet,

```
<HTML>
<HEAD><TITLE> Applet's Talking </TITLE></HEAD>
<BODY>
  <APPLET CODE="FooApplet.class" WIDTH=200 HEIGHT=50 NAME="foo"
                                 ARCHIVE="TwoApplets.jar"></APPLET>
  <APPLET CODE="BarApplet.class" WIDTH=200 HEIGHT=50 NAME="bar"
                                 ARCHIVE="TwoApplets.jar"></APPLET>
</BODY>
</HTML>
```

FIGURE 9.4.8   An HTML document that launches two applets.

```
import java.awt.*;
import java.awt.event.*;
import java.applet.*;
public class FooApplet extends Applet {
    public void init() {
        super.init();
        setLayout( new FlowLayout() );
        Button b = new Button( " Press me, please! " );
        b.addActionListener( new ActionListener() {
           public void actionPerformed( ActionEvent e ) {
              toggleColor();
           } } );
        b.setFont( new Font( "Dialog", Font.BOLD, 14 ) );
        add( b );
    }
    private void toggleColor() {
        Applet a = getAppletContext().getApplet( "bar" );
        if ( a == null )
          return;
        if ( toggle )
          a.setBackground( Color.black );
        else
          a.setBackground( Color.white );
        toggle = !toggle;
    }
    private boolean toggle;
}
```

FIGURE 9.4.9   One of two communicating applets launched from the
HTML document in Figure 9.4.8.

in turn, has a button to change the background color of the FooApplet. The
APPLET tags on the HTML page include an applet's NAME, which one applet can
use to access another applet. For example, the FooApplet executes the statement

```
Applet a = getAppletContext().getApplet( "bar" );
```

in order to obtain a reference to the `BarApplet`, whose background color then is changed by using the reference `a` to invoke the `setBackground` method. The `BarApplet` uses the same approach to change the `FooApplet`'s background. An applet's `AppletContext` also has a `getApplets` method that returns an `Enumeration` of other applets in the same context. Because the `FooApplet` and the `BarApplet` are launched from the *same* HTML document, the two applets share an applet context.

JAR Files

The example also illustrates the use of JAR (**J**ava **AR**chive) files. An **archive** is a file that aggregates other files. A JAR file, which uses the popular ZIP file format, typically compresses the archived files for efficiency. A JAR also may contain digital signatures. In Figure 9.4.8, each `APPLET` tag includes an `ARCHIVE` tag that names the JAR file containing the two applets. The JAR file *TwoApplets.jar* was created by

- Compiling the two applets in the usual way. For convenience, the applets were compiled in the same directory, which contained no other files.
- Issuing the command

```
$ jar -cf TwoApplets.jar *.class
```

to create a JAR file named *TwoApplets.jar* that includes all class files in the current directory. The flag c stands for **c**reate and the flag f stands for **f**ile. The Java Postscript lists the flags used with the JAR utility, which comes with the JDK.

JAR files are particularly attractive for a multimedia applet, which consists of a *class* file and associated video and audio files. The syntax

```
<APPLET CODE=JugglerApplet.class
  ARCHIVE="JugglerClasses.jar, JugImages.jar, JugSounds.jar"
```

shows how a single `ARCHIVE` tag can reference multiple JAR files. Finally, JAR files are a common way to aggregate Java beans or components (see Section 10.1). ■

Applet Security and the Sandbox

An applet, like any program downloaded from a server to execute on a client, poses a security risk to the client. To minimize the security risk, the standard security manager for applets restricts what an applet can do and throws a `SecurityException` if an applet violates any restriction. Because the applet security manager is strict, applets are said to reside in a **sandbox**, thereby suggesting that an applet has a well-defined area in which the applet may "play" but outside of which the applet must not venture. For example, the standard applet security manager prevents an applet from reading or writing the client machine's file system, from executing any program on the local machine, and from communicating with any host other than the host from which the applet was downloaded. Figure 9.4.10 contrasts default security restrictions for applets launched from a commercial browser and from the appletviewer. The figure also includes the default security restrictions for a Java application.

Operation	Commercial Browser	Appletviewer	Java Application
Query local file system	No	Yes	Yes
Read local file	No	Yes	Yes
Write local file	No	Yes	Yes
Delete local file	No	No	Yes
Execute local program	No	Yes	Yes
Connect with server	Yes	Yes	Yes
Connect with other host	No	Yes	Yes
Pop up a window	Yes	Yes	Yes

FIGURE 9.4.10 Sample security restrictions for applets and Java applications.

The security restrictions for an applet launched through the appletviewer require clarification. Although such an applet cannot directly delete a file, the applet could execute a local program that, in turn, could delete a file. The sandbox security that commercial browsers enforce therefore prevents an applet from executing a local program. Section 10.2 examines security in more detail.

Java Applications as Host Programs for Applets

An applet requires a host program, which need not be a browser or special utility such as the appletviewer. Indeed, a Java *application* can serve as the host program by providing basic applet support. The application as applet host should

- Implement the `AppletStub` interface, which includes methods such as `getCodeBase` to get the URL of applet's *class* file and `getDocumentBase` to get the URL of the HTML or comparable document with an APPLET tag. The application should set itself as applet's **stub**, that is, as the interface between the applet and the host environment in which the applet executes. The `AppletStub` interface also declares `getAppletContext`, which returns a reference to the applet's environment—the document with the APPLET tag, any other applets launched from the same document, and so on.
- Implement the `AppletContext` interface, which declares methods such as `getImage`, `getAudioClip`, `showDocument`, and `getApplets` to access other applets in the same context.

- Provide a framed window in which to display the applet.
- Invoke the applet's `init` method once the applet has been loaded and before the applet is shown.
- Invoke the applet's `start` method to start the applet's execution and the applet's `stop` method to stop the applet's execution.

■ **Example 9.4.6.**   The `AppletHost` application in Figure 9.4.11 serves as a host for an applet whose URL is given as a command-line argument. The application's main features can be summarized as follows:

- The `AppletHost` method `fetchClassFile` constructs a URL object to represent the applet *class* file's URL. The URL, in turn, is used to construct a `URLConnection`, an object that represents a communications link between the client and the applet server. A `URLConnection` has an associated input stream that can be used to read the bytecodes in the applet's class file. A `URLConnection` is a specialized client socket.
- Once the communications link to the applet server has been set up, the `getByteCodes` method reads the applet's bytecodes from an input stream into a `byte` array. The *class* file's size in bytes is unknown; hence, the bytecodes are read in chunks of 4,096 and copied into an array. The utility method `System.arraycopy` is used to copy byte chunks from a temporary `byte` array to the target `byte` array. Once all of the bytecodes have been read into the target array, the array is then written to a local file with the same name as the server file. For example, if the applet resides on the server in a file named *JugglingDuke.class*, the local file is also named *JugglingDuke.class*. At this point, the applet's *class* file has been copied to the client, that is, to the machine that executes the `AppletHost` application. The `AppletHost` program, as a Java *application*, is not confined to the sandbox and, therefore, can write a local file.

    In the current implementation, the `AppletHost` writes the applet's bytecodes to a *class* file on the local disk. The applet is then instantiated by reading from this *class* file. A more direct approach, left as a Programming Exercise, would be to construct the applet directly from the bytecodes stored in a `byte` array.

- Method `fetchClassFile` ends by constructing a `MyFrame` window, a subclass of a `Frame`. The `MyFrame` constructor first separates the applet's name (e.g., *JugglingDuke*) from the full *class* file name (e.g., *JugglingDuke.class*) by dropping the *class* extension. The applet's name as a string then becomes the argument for the powerful utility method `Class.forName`, which returns a reference to a `Class` object that represents a class such as *JugglingDuke*. The statement

```
a = (Applet) c.createInstance();
```

instantiates the class, in this example a `JugglingDuke` object whose reference is a. The cast is needed because `createInstance`'s return type is `Object`.

```
import java.awt.*;
import java.applet.*;
import java.net.*;
import java.io.*;
import java.util.*;
public class AppletHost {
   public static void main( String[ ] args ) throws Exception {
      if ( args.length < 1 )
         throw new Exception( "javac AppletHost <applet's URL>" );
      new AppletHost().fetchClassFile( args[ 0 ] );
   }
   private void fetchClassFile( String name ) throws Exception {
      InputStream in;
      URL u;
      URLConnection uc;
      String fileName = null;
      try {
         u = new URL( name );
      } catch( MalformedURLException e ) { throw e; }
      try {
         uc = u.openConnection();
         in = uc.getInputStream();
      } catch( IOException e ) { throw e; }
      byte[ ] theByteCodes = getByteCodes( in );
      try {
         //*** extract the file name from the URL string
         StringTokenizer st = new StringTokenizer( name, "/" );
         while ( st.hasMoreTokens() )
            fileName = st.nextToken();
         FileOutputStream out = new FileOutputStream( fileName );
         out.write( theByteCodes );
         out.close();
      } catch( IOException e ) { throw e; }
      new MyFrame( fileName, 400, 400 );
   }
   private byte[ ] getByteCodes( InputStream in ) throws Exception {
      byte[ ] buffer = new byte[ 0 ];
      byte[ ] chunk = new byte[ 4096 ];
      int count;
      try {
         while ( (count = in.read( chunk )) >= 0 ) {
            byte[ ] t = new byte[ buffer.length + count ];
            System.arraycopy( buffer, 0, t, 0, buffer.length );
```

FIGURE 9.4.11   A Java application that serves as a host program for an applet.

```
                 System.arraycopy( chunk, 0, t, buffer.length,count );
                 buffer = t;
              }
           } catch( Exception e ) { throw e; }
           return buffer;
       }
}
class MyFrame extends Frame implements AppletStub, AppletContext {
    public MyFrame( String s, int w, int h ) throws Exception {
        Applet a;
        StringTokenizer st = new StringTokenizer( s, "." );
        String name = st.nextToken(); //*** drop the ".class" extension
        try {
           Class c = Class.forName( name );
           a = (Applet) c.newInstance();
        } catch( ClassNotFoundException e ) { throw e; }
          catch( IllegalAccessException e ) { throw e; }
          catch( InstantiationException e ) { throw e; }
        setTitle( s );      //** applet's name is window's title
        setSize( w, h );    //** width and height
        add( "Center", a ); //** place applet in the center
        a.setStub( this );  //** the framed window is the stub
        a.init();           //** initialize the applet
        show();             //** show the window with the applet
        a.start();          //** start the applet
    }
    //** for now, trivial implementations of AppletStub and AppletContext
    public boolean isActive() { return true; }
    public URL getDocumentBase() { return null; }
    public URL getCodeBase() { return null; }
    public String getParameter( String s ) { return s; }
    public AppletContext getAppletContext() { return this; }
    public void appletResize( int w, int h ) { setSize( w, h ); }

    public AudioClip getAudioClip( URL url ) { return null; }
    public Image getImage( URL url ) { return null; }
    public Applet getApplet( String n ) { return null; }
    public Enumeration getApplets() { return null; }
    public void showDocument( URL url ) { }
    public void showDocument( URL url, String t ) { }
    public void showStatus( String s ) { }
}
```

FIGURE 9.4.11   A Java application that serves as a host program for an applet,
continued.

- Once the applet object has been instantiated, the `MyFrame` constructor
  - Sets the framed window's title to the applet's name.
  - Sets the framed window's width and height to the specified sizes.
  - Adds the applet to the center of the framed window.
  - Makes itself the applet's stub (i.e., interface to the run-time environment).
  - Initializes the applet by invoking its `init` method.
  - Shows the framed window.
  - Starts the applet by invoking its `start` method.

  At this point, the applet executes in the context of the `AppletHost` application. ∎

Having a Java application serve as a host program for an applet overcomes security restrictions imposed on applets that execute in the context of a commercial browser or even the appletviewer. The application as host program also underscores the flexibility and power of Java network programming.

EXERCISES

1. What is a *host program* for an applet?
2. Write an applet that prints your name to the screen. Provide an appropriate HTML document to launch the applet.
3. Explain how an applet behaves in the context of a client/server environment.
4. What is the relationship between the `Applet` and the `JApplet` classes?
5. Test the `HelloWorldWillTravel` applet of Figure 9.4.4.
6. Test the URL navigator applet of Figure 9.4.5.
7. Explain the typical roles of the applet methods `init`, `start`, and `stop`.
8. Write the `BarApplet` class that pairs with `FooApplet` (see Figure 9.4.9) in the communicating applets example.
9. Explain what is meant by *sandbox security*.
10. Do commercial browsers typically allow an applet to read from the local disk?
11. Can a Java *application* serve as a host program for an applet?
12. List the main responsibilities of a host program for an applet.

9.5   Sample Application: MACE as a Socketed Applet

Problem

Amend the Java application in Figure 7.3.3 to run as an applet. The original application displays a membership form for the **M**idwest **A**ssociation for **C**harisma **E**nhancement. A prospective member uses a graphical form to enter information for submission to the MACE administration. The applet should transmit the information back to the server from which the applet was downloaded.

Sample Input/Output

Figure 9.5.1 shows the MACE applet's form with test information provided. The program in Figure 9.5.2 is a test server, whose output is

```
J. Alfred Prufrock
pruf@wasteland.org
Missouri
married
I'm from Missouri. Show me.
```

after a click of the applet's *Submit* button causes the information to be transmitted to the test server.

Solution

The applet version of MACE uses AWT rather than Swing set graphics so that the applet can be run in as many commercial browsers as possible. Some browsers still do not support the Swing set. The applet's look-and-feel is essentially the same as the original application's. When the user clicks the *Submit* button, the applet opens a socket to the server from which the applet was downloaded and transmits the user's application information as a string. Recall that, even under the default applet security manager, an applet may communicate with the host from which the applet was downloaded. Information fields such as the user's name and e-mail address are delimited by the special symbol ! so that the server can easily break the transmitted string into the appropriate tokens.

Java Implementation

```java
import java.applet.*;
import java.awt.*;
import java.awt.event.*;
import java.io.*;
import java.net.*;
public class MaceApplet extends Applet
                        implements ActionListener {
    public void init() {
        buttons = new Panel( new FlowLayout() );
        misc = new Panel( new FlowLayout() );
        stList = new Panel();
        married = new Checkbox( "Married", false );
```

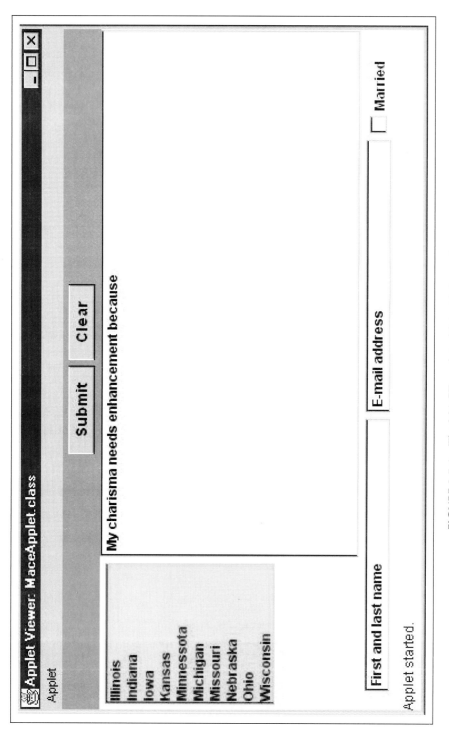

FIGURE 9.5.1 The MACE applet with test information.

```
import java.io.*;
import java.net.*;
import java.util.*;
public class TestServer {
   public static void main( String[ ] args ) {
      try {
         int port = 9876;
         ServerSocket servSock = new ServerSocket( port );
         while ( true ) {
            Socket sock = servSock.accept();
            BufferedReader br = new BufferedReader(
               new InputStreamReader( sock.getInputStream() ) );
            String t = br.readLine();
            StringTokenizer st = new StringTokenizer( t, "!" );
            while ( st.hasMoreTokens() )
               System.out.println( st.nextToken() );
         }
      } catch( IOException e ) { System.err.println( e ); }
   }
}
```

FIGURE 9.5.2 A test server for the MACE applet.

```
   email = new TextField( promptE );
   name = new TextField( promptN );
   reasons = new TextField( promptR );
   list = new List( states.length );
   initAux();
   setSize( w, h );
}
public void actionPerformed( ActionEvent e ) {
   String cmd = e.getActionCommand();
   if ( cmd.equals( submit ) )
     submitForm();
   else if ( cmd.equals( clear ) )
     clearForm();
}
private void initAux() {
   Font f = new Font( "Dialog", Font.BOLD, 12 );
   setLayout( new BorderLayout() );
   buttons.setBackground( Color.gray );
   email.setFont( f );
   name.setFont( f );
   reasons.setFont( f );
   married.setFont( f );
   misc.add( name );
```

```
      misc.add( email );
      misc.add( married );
      for ( int i = 0; i < states.length; i++ )
         list.add( states[ i ] );
      list.setFont( f );
      list.setBackground( Color.cyan );
      stList.add( list );
      addButton( submit );
      addButton( clear );
      add( buttons, BorderLayout.NORTH );
      add( reasons, BorderLayout.CENTER );
      add( stList, BorderLayout.WEST );
      add( misc, BorderLayout.SOUTH );
   }
   private void addButton( String name ) {
      Button b = new Button( name );
      b.setFont( new Font( "Dialog", Font.BOLD, 14 ) );
      b.addActionListener( this );
      buttons.add( b );
   }
   private void submitForm() {
      transmitData( name.getText() + "!" +
                    email.getText() + "!" +
                    list.getSelectedItem() + "!" +
                    ((married.getState()) ?
                       "married" : "not married") + "!" +
                    reasons.getText() + "!" );
   }
   private void clearForm() {
      reasons.setText( promptR );
      name.setText( promptN );
      email.setText( promptE );
      married.setState( false );
      list.deselect( list.getSelectedIndex() );
   }
   private void transmitData( String data ) {
      try {
         String hostName = getCodeBase().getHost();
         String hostAddress =
            InetAddress.getByName( hostName ).getHostAddress();
         Socket sock = new Socket( hostAddress, hostPort );
         PrintWriter ps =
            new PrintWriter( sock.getOutputStream() );
         ps.println( data );
         ps.flush();
```

```
            ps.close();
            sock.close();
        } catch( UnknownHostException ex ) { }
          catch( IOException ex ) { }
    }
    private Panel buttons, misc, stList;
    private List list;
    private Checkbox married;
    private TextField email, name;
    private TextField reasons;
    private final static int w = 600;
    private final static int h = 300;
    private final static String submit = "  Submit  ";
    private final static String clear = "  Clear  ";
    private final static String exit = "  Exit  ";
    private final static String promptN =
        "First and last name           ";
    private final static String promptE =
        "E-mail address                ";
    private final static String promptR =
       "My charisma needs enhancement because";
    private final static String[ ] states =
       { "Illinois", "Indiana", "Iowa", "Kansas",
         "Minnesota", "Michigan", "Missouri",
         "Nebraska", "Ohio", "Wisconsin" };
    private final static int hostPort = 9876;
}
```

Discussion

The changes to the original application of Figure 7.3.3 can be summarized as follows:

- The initialization originally done in a constructor is now done in the applet's init method. The panels, components, fonts, and colors are essentially the same, although AWT rather than Swing set components are used to promote compatibility with a wide range of browsers.

- The field in which the user gives reasons for wanting to join MACE has been changed from a multiline text area to a single-line text field in order to encourage brevity.

- When the user clicks the *Submit* button, a client socket is opened to the server. The server's IP address is computed in two steps:

```
        String hostName = getCodeBase().getHost();
        String hostAddress =
          InetAddress.getByName( hostName ).getHostAddress();
```

The `getCodeBase` method returns the URL for the applet's *class* file and `getHost` then returns the server's symbolic name such as *condor.depaul.edu*, which in turn is used to generate the server's IP address. A client socket is then constructed

```
Socket sock = new Socket( hostAddress, hostPort );
```

and the user's application information is written to the socket's output stream, in this case through a `PrintWriter`.

The MACE applet illustrates that an applet with a socket open to its server fits naturally into the client/server architecture of distributed systems. The applet is downloaded from the server to the client so that client rather than server resources such as CPU cycles are used for user input and related processing. The server is then free to service other clients. The socket allows information to be transmitted from the client back to the server. The server in turn might use the socket to send confirmation or other information back to the client.

EXERCISES

1. Run the MACE applet through a commercial browser. Recall that the applet can be tested on a standalone machine by using the reserved IP address *localhost* (see Section 9.2).
2. Is an applet confined to the sandbox allowed to open a connection to the host from which the applet was downloaded?
3. Is an applet confined to the sandbox allowed to open a connection to an arbitrary host?

9.6   Remote Method Invocation

A distributed system incurs a security risk whenever executable code moves from one machine to another. On the target machine, the code may cause mischief or serious damage, whether deliberately or inadvertently. Within the client/server architecture, some code ought to execute exclusively on the server. Consider the familiar case in which a client downloads an order form from a server. Once a user has filled in the form, the client machine might execute code to validate the order by checking, for example, whether required fields such as name and address have been filled in. An applet could be used for such processing. Suppose that the order form includes a field for a credit card number, which requires special validation. Such validation properly belongs on the server for at least security and perhaps even efficiency reasons, as the validation might require a lookup in a large database that could not be efficiently downloaded to the client.

Even when security is not an issue, offloading processing from one machine to another can be beneficial. Suppose that most of a scientific or engineering application runs perfectly well on a relatively slow desktop computer but that a critical part of an application would require hours or even days to complete on the desktop machine. It would be useful to partition the application so that most of it ran on the desktop machine but particularly time-consuming portions could be offloaded to a much faster machine.

RMI (**R**emote **M**ethod **I**nvocation) is a technology that allows a program executing on one machine to invoke a method that executes on a *different* machine. At the implementation level, a server constructs an object *Obj* and then makes a reference *refObj* to the object available to a remote client, which uses *refObj* to invoke *Obj* methods. The server's security manager ensures that client method invocations are allowed and throws a security exception if a client method invocation is improper. In this respect, the RMI server resembles an applet's host program. Just as the applet's host program restricts which operations an applet may perform on the host machine, so the RMI server restricts which operations a remote client may perform on the server machine. In RMI, the server and the client must be written in Java.[†]

A Sample RMI Server and Client

Figure 9.6.1 contains the source code for an RMI server and Figure 9.6.2 contains the source code for a client of this server. The RMI server provides a `HelloServer` object and provides clients with a reference to this object, which encapsulates a `sayHi` method that clients can invoke remotely. The class `HelloServer` implements a programmer-defined interface, which in this example is named `IHello`. The interface, which extends `java.rmi.Remote`, declares the method `sayHi`. Only the methods declared in the `IHello` interface are accessible to remote clients. Because the client code is simpler, we begin with it.

The RMI Client

The operations of RMI client in Figure 9.6.2 can be summarized as follows. The client

- Sets its security manager to an `RMISecurityManager`.
- Declares a reference of type `IHello`, which is the interface that the server implements. This interface is *registered* on the server's system under the name `hello`. A **registry** is a table that maps a URL such as

    ```
    rmi://kalinnt.cs.depaul.edu/hello
    ```

    to an object, in this case the `HelloServer` object that implements the `IHello` interface.

[†]Technically, the JNI (**J**ava **N**ative **I**nterface) could be used to work around the restriction so that a C-language function could be used in RMI. A later subsection on Jini elaborates.

```
//*** start of file IHello.java
import java.rmi.*;
public interface IHello extends Remote {
   public String sayHi() throws RemoteException;
}
//*** end of file IHello.java

//*** start of file HelloServer.java
import java.rmi.*;
import java.rmi.server.*;
import java.net.*;
public class HelloServer extends UnicastRemoteObject implements IHello {
   public HelloServer() throws RemoteException {
      hiMsg = "Hello, world!";
   }
   public String sayHi() throws RemoteException {
      return hiMsg;
   }
   public static void main( String[ ] args ) {
     try {
        Naming.rebind( "hello", new HelloServer() );
     } catch( RemoteException e ) { System.err.println( e ); }
       catch( MalformedURLException e ) { System.err.println( e ); }
   }
   private String hiMsg;
}
//*** end of file HelloServer.java
```

FIGURE 9.6.1   The source code in two *java* files for an RMI server.

- Sets the IHello reference, in this case named iface, to the remote object by invoking the lookup method of the java.rmi.Naming class with the registered name of the IHello interface as the URL. The URL begins with the protocol name rmi

    rmi://kalinnt.cs.depaul.edu/hello

to indicate that the resource to be located is an RMI object rather than, for example, an HTML document. The server machine in this example is

    kalinnt.cs.depaul.edu

and the resource to be located is registered under the name hello. The class Naming represents the registry and the lookup method performs the registry search. If the search fails, lookup throws the appropriate exception such as a MalformedURLException.

```
import java.rmi.*;
public class HelloClient {
   public static void main( String[ ] args ) {
      System.setSecurityManager( new RMISecurityManager() );
      try {
         IHello iface =
            (IHello) Naming.lookup( "rmi://kalinnt.cs.depaul.edu/hello" );
         System.out.println( "Client says " + iface.sayHi() );
      } catch( Exception e ) { System.err.println( e ); }
   }
}
```

FIGURE 9.6.2   A test RMI client for the server in Figure 9.6.1.

- Uses the `iface` reference to the remote object to invoke one of the object's methods, in this case the `sayHi` method, which returns a `String` that the client prints to the standard output.

Security Permissions

The client requires security permissions in order to search the server's registry with the `Naming.lookup` method. Such permissions can be granted in different ways, as Section 10.2 explains. One way, sufficient for now, is to follow these steps:

- Create the policy text file

```
grant {
  permission java.security.AllPermission;
};
```

and name the file, for example, *Hello.policy*. Any name will do.
- Execute the client with the command

```
$ java -Djava.security.policy=Hello.policy HelloClient
```

The -D flag and the parameter/value pair signal that the client has the permissions listed in the policy file. In this example, the client is granted all permissions for simplicity. A more realistic policy file would selectively grant permissions to a client.

The client code is relatively straightforward because the `Naming` class hides the implementation details of connecting to the server machine and obtaining a reference to a server object such as `HelloServer`. Because the reference's type is an `interface` such as `IHello`, the client is automatically restricted to invoking methods declared in the interface. If the client tried to invoke a server method not declared in the interface (e.g., `main`), the security manager would throw an exception. For basic security, RMI thus leverages the relationship between an interface such as `IHello` and a concrete class such as `HelloServer` that implements the interface. Only methods declared in the interface are exposed to RMI clients.

The RMI Server

The RMI server requires interface and implementation code together with some system configuration. The steps required to write and execute the server in Figure 9.6.1 can be summarized as follows:

- A public interface that extends `java.rmi.Remote` is created with methods that clients can invoke. In this example, the `IHello` interface declares a single method but might declare arbitrarily many more. Each declared method throws a `java.rmi.RemoteException`.
- A public, concrete server class that implements the interface is created and the interface's methods are appropriately defined. In this example, the `HelloServer` class thus implements the `IHello` interface and defines `sayHi`. In addition, the RMI server class typically extends the class `java.rmi.UnicastRemoteObject`, which handles low-level implementation details such as **marshalling**. Marshalling is the process of converting a remotely invoked method's arguments and return value to a byte stream. If the server does not extend `UnicastRemoteObject` directly or indirectly, the server then must handle these details itself.
- The server invokes the `Naming` method `bind` or `rebind` to register a server object under a symbolic name such as `hello` in this example. (The method `rebind` can change an already registered name/object binding, whereas the method `bind` cannot.) Every server constructor must throw a `RemoteException`.
- After the server has been compiled, the server **skeleton** and the client **stub** are generated by invoking the `rmic` utility. In this example, the commands

```
$ javac HelloServer.java
$ rmic HelloServer
```

would be invoked. The `rmic` command (the c stands for compile) generates the files

```
HelloServer_Skel.class
HelloServer_Stub.class
```

The RMI *skeleton* acts as a low-level proxy for the server, and the RMI *stub* acts as a low-level proxy for the client. The stub file is downloaded automatically from the server machine to the client machine so that the skeleton and the stub can handle transactions—remote method invocations—between the client and the server.

- The RMI registry is started on the server machine with the command

  ```
  $ rmiregistry
  ```

  The registry must be active in order for a client to perform a `lookup` operation. The default port for RMI is 1099. The registry command can specify a port number

  ```
  $ rmiregistry 9876
  ```

  in which case the client's URL would have to specify the same port

  ```
  Naming.lookup("rmi://kalinnt.cs.depaul.edu:9876/hello");
  ```

  when invoking the `lookup` method.
- The server is started and automatically waits for clients.

The server, like the client, requires security permissions. In particular, the server must be able to bind an object (in this example, a `HelloServer` object) and a registered name (in this example, `hello`). The server can use the same sample policy file given for the client. The server then is executed with the command

```
$ java -Djava.security.policy=Hello.policy HelloServer
```

RMI Activation

The sample RMI application requires that the remote server run all of the time so that a client can request services at any time. An alternative approach is have the remote server execute only when a client requests service. The `java.rmi.activation` package supports remote server activation "on demand" so that the remote server automatically executes only when a client requests services. The setup for activation is somewhat more complicated than the sample RMI application presented here. For an example of activation, see the JDK documentation under *RMI*.

RMI and Jini

RMI provides the infrastructure for **Jini Connection Technology**, which allows relatively simple digital devices such as cellular phones and software components to be mutually accessible through a network. Jini technology provides a registry mechanism through which a service provider, whether a hardware device or a software component, registers its availability as a Java *object*. A Jini client uses a lookup mechanism to request services, which the client accesses through a Java *object reference* to the server object. Because of the relative ease with which elements can be connected in a network, Jini technology supports an "impromptu community" of cooperating devices and software components. The key point is that RMI technology, like socket technology, can be leveraged to provide even higher-level networked services. For more information on Jini, see `http://www.sun.com/jini`.

EXERCISES

1. What does RMI stand for?
2. Under RMI, does a client receive an object instance or an object reference from the server?
3. Test the `HelloServer` and `HelloClient` applications of Figures 9.6.1 and 9.6.2, respectively. Recall that the test can be run a standalone machine by using the reserved IP address *localhost* (see Section 9.2).
4. Explain the role of the *registry* in RMI.
5. Do both the client and the server require security permissions under RMI?
6. Explain briefly the roles of the *skeleton* and the *stub* under RMI.
7. Can an RMI client invoke server methods that are *not* declared in an interface that the server exposes to clients?
8. Explain RMI activation.

9.7   Sample Application: Matrix Algebra Operations

Problem

Provide an RMI server for algebraic operations such as addition and multiplication on $N \times N$ integer matrices.

Sample Input/Output

For the input file

```
5
73 98 56 45 61
92 58 13 66 34
31 75 46 41 32
81 63 38 22 71
89 51 23 58 84
28 77 62 19 52
79 52 56 99 68
51 86 92 21 32
87 27 64 87 19
28 72 54 21 44
```

the sample RMI client in Figure 9.7.1 produces the output file

```
5
18265 21140 21340 17461 15791
14515 15448 16208 14219 11894
13602 13654 14706 13219 10371
13085 18487 17288 11979 13254
15092 19097 18738 14033 13630
```

```
import java.rmi.*;
import java.io.*;
import basicIO.*;
public class MatrixClient {
   public static void main( String[ ] args ) {
      if ( args.length < 1 ) {
        System.err.println( "MatrixClient <input file>" );
        return;
      }
      System.setSecurityManager( new RMISecurityManager() );
      try {
         IMatrix mm = (IMatrix)
            Naming.lookup( "rmi://condor.depaul.edu/matrix" );
         MatrixClient c = new MatrixClient();
         if ( c.readInput( args[ 0 ] ) )
            c.computeAndWrite( mm, args[ 0 ] );
      } catch( Exception e ) { System.err.println( e ); }
   }
   private boolean readInput( String fileName ) {
      try {
         BasicInput in = new BasicInput( fileName );
         int n = in.getInt();
         m1 = new int[ n ][ n ];
         m2 = new int[ n ][ n ];
         fillMatrix( in, m1, n );
         fillMatrix( in, m2, n );
         in.close();
      }
      catch( IOException e ) {
         System.err.println( e );
         return false;
      }
      return true; //*** successful I/O
   }
   private void fillMatrix( BasicInput in, int[ ][ ] m, int n ) {
      try {
         for ( int i = 0; i < n; i++ )
            for ( int j = 0; j < n; j++ )
               m[ i ][ j ] = in.getInt();
      }
      catch( IOException e ) {
         System.err.println( e );
         System.exit( 0 );
      }
   }
}
```

FIGURE 9.7.1   A sample RMI client for the MatrixServer.

```
   private void computeAndWrite( IMatrix mm, String fileName ) {
      try {
         int[ ][ ] product = mm.mult( m1, m2 );
         BasicOutput out = new BasicOutput( "OutputFor" + fileName );
         out.put( product.length );
         for ( int i = 0; i < product.length; i++ ) {
            out.putln();
            for ( int j = 0; j < product.length; j++ )
               out.put( product[ i ][ j ] + " " );
         }
         out.close();
      }
      catch( Exception e ) {
         System.err.println( e );
         return;
      }
   }
   private int[ ][ ] m1;
   private int[ ][ ] m2;
}
```

FIGURE 9.7.1   A sample RMI client for the `MatrixServer`, *continued.*

The sample client requests the multiplication of two 5×5 matrices. The input file's first record thus gives the number of rows and columns in each matrix. The next five records are the input values for the first matrix, and the last five records are the input values for the second matrix. The output file's first record is the number of rows and columns, and the following records are the product elements.

Solution

The `IMatrix` interface declares the methods `add` and `mult` for the matrix operations *addition* and *multiplication*, respectively. Let A and B be two $N \times N$ matrices. The *sum* of A and B is defined as

$$A + B = a_{i,j} + b_{i,j}$$

The sum of the two matrices is thus the sum of their corresponding elements. The *product* of A and B is defined as

$$AB = a_{i,1}b_{1,j} + a_{i,2}b_{2,j} + \ldots + a_{1,n}b_{n,j}$$

$$= \sum_{k=1}^{n} A_{i,k} B_{k,j}$$

If A and B are 3×3 matrices and A's *first row* consists of the elements 1, 2, 3 and B's *first column* consists of the elements 4, 5, 6, then the product element $P_{1,1}$ equals

$$(1 \times 4) + (2 \times 5) + (3 \times 6)$$

The `MatrixServer` class implements `IMatrix` and acts as **RMI** server for clients that request matrix addition and multiplication. The server's registered name is `matrix`.

Java Implementation

```
//*** start of IMatrix.java
import java.rmi.*;
public interface IMatrix extends Remote {
   public int[ ][ ] add( int[ ][ ] a, int[ ][ ] b )
      throws RemoteException;
   public int[ ][ ] mult( int[ ][ ] a, int[ ][ ] b )
      throws RemoteException;
}
//*** end of IMatrix.java

//*** start of MatrixServer.java
import java.rmi.*;
import java.rmi.server.*;
import java.net.*;
public class MatrixServer extends UnicastRemoteObject
                          implements IMatrix {
   public MatrixServer() throws RemoteException {
      super();
   }
   public int[ ][ ] add( int[ ][ ] a, int[ ][ ] b )
        throws RemoteException {
      int n = a.length;
      int[ ][ ] c = new int[ n ][ n ];
      for ( int i = 0; i < n; i++ )
         for ( int j = 0; j < n; j++ )
            c[ i ][ j ] = a[ i ][ j ] + b[ i ][ j ];
      return c;
   }
   public int[ ][ ] mult( int[ ][ ] a, int[ ][ ] b )
        throws RemoteException {
      int n = a.length;
      int[ ][ ] c = new int[ n ][ n ];
      for ( int i = 0; i < n; i++ )
         for ( int j = 0; j < n; j++ )
            for ( int k = 0; k < n; k++ )
               c[ i ][ j ] += a[ i ][ k ] * b[ k ][ j ];
      return c;
   }
```

```
public static void main( String[ ] args ) {
  try {
    Naming.rebind( "matrix", new MatrixServer() );
  } catch( RemoteException e )
      { System.err.println( e ); }
    catch( MalformedURLException e )
      { System.err.println( e ); }
  }
}
//**** end of MatrixServer.java
```

Discussion

The IMatrix interface declares two methods, one for matrix addition and another for matrix multiplication:

```
public interface IMatrix extends Remote {
  public int[ ][ ] add( int[ ][ ] a, int[ ][ ] b )
      throws RemoteException;
  public int[ ][ ] mult( int[ ][ ] a, int[ ][ ] b )
      throws RemoteException;
}
```

Each method expects references to two integer matrices as arguments and returns a reference to an integer matrix. The implementation of add is relatively straightforward because computing the matrix sum requires only the pairwise addition of matrix elements. By contrast, the mult implementation has three for loops

```
for ( int i = 0; i < n; i++ )
  for ( int j = 0; j < n; j++ )
    for ( int k = 0; k < n; k++ )
      c[ i ][ j ] += a[ i ][ k ] * b[ k ][ j ];
```

because each product element is computed by summing the products of elements from the ith row of the first matrix and the ith column of the second matrix.

The addition but especially the multiplication of large matrices can be time consuming. If the MatrixServer can be executed on a relatively fast machine, then it may make sense to distribute the task of matrix addition or multiplication between two machines. For example, the sample RMI client in Figure 9.7.1 can perform the input and output operations on a local machine such as a desktop computer but then distribute the multiplication to the remote and faster machine *condor.depaul.edu*, which is a high-performance workstation.

The Time Complexity of Matrix Addition and Multiplication

For the matrix addition, let a **time unit** be the amount of time required to perform the operation

```
c[ i ][ j ] = a[ i ][ j ] + b[ i ][ j ];
```

In adding two $N \times N$ matrices, this operation is performed approximately N^2 times, which thus requires approximately N^2 time units. The algorithm used here is therefore said to be *quadratic in N*.

For the matrix multiplication, a time unit is the amount of time required to perform the operation

```
c[ i ][ j ] += a[ i ][ k ] * b[ k ][ j ];
```

In multiplying two $N \times N$ matrices, this operation is performed approximately N^3 times, which thus requires approximately N^3 time units. The algorithm used here is therefore said to be *cubic in N*. The time complexity of matrix multiplication can be reduced significantly by using different algorithms or machines with special architectures. For example, a **systolic array processor** requires approximately N time units to multiply two $N \times N$ matrices. Such a machine thus reduces the time complexity of matrix multiplication from cubic to linear. For an introduction to systolic arrays processors and other special architectures for numeric computations, see J. B. Hayes, *Computer Architecture and Organization*, 3rd ed., (New York: McGraw-Hill, 1993). For a more advanced treatment of these topics, see F. T. Leighton, *Introduction to Parallel Algorithms and Architectures*, (San Mateo, CA: Morgan-Kauffman, 1992).

EXERCISES

1. Run the sample application and client.
2. Explain why the time complexity of matrix multiplication in particular is a good reason to consider an RMI solution.

9.8   Object Request Brokers and CORBA

RMI requires that the server and the client be written in the same language, Java. Alternative technologies for distributed computing remove this restriction. For example, DCE RPC (**D**istributed **C**omputing **E**nvironment **R**emote **P**rocedure **C**all) allows the server and the client to be written in different languages. An RPC server written in Java could provide services for clients written in Java, C, C++, Pascal, and so on. However, RPC is a procedural rather than an object-oriented technology. An object-oriented alternative to RMI is ORB (**O**bject **R**equest **B**roker) technology. As the name suggests, an ORB brokers client requests for services. Such brokers are sometimes described as **middleware**, that is, software that acts as an intermediary between clients that make requests and the remote servers that service these requests. An ORB enables **plug and play** interoperability among distributed software components written in various languages; that is, an arbitrary mixture of remote and local components can be "plugged" into an application and "played" or executed as if the application and all of these components were written in the same language and resided on the local machine. To enable plug and play, an ORB provides the infrastructure for the transparent integration of various distributed components—objects with their encapsulated methods and fields—into a application.

The OMG (**O**bject **M**anagement **G**roup) is an international consortium that promotes object-oriented approaches to distributed computing. The OMG has a software architecture (OMA, **O**bject **M**anagement **A**rchitecture) to which particular technologies are expected to conform. The OMG emphasizes collaboration on technologies that meet OMA standards. CORBA (**C**ommon **O**bject **R**equest **B**roker **A**rchitecture) is an OMA-compliant technology for the distribution of objects. At the core of CORBA is an ORB that supports **object transparency** at two levels:

- **Location transparency**. A client can access a CORBA object without needing to know the machine on which the object resides. CORBA provides a naming service for finding requested components.
- **Language transparency**. A CORBA object can be written in the designer's language of choice. In practice, however, languages such as Java, C, and C++ dominate in the construction of CORBA objects.

Because CORBA is an object-oriented technology and Java is an object-oriented language, the transition from Java to CORBA is relatively straightforward. Much of the vocabulary is common and CORBA can be viewed as a generalization and extension of RMI. On the practical level, the JDK provides several packages for CORBA programming, the main one of which is `org.omg.CORBA`.

A Sample CORBA Application

The sample CORBA application has a CORBA server that exposes two methods, `reverse` and `shuffle`, each of which expects a string argument. The `reverse` method returns the string with its characters reversed and the `shuffle` method returns the string with its characters shuffled. The details of writing a CORBA server and client should be viewed in light of CORBA's location and language transparency. The familiar concept of an *interface* is central to language transparency.

The IDL File

Figure 9.8.1 has the sample application's IDL (**I**nterface **D**efinition **L**anguage) file named *StringOps.idl*. The CORBA syntax is similar but not identical to Java syntax. The IDL file begins with the keyword `module`, which introduces a named module whose parts are interfaces. This IDL file defines a module `StringOpsMod` with a single interface, although the module can contain arbitrarily many interfaces. The module's `IStringOps` interface declares two methods, each of which expects a single string argument. Note that the argument type is `string` (a CORBA data type) rather than `String` (a Java data type). Because of language transparency, CORBA must support conversions of data types from one language (e.g., C) to another (e.g., Java). In the declarations of `reverse` and `shuffle`, each parameter is marked as `in` to signal that the argument is to be *read in* by the method rather than used to store a return value. A parameter marked as out would be used to store a value returned to the method's invoker. Finally, note that semicolons terminate the interface's body and the module's body.

```
module StringOpsMod {
  interface IStringOps {
    string reverse( in string s );
    string shuffle( in string s );
  };
};
```

FIGURE 9.8.1   The IDL file *StringOps.idl* for the sample CORBA application.

The *idltojava* utility[†] is used to generate Java code that supports underlying CORBA functionality for both the server and the clients. Running the utility

```
$ idltojava ServerOps.idl
```

on the file *ServerOps.idl* (see Figure 9.8.1) generates a subdirectory with five source files. The generated items can be described as follows:

- A subdirectory is created with the name *StringOpsMod*, which is the module's name in the IDL file *StringOps.idl*. Because *StringOpsMod* is a subdirectory, it thereby acts as a Java *subpackage*. Accordingly, the server and client both

    ```
    import StringOpsMod.*;
    ```

- The StringOpsMod subdirectory contains the five IDL-generated source files

    ```
    IStringOps.java
    IStringOpsHelper.java
    IStringOpsHolder.java
    _IStringOpsImplBase.java
    _IStringOpsStub.java
    ```

    Each file's name contains the string IStringOps, which is the interface in the IDL file *StringOps.idl*. The sample application code explicitly references only two of the five files:

    - The *server* (see Figure 9.8.2) has a class named ServerOpsImpl that extends the class _IStringOpsImplBase. The methods reverse and shuffle, which are declared in the IDL file's IStringOps interface, are

---

[†]The utility can be downloaded from Sun's Java Developer Connection (JDC). A link to the JDC is available from my web site or http://java.sun.com/products.

defined in `ServerOpsImpl`. The programmer can ignore the contents of
`_IStringOpsImplBase`, although Section 10.3 on Java *reflection* clarifies
the constructs used therein.

- The *client* (see Figure 9.8.3) invokes the `static` method `narrow` in the
`IStringOpsHelper` class in order to locate the ORB. The programmer
otherwise can ignore the contents of the IDL-generated file.

After the IDL file has been created and the *idltojava* utility has been run on this file to
generate the required *java* files, the client and server can be constructed. In this sample
application, the server and the client are written in Java. If the client were written in
C, for example, then an IDL utility that generated C code would be used on the client
side in place of the *idltojava* utility.

The Server

The server code (see Figure 9.8.2) divides roughly into two categories: CORBA
initialization, which provides an ORB with location transparency; and component
construction, which provides a CORBA component for clients to access. The first three
statements in the server's `try` block

```
//**** register the CORBA component
ORB orb = ORB.init( args, null );
StringOpsImpl corbaComp = new StringOpsImpl(); //** component
orb.connect( corbaComp );
```

construct the ORB and then construct and register the CORBA component, in
this case a `StringOpsImpl` object, which encapsulates the `reverse` and `shuffle`
methods declared in the `IStringOps` interface. This overload of the `static` method
`init` takes two arguments. The first argument, an array of references to `Strings`,
allows ORB-specific parameters to be passed as command-line arguments. The second
argument to `init` specifies ORB-specific `Properties`, which are persistent attributes
stored as key/value pairs. For simplicity, the sample application does not use command-
line arguments or ORB-specific `Properties`. The key point is that `init` returns a
reference to an ORB instance, which is critical for any CORBA application. The
second statement constructs the CORBA component, in this case a `StringOpsImpl`
object that the third statement connects to the ORB. The connected object is called
a **servant** because it serves clients. In summary, the server program is responsible for
setting up the ORB, constructing a servant, and connecting the servant to the ORB.

The CORBA Naming Service

Recall that location transparency is a key feature of CORBA. A CORBA client does
not need to know, for example, the server machine's IP address, the location of the
servant code on the server machine, and so forth. To enable location transparency, the
server uses the CORBA naming service. The five statements

```
import StringOpsMod.*;                    //** IDL-generated stubs
import org.omg.CORBA.*;                   //** general CORBA support
import org.omg.CosNaming.*;               //** naming service
import org.omg.CosNaming.NamingContextPackage.*; //** exceptions
import java.util.*;
public class StringOpsServer {
  public static void main( String[ ] args ) {
    try {
      //**** register the CORBA component
      ORB orb = ORB.init( args, null );
      StringOpsImpl corbaComp = new StringOpsImpl(); //** component
      orb.connect( corbaComp );
      //**** set up the naming context
      org.omg.CORBA.Object objRef =
         orb.resolve_initial_references( "NameService" );
      NamingContext ncRef = NamingContextHelper.narrow( objRef );
      //**** Bind the object reference in naming
      NameComponent nc = new NameComponent( "StringOps", " " );
      NameComponent[ ] path = { nc };
      ncRef.rebind( path, corbaComp );
      //**** wait for clients
      java.lang.Object lock = new java.lang.Object();
      synchronized( lock ) {
        lock.wait();
      }
    } catch( Exception e ) { System.err.println( e ); }
  }
}
//*** implementation of the IDL interface
class StringOpsImpl extends _IStringOpsImplBase {
  public String shuffle( String s ) {
    List l = new ArrayList();
    for ( int i = 0; i < s.length(); i++ )
       l.add( new Character( s.charAt( i ) ) );
    Collections.shuffle( l );
    String t = String.valueOf( l );
    StringBuffer b = new StringBuffer();
    for ( int i = 1; i < t.length() - 1; i++ ) {
       char next = t.charAt( i );
       if ( next != ',' && !Character.isWhitespace( next ) )
         b.append( next );
    }
    return new String( b );
  }
```

FIGURE 9.8.2 The sample CORBA server.

```
   public String reverse( String s ) {
     return new StringBuffer( s ).reverse().toString();
   }
}
```

FIGURE 9.8.2   The sample CORBA server, *continued.*

```
import StringOpsMod.*;      //** IDL-generated stubs
import org.omg.CORBA.*;     //** general CORBA support
import org.omg.CosNaming.*; //** naming service
public class StringOpsClient {
  public static void main( String[ ] args ) {
    try {
      //** initialize the ORB
      ORB orb = ORB.init( args, null );
      //** get the root naming context
      org.omg.CORBA.Object objRef =
         orb.resolve_initial_references( "NameService" );
      NamingContext ncRef = NamingContextHelper.narrow( objRef );
      //** resolve the naming context
      NameComponent nc = new NameComponent( "StringOps", " " );
      NameComponent[ ] path = { nc };
      IStringOps comp = IStringOpsHelper.narrow(ncRef.resolve( path ));
      //** test
      String s0 = "Then bright-eyed Pallas thought of one last thing.";
      String s1 = comp.reverse( s0 );
      String s2 = comp.shuffle( s0 );
      System.out.println( s0 );
      System.out.println( s1 );
      System.out.println( s2 );
    } catch(Exception e) { System.err.println( e );
                           e.printStackTrace( System.err ); }
  }
}
```

FIGURE 9.8.3   The sample CORBA client.

```
//**** set up the naming context
org.omg.CORBA.Object objRef =
   orb.resolve_initial_references( "NameService" );
NamingContext ncRef = NamingContextHelper.narrow( objRef );
//**** Bind the object reference in naming
NameComponent nc = new NameComponent( "StringOps", " " );
NameComponent[ ] path = { nc };
ncRef.rebind( path, corbaComp );
```

implement the location transparency for the `StringOps` component. The
`org.omg.CosNaming` package supports the CORBA COS (**C**ommon **O**bject **S**ervices)
naming service in which a `NamingContext` is a tree-like directory of object references.
A naming context is analogous to a hierarchical file system of directories, subdirectories, and nondirectory files. The code segment thus binds the CORBA component to
a location in a naming context so that the naming service can locate the component to
satisfy client requests for services.

Once the CORBA component has been constructed and placed in a naming
context, the server waits for clients. To ensure that the server's `main` does not exit, thus
destroying the ORB, the server enters an infinite wait, which requires a `synchronized`
block or method. In this example, the `synchronized` block

```
java.lang.Object lock = new java.lang.Object();
synchronized( lock ) {
    lock.wait();
}
```

is used. The fully qualified name `java.lang.Object` is required because the
`org.omg.CORBA` package also has an `Object` class.

Finally, the server's `ServerOpsImpl` class defines the two methods declared in
the IDL interface. A `ServerOpsImpl` object is the CORBA component connected to
the ORB by the code segment

```
StringOpsImpl corbaComp = new StringOpsImpl(); //** component
orb.connect( corbaComp );
```

After the server is written, it is compiled in the usual way.

The Client

The sample client's setup is similar to the server's setup: the ORB is constructed
and initialized after which the naming service is accessed and the naming context
is narrowed to the desired component's location. The major difference is that the
server constructs a component and makes the component available through the ORB,
whereas the client requests from the ORB a reference to the component. The request
code is

```
IStringOps comp =
    IStringOpsHelper.narrow( ncRef.resolve( path ) );
```

where `IStringOpsHelper` is an IDL-generated class and `ncRef` is a reference to the
naming context in which the component resides. Once the reference to the component
is obtained, the client uses the reference to invoke remote methods

```
String s0 =
  "Then bright-eyed Pallas thought of one last thing.";
```

```
String s1 = comp.reverse( s0 );
String s2 = comp.shuffle( s0 );
```

just as in RMI. In this example, the remote component's two exposed methods are
reverse and shuffle. On a sample run, the client produced the output

```
Then bright-eyed Pallas thought of one last thing.
.gniht tsal eno fo thguoht sallaP deye-thgirb nehT
tuyeboeth-nhnhlatgTreoiasPgfisdle.nahotgtlh
```

The implementation of shuffle randomly shuffles the characters and then removes
all whitespace characters.

Running the Application

This subsection first summarizes the steps required to build the sample server and
client and then explains how the ORB name server can be run.

- An IDL file, in this example *StringOps.idl* of Figure 9.8.1, is created. The
  file lists one or more CORBA interfaces that the component exposes. As in
  Java, each interface is named and contains method declarations. The CORBA
  syntax differs slightly from the Java syntax. In this example, the StringOps
  component exposes only one interface. The interfaces occur in a module, which
  likewise is named. When an IDL utility such as *idltojava* is executed

  ```
  $ idltojava StringOps.idl
  ```

  the utility generates various source files and places them in a subdirectory with
  the module's name, in this example StringOpsMod. In the current example,
  the IDL utility would be run *twice* on the *same IDL file*: once on the server
  machine and again on the client machine. The example requires that the server
  and the client use the *same* IDL file.
- The server and the client are written and then compiled in the usual way.
- The IDL name server is started with the command

  ```
  $ tnameserv -ORBInitialPort 1050
  ```

  The tnameserv name server is packaged with the JDK. The flag ORBInitial-
  Port and its value 1050 establish 1050 as the server port. By default, an ORB's
  initial port is 900. The syntax thus illustrates how an alternative port can be
  used. On some systems, a port number less than 1024 may be required.
- The server is executed with the statement

  ```
  $ java StringOpsServer -ORBInitialPort 1050
  ```

  Because the name server is specified to listen on port 1050, this port also is
  specified as the server's initial port.

- Clients are executed with the statement

      $ java StringOpsClient -ORBInitialPort 1050

  The statement again specifies 1050 as the ORB's initial port.

The Dynamic Invocation Interface

In the sample CORBA application, the client is a standalone Java *application* that is compiled using IDL-generated files. In ORB vocabulary, the sample client uses the *static* interface definitions that the IDL-generated files, called *stubs*, provide. Suppose, by contrast, that the client were an *applet*—that is, a *precompiled* program downloaded to a client machine—and that the applet was not compiled with the IDL stubs. The question is whether such an applet still could behave as a CORBA client. The answer is *yes*. CORBA's DII (**D**ynamic **I**nvocation **I**nterface) technology allows a client to discover a component's interfaces at run time. DII supports various mechanisms, one of which allows a client to convert a **stringified object reference**, that is, a string that names a CORBA component into a reference to the component. DII is similar to Java's own reflection technology (see Section 10.3). In any case, a CORBA client always requires access to a component interface in order to request component services. At issue is whether access to the interface is provided at compile time through IDL technology or at a run time through DII technology.

Summary of Networking Technologies

Java supports a range of networking technologies that are adaptable, flexible, extensible, and powerful. The technologies can be intermixed to meet the requirements of particular distributed systems. For example, serialization over sockets can occur in applets and be combined with RMI or CORBA services. An applet can act as a CORBA client (see the Java Postscript). The goal of this chapter is to explain the technical details of each technology while sketching the rich possibilities of its uses.

   Finally, work is underway for a convergence of RMI and CORBA technologies. The first step is a version of RMI that uses the Internet Inter-ORB Protocol (IIOP)[†] as well as an IDL extension that allows RMI constructs to specify CORBA rather than specifically RMI interfaces. The convergence makes sense because RMI and CORBA are fundamentally alike as technologies for object distribution.

EXERCISES

1. What does ORB stand for?
2. What does CORBA stand for?
3. What do OMG and OMA stand for?

[†]This technology is sometimes called *RMI-over-IIOP*.

4. Explain the relationship between CORBA and OMG.

5. What is meant by *location transparency* in the context of object request brokers?

6. What is meant by *language transparency* in the context of object request brokers?

7. Test the sample CORBA server and client. Recall that testing can be done on a standalone machine using the reserved IP address *localhost* (see Section 9.2).

8. What does DII stand for?

9. What is a *stringified object reference* and how is it used?

10. Briefly explain the difference between IDL and DII technology in CORBA.

JAVA POSTSCRIPT

The `jar` Utility

The `jar` command can be invoked with flags. Use of the JAR utility is illustrated in Sections 9.4 on applets and 10.1 on beans. The utility is typically invoked with the file flag **f** and whatever other flags are appropriate. For example, the command

```
$ jar -cf MyJar.jar *.class
```

creates a JAR archive file named *MyJar.jar* and puts in this file all *class* files in the current directory. By default, the archive is compressed. The command

```
$ jar -xf MyJar.jar
```

extracts the contents of the JAR file *MyJar.jar*. Here is a list of the flags together with a brief description of each:

Flag	Description
c	Creates a new archive.
t	Displays an archive's table of contents.
x	Extracts files from an archive.
f	Specifies the JAR file's name.
v	Generates verbose output.
m	Adds a manifest to a JAR file.
M	Does not create a manifest.
0	Disables compression.

Security Issues for Applets as CORBA Clients

A CORBA server's *location transparency* is in conflict with an applet's default *sandbox security manager*, which allows an applet to establish a connection only with the server machine from which the applet was downloaded. Protocols such as IIOP (**I**nternet

Inter-**O**RB **P**rotocol), an extension to TCP/IP, provide a workaround. An IIOP-enabled browser can act as a *forwarder* or *gateway* when an applet requests services from a location-transparent CORBA server. The underlying idea is that the IIOP-enabled browser forwards the applet's request to the target CORBA server, wherever the server may reside. In similar fashion, responses from the CORBA server are then sent back to the applet client via the IIOP gateway. In effect, an IIOP-enabled browser can act as a proxy CORBA server for applets confined to the sandbox.

COMMON ERRORS AND SAFE PRACTICES

1. To construct a client `Socket` in a program, the server's IP address and the port number of the service must be specified. Although the `Socket` class has a `protected` no-argument constructor, all of the `public` constructors require at least an IP address and a port number as arguments.

2. To get an `InetAddress`, a factory method such as `getByName` must be used. The `InetAddress` class does not expose any public constructors.

3. To construct a `ServerSocket` in a program, the constructor must specify at least a port number. The `ServerSocket` class does not expose a public no-argument constructor.

4. Only the `ServerSocket` class exposes an `accept` to listen for client connections.

5. Only client `Socket`s have associated input and output streams for reading from and writing to a socket, respectively. `ServerSocket`s are used exclusively to `accept` client connections, and the `accept` method returns a reference to a client `Socket`.

6. It is an error not to close a client or server socket that is no longer needed. Also, it is good practice to close a client socket's associated input and output streams when these are no longer needed.

7. It is an error to expect reliable transport from `DatagramSocket`s, which are UDP-based. By contrast, `ServerSocket`s and client `Socket`s are TCP-based.

8. Client `Socket`s have associated input and output steams. Reading from an associated input stream blocks until the stream has been written to. Accordingly, socket-based applications must ensure that writing to and reading from client `Socket`s is coordinated. In particular, it is an error to have a program read from a `Socket`'s input stream if no program is writing to the `Socket`'s output stream.

9. It is good practice to `flush` a client `Socket`'s output stream after writing so that any buffered output is indeed written to the stream.

10. Although `JApplet`s have the advantage of Swing set graphics, some browsers still do not handle `JApplet`s correctly. By contrast, most commercial browsers do handle `Applet`s correctly. Both are "heavyweight" components in any case.

11. An applet must be an instance of a *public* class.

12. Under RMI, a client and a server require a security manager.

13. It is an error for an RMI client to invoke a server method not declared in the interface that the server implements. For example, if a server implements IFace1 with methods m1 and m2, then a client may invoke only m1 and m2.

14. Under RMI, it is an error for either a client or a server to be written in a language other than Java.

15. An RMI client requires the server's IP address, although a CORBA client does not.

16. Under CORBA, a Java client requires an *idltojava* utility to create the appropriate stubs unless the client uses CORBA's DII technology.

PROGRAMMING EXERCISES

9.1. Write a client *ping* utility for checking whether a host with a specified IP address is reachable. The utility, originally developed under Unix, is now available on many systems. For example, the command

```
$ java ping condor.depaul.edu
```

should produce output such as

```
Pinging condor.depaul.edu [140.192.1.6]
Reply from 140.192.1.6
```

if the designated host is reachable and an appropriate message such as

```
Host not reachable: 140.192.1.6
```

if the designated host is not reachable. *Hint*: A datagram is sufficient for this application and port number 7 is typically reserved for the *ping* or *echo* service.

9.2. Write a socket-based port server application that responds to a client request for a particular port number on a specified host. For example, in response to a client request such as

```
$ java PortInfo condor.depaul.edu telnet
```

the server might respond with

```
telnet (remote login): port 23/tcp
```

In the request, condor.depaul.edu is the host and telnet is the service for which the port number is requested. In the response, the requested service (in this example, `telnet`) is listed together with the number of the server port through which the service is available and the associated protocol (in this example, `tcp` rather than `udp`). In response to a client request such as

```
$ java PortInfo condor.depaul.edu smtp
```

the server might respond with

```
smtp (simple mail transport protocol): port 25/tcp
```

If a requested service is not supported, the server should respond with an appropriate message. *Hint*: Figure 9.1.4 lists the typical port for services available on many systems.

9.3. Expand the `RecordSet` and `Database` applications of Programming Exercises 8.1 and 8.2, respectively, by adding a `Query` class whose objects are sent by a client to a database server to request records that match the query. For example, a query such as

```
Table: Flights
Filter: Origin='ORD'
```

requests records from `Flight` table where the `Origin` field's value is ORD, the traditional designation for Chicago's O'Hare International Airport. (The airport occupies land that once was an orchard.) The client and the server use serialization over sockets: the client serializes a `Query` to the server, which in turn serializes the resulting `RecordSet` to the client. The server application should be multithreaded. Write a test client that sends a `Query` to the server and prints the resulting `RecordSet` to the standard output.

9.4. Expand Programming Exercise 9.3 by allowing filter expressions to contain boolean operators such as *not*, *and*, and *or*. For example, the `Query`

```
Table: Flights
Filter: Origin='ORD' AND Destination='DIA'
```

requests records for flights that originate at ORD and terminate at DIA (Denver International Airport). Serialization over sockets again should be used for communication between the client and the server.

9.5. Write a multithreaded component server that accepts requests from clients for software components such as `TimeCards` (see Section 8.3), `Calculators` (see Programming Exercise 7.15), `Spreadsheets` (see Programming Exercise 7.12), and the like. When the server receives a client request, the server serializes back to the client a GUI that contains a list of available components. The client selects components from the list and then clicks the *Submit* button, which sends a request back to the server. The server responds to the request by serializing the requested components back to the client. The client then serializes the components to the local disk for later incorporation into an application.

9.6. Build several small applets that display images and perform simple animations. Package the applets in a *jar* file (see Example 9.4.5). Then test the download and execution of the applets in two ways:

- Launch the applet from an HTML document and run through a commercial browser
- Use a Java *application* as a host program (see Figure 9.4.11).

Hint: The `java.util.jar` package has classes for handling *jar* files.

9.7. Adapt Programming Exercise 9.6 by allowing the applets to communicate. For example, moving a scrollbar on one applet could increase or decrease the animation rate of another applet in the same context. The adaptation should cover the two cases in which a commercial browser and a Java *application* serve as the host program.

9.8. Build an applet in whose panel a user can draw simple figures or text by moving the mouse. *Hint*: Events such as *mouse down* and *mouse drag* may be useful.

9.9. Convert the tic-tac-toe application of Programming Exercise 7.13 to an applet.

9.10. Enhance the tic-tac-toe application of Programming Exercise 9.9 by providing a distributed version in which two players on distinct machines can play one another. *Hint*: The two players download the same applet, which contains the GUI. The applets communicate through sockets to the server, which maintains state information about the game such as the history of each player's moves.

9.11. Convert the multithreaded chip-gathering ant application of Programming Exercise 7.21 to an applet.

9.12. Adapt the multithreaded component server of Programming Exercise 9.5 so that the client can retrieve the list of available components as an applet. *Hint*: Because of the sandbox restrictions, an applet launched from a commercial browser could not serialize the retrieved components to the local disk. However, if a Java *application* were the applet's host program, then the sandbox restrictions would not apply.

9.13. Convert the card-playing application of Programming Exercise 7.14 to an applet.

9.14. Design an order form for an on-line catalog as an applet. The form should include lists of items (for instance, clothes, garden tools, and the like) together with text fields for the buyer's name, address, and other pertinent information. When the user clicks the *Submit* button, the data in the order form should be written to a socket back to the server, which in turn sends confirmation that the order has been received.

9.15. Profile the performance of the matrix algebra sample application of Section 9.7. In particular,

- Build a GUI that allows the user to enter the name of the input file.
- Perform matrix multiplication on a remote host using RMI, tracking the full amount of time required to invoke the remote method and to receive the product matrix from the server.
- Write a socket-based remote server to which the client serializes the matrices to be multiplied and deserializes the product matrix. Again track the full amount of time required to connect to the server, serialize the matrices to be multiplied, and deserialize the product matrix.
- Print an appropriate performance report to the GUI.

9.16. Modify the `AppletHost` program of Figure 9.4.11. The current version stores the applet's bytecodes, which are read from a remote host into a `byte` array, in a *class* file on the local disk. The modified version should construct the applet directly from the `byte` array. *Hint*: Extend `java.lang.ClassLoader` and use the inherited `defineClass` method, which returns a reference to a `Class` object.

9.17. Build an applet version of the matrix algebra sample application of Section 9.7. In the applet version, the server sends to the client not only the matrix algebra code but also the data, for example, two matrices to be multiplied. The applet performs the matrix operation and serializes the product matrix to the server, which prints the sum or product matrix to the standard output. The applet should display the sum or product matrix in the applet window.

9.18. Write a CORBA version of the matrix algebra sample application of 9.7. Ideally, the client and the server should be written in different languages to test CORBA's language transparency.

9.19. The JDK provides HTML documentation for standard packages and classes as well as HTML tutorials. Build an applet that delivers requested documentation to a client from a server with access to the JDK documentation. The client GUI should be designed to ease navigation through the packages and classes. For example, the GUI might present a list of standard packages. Clicking on a package might then generate another list of the package's classes and interfaces.

9.20. Make the browser application in Programming Exercise 7.3 functional by enabling downloads and displays of requested documents.

9.21. Implement a basic messaging system, where a **message** is structured data sent over a communications channel from one participating agent in the system to another. Assume that each agent participating in the system has a unique identifier that includes a particular IP address. Compared to object-oriented technologies such as RMI and CORBA, messaging systems are relatively simple and restrictive. Nonetheless, such systems are also efficient and flexible, particularly in environments in which object-oriented technologies are not available.

9.22. Revise the `DateBCast` program of Figure 9.2.8 so that the program reads a list of client IP addresses and port numbers from a file and then broadcasts the current `Date` to the clients.

10

Selected Topics

Chapter Outline

This chapter begins with a section **beans** or **software components**, that is, prebuilt software modules that can be integrated and assembled into an application. The section on beans also introduces the *bean box*, a utility for testing beans in a visual programming environment.

The section on security and cryptography examines the Java security model. After clarifying the model's various constructs such as the bytecode verifier and the class loader, the section focuses on how the programmer can design a security manager to fit an application's needs. The section also introduces basic cryptography with an emphasis on authentication.

Reflection is a technology used widely in object-oriented technologies such as CORBA. Java has modern, built-in support for reflection. The section focuses on practical uses of reflection technologies.

The section on servlets and database extends the networking material in Chapter 9. A common client/server system has a browser as a client interface to a database that resides on a remote server. The section shows how servlets and the `java.sql` package together support distributed systems with databases under the client/server model.

Beans

A component-based programming system should provide mechanisms for building, integrating, editing, saving, and distributing components. Java's object-oriented architecture in general and its event model in particular support component-based programming. For example, the distinction between *interface* and *implementation*, which is central to component-based programming, is likewise central to Java. An application that embeds a component object is required to know only the interfaces that the object's class implements rather than the implementation details. Indeed, if the component object's interfaces do not change, then changes in the object's implementation details do not impact the way in which an application manipulates the integrated component object.

The Java event model provides a powerful, flexible mechanism for component communication. For example, component C_1 can communicate with component C_2 by generating events that C_2 handles. C_2 can communicate with C_1 in the same way, which means that the communications model supports peer-to-peer rather than simply client-to-server or server-to-client communications. A component C_1 also might communicate, using the same basic event mechanism, with many other components C_2, C_3, ..., C_n. Components can unicast or multicast, as the situation requires.

If an application object is persistent, then so must be the components integrated into it. Serializing an object to a file is a straightforward way to make the object persistent. As minimal condition, a bean thus must be serializable. Because serialization works on *object graphs* (see Section 8.2) and not simply on isolated objects, an arbitrarily complex component is still serializable.

Dynamic Editing of Component Properties

Java already supports the run-time or dynamic editing of built-in AWT and Swing components, which provides a model for the run-time editing of programmer-built components. For example, every Component (which includes JComponents) has a *background* and a *foreground* property that can be accessed through the appropriate *get* methods (e.g., getBackground) and edited through the appropriate *set* methods (e.g., setBackground). In different words, a *get/set* method pair *specifies* a dynamically editable property such as *background*. If a graphical environment were able to detect *get/set* method pairs that specify a property, the graphical environment could support *visual* dynamic editing of a component's properties. The BDK (**B**ean **D**evelopment **K**it) has a *bean box* utility that supports visual dynamic editing.[†] In addition to the BDK, many commercial products are available for building, editing, integrating, and otherwise testing beans.

> ■ **Example 10.1.1.**   The TickerTape applet in Figure 10.1.1 is likewise a bean with several dynamically editable properties. The applet simulates a ticker tape by displaying a message whose *x* coordinate continually changes. A TickerThread sleeps between redisplays of the message so that the sleep length can be shortened to "speed up" the ticker tape or lengthened to "slow down" the ticker tape. The public methods getSpeed and setSpeed together define a *speed* property because the methods follow a bean convention:
>
> • The getSpeed method has int as the return type and takes no arguments.
> • The setSpeed method has a single int parameter and void in place of a return type.
> • The *get* method is *public*, which makes the property *readable*.
> • The *set* method is *public*, which makes the property *writable*.
>
> In general, then, method pairs such as
>
> ```
> public String getSomeProp() { /*...*/ }
> public void setSomeProp( String p ) { /*...*/ }
> ```
>
> define a property SomeProp of type String. Because both methods are public, SomeProp is readable and writable. If setSomeProp were private or nonexistent, SomeProp would be readable but not writable. If getSomeProp were private or nonexistent, SomeProp would be writable but not readable.
>   The ticker tape applet can be launched from an HTML document in the usual way. An Applet derives from a Component, which is Serializable; hence, a TickerTape is serializable. The next example illustrates bean serialization, and the following subsection then clarifies property changes and property change listeners. ■

[†]The BDK is available for download at Sun's Java Development Connection, a link to which is available from http://java.sun.com/products.

```java
import java.awt.*;
import java.applet.*;
import java.beans.*;
import java.io.*;
public class TickerTape extends Applet {
  //** message is read-write
  public String getMessage() { return message; }
  public void setMessage( String s ) {
    String old = message; message = s;
    fire( "message", old, message );
  }
  //** speed is read-write
  public int getSpeed() { return speed; }
  public void setSpeed( int s ) {
    int old = speed; speed = s;
    fire( "speed", new Integer( old ), new Integer( speed ) );
  }
  //** goRight is read-write
  public boolean isGoRight() { return goRight; }
  public void setGoRight( boolean f ) {
    boolean old = goRight; goRight = f;
    fire( "goRight", new Boolean( old ), new Boolean( goRight ) );
  }
  //** cycles is read-only
  public long getCycles() { return cycles; }
  private void setCycles( long c ) {
    long old = cycles;  cycles = c;
    fire( "cycles", new Long( old ), new Long( cycles ) );
  }
  public void init() {
    setFont ( new Font( "Dialog", Font.BOLD, 16 ) );
    setMessage( "What, me worry?" );
    setSpeed( 8 );
    setGoRight( false );
    setSize( getPreferredSize() );
    msgX = getSize().width / 2;
  }
  public void start() {
    if ( tt == null ) {
      tt = new TickerThread( this );
      tt.start();
    }
  }
}
```

FIGURE 10.1.1   A ticker tape applet that is also a bean.

```
  public void stop() {
    if ( tt != null ) {
      tt.setKeepTicking( false );
      tt = null;
    }
  }
  public void paint( Graphics g ) {
    len = getFontMetrics( getFont() ).stringWidth( getMessage() );
    msgX += ( ( goRight ) ? getSpeed() : -getSpeed() );
    if ( !goRight && ( ( msgX + len < 0 ) ) ) {
      msgX = getSize().width;
      setCycles( getCycles() + 1 );
    }
    else if ( goRight && ( msgX > getSize().width ) ) {
      msgX = -getSize().width;
      setCycles( getCycles() + 1 );
    }
    g.drawString( message, msgX, 20 );
  }
  public Dimension getPreferredSize()
    { return new Dimension( 350, 70 ); }
  public void addPropertyChangeListener(PropertyChangeListener l) {
    changes.addPropertyChangeListener( l );
  }
  public void removePropertyChangeListener(PropertyChangeListener l) {
    changes.removePropertyChangeListener( l );
  }
  private void fire( String prop, Object old, Object obj ) {
    changes.firePropertyChange( prop, old, obj );
  }
  private String              message; // what's displayed
  private int                 speed;   // ticker-tape speed
  private boolean             goRight; // true == right
  private long                cycles;  // count of message cycles
  private int                 msgX;    // where message starts
  private transient int       len;     // message length
  private transient TickerThread tt;   // ticker thread
  private PropertyChangeSupport changes =
    new PropertyChangeSupport( this ); // handles PropertyChange events
}
class TickerThread extends Thread {
  public TickerThread( TickerTape h ) {
    host = h;
    keepTicking = true;
  }
```

FIGURE 10.1.1   A ticker tape applet that is also a bean, *continued.*

```
   public TickerThread( TickerTape h, boolean t ) {
      host = h;
      keepTicking = t;
   }
   public void setKeepTicking( boolean t ) { keepTicking = t; }
   public void run() {
      while ( keepTicking ) {
         try { Thread.sleep( 100 ); }
         catch( InterruptedException e ) { System.err.println( e ); }
         host.repaint();
      }
   }
   private TickerTape host;
   private boolean keepTicking;
}
```

FIGURE 10.1.1   A ticker tape applet that is also a bean, *continued.*

■ **Example 10.1.2.**   The `TickerTest` program in Figure 10.1.2 illustrates three ways in which the `TickerTape` applet/bean of Figure 10.1.1 can be incorporated as a component. The program uses three panels with different background colors to display three ticker tapes. The top and bottom ticker tapes move right to left, whereas the middle ticker tape moves left to right. After the application loads each ticker tape, the application invokes the tape's `init` and `start` methods.

The `loadBeans` method loads each ticker tape. The tape in the top panel is loaded using two `Class` methods

```
Class c = Class.forName( "TickerTape" );
TickerTape tape1 = (TickerTape) c.newInstance();
```

The `static` method `forName` returns a reference to a `Class` object that represents the named class, in this case `TickerTape`. The method `newInstance` is then used to instantiate a `TickerTape` component. The first ticker tape is serialized in order to illustrate later deserialization of a bean.

The first method of loading the applet into the application does *not* involve deserialization. Instead, a `Class` object representing the `TickerTape` is created so that this `Class` object can be used to get a `TickerTape` instance. Deserialization would require prior serialization of a `TickerTape` object, as occurs in the next approach.

The ticker tape in the middle panel is deserialized from a disk file using the input stream's `readObject` method

```
ObjectInputStream is =
  new ObjectInputStream( new FileInputStream( serFile ) );
TickerTape tape2 = (TickerTape) is.readObject();
```

```
import java.awt.*;
import java.beans.*;
import java.io.*;
class TickerTest extends Frame {
   public static void main(String[ ] args) { new TickerTest().doIt(); }
   private void doIt() {
      setLayout( new BorderLayout() );
      top = new Panel(); mid = new Panel(); bot = new Panel();
      top.setBackground( Color.lightGray );
      mid.setBackground( Color.orange );
      bot.setBackground( Color.cyan );
      add( top, BorderLayout.NORTH );
      add( mid, BorderLayout.CENTER );
      add( bot, BorderLayout.SOUTH );
      setSize( 400, 300 ); loadBeans(); show();
   }
   private void loadBeans() {
      try {
        //*** Class.forName approach
        Class c = Class.forName( "TickerTape" );
        TickerTape tape1 = (TickerTape) c.newInstance();
        top.add( "Center", tape1 );
        tape1.init();
        tape1.start();
        serializeBean( tape1 );
        //*** Deserialization through readObject
        ObjectInputStream is =
          new ObjectInputStream( new FileInputStream( serFile ) );
        TickerTape tape2 = (TickerTape) is.readObject();
        is.close();
        mid.add( "Center", tape2 );
        tape2.init();
        tape2.setGoRight( true );
        tape2.start();
        //*** Beans.instantiate shortcut
        TickerTape tape3 =
          (TickerTape) Beans.instantiate( null, "TickerTape" );
        bot.add( "Center", tape3 );
        tape3.init();
        tape3.start();
      } catch( Exception e ) { System.err.println( e ); }
   }
```

FIGURE 10.1.2 A program that incorporates three TickerTapes.

```
   private void serializeBean( TickerTape t ) {
      try {
         ObjectOutputStream os =
            new ObjectOutputStream( new FileOutputStream( serFile ) );
         os.writeObject( t );
         os.close();
      } catch( Exception e ) { System.err.println( e ); }
   }
   private Panel top, mid, bot;
   private static final String serFile = "TickerTape.ser";
}
```

FIGURE 10.1.2   A program that incorporates three `TickerTapes`, *continued*.

The middle panel tape's `setGoRight` method is invoked with an argument of `true` so that this tape moves left to right for contrast with the tapes in the top and the bottom panels.

The ticker tape in the bottom panel is incorporated into the application by using the `java.beans.Beans` utility class's `instantiate` method

```
TickerTape tape3 =
   (TickerTape) Beans.instantiate( null, "TickerTape" );
```

The `instantiate` method looks for the named object first in a serialized file with a *ser* extension (e.g., *TickerTape.ser*) and then in a *class* file (e.g., *TickerTape.class*). The first argument specifies a class loader. If the first argument is `null`, as in this example, the system's class loader is used.

The example shows Java's flexibility with respect to incorporating beans into an application. The three approaches shown here can be used and intermixed as the situation requires. ∎

Property Change Events

The `TickerTape` applet/bean in Figure 10.1.1 has a `PropertyChangeSupport` field named `changes`

```
    private PropertyChangeSupport changes =
        new PropertyChangeSupport( this );
```

where `this` refers to the applet/bean object that encapsulates the field. The `TickerTape`'s four local properties—the *message* displayed, the *speed* at which the tape moves, the number of *cycles* the tape has made, and the *direction* in which the tape moves—are said to be **bound** because other objects can bind themselves to changes in these properties; that is, other objects can register themselves as *listeners* to `PropertyChangeEvents` that originate in a `TickerTape` object. Suppose, for example, that a `TickerTape`'s direction changes by having its `setGoRight` method

```
public void setGoRight( boolean f ) {
  boolean old = goRight; goRight = f;
  fire( "goRight", new Boolean( old ),
                    new Boolean( goRight ) );
}
```

invoked. The current value of goRight is saved in the local boolean variable old
after which goRight is assigned the parameter's value. The private method fire
is then invoked with the property's name (in this case, "goRight"), the old value
wrapped in a Boolean object, and the new value wrapped in a Boolean object. The
fire method

```
private void fire( String prop, Object old, Object obj ) {
  changes.firePropertyChange( prop, old, obj );
}
```

then invokes the PropertyChangeSupport field's method named fireProperty-
Change with the same three arguments. Any object that has registered as a listener
for a change in the bean's goRight property is thereby notified of the change. By the
way, the current implementation does not check whether the old and the new values
of a property are indeed different. This logic could be added so that listeners would be
notified only if the old and new values differed.

A listener registers for property change events by invoking the source object's ad-
dPropertyChangeListener method. An object can stop being a listener by invoking
the source object's removePropertyChangeListener. A listener must implement
the PropertyChangeListener interface and define the propertyChange method
declared in this interface. The interface belongs to the java.beans package.

■ **Example 10.1.3.**   The PropTest program in Figure 10.1.3 illustrates a
property change listener. The PropTest class implements the Property-
ChangeListener interface and defines propertyChange. The program has
two panels (see Figure 10.1.4). The bottom panel holds a TickerTape bean and
a top panel has a button that, when pushed, changes the tape's direction by causing the tape's setGoRight method to be invoked with the appropriate argument.
The PropTest object registers itself as a listener for changes in TickerTape
properties

```
tape.addPropertyChangeListener( this );
```

and changes its own background color

```
public void propertyChange( PropertyChangeEvent e ) {
  Color back = (mid.getBackground() == Color.lightGray) ?
                Color.white : Color.lightGray;
  mid.setBackground( back );
}
```

```
import java.awt.*;
import java.beans.*;
import java.io.*;
import java.awt.event.*;
class PropTest extends Frame implements PropertyChangeListener {
    public static void main( String[ ] args ) { new PropTest().test(); }
    public void propertyChange( PropertyChangeEvent e ) {
        Color back = (mid.getBackground() == Color.lightGray) ?
                      Color.white : Color.lightGray;
        mid.setBackground( back );
    }
    private void test() {
        setLayout( new BorderLayout() );
        mid = new Panel(); bot = new Panel();
        Button b = new Button( "Change Direction" );
        b.setFont( new Font( "Dialog", Font.BOLD, 14 ) );
        b.addActionListener( new ActionListener() {
            public void actionPerformed( ActionEvent e ) {
                tape.setGoRight( moveRight );
                moveRight = !moveRight;
            } } );
        mid.setLayout( new FlowLayout() );
        mid.setBackground( Color.lightGray );
        mid.add( b );
        bot.setBackground( Color.cyan );
        add( mid, BorderLayout.CENTER );
        add( bot, BorderLayout.SOUTH );
        try {
          tape = (TickerTape) Beans.instantiate( null, "TickerTape" );
          bot.add( "Center", tape );
          tape.init();
          tape.start();
          tape.addPropertyChangeListener( this );
        } catch( Exception e ) { System.err.println( e ); }
        setSize( 400, 200 );
        show();
    }
    private boolean moveRight = true;
    private TickerTape tape;
    private Panel mid, bot;
}
```

FIGURE 10.1.3   An object that listens for changes to TickerTape properties.

in response to changes in TickerTape properties. In the current implementation, PropTest changes only the *direction* of the ticker tape. Nonetheless, a change to any ticker tape property would cause propertyChange to be invoked as the callback. ∎

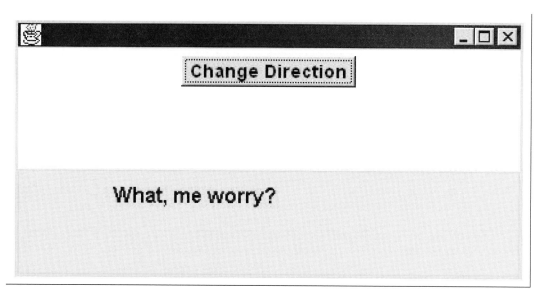

FIGURE 10.1.4   The GUI for the `PropTest` program of Figure 10.1.3.

Bound properties have a subtype known as **constrained** properties. A constrained property can change only if no listener rejects the proposed change. A listener for changes in constrained properties implements the `VetoableChangeListener` interface and defines the `vetoableChange` method declared therein. If a listener deems a proposed property change as unacceptable, the listener can veto the change by throwing a `PropertyVetoException`.

The Bean Box

The bean box is a container designed specifically for testing beans, in particular the visual editing of bean properties and the interaction of beans through event mechanisms. The bean box[†] has three main windows (see Figure 10.1.5). The left *ToolBox* window contains sample beans in JAR files. Other beans can be added to the *ToolBox* by clicking the middle window's *Load* and *Load Jar* menu items under the *File* menu. The middle window is the bean box *Container*. A bean selected from the *ToolBox* with a click can be inserted into the *Container* with another click. The right window is the *PropertySheet* for the currently selected bean in the container. In Figure 10.1.5, the *PropertySheet* lists the visually editable properties of the `TickerTape` bean, which has been inserted into the *Container*.

The bean box leverages the event model for bean interaction. Figure 10.1.6 shows the bean box's *Container* with the ubiquitous `Juggler` bean and two `ExplicitButton` beans, one of which is labeled `Start` and the other of which is labeled `Stop`. The following steps describe how the two button beans can interact with the `Juggler` bean:

[†]The Java Postscript explains how to run the bean box utility, load beans into it, and so on.

FIGURE 10.1.5 The bean box with a TickerTape bean in the container.

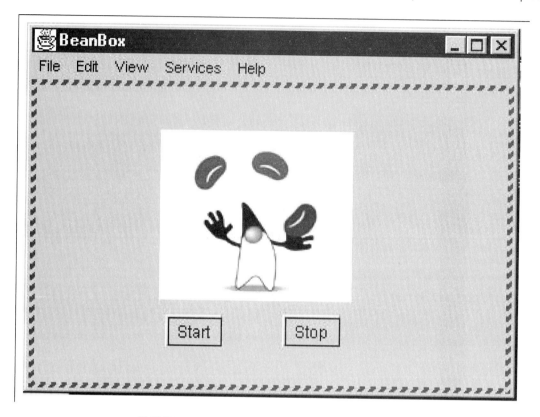

FIGURE 10.1.6   A juggler and two buttons in the bean box.

- One of the buttons (e.g., Stop) in the *Container* is selected with a click.
- Under the *Container* window's *Edit* menu, the *Events* item is clicked, which displays a list of the events that the selected button can generate. In this case, there are only two such events: a button push or a bound property change. The *button push* item is selected with a click, which causes a movable red line to appear with the selected button as its source.
- The red line is dragged onto the juggling duke and terminated there with a mouse click. A list of event callbacks appears, which includes the method stopJuggling. The choice is made with a mouse click.
- Clicking the Stop button now causes the juggler to stop juggling by invoking the Juggler's method stopJuggling.

In a similar manner, the Start button in the *Container* can be linked with the startJuggling operation of the Juggler.
   When the red line is dragged from the source bean (e.g., the Stop button bean) to the target bean (e.g., the Juggler bean), the bean box generates and compiles an *adapter class* that acts as an intermediary between the two beans (see Figure 10.1.7). In

this example, the `___Hookup_16104f7aa8` object generated by the bean box serves as a listener for `Start` button clicks. The listener then invokes the `Juggler` object's `startJuggling` method. The adapter class maps a source object's event (e.g., a push of the `Start` button) to a listener's callback (e.g., the `startJuggling` method encapsulated in the `Juggler`). The mechanism for bean interaction thus builds directly on Java's event model.

```
// Automatically generated event hookup file.
package tmp.sunw.beanbox;
import sunw.demo.juggler.Juggler;
import java.awt.event.ActionListener;
import java.awt.event.ActionEvent;
public class ___Hookup_16104f7aa8 implements
          java.awt.event.ActionListener, java.io.Serializable {
    public void setTarget(sunw.demo.juggler.Juggler t) {
        target = t;
    }
    public void actionPerformed(java.awt.event.ActionEvent arg0) {
        target.startJuggling(arg0);
    }
    private sunw.demo.juggler.Juggler target;
}
```

FIGURE 10.1.7   An adapter class generated to enable bean interaction.

Enterprise Java Beans

The Java 2 language is available in three development platforms, which differ in the scope of application domain for which the platform is suited. The platforms are

- **Java 2 Platform Micro Edition (J2ME).** This is the development platform for relatively small digital devices such as Palm Pilots and pagers. The virtual machine associated with J2ME is the KVM, a lightweight version of the JVM.

- **Java 2 Platform Standard Edition (J2SE).** This is the development platform for the standard JDK programming. The platform includes support for networking, graphics, multithreading, security, and so forth.

- **Java 2 Platform Enterprise Edition (J2EE).** This is the development platform for component-based applications on an enterprise scale. The J2EE extends the J2SE to support distributed computing for an enterprise—that is, for a large, diverse, and complex distributed environment. In particular, J2EE supports the deployment of components through application servers and the integration of Java components with enterprise-level technologies such as e-mail, messaging, and XML (**EX**tensible **M**arkup **L**anguage), a standard for structuring the content of electronic documents.

The J2EE platform addresses the special requirements that arise in the delivery of
components to applications spread across a large enterprise, which typically includes a
wide range of platforms, services, technologies, protocols, and vendors. In particular,
J2EE provides middleware infrastructure that allows clients to obtain services from
location-transparent components. EJBs (**E**nterprise **J**ava **B**eans) are precisely these
components, that is, the location-transparent components that servers provide for
enterprise-level applications. The distinctive feature of EJBs is thus their development
and deployment in the large, complex domain of enterprise computing. As the name
suggests, EJB extends bean technology to large-scale distributed systems.

EXERCISES

1. What is meant by a *software component*?
2. What is the Java term for a *software component*?
3. Why does it make sense for AWT and Swing set components such as buttons, lists,
   and checkboxes to be serializable?
4. Given the class declaration

   ```
   class C {
       public String getMys() { /*...*/ }
       private void setMys( String s ) { /*...*/ }
       //...
   }
   ```

   explain what *property* the pair of methods defines.
5. In Exercise 4, is the property *readable*, *writable*, or *both*?
6. Explain briefly why a bean should be serializable.
7. Explain briefly how a property change can be used for communication between
   two beans.
8. What is a *bound* property?
9. What is a *constrained* property?
10. Explain the basic purpose of the bean box utility.
11. Test the bean box utility by loading sample beans such as the Juggler and an
    ExplicitButton. In particular, make the beans interact.
12. What is an EJB?

10.2   Security and Cryptography

In a distributed system, modules such as applets or serialized objects may move from a
source machine to a target machine, thereby compromising the target machine whether
deliberately or inadvertently. A module that migrates to a target machine could tie

up resources such as the CPU, erase files, introduce viruses, or cause other mischief. In a distributed system, security is thus a critical issue. Even nondistributed systems may have security requirements, of course. Java's security constructs can be applied to distributed and local systems.

Java addresses security issues at various levels and with a variety of programming constructs. This section investigates the major security constructs and explains how encryption can contribute to system security.

Basic Security Constructs

Although this section focuses on the security manager and the closely related access controller, a brief look at all of the security mechanisms can provide context. Java supports security at various levels, some of which are already familiar:

- **Object-oriented design**. The private, package, and protected access modes can be used to restrict the visibility of class members. A well-designed class makes public only the members—typically constructors and high-level methods—required to deliver the class's core functionality. Low-level implementation details are hidden, thus reducing the security risks in such details. Good class design supports information hiding, which in turn can contribute to security. Further, classes themselves can be restricted in scope to the package in which they occur. In a class library implemented as a package, for example, only the main classes need to be given public scope. Information hiding at the member and class level represents a first level of security.

- **Compiler**. The compiler tests whether source code obeys the syntactic constraints that define Java. For example, the compiler ensures that uninitialized local variables are not used as source expressions in assignments, that invalid casts such as int to Object or boolean to int are not performed, that an object invoke only the methods encapsulated in it, and so forth. This level of security, often taken for granted, is an important defense against inadvertent security breaches.

- **Bytecode verifier**. The JVM has a bytecode verifier that performs run-time checks on the bytecodes of all classes except those in Java's core packages. For example, the bytecode verifier checks that a *class* file loaded into the JVM has the correct format, that every class except Object has exactly one superclass, that invalid run-time casts or other data conversions do not occur, that method invocations are type safe, and so forth. Although the bytecode verifier cannot be made foolproof, it provides run-time assurance that executed instructions satisfy fundamental language constraints.

- **Class loader**. The class loader works closely with the security manager to enforce security policy. For example, when the class loader loads an applet *class* over a network connection, the class loader notifies the security manager, which in turn enforces the appropriate security restrictions. An applet thus cannot write to the local disk or open a network connection except to the host from which the applet came.

- **Security manager**. The security manager determines at run time which operations a program should be allowed to perform and prevents a program from performing proscribed operations. The security manager uses an **access controller** to implement a security policy in intuitive terms such as permissions and policies. For the programmer, there are advantages of articulating and implementing a security policy through an access controller rather than directly through a security manager. In any case, the security manager and its access controller provide flexible mechanisms that the programmer can use to articulate and enforce security policies.

The major security constructs have class representations. For example, the java.lang package provides a SecurityManager class and the java.security package and subpackages provide classes such as AccessController, Policy, and Permission. The programmer can even enforce security at the class loader level. The java.lang package has a ClassLoader class and the java.security package has a SecureClassLoader class that can be extended. This subsection focuses on programmable security at the higher level of the security manager and access controller.

Finally, security *within* Java determines the operations that the JVM can perform. The host platform's underlying security cannot be disabled through Java security. For example, a host operating system commonly restricts access to selected files. Such restrictions cannot be set aside through Java's security constructs. In effect, Java security allows the programmer to impose *additional* security restrictions on Java programs.

The Security Manager

Program types differ with respect to security managers. An applet normally runs under the browser's security manager, which prohibits the applet from, for instance, reading or writing the local disk. An RMI application requires a security manager, whereas a general Java *application* does not require any security manager at all.

■ **Example 10.2.1.** The AppletEx applet in Figure 10.2.1 throws an Access-ControlException, a subtype of SecurityException, because the applet tries to open a file. When launched with the *appletviewer* utility, the error message is

```
java.security.AccessControlException: access denied
(java.io.FilePermission noChance.dat write)
```

A general Java *application* normally has no security manager, although the programmer can invoke the System class's setSecurityManager method to provide

```
import java.applet.*;
import java.io.*;
public class AppletEx extends Applet {
   public void init() {
      try {
         FileOutputStream os = new FileOutputStream( "noChance.dat" );
         os.close();
      } catch( IOException e ) { System.err.println( e ); }
   }
}
```

FIGURE 10.2.1   An applet that throws an `AccessControlException`.

an application with a security manager. By default, then, an application can perform any operation that the host system permits. The `SecurityManager` class can be extended to make a Java *application* behave more like an applet.

■ **Example 10.2.2.**   The `SecureApplication` program in Figure 10.2.2, which is a Java *application* rather than an applet, throws a `SecurityException` and generates the error message

```
Exception in thread "main" java.lang.SecurityException:
No file writing allowed!
```

because the application tries to open a `FileOutputStream`. The application's `MySecurity` class extends `SecurityManager` and overrides the latter's two overloads of `checkWrite`, a method that checks whether the application should be allowed to write to a file. The `SecurityManager` class has various other check methods such as `checkRead` and `checkPrintJobAccess` that throw a `SecurityException` if the specified operation is disallowed.

The application invokes the `System` class's `static` method `setSecurityManager`

```
MySecurity ms = new MySecurity();
System.setSecurityManager( ms );
```

with a `MySecurity` object as the argument, which sets the application's `SecurityManager` to a `MySecurity` object. Once an application's security manager has been set, typically as the first statement in `main`, the security manager cannot be reset. Before attempting to write to the local disk, the application invokes the security manager's `checkWrite` method, which throws a `SecurityException` in order to prevent writing. In this security respect, the *application* in Figure 10.2.2 behaves like the applet in Figure 10.2.1.

```
import java.io.*;
class SecureApplication {
   public static void main( String[ ] args ) {
      MySecurity ms = new MySecurity();
      System.setSecurityManager( ms );
      try {
        String fileName = "noChance.dat";
        FileOutputStream os = new FileOutputStream( fileName );
        ms.checkWrite( fileName ); //**** SecurityException thrown
        //...writing never occurs
        os.close(); //...never occurs
      } catch( IOException e ) { System.err.println( e ); }
   }
}
class MySecurity extends SecurityManager {
   public void checkWrite( String fileName ) {
      disallow();
   }
   public void checkWrite( FileDescriptor fileDes ) {
      disallow();
   }
   private void disallow() throws SecurityException {
      throw new SecurityException( "No file writing allowed!" );
   }
}
```

FIGURE 10.2.2   An application that is not allowed to write to the local disk.

Example 10.2.3.   An RMI client application requires a security manager. For example, the RMI client in Figure 9.6.2 sets a security manager

```
System.setSecurityManager( new RMISecurityManager() );
```

as the first statement in main.

The Access Controller

Example 10.2.2 illustrates how an application's security might be managed by extending the SecurityManager class and overriding the appropriate check methods. Java 2's introduction of the **access controller** supports a more intuitive customization of security, however. The java.security package's AccessController class represents an access controller, which has three main roles:

- **Access to critical system resources**. The access controller determines whether a program should have access to critical system resources such as the file system or sockets. An underlying *security policy* determines whether a program has *permission* for such access. For example, a browser might enforce a sandbox security policy on applets by not allowing them to read or write the local file system, to execute another program, to open a network connection to an arbitrary host, and so forth.

- **Privileged code**. The access controller can be used to mark code segments as *privileged*, which impacts the access permissions accorded such code. For example, privileged code might be allowed to write the local file system, whereas other code would not be given such access.

- **Context management**. The access controller can obtain and save a "snapshot" of a program's current execution context so that this saved context can be used to make access decisions. Suppose, for example, that a program is multithreaded and that thread T_1 takes a "snapshot" S of the current execution environment. Some other thread T_2, executing in an altogether different context, could check access permissions against the saved S rather than against T_2's own execution context. In different terms, particular code segments might be *privileged* in one context but not in another. Access control thus can be tailored even to programs that have sophisticated security requirements.

The `AccessController` class has intuitive methods such as `getContext`, `checkPermission`, and `doPrivileged` that support security customization. Further, the access controller allows security policy to be set through text files of the sort illustrated in an earlier RMI example (see Section 9.6). The concept of a *permission* is central to the access controller.

Permissions

A **permission** allows a program to perform an operation. The abstract class `Permission` (in `java.security`) and its concrete subclasses such as `FilePermission` (in `java.io`) are used to indicate whether a program has permission to perform a particular operation. In general, a `Permission` has three properties:

- **Type**. Permissions differ by type such as `FilePermission` and `Socket-Permission`. For example, the statement

```
FilePermission rw =
  new FilePermission( "Foo.class", "read,write" );
```

constructs a `FilePermission` object, whereas the statement

```
SocketPermission sp =
  new SocketPermssion( "condor:2048", "connect" );
```

constructs a `SocketPermission` object. The abstract `Permission` class and its subclasses can be extended to articulate permissions appropriate to a particular application.

- **Target Name**. A permission target has a symbolic name, which differs in syntax depending on the permission type. For example, the target name of a `FilePermission` can be a file's name. In the statement

```
FilePermission rw =
   new FilePermission( "Foo.class", "read,write" );
```

the named target is the file *Foo.class*. By contrast, the target name of a `SocketPermission` is a *hostname:port* pair such as *condor:2048*, where *condor* maps to an IP address such as 140.192.2.8. In the statement

```
SocketPermission sp =
   new SocketPermssion( "condor:2048", "connect" );
```

the named target is port *2048* on host *condor*.

- **Permitted Actions**. The syntax of permitted actions depends on the particular permission. For example, the statement

```
FilePermission rw =
   new FilePermission( "Foo.class", "read, write" );
```

enables *read* and *write* actions on the named target *Foo.class*. However, the statement does not grant permission to *delete* the file. Some permissions do not have explicitly named actions because a particular action is implied by the target. For example, the statement

```
RuntimePermission halt =
   new RuntimePermission( "exitVM" );
```

has exiting the JVM as a named target but does not explicitly specify an action, in this case the implied action of halting the JVM. If a permission is boolean in nature, then explicit actions are not provided. For example, a program can either exit the JVM or it cannot. The named target `exitVM` therefore does not require an explicit list of two actions. By contrast, the named target of a file permission has many possible combinations of action: readable only, readable and writable, writable only, and so on.

Example 10.2.4. The `RunAndCopy` application in Figure 10.2.3 invokes the Runtime class's `static` method `getRuntime` and this class's instance method `exec` to execute, as a separate process, a program whose name is given as a command-line argument. In a Windows environment, for example, the name of a file with an *exe* extension could be given as a command-line argument. After executing the program, the `RunAndCopy` application then copies the executable file to another file whose name is given as a second command-line argument. Given the executable file *welcome.exe*, the command

```
$ java RunAndCopy welcome.exe welcome.bak
```

```
import java.io.*;
class RunAndCopy {
   public static void main( String[ ] args ) {
      if ( args.length < 2 ) {
        System.err.println( "java RunAndCopy <program file> " +
                                            "<destination file>" );
        return;
      }
      try {
         Runtime.getRuntime().exec( args[ 0 ] );
         FileInputStream in = new FileInputStream( args[ 0 ] );
         FileOutputStream out = new FileOutputStream( args[ 1 ] );
         int next;
         while ( (next = in.read()) != -1 )
            out.write( next );
         in.close(); out.close();
      } catch( Exception e ) { System.err.println( e ); }
   }
}
```

FIGURE 10.2.3   An application that executes another program.

would execute the *welcome* program and then copy the file *welcome.exe* to the file *welcome.bak*.

Suppose that the RunAndCopy application were run under password protection. Some passwords would allow RunAndCopy to execute but not copy a program, whereas other passwords would allow the application to execute and copy a program. Various security approaches could be taken. The RunAndCopySecure program in Figure 10.2.4 uses the access controller and FilePermissions. A FilePermission extends the abstract Permission class, as do related concrete classes such as BasicPermission and SocketPermission. Among the methods that these subclasses implement is getActions, which returns a string representation of the permitted actions. Depending on the password, the RunAndCopySecure application constructs a FilePermission whose target should be an executable file and whose permitted actions are some fix of read, write, execute, and delete. For example, the statement

```
FilePermission fp =
  new FilePermission( "welcome.exe", "ExecuTe, rEAD" );
```

gives read and execute permissions on the target file *welcome.exe*. The subsequent statement

```
fp.getActions();
```

```
import java.io.*;
class RunAndCopySecure {
   public static void main( String[ ] args ) {
      if ( args.length < 2 ) {
         System.err.println( "java RunAndCopy <password> " +
                  "<program file> <destination file>" );
         return;
      }
      RunAndCopySecure self = new RunAndCopySecure();
      self.actOnPermissions( self.getPermission( args[ 0 ] ),
                                 args[ 1 ], args[ 2 ] );
   }
   private void actOnPermissions( int permission,
                                 String src, String dst ) {
      if ( permission == Run )
        fp = new FilePermission( src, "execute" );
      else if ( permission == RunCopy )
        fp = new FilePermission( src, "read,execute" );
      if ( fp == null ) { //*** no permissions at all
        System.err.println( "No permission to run and copy " + src );
        return;
      }
      try {
         if ( fp.getActions().endsWith( "execute" ) )
           Runtime.getRuntime().exec( src );
         if ( fp.getActions().startsWith( "read,execute" ) ) {
           FileInputStream in = new FileInputStream( src );
           FileOutputStream out = new FileOutputStream( dst );
           int next;
           while ( (next = in.read()) != -1 )
             out.write( next );
           in.close(); out.close();
         }
      } catch( Exception e ) { System.err.println( e ); }
   }
   private int getPermission( String password ) {
      if ( password.equals( "Manon" ) )
        return Run;
      else if ( password.equals( "Isolde" ) )
        return RunCopy;
      else
        return None;
   }
}
```

FIGURE 10.2.4 A program that illustrates a FilePermission.

```
    private final static int None  =    -1;
    private final static int Run   =    -2;
    private final static int RunCopy = -3;
    private FilePermission fp; //*** null by default
}
```

FIGURE 10.2.4   A program that illustrates a `FilePermission`, *continued.*

would return the string `read,execute`. The `getActions` method returns the permissions in a canonical order and representation. As the example shows, the permissions are returned in *lowercase* and the canonical order is `read,write,execute,delete` with commas separating the terms. To enable execution of a program named in a command-line argument, the application gives `execute` permission. To enable copying of the executed program, the application gives `read,execute` permission on the *source* file, which is the file in which the executed program resides.   ■

There are standard `Permissions`, each implemented as a concrete class. The concrete permission classes reside in packages appropriate to the permission types. For instance, `FilePermission` is in the `java.io` package, whereas `SocketPermission` is in the `java.net` package. Figure 10.2.5 lists many of the common permission classes. In the figure, permissions without actions such as `RuntimePermission` have *yes* and *no* listed in the *Action* column. Recall that a `RuntimePermission` such as `exitVM` is either allowed or not allowed so that such a permission has no explicit actions associated with a target operation.

Class	*Target*	*Actions*
`java.awt.AWTPermission`	Graphics	*yes, no*
`java.io.FilePermission`	Files	Read, write, delete, execute.
`java.io.SerializablePermission`	Objects	*yes, no*
`java.lang.ReflectPermission`	Operations	*yes, no*
`java.lang.RuntimePermission`	Operations	*yes, no*
`java.net.NetPermission`	Authentications	*yes, no*
`java.net.SocketPermission`	Sockets	Accept, connect, listen, resolve
`java.security.AllPermission`	All	*yes, no*
`java.security.AbstractPermssion`	NA	Abstract parent class
`java.security BasicPermission`	All	Standard named permission
`java.security.SecurityPermission`	Operations	*yes, no*
`java.security.UnresolvedPermission`	Policies	*yes, no*
`java.util.PropertyPermission`	Properties	Read (get), write (set)

FIGURE 10.2.5   The standard `Permission` classes. NA means *Not Applicable.*

Security Policy Files

A **security policy** is a set of permissions applied to a set of programs. Security policy typically takes into account a program's *source*. For example, an applet downloaded from a remote host typically has fewer permissions than an application residing on the local machine. The same security policy thus can treat an applet in one way with respect to security permissions and an application in an altogether different way.

Although the `java.security.Policy` class that encapsulates a security policy can be extended, a more straightforward and intuitive way to articulate and implement a security policy is through *security policy files*. Two files are particularly important:

- *java.security*. This is a text file with extensive documentation (marked by the symbol # as the first character in a line) for about a half dozen statements, the most important of which are shown in Figure 10.2.6. The five statements

```
# List of providers and their preference orders:
security.provider.1=sun.security.provider.Sun
# Name of class file to instantiate Policy object:
policy.provider=sun.security.provider.PolicyFile

# Default is a single system-wide policy file in user's home directory:
policy.url.1=file:${java.home}/lib/security/java.policy
policy.url.2=file:${user.home}/.java.policy

# Allow specification of policy file with -D command-line option:
policy.allowSystemProperty=true
```

FIGURE 10.2.6   Important statements in the *java.security* file.

in Figure 10.2.6 are in three groups, with blank lines separating the groups for ease of reference. The statements in each group can be clarified as follows:

- The first statement sets the default security provider, in this case Sun. Typically only one security provider is named, although the multiple providers can be listed and ordered 1, 2,. . . , *N*.
- The second statement specifies Sun's *PolicyFile.class* as the class file from which a `Policy` object is to be instantiated. The `Policy` object, in turn, represents the system's security policy.
- The third and fourth statements specify the location of the *system-wide* and the *user* security policy files, respectively. The user's security file resides by default in the user's home directory.
- The last statement indicates that the *first* security file to be read is a file specified on the command line with the -D option. For example, the sample RMI client in Section 9.6 was executed with the command

```
java -Djava.security.policy=Hello.policy HelloClient
```

where *Hello.policy* is a security file. (The syntax of security files is explained shortly.) In this example, the *Hello.policy* file thus states the security policy for the `HelloClient`'s execution.

- *java.policy*. The default policy file determines the permissions for code sources. For example, the *Hello.policy* file for the sample RMI client in Section 9.6

```
grant {
   permission java.security.AllPermission;
};
```

grants `AllPermissions` to the client. By contrast, a policy file entry such as

```
grant codeBase http://condor.depaul.edu/applets/ {
   permission java.io.FilePermission
      "${user.home}${/}localDir${/}-", "read", "write";
};
```

specifies that code loaded from the *applets* directory on the machine *condor.depaul.edu* is allowed to read and write files on the user's *localDir* directory. Granting *write* permissions to applets is risky, of course. Figure 10.2.7 lists some of the default *java.policy* file that comes with Java 2. Note that this policy file grants all code the permission to invoke `Thread.stop` but recommends that the permission be revoked (see Java Postscript, Chapter 8).

The -D option means that a security policy can be tailored to each program, if necessary. Caution dictates that the system-wide security file should be relatively strict, with -D security files providing relief as necessary.

Cryptography

Cryptography is the science of secret writing in which an original message in *plaintext* is transformed into *ciphertext*. The transformation is such that a special piece of information known as a **key** must be used to decrypt the encrypted message. **Cryptanalysis** is the science of breaking ciphers. **Cryptology** is the discipline that combines cryptography and cryptanalysis.

Cryptography has various uses within the broad field of computer security and the even broader field of information security. This subsection focuses on Java support for **digital signatures** in a distributed environment. Consider the case in which a client machine *C* is to download a program *P* from a host machine *S*, which is a *trusted source* from which to download programs. *C* needs to verify that *P* comes from *S* rather than, for example, a server pretending to be *S*. A digital signature can be used to assure *C* that *P* indeed comes from *S*.

```
grant {
   // Allows any thread to stop itself using the java.lang.Thread.stop()
   // method that takes no argument.
   // Note that this permission is granted by default only to remain
   // backwards compatible.
   // It is strongly recommended that you either remove this permission
   // from this policy file or further restrict it to code sources
   // that you specify, because Thread.stop() is potentially unsafe.
   // See "http://java.sun.com/notes" for more information.
   permission java.lang.RuntimePermission "stopThread";
   // allows anyone to listen on un-privileged ports
   permission java.net.SocketPermission "localhost:1024-", "listen";
   // "standard" properties that can be read by anyone
   permission java.util.PropertyPermission "java.version", "read";
   permission java.util.PropertyPermission "java.vendor", "read";
   permission java.util.PropertyPermission "java.vendor.url", "read";
   //... other properties
   permission java.util.PropertyPermission "java.vm.vendor", "read";
   permission java.util.PropertyPermission "java.vm.name", "read";
};
```

FIGURE 10.2.7   Part of the default *java.policy* file.

Message Digests and Digital Signatures

The `java.security` package has classes that encapsulate security mechanisms such as message digests and digital signatures. Because a digital signature is an *encrypted* message digest, the discussion begins with message digests. As the name suggests, a **message digest** produces a short or "digested" form of message data. The class `java.security.MessageDigest` encapsulates a message digest.

■ **Example 10.2.5.**   The `Digest` program in Figure 10.2.8 creates a message digest for a file named as a command-line argument. A `MessageDigest` object

```
md = MessageDigest.getInstance( "MD5" );
```

is constructed by invoking the `static` method `getInstance` with the name of message digest algorithm, in this case MD5 (**M**esssage **D**igest Version **5**). The program reads bytes from the input file into the buffer `buf` and then updates the message digest's input data

```
md.update( buf );
```

with the contents of the input buffer and writes the digest to an output file

```
out.write( md.digest() );
```

```
import java.io.*;
import java.security.*;
public class Digest {
    public static void main( String[ ] args ) {
        if ( args.length < 1 ) {
            System.err.println( "java Digest <name of file to digest>" );
            return;
        }
        MessageDigest md = null;
        try {
            md = MessageDigest.getInstance( "MD5" );
        } catch( NoSuchAlgorithmException e ) { System.err.println( e ); }
        byte[ ] buf = new byte[ 4096 ];
        int n = 0, k = 0;
        try {
            FileInputStream in = new FileInputStream( args[ 0 ] );
            while ( (n = in.read( buf )) != -1 )
                k += n;
            md.update( buf );
            in.close();
            FileOutputStream out =
                new FileOutputStream( args[ 0 ] + ".DIGEST" );
            out.write( md.digest() );
            out.close();
        } catch( IOException e ) { System.err.println( e ); }
        System.out.println( "Digest from " + args[ 0 ] + " with " + k +
                    " bytes using " + md.getAlgorithm() + " has " +
                    md.getDigestLength() + " bytes." );
    }
}
```

FIGURE 10.2.8   A program to illustrate a `MessageDigest`.

The digest's `getAlgorithm` and `getDigestLength` methods are used to print information about the process to the standard output. On a sample run, the file *Digest.class* with 1,603 bytes yielded a digest of 16 bytes. On another sample run, the file *hi.exe* with 53,248 bytes also yielded a digest of 16 bytes. Whatever the byte length of the input file, the MD5 digest has a fixed length of 16 bytes.   ■

In technical language, a message digest is a *secure one-way function* that takes the arbitrary-size data of the message as input and produces a fixed-length hash value as output. The *one-way* attribute means that the original message cannot be recomputed directly from the digest even if the underlying digest algorithm is known.

A message digest illustrates the principle of identifying a message with a special byte sequence, that is, the digest itself. A digital signature is an encrypted message digest so that the signature can be used to authenticate messages sent

across even insecure networks. In detail, a **digital signature** for a message is constructed by

  • Generating a message digest from input data.
  • Encrypting the message digest using a key.

The encrypted message digest is the digital signature. The `Signature` class's methods
hide these implementation details. In particular, the `Signature` hides the underlying
message digest that is encrypted to form the digital signature. Figure 10.2.9 illustrates
the process.

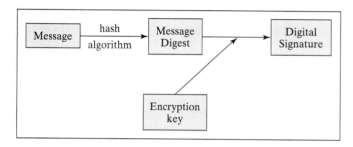

FIGURE 10.2.9   Generating a
digital signature from a message
digest and key.

Private and Public Key Systems

The encryption key is critical for constructing digital signatures. A good key has
mathematical properties that give it high security value, although the specific properties
differ across encryption systems. For example, in a **secret key** or **symmetric key** system,
a key should have properties that make it extremely difficult to guess or forge. A
secret key system has the disadvantage that the sender and receiver of an encrypted
message must either share the same key or have keys that are derivable from each
other. Alternative systems rely upon key pairs, one used for encryption and the other
used for decryption. Such systems are called **public key** systems. Standard digital
signature algorithms such as DSA (**D**igital **S**ignature **A**lgorithm) and RSA (**R**ivest
Shamir **A**dleman) rely upon key pairs for signature generation and verification.
    Public key systems are convenient in that a *public* key can be published globally
without compromising security. Suppose that person P publishes a public key globally.
Anyone wishing to send a sensitive message M to P encrypts M using P's public key.
P retains a *private* key that alone can decrypt M. Note that P's private key need
not—indeed, should not—be published. For digital signatures, the same principle
applies. Suppose that sender S transmits a digitally signed message M to receiver R,
who needs to authenticate that M comes from S. S signs M with a digital signature
generated with S's *private* key. R then uses S's *public* key to verify the signature, that is,
to verify that M comes from S. S can publish the public key so that M, in principle, can
be broadcast globally and all receivers can use S's public key to verify that M comes
from S.

Generating and Verifying a Digital Signature

The `java.security` package has high-level support for digital signatures. The package's `Signature` class is an **engine class** for digital signatures, that is, an abstract class that specifies the desired functionality but does not provide an implementation of a particular algorithm such as DSA or RSA. The package also provides a `KeyPair` class as well as `PublicKey` and `PrivateKey` interfaces. These classes and interfaces simplify the task of authenticating code such as applets through digital signatures. Before working through an example, it may be useful to summarize the steps required for generating and verifying a digital signature:

- The `KeyPairGenerator` class's `getInstance` method is used to get a key pair generator for a particular algorithm such as DSA. This generator can be initialized with, for example, a `SecureRandom` number.
- The `KeyPairGenerator`'s instance method `generateKeyPair` is invoked to get a `KeyPair`, which in turn has `getPrivate` and `getPublic` methods to access the private and public keys in the pair.
- The sender's *private* key is used to *generate* a digital signature.

  - The `Signature` class's `static` method `getInstance` is invoked to get a `Signature` object for a particular algorithm such as DSA or RSA.
  - The `Signature`'s instance method `initSign` is invoked with a `PrivateKey` argument to initialize the digital signature.
  - The `Signature`'s instance method `update` provides the input for the message digest that, once encrypted, is the digital signature.
  - The `Signature`'s instance method `sign` is invoked to convert the signature into an array of `bytes`, which then can be transmitted to a receiver through, for example, a socket.

- The sender's *public* key, once distributed to potential recipients of messages from the sender, is used to *verify* the digital signature.

  - The `Signature` class's `static` method `getInstance` again is invoked to get a `Signature` object that represents a named signature algorithm.
  - The `Signature` object's instance method `initVerify` is invoked to initialize the signature object with a `PublicKey` argument.
  - The `Signature` object's instance method `update` again is invoked to provide the data for the message digest, which in encrypted form is the digital signature. The sender and the receiver must invoke `update` on the *same* input data in order for the receiver to verify the sender's signature.
  - The `Signature` object's instance method `verify` is invoked on the signature that the sender transmits. The method returns `true`, if the signature constructed with the private key (i.e., the sender's computed signature) matches the signature constructed with the public key (i.e., the receiver's computed signature), and `false`, if the two signatures do not match.

Examples now can illustrate the process of generating, using, and verifying a digital signature.

```
import java.security.*;
import java.io.*;
public class MakeKeyPair {
   public static void main( String[ ] args ) {
      if ( args.length < 1 ) {
        System.err.println(
            "java MakeKeyPair <save file (no extension)>" );
        return;
      }
      try {
        //*** Generate a key pair
        KeyPairGenerator kpg = KeyPairGenerator.getInstance( alg );
        kpg.initialize( keyLen );
        KeyPair pair = kpg.generateKeyPair();
        //*** Serialize the pair.
        ObjectOutputStream os =
          new ObjectOutputStream( new FileOutputStream( args[ 0 ] +
                                  ".ser" ) );
        os.writeObject( pair );
        os.close();
        System.out.println( "Pair written to " + args[ 0 ] + ".ser" );
      } catch( NoSuchAlgorithmException e ) { System.err.println( e ); }
        catch( IOException e ) { System.err.println( e ); }
   }
   private static final int    keyLen = 1024;
   private static final String alg = "DSA";
}
```

FIGURE 10.2.10 A program that generates and serializes a KeyPair.

■ **Example 10.2.6.** The MakeKeyPair program in Figure 10.2.10 above generates and serializes a key pair. The program first gets an instance of a KeyPairGenerator for the DSA algorithm and then initializes the generator by specifying a key size of 1,024 bits. In general, the longer the key is, the more secure the key is. Next a KeyPair is generated and serialized to a file whose name is given as a command-line argument. ■

■ **Example 10.2.7.** The AdviceServer program in Figure 10.2.11 is a socket-based, investment advice server. When the server accepts a client request for advice, the server serializes a digitally signed InvestAdvice object to the client socket. In a more realistic implementation, the server would require confirmation that the client was registered to receive advice.

```java
import java.net.*;
import java.util.*;
import java.io.*;
import java.security.*;
class AdviceServer {
  public static void main( String[ ] args ) {
    try {
      //*** Create a digital signature for the data to be sent
      Signature ds = Signature.getInstance( "DSA" );
      //** get the private key from the serialized key pair
      ObjectInputStream is =
        new ObjectInputStream( new FileInputStream( keyFile ) );
      KeyPair kp = (KeyPair) is.readObject();
      is.close();
      //** initialize the signature with the private key
      ds.initSign( kp.getPrivate() );
      //** update and sign the data
      ds.update( whatToDo.getBytes() );
      byte[ ] sig = ds.sign();
      //** construct an InvestAdvice object for clients
      InvestAdvice ia = new InvestAdvice( whatToDo, sig );
      ServerSocket sSock = new ServerSocket( port );
      while ( true ) { //** service clients indefinitely
          Socket sock = sSock.accept();
          ObjectOutputStream os =
            new ObjectOutputStream( sock.getOutputStream() );
          os.writeObject( ia ); os.flush(); sock.close();
      }
    } catch( ClassNotFoundException e ) { System.err.println( e ); }
      catch( InvalidKeyException e ) { System.err.println( e ); }
      catch( SignatureException e ) { System.err.println( e ); }
      catch( SocketException e ) { System.err.println( e ); }
      catch( NoSuchAlgorithmException e ) { System.err.println( e ); }
      catch( IOException e ) { System.err.println( e ); }
  }
  private final static int port = 9876;
  private final static String whatToDo = "Buy low, sell high!";
  private final static String keyFile = "kp.ser";
}
class InvestAdvice implements Serializable {
  public InvestAdvice( String a, byte[ ] s ) {
     setAdvice( a ); setSignature( s );
  }
```

FIGURE 10.2.11   A program that sends a digitally signed message.

```
    public void setAdvice( String s ) { adv = s; }
    public String getAdvice() { return adv; }
    public void setSignature( byte[ ] s ) { sig = s; }
    public byte[ ] getSignature() { return sig; }
    private String adv;
    private byte[ ] sig;
}
```

FIGURE 10.2.11   A program that sends a digitally signed message, *continued*.

The program creates a digital signature using the DSA algorithm. A KeyPair is deserialized so that the digital signature can be initialized with the Private key from the pair

```
ds.initSign( kp.getPrivate() );
```

where ds is a reference to the Signature. (For this example, the deserialized KeyPair is the pair serialized by the MakeKeyPair program in Figure 10.2.10.) The digital signature is updated with the data to be sent, in this example, the bytes from a String that represents that advice:

```
ds.update( whatToDo.getBytes() );
byte[ ] sig = ds.sign();
```

At present, all clients receive the same investment advice: *Buy low, sell high!*. The program has six catch statements to highlight which exceptions can be thrown. ∎

■ **Example 10.2.8.**   The AdviceClient program in Figure 10.2.12 is a client for the investment advice server in Figure 10.2.11. With respect to signature generation, the main difference between the server and the client is that the server invokes initSign to initialize the signature with the server's *private* key, whereas the client invokes initVerify with the server's *public* key. After initializing the signature and providing the signature's input data with a call to update, the client then calls verify to check whether the server's transmitted signature matches the signature that the client generated.

Example 10.2.8 does not explain how the public key from the server's KeyPair is distributed to the client, a critical step in client authentication. In some cases, a technology as simple as e-mail is used to distributed public keys to clients. The Java 2 packages provide more sophisticated support for key distribution. For a discussion of key distribution and related key management issues, see Scott Ochs, *Java Security* (Cambridge: O'Reilly and Associates, 1998).

```java
import java.net.*;
import java.io.*;
import java.security.*;
class AdviceClient {
  public static void main( String[ ] args ) {
     if ( args.length < 1 ) {
       System.err.println( "AdviceClient <IP address of server>" );
       return;
     }
     try {
       Socket sock = new Socket( args[ 0 ], port );
       ObjectInputStream ois =
          new ObjectInputStream( sock.getInputStream() );
       InvestAdvice adv = (InvestAdvice) ois.readObject();
       sock.close();
       //*** get the KeyPair and use the Public key
       ObjectInputStream is =
        new ObjectInputStream( new FileInputStream( keyFile ) );
       KeyPair kp = (KeyPair) is.readObject();
       is.close();
       //*** verify the signature
       Signature ds = Signature.getInstance( "DSA" );
       ds.initVerify( kp.getPublic() );
       ds.update( adv.getAdvice().getBytes() );
       if ( ds.verify( adv.getSignature() ) )
         System.out.println( "Signature verified. Advice is\n*** " +
                             adv.getAdvice() );
       else
         System.out.println( "Verification failed. No advice." );
     } catch( Exception e ) { System.err.println( e ); }
  }
  private static final int port = 9876;
  private static final String keyFile = "kp.ser";
}
class InvestAdvice implements Serializable {
  public InvestAdvice( String a, byte[ ] s ) {
     setAdvice( a ); setSignature( s );
  }
  public void setAdvice( String s ) { adv = s; }
  public String getAdvice() { return adv; }
  public void setSignature( byte[ ] s ) { sig = s; }
  public byte[ ] getSignature() { return sig; }
  private String adv;
  private byte[ ] sig;
}
```

FIGURE 10.2.12   A client for the investment advice server in
Figure 10.2.11.

The Java Cryptography Extension

The `java.security` package provides thorough support for security in general
and partial support for cryptography in particular. Because of U.S. export control
regulations, implementations of encryption algorithms, key exchange mechanisms, and
message authentication codes are packaged separately in the JCE (**J**ava **C**ryptography
Extension). So the `java.security` package and JCE together support cryptography
in Java.

EXERCISES

   1. Does the bytecode verifier perform compile-time or run-time security checks?
   2. What is the relationship between a security manager and an access controller?
   3. Does a Java *application* other than an RMI application require a security manager?
   4. Can the programmer provide a general Java *application* with a security manager?
   5. Does an RMI application require a security manager?
   6. Test whether the `AppletEx` applet in Figure 10.2.1 throws a security exception
      when launched from a commercial browser.
   7. Confirm that the `SecureApplication` program in Figure 10.2.2 throws a security
      exception.
   8. What is the role of a *permission*?
   9. Confirm that the `RunAndCopySecure` program in Figure 10.2.4 limits permissions
      depending on the user's password.
  10. What is a *security policy*?
  11. Locate and print the *java.security* file shipped with the JDK.
  12. Locate and print the *java.policy* file shipped with the JDK.
  13. Write policy file that grants all permissions.
  14. What is *cryptography*?
  15. What is *cryptanalysis*?
  16. What is a *message digest*?
  17. Explain the relationship between a *digital signature* and a *message digest*.
  18. Briefly explain the advantage of a public key system over a private key system.
  19. Run the `Digest` program of Figure 10.2.8 several times to create message digests
      for different files. Confirm that the digests have the same byte length.
  20. In an authentication scheme using digital signatures, does the sender use a public
      or private key to sign the message?
  21. In an authentication scheme using digital signatures, does the receiver use a public
      or private key to verify a message signature?
  22. Test the investment advice server and client in Figures 10.2.11 and 10.2.12,
      respectively.

10.3   Reflection

The java.lang.Class class and the java.lang.reflect package together provide programming constructs for obtaining run-time **reflective information** about classes and objects, that is, information about a class's scope, its superclass, its members, its interfaces, and so on. This section clarifies reflection through examples.

Testing for Serializability

■ **Example 10.3.1.**   The SerializableTester utility class in Figure 10.3.1 tests whether an object is serializable by determining whether the object's class or any ancestor class implements the Serializable interface. The utility class has a single static method named isSerializable, which returns true, if a specified object is serializable, and false otherwise. For example, the expression

SerializableTester.isSerializable(new java.util.Date())

evaluates to true because a Date object is serializable, whereas the expression

SerializableTester.isSerializable(new Object())

evaluates to false because an Object instance is not serializable.

The utility class uses methods only from java.lang.Class, whose objects encapsulate information about the class that a particular object instantiates. The utility can be clarified by tracing how it determines whether, for example, an Applet is serializable.

```
import java.io.Serializable;
public class SerializableTester {
   public static boolean isSerializable( Object obj ) {
      if ( obj == null )
        return false;
      Class c = obj.getClass();
      do {
        Class[ ] ifaces = c.getInterfaces();
        for ( int i = 0; i < ifaces.length; i++ )
          if ( serial.equals( ifaces[ i ].getName() ) )
            return true;
        c = c.getSuperclass();
      } while ( c != null ); // loop until class is Object
      return false;
   }
   private static final String serial = "java.io.Serializable";
}
```

FIGURE 10.3.1   A utility class to test whether an object is serializable.

The isSerializable method first checks for a null argument. In this example, the argument is not null but rather an Applet reference; hence, the object's Class is obtained

```
Class c = obj.getClass();
```

to represent the Applet to which obj refers. The public method getClass is encapsulated in Object and, therefore, is available in any object.

Once a Class object is available to represent the Applet, the next step is to invoke Class's instance method getInterfaces

```
Class[ ] ifaces = c.getInterfaces();
```

to get an array of interfaces that class Applet implements. Each interface in the array is checked against java.io.Serializable. If there is a match, isSerializable returns true. However, class Applet does *not* implement Serializable. The process therefore continues by getting Applet's superclass

```
c = c.getSuperclass();
```

and continuing the search. The do while terminates when either a class has been found that implements Serializable, or the class currently under consideration has no superclass. Only Object has no superclass; hence, the search proceeds from a class such as Applet up the hierarchy until Object is reached. If no class along the search path is found to implement Serializable, the method isSerializable returns false.

In the case of Applet, the search goes from Applet to Panel to Container to Component, which does implement Serializable. An Applet object is thus serializable because class Applet descends from class Component.

Obtaining Run-Time Class Information

Suppose that a program loads a *class* file and needs to get information about the class. The java.lang.reflect has classes such as Constructor, Field, and Modifier to represent class members and their attributes.

Example 10.3.2.   The ClassInfo program in Figure 10.3.2 expects class names as command-arguments. An invocation such as

```
$ java ClassInfo DiningPhilosophers Philosopher
```

produces the output in Figure 10.3.3. (The ClassInfo program also outputs reflective information about the Philosopher class, which is not shown in Figure 10.3.3.) As the sample invocation shows, more than one class can be given as a command-line argument.

```java
import java.lang.reflect.*;
public class ClassInfo {
   public static void main( String[ ] args ) throws
                                ClassNotFoundException {
      if ( args.length < 1 ) return; // exit if no classes given
      for ( int i = 0; i < args.length; i++ ) {
         new ClassInfo().printInfo( args[ i ] );
         System.out.println();
      }
   }
   private void printInfo( String s ) throws ClassNotFoundException {
      Class c = Class.forName( s );
      String modifiers = stringifyModifiers( c.getModifiers() );
      String name = c.getName();
      if ( c.isInterface() )
        System.out.print( modifiers + name );
      else
        System.out.print( modifiers + " class " + name + " extends " +
                          c.getSuperclass().getName() );
      Class[ ] interfaces = c.getInterfaces();
      if ( interfaces != null && interfaces.length > 0 ) {
        if ( c.isInterface() ) System.out.print( " extends " );
        else System.out.print( " implements " );
        for ( int i = 0; i < interfaces.length; i++ ) {
          if ( i > 0 )
            System.out.print( ", " );
          System.out.print( interfaces[ i ].getName() );
        }
      }
      System.out.println( " {" );
      System.out.println( indent +  "// Constructors" );
      Constructor[ ] constructors = c.getDeclaredConstructors();
      for ( int i = 0; i < constructors.length; i++ )
         printMethod( constructors[ i ] );
      System.out.println( indent + "// Other methods " );
      Method[ ] methods = c.getDeclaredMethods();
      for ( int i = 0; i < methods.length; i++ )
         printMethod( methods[ i ] );
      System.out.println( indent + "// Fields " );
      Field[ ] fields = c.getDeclaredFields();
      if ( fields != null )
        for ( int i = 0; i < fields.length; i++ )
           printField( fields[ i ] );
      System.out.println( "}" );
   }
```

FIGURE 10.3.2   The ClassInfo program.

```
private void printMethod( Member m ) {
   Class rt = null;
   Class[ ] params, exceptions;
   if ( m instanceof Method ) { // nonconstructor method
     Method method = (Method) m;
     rt = method.getReturnType();
     params = method.getParameterTypes();
     exceptions = method.getExceptionTypes();
   }
   else { // a constructor
     Constructor c =  (Constructor) m;
     params = c.getParameterTypes();
     exceptions = c.getExceptionTypes();
   }
   System.out.print( indent + stringifyModifiers( m.getModifiers() )
           + " " + (( rt != null ) ? getTypename( rt ) + " " : "" )
           + m.getName() + "( " );
   for ( int i = 0; i < params.length; i++ ) {
      if ( i > 0 )
        System.out.print( ", " );
      System.out.print( getTypename( params[ i ] ) );
   }
   if ( params.length > 0 )
     System.out.print( " )" );    // at least 1 param
   else
     System.out.print( ")" );     // no params
   if ( exceptions.length > 0 )
     System.out.print( " throws" );
   for ( int i = 0; i < exceptions.length; i++ ) {
      if ( i > 0 )
        System.out.print( ", " );
      System.out.print( getTypename( exceptions[ i ] ) );
   }
   System.out.println( ";" );
} //*** printMethod
private void printField( Field f ) {
   System.out.println( indent +
                       stringifyModifiers( f.getModifiers() ) +
                       " " + getTypename( f.getType() ) +
                       " " + f.getName() + ";" );
}
private String stringifyModifiers( int i ) {
   return (i == 0) ? "" : Modifier.toString( i );
}
```

FIGURE 10.3.2   The ClassInfo program, *continued.*

```
   private String getTypename( Class c ) {
      String b = "";
      while( c.isArray() ) {
        b += "[ ]";
        c = c.getComponentType();
      }
      return c.getName() + b;
   }
   private static String indent = "    ";
}
```

FIGURE 10.3.2   The ClassInfo program, *continued*.

```
public class DiningPhils extends java.lang.Object {
   // Constructors
   public DiningPhils( );
   // Other methods
   public void dumpStatus( );
   public int generateTimeSlice( );
   public boolean getChopstick( int );
   public int getCount( );
   private void init( int );
   private void initPhils( );
   public static void main( java.lang.String[] );
   private boolean moreToStart( );
   public void setChopstick( int, boolean );
   // Fields
   private int n;
   private Philosopher[ ] phils;
   private boolean[ ] chops;
   private java.util.Random r;
   private static final int maxPhils;
   private static final int maxEat;
   private static final int minEat;
}
```

FIGURE 10.3.3   Sample output from the ClassInfo program of Figure 10.3.2.

In the printInfo method, the program first gets a Class object to represent a class whose name is provided as a command-line argument. For the invocation

```
$ java ClassInfo DiningPhilosophers Philosopher
```

the first call to `printInfo` would invoke

```
Class c = Class.forName( s );
```

where s refers to the string `DiningPhilosophers`. The program then determines class modifiers such as `public` and determines whether, for example,
`DiningPhilosophers` is a `class` or an `interface`. The program invokes
the methods `getDeclaredConstructors` and `getDeclaredMethods` to get
lists of the constructors and methods encapsulated in the class, together with
their attributes, argument types, and any exceptions that the constructors and
methods may throw. Finally, the program gets and prints a list of a target class's
`Fields`.

The `ClassInfo` utility produces *declarations* rather than definitions of the
constructors and methods encapsulated in a target class. Commercial products
are available fully to reconstruct a *java* source file from a compiled *class* file,
including constructor and method *definitions*.

Reflection and Beans

Reflection plays a key role in beans, particularly in constructing the property sheet (see
Section 10.1) that allows a bean's properties to be edited visually. Recall that a pair of
methods such as

```
public void setLName( String lname ) { /*...*/ }
public String getLName() { /*...*/ }
```

define a *readable* and *writable* property called `LName`. Utilities such as the bean box
need reflective information in order to construct a property sheet from a bean's
property-defining methods.

EXERCISES

1. Give an example of *reflective information* about a class.
2. Test the utility `SerializableTester` of Figure 10.3.1 against several classes whose
   instantiations are and are not serializable.
3. Write the declaration for the `getClass` method in the `Object` class.
4. Write a statement that prints the name of a `Date` object's class.
5. Run the `ClassInfo` program in Figure 10.3.2 against the file *ClassInfo.class* and
   check the output against the source code.
6. Does the `ClassInfo` program in Figure 10.3.2, which relies exclusively upon
   standard packages and classes, reconstruct constructor and method *definitions* or
   declarations?

10.4   Servlets and Database

Modern client/server applications often use a Web browser as the client's interface and a database application as a server backend. Figure 10.4.1 depicts the steps in a familiar ordering system in which

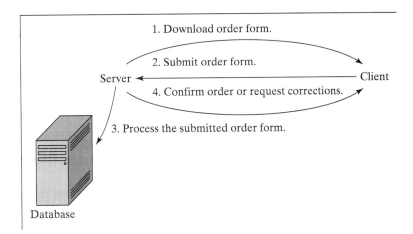

FIGURE 10.4.1   A client/server online ordering system.

- The client downloads an HTML or equivalent document that contains an order form for goods or services that the server provides. Most Web users are familiar with order forms for books, videos, automobiles, vacations, astrological readings, investment advice, and so on. As an example, suppose that the client downloads a book order form. This is Step 1 in Figure 10.4.1
- The client fills in and submits the form, which is returned to the server. This is Step 2 in Figure 10.4.1.
- The server checks a database for product availability, places the order itself in a database, and performs whatever other server-side actions are appropriate. This is Step 3 in Figure 10.4.1.
- The server sends back to the receiver an HTML or similar confirmation or, in the case of problems, an HTML or similar response that calls for order resubmission. This is Step 4 in Figure 10.4.1.

Various technologies are available for building client/server applications of the type just described. For example, CGI (**C**ommon **G**ateway **I**nterface) with Perl or C scripts for server-side processing is widely used for generating **dynamic Web content**, that is, Web content such as HTML documents that are customized to a particular client transaction. ASP (**A**ctive **S**erver **P**ages) is a proprietary technology from Microsoft that is functionally similar to CGI. Java has several technologies suitable for such applications, including JSP (**J**ava **S**erver **P**ages, modeled after ASP) and servlets. This section focuses on servlets to generate dynamic Web content and JDBC for database programming. Originally, JDBC stood for **J**ava **D**ata**B**ase **C**onnectivity, although the term no longer is treated as an acronym.

Servlet Basics

A servlet, like an applet, typically is launched from an HTML or comparable document. On a technical level, a servlet must instantiate a class that implements the Servlet interface. An HTTP[†] servlet located on a Web site extends the concrete HttpServlet class, which in turn extends the abstract GenericServlet class, which in turn implements the Servlet interface. The javax.servlet package and its subpackages support servlet programming. Further details are best clarified through examples.

■ **Example 10.4.1.**   The HTML document in Figure 10.4.2 launches a servlet named HelloWorld whose source code appears in Figure 10.4.3. When the

```
<html><head><title>HelloWorld</title></head>
<body>
  <center>
     <h1>HelloWorld Demo</h1>
     <form method="get" action="/servlet/HelloWorld">
       <input type=submit value="Push me!">
     </form>
  </center>
</body></html>
```

FIGURE 10.4.2   The HTML document that launches the HelloWorld servlet in Figure 10.4.3.

HTML documented is loaded into the client's browser and the button labeled *Push me!* is clicked, the message

```
Hello, world!
```

then appears in the client's browser. The Java Postscript explains where the HTML and *class* files should be located on the server machine and how the server software can be downloaded and run.

The Action Tag

The HTML document in Figure 10.4.2 has special syntax called an action tag

```
action="/servlet/HelloWorld"
```

[†]For a review of HTTP and related protocols, see Section 9.1.

```
import java.io.*;
import javax.servlet.*;
import javax.servlet.http.*;
public class HelloWorld extends HttpServlet {
    public void doGet( HttpServletRequest request,
                       HttpServletResponse response )
       throws IOException, ServletException {
          response.setContentType( "text/html" );   //** 1
          PrintWriter out = response.getWriter();    //** 2
          out.println( "<html>" );                   //** 3
          out.println( "<body>" );                   //** 4
          out.println( "Hello, world!" );            //** 5
          out.println( "</body>" );                  //** 6
          out.println( "</html>" );                  //** 7
    }
}
```

FIGURE 10.4.3   The HelloWorld servlet launched by the HTML
document in Figure 10.4.2.

to specify that the HelloWorld servlet should be executed *on the server* when
the user clicks the *Push me!* button. When the user clicks the button, an HTTP
request goes from the client browser to the server. Such a request typically
uses one of two methods, commonly known as *GET* and *POST*. The name
GET is meant to suggest *getting information* and the name *POST* is meant to
suggest *posting information*. Nonetheless, either method may be used to send
request information from the client to the server. At the implementation level,
GET and *POST* differ. The *GET* method appends request information to the
URL. When *GET* is used, the request information is known as a *query string*,
which appears in the browser appended to the URL. When *POST* is used,
the request information is known as a *form* and does *not* appear appended
to the URL. In this example, the *GET* method is specified in the HTML
document.

The doGet and doPost **Callbacks**

The HttpServlet class has protected doGet and doPost methods, at least one
of which should be overriden as a *public* method in a servlet. The *do* methods
behave as callbacks. When the request information is passed from the client
to the server, the server invokes the servlet's doGet method, if the HTML
document specifies *GET*; and the server invokes the servlet's doPost method, if
the HTML document specifies *POST*. In either case, the request information is
encapsulated in an HttpServletRequest argument. The HelloWorld servlet
in Figure 10.4.3 overrides doGet because the HTML document in Figure 10.4.2
specifies *GET*.

The `HelloWorld` servlet in Figure 10.4.3 does not use any request information but simply generates an HTML document that constitutes the server's *response information*. In this example, the response information is the message

`Hello, world!`

displayed on the client's browser. The `HttpServletResponse` argument encapsulates an HTTP response.

In Figure 10.4.3, the source lines of the `SimpleHelloWorld` servlet are numbered for reference. For example, source line 1 invokes the `response` method `setContentType` with a `text/html` argument to signal that the response to the client will take the form of an HTML document, which the client's browser displays. Source lines 3, 4, 6, and 7 generate HTML tags such as `<body>` and `<\body>`, which enclose the body of the response information. Source line 5 generates the response message. All of the response information is conveniently written using a `PrintWriter` returned from the `response` argument's `getWriter` method. The familiar method `println` is used for source lines 3 through 7. The servlet generates the HTML

```
<html>
<body>
Hello, world!
</body>
</html>
```

The servlet code could be simplified by combining several or even all of the `println` statements into one statement.   ■

■ **Example 10.4.2.**   The HTML document in Figure 10.4.4 launches a `Greetings` servlet (see Figure 10.4.5) that uses an `HttpServletRequest` object to get the user's name from a text box provided on the HTML form. The text box's contents are part of the response information sent to the server when the user clicks the *Submit* button.

```
<html><head><title>Greetings</title></head>
<body><center>
    <h1>Greetings Demo</h1>
    <form method="post" action="/servlet/Greetings">
    <pre>Name <input type="text" name="name"></pre>
      <input type=submit value="Submit">
    </form>
</center></body>
</html>
```

FIGURE 10.4.4   The HTML document that launches the `Greetings` servlet in Figure 10.4.5.

```
import java.io.*;
import javax.servlet.*;
import javax.servlet.http.*;
public class Greetings extends HttpServlet {
    public void doGet( HttpServletRequest req,
                       HttpServletResponse res )
      throws IOException, ServletException { greet( req, res ); }
    public void doPost( HttpServletRequest req,
                        HttpServletResponse res )
      throws IOException, ServletException { greet( req, res ); }
    private void greet( HttpServletRequest req,
                        HttpServletResponse res )
      throws IOException, ServletException {
        res.setContentType( "text/html" );
        PrintWriter out = res.getWriter();
        out.println( "<html><body>" );
        out.println( "Greetings, " + req.getParameter( "name" ) );
        out.println( "</body></html>" );
    }
}
```

FIGURE 10.4.5   The Greetings servlet launched from the HTML
document in Figure 10.4.4.

The Greetings servlet overrides doGet and doPost so that it can handle
either *GET*s or *POST*s. The server invokes the HttpServletRequest object's
getParameter method to get the contents of the specified control, in this case a
text box labeled name, on the HTML form. The getParameter method returns
as a String the text that the user enters on the HTML form. On a sample run,
the servlet generated the HTML

```
<html><body>
Greetings, J. Alfred Prufrock
</body></html>
```

to display a response in the client's browser. The user initially entered J. Alfred
Prufrock in the HTML form's text box and then hit the *Submit* button.

A servlet can execute arbitrary code, which makes servlet technology very flexible.
The next section introduces JDBC so that this database technology can be combined
with servlet technology in a Web-based, client/server application.

JDBC Basics

The java.sql package contains the JDBC classes for programmatic manipulation
of relational databases. JDBC provides a framework in which a program can use
different database "drivers"—software that allows JDBC methods to interact with

vendor-specific databases—to create tables, execute queries, and perform other standard relational database operations. The `sql` in the package's name stands for **S**tructured **Q**uery **L**anguage, the industry standard language for relational databases. JDBC has interfaces such as `Connection`, `Statement`, and `ResultSet` that declare methods for connecting to a database, executing queries against a database, and accessing table data generated from queries. JDBC also has classes such as `DriverManager` for managing vendor-specific database drivers and `Timestamp`, which encapsulates the SQL TIMESTAMP value.

■ **Example 10.4.3.** The `ListShippers` program in Figure 10.4.6 executes a query against the Northwind database, a sample database in Microsoft's Access database management system. The Java Postscript explains how to enable programmatic access to Northwind.

The program first loads a *class* file from a Sun package that implements a driver suitable for the Northwind database. The `static` method `forName` in the class `Class`

```
Class.forName( "sun.jdbc.odbc.JdbcOdbcDriver" );
```

is used for loading. The driver is Sun's **bridge** from JDBC to ODBC (**O**pen **D**ata**B**ase **C**onnectivity), a Microsoft driver manager. A *bridge* allows the two

```
import java.sql.*;
class ListShippers {
   public static void main( String[ ] args ) {
      Connection conn = null;
      try {
         Class.forName( "sun.jdbc.odbc.JdbcOdbcDriver" );
         conn = DriverManager.getConnection( "jdbc:odbc:northwind" );
         Statement stmt = conn.createStatement();
         String query = "Select * from Shippers";
         ResultSet rs = stmt.executeQuery( query );
         while ( rs.next() )
            System.out.println( rs.getString( 1 )   + " " +
                                rs.getString( 2 ) + " " +
                                rs.getString( 3 ) );
      } catch( Exception e ) { e.printStackTrace( System.err ); }
      finally {
         try {
            conn.close();
         } catch( Exception e ) { e.printStackTrace( System.err ); }
      }
   }
}
```

FIGURE 10.4.6   A program that executes a query against the Northwind database.

technologies to interact transparently. Drivers for other commercial databases such as DB2, Oracle, and Sybase are also available.

Once the driver has been loaded, a `Connection` to the database is opened through the `DriverManager`

```
Connection conn =
  DriverManager.getConnection( "jdbc:odbc:northwind" );
```

The string argument to `getConnection`, in this case `jdbc:odbc:northwind`, is a database URL that has the form

jdbc :subprotocol :subname

The `Connection` object is used to create a `Statement`

```
Statement stmt = conn.createStatement();
```

that is used in turn to execute an SQL query

```
ResultSet rs = stmt.executeQuery( query );
```

In this example, the SQL query

```
Select * from Shippers;
```

selects all of the rows from the Northwind table named *Shippers*.

The executed query returns a reference to a `ResultSet`, which in this example consists of the records selected from the *Shippers* table. A `while` loop then is used to print each record by printing each record's three fields. The syntax

```
rs.getString( 1 )
```

returns the *first* field's value as a string, in this case the shipper's integer identifier. Another overload of the `getString` method takes the field's name rather than column position as an argument. On a sample run, the output was

```
1 Speedy Express (503) 555-9831
2 United Package (503) 555-3199
3 Federal Shipping (503) 555-9931
```

The database `Connection` is closed in a `finally` clause to ensure closing regardless of whether an exception is thrown. All of the program's `catch` clauses print a stack trace to the standard error to facilitate debugging. ∎

The `ListShippers` program in Figure 10.4.6 illustrates basic JDBC programming. JDBC provides constructs such as `java.sql.Date` to access SQL datatypes such as `DATE` and `Statement` subtypes such as `PreparedStatement` to allow statements to be precompiled and saved for multiple use. Yet the basic structure of a JDBC program is

Chap. 10   Selected Topics

- Load the appropriate driver.
- Open a connection through the `DriverManager` to a database.
- Construct statements that can be executed against the database.
- If appropriate, process a `ResultSet` returned from an executed query.
- Close the connection to the database.

The servlet and JDBC technologies can be combined in flexible, powerful ways so that clients can access server databases through the ubiquitous Web browser. The next section illustrates.

EXERCISES

1. Give an informal description of a *servlet*.
2. Give a formal description of a *servlet* as a Java program type.
3. Does a *servlet* execute on a server or on a client?
4. Test the `SimpleHelloServlet` in Figure 10.4.3.
5. Is `Servlet` an interface, abstract class, or concrete class?
6. Is `HttpServlet` an interface, abstract class, or concrete class?
7. Explain the relationship between the `doGet` and `doPost` servlet methods and the HTML action tags *GET* and *POST*.
8. Explain the role of an `HttpServletRequest` argument in a `doGet` or `doPost` method.
9. Explain the role of an `HttpServletResponse` argument in a `doGet` or `doPost` method.
10. What is the standard package that supports JDBC?
11. Explain the role of a `ResultSet` in relation to a database query.
12. What are the typical steps for interacting with a database from within a Java program?
13. Test the `ListShippers` program in Figure 10.4.6.
14. What is a standard interface that declares the `executeQuery` method?
15. Explain why the `ListShippers` program in Figure 10.4.6 closes the database `Connection` in a `finally` clause rather than in a `catch` clause.

10.5   Sample Application: Database Webification

Problem

Provide Web access to a database such as Microsoft's Northwind that stores information about a firm's products and the customers who purchase them. The application's user should be presented with a Web document that lists available products. When the user selects a product and submits a request, a list of customers who purchased the product should be displayed as a Web document. The product and customer lists should be current to the day.

Sample Input/Output

Figure 10.5.1 shows the HTML document from which the user selects a product and Figure 10.5.2 shows the underlying HTML code that the Products servlet generates. Figure 10.5.3 shows the customer list constructed by the SalesServlet for the Aniseed Syrup product.

Solution

The application has two servlets that interact as follows:

- The user enters the Products servlet's URL in a browser. For example, if the servlet resides on the *kalinnt* machine in the *servlets* directory, the URL would be

        http://kalinnt:8080/servlet/Products

  for a servlet server listening on port 8080.
- The Products servlet generates as *response information* the HTML document shown in Figure 10.5.1. The document's underlying code is shown in Figure 10.5.2. The user can select and submit a product from this list. If a submit occurs without a select, the first product in the list is the default selection.
- The SalesServlet handles the client request for customer information by generating a customer list as an HTML document, which is displayed on the client's browser.

Both servlets use JDBC to access tables in Microsoft's Northwind database. The Products servlet simply reads records from the database's *Products* table, whereas the SalesServlet servlet performs a complex *join* operation (see the Discussion Section) to assemble the customer list.

Java Implementation

```
//*************** start of Products.java
import java.io.*;
import java.sql.*;
import java.util.*;
import javax.servlet.*;
import javax.servlet.http.*;
public class Products extends HttpServlet {
  public void doGet( HttpServletRequest req,
                     HttpServletResponse res )
```

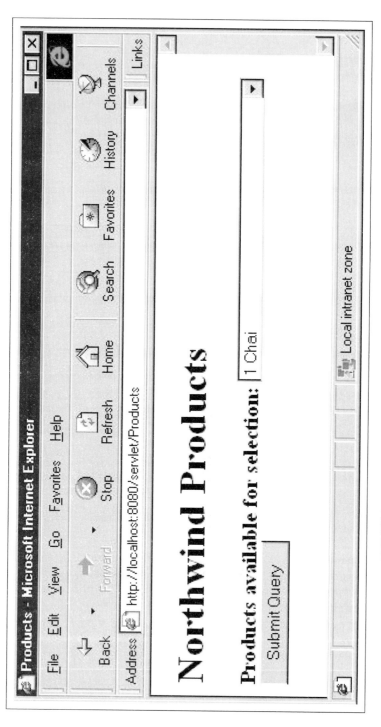

FIGURE 10.5.1 The displayed HTML document that lists products.

```
<html><head><title>Product List</title></head>
<body><h1>Northwind Products</h1>
<form action="http://kalinnt:8080/servlet/SalesServlet" method="post">
<h3>Products available for selection: <select name="product"></h3>
<option>1 Chai
<option>2 Chang
<option>3 Aniseed Syrup
<option>4 Chef Anton's Cajun Seasoning
...
</select><br><input type="submit"></form></body></html>
```

FIGURE 10.5.2   The HTML code for the document in Figure 10.5.1.

```
  throws IOException, ServletException { showProds( res ); }
public void doPost( HttpServletRequest req,
                    HttpServletResponse res )
 throws IOException, ServletException { showProds( res ); }
private void showProds( HttpServletResponse res ) {
  if ( records == null ) //*** 1st time?
    getRecs();          //*** if so, fetch the records
  displayRecs( res ); //*** display the records
}
private void getRecs() {
  Connection conn = null;
  String urlFile =
    getServletConfig().getServletContext().getRealPath( "/" ) +
    "dbURL.url";
  try {
     //*** get URL of servlet that accesses database
     InputStreamReader isr =
       new InputStreamReader( new FileInputStream( urlFile ) );
     BufferedReader br = new BufferedReader( isr );
     servletURL = br.readLine();
     br.close();
     //*** get the ResultSet with the products
     Class.forName( "sun.jdbc.odbc.JdbcOdbcDriver" );
     conn = DriverManager.getConnection( "jdbc:odbc:northwind" );
     String query = "Select * from Products";
     ResultSet rs =
      conn.createStatement().executeQuery( query );
     records = new Vector();
     while ( rs.next() )
        records.addElement( "<option>" + rs.getString( 1 ) +
                                " " + rs.getString( 2 ) );
     rs.close();
```

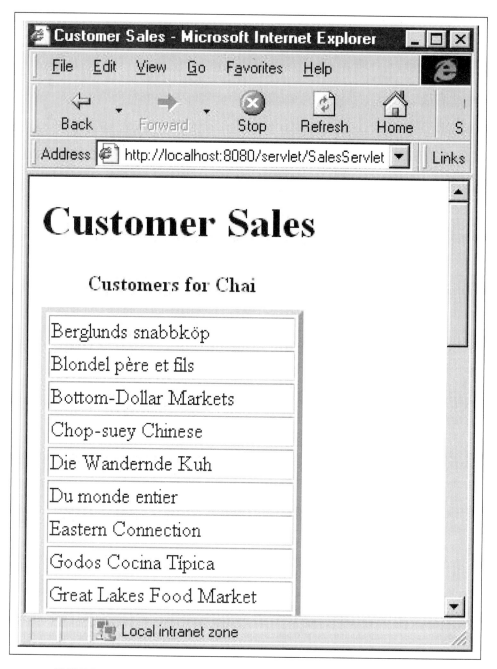

FIGURE 10.5.3   The HTML customer list generated for the Aniseed Syrup product.

```java
    } catch( Exception e ) { e.printStackTrace( System.err ); }
      finally {
        try { conn.close(); }
        catch( Exception e ) { e.printStackTrace( System.err ); }
      }
  }
  private void displayRecs( HttpServletResponse res ) {
    try {
      //*** generate HTML: list of products to pick from
      res.setContentType("text/html");
      PrintWriter out = res.getWriter();
      out.println("<html><head><title>Products</title></head>");
      out.println("<body><h1>Northwind Products</h1>");
      out.println("<form action=\"" + servletURL + "\"" +
                  " method=" + "\"post\"> ");
      out.println("<h3>Products available for selection: " +
                  "<select name=\"product\"></h3>");
      Enumeration e = records.elements();
      while ( e.hasMoreElements() )
        out.println( e.nextElement() );
      out.println("</select><br><input type=" +
                  "\"submit\"></form></body></html>" );
      out.close();
    } catch( Exception e ) { e.printStackTrace( System.err ); }
  }
  private Vector records;
  private String servletURL;
}
//*************** end of Products.java

//*************** start of SalesServlet.java
import java.io.*;
import java.sql.*;
import java.util.*;
import javax.servlet.*;
import javax.servlet.http.*;
public class SalesServlet extends HttpServlet {
  public void doGet( HttpServletRequest req,
                     HttpServletResponse res )
    throws IOException, ServletException { showSales( req, res ); }
  public void doPost( HttpServletRequest req,
                      HttpServletResponse res )
    throws IOException, ServletException { showSales( req, res ); }
  private void showSales( HttpServletRequest req,
                          HttpServletResponse res ) {
```

```
      getProdIdAndName( req );
      if ( productID != null ) {
        getRecs();              //*** retrieve records
        displayRecs( res ); //*** display the records
      }
    }
    private void getProdIdAndName( HttpServletRequest req ) {
      StringTokenizer st =
        new StringTokenizer( req.getParameter( "product" ) );
      productID = st.nextToken();
      productName = st.nextToken();
    }
    private void getRecs() {
      Connection conn = null;
      try {
        //*** get the ResultSet with the products
        if ( !driverLoaded ) {
          Class.forName( "sun.jdbc.odbc.JdbcOdbcDriver" );
          driverLoaded = true;
        }
        conn = DriverManager.getConnection("jdbc:odbc:northwind");
        String query = "SELECT Customers.CompanyName " +
          "FROM Products INNER JOIN ((Customers INNER JOIN " +
          "Orders ON Customers.CustomerID = Orders.CustomerID) " +
          "INNER JOIN [Order Details] ON Orders.OrderID = " +
          "[Order Details].OrderID) ON Products.ProductID = " +
          "[Order Details].ProductID " +
          "GROUP BY Products.ProductID, Customers.CompanyName " +
          "HAVING (((Products.ProductID)= " + productID + "))";
        ResultSet rs =
         conn.createStatement().executeQuery( query );
        records = new Vector();
        while ( rs.next() )
          records.addElement("<td>" + rs.getString(1) + "</td>");
        rs.close();
    } catch( Exception e ) { e.printStackTrace(System.err); }
        finally {
          try { conn.close(); }
          catch( Exception e ) { e.printStackTrace(System.err); }
        }
    }
    private void displayRecs( HttpServletResponse res ) {
      try {
        //*** generate HTML: products sold to customers
        res.setContentType("text/html");
```

```
        PrintWriter out = res.getWriter();
        out.println("<html><head><title>Customer Sales" +
                "</title></head>");
        out.println("<body><h1>Customer Sales</h1>");
        out.println("<table border=4><caption><b>" +
                "Customers for  " + productName +
                "</b></caption>");
        Enumeration e = records.elements();
        while ( e.hasMoreElements() )
          out.println( "<tr>" + e.nextElement() + "</tr>" );
        out.close();
    } catch( Exception e ) { e.printStackTrace( System.err ); }
  }
  private Vector records;
  private String servletURL;
  private String productID;
  private String productName;
  private boolean driverLoaded;
}
//*************** end of SalesServlet.java
```

Discussion

A user initiates the application from a browser by entering the `Products` servlet's URL, for example

```
http://kalinnt:8080/servlet/Products
```

Although the file *Products.class* resides in the *servlets* directory, the URL must specify *servlet* rather than *servlets* as the directory. After the server loads the `Products` servlet for the first time, the servlet remains loaded for efficiency; that is, the server need not reload the servlet on every new client request. The application requires only that product information be current on a daily basis. The assumption, then, is that a system administrator manually or programmatically stops and restarts the server program at least once a day.

The `Products` Servlet

The `Products` servlet overrides `doGet` and `doPost` so that the servlet could be launched from an HTML document using either the *GET* or the *POST* method. Two private methods perform the required work:

- `getRecs`. The first time the servlet is loaded in response to a client request, `getRecs` reads from a text file the URL of the `SalesServlet`, which produces the customer list for a product selected from the product list that the `Products` servlet generates. In the current implementation, the URL is

```
http://kalinnt:8080/servlet/SalesServlet
```

although the `SalesServlet` could reside in a different directory than the `Products` servlet or even on physically distinct machine. The `getRecs` method also reads the records from Northwind's *Products* table into a `Vector`. The query

```
Select * from Products
```

is executed against Northwind to obtain the records through JDBC. The `Vector` holds strings such as

```
<option>3 Aniseed Syrup
```

The `<option>` is an HTML tag that signifies a list member. In this example, 3 is a product's identifying number or **database key** and `Aniseed Syrup` is the product's name. The `getRecs` method closes the JDBC `ResultSet` and `Connection` once the records have been read.

- `displayRecs`. This method generates the servlet's response, which consists of an HTML list of products together with a *Submit* button. The `displayRecs` method is invoked each time a client submits the `Products` servlet's URL. Clicking the *Submit* button launches the `SalesServlet`, which in turn generates the customer list for the selected product.

The `SalesServlet`

The `SalesServlet` is similar in structure to the `Products` servlet. For example, the `SalesServlet` overrides `doGet` and `doPost` so that the servlet can be launched using either a *GET* or a *POST*. The `SalesServlet` always does a database read through JDBC. The `SalesServlet` performs three major operations, each implemented as a private method:

- `getProdIdAndName`. This method uses the `HttpServletRequest` argument passed to either `doGet` or `doPost` to extract the user's product selection, for example,

```
3 Aniseed Syrup
```

A `StringTokenizer` is used first to extract 3, which is the product's database key. The key is required for the query that generates the customer list. The tokenizer next is used to extract `Aniseed Syrup`, which occurs in the response HTML document. The response document, which contains a list of customers, would begin in this example with

```
Customers for Aniseed Syrup
```

The product name is thus used to customize the response document.

- `getRecs`. This method is invoked to get the customer records for a particular client request. The method generates a query, which is run against the database. The query performs a *join* in which fields from various tables—*Products*, *Customers*, *Orders*, and *Order Details*—are compared. A *join* operation is required because the *Products* and *Customers* are not directly linked. The link is indirect: a product belongs to an order, which has detailed information about quantity and price; and this detailed information is linked to a particular customer. For this application, the query was generated using Microsoft Access's QBE (**Q**uery **B**y **E**xample) editor, which allows the user to create queries in an intuitive point-and-click environment. The Access database system has a translator that converts QBE into SQL, which was copied into the `SalesServlet` program.

  The `getRecs` method stores the retrieved records together with HTML formatting in a `Vector`. The database connection and the result set are closed after each transaction.
- `displayRecs`. This method generates the HTML response document. The customer records are placed in an HTML table (see Figure 10.5.3) for convenient viewing.

The `Servlet` and JDBC constructs greatly simplify the task of making a server database accessible to clients through their browsers. This application also illustrates how two servlets can interact seamlessly. The application could be extended to allow, for example, database editing through a browser. Servlets, JDBC, and the Web provide a powerful, flexible infrastructure for client/server database applications.

EXERCISES

1. What advantage results from overriding both `doGet` and `doPost` in a servlet?
2. Test the sample application, at least on the local machine using the reserved IP address *localhost*.
3. What advantage results from having a browser as the frontend for a database such as Northwind?
4. What is the default port for the servlet server?

JAVA POSTSCRIPT

The Bean Box Utility

The BDK (**B**ean **D**evelopment **K**it) can be downloaded from Sun at

    http://java.sun.com/products

Installation is straightforward. For example, the Windows version is a self-extracting ZIP file. Once installed, *beanbox* is a subdirectory of the install directory. For example, if the user selects *bdk* as the directory in which to install the BDK, then *beanbox* is a subdirectory of *bdk*. The *beanbox* directory contains a *run* command that launches the bean box.

The bean box utility comes with sample beans in *jar* files, which are Java's version of the familiar *zip* file. A user can add beans to the bean box. The preferred method is create a *jar* file with the bean's constituent *class* files and a manifest, a text file that describes the *jar* file's contents. For the `TickerTape` bean of Section 10.1, the manifest file (e.g., *tick.mf*) would be

```
Manifest-Version: 1.0
Name: TickerTape.class
Java-Bean: true

Name: TickerThread.class
Java-Bean: false
```

because only the `TickerTape` is serializable and, therefore, a bean. The `TickerThread` is a utility class for the `TickerTape`. The command

```
$ jar cfmv my.jar tick.mf TickerTape.class TickerThread.class
```

would create the file *my.jar* whose contents would be the two *class* files and the manifest file. The flag `c` stands for create, the flag `f` for file name, the flag `m` for manifest file name, and the flag `v` for verbose output. The file *my.jar* now can be loaded into the bean box using the *Load Jar* option under the *File* menu.

The Java Servlet Development Kit

The JSDK can be downloaded from

```
http://java.sun.com/products
```

and installed on Windows, Unix, and other platforms. The JSDK includes the `javax` classes and interfaces for servlets. The `CLASSPATH` variable should be updated to include the *jar* file that contains the `javax` package. In the current implementation, the file is *servlet.jar* and it resides in the root install directory (e.g., *jsdk*). The root install directory also includes *startserver* and *stopserver* commands to start and stop, respectively, the test server. This server expects requests on port 8080, as the examples in Sections 10.4 and 10.5 illustrate.

The root install directory has a subdirectory named *webpages*, which can hold HTML or other documents used to launch servlets. In the current implementation, *webpages* has a *WEB-INF* subdirectory, which in turn has a *servlets* directory that is the default location for servlets. The *class* files for servlets such as the `Products` and `SalesServlet` programs of Section 10.5 should be placed in *servlets*. The directories *webpages* and *servlets* are *not* specified in a URL. Two examples will illustrate.

Suppose that the HTML file *hello.htm* (see Figure 10.4.4) is placed in the *webpages* directory. To test access to this document, the server is started (*startserver*) and the URL

```
http://localhost:8080/hello.htm
```

is specified in a browser on the local machine. Note that *webpages* is not part of the URL.

Suppose that the servlet file *Products.class* is placed in the directory *servlets* and that the server is started. To test access to the servlet, the URL

```
http://localhost:8080/servlet/Products
```

is entered in a browser on the local machine. Note that the URL specifies the directory as *servlet* even though the directory's actual name is *servlets*.

Setting Up the Northwind Database for the JDBC-to-ODBC Bridge

Microsoft's Northwind database can be accessed through the Sun-supplied driver `JdbcOdbcDriver`, which is illustrated in the program of Figure 10.4.6 and the Sample Application of Section 10.5. The Northwind database ships with Microsoft's Access Database Management System. The setup steps are:

- Open the Windows *ControlPanel* application and the *ODBC* utility listed there.
- Click the *System DSN* tab. *DSN* stands for Data Source Name. If *northwind* or an equivalent (e.g., *nwind*) is already listed, exit and test an application such as the program in Figure 10.4.6.
- Click the *Add* button and select *Microsoft Access Driver* as the software driver for accessing Northwind.
- Once the *Add* operation completes, a dialog window opens in which to specify the DSN. Enter *northwind* as the DSN.
- In the *Database* section, browse if necessary for the file *Northwind.mdb*, which contains the Northwind database. Select this file to complete the setup.

COMMON ERRORS AND SAFE PRACTICES

1. A software module designed to be a bean or component should be serializable so that the bean can be integrated into a serializable container.
2. The `static` method `Beans.instantiate` attempts first to deserialize the named bean from a *ser* file and then to load the bean from a *class* file.
3. A listener to property change events must implement the `PropertyChange-Listener` interface and define the `propertyChange` method declared therein.

4. It is an error for any Java program to perform operations that a security manager disallows. For this reason, *applets* launched from a commercial browser cannot read from or write to the local disk, launch another program, open a socket to an arbitrary host, and so forth.

5. Although the `java.security` package has generic security classes such as `AllPermission`, permissions for particular actions reside in the appropriate package. For example, the `FilePermission` class resides in the `java.io` package.

6. Java security mechanisms are additions to rather than replacements for the security of the host system. For example, if the host system denies all user programs access to a particular file, the Java security mechanisms cannot be used to overcome this restriction.

7. System-wide security policy for Java programs should be articulated in the *java.security* and *java.policy* files, with the −D runtime option used to tailor security policy for a particular program.

8. In a public-key authentication system, the sender's *private* key is used to sign a message and the receiver's *public* key is used to verify the signature. At the code level, the keys must come from the same `KeyPair` and the signature's `update` method must be invoked on the same input data for the authentication to work.

9. A typical servlet does not implement the `Servlet` interface but rather extends a concrete class such as `HttpServlet`, which in turn implements the interface.

10. A servlet to be launched from an HTML document should extend the concrete `HttpServlet` class.

11. When a servlet is launched from an HTML document, the servlet callback for a *GET* action is `doGet` and the callback for a *POST* action is `doPost`. It is thus advisable to override both methods so that a servlet can service requests under either HTML action.

12. The servlet server, whose default listening port is 8080, searches for servlets and web pages in a predefined path. Accordingly, the server documentation should be consulted to ensure that servlets and supporting web pages are placed in the appropriate directories.

13. To use JDBC, a program must load a driver suited to a particular database. The driver is then used to open a `Connection` to the database.

14. A database connection should be closed in a `finally` clause to ensure that the connection gets closed through any execution path.

PROGRAMMING EXERCISES

10.1. Create a bean that generates an applet host for a specified applet. In effect, the bean should convert an applet into a standalone *application*. *Hint*: Review the `AppletHost` program of Figure 9.4.11. For a specified applet, the bean would generate a class like `AppletHost`, which is a standalone application.

10.2. Create a collection of network utility beans, including a port tester (see Figure 9.2.2), a *finger* utility (see Figure 9.2.3), and a *ping* utility (see Programming Exercise 9.1). Each bean should have a property sheet for the visual editing of its properties. *Hint*: The `java.beans` package has classes such as `BeanDescriptor` and `SimpleBeanInfo` to provide information about beans.

10.3. Provide a property sheet for the `TickerTape` bean of Figure 10.1.1. *Hint*: The `java.beans` package has classes such as `BeanDescriptor` and `SimpleBeanInfo` to provide information about beans.

10.4. Create a `StdGUI` bean that provides a standard GUI for a desktop machine. The `StdGUI` could contain a mix of simple components such as buttons and lists for launching applications as well as other beans (e.g., the network utility collection of Programming Exercise 10.2). In the initial phase of GUI design, the buttons can have stub methods as callbacks. Recall that a Java program can launch applications as separate processes through the `Runtime`'s method `exec` (see Figure 10.2.3). The `StdGUI` bean should be available to clients through serialization over sockets from a server.

10.5. Adapt the order-form applet of Programming Exercise 9.14 so that this component has a property sheet for visually editing its properties. Recall that an applet is technically a bean because the `Applet` class has `Component`, which implements `Serializable`, as an ancestor.

10.6. Create a bean that produces a message digest for a file that the user selects a list. The bean should have a GUI to facilitate user interaction, including selection of a message digest algorithm.

10.7. Change the `MakeKeyPair` application of Figure 10.2.10 into a bean whose property sheet allows the user to specify the algorithm and key length. The bean also should have a list of clients to which the public key in the pair should be sent. In other words, the bean should be able to distribute the public key in an appropriate fashion.

10.8. Implement a version of the bean box that allows beans packed in *jar* files to be loaded into a container and selected with a mouse click. A selected bean's property sheet should appear for visual editing. *Hint*: The `java.util.jar` class has support for reading from *jar* files.

10.9. Extend Programming Exercise 10.8 to allow bean interaction through the event model. The user should be able to select the interacting beans with mouse clicks, as in the BDK's bean box utility. *Hint*: Use Figure 10.1.7 to review the adapter class that the bean box utility generates for bean interaction.

10.10. Adapt the tic-tac-toe application of Programming Exercise 7.13 to a servlet-based application in which the human player's interface is a series of HTML documents that display the current board and allow the player to enter a move.

10.11. Build a servlet-based version of the matrix algebra sample application of Section 9.7. The user submits an HTML form with appropriate controls to enter the data and to select either addition or multiplication as the operation. After performing the matrix operation, the servlet responds with an HTML form that displays the sum or product matrix.

10.12. Build a servlet-based database application in which users enter weather data from various locations into an HTML form, which includes fields to enter the user's unique identification number, the region (e.g., *northeast, midwest, rockymountains*, and the like), the time, the current temperature, and the current conditions (e.g., *rainy, partly cloudy*, and the like). The servlet handles the submission by extracting the data and constructing a record stored in a database table. The servlet then generates an HTML summary report about the submitting region's weather, which is sent back to the client both as confirmation and as a synopsis of other reports from the same region.

10.13. Design an HTML form that an investment specialist fills out and submits using a commercial browser. The form lists a stock, its current price, and a recommendation about whether the stock should be purchased. A servlet handles the submission by extracting the relevant data from the form and e-mailing the data to a list of clients. *Hint*: The JavaMail API available at

```
http://java.sun.com/products/javamail
```

supports e-mail. Sun also provides an `SmtpClientClass` with the JDK in the package `sun.net.smtp`. If these technologies are not available, simulate an e-mail system with sockets.

10.14. Design an HTML order form for products listed in a database such as Northwind. When the user submits the order, a servlet handles the submission by recording the order in the database and by generating a confirmation document that is sent back to the customer. *Hint*: If Northwind is available, examine its table structure. In particular, Northwind stores order information in two separate tables, an *Orders* table that records basic information about the product and the customer and an *OrderDetails* table that records information about prices, quantity, and discounts.

Hints and Solutions to Odd-Numbered Exercises

Section 1.1

1. Program modules are parts that can be designed, coded, and tested separately and then assembled to form a program.

3. A procedure such as a function.

5. A subproblem that is not further decomposed but rather solved directly.

7. Collections of objects.

9. As fields encapsulated in the class.

11.
```
class Student {
     String id;
     String lname;
     String fname;
     String mname;
     int age;
     int majorCode;
     int minorCode;
     float gpa;
     List coursesTaken;
     List coursesRequired;
     //... other properties
```

```
        float computeGPA() { /*...*/ }
        List computeCoursesToBeTaken() { /*...*/ }
        void requestMoreAllowance() { /*...*/ }
        //...other operations
    }
```

13. A *Novel* is a *LiteraryForm*.

15. A constructor is a function used to construct or create objects by instantiating a class, whereas a method is a function that implements an operation appropriate to a class and its instances. For example, a *Student* constructor would be used to construct a *Student* object, whereas a *computeGPA* method would be used to compute a *Student*'s grade point average.

Section 1.2

1. A class's interface publishes the services that the class provides to clients.

3. A class's interface is public—*open*, *available*, or *accessible*—to potential clients.

5. A class can designate members (constructors, methods, and fields) as nonpublic in order to limit access to such members.

7. Yes.

9. Clients can request a class's services without concern for low-level implementation details. Also, a class's hidden implementation can be changed without impacting clients. Information hiding also can be used for security.

11. An abstract data type allows users to abstract from—that is, to ignore—low-level implementation details and to attend instead to high-level functionality.

13. The programmer can ignore low-level implementation details such as range in the case of the abstract data type *Integer* but not in the case of the primitive data type *int*.

Section 1.3

1. Classes and their instances are *servers* that provide the services published in their interfaces. *Clients* are programs that use the services that classes and their instances provide.

3. Fields commonly are a part of a class's low-level implementation details. By contrast, a class's interface typically consists of high-level methods.

5. A message is sent to an object by invoking one of its methods. For example, invoking the *length* method of a *String* object would send the *String* a message that requests the number of characters in the *String*.

7. A well-designed class should expose its functionality to clients in a clear, straightforward, and easy-to-use manner. Therefore, high-level methods are generally the core of a class's interface.

Section 1.4

1. *Java* is a *ProgrammingLanguage*.

3. No.

5. A child class redefines—overrides—the inherited method in some appropriate manner.

7. Inheritance is a requirement for polymorphism.

Section 1.5

1. Declared.

3. Yes.

5. A software component is a prebuilt module that can be integrated as a part of an application.

7. Yes.

Section 1.6

1. Unified Modeling Language.

3. No.

5. *Structure* and *Behavior*.

7. A diagram is a graphical depiction of things and their relationships.

9. In the *Parent* to *Child* relationship, the *Child* has an associated multiplicity of one or more because a parent as such must have at least one child. The *Parent* has an associated multiplicity of two because a child requires exactly two (biological) parents.

11. A *Team* consists of two or more *Players*, each of whom may belong to arbitrarily many *Teams*.

13. Yes.

15. Yes.

Section 2.1

1.
```
class MyHi {
    public static void main( String[ ] a ) {
      System.out.println( "Martin Kalin" );
    }
}
```
3.
```
class MyHi {
    public static void main( String[ ] a ) {
      System.out.println( "Martin\nKalin" );
    }
}
```
5. System is a standard class, out is a `static` field that refers to a `PrintStream` object, and `println` is a method encapsulated in `PrintStream`.

7. `"Hello, world!"`

Section 2.2

1. There should be a `void` immediately to the left of `main`.

3. No. A `static` method may access only `static` members in its encapsulating class.

5.
```
0
1
2
3
```

```
4
5
6
7
8
9
```

7. No.

9. No.

11. 1

13. `double[ ] doubs = new double[ 500 ];`

15. `Arrays.sort( ar );`

Section 2.3

1. Yes.

3. Yes.

5.
```
class Test {
    public static void main( String[ ] args ) {
        String s = "FOO";
        s.toLowerCase();
        System.out.println( s );
    }
}
```

7. `String s = String.valueOf( 3.14 );`

9. A String is immutable, whereas a StringBuffer is not.

11. `String s = new StringBuffer( "foo" ).toString();`

Section 2.4

1.
```
Emp e1 = new Emp();
Emp e2 = new Emp( "maria", "callas" );
Emp e3 = new Emp( "bjoern", "daehlie", 1234 );
```

3. Assuming that an int field named id has been added to the Emp class, the code segment

```
Emp maria = new Emp( "maria", "callas" );
maria.setId( 9876 );
System.out.println( maria.getId() );
```

can be added to the test client of Figure 2.4.2.

Section 2.5

1. An *input stream* is a sequence of data with a source such as a disk file. An *output stream* is a sequence of data with a destination such as a disk file.

3. char

5. An exception is an unusual condition that arises during a program's execution. An example is integer division by zero.

7. Trying to construct an input stream such as a `FileInputStream` with a nonexistent file as the source would cause an `IOException`.

9. A `FileInputStream` is a type of *binary* stream, that is, an input stream of bytes. A `FileReader` is a type of *character* stream, that is, an input stream of chars.

11. `BufferReader br =`
   `new BufferedReader( new FileReader( "input.dat" ) );`

Section 2.6

1. The tokens are a, b, cef, and h.

3. `StringTokenizer st = new StringTokenizer( "foo bar baz" );`

5. An array has a fixed size that does not change as elements are added and removed. By contrast, a `Vector` grows in size as elements are added and shrinks in size as elements are removed. An array's elements can be of a primitive type such as `int` but a `Vector`'s elements cannot be of a primitive type.

7. The `int` could be "wrapped" in an `Integer`, as a `Vector` cannot store primitive types such as `int`.

9. A `Hashtable` is a collection of key/value *pairs*, whereas a `Vector` is a collection of elements that do not occur in pairs.

Section 3.1

1. Java Virtual Machine.

3. Yes.

5. The *java* utility implements the JVM as a run-time interpreter.

7. The JVM *bytecode* instructions are translated into native instructions for execution on the local platform.

9. A Java *application* is a program that requires only the JVM to execute. Unlike an *applet*, for example, an *application* does not require a host program.

11. A *servlet* is a program typically launched through a Web document. A servlet executes on the server rather than the client machine.

13. Server.

15. Shallow. For instance, every applet is likewise a bean.

Section 3.2

1. The extension for source files is *java*.

3. Three: *A.class*, *K.class*, and *Z.class*.

5. Files with a *class* extension.

Section 3.3

1. A package is a collection of *class* files.

3. Extension.

5. No.

7. A fully qualified name such as `java.util.Date` gives the package(s) and the class, with periods as separators. The class name always occurs in the rightmost position.

9. Every *class* file occurs in a package. If the corresponding source file does not contain a `package` statement, then the *class* files produced through compilation reside in a default or unnamed package.

11. The `CLASSPATH` environment variable allows utilities such as *javac* and *java* to locate programmer-defined packages.

Section 3.4

1. The `Random` field is not accessed by clients but only the `RandNN` constructor and the `nextInt` method. The field thus belongs to the class's hidden implementation.

3.
```
public int nextInt( boolean nonneg ) {
    if ( nonneg )           //** only nonnegative integer?
      return nextInt();     //** other RandNN overload
    else                    //** otherwise,
      return r.nextInt();   //** could be negative
}
```

Section 4.1

1. (a) yes   (e) no: has a dash, –   (i) no: has a #
    (b) yes   (f) yes   (j) no: has a #
    (c) yes   (g) no: starts with 2   (k) no: has a ,
    (d) yes   (h) yes   (l) no: has a blank

3. Local variable x, which is part of the target expression in an assignment statement, has not been assigned a value.

5. Zero (0.0).

7. `null`

9. Because field `size` is `final`, `size` cannot be assigned 100 in method `f`.

Section 4.2

1. A constructor must not have a return type or `void` in place of one.

3. Yes, as constructors and methods.

5. No. In Java, unlike some other object-oriented languages, there is a technical distinction between a constructor and a method.

7. Yes.

9. Method m must return an `int`.

11. Yes. Indeed, constructors *must* have the same name: the class's name.

13. Yes.

15. No.

17. Yes.

Section 4.3

1. No.
3. Names of the primitive data types begin with lowercase letters (e.g., `char`), whereas names of standard classes begin with uppercase letters (e.g., `Character`).
5. $-2,187,483,648$ to $2,187,483,647$.
7. $-9,223,372,036,854,775,808$ to $9,223,372,036,854,775,807$.
9. $1.40239846E - 45$ to $3.40282347E + 38$.
11. The integer types such as `byte` and `int` are *signed*, whereas the `char` type is *unsigned*.
13. No.
15. 0x18.
17. A floating-point literal such as 3.1415 is of type `double`. Therefore, this value must be cast to `float` to be assigned to the `float` variable `pi`. By contrast, the literal 3.1415F or 3.1415f is of type `float`.
19. Yes.
21. 1
    3
23. Yes.
25. no

Section 4.4

1. The storage can be allocated with the operator `new` or by providing initializing values in the array's declaration. The code segment

```
int[ ] a1 = new int[ 3 ];   // size is three
int[ ] a2 = { 9, 8, 7 };    // size is three
```

   illustrates.
3. 10.
5. 10.
7. No.

Section 4.5

1. No.
3.
```
if ( c == 'n' )
   System.out.println( "Never married." );
else if ( c == 'm' )
   System.out.println( "Married." );
else if ( c == 'd' )
   System.out.println( "Divorced." );
else if ( c == 'w' )
   System.out.println( "Widowed." );
else
   System.out.println( "Invalid marital code." );
```

5. The code segment has a dangling `else` because the `if` clause's body is not enclosed in braces. The correct code is

```
int x = 1, y = 2;
if ( x > y ) {
   x = x * 2;
   y = y * 3;
}
else
   x = 0;
```

7. Yes.

9. 1
2
3
5

Section 4.7

1. An exception is an unexpected condition that arises during a program's execution.

3. The program terminates.

5. The `throws` clause indicates that an exception may be thrown when the constructor's or the method's body is executed.

7. Yes.

Section 5.1

1. A top-level class cannot have `protected` scope.

3. Package and public.

5. Package.

7. Only within the encapsulating class.

9. To other classes in the same package and in subclasses, whether in the same package or a different package.

11. Because field x is `private` in class `Alpha`, the `Beta` method m cannot access the `Alpha` object's field x.

Section 5.2

1. Yes.

3. A constructor's main roles are to construct objects (i.e., to instantiate the class in which the constructor is encapsulated) and to perform appropriate initialization operations on a constructed object.

5. A constructor does not have a return type or `void` in place of one.

7. Because class `Alpha` defines a constructor, the compiler does *not* provide a public no-argument constructor. Therefore, the statement

```
Alpha a1 = new Alpha();
```

in the `Zeta` constructor is an error.

9. Yes.

11. Every method must have a return type or `void` in place of one. Method m's definition is thus in error.

13. To define operations appropriate to the encapsulating class and its instances.

15. Yes.

17. Zero (0).

19. The syntax shows that `red` is associated with the `Color` class rather than with a `Color` instance or object.

21. No.

23. A deprecated language feature is still available but unsuitable for continued use.

Section 5.3

1. As packages.

3. Yes.

5. If the client application needed services from the class or its objects.

7. The method's signature: its name, argument types, return type or `void` in place of one, and any exceptions that the method might throw.

11. `static`

Section 5.4

1. The two classes repackage for ease of use the functionality already available in other classes, in this case standard input/output classes from the `java.io` library.

3. Readers and writers handle *character* input and output, respectively, whereas input streams and output streams handle *binary* input and output, respectively.

5. The `BasicInputTester` program in Figure 5.4.1 tests all of the public constructors and methods except for `getByte`. Adding the statement

```
System.out.println( stdin.getByte() );
```

to the program completes the test of `BasicInput` functionality.

7. The missing primitive types are `boolean`, `float`, and `short`. Adding the methods

```
public boolean getBoolean() throws IOException {
    resetBuffer();
    return Boolean.getBoolean( st.nextToken() );
}
public float getFloat() throws IOException {
    resetBuffer();
    return Float.parseFloat( st.nextToken() );
}
public short getShort() throws IOException {
    resetBuffer();
    return Short.parseShort( st.nextToken() );
}
```

to the `BasicInput` class completes the coverage of primitive types.

Section 5.5

1. Abstract **W**indow **T**oolkit.

Section 6.1

1. No.
3. `class Sample extends Object { /*...*/ }`
5. No.
7. The compiler automatically invokes the `toString` method so that the statement is equivalent
to

```
System.out.println( new Vector().toString() );
```

9. Yes.
11. The required change is

```
public void m( int p ) {
   n = p;        // local n
   super.n = p; // inherited n
}
```

13. `Date` and `Vector` are peer classes, that is, neither is an ancestor of the other. Therefore, it
is an error to cast a `Date` type to a `Vector` type.
15. `Alpha`
`Beta`

Section 6.2

1. Yes.
3. `Alpha`
`Zeta`
5. No.
7. Yes.
9. Yes.
11. `public final void m() { /*...*/ }`

Section 6.3

3. A subclass (e.g., `Mang`) delegates to its superclass (e.g., `Emp`) the task of doing superclass-
appropriate input such as reading values for superclass fields. The subclass then does
subclass-specific input such as reading values for local fields. This modular design means
that a subclass `read` need not be rewritten if the superclass input requirements change.

Section 6.4

1. Package and public.

3. The keyword `abstract` signals that an interface, unlike a concrete class, cannot be instantiated as an object. In specific terms, the keyword signals that an interface contains method *declarations* rather than definitions.

5. Declarations.

7. Yes.

9. To implement an interface is to *define* the methods declared therein. An interface only *declares* rather than defines methods.

11.
```
Enumeration e = v.elements();
while ( e.hasMoreElements() )
    System.out.println( e.nextElement() );
```

13. **A**pplication **P**rogram **I**nterface.

Section 6.5

1. A concrete class can be instantiated as an object but an abstract class cannot. A concrete class contains only method *definitions*, whereas an abstract class may contain a mix of method definitions and declarations.

3. Yes.

5. `abstract class Kappa { /*...*/ }`

7. Yes.

9. Yes.

11. If class `Alpha` implements an interface but fails to define all of the methods declared in the interface, `Alpha` is abstract.

Section 7.1

1. A heavyweight graphical component is one whose native peer has features and operations beyond those that the component requires. The component is thus heavyweight in the sense that its native peer carries "extra baggage" that the component does not need.

3. A Java graphical component such as a `Framed` window has a graphical peer on the host system. A `Frame`'s native peer thus would differ on, for example, a Windows system and a Unix system.

5. **J**ava **F**oundation **C**lasses.

7. `java.awt`

9. Lightweight.

11. All Java windows have a `setBackground` method to set the window's background color and a `getBackground` method to get a window's background color.

Section 7.2

1. A pure callback is a method that the programmer writes but never invokes. Instead, the system invokes or "calls back" the method in response to an appropriate event.

3. An object that has been delegated to handle particular events such as button pushes by providing the appropriate callback method.

5. `public void actionPerformed( ActionEvent e )`

7. `ContainerEvent`

9. `b1.addActionListener( this );`

11. `java.awt.event`

Section 7.3

1. A prebuilt part of a larger application. For example, a button or menu might be part of graphical application.

3. Yes.

5. A layout manager determines how the components in a container are organized and arranged.

7. A container.

9. Invisible.

11. `jf.getContentPane()`

13. A trivial implementation of a method provides an *empty* body, whereas a default implementation provides a nonempty body that defines the method's default operation.

15. A menu is attached to a menu bar, whereas a popup menu is "free floating" or unattached.

17. A specified key that represents a menu item. For example, the key *E* might be the shortcut for the menu item *Exit*.

19. Yes.

21. If a dialog window were needed only once, the `JOptionPane`'s `static` methods are a convenient way to open the dialog window. If such a window were to be used repeatedly, it would be more efficient to construct the dialog as an object that could be shown and hidden as needed.

Section 7.4

1. Because a modern file system has a hierarchical or *tree* structure.

3. `MouseListener` is an interface that declares methods such as `mouseClicked`. `MouseAdapater` is a class that implements the interface but provides only trivial (i.e., empty) implementations of the `MouseListener` interface. A programmer can extend `MouseAdapter` and, in the extended class, provide nontrivial implementations of selected `MouseListener` methods.

5. The code segment

```
JOptionPane msgDialog = new JOptionPane();
msgDialog.setMessage( "This is a message!" );
msgDialog.show();
```

illustrates how the required changed would be implemented.

Section 7.5

1. A JScrollBar's model stores state information such as the scrollbar's current position, the range of values for its position, and the extent of the scrollbar's thumb. The view provides a graphical representation of the scrollbar's state and a graphical interface for altering the state. For example, if a scrollbar's current position is 0 in a range of 0 through 100, the scrollbar thumb is at its leftmost position. Moving the thumb changes the current position, which is thus alters the model. The controller handles the event-driven interactions between the view and the model. For instance, the controller is responsible for mapping changes in the thumb's position to changes in the scrollbar's model.

3. The view and the controller.

5. A graphics context encapsulates information about drawing such as line width and style.

7. The `paint` method is a callback invoked whenever a container such as a window requires redrawing, for example, because of an exposure event. The method expects a single argument of type `Graphics`. If a program needs to repaint a container, the program should invoke `repaint`, which expects no arguments. The `repaint` method invokes `update`, which in turn invokes `paint`.

9. A component's `validate` method is invoked to ensure that the component is displayed properly. For instance, if a button is added dynamically to a window, the window's `validate` method might be invoked to ensure that the button is displayed. A component's `invalidate` method is invoked to signal that the component has changed in a way that might impact its display. For example, if an already displayed button's font were changed, the button's `invalidate` method might be invoked to ensure that the button displayed with a size appropriate to the new font.

Section 7.6

3. So that scrollbars are available if the `JTable`'s records do not all fit onto the screen at once.

Section 8.1

1. Copying a reference need not copy the object to which reference refers. Cloning an object produces an exact and distinct copy of the original.

3. 125
   512

5. In the program in Figure 8.1.4, the `Zeta` objects to which `z1` and `z2` refer are *not* independent after the `z2`-object has been cloned from the `z1`-object.

7. A class's `clone` override can throw a `CloneNotSupportedException`.

9. A maker interface is empty; hence, its purpose is to signal that an implementing class has some distinctive feature.

11. The advantage is that a C object cannot be cloned outside the inheritance hierarchy rooted in C unless the designer of C overrides `clone` as a public method. Presumably the designer would provide such an override only after considering whether C objects ought to be clonable.

Section 8.2

1. None. `Serializable` is a marker interface.
3. Serialization is the process of writing an in-memory object to a byte stream, whereas deserialization is the inverse process of reading an object from a byte stream to which the object previously was written.
5. Class `Alpha` must implement `Serializable` because `Object` does *not* implement this interface.
7. The subclass must implement `Serializable` and `Alpha` must have an accessible no-argument constructor.
9. No, but they can be written to and read from byte streams.
11. An object is serialized to an `ObjectOutputStream`.
13. `readObject`
15. A `static` field is not serialized or deserialized.
17. A field marked as `transient` is restored to its default value during deserialization. In effect, marking a field as `transient` signals that the field is not involved in serialization.
19. A class that needs completely customized serialization can implement `Externalizable` and define the `writeObject` and `readObject` methods declared therein.
21. When an object is serialized, a `long` integer that identifies the object's class is written with the object.

Section 8.3

3. During deserialization, the application needs to construct a `Date` to represent the current date and time, construct the GUI, and display the appropriate values in the three GUI fields.

Section 8.4

1. A sequence of instructions.
3. No.
5. No.
7. A GUI commonly has one thread "listen" for user inputs such as mouse clicks and separate threads to perform other tasks such as drawing or input and output.
9. One, the method `public void run()`.
11. The inherited `run` method returns immediately.
13. A user thread can sustain an application but a daemon thread cannot. In this sense, a daemon thread is meant to be a "helper" thread for a user thread.
15. To be effective, the `setDaemon` method must be invoked *before* the `start` method is invoked.
17. Yes.
19. Higher-priority threads are scheduled ahead of and can preempt lower-priority threads.
21. After the thread has been constructed but before it has been started.
23. Once the thread exits the `run` method or has `stop` invoked on it.

25. No.

27. A collection of threads with methods that operate on all threads in the group.

29. No.

31. A primitive type cannot be the argument in a `synchronized` clause.

33. Mutual exclusion is a condition under which only one thread at a time can execute a code segment. Mutual exclusion should be enforced on *critical sections*, that is, sections of code that require one-thread-at-a-time execution.

35. The `notify` and `notifyAll` methods are used to awaken an arbitrary `waiting` thread or all `waiting` threads, respectively.

37. No.

Section 8.5

3. The nonsynchronized `takeChopsticks` is invoked only from within the synchronized `grabChopsticks` method.

5. The *main thread* stops after starting all of the philosopher threads.

7. So that the *main thread* can construct and start *all* of the philosopher threads before any of the philosopher threads begins executing. The goal is to promote fairness.

9. Yes.

11. The simulation promotes fairness in several ways but does not guarantee fairness. First, no philosopher thread begins executing until all of the philosopher threads have been started. Second, the philosopher threads are started in random order. Third, philosopher threads eat and think for random intervals.

Section 9.1

1. Internet Protocol.

3. ftp (**f**ile **t**ransfer **p**rotocol).

5. Access to a particular physical network such as Ethernet.

7. 32 bits.

9. Because the address is a class B address, the net portion is 140.192 (leftmost octets) and the host portion is 1.1 (rightmost octets).

11. A port number on a particular machine associates with a specific application.

13. A software/hardware configuration that isolates an internal network from external networks.

Section 9.2

1. `Socket s = new Socket( "140.192.1.1", 23 );`

5. `InetAddress a =`
    `InetAddress.getByName( "140.192.1.1" );`

7. A plain socket server is a `ServerSocket` constructed with the default socket implementation.

9. A client `Socket` is associated with TCP, whereas a `DatagramSocket` is associated with UDP.

Section 9.3

1. The *main thread* can simply await client connections and offload the client servicing to a `ClientHandler` thread.

3. The server and client would need to agree upon a delimiter character such as a #, which then could be sent by the server at the end of each cliche.

Section 9.4

1. The host program provides the environment or context in which the applet executes.

3. The applet's bytecodes are downloaded from the server to the client and then executed on the client's JVM.

7. The `init` method typically does initialization such as setting fonts and colors. If the applet is multithreaded, the `start` method typically constructs and starts threads and the `stop` method typically stops these started threads.

9. An applet is highly restricted on the operations that it can perform. For example, the standard security manager used in commercial browsers prevents an applet from reading or writing the local disk, from launching another program, or from opening a connection to an arbitrary host. An applet is thus confined to a "sandbox" in which the applet must "play" and beyond which the applet must not venture.

11. Yes.

Section 9.5

3. No.

Section 9.6

1. **R**emote **M**ethod **I**nvocation.

5. Yes.

7. No.

Section 9.8

1. **O**bject **R**equest **B**roker.

3. **O**jbect **M**anagement **G**roup and **O**bject **M**anagement **A**rchitecture.

5. A client is not required to know the IP address of server on which the requested object resides.

9. Under CORBA Dynamic Invocation Interface, a client can convert the string that names a CORBA component into a reference to the component.

Section 10.1

1. A software component is a prebuilt module that can be integrated into an application.

3. Beans are meant to be parts of larger applications. If the larger application is serializable, then so should be the beans contained therein. Also, it may be convenient to construct individual beans through deserialization.

5. Readable.

7. If a property in one object changes, then any object registered as a property change listener is automatically notified of the property change. For example, changing the `salary` property in an Employee object could cause the appropriate `RetirementPlan` object to be notified.

9. A constrained property can be changed only if no listener objects to the change.

Section 10.2

1. Run time.

3. No.

5. Yes.

13. `grant {`
    `permission java.security.AllPermission;`
`};`

15. The science of breaking ciphers.

17. A digital signature is an *encrypted* message digest.

21. Public key.

Section 10.3

1. A list of all of a class's fields and their attributes.

3. `public Class getClass();`

Section 10.4

1. A servlet is a Java program, typically launched from a Web document, that executes on a server rather than a client machine.

3. Server.

5. Interface.

7. The `doGet` method is the callback for an HTTP request launched with *GET*, whereas the `doPost` method is the callback for an HTTP request launched with *POST*.

9. The `HttpServletResponse` argument encapsulates information that the server sends to client.

11. A `ResultSet` is the set of records typically generated from an SQL query against a database.

15. The database connection should be closed regardless of whether an exception is thrown.

Section 10.5

1. The servlet then works regardless of whether the HTTP method is *GET* or *POST*.

3. Browsers are standard, widely available, and typically free software products.

Index

EXHIBIT A

INPRISE-AUTHORIZED ELIGIBLE END USER LICENSE STATEMENT AND LIMITED WARRANTY FOR TITLES

IMPORTANT—READ CAREFULLY

This license statement and limited warranty constitutes a legal agreement ("License Agreement") for the software product ("Software") identified above (including any software, media, and accompanying on-line or printed documentation supplied by Inprise) between you (either as an individual or a single entity), the Book Publisher from whom you received the Software ("Publisher"), and Inprise International, Inc. ("Inprise").

BY INSTALLING, COPYING, OR OTHERWISE USING THE SOFTWARE, YOU AGREE TO BE BOUND BY ALL OF THE TERMS AND CONDITIONS OF THE LICENSE AGREEMENT. If you are the original purchaser of the Software and you do not agree with the terms and conditions of the License Agreement, promptly return the unused Software to the place from which you obtained it for a full refund.

Upon your acceptance of the terms and conditions of the License Agreement, Inprise grants you the right to use the Software solely for educational or training purposes. No rights are granted for deploying or distributing applications created with the Software.

This Software is owned by Inprise or its suppliers and is protected by copyright law and international copyright treaty. Therefore, you must treat this Software like any other copyrighted material (e.g., a book), except that you may either make one copy of the Software solely for backup or archival purposes or transfer the Software to a single hard disk provided you keep the original solely for backup or archival purposes.

You may transfer the Software and documentation on a permanent basis provided you retain no copies and the recipient agrees to the terms of the License Agreement. Except as provided in the License Agreement, you may not transfer, rent, lease, lend, copy, modify, translate, sublicense, time-share or electronically transmit or receive the Software, media or documentation. You acknowledge that the Software in source code form remains a confidential trade secret of Inprise and/or its suppliers and therefore you agree not to modify the Software or attempt to reverse engineer, decompile, or disassemble the Software, except and only to the extent that such activity is expressly permitted by applicable law notwithstanding this limitation.

Though Inprise does not offer technical support for the Software, we welcome your feedback.

This Software is subject to U.S. Commerce Department export restrictions, and is intended for use in the country into which Inprise sold it (or in the EEC, if sold into the EEC).

LIMITED WARRANTY

The Publisher warrants that the Software media will be free from physical defects in materials and workmanship for a period of ninety (90) days from the date of receipt. Any implied warranties on the Software media are limited to ninety (90) days. Some states/jurisdictions do not allow limitations on duration of an implied warranty, so the above limitation may not apply to you.

The Publisher's, Inprise's, and the Publisher's or Inprise's suppliers' entire liability and your exclusive remedy shall be, at the Publisher's or Inprise's option, either (a) return of the price paid, or (b) repair or replacement of the Software media that does not meet the Limited Warranty and which is returned to the Publisher with a copy of your receipt. This Limited Warranty is void if failure of the Software has resulted from accident, abuse, or misapplication. Any replacement Software will be warranted for the remainder of the original warranty period or thirty (30) days, whichever is longer. **Outside the United States, neither these remedies nor any product support services offered are available without proof of purchase from an authorized non-U.S. source.**

TO THE MAXIMUM EXTENT PERMITTED BY APPLICABLE LAW, THE PUBLISHER, INPRISE, AND THE PUBLISHER'S OR INPRISE'S SUPPLIERS DISCLAIM ALL OTHER WARRANTIES AND CONDITIONS, EITHER EXPRESS OR IMPLIED, INCLUDING, BUT NOT LIMITED TO, IMPLIED WARRANTIES OF MERCHANTABILITY, FITNESS FOR A PARTICULAR PURPOSE, TITLE, AND NON-INFRINGEMENT, WITH REGARD TO THE SOFTWARE, AND THE PROVISION OF OR FAILURE TO PROVIDE SUPPORT SERVICES. THIS LIMITED WARRANTY GIVES YOU SPECIFIC LEGAL RIGHTS. YOU MAY HAVE OTHERS, WHICH VARY FROM STATE/JURISDICTION TO STATE/JURISDICTION.

LIMITATION OF LIABILITY

TO THE MAXIMUM EXTENT PERMITTED BY APPLICABLE LAW, IN NO EVENT SHALL THE PUBLISHER, INPRISE, OR THE PUBLISHER'S OR INPRISE'S SUPPLIERS BE LIABLE FOR ANY SPECIAL, INCIDENTAL, INDIRECT, OR CONSEQUENTIAL DAMAGES WHATSOEVER (INCLUDING, WITHOUT LIMITATION, DAMAGES FOR LOSS OF BUSINESS PROFITS, BUSINESS INTERRUPTION, LOSS OF BUSINESS INFORMATION, OR ANY OTHER PECUNIARY LOSS) ARISING OUT OF THE USE OF OR INABILITY TO USE THE SOFTWARE PRODUCT OR THE PROVISION OF OR FAILURE TO PROVIDE SUPPORT SERVICES, EVEN IF INPRISE HAS BEEN ADVISED OF THE POSSIBILITY OF SUCH DAMAGES. IN ANY CASE, INPRISE'S ENTIRE LIABILITY UNDER ANY PROVISION OF THIS LICENSE AGREEMENT SHALL BE LIMITED TO THE GREATER OF THE AMOUNT ACTUALLY PAID BY YOU FOR THE SOFTWARE PRODUCT OR U.S. $25. BECAUSE SOME STATES AND JURISDICTIONS DO NOT ALLOW THE EXCLUSION OR LIMITATION OF LIABILITY, THE ABOVE LIMITATION MAY NOT APPLY TO YOU.

HIGH RISK ACTIVITIES

The Software is not fault-tolerant and is not designed, manufactured or intended for use or resale as on-line control equipment in hazardous environments requiring fail-safe performance, such as in the operation of nuclear facilities, aircraft navigation or communication systems, air traffic control, direct life support machines, or weapons systems, in which the failure of the Software could lead directly to death, personal injury, or severe physical or environmental damage ("High Risk Activities"). The Publisher, Inprise, and their suppliers specifically disclaim any express or implied warranty of fitness for High Risk Activities.

U.S. GOVERNMENT RESTRICTED RIGHTS

The Software and documentation are provided with RESTRICTED RIGHTS. Use, duplication, or disclosure by the Government is subject to restrictions as set forth in subparagraphs (c)(1)(ii) of the Rights in Technical Data and Computer Software clause at DFARS 252.227-7013 or subparagraphs (c)(1) and (2) of the Commercial Computer Software-Restricted Rights at 48 CFR 52.227-19, as applicable.

GENERAL PROVISIONS

This License Agreement may only be modified in writing signed by you and an authorized officer of Inprise. If any provision of this License Agreement is found void or unenforceable, the remainder will remain valid and enforceable according to its terms. If any remedy provided is determined to have failed for its essential purpose, all limitations of liability and exclusions of damages set forth in the Limited Warranty shall remain in effect.

This License Agreement shall be construed, interpreted and governed by the laws of the State of California, U.S.A. This License Agreement gives you specific legal rights; you may have others which vary from state to state and from country to country. Inprise reserves all rights not specifically granted in this License Agreement.

LICENSE AGREEMENT AND LIMITED WARRANTY